PHILOSOPHICAL TROUBLES

Philosophical Troubles

Collected Papers, Volume I

SAUL A. KRIPKE

OXFORD
UNIVERSITY PRESS

Oxford University Press

Oxford University Press, Inc., publishes works that further
Oxford University's objective of excellence
in research, scholarship, and education.

Oxford   New York
Auckland   Cape Town   Dar es Salaam   Hong Kong   Karachi
Kuala Lumpur   Madrid   Melbourne   Mexico City   Nairobi
New Delhi   Shanghai   Taipei   Toronto

With offices in
Argentina   Austria   Brazil   Chile   Czech Republic   France   Greece
Guatemala   Hungary   Italy   Japan   Poland   Portugal   Singapore
South Korea   Switzerland   Thailand   Turkey   Ukraine   Vietnam

Copyright © 2011 Saul A. Kripke

Published by Oxford University Press, Inc.
198 Madison Avenue, New York, New York 10016

www.oup.com

Oxford is a registered trademark of Oxford University Press

All rights reserved. No part of this publication may be reproduced,
stored in a retrieval system, or transmitted, in any form or by any means,
electronic, mechanical, photocopying, recording, or otherwise,
without the prior permission of Oxford University Press.

Library of Congress Cataloging-in-Publication Data
Kripke, Saul A., 1940–
[Selections. 2011]
Philosophical troubles : collected papers / Saul A. Kripke.
p. cm.
"Includes a selection of published and unpublished papers"–Introd.
Includes bibliographical references and index.
ISBN 978-0-19-973015-5 (alk. paper)
1. Philosophy. I. Title.
B945.K79 2011
191—dc22

1 3 5 7 9 8 6 4 2

Printed in the United States of America
on acid-free paper

To Netta

Contents

Introduction ix
Acknowledgments xiii

1. Identity and Necessity 1
2. On Two Paradoxes of Knowledge 27
3. Vacuous Names and Fictional Entities 52
4. Outline of a Theory of Truth 75
5. Speaker's Reference and Semantic Reference 99
6. A Puzzle about Belief 125
7. Nozick on Knowledge 162
8. Russell's Notion of Scope 225
9. Frege's Theory of Sense and Reference: Some Exegetical Notes 254
10. The First Person 292
11. Unrestricted Exportation and Some Morals for the Philosophy of Language 322
12. Presupposition and Anaphora: Remarks on the Formulation of the Projection Problem 351
13. A Puzzle about Time and Thought 373

Index 381

Introduction

The present volume includes a selection of published and unpublished papers. I have not followed a single criterion for making the selections. In fact, I have followed several different and perhaps even conflicting criteria. This may amount to saying that I have followed no criterion at all, but a number of considerations have crossed my mind (or my editors' minds) in arriving at a final list. Some of them might be worth mentioning.

One of the first decisions we made was to exclude my published papers on modal logic, thinking that with some new additions they might make a nice volume on their own. This decision led us to a more general attitude of favoring philosophically oriented papers over work that is predominantly technical. Among my previously published papers we have selected a group of older papers that have already been the subject of a great deal of discussion: "Identity and Necessity" (1971), "Outline of a Theory of Truth" (1975), "Speaker's Reference and Semantic Reference" (1977), and "A Puzzle about Belief" (1979). To these we have added my more recent publications: "Russell's Notion of Scope" (2005), "Frege's Theory of Sense and Reference: Some Exegetical Notes" (2008), and "Presupposition and Anaphora: Remarks on the Formulation of the Projection Problem" (2009). "Outline" is, of course, an exception to the "no-technical-papers" rule, but it is an old favorite of mine and I felt it also belongs among my more strictly philosophical papers. It was, in fact, originally published in a general philosophical journal (*The Journal of Philosophy*) and was intended to make some sense to a general philosophical audience.

The selection of the unpublished papers is meant to be in keeping with the principle of excluding technical work. But this hardly simplified the process of coming up with a final list. The papers chosen represent a very small portion of the unpublished work I have accumulated over the years, and I am sure many of the omitted manuscripts would have been equally appropriate for the present volume. But size and length of preparation time were also important factors in the selection process, and decisions had to be made. I had to content myself with the thought that the numerous manuscripts that were passed over will find a home in a future collection. Of the papers chosen, some originated in relatively recent talks and lectures, addressing topics that for some reason or other I found myself thinking about again. These include "The First Person" and "Unrestricted Exportation and Some Morals for the Philosophy of Language." Some of the older unpublished papers, such as "On Two Paradoxes of Knowledge" and "Vacuous Names and Fictional Entities," reflect the preferences of people working with me in this project. And still others, such as "Nozick on

Knowledge," were included because the original manuscripts seemed to need little work. Or so we thought then, anyway.

As has become usual with my work, most of the selected unpublished papers are based on transcriptions of lectures. Only two of them have been essays since their conception—"A Puzzle about Time and Thought" and "Nozick on Knowledge" (originally commissioned, by Hector Castañeda, as a review of Robert Nozick's *Philosophical Explanations* for *Noûs*). Strangely enough, the only paper especially written for this volume—"A Puzzle about Time and Thought"—is also, at least in a loose and elementary sense of "technical," arguably an exception to the "no technical papers" policy. I first thought of the paradox presented there several decades ago, and found myself thinking about it again in connection with Kaplan's paradox about possible world semantics.

All the unpublished papers underwent considerable rewriting (or writing!), and I have only very rarely pointed out that an addition or change has been made. Sometimes, even though not explicitly stated, such modifications will be obvious to the reader, but in most cases they will not. Having said that, I should add that the basic ideas have not been altered, and the core of each paper remains the same as when it was originally presented or written. Those who heard me give the lectures or have had access to the manuscripts will no doubt be familiar with the main ideas of the papers.

Indeed, even though the unpublished papers had not, alas, been published, some of them have been widely circulated. This remark applies more to the older material, such as "Vacuous Names and Fictional Entities," a precursor to my John Locke Lectures at Oxford, and "On Two Paradoxes of Knowledge." Both papers have in fact been discussed in print; many writers, including such distinguished philosophers as Gilbert Harman, David Lewis, and Robert Nozick, have tried to give a solution to the dogmatism paradox presented in "On Two Paradoxes of Knowledge." The "red barn" counterexample given in "Nozick on Knowledge" has also become a standard criticism of counterfactual theories of knowledge, though the paper as whole, a quite long and detailed analysis of Nozick's views, is not nearly as well known.

In general, I have not tried to reply to criticisms or alternative proposals. "On Two Paradoxes of Knowledge" is, however, an exception. I have added an appendix that contains a discussion of the self-referential approach to the surprise exam and a letter I wrote to Frederick Fitch in 1972 concerning these issues (come to think of it, another exception to the "no-technical papers" rule). Also, since many people learned of the dogmatism paradox from Gilbert Harman's presentation of it in *Thought*, I thought I should add a comment as to why his treatment does not seem to me to settle the matter.

In contrast to my unpublished manuscripts, I have adopted a very conservative policy regarding my previously published papers. They all appear here in their original form, and I have only occasionally added a note or footnote making specific additions. The fact that I have not tried to make corrections doesn't, of course, mean that I have no corrections to make. One of my excuses is that some of the published papers, especially the earlier ones, have generated an enormous amount of commentaries and replies, and it seemed to me unfair to my readers and commentators to introduce modifications to the original texts. The truth is that I would not dare tamper with them. And adding postscripts discussing reactions and my own modifications seemed to me to threaten to prolong a project long delayed—not to mention the added danger of their becoming longer than the original papers, separate pieces in their own right (or at least that has been my experience with a several-hundred-page transcription of a seminar recording reactions and modifications to "Outline of a Theory of Truth").

I hope my readers won't be disappointed with the decision to concentrate my efforts on the unpublished material. I can say that even though I would now perhaps change an emphasis here or there, try to be clearer in certain passages, or make certain corrections, I do stand with the main ideas presented in my previously published papers. As I said before, I would probably have something to add to each paper, published or unpublished. The process, however, can certainly go on and, indeed, did go on much longer than we had originally anticipated. Some of the papers had to wait too long to come to an end, and there was a certain sense of urgency, shared with the people working with me, that they finally appear.

The result is a volume with papers ranging over many topics: epistemology, linguistics, pragmatics, philosophy of language, history of analytic philosophy, theory of truth, metaphysics, and so on. People have noted that a significant part of the selection reflects a certain fondness for philosophical puzzles and paradoxes. In general, thinking about philosophy and logic has always been for me the fun part of my work. I can get gripped by certain problems. Writing them up is, unfortunately, neither as much fun nor as gripping, though I do find that sometimes one does not really know one's own thoughts precisely until they have been either properly presented in lectures or even written down. I hope that it has been worth the effort and that others will find the philosophical problems discussed in these pages as engaging as I have.

Many people have helped, directly or indirectly, bring this volume to light. The establishment of the Saul Kripke Center (SKC) at the City University of New York, Graduate Center, was crucial to its realization. For that reason I want to thank in the first place Chancellor Matthew Goldstein, President Bill Kelly, and Provost Chase Robinson for their enthusiasm for my work and for making the Center a reality. Michael Devitt, John Greenwood, Brian Schwartz, and Iakovos Vasiliou also deserve special thanks for their work in the establishment and continuing progress of the Center. I deeply appreciate their support.

The SKC team has provided invaluable help. Gary Ostertag, the Center's director, and Jeff Buechner have carefully read, commented on, and edited several versions of the previously unpublished papers. Monique Whitaker and Ben Phillips helped with the proofreading and checked references. Michael

Devitt has closely followed the book's progress, giving advice and suggesting deadlines, depending on what the situation called for, at several points. Finally, Romina Padró had the original idea for this book and pushed for it all the way, doing most of the editorial work, providing comments, suggestions, and encouragement throughout the selection and rewriting processes; it is indeed very doubtful that this book would exist without her help. I am extremely thankful for having been able to work with this excellent group of people and hope to continue doing so in the future.

The papers included in this volume were conceived and written or presented during a period spanning more than forty years. Many colleagues and friends who may not have been directly involved in the production of this book have made contributions to the individual papers contained here. I have tried to thank and give credit to them in the relevant papers, but I also want to stress my thanks to them here. Special thanks go to Harold Teichman, who has kindly given many hours of his time to edit the original manuscripts, and to Fernando Birman and Pegg Nadler for suggesting the title of the book. I am grateful to my editor at Oxford University Press, Peter Ohlin, and his staff, especially Natalie Johnson, for their support and helpfulness.

Finally I want to thank my family and especially my father, Rabbi Myer S. Kripke, for his generous support of me and the Center.

Saul Kripke
October 12, 2010

Acknowledgments

The author gratefully acknowledges the editors and publishers who have granted permission to reprint the following papers:

Chapter 1, "Identity and Necessity." First published in *Identity and Individuation*, edited by Milton K. Munitz (New York: New York University Press, 1971), 135–64.

Chapter 4, "Outline of a Theory of Truth." First published in *Journal of Philosophy* 72 (1975):690–716.

Chapter 5, "Speaker's Reference and Semantic Reference." First published in *Midwest Studies in Philosophy* 2 (1977):255–76.

Chapter 6, "A Puzzle About Belief." First published in *Meaning and Use*, edited by A. Margalit (Dordrecht, Netherlands: D. Reidel, 1979), 239–83.

Chapter 8, "Russell's Notion of Scope." First published in *Mind* 114 (2005): 1005–37 (Special Edition on the 100th anniversary of "On Denoting").

Chapter 9, "Frege's Theory of Sense and Reference: Some Exegetical Notes." *Theoria* 74 (2008):181–218.

Chapter 12, "Presupposition and Anaphora: Remarks on the Formulation of the Projection Problem." *Linguistic Inquiry* 40 (2009):367–86.

Chapters 2, 3, 7, 10, 11, and 13 are previously unpublished and appear here for the first time.

1

Identity and Necessity

A problem which has arisen frequently in contemporary philosophy is: "How are *contingent* identity statements possible?" This question is phrased by analogy with the way Kant phrased his question "How are synthetic a priori judgments possible?" In both cases, it has usually been taken for granted in the one case by Kant that synthetic a priori judgments were possible, and in the other case in contemporary philosophical literature that contingent statements of identity are possible. I do not intend to deal with the Kantian question except to mention this analogy: After a rather thick book was written trying to answer the question how synthetic a priori judgments were possible, others came along later who claimed that the solution to the problem was that synthetic a priori judgments were, of course, impossible and that a book trying to show otherwise was written in vain. I will not discuss who was right on the possibility of synthetic a priori judgments. But in the case of contingent statements of identity, most philosophers have felt that the notion of a contingent identity statement ran into something like the following paradox. An argument like the following can be given against the possibility of contingent identity statements:[1]

First, the law of the substitutivity of identity says that, for any objects x and y, if x is identical to y, then if x has a certain property F, so does y:

---

[1] This paper was presented orally, without a written text, to a New York University lecture series on identity. The lecture was taped, and the present paper represents a transcription of these tapes, edited only slightly with no attempt to change the style of the original. If the reader imagines the sentences of this paper as being delivered, extemporaneously, with proper pauses and emphases, this may facilitate his comprehension. Nevertheless, there may still be passages which are hard to follow, and the time allotted necessitated a condensed presentation of the argument. (A longer version of some of these views, still rather compressed and still representing a transcript of oral remarks, appeared in *Semantics of Natural Language*, ed. by Donald Davidson and Gilbert Harman, [Dordrecht: D. Reidel, 1972]; it subsequently appeared as a monograph, titled *Naming and Necessity* [Cambridge: Harvard University Press, 1980].) Occasionally, reservations, amplifications and gratifications of my remarks had to be repressed, especially in the discussion of theoretical identification and the mind-body problem. The footnotes, which were added to the original, would have become even more unwieldy if this had not been done.

(1) $(x)(y)[(x = y) \supset (Fx \supset Fy)]$

On the other hand, every object surely is necessarily self-identical:

(2) $(x)\Box(x = x)$

But

(3) $(x)(y)(x = y) \supset [\Box(x = x) \supset \Box(x = y)]$

is a substitution instance of (1), the substitutivity law. From (2) and (3), we can conclude that, for every x and y, if x equals y, then, it is necessary that x equals y.

(4) $(x)(y)((x = y) \supset \Box(x = y))$

This is because the clause $\Box(x = x)$ of the conditional drops out because it is known to be true.

This is an argument which has been stated many times in recent philosophy. Its conclusion, however, has often been regarded as highly paradoxical. For example, David Wiggins, in his paper, "Identity-Statements," says,

> Now there undoubtedly exist contingent identity-statements. Let $a = b$ be one of them. From its simple truth and (5) [= (4) above] we can derive '$\Box(a = b)$'. But how then can there be any contingent identity-statements?[2]

He then says that five various reactions to this argument are possible, and rejects all of these reactions, and reacts himself. I do not want to discuss all the possible reactions to this statement, except to mention the second of those Wiggins rejects. This says,

> We might accept the result and plead that provided 'a' and 'b' are proper names nothing is amiss. The consequence of this is that no contingent identity-statements can be made by means of proper names.

And then he says that he is discontented with this solution and many other philosophers have been discontented with this solution, too, while still others have advocated it.

What makes the statement (4) seem surprising? It says, for any objects x and y, if x is y, then it is necessary that x is y. I have already mentioned that someone might object to this argument on the grounds that premise (2) is already false, that it is not the case that everything is necessarily self-identical. Well, for example, am I myself necessarily self-identical? Someone might argue that in some situations which we can imagine I would not even have existed and therefore the statement "Saul Kripke is Saul Kripke" would have been false or it would not be the case that I was self-identical. Perhaps, it would have been neither true nor false, in such a world, to say that Saul Kripke is self-identical.

---

[2] R. J. Butler, ed., *Analytical Philosophy, Second Series* (Oxford: Blackwell, 1965), p. 41.

Well, that may be so, but really it depends on one's philosophical view of a topic that I will not discuss, that is, what is to be said about truth values of statements mentioning objects that do not exist in the actual world or any given possible world or counterfactual situation. Let us interpret necessity here weakly. We can count statements as necessary if whenever the objects mentioned therein exist, the statement would be true. If we wished to be very careful about this, we would have to go into the question of existence as a predicate and ask if the statement can be reformulated in the form: For every x it is necessary that, if x exists, then x is self-identical. I will not go into this particular form of subtlety here because it is not going to be relevant to my main theme. Nor am I really going to consider formula (4). Anyone who believes formula (2) is, in my opinion, committed to formula (4). If x and y are the same things and we can talk about modal properties of an object at all, that is, in the usual parlance, we can speak of modality *de re* and an object *necessarily* having certain properties as such, then formula (1), I think, has to hold. Where x is any property at all, including a property involving modal operators, and if x and y are the same object and x had a certain property F, then y has to have the same property F. And this is so even if the property F is itself of the form of necessarily having some other property G, in particular that of necessarily being identical to a certain object. Well, I will not discuss the formula (4) itself because by itself it does not assert, of any particular true statement of identity, that it is necessary. It does not say anything about *statements* at all. It says for every *object* x and *object* y, if x and y are the same object, then it is necessary that x and y are the same object. And this, I think, if we think about it (anyway, if someone does not think so, I will not argue for it here), really amounts to something very little different from the statement (2). Since x, by definition of identity, is the only object identical with x, $(y)(y = x \supset Fy)$ seems to me to be little more than a garrulous way of saying 'Fx', and thus $(x)(y)(y = x \supset Fx)$ says the same as $(x)Fx$ no matter what 'F' is—in particular, even if 'F' stands for the property of necessary identity with x. So if x has this property (of necessary identity with x), trivially everything identical with x has it, as (4) asserts. But, from statement (4) one may apparently be able to deduce that various particular statements of identity must be necessary and this is then supposed to be a very paradoxical consequence.

Wiggins says, "Now there undoubtedly exist contingent identity-statements." One example of a contingent identity statement is the statement that the first Postmaster General of the United States is identical with the inventor of bifocals, or that both of these are identical with the man claimed by the *Saturday Evening Post* as its founder (*falsely* claimed, I gather, by the way). Now some such statements are plainly contingent. It plainly is a contingent fact that one and the same man both invented bifocals and took on the job of Postmaster General of the United States. How can we reconcile this with the truth of statement (4)? Well, that, too, is an issue I do not want to go into in detail except to be very dogmatic about it. It was I think settled quite well by Bertrand Russell in his notion of the scope of a description. According to Russell, one can, for example, say with propriety that the author of *Hamlet* might not have written *Hamlet*, or even that the author of *Hamlet* might not have been the author of *Hamlet*. Now here, of course, we do not deny the necessity of the identity of an object with itself; but we say it is true concerning a certain man that he in fact was the unique person to have written *Hamlet* and secondly that the man, who in fact was the man who wrote *Hamlet*, might not have written *Hamlet*. In other words, if Shakespeare had decided not to write tragedies, he might not have written *Hamlet*. Under these circumstances, the man who in fact wrote *Hamlet* would not have written *Hamlet*. Russell brings this out by saying that in such a statement, the first occurrence of the description "the author of *Hamlet*" has large scope.[3] That is, we say "The author of *Hamlet* has the following property: that he might not have written *Hamlet*." We *do not* assert that the following statement might have been the case, namely that the author of *Hamlet* did not write *Hamlet*, for that is not true. That would be to say that it might have been the case that someone wrote *Hamlet* and yet did not write *Hamlet*, which would be a contradiction. Now, aside from the details of Russell's particular formulation of it, which depends on his theory of descriptions, this seems to be the distinction that any theory of descriptions has to make. For example, if someone were to meet the President of Harvard and take him to be a Teaching Fellow, he might say: "I took the President of Harvard for a Teaching Fellow." By this he does not mean that he took the proposition "The President of Harvard is a Teaching Fellow" to be true. He could have meant this, for example, had he believed that some sort of democratic system had gone so far at Harvard that the President of it decided to take on the task of being a Teaching Fellow. But that probably is not what he means. What he means instead, as Russell points out, is "Someone is President of Harvard and I took him to be a Teaching Fellow." In one of Russell's examples someone says, "I thought your yacht is much larger than it is." And the other man replies, "No, my yacht is not much larger than it is."

Provided that the notion of modality *de re*, and thus of quantifying into modal contexts, makes any sense at all, we have quite an adequate solution to the problem of avoiding paradoxes if we substitute descriptions for the universal quantifiers in (4) because the only consequence we will draw,[4] for example, in the bifocals case, is that there is a man who both happened to have invented bifocals

---

[3] The second occurrence of the description has small scope.

[4] In Russell's theory, $F(\imath x Gx)$ follows from (x) Fx and $(\exists ! x)$ Gx, provided that the description in $F(\imath x Gx)$ has the entire context for its scope (in Russell's 1905 terminology, has a 'primary occurrence'). Only then is $F(\imath x Gx)$ 'about' the denotation of '$\imath x Gx$'. Applying this rule to (4), we get the results indicated in the text. Notice that, in the ambiguous form $\Box(\imath x Gx = \imath x Hx)$, if one or both of the descriptions have 'primary occurrences' the formula does not assert the necessity of $\imath x Gx = \imath x Hx$; if both have secondary occurrences, it does. Thus in a language without explicit scope indicators, descriptions must be construed with the smallest possible scope—only then will $\sim A$ be the negation of A, $\Box A$ the necessitation of A, and the like. See Chapter 8.

and happened to have been the first Postmaster General of the United States, and is necessarily self-identical. There is an object x such that x invented bifocals, and as a matter of contingent fact an object y, such that y is the first Postmaster General of the United States, and finally, it is necessary, that x is y. What are x and y here? Here, x and y are both Benjamin Franklin, and it can certainly be necessary that Benjamin Franklin is identical with himself. So, there is no problem in the case of descriptions if we accept Russell's notion of scope.[5] And I just dogmatically want to drop that question here and go on to the question about names which Wiggins raises. And Wiggins says he might accept the result and plead that, provided a and b are proper names, nothing is amiss. And then he rejects this.

Now what is the special problem about proper names? At least if one is not familiar with the philosophical literature about this matter, one naively feels something like the following about proper names. First, if someone says "Cicero was an orator," then he uses the name 'Cicero' in that statement simply to pick out a certain object and then to ascribe a certain property to the object, namely, in this case, he ascribes to a certain man the property of having been an orator. If someone else uses another name, such as, say, 'Tully', he is still speaking about the same man. One ascribes the same property, if one says "Tully is an orator," to the same man. So to speak, the fact, or state of affairs, represented by the statement is the same whether one says "Cicero is an orator" or one says "Tully is an orator." It would, therefore, seem that the function of names is *simply* to refer, and not to describe the objects so named by such properties as "being the inventor of bifocals" or "being the first Postmaster General." It would seem that Leibniz' law and the law (1) should not only hold in the universally quantified form, but also in the form "if $a = b$ and Fa, then Fb," wherever 'a' and 'b' stand in

---

[5] An earlier distinction with the same purpose was, of course, the medieval one of *de dicto-de re*. That Russell's distinction of scope eliminates modal paradoxes has been pointed out by many logicians, especially Smullyan.

So as to avoid misunderstanding, let me emphasize that I am of course not asserting that Russell's notion of scope solves Quine's problem of 'essentialism'; what it does show, especially in conjunction with modern model-theoretic approaches to modal logic, is that quantified modal logic need not deny the truth of all instances of $(x)(y)(x = y \cdot \supset \cdot Fx \supset Fy)$, nor of all instances of '(x) $(Gx \supset Ga)$' (where 'a' is to be replaced by a nonvacuous definite description whose scope is all of 'Ga'), in order to avoid making it a necessary truth that one and the same man invented bifocals and headed the original Postal Department. Russell's contextual definition of description need not be adopted in order to ensure these results; but other logical theories, Fregean or other, which take descriptions as primitive must somehow express the same logical facts. Frege showed that a simple, non-iterated context containing a definite description with small scope, which cannot be interpreted as being 'about' the denotation of the description, can be interpreted as about its 'sense'. Some logicians have been interested in the question of the conditions under which, in an intensional context, a description with small scope is equivalent to the same one with large scope. One of the virtues of a Russellian treatment of descriptions in modal logic is that the answer (roughly that the description be a 'rigid designator' in the sense of this lecture) then often follows from the other postulates for quantified modal logic: no special postulates are needed, as in Hintikka's treatment. Even if descriptions are taken as primitive, special postulation of when scope is irrelevant can often be deduced from more basic axioms. (See Chapter 11.)

place of names and '*F*' stands in place of a predicate expressing a genuine property of the object:

$(a = b \cdot Fa) \supset Fb$

We can run the same argument through again to obtain the conclusion where '*a*' and '*b*' replace any names, "If $a = b$, then necessarily $a = b$." And so, we could venture this conclusion: that whenever '*a*' and '*b*' are proper names, if *a* is *b*, that it is necessary that *a* is *b*. Identity statements between proper names have to be necessary if they are going to be true at all. This view in fact has been advocated, for example, by Ruth Barcan Marcus in a paper of hers on the philosophical interpretation of modal logic.[6] According to this view, whenever, for example, someone makes a correct statement of identity between two names, such as, for example, that Cicero is Tully, his statement has to be necessary if it is true. But such a conclusion *seems* plainly to be false. (I, like other philosophers, have a habit of understatement in which "it seems plainly false" means "it is plainly false." Actually, I think the view is true, though not quite in the form defended by Mrs. Marcus.) At any rate, it seems plainly false. One example was given by Professor Quine in his reply to Professor Marcus at the symposium: "I think I see trouble anyway in the contrast between proper names and descriptions as Professor Marcus draws it. The paradigm of the assigning of proper names is tagging. We may tag the planet Venus some fine evening with the proper name 'Hesperus'. We may tag the same planet again someday before sun rise with the proper name 'Phosphorus'." (Quine thinks that something like that actually was done once.) "When, at last, we discover that we have tagged the same planet twice, our discovery is empirical, and not because the proper names were descriptions." According to what we are told, the planet Venus seen in the morning was originally thought to be a star and was called "the Morning Star," or (to get rid of any question of using a description) was called 'Phosphorus'. One and the same planet, when seen in the evening, was thought to be another star, the Evening Star, and was called "Hesperus." Later on, astronomers discovered that Phosphorus and Hesperus were one and the same. Surely no amount of a priori ratiocination on their part could conceivably have made it possible for them to deduce that Phosphorus is Hesperus. In fact, given the information they had, it might have turned out the other way. Therefore, it is argued, the statement 'Hesperus is Phosphorus' has to be an ordinary contingent, empirical truth, one which might have come out otherwise, and so the view that true identity statements between names are necessary has to be false. Another example which Quine gives in *Word and Object* is taken from Professor Schrödinger, the famous pioneer of quantum mechanics: A certain mountain can be seen from

---

[6] "Modalities and Intensional Languages," *Boston Studies in the Philosophy of Science*, Vol. 1 (New York: Humanities Press, 1963), pp. 71ff. See also the "Comments" by Quine and the ensuing discussion.

both Tibet and Nepal. When seen from one direction it was called 'Gaurisanker'; when seen from another direction, it was called 'Everest'; and then, later on, the empirical discovery was made that Gaurisanker *is* Everest. (Quine further says that he gathers the example is actually geographically incorrect. I guess one should not rely on physicists for geographical information.)

Of course, one possible reaction to this argument is to deny that names like 'Cicero', 'Tully', 'Gaurisanker', and 'Everest' really are proper names. Look, someone might say (someone has said it: his name was 'Bertrand Russell'), just because statements like "Hesperus is Phosphorus" and "Gaurisanker is Everest" are contingent, we can see that the names in question are not really purely referential. You are not, in Mrs. Marcus' phrase, just 'tagging' an object; you are actually describing it. What does the contingent fact that Hesperus is Phosphorus amount to? Well, it amounts to the fact that *the* star in a certain portion of the sky in the evening is *the* star in a certain portion of the sky in the morning. Similarly, the contingent fact that Guarisanker is Everest amounts to the fact that the mountain viewed from such and such an angle in Nepal is the mountain viewed from such and such another angle in Tibet. Therefore, such names as 'Hesperus' and 'Phosphorus' can only be abbreviations for descriptions. The term 'Phosphorus' *has* to mean "the star seen . . . ," or (let us be cautious because it actually turned out not to be a star), "the *heavenly body* seen from such and such a position at such and such a time in the morning," and the name 'Hesperus' has to mean "the heavenly body seen in such and such a position at such and such a time in the evening." So, Russell concludes, if we want to reserve the term "name" for things which really just name an object without describing it, the only real proper names we can have are names of our own immediate sense data, objects of our own 'immediate acquaintance'. The only such names which occur in language are demonstratives like "this" and "that." And it is easy to see that this requirement of necessity of identity, understood as exempting identities between names from all imaginable doubt, can indeed be guaranteed only for demonstrative names of immediate sense data; for only in such cases can an identity statement between two different names have a general immunity from Cartesian doubt. There are some other things Russell has sometimes allowed as objects of acquaintance, such as one's self; we need not go into details here. Other philosophers (for example, Mrs. Marcus in her reply, at least in the verbal discussion as I remember it—I do not know if this got into print, so perhaps this should not be 'tagged' on her[7]) have said, "If names are really just tags, genuine tags, then a good dictionary should be able to tell us that they are names of the same object." You have an object *a* and an object *b* with names 'John' and 'Joe'. Then, according to Mrs. Marcus, a dictionary should be able to tell you whether or not 'John' and 'Joe' are names of the same object. Of course, I do not

---

[7] It should. See her remark on p. 115, *Boston Studies in the Philosophy of Science*, Vol. 1, in the discussion following the papers.

know what ideal dictionaries should do, but ordinary proper names do not seem to satisfy this requirement. You certainly *can*, in the case of ordinary proper names, make quite empirical discoveries that, let's say, Hesperus is Phosphorus, though we thought otherwise. We can be in doubt as to whether Gaurisanker is Everest or Cicero is in fact Tully. Even now, we could conceivably discover that we were wrong in supposing that Hesperus was Phosphorus. Maybe the astronomers made an error. So it seems that this view is wrong and that if by a name we do not mean some artificial notion of names such as Russell's, but a proper name in the ordinary sense, then there can be contingent identity statements using proper names, and the view to the contrary seems plainly wrong.

In recent philosophy a large number of other identity statements have been emphasized as examples of contingent identity statements, different, perhaps, from either of the types I have mentioned before. One of them is, for example, the statement "Heat is the motion of molecules." First, science is supposed to have discovered this. Empirical scientists in their investigations have been supposed to discover (and, I suppose, they did) that the external phenomenon which we call "heat" is, in fact, molecular agitation. Another example of such a discovery is that water is H_2O, and yet other examples are that gold is the element with such and such an atomic number, that light is a stream of photons, and so on. These are all in some sense of "identity statement" identity statements. Second, it is thought, they are plainly contingent identity statements, just because they were scientific discoveries. After all, heat might have turned out not to have been the motion of molecules. There were other alternative theories of heat proposed, for example, the caloric theory of heat. If these theories of heat had been correct, then heat would not have been the motion of molecules, but instead, some substance suffusing the hot object, called "caloric." And it was a matter of course of science and not of any logical necessity that the one theory turned out to be correct and the other theory turned out to be incorrect.

So, here again, we have, apparently, another plain example of a contingent identity statement. This has been supposed to be a very important example because of its connection with the mind-body problem. There have been many philosophers who have wanted to be materialists, and to be materialists in a particular form, which is known today as "the identity theory." According to this theory, a certain mental state, such as a person's being in pain, is identical with a certain state of his brain (or, perhaps, of his entire body, according to some theorists), at any rate, a certain material or neural state of his brain or body. And so, according to this theory, my being in pain at this instant, if I were, would be identical with my body's being or my brain's being in a certain state. Others have objected that this cannot be because, after all, we can imagine my pain existing even if the state of the body did not. We can perhaps imagine my not being embodied at all and still being in pain, or, conversely, we could imagine my body existing and being in the very same state even if there were no pain. In fact, conceivably, it could be in this state even though there were no mind 'back of it', so to speak, at all. The usual reply has been to concede that all of these things might have been the case, but to argue that these are irrelevant to the question of the identity of the mental state and the physical state. This identity, it is said, is just another contingent scientific identification, similar to the identification of heat with molecular motion, or water with H_2O. Just as we can imagine heat without any molecular motion, so we can imagine a mental state without any corresponding brain state. But, just as the first fact is not damaging to the identification of heat and the motion of molecules, so the second fact is not at all damaging to the identification of a mental state with the corresponding brain state. And so, many recent philosophers have held it to be very important for our theoretical understanding of the mind-body problem that there can be contingent identity statements of this form.

To state finally what *I* think, as opposed to what seems to be the case, or what others think, I think that in both cases, the case of names and the case of the theoretical identifications, the identity statements are necessary and not contingent. That is to say, they are necessary if *true*, of course, false identity statements are not necessary. How can one possibly defend such a view? Perhaps I lack a complete answer to this question, even though I am convinced that the view is true. But to begin an answer, let me make some distinctions that I want to use. The first is between a *rigid* and a *nonrigid designator*. What do these terms mean? As an example of a nonrigid designator, I can give an expression such as 'the inventor of bifocals'. Let us suppose it was Benjamin Franklin who invented bifocals, and so the expression, 'the inventor of bifocals', designates or refers to a certain man, namely, Benjamin Franklin. However, we can easily imagine that the world could have been different, that under different circumstances someone else would have come upon this invention before Benjamin Franklin did, and in that case, *he* would have been the inventor of bifocals. So, in this sense, the expression 'the inventor of bifocals' is nonrigid: Under certain circumstances one man would have been the inventor of bifocals; under other circumstances, another man would have. In contrast, consider the expression 'the square root of 25'. Independently of the empirical facts, we can give an arithmetical proof that the square root of 25 is in fact the number 5, and because we have proved this mathematically, what we have proved is necessary. If we think of numbers as entities at all, and let us suppose, at least for the purpose of this lecture, that we do, then the expression 'the square root of 25' necessarily designates a certain number, namely 5. Such an expression I call 'a *rigid* designator'. Some philosophers think that anyone who even uses the notions of rigid or nonrigid designator has already shown that he has fallen into a certain confusion or has not paid attention to certain facts. What do I mean by 'rigid designator'? I mean a term that designates the same object in all possible worlds. To get rid of one confusion which certainly is not mine, I do not use "might have designated a different object" to refer to the fact that language might have been used differently. For example, the expression 'the inventor of bifocals' might have been used by inhabitants of this planet always to refer to the man who corrupted Hadleyburg. This would have been the case, if, first, the people on this planet had not spoken English, but some other language, which phonetically overlapped with English; and if, second, in that language the expression 'the inventor of bifocals' meant the 'man who corrupted Hadleyburg'. Then it would refer, of course, in their language, to whoever in fact corrupted Hadleyburg in this counterfactual situation. That is not what I mean. What I mean by saying that a description might have referred to something different, I mean that in *our* language as *we* use it in describing a counterfactual situation, there might have been a different object satisfying the descriptive conditions *we* give for reference. So, for example, we use the phrase 'the inventor of bifocals', when we are talking about another possible world or a counterfactual situation, to refer to whoever in that counterfactual situation would have invented bifocals, not to the person whom people *in* that counterfactual situation would have called 'the inventor of bifocals'. *They* might have spoken a different language which phonetically overlapped with English in which 'the inventor of bifocals' is used in some other way. I am *not* concerned with that question here. For that matter, they might have been deaf and dumb, or there might have been no people at all. (There still could have been an inventor of bifocals even if there were no people—God, or Satan, will do.)

Second, in talking about the notion of a rigid designator, I do not mean to imply that the object referred to has to exist in all possible worlds, that is, that it has to necessarily exist. Some things, perhaps mathematical entities such as the positive integers, if they exist at all, necessarily exist. Some people have held that God both exists and necessarily exists; others, that He contingently exists; others, that He contingently fails to exist; and others, that He necessarily fails to exist:[8] all four options have been tried. But at any rate, when I use the notion of rigid designator, I do not imply that the object referred to necessarily exists. All I mean is that in any possible world where the object in question *does* exist, in any situation where the object *would* exist, we use the designator in question to designate that object. In a situation where the object does not exist, then we should say that the designator has no referent and that the object in question so designated does not exist.

As I said, many philosophers would find the very notion of rigid designator objectionable per se. And the objection that people make may be stated as follows: Look, you're talking about situations which are counterfactual, that is to say, you're talking about other possible worlds. Now these worlds are completely disjoint, after all, from the actual world which is not just another possible world; it is the actual world. So, before you talk about, let us say, such an object as Richard Nixon in another possible world at all, you have to say which object in this other possible world would *be* Richard Nixon. Let us talk about a

---

[8] If there is no deity, and especially if the nonexistence of a deity is *necessary*, it is dubious that we can use "He" to refer to a deity. The use in the text must be taken to be non-literal.

situation in which, as *you* would say, Richard Nixon would have been a member of SDS. Certainly the member of SDS you are talking about is someone very different in many of his properties from Nixon. Before we even can say whether this man would have been Richard Nixon or not, we have to set up criteria of identity across possible worlds. Here are these other possible worlds. There are all kinds of objects in them with different properties from those of any actual object. Some of them resemble Nixon in some ways, some of them resemble Nixon in other ways. Well, which of these objects is Nixon? One has to give a criterion of identity. And this shows how the very notion of rigid designator runs in a circle. Suppose we designate a certain number as the number of planets. Then, if that is our favorite way, so to speak, of designating this number, then in any other possible worlds we will have to identify whatever number is the number of planets with the number 9, which in the actual world is the number of planets. So, it is argued by various philosophers, for example, implicitly by Quine, and explicitly by many others in his wake, we cannot really ask whether a designator is rigid or nonrigid because we first need a criterion of identity across possible worlds. An extreme view has even been held that, since possible worlds are so disjoint from our own, we cannot really say that any object in them is the *same* as an object existing now but only that there are some objects which resemble things in the actual world, more or less. We, therefore, should not really speak of what would have been true of Nixon in another possible world but, only of what 'counterparts' (the term which David Lewis uses[9]) of Nixon there would have been. Some people in other possible worlds have dogs whom they call 'Checkers'. Others favor the ABM but do not have any dog called Checkers. There are various people who resemble Nixon more or less, but none of them can really be said to be Nixon; they are only *counterparts* of Nixon, and you choose which one is the best counterpart by noting which resembles Nixon the most closely, according to your favorite criteria. Such views are widespread, both among the defenders of quantified modal logic and among its detractors.

All of this talk seems to me to have taken the metaphor of possible worlds much too seriously in some way. It is as if a 'possible world' were like a foreign country, or distant planet way out there. It is as if we see dimly through a telescope various actors on this distant planet. Actually David Lewis' view seems the most reasonable if one takes this picture literally. No one far away on another planet can be strictly identical with someone here. But, even if we have some marvelous methods of transportation to take one and the same person from planet to planet, we really need some epistemological criteria of identity to be able to say whether someone on this distant planet is the same person as someone here.

All of this seems to me to be a totally misguided way of looking at things. What it amounts to is the view that counterfactual situations have to be described

---

[9] David K. Lewis, "Counterpart Theory and Quantified Modal Logic," *Journal of Philosophy*, LXV (1968), 113ff.

purely qualitatively. So, we cannot say, for example, "If Nixon had only given a sufficient bribe to Senator X, he would have gotten Carswell through" because that refers to certain people, Nixon and Carswell, and talks about what things would be true of them in a counterfactual situation. We must say instead "If a man who has a hairline like such and such, and holds such and such political opinions had given a bribe to a man who was a senator and had such and such other qualities, then a man who was a judge in the South and had many other qualities resembling Carswell would have been confirmed." In other words, we must describe counterfactual situations purely qualitatively and then ask the question, "Given that the situation contains people or things with such and such qualities, which of these people is (or is a counterpart of) Nixon, which is Carswell, and so on?" This seems to me to be wrong. Who is to prevent us from saying "Nixon might have gotten Carswell through had he done certain things"? We are speaking of *Nixon* and asking what, in certain counterfactual situations, would have been true of *him*. We can say that if Nixon had done such and such, he would have lost the election to Humphrey. Those I am opposing would argue, "Yes, but how do you find out if the man you are talking about is in fact Nixon?" It would indeed be very hard to find out, if you were looking at the whole situation through a telescope, but that is not what we are doing here. Possible worlds are not something to which an epistemological question like this applies. And if the phrase 'possible worlds' is what makes anyone think some such question applies, he should just *drop* this phrase and use some other expression, say 'counterfactual situation,' which might be less misleading. If we say "If Nixon had bribed such and such a Senator, Nixon would have gotten Carswell through," what is *given* in the very description of that situation is that it is a situation in which we are speaking of Nixon, and of Carswell, and of such and such a Senator. And there seems to be no less objection to *stipulating* that we are speaking of certain *people* than there can be objection to stipulating that we are speaking of certain *qualities*. Advocates of the other view take speaking of certain qualities as unobjectionable. They do not say, "How do we know that this quality (in another possible world) is that of redness?" But they do find speaking of certain *people* objectionable. But I see no more reason to object in the one case than in the other. I think it really comes from the idea of possible worlds as existing out there, but very far off, viewable only through a special telescope. Even more objectionable is the view of David Lewis. According to Lewis, when we say "Under certain circumstances Nixon would have gotten Carswell through," we really mean "Some man, other than Nixon but closely resembling him, would have gotten some judge, other than Carswell but closely resembling him, through." Maybe that is so, that some man closely resembling Nixon could have gotten some man closely resembling Carswell through. But *that* would not comfort either Nixon or Carswell, nor would it make Nixon kick himself and say "*I* should have done such and such to get Carswell through." The question is whether under certain circumstances Nixon *himself* could have gotten *Carswell* through. And I think the objection is simply based on a misguided picture.

Instead, we can perfectly well talk about rigid and nonrigid designators. Moreover, we have a simple, intuitive test for them. We can say, for example, that the number of planets might have been a different number from the number it in fact is. For example, there might have been only seven planets. We can say that the inventor of bifocals might have been someone other than the man who *in fact* invented bifocals.[10] We cannot say, though, that the square root of 81 might have been a different number from the number it in fact is, for that number just has to be 9. If we apply this intuitive test to proper names, such as for example 'Richard Nixon', they would seem intuitively to come out to be rigid designators. First, when we talk even about the counterfactual situation in which we suppose Nixon to have done different things, we assume we are still talking about Nixon himself. We say, "If Nixon had bribed a certain Senator, he would have gotten Carswell through," and we assume that by 'Nixon' and 'Carswell' we are still referring to the very same people as in the actual world. And it seems that we cannot say "Nixon might have been a different man from the man he in fact was," unless, of course, we mean it metaphorically: He might have been a different *sort* of person (if you believe in free will and that people are not inherently corrupt). You might think the statement true in that sense, but Nixon could not have been in the other literal sense a different person from the person he, in fact, is, even though the thirty-seventh President of the United States might have been Humphrey. So the phrase "the thirty-seventh President" is nonrigid, but 'Nixon', it would seem, is rigid.

Let me make another distinction before I go back to the question of identity statements. This distinction is very fundamental and also hard to see through. In recent discussion, many philosophers who have debated the meaningfulness of various categories of truths, have regarded them as identical. Some of those who identify them are vociferous defenders of them, and others, such as Quine, say they are all identically meaningless. But usually they're not distinguished. These

---

[10] Some philosophers think that definite descriptions, in English, are ambiguous, that sometimes 'the inventor of bifocals' rigidly designates the man who in fact invented bifocals. I am tentatively inclined to reject this view, construed as a thesis about English (as opposed to a possible hypothetical language), but I will not argue the question here.

What I do wish to note is that, contrary to some opinions, this alleged ambiguity cannot replace the Russellian notion of the scope of a description. Consider the sentence, "The number of planets might have been necessarily even." This sentence plainly can be read so as to express a truth; had there been eight planets, the number of planets would have been necessarily even. Yet without scope distinctions, both a 'referential' (rigid) and a non-rigid reading of the description will make the statement false. (Since the number of planets is nine, the rigid reading amounts to the falsity that nine might have been necessarily even.)

The 'rigid' reading is equivalent to the Russellian primary occurrence; the non-rigid, to innermost scope—some, following Donnellan, perhaps loosely, have called this reading the 'attributive' use. The possibility of intermediate scopes is then ignored. In the present instance, the intended reading of $\Diamond\Box$ (the number of planets is even) makes the scope of the description $\Box$ (the number of planets is even), neither the largest nor the smallest possible. (See also Chapter 8, section 2a.)

are categories such as 'analytic', 'necessary', 'a priori', and sometimes even 'certain'. I will not talk about all of these but only about the notions of a prioricity and necessity. Very often these are held to be synonyms. (Many philosophers probably should not be described as holding them to be synonyms; they simply *use* them interchangeably.) I wish to distinguish them. What do we mean by calling a statement *necessary?* We simply mean that the statement in question, first, is true, and, second, that it could not have been otherwise. When we say that something is *contingently* true, we mean that, though it is in fact the case, it could have been the case that things would have been otherwise. If we wish to assign this distinction to a branch of philosophy, we should assign it to metaphysics. To the contrary, there is the notion of an *a priori truth*. An a priori truth is supposed to be one which can be *known* to be true independently of all experience. Notice that this does not in and of itself say anything about all possible worlds, unless this is put into the definition. All that it says is that it can be known to be true of the actual world, independently of all experience. It may, by some philosophical argument, follow from our knowing, independently of experience, that something is true of the actual world, that it has to be known to be true also of all possible worlds. But if this is to be established, it requires some philosophical argument to establish it. Now, *this* notion, if we were to assign it to a branch of philosophy, belongs, not to metaphysics, but to epistemology. It has to do with the way we can know certain things to be in fact true. Now, it may be the case, of course, that anything which is necessary is something which *can* be known a priori. (Notice, by the way, the notion a priori truth as thus defined has in it *another* modality: it *can* be known independently of all experience. It is a little complicated because there is a double modality here.) I will not have time to explore these notions in full detail here, but one thing we can see from the outset is that these two notions are by no means trivially the same. If they are coextensive, it takes some philosophical argument to establish it. As stated, they belong to different domains of philosophy. One of them has something to do with *knowledge*, of what can be known in certain ways about the *actual* world. The other one has to do with *metaphysics*, how the world *could* have been; given that it is the way it is, could it have been otherwise, in certain ways? Now I hold, as a matter of fact, that neither class of statements is contained in the other. But, all we need to talk about here is this: Is everything that is necessary knowable a priori or known a priori? Consider the following example: the Goldbach conjecture. This says that every even number is the sum of two primes. It is a mathematical statement and if it is true at all, it has to be necessary. Certainly, one could not say that though in fact every even number is the sum of two primes, there could have been some extra number which was even and not the sum of two primes. What would that mean? On the other hand, the answer to the question whether every even number *is* in fact the sum of two primes is unknown, and we have no method at present for deciding. So we certainly do not know, a priori or even a posteriori, that every even number is the sum of two primes. (Well, perhaps we have some evidence in that no counterexample has been found.) But we certainly do not know a priori anyway, that every even number is, in fact, the sum of two primes. But, of course, the definition just says "*can* be known independently of experience," and someone might say that if it is true, we *could* know it independently of experience. It is hard to see exactly what this claim means. It might be so. One thing it might mean is that if it were true we could *prove* it. This claim is certainly wrong if it is generally applied to mathematical statements and we have to work within some fixed system. This is what Gödel proved. And even if we mean an 'intuitive proof in general' it might just be the case (at least, this view is as clear and as probable as the contrary) that though the statement is true, there is just no way the human mind could ever prove it. Of course, one way an *infinite* mind might be able to prove it is by looking through each natural number one by one and checking. In this sense, of course, it can, perhaps, be known a priori, but only by an infinite mind, and then this gets into other complicated questions. I do not want to discuss questions about the conceivability of performing an infinite number of acts like looking through each number one by one. A vast philosophical literature has been written on this: Some have declared it is logically impossible; others that it is logically possible; and some do not know. The main point is that it is not trivial that just because such a statement is necessary it can be known a priori. Some considerable clarification is required before we decide that it can be so known. And so this shows that even if everything necessary is a priori in some sense, it should not be taken as a trivial matter of definition. It is a substantive philosophical thesis which requires some work.

Another example that one might give relates to the problem of essentialism. Here is a lectern. A question which has often been raised in philosophy is: What are its essential properties? What properties, aside from trivial ones like self-identity, are such that this object has to have them if it exists at all,[11] are such that if an object did not have it, it would not be this object?[12] For example, being

---

[11] This definition is the usual formulation of the notion of essential property, but an exception must be made for existence itself: on the definition given, existence would be trivially essential. We should regard existence as essential to an object only if the object necessarily exists. Perhaps there are other recherché properties, involving existence, for which the definition is similarly objectionable. (I thank Michael Slote for this observation.)

[12] The two clauses of the sentence footnoted give equivalent definitions of the notion of essential property, since $\Box\ ((\exists x)(x=a) \supset Fa)$ is equivalent to $\Box(x)(\sim Fx \supset x \neq a)$. The second formulation, however, has served as a powerful seducer in favor of theories of 'identification across possible worlds'. For it suggests that we consider 'an object *b* in another possible world' and test whether it is identifiable with *a* by asking whether it lacks any of the essential properties of *a*. Let me therefore emphasize that, although an essential property is (trivially) a property without which an object cannot be *a*, it by no means follows that the essential, purely qualitative properties of *a* jointly form a sufficient condition for being *a*, nor that *any* purely qualitative conditions are sufficient for an object to be *a*. Further, even if necessary and sufficient qualitative conditions for an object to be Nixon may exist, there would still be little justification for the demand for a purely qualitative description of all counterfactual situations. We can ask whether Nixon might have been a Democrat without engaging in these subtleties.

made of wood, and not of ice, might be an essential property of this lectern. Let us just take the weaker statement that it is not made of ice. That will establish it as strongly as we need it, perhaps as dramatically. Supposing this lectern is in fact made of wood, could this very lectern have been made from the very beginning of its existence from ice, say frozen from water in the Thames? One has a considerable feeling that it could *not*, though in fact one certainly could have made a lectern of water from the Thames, frozen it into ice by some process, and put it right there in place of this thing. If one had done so, one would have made, of course, a *different* object. It would not have been *this very lectern*, and so one would not have a case in which this very lectern here was made of ice, or was made from water from the Thames. The question of whether it could afterward, say in a minute from now, turn into ice is something else. So, it would seem, if an example like this is correct—and this is what advocates of essentialism have held—that this lectern could not have been made of ice, that is in any counterfactual situation of which we would say that this lectern existed at all, we would have to say also that it was not made from water from the Thames frozen into ice. Some have rejected, of course, any such notion of essential property as meaningless. Usually, it is because (and I think this is what Quine, for example, would say) they have held that it depends on the notion of identity across possible worlds, and that this is itself meaningless. Since I have rejected this view already, I will not deal with it again. We can talk about *this very object*, and whether it could have had certain properties which it does not in fact have. For example, it could have been in another room from the room it in fact is in, even at this very time, but it could not have been made from the very beginning from water frozen into ice.

If the essentialist view is correct, it can only be correct if we sharply distinguish between the notions of a posteriori and a priori truth on the one hand, and contingent and necessary truth on the other hand, for although the statement that this table, if it exists at all, was not made of ice, is necessary, it certainly is not something that we know a priori. What we know is that first, lecterns usually are not made of ice, they are usually made of wood. This looks like wood. It does not feel cold and it probably would if it were made of ice. Therefore, I conclude, probably this is not made of ice. Here my entire judgment is a posteriori. I could find out that an ingenious trick has been played upon me and that, in fact, this lectern is made of ice; but what I am saying is, given that it is in fact not made of ice, in fact is made of wood, one cannot imagine that under certain circumstances it could have been made of ice. So we have to say that though we cannot know a priori whether this table was made of ice or not, given that it is not made of ice, it is *necessarily* not made of ice. In other words, if P is the statement that the lectern is not made of ice, one knows by a priori philosophical analysis, some conditional of the form "if P, then necessarily P." If the table is not made of ice, it is necessarily not made of ice. On the other hand, then, we know by empirical investigation that P, the antecedent of the conditional, is true—that this table is not made of ice. We can conclude by *modus ponens*:

$P \supset \Box P$

P
___
$\Box P$

The conclusion—'$\Box P$'—is that it is necessary that the table not be made of ice, and this conclusion is known a posteriori, since one of the premises on which it is based is a posteriori. So, the notion of essential properties can be maintained only by distinguishing between the notions of a priori and necessary truth, and I do maintain it.

Let us return to the question of identities. Concerning the statement 'Hesperus is Phosphorus' or the statement 'Cicero is Tully', one can find all of these out by empirical investigation, and we might turn out to be wrong in our empirical beliefs. So, it is usually argued, such statements must therefore be contingent. Some have embraced the other side of the coin and have held "Because of this argument about necessity, identity statements between names have to be knowable a priori, so, only a very special category of names, possibly, really works as names; the other things are bogus names, disguised descriptions, or something of the sort. However, a certain very narrow class of statements of identity are known a priori, and these are the ones which contain the genuine names." If one accepts the distinctions that I have made, one need not jump to either conclusion. One can hold that certain statements of identity between names, though often known a posteriori, and maybe not knowable a priori, are in fact necessary, if true. So, we have some room to hold this. But, of course, to have some room to hold it does not mean that we should hold it. So let us see what the evidence is. First, recall the remark that I made that proper names seem to be rigid designators, as when we use the name 'Nixon' to talk about a certain man, even in counterfactual situations. If we say, "If Nixon had not written the letter to Saxbe, maybe he would have gotten Carswell through," we are in this statement talking about Nixon, Saxbe, and Carswell, the very same men as in the actual world, and what would have happened to them under certain counterfactual circumstances. If names are rigid designators, then there can be no question about identities being necessary, because 'a' and 'b' will be rigid designators of a certain man or thing x. Then even in every possible world, a and b will both refer to this same object x, and to no other, and so there will be no situation in which a might not have been b. That would have, to be a situation in which the object which we are also now calling 'x' would not have been identical with itself. Then one could not possibly have a situation in which Cicero would not have been Tully or Hesperus would not have been Phosphorus.[13]

---

[13] I thus agree with Quine, that "Hesperus is Phosphorus" is (or can be) an empirical discovery; with Marcus, that it is necessary. Both Quine and Marcus, according to the present standpoint, err in identifying the epistemological and the metaphysical issues.

Aside from the identification of necessity with a priority, what has made people feel the other way? There are two things which have made people feel the other way.[14] Some people tend to regard identity statements as metalinguistic statements, to identify the statement "Hesperus is Phosphorus" with the metalinguistic statement, "'Hesperus' and 'Phosphorus' are names of the same heavenly body." And that, of course, might have been false. We might have used the terms 'Hesperus' and 'Phosphorus' as names of *two* different heavenly bodies. But, of course, this has nothing to do with the necessity of identity. In the same sense "2 + 2 = 4" might have been false. The phrases "2 + 2" and "4" might have been used to refer to two different numbers. One can imagine a language, for example, in which "+", "2", and "=" were used in the standard way, but "4" was used as the name of, say, the square root of minus 1, as we should call it, "*i*." Then "2 + 2 = 4" would be false, for 2 plus 2 is not equal to the square root of minus 1. But this is not what we want. We do not want just to say that a certain statement which we in fact use to express something true could have expressed something false. We want to use the statement in *our* way and see if it could have been false. Let us do this. What is the idea people have? They say, "Look, Hesperus might not have been Phosphorus. Here a certain planet was seen in the morning, and it was seen in the evening; and it just turned out later on as a matter of empirical fact that they were one and the same planet. If things had turned out otherwise, they would have been two different planets, or two different heavenly bodies, so how can you say that such a statement is necessary?"

Now there are two things that such people can mean. First, they can mean that we do not know a priori whether Hesperus is Phosphorus. This I have already conceded. Second, they may mean that they can actually imagine circumstances that they would call circumstances in which Hesperus would not have been Phosphorus. Let us think what would be such a circumstance, using these terms here as *names* of a planet. For example, it could have been the case that Venus did indeed rise in the morning in exactly the position in which we saw it, but that on the other hand, in the position which is in fact occupied by Venus in the evening, Venus was not there, and Mars took its place. This is all counterfactual because in fact Venus is there. Now one can also imagine that in this counterfactual other

---

[14] The two confusions alleged, especially the second, are both related to the confusion of the metaphysical question of the necessity of "Hesperus is Phosphorus" with the epistemological question of its a prioricity. For if Hesperus is identified by its position in the sky in the evening, and Phosphorus by its position in the morning, an investigator may well know, in advance of empirical research, that Hesperus is Phosphorus if and only if one and the same body occupies position x in the evening and position y in the morning. The a priori material equivalence of the two statements, however, does not imply their strict (necessary) equivalence. (The same remarks apply to the case of heat and molecular motion below.) Similar remarks apply to some extent to the relationship between "Hesperus is Phosphorus" and "'Hesperus' and 'Phosphorus' name the same thing." A confusion that also operates is, of course, the confusion between what *we* say of a counterfactual situation and how people *in* that situation would have described it; this confusion, too, is probably related to the confusion between a prioricity and necessity.

possible world, the earth would have been inhabited by people and that they should have used the names 'Phosphorus' for Venus in the morning and 'Hesperus' for Mars in the evening. Now, this is all very good, but would it be a situation in which Hesperus was not Phosphorus? Of course, it is a situation in which people would have been able to *say*, truly, "Hesperus is not Phosphorus"; but we are supposed to describe things in our language, not in theirs. So let us describe it in our language. Well, how could it actually happen that Venus would not be in that position in the evening? For example, let us say that there is some comet that comes around every evening and yanks things over a little bit. (That would be a very simple scientific way of imagining it: not really too simple—that is very hard to imagine actually.) It just happens to come around every evening, and things get yanked over a bit. Mars gets yanked over to the very position where Venus is, then the comet yanks things back to their normal position in the morning. Thinking of this planet which we now call 'Phosphorus', what should we say? Well, we can say that the comet passes it and yanks Phosphorus over so that it is not in the position normally occupied by Phosphorus in the evening. If we do say this, and really use 'Phosphorus' as the name of a planet, then we have to say that, under such circumstances, Phosphorus in the evening would not be in the position where we, in fact, saw it; or alternatively, Hesperus in the evening would not be in the position in which we, in fact, saw it. We might say that under such circumstances, we would not have called Hesperus 'Hesperus' because Hesperus would have been in a different position. But that still would not make Phosphorus different from Hesperus; but what would then be the case instead is that Hesperus would have been in a different position from the position it in fact is and, perhaps, not in such a position that people would have called it 'Hesperus'. But that would not be a situation in which Phosphorus would not have been Hersperus.

Let us take another example which may be clearer. Suppose someone uses 'Tully' to refer to the Roman orator who denounced Cataline and uses the name 'Cicero' to refer to the man whose works he had to study in third-year Latin in high school. Of course, he may not know in advance that the very same man who denounced Cataline wrote these works, and that is a contingent statement. But the fact that this statement is contingent should not make us think that the statement that Cicero is Tully, if it is true, and it is in fact true, is contingent. Suppose, for example, that Cicero actually did denounce Cataline, but thought that this political achievement was so great that he should not bother writing any literary works. Would we say that these would be circumstances under which he would not have been Cicero? It seems to me that the answer is no, that instead we would say that, under such circumstances, Cicero would not have written any literary works. It is not a necessary property of Cicero—the way the shadow follows the man—that he should have written certain works; we can easily imagine a situation in which Shakespeare would not have written the works of Shakespeare, or one in which Cicero would not have written the works of Cicero.

What may be the case is that we *fix the reference* of the term 'Cicero' by use of some descriptive phrase, such as 'the author of these works'. But once we have this reference fixed, we then use the name 'Cicero' *rigidly* to designate the man who in fact we have identified by his authorship of these works. We do not use it to designate whoever would have written these works in place of Cicero, if someone else wrote them. It might have been the case that the man who wrote these works was not the man who denounced Cataline. Cassius might have written these works. But we would not then say that Cicero would have been Cassius, unless we were speaking in a very loose and metaphorical way. We would say that Cicero, whom we may have identified and come to know by his works, would not have written them, and that someone else, say Cassius, would have written them in his place.

Such examples are not grounds for thinking that identity statements are contingent. To take them as such grounds is to misconstrue the relation between a *name* and a *description used to fix its reference,* to take them to be *synonyms.* Even if we fix the reference of such a name as 'Cicero' as the man who wrote such and such works, in speaking of counterfactual situations, when we speak of Cicero, we do not then speak of whoever in such counterfactual situations *would* have written such and such works, but rather of Cicero, whom we have identified by the contingent property that he is the man who in fact, that is, in the actual world, wrote certain works.[15]

I hope this is reasonably clear in a brief compass. Now, actually I have been presupposing something I do not really believe to be, in general, true. Let us suppose that we do fix the reference of a name by a description. Even if we do so, we do not then make the name *synonymous* with the description, but instead we use the name *rigidly* to refer to the object so named, even in talking about counterfactual situations where the thing named would not satisfy the description in question. Now, this is what I think in fact is true for those cases of naming where the reference is fixed by description. But, in fact, I also think, contrary to most recent theorists, that the reference of names is rarely or almost never fixed by means of description. And by this I do not just mean what Searle says: "It's not

---

[15] If someone protests, regarding the lectern, that it *could* after all have *turned out* to have been made of ice, and therefore could have been made of ice, I would reply that what he really means is that *a lectern* could have looked just like this one, and have been placed in the same position as this one, and yet have been made of ice. In short, I could have been in the *same epistemological situation* in relation to *a lectern made of ice* as I actually am in relation to *this* lectern. In the main text, I have argued that the same reply should be given to protests that Hesperus could have turned out to be other than Phosphorus, or Cicero other than Tully. Here, then, the notion of 'counterpart' comes into its own. For it is not this table, but an epistemic 'counterpart', which was hewn from ice; not Hesperus-Phosphorus-Venus, but two distinct counterparts thereof, in two of the roles Venus actually plays (that of Evening Star and Morning Star), which are different. Precisely because of this fact, it is not *this table* which could have been made of ice. Statements about the modal properties of *this table* never refer to counterparts. However, if someone confuses the epistemological and the metaphysical problems, he will be well on the way to the counterpart theory Lewis and others have advocated.

a single description, but rather a cluster, a family of properties which fixes the reference." I mean that properties in this sense are not used *at all*. But I do not have the time to go into this here. So, let us suppose that at least one half of prevailing views about naming is true, that the reference is fixed by descriptions. Even were that true, the name would not be synonymous with the description, but would be used to *name* an object which we pick out by the contingent fact that it satisfies a certain description. And so, even though we can imagine a case where the man who wrote these works would not have been the man who denounced Cataline, we should not say that that would be a case in which Cicero would not have been Tully. We should say that it is a case in which Cicero did not write these works, but rather that Cassius did. And the identity of Cicero and Tully still holds.

Let me turn to the case of heat and the motion of molecules. Here surely is a case that is contingent identity! Recent philosophy has emphasized this again and again. So, if it is a case of contingent identity, then let us imagine under what circumstances it would be false. Now, concerning this statement I hold that the circumstances philosophers apparently have in mind as circumstances under which it would have been false are not in fact such circumstances. First, of course, it is argued that "Heat is the motion of molecules" is an a posteriori judgment; scientific investigation might have turned out otherwise. As I said before, this shows nothing against the view that it is necessary—at least if I am right. But here, surely, people had very specific circumstances in mind under which, so they thought, the judgment that heat is the motion of molecules would have been false. What were these circumstances? One can distill them out of the fact that we found out empirically that heat is the motion of molecules. How was this? What did we find out first when we found out that heat is the motion of molecules? There is a certain external phenomenon which we can sense by the sense of touch, and it produces a sensation which we call "the sensation of heat." We then discover that the external phenomenon which produces this sensation, which we sense, by means of our sense of touch, is in fact that of molecular agitation in the thing that we touch, a very high degree of molecular agitation. So, it might be thought, to imagine a situation in which heat would not have been the motion of molecules, we need only imagine a situation in which we would have had the very same sensation and it would have been produced by something other than the motion of molecules. Similarly, if we wanted to imagine a situation in which light was not a stream of photons, we could imagine a situation in which we were sensitive to something else in exactly the same way, producing what we call visual experiences, though not through a stream of photons. To make the case stronger, or to look at another side of the coin, we could also consider a situation in which we *are* concerned with the motion of molecules but in which such motion does not give us the sensation of heat. And it might also have happened that we, or, at least, the creatures inhabiting this planet, might have been so constituted that, let us say, an increase in the motion of molecules did not give us this sensation but that, on the contrary, a slowing down of the molecules did give us the very same sensation. This would be a situation, so it might be thought, in which heat would not be the motion of molecules, or, more precisely, in which temperature would not be mean molecular kinetic energy.

But I think it would not be so. Let us think about the situation again. First, let us think about it in the actual world. Imagine right now the world invaded by a number of Martians, who do indeed get the very sensation that we call "the sensation of heat" when they feel some ice which has slow molecular motion, and who do not get a sensation of heat—in fact, maybe just the reverse—when they put their hand near a fire which causes a lot of molecular agitation. Would we say, "Ah, this casts some doubt on heat being the motion of molecules, because there are these other people who don't get the same sensation"? Obviously not, and no one would think so. We would say instead that the Martians somehow feel the very sensation we get when we feel heat when they feel cold and that they do not get a sensation of heat when they feel heat. But now let us think of a counterfactual situation.[16] Suppose the earth had from the very beginning been inhabited by such creatures. First, imagine it inhabited by no creatures at all: then there is no one to feel any sensations of heat. But we would not say that under such circumstances it would necessarily be the case that heat did not exist; we would say that heat might have existed, for example, if there were fires that heated up the air.

Let us suppose the laws of physics were not very different: Fires do heat up the air. Then there would have been heat even though there were no creatures around to feel it. Now let us suppose evolution takes place, and life is created, and there are some creatures around. But they are not like us, they are more like the Martians. Now would we say that heat has suddenly turned to cold, because of the way the creatures of this planet sense it? No, I think we should describe this situation as a situation in which, though the creatures on this planet got our sensation of heat, they did not get it when they were exposed to heat. They got it when they were exposed to cold. And that is something we can surely well imagine. We can imagine it just as we can imagine our planet being invaded by creatures of this sort. Think of it in two steps. First there is a stage where there are no creatures at all, and one can certainly imagine the planet still having both heat and cold, though no one is around to sense it. Then the planet comes through an evolutionary process to be peopled with beings of different neural

---

[16] Isn't the situation I just described also counterfactual? At least it may well be, if such Martians never in fact invade. Strictly speaking, the distinction I wish to draw compares how we *would* speak *in* a (possibly counterfactual) situation, *if* it obtained, and how we *do* speak *of* a counterfactual situation, knowing that it does not obtain—i.e., the distinction between the language we would have used in a situation and the language we *do* use to describe it. (Consider the description: "Suppose we all spoke German." This description is in English.) The former case can be made vivid by imagining the counterfactual situation to be actual.

structure from ourselves. Then these creatures could be such that they were insensitive to heat; they did not feel it in the way we do; but on the other hand, they felt cold in much the same way that we feel heat. But still, heat would be heat, and cold would be cold. And particularly, then, this goes in no way against saying that in this counterfactual situation heat would still *be* the molecular motion, *be* that which is produced by fires, and so on, just as it would have been if there had been no creatures on the planet at all. Similarly, we could imagine that the planet was inhabited by creatures who got visual sensations when there were sound waves in the air. We should not therefore say, "Under such circumstances, sound would have been light." Instead we should say, "The planet was inhabited by creatures who were in some sense visually sensitive to sound, and maybe even visually sensitive to light." If this is correct, it can still be and will still be a necessary truth that heat is the motion of molecules and that light is a stream of photons.

To state the view succinctly: we use both the terms 'heat' and 'the motion of molecules' as rigid designators for a certain external phenomenon. Since heat is in fact the motion of molecules, and the designators are rigid, by the argument I have given here, it is going to be *necessary* that heat is the motion of molecules. What gives us the illusion of contingency is the fact we have identified the heat by the contingent fact that there happen to be creatures on this planet—(namely, ourselves) who are sensitive to it in a certain way, that is, who are sensitive to the motion of molecules or to heat—these are one and the same thing. And this is contingent. So we use the description, 'that which causes such and such sensations, or that which we sense in such and such a way', to identify heat. But in using this fact we use a contingent property of heat, just as we use the contingent property of Cicero as having written such and such works to identify him. We then use the terms 'heat' in the one case and 'Cicero' in the other *rigidly* to designate the objects for which they stand. And of course the term 'the motion of molecules' is rigid; it always stands for the motion of molecules, never for any other phenomenon. So, as Bishop Butler said, "everything is what it is and not another thing." Therefore, "Heat is the motion of molecules" will be necessary, not contingent, and one only has the *illusion* of contingency in the way one could have the illusion of contingency in thinking that this table might have been made of ice. We might think one could imagine it, but if we try, we can see on reflection that what we are really imagining is just there being another lectern in this very position here which was in fact made of ice. The fact that we may identify this lectern by being the object we see and touch in such and such a position is something else.

Now how does this relate to the problem of mind and body? It is usually held that this is a contingent identity statement just like "Heat is the motion of molecules." That cannot be. It cannot be a contingent identity statement just like "Heat is the motion of molecules" because, if I am right, "Heat is the motion of molecules" is not a contingent identity statement. Let us look at this statement. For example, "My being in pain at such and such a time is my being in such and such a brain state at such and such a time," or, "Pain in general is such and such a neural (brain) state."

This is held to be contingent on the following grounds. First, we can imagine the brain state existing though there is no pain at all. It is only a scientific fact that whenever we are in a certain brain state we have a pain. Second, one might imagine a creature being in pain, but not being in any specified brain state at all, maybe not having a brain at all. People even think, at least prima facie, though they may be wrong, that they can imagine totally disembodied creatures, at any rate certainly not creatures with bodies anything like our own. So it seems that we can imagine definite circumstances under which this relationship would have been false. Now, if these circumstances are circumstances, notice that we cannot deal with them simply by saying that this is just an illusion, something we can apparently imagine, but in fact cannot in the way we thought erroneously that we could imagine a situation in which heat was not the motion of molecules. Because although we can say that we pick out heat contingently by the contingent property that it affects us in such and such a way, we cannot similarly say that we pick out pain contingently by the fact that it affects us in such and such a way. On such a picture there would be the brain state, and we pick it out by the contingent fact that it affects us as pain. Now that might be true of the brain state, but it cannot be true of the pain. The experience itself has to be *this experience*, and I cannot say that it is a contingent property of the pain I now have that it is a pain.[17] In fact, it would seem that both the terms, 'my pain' and 'my being in such and such a brain state' are, first of all, both rigid designators. That is, whenever anything is such and such a pain, it is essentially that very object, namely, such and such a pain, and wherever anything is such and such a brain

---

[17] The most popular identity theories advocated today explicitly fail to satisfy this simple requirement. For these theories usually hold that a mental state is a brain state, and that what makes the brain state into a mental state is its 'causal role', the fact that it tends to produce certain behavior (as intentions produce actions, or pain, pain behavior) and to be produced by certain stimuli (e.g., pain, by pinpricks). If the relations between the brain state and its causes and effects are regarded as contingent, then *being such-and-such-a-mental-state* is a contingent property of the brain state. Let X be a pain. The causal-role identity theorist holds (1) that X is a brain state, (2) that the fact that X is a pain is to be analyzed (roughly) as the fact that X is produced by certain stimuli and produces certain behavior. The fact mentioned in (2) is, of course, regarded as contingent; the brain state X might well exist and not tend to produce the appropriate behavior in the absence of other conditions. Thus (1) and (2) assert that a certain pain X might have existed, yet not have been a pain. This seems to me self-evidently absurd. Imagine any pain: is it possible that *it itself* could have existed, yet not have been a pain?

If $X = Y$, then X and Y share all properties, including modal properties. If X is a pain and Y the corresponding brain state, then *being a pain* is an essential property of X, and *being a brain state* is an essential property of Y. If the correspondence relation is, in fact, identity, then it must be *necessary* of Y that it corresponds to a pain, and *necessary* of X that it correspond to a brain state, indeed to this particular brain state, Y. Both assertions seem false; it *seems* clearly possible that X should have existed without the corresponding brain state; or that the brain state should have existed without being felt as pain. Identity theorists cannot, contrary to their almost universal present practice, accept these intuitions; they must deny them, and explain them away. This is none too easy a thing to do.

state, it is essentially that very object, namely, such and such a brain state. So both of these are rigid designators. One cannot say this pain might have been something else, some other state. These are both rigid designators.

Second, the way we would think of picking them out—namely, the pain by its being an experience of a certain sort, and the brain state by its being the state of a certain material object, being of such and such molecular configuration—both of these pick out their objects essentially and not accidentally, that is, they pick them out by essential properties. Whenever the molecules *are* in this configuration, we *do* have such and such a brain state. Whenever you feel *this*, you do have a pain. So it seems that the identity theorist is in some trouble, for, since we have two rigid designators, the identity statement in question is necessary. Because they pick out their objects essentially, we cannot say the case where you seem to imagine the identity statement false is really an illusion like the illusion one gets in the case of heat and molecular motion, because that illusion depended on the fact that we pick out heat by a certain contingent property. So there is very little room to maneuver; perhaps none.[18] The identity theorist, who holds that pain is the brain state, also has to hold that it necessarily is the brain state. He therefore cannot concede, but has to deny, that there would have been situations under which one would have had pain but not the corresponding brain state. Now usually in arguments on the identity theory, this is very far from being denied. In fact, it is conceded from the outset by the materialist as well as by his opponent. He says, "Of course, it *could* have been the case that we had pains without the brain states. It is a contingent identity." But that cannot be. He has to hold that we are under some illusion in thinking that we can imagine that there could have been pains without brain states. And the only model I can think of for what the illusion might be, or at least the model given by the analogy the materialists

---

[18] A brief restatement of the argument may be helpful here. If "pain" and "C-fiber stimulation" are rigid designators of phenomena, one who identifies them must regard the identity as necessary. How can this necessity be reconciled with the apparent fact that C-fiber stimulation might have turned out not to be correlated with pain at all? We might try to reply by analogy to the case of heat and molecular motion; the latter identity, too, is necessary, yet someone may believe that, before scientific investigation showed otherwise, molecular motion might have turned out not to be heat. The reply is, of course, that what really is possible is that people (or some rational or sentient beings) could have been in the *same epistemic situation* as we actually are, and identify *a phenomenon* in the same way we identify heat, namely, by feeling it by the sensation we call "the sensation of heat," without the phenomenon being molecular motion. Further, the beings might not have been sensitive to molecular motion (i.e., to heat) by any neural mechanism whatsoever. It is impossible to explain the apparent possibility of C-fiber stimulations not having been pain in the same way. Here, too, we would have to suppose that we could have been in the same epistemological situation, and identify something in the same way we identify pain, without its corresponding to C-fiber stimulation. But the way we identify pain is by feeling it, and if a C-fiber stimulation could have occurred without our feeling any pain, then the C-fiber stimulation would have occurred without there *being* any pain, contrary to the necessity of the identity. The trouble is that although 'heat' is a rigid designator, heat is picked out by the contingent property of its being felt in a certain way; pain, on the other hand, is picked out by an essential (indeed necessary and sufficient) property. For a sensation to be *felt* as pain is for it to *be* pain.

themselves suggest, namely, heat and molecular motion, simply does not work in this case. So the materialist is up against a very stiff challenge. He has to show that these things we think we can see to be possible are in fact not possible. He has to show that these things which we can imagine are not in fact things we can imagine. And that requires some very different philosophical argument from the sort which has been given in the case of heat and molecular motion. And it would have to be a deeper and subtler argument than I can fathom and subtler than has ever appeared in any materialist literature that I have read. So the conclusion of this investigation would be that the analytical tools we are using go against the identity thesis and so go against the general thesis that mental states are just physical states.[19]

The next topic would be my own solution to the mind-body problem, but that I do not have.

---

[19] All arguments against the identity theory which rely on the necessity of identity, or on the notion of essential property, are, of course, inspired by Descartes' argument for his dualism. The earlier arguments which superficially were rebutted by the analogies of heat and molecular motion, and the bifocals inventor who was also Postmaster General, had such an inspiration: and so does my argument here. R. Albritton and M. Slote have informed me that they independently have attempted to give essentialist arguments against the identity theory, and probably others have done so as well.

The simplest Cartesian argument can perhaps be restated as follows: Let 'A' be a *name* (rigid designator) of Descartes' body. Then Descartes argues that since he could exist even if A did not, $\Diamond$(Descartes $\neq$ A), hence Descartes $\neq$ A. Those who have accused him of a modal fallacy have forgotten that 'A' is rigid. His argument is valid, and his conclusion is correct, provided its (perhaps dubitable) premise is accepted. On the other hand, provided that Descartes is regarded as having ceased to exist upon his death, "Descartes $\neq$ A" can be established without the use of a modal argument; for if so, no doubt A survived Descartes when A was a corpse. Thus A had a property (existing at a certain time) which Descartes did not. The same argument can establish that a statue is not the hunk of stone, or the congery of molecules, of which it is composed. Mere non-identity, then, may be a weak conclusion. (See D. Wiggins, *Philosophical Review*, LXXVII [1968], 90ff.) The Cartesian modal argument, however, surely can be deployed to maintain relevant stronger conclusions as well.

2

On Two Paradoxes of Knowledge*

I suppose that we have all heard the puzzle about the surprise execution or the surprise examination. I will state the paradox in terms of the examination; the execution, of course, puts the situation in more dramatic colors.[1]

The paradox can be stated in the following way. A teacher announces that he will give an examination within the month. Examinations are always given at noon. He also announces that the exam will be a surprise exam: no student will know on the day before the exam is given that it will be given the next day. A student can then reason as follows:

The teacher, if he intends to fulfill his announced promise, cannot give the exam on the very last day. If he did, after noon had passed on the previous day, we (the students) would know that only the last day was left and that it had to be the day of the examination. This would be a plain contradiction of the announcement that it was to be a surprise exam, so that day can be crossed off the calendar. But then it cannot be given on the second-to-last day either because, after noon of the day before has passed and the exam still has not been given, we will realize that only two days are left, and that since the

---

* The present paper is based on a transcript of a recorded lecture given at Cambridge University to the Moral Sciences Club in 1972. The transcript appears to be known at least to B. Phil. students at Oxford, where it has been listed as part of their syllabus. The conversational tone of the paper, as in some other publications of mine, may sometimes reflect its origins. I have made changes and additions and included an appendix, but my solution to the surprise-exam paradox remains as it was presented in 1972 (and probably even earlier elsewhere).

[1] We now have in Sorensen (1988a: ch. 7) a history of the origins of this puzzle. Sorensen goes through much of the philosophical literature on the subject, including early occurrences. But also, basing himself on others whom he cites in the beginning of the chapter, Sorensen traces it to an actual civil defense exercise in Sweden during World War II (sometime in 1943–44) that was to be held within the week on a day not to be known in advance. A Swedish mathematician, Lennart Ekbom, detected a problem. His role in originating the paradox has been lost to the subsequent philosophical literature, but it is mentioned in some sources Sorensen cites.

Although when I gave the talk I appear to have been aware only of the hanging and examination versions, in Quine (1953) a surprise air-raid drill version is explicitly mentioned in the first paragraph, and this may have its origin in the actual event. More important, the date 1943–44 would appear to establish the surprise paradox as the earliest "backward induction" paradox, earlier than the (finitely) iterated prisoner's dilemma and Selten's chain-store paradox, both well-known to game theorists and probably to economists in general. I don't make any claims here as to how to analyze these.

last day is ruled out, the exam must be given on the second-to-last day. But then we would know in advance that that is the day of the exam, which is again a contradiction.

The student can continue the same reasoning backward: as soon as she crosses out one day from the calendar, the last remaining day is as if it were the last day, and so it can be ruled out by the same type of reasoning. There will, finally, be no days left. The student is then in a position to conclude that either the exam will not be given or it will not be a surprise.

As I said before, this problem is sometimes presented in terms of the hangman or judge who announces the execution of a prisoner under the same conditions. I wanted to present the puzzle as concerned with teachers and examinations because it should be realized that this is an everyday occurrence. Teachers *do* announce surprise examinations and no such contradictions seem to arise: it does not seem impossible for a teacher to fulfill his or her promise to give a surprise examination.[2]

It is interesting that this kind of problem is discussed as if it were a philosophical problem at all. How philosophical it actually is depends on whatever philosophical morals we may draw from it. Graham Greene classifies his works into novels, entertainments, and some other works: a novel is supposed to be a more serious work, but the entertainments are often the best. A problem like this might be classified as an entertainment in this sense. But it can have aspects of a "novel" if conclusions concerning our basic concepts of knowledge may be drawn from it. Here, more so than with typical philosophical problems, we are in the kind of "intellectual cramp" that Wittgenstein describes—one in which all the facts seem to be before us, there does not seem to be any new information to be gained, and yet we don't quite know what is going wrong with our picture of the problem.

I once did the following "scientific experiment," which can be a model for the problem. The experimenter announces to the subject that he has a deck of cards (which is finite)—it might be the whole deck or just part of it, but it includes the ace of spades. The cards are going to be turned over in order one by one, and the experimenter further tells the subject that he (the subject) will not know in advance when the ace of spades will turn up.[3]

Now suppose the deck consists of only one card. The experimenter says: "This card is the ace of spades, but you will not know which card it is until it has been turned over." The subject will think that this is obvious nonsense. Many people who have discussed the surprise-exam paradox have assumed that the significant

---

[2] We all know that in contemporary death penalty jurisprudence people are often not sure when they will be executed—last-minute appeals and the like make the execution date uncertain. But sadistic judges who announce that they have chosen a "surprise" date to execute a prisoner, are, I hope, very rare.

[3] I really think this should be done in a serious psychological laboratory; I did it as a student in college with a fellow student. One can try variations on the number of cards, and also vary whether subjects have heard of the "surprise exam" problem before the card experiment, or whether they have not been told about it before (but may or may not start going through the reasoning themselves during the experiment).

transition comes between the cases of one and two days (or rather, between ruling out the last day and the second-to-last day, as long as there are two or more). Maybe in some sense this is right. But suppose now that there are two cards in the deck, the ace of spades and another one, and the experimenter again announces: "You will not know in advance when the ace of spades will be turned over." When I tried the experiment, the subject,[4] who had heard of the paradox, reacted along the following lines: "There is still something very strange about this announcement. If you have put the ace on the bottom, I will not be surprised after you have turned up the first card. So, if you really mean to do what you say, you can't have put the ace on the bottom. But now I have proved that it must be the top card, and so again will not be surprised. I *do* know in advance."

Consider the case where all fifty-two cards, or at least a large number, are in the deck. Imagine that the experimenter, without telling the subject where it is, assures the subject that he has put the ace somewhere in the deck, and that the subject will not know in advance when the ace will come up if the cards are turned up one by one. Can the experimenter guarantee this? It seems clear that he can, say, by putting the ace somewhere in the middle.[5]

The subject can still go through the same kind of reasoning as in the case of the two cards. It *seems* that the reasoning may be generalized. However, it sounds very *un*convincing in this case. One therefore gets the impression that the reasoning gets weaker and weaker the more cards there are. This in itself is strange because it is the same piece of reasoning applied again and again.

Of course we are familiar with this kind of phenomenon from the paradox of the heap: if someone has only £1 to his or her name, she is poor; and if someone with only £N to his or her name is poor, so is someone with just £(N+1). Therefore, by mathematical induction, no matter how many pounds she has, she

---

[4] The subject was Richard Speier. If my memory is right, we were both undergraduates (so about 1960). I now (2009) find that Ayer (1973) mentions a card model, but it differs somewhat from the original problem, as in the case of the next footnote (though it is not quite the same as that one either).

[5] In the original version of this lecture I imagined that the experimenter put the ace somewhere in the middle right in front of the subject. But this is not the appropriate model for the examination version. Though no doubt the subject will not know in advance when the ace will turn up, neither will the experimenter. In the original examination problem the teacher has decided on a particular day to give the surprise exam, which makes the situation very different. If the experimenter acts as I described in the earlier version, the last card is excluded all right, but the reasoning of the surprise-exam paradox is superfluous, since everyone sees that the ace has been inserted somewhere in the middle. Similarly for the second-to-the-last card, and so on. (Actually, in the same original version, I eventually mentioned this point of disanalogy. But then I shouldn't have introduced this procedure as if it were an analogue in the first place). Exactly where the exclusion stops is somewhat indeterminate, and in contrast with what I say about the problem below in the text, something like vagueness may be involved. But here, whether or not it applies elsewhere (and I find the view rather dubious in general), it would be vagueness only in the sense of something like the now well-known characterization of Timothy Williamson (1994), since, after all, the card is in some definite place. Its exact position is simply unknown to both people, and the vagueness is merely epistemic (though in this case they could eventually find out the card's location).

is poor. It is a familiar philosophical problem that there must be something wrong with this, but it is hard to say exactly what. The heap/poverty problem involves reasoning with a vague predicate, but it is not clear that the issue in the present problem involves any question of vagueness.

What are the premises of the reasoning in this problem? The student is not to know on the day before the exam that it will be given. Let there be N days in which the exam may be given and let E_i mean that the exam will be given on day i. The teacher announces that the exam will be given on one of the first N days:

(1) E_i for some i, $1 \leq i \leq N$ (equivalently, $E_1 \vee \ldots \vee E_N$)

The exam is going to be given on exactly one day; that is, it is not the case that it is going to be given on two distinct days:

(2) $\neg(E_i \wedge E_j)$ for any $i \neq j$, $1 \leq i, j \leq N$

Then there is the announcement that the examination is to be a surprise. Let $K_i(p)$, for any statement "p," mean that the student knows on day i that p is true. So we can say that it is not the case that the student knows on day $i-1$ that the exam will be given on day i:

(3) $\neg K_{i-1}(E_i)$ for each i, $1 \leq i \leq N$

If i is 1, then $i-1$ is 0, which means that she does not know in advance of the whole series (that is, before the first day) that the exam will be given on the first day.

We now have an additional premise. If the exam has not been given on one of the first $i-1$ days, then the student knows this on day $i-1$, as soon as noon has passed:

(4) $(\neg E_1 \wedge \neg E_2 \wedge \ldots \wedge \neg E_{i-1}) \supset K_{i-1}(\neg E_1 \wedge \neg E_2 \wedge \ldots \wedge \neg E_{i-1})$
for each i, $1 \leq i \leq N$

Given premise (2), we can conclude that if the exam is going to be held on the ith day, it cannot have been given on any previous day. Hence, it follows from (4) and (2) that if the exam is to be given on the ith day, the student will know on the $(i-1)$th day that the exam has not been given on any of the first $i-1$ days:

(5) $E_i \supset K_{i-1}(\neg E_1 \wedge \neg E_2 \wedge \ldots \wedge \neg E_{i-1})$ for each i, $1 \leq i \leq N$

So, these are the premises that are alleged to lead to a paradox. There may be some additional premises about knowledge itself that are required to carry out the reasoning. Obvious premises include: if a student knows any statement on day i, then it is true:

(6) $K_i(p) \supset p$ for each i, $1 \leq i \leq N$

Also, we may require the "deductive closure of knowledge": if a student knows that p on day i, and knows that if p then q on day i, then she knows that q on day i:

(7) $(K_i(p) \wedge K_i(p \supset q)) \supset K_i(q)$ for each $i, 1 \leq i \leq N$

This premise is, in general, false—people may know all the premises of a deductive argument without knowing the conclusion. Mathematics would be a trivial subject if everyone's knowledge were deductively closed. It would be the easy way out, as the president of the United States would say,[6] to solve this problem by denying such a premise; but we can make the simplifying assumption that these particular students are clever enough to draw all the consequences of the things they know. This is not what is in question.[7]

We must also assume that, on any day, a student knows all principles of logic, including all propositional tautologies. This, again, is not true of students in practice, as anyone who has given a logic course knows. However, we can assume that it is true of these students, so they may do any kind of deductive reasoning. Let us symbolize this schema as follows:

(8) Taut $\supset K_i$(Taut) for each $i, 1 \leq i \leq N$

Can we now deduce a contradiction—that the exam cannot be given by surprise at all, which contradicts premise (1)—from all these premises? We start the reasoning by trying to show that the exam cannot be given on the last day. This reasoning must try to state that if the exam were to be given on the Nth day, the student will know on the $(N–1)$th day that the exam will be given on the Nth day (the last day), thus showing by *reductio ad absurdum* that the exam cannot be held on the Nth day. By substituting N for i in premise (5), we find that the student knows that the exam has not been given on one of the first $N–1$ days *on the $(N–1)$th day*. She knows from premise (1) that it must be given on one of the first N days, and so concludes on day $N–1$ that it must be given on the Nth day (i.e., $K_{N-1}(E_N)$). But this is an immediate contradiction of the relevant instance of premise (3) (viz. $\neg K_{N-1}(E_N)$). She then concludes that her initial hypothesis, (E_N), has been disproved by *reductio ad absurdum*, and thus that the exam cannot be given on the last day.

---

[6] The president was Richard Nixon when this talk was given.

[7] By the time I spoke, at least Fred Dretske (see 1970, 1971) had already denied that knowledge is always deductively closed, even for people able to make the deduction. Since then he has been followed by many others. This was supposed to protect against some problems of philosophical skepticism. But presumably these writers (who may or may not give the required restrictions) must think that only in very exceptional cases having to do with skepticism should the relevant principles of deductive closure fail. Otherwise, one person could accuse another of making the well-known fallacy of giving a valid deductive argument (from accepted premises) for his views!

I was probably unaware of Dretske's papers when I gave this lecture. However, I was fortunate enough to have Dretske in the audience when I gave a version of this lecture, and he was not only disinclined to object, but found the paper very convincing. See Chapter 7 for some discussion on this issue.

But this has a fallacy in it: all premise (1) says is that the exam will be given on one of the first N days, not that the student *knows* that fact. To reach the conclusion, we must also have the premise that the student knows on day N–1 that the exam will be given on one of the first N days (i.e., K_{N-1} (E_i) for some i, $1 \leq i \leq N$). But we cannot obtain this from our premises. This is Quine's solution to the paradox in his article "On a So-Called Paradox" (Quine 1953). (He chooses the version in which a prisoner is to be hanged.) The prisoner is supposed to know that the judge's decree that he is to be hanged will be fulfilled. But how does he know this? Maybe the judge is a liar. As Quine puts it:

It is notable that K [the prisoner] acquiesces in the conclusion (wrong, according to the fable of the Thursday hanging) that the decree will not be fulfilled. If this is a conclusion that he is prepared to accept (though wrongly) in the end as a certainty, it is an alternative which he should have been prepared to take into consideration from the beginning as a possibility.

K's fallacy may be brought into sharper relief by taking n as 1 and restoring the hanging motif. The judge tells K on Sunday afternoon that he, K, will be hanged the following noon and will remain ignorant of the fact till the intervening morning. It would be like K to protest at this point that the judge was contradicting himself. And it would be like the hangman to intrude upon K's complacency at 11.55 next morning, thus showing that the judge had said nothing more self-contradictory than the simple truth. If K had reasoned correctly, Sunday afternoon, he would have reasoned as follows. "We must distinguish four cases: first, that I shall be hanged tomorrow noon and I know it now (but I do not); second, that I shall be unhanged tomorrow noon and know it now (but I do not); third, that I shall be unhanged tomorrow noon and do not know it now; and fourth, that I shall be hanged tomorrow noon and do not know it now. The latter two alternatives are the open possibilities, and the last of all would fulfil the decree. Rather than charging the judge with self-contradiction, therefore, let me suspend judgment and hope for the best." (Quine 1953:20, 21)[8]

Quine's solution to this problem has never seemed to me to be quite satisfactory: consider again the card experiment. It does seem strange, even though not literally contradictory, to take a card (face down) and say, "This is the ace of

---

[8] Two things to add, summarizing Quine's discussion. First, Quine originally discusses the case of many days and argues that the idea that the decree cannot be fulfilled if the hanging takes place on the last day is wrong; he also discusses it in a more abstract way—hence the phrase "restoring the hanging motif." He then goes on to draw the more extreme conclusion quoted in the text, that is, that even in the case of only one day there is no problem in the judge's announcement.

Second, one might elaborate on Quine's remark that "if this is a conclusion that he is prepared to accept (though wrongly) in the end as a certainty, it is an alternative which he should have been prepared to take into consideration from the beginning as a possibility" (1953:65). He says: "The tendency to be deceived by the puzzle is perhaps traceable to a wrong association of K's argument with *reductio ad absurdum*. It is perhaps supposed that K is quite properly assuming fulfillment of the decree, for the space of his argument, in order to prove that the decree will not be fulfilled" (66). Quine goes on to say that the argument of the puzzle requires not only the supposition that the decree will be fulfilled, but that the prisoner *knows* that it will be. This destroys any idea that this is a valid *reductio ad absurdum* argument, where only the weaker assumption would be allowed.

spades, but you do not know that this is the ace of spades."[9] In the second half of my utterance, am I inviting you to suppose that I cannot be trusted? Wasn't I communicating knowledge to you in the first half? Indeed, in this case (analogous to the one with only one day in the examination or hanging period), the hearer will not know what to believe, given the strangeness of the performance, and therefore would not know, though the strangeness does not persist if there are many cards.

Quine says that the fallacy derives from the fact that the prisoner does not *know* that the judge is telling the truth, or that the student does not *know* that there will be an exam given at all. But often, I think, you do *know* something simply because a good teacher has told you so. If a teacher were to announce a surprise exam to be given within a month, a student who did badly could not excuse herself by saying that she did not *know* that there was going to be an exam. If there is only one day, we have the anomalous situation I have just mentioned. But if there are many days, then it is natural to give the students knowledge on the basis of what the teacher tells them.

Clearly, we are justified in changing premise (1) to allow that a student *knows* from the beginning that an exam will be given on one of the first N days.

(1') $K_0(E_i)$ for some $i, 1 \leq i \leq N$ (in other words $K_0(E_i \vee ... \vee E_N)$)

Similarly, we may allow that she *knows* at the beginning that the exam will not be given on two days and that it will be a surprise:

(2') $K_0(\neg(E_i \wedge E_j))$ for any $i \neq j, 1 \leq i, j \leq N$

(3') $K_0(\neg K_{i-1}(E_i))$ for each $i, 1 \leq i \leq N$

Can we now derive the paradox? We need two further premises. First, that if a student knows a statement on day i, she knows it on any later day:

(9) $K_i(p) \supset K_j(p)$ for any i, j such that $0 \leq i \leq j \leq N$

On its face this simply means that we are assuming that the student does not forget anything that she knows. Second, we need (though its use could perhaps be avoided) what has been called the double-K principle: that if a student knows on day i that p, then the student knows on day i that she knows on day i that p:

(10) $K_i(p) \supset K_i(K_i(p))$ for any $i, 0 \leq i \leq N$

---

[9] See Moore's paradox ("p, but it is not the case that I believe that p"). As is well known, statements of this form are not contradictory, and may sometimes even be true, but anyone who utters one has made a strange performance. The case is similar here, with appropriate changes. Suppose someone asked me my name and I said, "It is Saul Kripke, but you still don't know what my name is." This may not literally be a contradiction, but is obviously very odd.

This latter is a controversial principle in the logic of knowledge; so one might think that that is what is going wrong and try to avoid the use of it. I will, however, make a few preliminary remarks about it. Is it the case that if someone knows something, she knows that she knows it? There have been two attitudes about this in recent philosophy. One is that all that is meant by knowing that you know something is that you know it. This sort of extreme attitude is stated, according to Hintikka (1962:108–10), by Schopenhauer, and is further argued by Hintikka himself. At the opposite extreme is the view[10] that, maybe we know many things: that Nixon is president of the United States, that the Russians had a revolution in 1917, that the sun is mostly gas—things which epistemological skeptics alone would deny. We do not, however, really *know* that we know them because that would involve a very high degree of certainty. Maybe our evidence does not constitute knowledge (though in fact it does, I guess, if we are lucky). To know that you know something is to perform a very great epistemological feat, which is not comparable to just knowing it—since you can't distinguish knowledge from mere justified belief in something false. It is very hard to adjudicate between these two positions, or even find a position in between, because "I know that I know that p" is not a sentence that we often find on our lips.

I would suggest the following in favor not of the principle being true, but of its being *nearly* true: true enough for all practical purposes. Suppose I know something—for example, I know that Nixon is the president of the United States now. The following is an argument for the double-K principle in this instance. Certainly *you* (in the audience) know that I know that Nixon is the president. For one thing, I have just said this, presumably basing my statement on newspapers, television, and so on. Even if I had not said this, if you knew me, you would presume that I knew the fact on the same basis. Surely, I am not normally in a worse position than *you* to judge this matter. Is there a principle of privileged non-self-access here? I would suppose that normally, if someone else can know that I know something, then I myself can know it at least on the same basis, though perhaps I do not need to use this basis. (I do not myself *need* to argue: well, I have said that Nixon is president, I read the newspapers, and so on; but if you can know that I know this on such a basis, it would be surprising that I am singularly worse off.)

In fact, the argument can be strengthened. For I know that you know that I know that Nixon is president. After all, I just said so. But knowledge implies truth. So if I know that you know something, I must know it myself. Hence, I know that I know that Nixon is president.

---

[10] The truth is that now (in 2009) I am not sure who in "recent philosophy" (i.e., in 1972) I might have had in mind as holding this opposite extreme. One could certainly imagine the plausibility that someone might hold such a view. However, the claim that knowing implies knowing that one knows can certainly be doubted, and has been doubted by many philosophers.

Yet another variation: I know that everyone who reads the newspapers knows that Nixon is president, and I know that I myself read the newspapers. Therefore, I know that I must know that Nixon is president. Once again, in the case of these variations, it is artificial to suppose that I need to go through the reasoning given, but nevertheless it is valid and implies the appropriate case of the double-K principle.

No doubt there may be exceptions where arguments such as these are not applicable, but the arguments should be acceptable in a very wide range of cases. I would, however, like to distinguish myself from Hintikka and others who advocate such a principle universally and as a near tautology (in Hintikka's case, on the basis of what appears to me to be a circular argument). However, because of the arguments I have given, I believe that one should have no doubt of the principle in the present case. Therefore, I think that the fallacy does not lie here at all. We may, therefore, put any number of Ks before the premises—not only does a student know on a given day that they are true, but she also knows that she knows on that given day that they are true, and so on.

One can now derive the contradiction from these premises plus the principle we have just discussed. Yet it seems very strange that even if the announcement that the exam will be given is true, the student cannot possibly *know* that it will be: for students surely do know that such exams will be given. Let us look again at premise (9), that if a student knows something on a given day, she knows it on any later day. Is this a generally true principle of epistemology? It is true that she can forget, but this is not what is in question: we may suppose that her memory is good enough not to forget any significant detail. Then, will it be true?

Many of you will know that I have written articles on modal logic; suppose I came to one of you and sadly denied that, and claimed ("admitted") they were written by someone named "Schmidt" and that I merely signed them. Suppose I even showed you a manuscript in Schmidt's handwriting. After a certain amount of persuading you might well be convinced that I did not write any articles on modal logic. So you would not, at that later date, even believe it, let alone know it. You may say that this means that you did not *know* it at the earlier time. This may be so if I am now telling the truth and have not written any articles on modal logic. But suppose now that I was lying, as some form of English joke, and really had written the articles. You would then have been correct in your initial belief, and, assuming that you were in a good enough position to support your belief rationally, and so on, it would seem you did know this at the earlier date but were rationally persuaded to change your mind. If you wanted to argue that you did *not* know at the earlier date, then you would have to say that you do not know a certain fact if at some future date someone produces phony evidence to change your mind. Thus, what is true for you now would be vulnerable to what might happen later. I think that I would rather say that one can know something now but *lose* that knowledge at a later date on the basis of further misleading evidence. (It must be *misleading* evidence; if it were genuine, then your supposed knowledge would in fact have been mistaken belief.)

What happens in the particular case of the paradox? Let us again try to rule out the last day. We say, for the *reductio ad absurdum*, that the exam will be given on the Nth day. It will not have been given on any of the first $N-1$ days; the student therefore *knows* it will not have been given on the first $N-1$ days and, according to premise (4), knows this on day $N-1$. The student knew at the outset that it will be given on one of the first N days. So we can conclude that if she knew it was not given on one of the first $N-1$ days, then she knew that it must be given on the Nth, which contradicts premise (3). But there is a missing step in the argument, which is that just because she knows on day 0 that it will be given on one of the first N days, she must therefore know this on day $N-1$. This does not in fact follow without using premise (9), and would be false if the student later doubted that the exam was to be given at all.

Is it plausible to call this "a missing step"? Is it clear, in this case, that what the student knew on day 0 she would still know at any future date? The teacher has announced that the exam is going to be given on one of the N following days and that it is to be a surprise. What then will the students think when all the available days but one have passed? Perhaps that something has gone wrong, since, if the teacher still intends to give an exam, it will not be a surprise: they may therefore fall into doubt and say, "Look, maybe the teacher isn't intending to give us an exam now; maybe he's changed his mind." This would be a case of having had knowledge at one time but losing it at some later time. The student has the knowledge that the exam will be given at the outset, but she no longer has it at the end of the examination period. This seems to me to be fairly straightforward common sense, and so it is a fallacy to assume that the student retains this knowledge. Thus, the step of the argument which says that the last day can be ruled out is, in fact, erroneous, and so the whole argument never gets going. This is the basic fallacy in the argument.

This explanation, however, does not yield one feature of the problem which I have mentioned before—that, somehow, the more days there are, the worse the argument becomes. Perhaps we can in some way reinstate the argument by ruling out the last day. We cannot appeal to premise (9), since it is clearly false in this case. But we could add an extra premise: that the student knows, even on day $N-1$, that the exam will be given. We can make this plausible by saying that it is a rule of the school that a grade must be given for the course and that grades are always given on the basis of exams. Then the students would think on day $N-1$, when the exam still had not been given, "Something has gone wrong, but it cannot be that the teacher has decided not to give us an exam: it must be that he has decided not to bother making it a surprise."

Now we really can rule out the last day—rule it out in the sense that the premises contradict the supposition that the examination will be given on the last day, for the premises include that the exam, when given, will be a surprise. How do we rule out the second-to-last day? The intuitive reasoning is something like this: knowing that the examination will not be given on the last day, the $(N-1)$th is the last possible day left, and then we go through the very same reasoning for that day as we did for the Nth day; we therefore will not need any more premises to allow us to rule out each day one-by-one going backward. But, as we have explicitly argued so far, this is a fallacy: we have not yet concluded that anyone *knows on any particular day* that the examination will not be given on the last day; we have merely concluded that it will not *in fact* be given on the last day.

What do we need for the student to reason? We have to know that on day $N-2$ she says "I know the exam cannot be on the last day, so there is only one day left for the exam, the $(N-1)$th." Then that day may be treated as if it were a new last day, and the supposition that it will be given on that day can be ruled out as contradicting the assumption that the exam will be a surprise. But this is fallacious, as things stand, because all we know is that *in fact* the examination will not be given on the Nth day, not that the student knows it on day $N-2$ (i.e., that $K_{N-2}(\neg E_N)$). A student whose knowledge is deductively closed will know this provided that she knows (on any given day) all the premises on which that conclusion was based. What premise did we use? We demanded that the student know on day $N-1$ that the exam was still going to be given. But now we need the stronger premise that she will know on day $N-2$ that she will know on day $N-1$ that the exam is still going to be given. This is acceptable in the situation I described, where exams are a rule of the school. But another premise used was that the exam will be a surprise: that the student was not to know on day $N-1$ that the exam would be given on day N (this is the particular case that we used). For the student to use this on day $N-2$, she will have to know on day $N-2$ that she will not know on day $N-1$ that the examination will be given on day N, that is, that $K_{N-2}(\neg K_{N-1}(E_N))$. She knows this on day 0, from premise (3), but $N-2$ need not be 0. If we accept premise (9), then since she knows on day 0 that $\neg K_{N-1}(E_N)$, then she must know it on day $N-2$. Is the principle plausible in this case? Well, what does the student think on day $N-2$ if the exam has not yet been given? "There is going to be an exam—it's a rule of the school. But is it really going to be a surprise? If I *knew* it were going to be a surprise, then I would know the exam would have to be tomorrow, in which case it would not be a surprise at all. Therefore, I do not *know* that it is going to be a surprise. Maybe the teacher is going to stick to it being a surprise and maybe he is not going to bother and just give the exam on the last day." So, although the student knew at the outset that it was to be a surprise, she may not know it on day $N-2$; she may still be said to have known this at the outset, provided that it still will be a surprise—that is, that it is given on the $(N-1)$th day rather than the Nth. Again, it is premise (9) that is causing the fallacy—only now about the surprise element rather than about whether the exam will be given.

Thus we cannot use premise (9) to conclude from what the student knows initially to what she knows on day $N-2$; we would need an extra premise to say that the student still knows on day N–2 that the exam will be a surprise. When will this extra premise be plausible? Well, one case is the case where N=2, that is, where the entire class period has only two days. Then premise (9) is not needed, since what the student is supposed to know initially suffices; there is not time for the knowledge to be lost. However, in this case the teacher's announcement has the Moore's paradoxical flavor we already noted in Quine's analysis of the one-day case. This is exactly what happened when I tried the card experiment on a fellow undergraduate, as I have mentioned above. Therefore, as I have already said, the difference between the last day and the penultimate day is not always the crucial one.

What if there are many days? Then to exclude day N–1, one needs another argument: that the student still would know on day N–2 that the exam will be given and will be a surprise (not known in advance). Once again, we could invoke the "rule of the school" device. We can suppose that it is long-settled school policy that the exam must be given on a day when the students do not know that it will be given, even on the day before. And, of course, we also suppose that school policy demands an exam. Given these things, the supposition that the exam will be given on day N–1 will lead to a contradiction of the appropriate premises. This type of idea could be iterated to exclude successive days from the list. The rule of the school will get successively more complicated and involve iterations of knowledge about knowledge, lack of knowledge, and the preservation of the situation.[11]

Let me generalize this argument by describing how the reasoning is iterated. In each case, we conclude that the exam cannot be given on a given day, the Jth day; we then try to rule out the $(J$–1$)$th day. To do this we have to assume not only that the previous premises are true but also that the student knows on the previous day, the $(J$–2$)$th day, that all these previous premises are true. Only then can the student conclude, on the basis of her knowledge on day J–2, that the exam is not going to be given on days from J onward and so say that it must be given on the $(J$–1$)$th day, contradicting the premise that it is a surprise. Thus, we always require not only that the previous premises shall be true and known to be true at the outset but also that they shall remain known to be true on day J–2, whatever day that is, and this is *always* an extra premise, since we have not accepted

---

[11] One could think vaguely that it is school policy to allow enough of these iterations in each case to generate the paradox. Then there *would* be a vagueness question.
In the original version of this talk, I mentioned the case already discussed in note 5, where the experimenter randomly sticks the card somewhere in the middle of the deck. Then it might seem (at least again thinking vaguely) that enough iterations of the knowledge involved will always be available to rule out successive days from the end. But in the original transcript, I explicitly say that it would be valid but superfluous to use this reasoning to rule out the second-from-the-last card, since the subject can see that the card is not being placed near the bottom. I should have gone on to conclude, as I did in note 5, that this model considerably changes the original problem.

premise (9) as generally true but rather as something that must be argued separately in each case.

Thus where we thought that we were only applying the same reasoning again and again, we were in fact adding tacit extra premises at each stage. The feeling of the heap—that the more days that are involved, the weaker the reasoning becomes—derives from these extra premises piling up, which in fact need special arguments to justify them.

This is all I want to say about this paradox. I do not know if it is really solved; I am sure that there are more things one could say about it.

I would like here to go on to consider the principle that *if you know something now you will know it at any later date*. It was assumed (premise (9)) in the fallacious argument for the paradox above, and it is also assumed by Quine:

If this [that the decree will not be fulfilled] is a conclusion which he is prepared to accept... in the end as a certainty, it is an alternative which he should have been prepared to take into consideration from the beginning as a possibility. (Quine 1953: 20)

That is to say, if she knew in the beginning that the exam will be given, then she cannot, at any later stage, fall into doubt or denial of this: and this is what I am denying. Quine, on the contrary, seems to consider it obvious that if she is willing to accept at a later stage that the exam will not be given, then at no earlier date could she have *known* that the exam will be given.

Again, Hintikka says:

What exactly is implied in the requirement that the grounds of knowledge in the full sense of the word must be *conclusive*? For our purposes it suffices to point out the following obvious consequence of this requirement: If somebody says "I know that p" in this strong sense of knowledge, he implicitly denies that any further information would have led him to alter his view. He commits himself to the view that he would still persist in saying that he knows that p is true—or at the very least, persists in saying that p is, in fact true—even if he knew more than he now knows. (Hintikka 1962:20–21; emphasis in text)

Of course, in a way, what Hintikka is saying here is obviously true because he says, "He commits himself to the view that he would still persist in saying that he knows that p is true ... even if he knew more than he now knows." As stated, this is not a substantive principle. "Knows that" could be replaced by any propositional attitude verb, say, "believes that" or even "doubts that," and the resulting principle still would be true—that is, it would still be true that someone would persist in saying that he doubts that p, say, even if he would come to doubt more than he now doubts. But what Hintikka really means here, presumably, is that it is a characteristic of knowledge that even if I have more evidence than I now have, I will still know that p; and this is what I have been denying in giving my counterexamples. You may know something now, but, on the basis of further evidence—without any loss of evidence or forgetfulness—be led to fall into doubt about it later.

Hintikka says that the principle is true only for the "strong sense of knowledge." This implies that there are two senses of the phrase "to know": a strong one and, perhaps, a weak one for which the principle is not really true. There is something in Malcolm (1952) about this too: Malcolm admits that there are cases where you can know something but, later on, on the basis of extra evidence, conclude that you did not know it. He gives the following example: if you *know* that the sun is about 90 million miles from the Earth, you might later, on the basis of learned astronomers saying (perhaps falsely—he is not clear on this point) that an error had been made and that the correct distance was 20 million miles, be persuaded that you were wrong. The astronomers might be saying something false (e.g., if an astronomers' convention had decided to play a trick on the public), but if they were right, then, of course, you did not know it beforehand.[12]

But Malcolm argues that this is not always true, citing another example: suppose there is an ink bottle in front of you, on your desk. Can it be the case that some *later information would lead* you to change your mind? Malcolm writes:

It could happen that in the next moment the ink-bottle will suddenly vanish from sight; or that I should find myself under a tree in the garden with no ink-bottle about;[13] or that one or more persons should enter this room and declare with apparent sincerity that they see no ink-bottle on this desk. . . . Having admitted that these things *could* happen, am I compelled to admit that if they did happen then it would be proved that there is no ink-bottle here *now*? Not at all! I could say that when my hand seemed to pass through the ink-bottle I should *then* be suffering from hallucination; that if the ink-bottle suddenly vanished it would have miraculously ceased to exist . . .

. . . No future experience or investigation could prove to me that I am mistaken. Therefore, if I were to say "I know that there is an ink-bottle here," I should be using "know" in the strong sense. . . .

In saying that I should regard nothing as evidence that there is no ink-bottle here now, I am not *predicting* what I should do if various astonishing things happened. If other members of my family entered this room and, while looking at the top of this desk, declared with apparent sincerity that they see no ink-bottle, I might fall into a swoon or become mad. I *might* even come to believe that there is not and has not been an ink-bottle here. I cannot foretell with certainty how I should react. But if it is *not* a prediction what is

---

[12] See Malcolm (1952:184). Since knowledge implies truth, then if Malcolm is really giving an example where knowledge is lost, the announcement by the astronomers must be wrong—after all, you did once know that the sun is about 90 million miles from the Earth. Things would be different if the discussion were one of certainty, justified conviction, or whatever, where these are not construed as implying truth. The same is true of much of my previous discussion in this paper. Everything would be different if knowledge were replaced by a concept that does not imply truth. For example, I wouldn't have had to give an example where I *falsely* convince someone that I never wrote on modal logic. However, other arguments that used the fact that knowledge implies truth would go.

[13] He was in his room at his desk.

the meaning of my assertion that I should regard nothing as evidence that there is no ink-bottle here?

That assertion describes my *present* attitude towards the statement that here is an ink-bottle. It does not prophesy what my attitude *would* be if various things happened. My present attitude toward that statement is radically different from my present attitude toward those other statements (e.g., that I have a heart).[14] I do *now* admit that certain future occurrences would disprove the latter. Whereas no imaginable future occurrence would be considered by me *now* as proving that there is not an ink-bottle here.

These remarks are not meant to be autobiographical. They are meant to throw light on the common concepts of evidence, proof, and disproof. (Malcolm 1952:185–86; emphasis in text)

He includes the statement "three plus two is five" in the same batch as the ink-bottle case. I am not sure that the ink-bottle case is a good example—a magician might persuade you that you had been tricked.[15]

---

[14] The statement that he himself has a heart Malcolm supposes to be a statement he knows only in the weak sense since he could be persuaded later of its falsity.

[15] Malcolm is surely right that ordinarily we would regard the presence of an ink bottle in the room as conclusive, not merely probable. Malcolm quotes Ayer to the effect that "no proposition, other than a tautology, can possibly be anything more than a probable hypothesis" (1952:183, note 4). (See also Malcolm's quotations from Descartes and Locke on the same page.) Actually, Hume already states that some empirical statements are not really just probable. He writes: "One would appear ridiculous, who would say that it is only probable the sun will rise to-morrow, or that all men must dye; though it is plain we have no further assurance of these facts, than what experience affords us" (2000: Book 1, Part III, Sec. XI). (However, Hume goes on to reserve the term "knowledge," following previous authors, for a priori knowledge, and uses "proofs" for arguments giving empirically certain knowledge; I take this to be a bit of technical terminology, not really a denial of what Malcolm affirms against Ayer.)

In Malcolm's case of the ink bottle, indeed I may be certain that there is an ink bottle here, but I will be equally certain that the extraordinary future events Malcolm describes will not happen. If I seriously entertain the idea that some of them will or even may happen, then I am entertaining the idea that perhaps a clever magician is deceiving me, or some other even more *outré* case. What Malcolm says does not seem to me to describe my present attitude toward the bizarre possibilities he mentions.

My own intuitions differ from Malcolm's in the opposite direction about some other cases. The statement that I have a heart in the quoted material refers to his claim earlier in the paper that if astonished surgeons told him that when they operated on him they found that he had none, he would believe them, in contrast to the case involving the ink bottle. But I find this belief much harder to give up, even under extraordinary circumstances (I would probably think that the surgeons must be putting me on).

In my discussion of the astronomer's case, I was worried that if the distance from the earth to the sun was *knowledge,* the astronomers must be tricking us (by definition). But let us just speak of what would lead me to give up my *belief* about the distance between the sun and the earth. An extraordinary error such as Malcolm describes would be very hard to swallow without an elaborate explanation. I might wonder whether astronomy is much of a science after all. A slighter error would be better and might be easier to explain. I simply would not believe a committee of astronomers who announced that the earth is flat after all.

Malcolm says at the end of the paper (189) that the ideas in this paper derive from discussion with Ludwig Wittgenstein, something I may not have noticed in 1972. If so, they appear to be based on Wittgenstein's exposition to him of some of the ideas that are now published in *On Certainty* (Wittgenstein 1969). I am not sure, however, that the Wittgenstein of that book would agree with the way Malcolm puts various matters.

I may be in no doubt now as to whether there is an ink-bottle in front of me and yet it seems to me compatible with this to suppose that future evidence could persuade me that there is no ink-bottle. There seem to me to be two different questions here: whether I have the kind of certainty characterized by there being no doubt now, and whether I take the attitude that no future evidence could disprove this. But let this distinction, and the question as to whether this particular example is correct, be set aside—there may be correct examples. The strange—and unargued—thing here is, why does this show that there is a strong sense of "know" for which this is true? Suppose there are some cases of knowledge in which no future evidence will lead me to change my mind, and *other* cases of knowledge in which I would change my mind. That does not show that the word "know" is being used in two *senses* anymore than there being Americans who are rich and Americans who are poor shows that the word "American" is being used in two senses. Any class may, in various interesting ways, divide up into subclasses. Why not instead say that, in general, knowing does not imply that no future evidence would lead me to lose my knowledge, but in some cases, where I do know, it just is in fact the case (and not because of some special sense of "know") that no future evidence would lead me to change my mind?

One would need some additional—say, linguistic—evidence that this shows that "know" is being used in two senses. After all, is it likely that, in Ubangi or Swahili, two different words are used for these two different senses of "know"? There are, of course, different senses of the word "know" in English: those that would be translated as *connaître* as opposed to *savoir*, *kennen* as opposed to *wissen*. These are different senses of knowing: you *know a person* as opposed to *knowing that p is true*. These are indeed different senses of "to know," and this fact is exhibited by the fact that other languages differentiate between them. We all, of course, have heard of the "biblical sense" of "to know," which in English derives from the King James Bible's translation of the corresponding classical Hebrew, and is perhaps similarly distinct in some other languages. But why should there be different kinds of propositional or factual knowledge? Prima facie, it seems to me that the idea that factual-propositional knowledge has two different senses is a red herring. So, what can these people have in mind? Why do they not just say that there are two cases?

I think what they have in mind is this.[16] First, there are obvious principles about knowledge which seem to them to imply that, in general, if you know something, no future evidence could lead you to change your mind—the grounds must be conclusive. But then there are counterexamples; this conclusion does not seem to be correct. So then they argue: well, that must be a weaker sense of "to know." But why not accept counterexamples as counterexamples? Why

---

[16] Even though there has been a recent resurgence of interest in the question of whether "knows" has different senses, I have chosen not to incorporate the ever-growing recent literature on this subject.

invoke a doctrine of different senses of "know"? Should there really be different dictionary entries? But there must be something behind the idea that "know" has a sense in which knowledge cannot be lost (Hintikka) or at least that our present attitude toward the statement is that the knowledge cannot be lost (Malcolm). This is to be our second paradox. Unlike my treatment of the first paradox, I shall merely state it, and not attempt to solve it—because I discovered it!

I want to try to prove the principle that I earlier declared to be false: that if you know something now, you have got to know it later. One cannot really prove it in such a simple form. You might forget, and so on. But one can try to prove the more careful principle suggested by Malcolm's discussion of the alleged strong sense of "know": that if I know something now, I should, as a rational agent, adopt a resolution not to allow any future evidence to overthrow it. But this does not seem to be our attitude toward statements that we know—nor does it seem to be a rational attitude.

Consider the following. First, the deductive closure of knowledge:

(*i*) If A knows that p and A knows that p entails q, and, on the basis of such knowledge, A concludes that q, then A knows that q.

And then (let "p" be any statement):

(*ii*) p entails the following hypothetical: any evidence against p is misleading (where misleading is to mean *leads to a false conclusion*).

If p is true—notice that (*ii*) does not say anything about knowledge—any evidence against it is misleading, that is, leads to the false conclusion that not-p. Now, suppose that

(*iii*) The subject A knows that p, and A knows (*ii*).

Then, provided that he carries out the appropriate deduction, it follows from premise (*ii*) that we can conclude:

(*iv*) A knows that any evidence against p is misleading.

(The statement applies to any evidence, arising now or in the future, but naturally we are most interested in the future.) This already seems very strange: that just by knowing some common or garden-variety statement, which I am calling p, one knows a sweeping thing: that any future evidence against p will be misleading.

We might have as a general principle something like this (though it is very hard to state in a nice, rigorous way, especially giving it the necessary generality):

(*v*) If A knows that taking an action of type T leads to consequence C, and A wishes above all else to avoid C (i.e., this is the only relevant issue), then A should resolve now not to take any action of type T.

This, too, is a very sweeping statement, but we are considering the case where *A* knows, at a certain time, that if he does anything of a certain kind in the future, it will lead to some consequence that he thinks bad, there being no other relevant consequences which would override it. For example, suppose he knows that if he opens the door, someone standing outside is going to shoot him. It would then be a reasonable thing for him to resolve not to open the door.

So, he should resolve not to take any action of type *T*. Let the action of type *T* be accepting evidence against *p*—that is, doubting or denying that *p* on the basis of some future evidence. The consequence *C* is gaining a false belief—or at least losing a true one, if we merely fall into doubt—and this is something that we do not want. Then one may conclude:

(*vi*) *A* should resolve not to be influenced by any evidence against *p*.

To make the argument clearer, notice there are two ways in which one can make this resolution. In the first place, one can resolve not to *look at* any alleged evidence against *p*. For example, I might resolve not to read books of a certain type. I think that, in practice, this is the most important case. It is not possible to keep to such a resolution in the case of the surprise exam (see also note 17), nor does it seem to be what some of the authors I have mentioned have in mind. In the second place, one could conceivably resolve that, if one is faced, regardless of whether one wanted it, with particular evidence against *p*, one should nevertheless ignore it, since one knows that it must be misleading, given that one knows that *p*. Neither of these things seems to be our attitude toward future evidence in cases where we know something. I think it is from such an argument that the idea of a strong sense of "know" may come; that, in some special cases, these conclusions are true. But if you look at the premises and reasoning, there does not seem to be any "super" sense of "know" being supposed, just "know" in the ordinary sense. So there must be something else wrong, and this is the question—what *is* wrong?

Some political or religious leaders have indeed argued along some lines such as those of (*vi*). They have argued on this basis that if their followers or subjects are not strong enough to stick to the resolution themselves, they—the leaders—ought to help them avoid contact with the misleading evidence. For this reason, they have urged or compelled people not to read certain books, writings, and the like. But many people need no compulsion. They avoid reading things, and so on.

If the conclusion of this argument were accepted, our solution to the first paradox would in some sense go by the board, since the student should resolve that, no matter how things appear in the future, she should never lose any of her beliefs in the teacher's announcements. That is a trivial special case of principle (*vi*), but it is the genesis of my considering this second problem and this particular set of premises. And they have their own sort of importance in epistemology. One can be led in two directions by them: first, one can think that conclusion (*vi*) is correct, and so to know something means that no possible future evidence should lead me to change my mind. But since that is almost never the case, we know almost nothing. This is the skeptical attitude. Alternatively, one might be lead to the corresponding dogmatic view—that, since we know all sorts of things, we should now make a resolution not to be swayed by any future evidence.[17]

The commonsense view is, for example, that you *do* know that I have written certain papers on modal logic but that future evidence could lead you to change your mind about this. So, you should rationally leave yourself open to such changings-of-mind, even though it is the case that you *know* that I wrote these papers. The question is, why?[18,19]

APPENDIX I

In a recent class discussion,[20] Fred Michael remarked that Quine's move, at least as to the last day, could be avoided by a simple change in the notion of "surprise." Regard an exam (or hanging) as a surprise if one cannot know in advance of a given day that *if* the event (exam or hanging) will occur at all, the event must occur on that day. Then the question of whether one knows in advance that there will be an exam (a hanging) becomes irrelevant.[21] One could try to complicate the definition of surprise corresponding to the successive elimination of days, but eventually the pileup of extra knowledge assumptions in my main discussion will go over into more and more complicated conditionals with more and more antecedents, and very artificial notions of "surprise."

---

[17] Although I was in fact led to the second paradox by my consideration of the first (the surprise-exam paradox), in one way taking this case as paradigmatic is misleading. In the case of the surprise exam, the student experiencing the passing of successive days (and perhaps seeing no exam until nearly the end) cannot avoid facing the future evidence, and may not be able to stick to her resolution. The same is not true of what I had in mind for many typical cases of the paradox, where one may avoid contact with the "misleading" counterevidence altogether—for example, by avoiding reading certain books or articles.

The corresponding cases of Malcolm (1952) are at least similar in that it was important to me to phrase the problem in terms of a resolution at the present time, rather than as a prediction as to what I would do. However, in all of Malcolm's cases the idea that one might avoid the misleading counterevidence altogether is not there. (And, as I said above, for some of his cases it is not clear that Malcolm regards the counterevidence as misleading.)

[18] But see also my note 12 above. Since the authors I was concerned with (Hintikka and Malcolm), as well as the previous discussion of the surprise exam, were discussing knowledge, and since knowledge is the subject of the present paper, this second problem has been put in terms of knowledge. But there could be parallel problems for certainty, rationally justified conviction, and so on.

[19] My thanks to the late G. E. M. (Elizabeth) Anscombe and the Cambridge Moral Sciences Club for transcribing this lecture. Thanks to Jeff Buechner, Gary Ostertag, Harold Teichman, and especially to Romina Padró for their help in producing the present version. This paper has been completed with support from the Saul A. Kripke Center at the City University of New York, Graduate Center.

[20] In my spring 2009 seminar at the CUNY Graduate Center.

[21] I now find that a similar remark is made in Ayer (1973:125).

However, we owe to Shaw (1958) the proposal that the teacher's announcement be taken to be *self-referential*: one cannot derive in advance *from the present announcement* when the exam will be given. Done that way, any pileup is avoided, either in knowledge assumptions or in antecedents. The formulation I prefer of this self-referential approach to the surprise exam is in a paper by Frederic B. Fitch (1964).[22, 23] Given enough material to formalize the kind of self-reference involved in Gödel's first incompleteness theorem (say, by quoting syntax into elementary number theory), one can formalize the problem in terms of deducibility and eliminate any notion of knowledge. That is, the announcement (A) can be that the exam will be given on a day such that one cannot deduce from (A) itself, plus the fact that it has not been given on previous days, that it will be given on that very day. Fitch simply accepts that such an announcement, so formulated, leads to a contradiction. The reasoning follows that of the usual surprise exam argument, successively eliminating the days starting from the last. However, he argues that a slightly weaker version is "apparently self-consistent" (1964:163). This modifies the announcement so that "what is intended in practice is not that the surprise event will be a surprise *whenever* it occurs, but only when it occurs on some day *other than the last*" (163). He

---

[22] Shaw (1958) seems to think that the self-reference makes the problem dubious, like the liar paradox, but Fitch's Gödelian formulation is beyond logical doubt. Shaw is also somewhat sloppy in his formulation. The deduction in advance that is ruled out involves not only the announcement itself, but also that the exam has not been given yet.

[23] See also Kaplan and Montague (1960). Their version is still about knowledge, whereas that of Fitch shows that the notion of knowledge can be eliminated in favor of deduction. Kaplan and Montague have both done justly esteemed and famous work, and the present paper is formally unexceptionable. However, I see some problems in it. For example, is it really one of our "intuitive epistemological principles" that "one cannot know a non-analytic sentence about the future" (81–82)? No wonder one cannot know anything about the exam (hanging) in advance; it will be just as much a surprise as the rising of the sun! (See also note 15 above.)

But the main problem with their paper is this: in order to obtain Gödelian self-reference, they take knowledge as a predicate, rather than an intensional operator (see their excuse at the end of the first paragraph on 80). They then reduce the problem to an analogue of the liar paradox (which they call "the Knower," 88). Basically, it is "my negation is known" (87, formula (1)), from which they derive a contradiction using intuitive principles about knowledge. But then the entire original flavor of the surprise exam (hanging) is lost. One could blame everything on the use of a knowledge predicate. In a subsequent paper, Montague (1963) himself, inspired by this one, argues that if modality is treated as a predicate, customary modal laws cannot be maintained, precisely because of the possibility of Gödelian self-reference.

There is an important difference between the goals of Kaplan–Montague and those of Fitch. Kaplan and Montague are looking for "a genuinely paradoxical decree" (1960:85), that is, one that apparently can be proved to be both true and false. Fitch, on the other hand, avoids the possibility of any paradox almost by the definition of his enterprise. The whole argument can be formalized in first-order arithmetic ("Peano Arithmetic"), or strictly speaking, an extension of that system, by adding finitely many propositional constants corresponding to the $E_1, \ldots, E_N$. By definition, there can be no contradiction as long as Peano Arithmetic is consistent (the added propositional constants change nothing).

Given that we are looking for a self-referential interpretation, I think Fitch's perspective to be better than that of Kaplan and Montague. The problem is not to find a paradox like the liar, but simply a highly counterintuitive conclusion that it is impossible to announce a surprise exam (or decree a surprise hanging) within a certain time limit. One case in Kaplan and Montague (the decrees D_2 and D_3) (82–84), which they consider merely to be a decree that cannot be fulfilled (and thus not genuinely paradoxical), in fact comes closer to capturing the right flavor than the subsequent modification to get a "genuinely paradoxical decree".

includes in the modified announcement that the last day "will be a surprise in the *weak* sense of being not provably implied by the prediction itself" (163).[24]

APPENDIX 2: LETTER TO FITCH

I now append a letter that I wrote to Fitch.[25] Were I to have written it today, I would not have started with Löb's theorem, but with Gödel's second incompleteness theorem, which is the main point.[26] The point is that Fitch's modified announcement implies that various things cannot be derived from it, namely things about when the exam will be given. *A fortiori*, it implies its own consistency. But, by Gödel's second incompleteness theorem, any statement implying its own consistency must itself be inconsistent, contrary to Fitch's guess about his modified announcement.

As I conclude in the letter to Fitch, I do not think that the self-referential interpretation of the problem is a very natural one.

[UCLA]

Los Angeles, California
Department of Philosophy
August 4, 1972

Prof. Frederick Fitch
Department of Philosophy
Yale University
New Haven, Connecticut 06520

Dear Fred:
You may be interested in the following observation related to your article on the Prediction Paradox in the *APQ* for April 1964. The statement in (16) [and the one in (17) also] which you call "apparently self-consistent" is actually refutable. The reason: call the statement "P." P implies $\sim$Bew#$\sim$P, since if Bew#$\sim$P then, of course, Bew#[P $\supset$ Q$_1$] and Bew#[P $\supset$ Q$_2$]. So P $\supset$ $\sim$Bew#$\sim$P is provable. So Bew# $\sim$P $\supset$ $\sim$P is provable. By the famous theorem of Löb (*viz*, if Bew#A $\supset$ A is provable, so is A; *JSL* 1955 pp. 115–8), $\sim$P is provable [Löb 1955].

The situation should really be looked at this way: let P be any statement which implies that it itself is not refutable. Then, Z plus P, where Z is elementary number theory, is a system which can prove its own consistency, and therefore is inconsistent by Gödel's Second Incompleteness Theorem. Hence, P must be refutable in Z. Your statement P is a statement

---

[24] See his formulae (16) (for two days) and (17) (for three days). (There appears to me to be a subtle error involving the use of exclusive "or" in the formulation of (17) that I hope to discuss elsewhere, not particularly in connection with Fitch's paper.)

[25] Fitch replied to this letter simply saying that he could find nothing wrong with it.

[26] As I mentioned in the letter, I have shown that Löb's theorem, proved by Löb in a different way, is actually a simple corollary of Gödel's second incompleteness theorem. See, for example, Smullyan (1992:110), and Boolos and Jeffrey (1980: ch. 16). In the letter to Fitch, I actually give the argument, and maybe this is why I mention Löb's theorem.

which implies its own irrefutability, since it implies that various things cannot be deduced from it, and is therefore refutable. The same argument easily establishes that Löb's theorem, cited above, is a simple consequence of Gödel's Second Incompleteness Theorem, as I observed in a short unpublished paper. Simply take P in the preceding paragraph to be ∼A.

The same observations show that much of what Bennett says in his review (*JSL* 1965) of your paper and others is wrong. Some of the statements which he declares to be self-consistent or even logically true can be shown to be refutable by the same argument, at least if they are interpreted in terms of Gödelian self-reference.

Since any statement whatsoever which implies its own self-consistency (and therefore any statement which implies that something else cannot be deduced from it) is refutable, it seems to me that interpretations of the Prediction Paradox in terms of Gödelian self-reference and deducibility in number theory do not really capture the spirit of the original paradox. For, surely the original paradox was not meant to follow from such general considerations. My own view of the paradox is different, but that's another story.

Best,
Saul Kripke

APPENDIX 3: COMMENTS ON THE SECOND PARADOX

There has been a considerable secondary literature on my second paradox, which has come to be known as the dogmatism paradox. As I said, it can be discussed for other epistemic concepts such as certainty, rational belief, and so on; and indeed there is literature on some other forms. Moreover, one might distinguish between first and third person formulations of the problem, and in the latter case, whether it is a subject who really knows or merely *thinks* he or she knows. Here I am discussing a subject S who genuinely knows that p.

In the published literature the first discussion of my second paradox is in Gilbert Harman's well-known book *Thought* (Harman 1973:147ff), and I emphasize this version. I hope I have understood Harman correctly. To discuss his treatment of the problem, one should remember that my point is about a resolution *made in advance* to ignore certain types of evidence. Mostly the strategy followed is that of failing to read literature of a certain type, and so on. One might make a resolution to ignore particular evidence even when one is forcibly confronted with it, but this is often more difficult to keep.[27]

People who follow these strategies are, after all, not uncommon at all, as I have mentioned in the paper. Often, however, we think of them for this reason as dogmatists who do not really know. Here, however, the premise was that we are dealing with a subject who really knows. We are arguing that such a subject ought to maintain the dogmatic attitude because any counterevidence really is misleading. (In my own discussion, I imagine trying to convince people, falsely, that I never worked on modal logic after all, so that some prior knowledge would be lost.)

---

[27] Those who followed the main strategy might be compared to what Ulysses would have done if he had decided to put wax in his ears or follow another route. Tying oneself to the mast is something of an analogue of the second strategy some might follow if forced to confront the evidence (the sirens). Think also of cases of trying to avoid addictive substances (I have heard the comparison made between dangerous—misleading—books and dangerous drugs) and what an addict may warn his friends about his behavior before he tries to withdraw.

Harman's discussion goes like this, where we replace his particular example with the letter "*p*." He says, "Since I now know that *p*, I now know that any evidence that appears to indicate something else is misleading. That does not warrant me in simply disregarding any further evidence, since getting that further evidence can change what I know. In particular, after I get such further evidence I may no longer know that it is misleading. For having the new evidence can make it true that I no longer know that *p*; if I no longer know that, I no longer know that the new evidence is misleading" (1973:148–49).

Well, one need not disagree with what Harman says about the acquisition of the new evidence (at least for typical cases). But remember that I was talking about a resolution to be made in advance. Just because the subject wishes to avoid a loss of knowledge such as Harman describes, so for that reason she or he makes the resolution. Usually, this resolution is to avoid certain types of contact with alleged evidence, such as reading the wrong books (for they can contain nothing but sophistry and illusion), associating with the wrong people, and so on. Moreover, by hypothesis, the books and so on, *are* misleading, and the subject knows they are.

One should certainly construe the resolution to include a more specific form, avoiding contact with some specific counterevidence to *p*, though usually one will not know of it. Harman is right to say that if such contact nevertheless occurs, one may well lose the knowledge that *p*, and hence no longer know that the counterevidence is misleading. But just this is why the subject resolves not to get into such a situation![28]

I should add something I was probably not aware of when I originally gave this lecture, which is that sometimes the dogmatic strategy is a rational one. I myself have not read much defending astrology, necromancy, and the like (I remember Stephen Weinberg making the same remark). Even when confronted with specific alleged evidence, I have sometimes ignored it although I did not know how to refute it. I once read part of a piece of writing by a reasonably well-known person defending astrology.[29] Another time, I saw an advertisement professing to prove that Vincent Foster had been murdered (presumably on orders of the Clintons, though this was not stated explicitly). I was not in a position to refute specific claims but assumed that this was a piece of no value.[30, 31] One epistemological problem is to delineate the cases when the dogmatic attitude is justified.

---

[28] I am assuming that we are dealing with a subject who wishes to avoid losing knowledge. Sometimes there are people who "don't want to know" or do wish to lose knowledge that they have, sometimes for arguably good reasons. They are not in question here.

[29] What I had glanced at was a piece by Hans Eysenck professing to prove the theories of a particular French astrologer.

[30] My reaction was amply confirmed by several investigations, including even one headed by Kenneth Starr. If someone doesn't like this example, try, say, holocaust denial.

[31] It is a merit of Robert Nozick's discussion of the problem (1981:237–39) that he recognizes that there are cases where alleged evidence for dubious or crackpot views contrary to what we know may be ignored (239). The rest of his discussion, in this respect like Harman's, imagines us confronted with a particular piece of evidence *e*, purporting to undermine, or even contradict, the knowledge that *p*. Nozick bases his rather detailed discussion of this matter on his view that knowledge fails to be closed under Universal Instantiation (UI). Even though *S* may know that all evidence against *p* is misleading, according to Nozick that does not show that *S* knows that some specific evidence *e* against *p* is misleading, and therefore can be disregarded. He then adds a subtle discussion of this particular case. Many (including me) might find Nozick's rejection of the closure of knowledge under UI in and of itself implausible. But I have discussed Nozick's theory in some detail in the present volume and hope to be pardoned for omitting any further discussion of its application to this case. (For more discussion of Nozick's views on deductive closure, see Chapter 7.) David Lewis also developed an epistemological theory stating that whether a subject knows that

REFERENCES

Ayer, A. J. (1973). "On a Supposed Antinomy." *Mind* 82:125–26.
Bennett, J. (1965). "Review of R. Shaw, *The Paradox of the Unexpected Examination.*" *Journal of Symbolic Logic* 30:101–12.
Boolos, G., and R. Jeffrey (1980). *Computability and Logic*, 2nd ed. Cambridge: Cambridge University Press.
Dretske, F. (1970). "Epistemic Operators." *Journal of Philosophy* 67:1007–23.
———. (1971). "Conclusive Reasons." *Australasian Journal of Philosophy* 49:1–22.
Fitch, F. (1964). "A Goedelized Formulation of the Prediction Paradox." *American Philosophical Quarterly* 1:161–64.
Harman, G. (1973). *Thought*. Princeton: Princeton University Press.
Hawthorne, J. (2004). *Knowledge and Lotteries*. Oxford: Oxford University Press.
Hintikka, J. (1962). *Knowledge and Belief: An Introduction to the Logic of the Two Notions*. Ithaca, NY: Cornell University Press.
Hume, D. (2000). *Treatise of Human Nature*. Ed. David Fate Norton. Oxford: Oxford University Press. First published 1740.
Kaplan, D., and R. Montague (1960). "A Paradox Regained." *Notre Dame Journal of Formal Logic* 1:79–90.
Lewis, D. (1996). "Elusive Knowledge." *Australasian Journal of Philosophy* 74:549–67.
Löb, M. H. (1955). "Solution to a Problem of Leon Henkin." *Journal of Symbolic Logic* 20:115–18.
Malcolm, N. (1952). "Knowledge and Belief." *Mind* 61:178–89.
Montague, R. (1963). "Syntactical Treatments of Modality, with Corollaries on Reflexion Principles and Finite Axiomatizability." *Acta Philosophica Fennica* 16:153–67; reprinted in Montague (1974).
———. (1974). *Formal Philosophy: Selected Papers of Richard Montague*. Ed. R. Thomason. New Haven, CT: Yale University Press.
Nozick, R. (1981). *Philosophical Explanations*. Cambridge, MA: Harvard University Press.
Quine, W. V. O. (1953). "On a So-Called Paradox." *Mind* 62:65–67. Reprinted under the title "On a Supposed Antinomy," in *The Ways of Paradox and other Essays*. Cambridge, MA: Harvard University Press, 1966, 19–21; page references are to the reprint.
Shaw, R. (1958). "The Paradox of the Unexpected Examination." *Mind* 67:382–84.
Smullyan, R. (1992). *Gödel's Incompleteness Theorems*. Oxford: Oxford University Press.
Sorensen, R. (1988a). *Blindspots*. Oxford: Clarendon.

---

p can depend on the conversational context, notably whether traditional skeptical philosophical doubts have been brought into the discussion (see Lewis 1996). In the case of the present paradox, he thinks that merely hearing that there is purported counterevidence is enough to create a context in which one no longer knows that p, and hence that such counterevidence is misleading. (It is unclear to me whether Lewis means that we are aware of what the purported counterevidence is, or aware merely of its existence.) We have seen that this is in general too strong, but I think Lewis is probably not really unaware of this. I can't go into Lewis's contextual theory here, though my inclination is not to agree. Other philosophers, such as Hawthorne (2004) and Sorensen (1988b), have discussed the problem. I will not discuss their views here.

———. (1988b). "Dogmatism, Junk Knowledge, and Conditionals." *Philosophical Quarterly* 38:433–54.
Williamson, T. (1994). *Vagueness.* London: Routledge.
Wittgenstein, L. (1969). *On Certainty.* Ed. G. E. M. Anscombe and G. H. von Wright. Trans. G. E. M. Anscombe and D. Paul. Oxford: Blackwell.

3

Vacuous Names and Fictional Entities*

One of the main concerns of my previous work (Kripke 1980)[1] is the semantics of proper names and natural kind terms. A classical view which Putnam mentioned, advocated by Mill, states that proper names have as their function simply to refer; they have denotation but not connotation. The alternative view, which until fairly recently has dominated the field, has been that of Frege and Russell. They hold that ordinary names[2] have connotation in a very strong sense: a proper name such as 'Napoleon' simply means *the man having most of the properties we commonly attribute to Napoleon, such as being Emperor of the French, losing at Waterloo, and the like*. Of course, intermediate views might be suggested, and perhaps have been suggested.

For various general terms, such as 'cow' and 'tiger' or 'elm' and 'beech', not only Frege and Russell, but Mill as well (probably more explicitly than the other two), held that they have connotation in the sense that we learn what it is to be a tiger by being given some list of properties which form necessary and sufficient conditions for being a tiger. In both these cases, both where Mill and Frege–Russell disagree and where Mill and Frege–Russell agree, I have advocated the

---

* The present paper (essentially a precursor of my John Locke Lectures at Oxford) was delivered at the conference 'Language, Intentionality, and Translation Theory', held at the University of Connecticut in March of 1973 and organized by Sam Wheeler and John Troyer. The other papers in the conference, together with the discussions afterward, were published in *Synthese* 27, 1974. The version here is based on a transcription made by the conference organizers. A general discussion of my own paper was printed in the *Synthese* volume mentioned (509–21), even though the paper itself was not. Papers were presented by many distinguished philosophers of language, who also participated in the discussion.

[1] Now this work is well known, but the present paper should be read bearing in mind that it was fairly new at the time, and hence was summarized again in part.

[2] Russell also speaks of so-called logically proper names. For these, his views are close to those of Mill, but he argues that what we normally call 'names' are not, in fact, logically proper names. It is with ordinary names that I am concerned when I speak of Russell's views on names, and I will henceforth omit the qualification 'ordinary', even though according to Russell they are not 'genuine' names. See the discussion mentioned in note 14 below, and Russell (1918–19) generally.

view that the consensus is largely wrong; that it is reference which is much more important here than any supposed sense.³

I want to discuss one aspect of this problem today, since no consideration in favor of the Frege–Russell view of proper names has seemed more conclusive than the fact that names can sometimes be empty—that, for example, they can occur in fiction. Also, even if they do in fact refer, it is intelligible to raise the question of whether the alleged referent really exists. For instance, we ask whether Moses as a historical character really existed and the like. What can we mean by this? If the function of naming were simply reference, then empty names would seem to have no semantic function at all, but plainly they do not fail to have a semantic function, as anyone who enjoys a good work of fiction can attest. And even if they do have referents, we can ask whether, say, Moses or Napoleon really existed. When we do so we are not asking whether *that person* really existed. We are not questioning *of him* whether he really existed, because if we were asking such a question, the answer should be evident. Since everyone really exists, *that* person does also. It is unintelligible, as Russell and Frege have emphasized, to ask of a person whether he really exists.

Now to this problem the Frege–Russell analysis, and its modifications, provides a neat solution. If we have a story—for example, one involving Sherlock Holmes—to say that Sherlock Holmes really exists is to say that someone or other uniquely satisfies the conditions of the story, or at any rate, most or enough of them. To say that he does not exist is to say that this is not the case. Presumably, if this is to be the analysis of the statement, it should apply to counterfactual situations also. To say, 'Sherlock Holmes would have existed (or might have existed) under certain circumstances' is to say that some person would have uniquely played the role of the detective in the Sherlock Holmes story, or might have played it under those circumstances. And to say that he would not have existed in certain circumstances is to say that the story would not have been true of any such detective under those circumstances. We can then replace the names in these sentences by existential quantifiers, replacing 'Sherlock Holmes existed' with 'There exists a man uniquely satisfying the conditions of the story'. And these are supposed to be necessary and sufficient conditions both about the actual world and about every possible world.

Some of you will know that I distinguish between the questions of what is necessary, whether something would have been true in a possible world, and the epistemological question of whether we know a priori that certain conditions

---

³ There are more recent modifications, but here I am going to lump them together with Frege and Russell: many writers—Wittgenstein (1953), Searle (1958), and others—have held that instead of a fixed list of properties forming necessary and sufficient conditions for being Napoleon or being a tiger, one should instead use a cluster of properties, most of which must roughly hold of the object. Not all of them—or at least not a lot of them—could fail. In Kripke (1980) I argued that this modification, no matter what those who made it thought, does not really overcome the most important objections to the classical view (see 31–33, 60–61, and 74–75).

must be true of the actual world. Therefore there are two questions here about the Frege–Russell analysis. First, is it true that to ask whether Moses exists in a given counterfactual situation, or whether Sherlock Holmes exists, is to ask whether the things commonly said about them would have been true in that situation? Secondly, do we know a priori, or with some sort of advance certainty about the actual world, that the existence of Moses or of Sherlock Holmes is materially equivalent in the actual world to the question of the existence of some unique person satisfying the conditions in the story? These questions are separable and distinct; Frege and Russell could be right on one and wrong on the other. At any rate, they seem to have a neat solution to all these problems that seems to fit into what we actually ask when we ask whether there really was a Sherlock Holmes—or so it may seem at first blush.

Those familiar with my previous work will know that I believe, from a battery of examples, that the Frege–Russell analysis is erroneous, as applied to natural language, for both cases. It is wrong in general about the counterfactual situations, and it is wrong about what we can say a priori about the actual world. Surely, for example, to ask whether under certain circumstances Moses would have existed is not to ask whether under these circumstances such-and-such events would have taken place. For, first, presumably Moses might have existed yet not gone into religion or politics, and therefore not done any of these great deeds. Nor need anyone else, of course, have done them in his place. Second, even had Moses never existed, perhaps someone of comparable stature would have come along to do exactly these great deeds. The statements (that is, one containing 'Moses' and the other containing a description typically associated with that name), which are supposed to have the same truth-value in all possible worlds, are such that neither one entails the other in a possible world. One can be true and the other false in both directions.[4] Of course, there might be certain (extremely implausible, maybe never held) views in the philosophy of history which assert that there are great individuals uniquely called forth to perform certain tasks. This should hardly be assumed simply to follow from an analysis of existential statements and of proper names. I think then that in this case the Frege–Russell analysis must be rejected. In particular, to describe a counterfactual situation as one in which Moses would or would not have existed is not to ask whether any properties would have been instantiated.[5] This is to oppose the

---

[4] Note that in this case I am taking 'Moses' as the name of a real person, and even perhaps assuming the essential accuracy (if not entire accuracy) of the Pentateuchal account. I am then talking about counterfactual situations, and arguing that the existence of someone satisfying the Pentateuchal account has little to do with whether Moses would have existed in a given counterfactual situation. (The case of Moses was discussed in Kripke [1980:66–67], based on Wittgenstein's use of this example [1953:§79].)

[5] Of course, one could invent a property, 'Mosesizing', as frequently proposed by Quine. See Quine (1940:149–50) and Quine (1960:176–80), and my comment in Kripke (1980:29). Such an artificially invented property is not in question here, and is not in and of itself objectionable.

technical meaning that Frege gave to the doctrine that existence is not a predicate. An apparent singular statement of the form 'Moses exists' is *not* equivalent to any statement of the form 'Such-and-such properties are instantiated', unless you take the property of being Moses as the property in question. But if you did so, this would be written out in the form that Frege did not like. It would mean, essentially, 'There is a y, such that y is Moses'.

Russell also held that existence is not a predicate.[6] Explicitly what bothered him about this property is that it would be trivially true of everything. As Russell says, 'There is no sort of point in a predicate which could not conceivably be false. I mean, it is perfectly clear that, if there were such a thing as this existence of individuals that we talk of, it would be absolutely impossible for it not to apply, and that is the characteristic of a mistake' (Russell 1918–19:211). The premise Russell is using here can be construed to be correct. It *is* necessary that everything exists, or that for every x there is a y, such that y is x. It by no means follows that existence is a trivial property, in the sense that everything has necessary existence. Symbolically, the difference is between $\Box(x)Ex$ (the fact that Russell invokes) and $(x)\Box Ex$, which does not follow. Only if the second formula were true would the predicate attributing existence to individuals be trivial. I have discussed this confusion as a modal fallacy in a technical paper on modal logic (Kripke 1971:70)[7] If, in fact, the existence of a particular object is contingent, we can say of that object that it might not have existed and *would* not have existed under certain specified conditions. For example, I would not have existed if my parents had never met. So Moore is right in saying, as against Russell, that one can say of a particular that it might not have existed under certain circumstances and mean nothing that has to be analyzed out in terms of whether certain properties might or might not have been instantiated.[8]

---

[6] Both Frege and Russell think that existence cannot be a predicate of individuals but identify it with the 'higher level' property expressed when we attach an existential quantifier to a one-place predicate. Frege said that the error of regarding existence as a predicate of individuals rather than (in his terminology) a second-level concept is the fundamental error of the ontological argument (see Frege 1997:146, note H). Russell's view is in fact similar to Frege's, though formulated in terms of his theory of descriptions, so that the illusion that there is a predicate of individuals can be connected to the illusion that the descriptions are terms referring to objects. This is clear from Quine, who writes: 'Russell undertook to resolve the anomalies of existence by admitting the word "exists" only in connection with descriptions, and explaining the whole context "$(\imath x)(\ldots x \ldots)$ exists" as short for '$(\exists y)(x)(x = y. \equiv. \ldots x \ldots)$' ... This course supplies a strict technical meaning for Kant's vague declaration that "exists" is not a predicate; namely, "exists" is not grammatically combinable with a variable to form a matrix "y exists"' (1940:151, citations omitted). But it is hard to see how Frege or Russell could deny that '$(\exists y)(y = x)$' is a 'first-level concept' (or predicate of individuals) that defines existence. See the discussion below about necessary existence, and Moore's argument against Russell in note 8.

[7] As I said in Kripke (1980:157–58), in which some of the views I am now stating are already summarized, the use of 'Sherlock Holmes' as the name of an actual but not possible individual now seems to me to be mistaken.

[8] Moore writes:

[I]n the case of every sense-datum which any one ever perceives, the person in question could always say with truth of the sense-datum in question 'This might not have existed'; and I cannot see how

Now turn to the actual world. The view of Frege and Russell would assert that to ask whether Sherlock Holmes really existed is to ask whether the story was substantially true of someone (uniquely); and to ask whether Moses existed is to ask whether the story was substantially true of someone. Let's first take the case where it is not a work of fiction, where historians have concluded that the characters really existed. I have discussed this case in Kripke (1980:67–68). In the case of Moses existing, does an affirmative answer imply that the story was substantially true of someone? I think that here again Frege and Russell have gone wrong, even in talking about the actual world. They fail to distinguish between a legend that is completely a tissue of whole cloth about a mythical character and a legend that grew up about an actual character. In the latter case we may say that the stories which have reached us are legendary and were true of no one, yet Moses or whoever else is mentioned in the story really existed. In fact, I quoted a biblical scholar who says exactly that about Jonah.[9]

As I have emphasized about these cases, the reason that we can say that Jonah really existed, though the stories which have reached us about him are substantially false, is that there is a historical chain of communication in which the name, with perhaps linguistic changes, has reached us, leading back to the man Jonah himself and the stories which were erroneously asserted about him.

Suppose the Sherlock Holmes stories were all true of one unique detective: does that amount to concluding that Sherlock Holmes really existed? The dustjackets of many books of this type contradict such a thesis. The opening page may say 'The characters in this work are fictional and any resemblance to anyone living or dead is purely coincidental'. What is meant by this is that even if by some bizarre accident the stories told in this work are substantially true of some particular people, and even true of them uniquely, the resemblance is purely fortuitous and was unknown to the author. (Actually, we might be suspicious of such a claim, but surely it is not conceptually impossible.) They are not the referents of the names that occur in the story, and it is just a coincidence that the story is substantially true of them. If one of these people about whom the story was true sued in court for invasion of privacy, or perhaps slander or libel, he would not win the case *solely* on the basis of establishing that the story was

---

this could be true, unless the proposition 'This does in fact exist' is also true, and therefore the words 'This exists' significant (1959:126).

Moore's argument would obviously apply to a much larger class of objects than sense-data. (I think the reason he is concerned with sense-data involves Russell's ideas on logically proper names, in particular that 'this' is always used as a logically proper name of a sense-datum.) And if one thought that some objects (say, numbers) *did* have necessary existence, this would be a significant fact about each such object and should imply a fortiori that the object exists.

[9] I could have stuck to Moses himself. The famous biblical scholar Martin Noth believed that there really was a Moses but that (in contrast to Wittgenstein 1953:§79, quoted in Kripke 1980:31) he had nothing to do with the exodus from Egypt or most of the best-known things related of him in the Pentateuch. (The true core about him is 'guidance into the arable land'.) This information was probably unknown to me when I gave the present paper.

substantially true of him. The judge, if the coincidence were really established, would rule against the plaintiff and against Frege, Russell, Wittgenstein, and Searle.[10] The reason, once again, lies in the lack of any historical connection to an actual person, even though the beliefs are substantially true of the person.

This is enough by way of softening up. If the Frege–Russell theory is wrong, then, of course, some account must be put forward in its place. But if their theory (as standardly conceived) does not give an account of the problems of existence and apparently empty names that is intuitively correct, then these problems do not, in themselves, argue in favor of their theory as opposed to one emphasizing reference rather than descriptive sense.

Let me take a stab at what a true account should be. There are really two different issues. One is what kind of proposition is expressed using an actual name, a name that really has reference: what is expressed when we make an existential statement using that name? Assume that the name 'Moses' refers to a certain man. When we say truly that Moses did exist, or if we said falsely that Moses did not exist, or counterfactually, what would have happened if Moses had not existed, we are always talking about *that man*. Existence is in this sense a predicate. Of course, if the man is around he has got to satisfy the predicate, and that makes it is a very special one. But although we could analyze this as '($\exists y$) (y = Moses),' we shouldn't try to replace it by anything involving instantiation of properties. When we say, 'Moses might not have existed and under certain circumstances would not have existed', we are saying something about a certain person, not about whether his deeds would have been accomplished under certain circumstances. Quantified sentences, such as 'Every (actual) person might not have existed at all', make perfect sense, and existence is a predicate governed by a quantifier.

As I have warned with respect to analogous cases in Kripke (1980), it doesn't matter that if Moses had not existed, people would not have been able to make the negative existential assertion. Rather, since we can refer to Moses, we can describe a counterfactual situation in which Moses wouldn't have existed. It matters not at all that in that situation people would not have been able to say, 'Moses does not exist', at least using 'Moses' the way we are using it here. Indeed, I can describe a counterfactual situation in which I would not have existed, even though if that were the case I wouldn't be around to say it. It would be wrong to identify the language people *would have*, given that a certain situation obtained, with the language that *we use to describe how circumstances would have been* in that situation. (I have sometimes run across this confused identification, both in the published literature and in discussion.)

---

[10] I have later been told that my assertion would not be true in English libel law, which is very favorable to plaintiffs, but would be true in U.S. law. I have not checked up on the matter. The conceptual point I am making is not really affected (even if English law imposes something like 'strict liability' here).

What happens in the case of a work of fiction? A work of fiction, generally speaking of course, is a pretense that what is happening in the story is really going on. To write a work of fiction is to imagine—spin a certain romance, say—that there really is a Sherlock Holmes, that the name 'Sherlock Holmes' as used in this story really refers to some man, Sherlock Holmes, and so on. It is therefore presumably part of the pretense of the story that the name 'Sherlock Holmes' is really a name and really has the ordinary semantic function of names. If one mistakenly believed the name to be non-empty rather than empty, it would be part of the mistake that this is a name having the ordinary semantic function of names. This principle I have roughly stated here, just as applied to works of fiction, we can call the pretense principle. What goes on in a work of fiction is a pretense that the actual conditions obtain.[11] A work of fiction need not even say that the names used in it are the 'real names' of the characters, the names that their parents gave them or the correct 'family name', or what their friends call them, and so on. In *Lolita* (Nabokov 1955),[12] in fact, it is stated that the names have been changed to protect the innocent. And that, too, is part of the pretense.

---

[11] Many other people have held something like this. But when I gave this talk, and even the subsequent John Locke Lectures, I was simply unaware that this principle is enunciated by Frege. See the following passage:

Names that fail to fulfill the usual role of a proper name, which is to name something, may be called mock proper names [*Scheineigennamen*]. Although the tale of William Tell is a legend and not history and the name 'William Tell' is a mock proper name, we cannot deny it a sense. But the sense of the sentence 'William Tell shot an apple off his son's head'. . . I characterize . . . as fictitious.

Instead of speaking of 'fiction', we could speak of 'mock thoughts' ['*Scheingedanke*]. . . . Even the thoughts are not to be taken seriously as in the sciences: they are only mock thoughts. If Schiller's *Don Carlos* were to be regarded as a piece of history, then to a large extent the drama would be false. But a work of fiction is not meant to be taken seriously in this way at all: it is all play. Even the proper names in the drama, though they correspond to names of historical persons, are mock proper names; they are not meant to be taken seriously in the work. . . .

The logician does not have to bother with mock thoughts, just as a physicist, who sets out to investigate thunder, will not pay any attention to stage-thunder. (Frege 1897:229–30)

There are various puzzles created by this passage, but the exegesis of Frege is not the main point here. Three things, however, should be noted. First, Frege is the first author I am aware of to have emphasized that empty names in fiction, and the sentences that contain them, are pretenses. Second, were the passage I am quoting to be given in full and expounded, it would not be clear that what I am calling the 'Frege–Russell' view was really Frege's view of the senses of names in fiction. Something like it does appear to be Frege's view of names of historical characters; it also appears to be the view of certain contemporary Fregeans, such as Alonzo Church, for legend and fiction (see his remarks about 'Pegasus' in Church 1956: 7, note 18). However, the view of names in fiction one might deduce from the passage quoted will be considerably different. (There is some difficulty understanding the passage, making it self-consistent or consistent with what Frege says elsewhere.) Third, in the passage Frege says that when a historical figure appears even by name in a fictional work, the name is only a "mock proper name". If this means that it is not truly a name of the figure in question, or that it fails to refer to him or her, I don't think this is right. When in *War and Peace* Tolstoy mentions Napoleon, and has him as a character in the work, he is talking about Napoleon (See Chapter 9.)

[12] In the preface, the supposed editor of the manuscript says that the names are not real. For example, 'Humbert Humbert', the name of the narrator and main character, is a pseudonym.

If this is so, the name, of course, doesn't *really* have any referent, it is *pretended* to have a referent; and if some view like Mill's is right, and the semantic function of naming is reference, then it follows that here we are only *pretending* to refer to a certain person and say something about him. The propositions that occur in the story, then, are not genuine propositions saying something about some particular person; they are instead merely *pretended propositions*. This is not to say that the sentences that occur in the story are meaningless in the strongest possible sense, because one knows, so to speak, what kind of propositions they are pretending to express. It could be (though maybe the supposition is fantastic) that in fact Doyle had not written stories but historical accounts of actual events. In this case we would be mistaken in believing that these sentences expressed no proposition. In fact, we could in principle say that they did express a proposition. But they don't, on the view I'm suggesting, express any proposition at all if in fact the names don't refer. In particular, it should be required of a genuine proposition that we should be able to say, of each possible world, whether the proposition allegedly expressed by the sentence would or would not have been true under the circumstances in question. If this test fails for the sentences in fiction, then they do not express genuine propositions. And to my mind this test does fail for the sentences in fiction.

Under what circumstances, to mention the case that I noted before, would Sherlock Holmes have existed, given that the name in fact has no referent? Well, not simply if someone or other would have done these things in the story, because the name 'Sherlock Holmes' is supposed to refer to a particular person rigidly. One cannot say, 'Well, it does not designate a real person, but just a (merely) possible person', whether one likes such an ontology or not, because many possible people might have done the things in the story. In fact, some actual people might have done the things in the story, if the circumstances had been different, in another possible world. Charles Darwin, if had he decided to go into another line of work, might have made an excellent detective around London at the time and fought with some analogue of Moriarty. This is not to say of him, or of anyone else, that he would have been Sherlock Holmes or might have been Sherlock Holmes. He could have *played the role* of Sherlock Holmes, he could have fulfilled the stories that are told about Sherlock Holmes. But if the pretense about Sherlock Holmes is that 'Sherlock Holmes' designates someone rigidly, one cannot say which person would have been designated. There is no criterion to pick out one as opposed to another; one should just say that this name does not designate.[13]

I want to say something further about this question of pretense. Aside from the philosophical doctrine of pretended propositions that I have, it seems to me

---

[13] See Kripke (1980:156–58). Recall that when this talk was given, the lectures were fairly recent. This section begins with a mythical natural kind term ('unicorn'), but continues with 'Sherlock Holmes'.

obvious that any theory has got to start with the fact that these pretenses in fiction are pretenses. It seems that people have worried and puzzled about empty names as if their existence is a great paradox, and that it is very hard to find a theory that can possibly account for the possibility of such things. 'If the function of naming is reference, how could we have empty names?' On the contrary, one has virtually *got* to have empty names because given any theory of reference—given *any* theory of how the conditions of reference are fulfilled—one can surely *pretend* that these conditions are fulfilled when in fact they are not. Thus the existence of pretended names (in fiction) cannot possibly adjudicate among different theories of names.

The question of whether empty names are possible particularly agitated Russell. He wanted to get rid of the possibility of an empty name (for his notion of logically proper names; names in the ordinary sense were supposed to be abbreviated definite descriptions, could be empty, and were not really names; see note 2). He restricted logically proper names to names of our immediate sense-data, whose existence was supposed to be indubitable, but was also very fleeting.[14] It was then an indubitable truth that the things so named exist. Wittgenstein in the *Tractatus* (1961) makes the objects his names refer to part of the necessary furniture of the world. Thus it is not possible that the things in question should have failed to exist. These two strategies come from, of course, the same motivation: in fact, as we know, they were working together.

It is interesting to point out that the conclusions to which they were led are not identical but, in fact, incompatible and show the trouble of switching from epistemic to metaphysical considerations. For surely our own immediate sense-data do not have any kind of necessary existence. Their existence is as contingent as anything could be. I right now am receiving all sorts of visual impressions. Had I not entered this room at all, or had I entered it blindfolded, these visual impressions would never have existed. Their existence is therefore contingent.

---

[14] As the following exchange shows:

Q.: If the proper name of a thing, a 'this', varies from instant to instant, how is it possible to make any arguments?
Mr. Russell: You can keep 'this' going for about a minute or two. I made that dot [he had then put a dot on the blackboard] and talked about it for some little time. I mean it varies often. If you argue quickly, you can get some little way before it is finished. I think things last for a finite time, a matter of some seconds or minutes or whatever it may happen to be.
Q.: You do not think that air is acting on that and changing it?
Mr. Russell: It does not matter about that if it does not alter its appearance enough for you to have a different sense-datum. (Russell 1918–19:180)

Russell already thought in 'On Denoting' (1905) that the constituents of our propositions must be objects of acquaintance, but what we are allowed to be acquainted with gradually became more and more restricted as his work progressed. So-called names of things that are not objects of our acquaintance are really disguised descriptions. The theory proposed in Russell (1918–19) is more restrictive than earlier ideas. To Gideon Makin (well after this lecture was delivered) I owe the point that for Russell sense-data were actually something physical, not strictly speaking to be identified with visual impressions, as I tend to do in the text. This doesn't affect the point that they are fleeting entities, as the cited interchange attests.

Lots of exegetes have wondered whether the objects of the *Tractatus* were in fact the Russellian sense-data. Aside from internal evidence, one thing we can say is that if they were, they would not fulfill the conditions laid down for objects in the *Tractatus*.

At any rate, Russell hardly succeeds in avoiding the mere possibility of empty names. If names are restricted to our own immediate sense-data, perhaps it is the case then that one cannot doubt whether objects so-called exist. But one can still spin a story, imagining oneself naming sense-data using pretended names, which in the story are stated to be Russellian logically proper names, though in fact they are the names of sense-data that one doesn't have. Suppose, for example, one such name were 'Harry', and 'Harry' is the name of some particular sense-datum. It will then be true for me to say outside the story that Harry does not exist, that there is no such sense-datum as Harry. So even Russell's theory does not avoid this difficulty. It seems to me impossible to imagine that this difficulty could conceivably have been avoided; given that we have a theory of reference, it can be part of the pretense of a story that the conditions for this theory are fulfilled, even when in fact they are not. (It might be possible to avoid any mistake as to whether one is really naming, but not the possibility of fiction or pretense.)

So to get clearer about this problem, one must stop tying oneself up in knots; one must recognize that pretenses that the conditions for semantic reference are fulfilled will always be possible, regardless of what theory of reference one may espouse. The degree of meaningfulness that a story has depends on our knowing what is being pretended. In the case of Sherlock Holmes it is being pretended that the name refers to a certain man and that certain things are being said about him. That is not to say that the sentences which occur in the story express genuine propositions in the sense that we can say under which counterfactual circumstances they would have been true, because we cannot. What I'm saying about pretense could be applied, *mutatis mutandis,* to mistakes and other cases like that—error as opposed to pretense or fiction. (Russell does, perhaps, by his certainty condition, avoid the possibility of mistake.) And one should not regard it as strange that such errors can exist—one should regard it as natural and inevitable.

Now to get a correct view on this matter, one has to separate the case of names occurring in fiction—where, using them correctly, we can say that the character doesn't exist: for example, 'Sherlock Holmes does not exist'—from cases where, on the contrary, the name 'Sherlock Holmes' is used in such a way that it is true to say that Sherlock Holmes does exist. It has been argued in the literature—for example, by Hintikka (1962)—that, regarded as a logical inference, 'I think, therefore I am', as stated by Descartes, would be fallacious. For, Hintikka says, replace 'I' with 'Hamlet'. Hamlet thought many things, but does it follow that Hamlet existed? The sort of usage that Hintikka presumably has in mind is on a true–false English test, where one asks:

Hamlet was married—true or false?
Hamlet was indecisive—true or false?
Hamlet thought—true or false?

To mark the latter one false would be to call him a mindless character, which is not the intent of the play. But what Hintikka's argument fails to recognize is that in this sense—in this special usage, where one is reporting on the play—'Hamlet existed' would be true also, because within the play there really was such a person as Hamlet. This is not trivial; sometimes on such a true–false test such a statement should be marked 'false'. For example, it is probable that according to the play Macbeth's dagger did not exist. Was the ghost of Hamlet's father real, or was Hamlet merely imagining things? In that case, I think the intent of the play is that the ghost was real. In this sense, surely Hamlet really did exist, though if he really thought there was a rat behind a curtain, there was no such rat. So the inference '*A* thinks, therefore *A* exists' holds up perfectly well against this alleged counterexample to the inference pattern.[15]

In the play *Hamlet* they put on a play called *The Murder of Gonzago*. Let's suppose that, according to the play *Hamlet*, this isn't supposed to be about any historical character.[16] One can then say, speaking within the play *Hamlet*, that such a real person as Gonzago never existed and that Gonzago was merely a fictional character. Since Hamlet was a real person within the play, it would be false to say that about Hamlet. So Gonzago was merely fictional; Hamlet was a real person. Whatever reasons there may be for free logic, the case of Hamlet (as cited in Hintikka's paper) is not one of them.[17]

Sometimes we say not that 'Hamlet' is an empty name, but that 'Hamlet' is the name of a fictional character. That seems to give the name a referent. Now, should we take this as a misleading mode of speaking, or should we attribute to ordinary language an ontology of things called 'fictional characters'? Well, the scary phrase 'things called "fictional characters"' suggests a negative answer. Are there going to be ghostly entities around?

Now actually I think that the answer to my question is yes, and that fictional characters are *not* ghostly entities or merely possible entities—they are entities of a certain sort that exist in the real world. We seem to existentially quantify over

---

[15] H. P. Grice told me that this was his view also, though I do not vouch for every detail.
[16] When I made such a supposition, I was only showing my own ignorance. Apparently, in fact, the House of Gonzaga was an important group of Italian noblemen who ruled in Mantua and elsewhere. (Why it is spelled 'Gonzago' in Shakespeare is unclear to me.) Years ago I talked to a Shakespeare expert, who told me that a real Gonzago (presumably, a member of the House) was, in fact, murdered, though there was no such play as *The Murder of Gonzago* as far as anyone knows. However, I have been unable to verify this conclusively. In the text, I have let stand my supposition that historically there was neither a murdered Gonzago, nor a play about such a murder.
[17] In free logic the general inference pattern $Fa \therefore (\exists x) Fx$ is invalid. Also, $(\exists x)(x=a)$ is neither valid nor does it follow in general from Fa. Whatever the motivations may be, the case of 'Hamlet thinks', taken within the play, is no confirmation of the need for free logic.

them when we say, 'There was such a fictional character as Hamlet'. Statements of this form—they are not within the story, because within the story Hamlet is not a fictional character, though Gonzago is—are also not trivial, just as within the story the affirmative existence statements using 'Hamlet' are not trivial. Here we can ask, 'Was there such a fictional character as Hamlet?', and the answer is 'Yes'. Was there such a fictional character as Gonzago? The answer is 'No', because it is only the play *Hamlet* that says that there is a play *The Murder of Gonzago*. There really isn't any such play, and therefore there isn't any such dramatic character as Gonzago to appear in *The Murder of Gonzago*. Speaking inside the play, we would say that Hamlet is a real person and Gonzago a fictional character. Speaking *outside* the play, we say that Hamlet is a fictional character and not a real person; Gonzago, on the other hand, is not a fictional character. That is, in a work of fiction there is said to be such a fictional character, but not outside that work of fiction.

It is important to see that fictional characters so called are not shadowy possible people. The question of their existence is a question about the actual world. It depends on whether certain works have actually been written, certain stories in fiction have actually been told. The fictional character can be regarded as an abstract entity which exists in virtue of the activities of human beings, in the same way that nations are abstract entities which exist in virtue of the activities of human beings and their interrelations.[18] A nation exists if certain conditions are true about human beings and their relations; it may not be reducible to them because we cannot spell them out exactly (or, perhaps, without circularity). Similarly, a fictional character exists if human beings have done certain things, namely, created certain works of fiction and the characters in them.

In ordinary language, we very often quantify over fictional characters. Perhaps such quantification could be eliminated if it were always possible to replace the original (quantified) sentence with a sentence describing the activities of people.[19] But, for example, here is a conversation I once had. You have probably heard how in the Bible the Israelites are often condemned to sacrificing their children to an evil deity called 'Moloch'. There are biblical scholars who hold that taking 'Moloch' to be the proper name of a deity was a mistake.[20] There was

---

[18] Van Inwagen (1977, 1983) seems to have rediscovered a very similar theory. I myself now vaguely recall hearing a lecture by Michael Dummett that mentioned a distinction between empty names and names of fictional characters. If my recollection is correct, it could well have influenced my ideas. Also, already in his paper 'Imaginary Objects', Moore (arguing against Ryle) says that, of course, various fictional statements of Dickens really are 'about Mr. Pickwick', but does not draw any explicit conclusion about an ontology of fictional characters. Nor does he seem to be defending a Meinongian ontology. See Moore (1959:105).

[19] Nevertheless, it is true that there are fictional characters with certain properties, and anyone who denies this is wrong.

[20] In fact, among them was Otto Eissfeldt, and those who accepted his theory (see Eissfeldt 1935). I think that Eissfeldt's theory may be less popular now than it was when I spoke, but this in no way affects the example. The much earlier theory, attributed by Eissfeldt to Abraham Geiger,

not, in fact, any such pagan deity, and 'Moloch' meant a type of sacrifice, like a burnt offering.[21] And 'to Moloch' should really be translated 'as a Moloch', the kind of sacrifice. So the idea that there was such a pagan deity was just a mistake. I was explaining this to someone[22] once and saying that on this account there was no such god, and he said to me, 'Of course there was not such a god. You don't believe in pagan deities, do you?' This response reveals an ambiguity in what I had said: one construal involves quantification over real gods, in which it is presumably already guaranteed that there is no such a god as Moloch; the other construal involves quantification over mythical entities, as in 'Was there such a (mythical) god?' The answer might have been 'yes', but according to this particular theory, turns out to be 'no'. The term 'god' turns out to be ambiguous. It may be used in such a way that only a pagan believer of the right kind would recognize the existence of the gods on Mount Olympus. But usually we use it otherwise—for example, when we ask, 'How many Greek gods were there?', 'Can you name any of the Greek gods?', and the like.

Phrasing the question in terms of the existence of fictional characters, the answer to the question 'Did Hamlet exist?' is affirmative, and we are not reporting on what the story says. In the same way, the answer to the question 'Was there such a deity as Moloch?' may be affirmative, contrary to Eissfeldt. One has to make sure what kind of entity one is talking about here. If one asks, 'Was there such a fictional character as Hamlet?' the answer is 'yes'. And, of course, one can ask of a fictional character referred to as *A* and a fictional character referred to as *B* whether they are the same fictional character; that makes sense, too. In a rough and ready way the apparatus of quantification and identity over these fictional characters is available to us in ordinary language. They are *not* ghostly possible entities; they are abstract entities of a certain sort that exist in virtue of the activities of people.

Many people have gotten confused about these matters because they have said, 'Surely there are fictional characters who fictionally do such-and-such things; but fictional characters don't exist; therefore, some view like Meinong's, with a first-class existence and a second-class existence, or a broad existence and a narrow existence, must be the case'.[23] This is not what I am saying here. The name 'Hamlet' as used in the story is not purporting to refer to a fictional character, it is purporting to refer to a person; and only when we speak *outside* the story can we

---

would also have the consequence that 'Moloch' was not the name of a pagan deity but came from a misvocalization of 'melech' ('king' in Hebrew). Some recent commentators I have read (long after this paper was delivered) accept that 'Moloch' did indeed name a pagan deity.

[21] In fact, as I recall, it meant human sacrifice.
[22] Harry Frankfurt.
[23] At any rate, this is how Meinong is characterized by Russell in 'On Denoting'. I confess that I have never read Meinong and don't know whether the characterization is accurate. It should be remembered that Meinong is a philosopher whom Russell (at least originally) respected; the characterization is unlikely to be a caricature.

say that no such person exists. When we say 'There was such a fictional character as Hamlet', we are not referring to a ghostly person—we are referring to a fictional character, one who really does exist, because people have written works of a certain sort. As I said, fictional characters are abstract entities of a certain kind. There are also alleged fictional characters that don't exist—Gonzago is an example. However, there can be *fictional* fictional characters, such as Gonzago. The predicate 'fictional' can be iterated, and Gonzago is a genuine fictional fictional character. There really is such a fictional fictional character, even though there is no such fictional character.[24]

The properties of fictional characters can be various. Many are not those of people (Meinongian or otherwise). Thus a fictional character can be widely popular or little read about, much discussed by literary critics, found in several Shakespeare plays, invented by Conan Doyle, and so on. On the other hand, a convention of our language allows us to elliptically[25] attribute to them properties in the works where they occur. Thus there was a fictional detective who lived on Baker Street, could draw conclusions from small details, and so on. There is a fictional character who was given a mission to kill his uncle, but there isn't one given a mission to kill his great-grandmother. (Or maybe there is; too many works have been written, and quite likely I just haven't heard about a relevant work. Still, if there is such a work, I can say with confidence that the respective fictional characters are not equally famous.)

Two sorts of things remain. First, I should mention, especially in light of the fact that Putnam emphasized these cases, my views about imaginary substances, as, for example, a magic elixir or unicorns. There, too, I would hold that one cannot intelligibly say, as is usually said in the literature, that though there are in fact no unicorns, unicorns might have existed. Why do I say that we cannot say this? Well, unicorns in the myth are supposed to refer to a certain species, a certain natural kind of animals. The term 'tiger' does not just mean 'any old animal that is yellow in color with black stripes'. An animal, whether existing in fact or only counterfactually, even though it looked just like a tiger on the outside, would not, if it were a reptile on the inside, be a tiger, as I have emphasized (Kripke 1980:119–21, and elsewhere).[26] Similarly, of course, something with a different chemical composition from water would not be water. Hence the statement 'water is H_2O' is a necessary truth.

If one is referring to an actual animal, one may of course pick it out by what Putnam calls a 'stereotype' (Putnam 1975a), without knowing what its internal structure is or how to differentiate it from other bogus things like fool's gold or

---

[24] Recall (see note 16) that the example is apparently incorrect, but I have kept up the pretense that it is correct. Correct examples plainly do exist. Note that if Eissfeldt is right there is no such fictional character (god) as Moloch, but there is no such fictional fictional character either.

[25] I mean that such a phrase as 'in the relevant stories' can be, and usually is, omitted.

[26] The dictionary definition to which I refer is given there in full.

fool's tiger. David Lewis once mentioned marsupial tigers to me, which might come along. One need not be able to make the differentiation as a layperson, and one may leave it up to the scientists, who may take a long time to do so, but we can still refer to tigers. That is because tigers are around; we have historical causal connections to them in the real world by virtue of which we can refer to them. Those properties that determine their essence can be discovered empirically later; when they are discovered, we can say which possible (or actual) animals resembling tigers wouldn't have been (or are not) tigers.

The same thing, I say, holds of unicorns. If the story about unicorns had really been true, then of course the animals would really be around and we could refer to them and discover their internal structure later. But suppose the story is completely false, that there is no connection with any actual animal. Then one should not say that 'unicorn' in this story simply means (let's say this is all the story tells us) 'that animal which looks like a horse and has a single horn'. One should not say that 'unicorn' simply means *any old animal like that* because then it would not be a pretended name of a species. In fact, one might well discover a new fragment of the story that explains how sometimes people were misled by animals that looked just like unicorns and mistook them for unicorns. These fool's unicorns commanded a high price on the market until their internal structure was discovered. The story, however, does not specify the differences in internal structure. 'Unicorn' is supposed to be the name of a particular species. We are given a partial identification of them; there are other criteria that would pick them out from fool's unicorns, but we are not told what these criteria are. Nor can we say 'Well, let's wait for the biologists to find out', because biologists cannot find anything out about unicorns. Thus of no possible animal can we say that it would have been a unicorn. One can merely say that it would look the way unicorns are supposed to. If a possible world contained two very different species, both fully conforming to the aforementioned story, one could not say which of them would have been unicorns.

Speaking of the actual world, I want similarly to say that a mere discovery that there were animals that answered entirely to whatever the myth says about unicorns would not, in and of itself, constitute a discovery that unicorns really existed. The connection, unlikely though this may be, could be purely coincidental. In fact the myth may say, 'The species mentioned in this myth is mythical, and any resemblance to any species extant or extinct is purely coincidental'. Let us suppose it does in fact say this. This shows that what one needs is not merely the fact that the animals in the unmodified myth satisfy everything that unicorns are supposed to satisfy, but that the myth was *about* them, that the myth was saying these things about them because the people had some historical and actual connection with them.

There are, then, two distinct theses here. First, we could find out that unicorns actually existed, but to find this out we would not just have to find out that certain animals have the properties mentioned in the myth. We would have to discover a real connection between the species and the myth—at least in the case of a species that is highly biologically unspecified. If a precise biological specification of it were given, the answer might be different. A complete description of the internal structure (and perhaps a specification of its place on the evolutionary tree, genetic inheritance, and the like) might lead us to say, 'By accident it turns out that there is a species exactly like that'. But that is not what usually goes on in stories and myths. Moreover, the way I have been putting it may be too epistemic. I am not really talking about what we could 'find out'. I am giving requirements for it to be *true* that unicorns actually existed, contrary to what we normally think.[27] However, were the specifications precise in the terms that I have just mentioned, then, if a kind meeting these specifications (structure, position on the evolutionary tree, etc.) actually existed, the story might arguably be true, and genuine propositions about the kind in question might be expressed, even in the (unlikely) case that the connection is purely coincidental.

Secondly—and this is another thesis—given that there are no unicorns, we *cannot* say that unicorns might have existed or would have existed under certain circumstances. Statements about unicorns, like statements about Sherlock Holmes, just *pretend* to express propositions. They do not really express, but merely purport to express, propositions. In the case of species, at least, this is true when the myth has not fully specified a hypothetical species, as I have mentioned in the previous paragraph. One cannot say when these sentences would have been true of a counterfactual situation, and therefore no proposition can have been expressed.[28]

However, something else should be said. Just as Sherlock Holmes was a fictional character, and there might or might not have been a mythical god referred to by the biblical 'Moloch',[29] so there really is such a mythical kind of animal as 'the unicorn'. This does not name a natural kind—even a Meinongian

---

[27] If the term 'unicorn' does in fact go back to some real kind of animal, there are two possibilities. One would be that unicorns really existed after all. Another is that a mythical kind of animal is historically connected to a real kind. In the case of individual people, an analogue is Santa Claus, a mythical character tracing back to a real historical person, Saint Nicholas (see Kripke 1980:93). Exactly when we should say, in the case either of animal kinds or of persons, that what is now a mythical case grew out of a real one or whether misconceptions grew up about an actual historical person or kind of animal is delicate. There may be borderline cases. We need not deal with this further here.

[28] Probably I ignored a nest of special technicalities when here, and in Kripke (1980), I talked very informally of animal natural kinds, and even used the term 'species' in a relatively informal way. There have been problems and disputes in the taxonomic literature on how 'species' should be defined and how larger and smaller natural kinds of animals should be defined. Moreover, I pay no attention to species where the male and the female may have very different internal structures (there is always going to be some difference). Although I am not an expert in the chemical case either, talk of chemical substances probably involves fewer issues. But here the examples of mythical species are too good to pass up, and I hope that a rough and ready treatment gives a reasonable idea for these cases.

[29] Outside the Pentateuch itself, probably 'Moloch' occurs in later religious literature and *is* used for a mythical god. My statements really should be confined to the Pentateuchal usage.

natural kind—but once again an actual abstract entity, a 'mythical beast', as I think I have seen in one dictionary.

Let me mention perhaps the stickiest point about the doctrine of pretending to express a proposition. One may feel, very strongly, 'How can the statement that unicorns exist not really express a proposition, given that it is false?' Against this, I would say first that it is not sufficient just to be able to say that it is false; one has to be able to say under what circumstances it would have been true, if any. And there seems to be no clear criterion here. Nevertheless, there remains the question of why we call this false. Why do we *say* 'unicorns don't exist'? Similarly, of course, in the case of Sherlock Holmes.

I am not entirely sure of the answer to this, but I will say what I can. First, I think the argument that 'unicorns exist' cannot express a proposition, or that 'Sherlock Holmes really exists' cannot express a proposition, is fairly conclusive. Here, when I talk about 'Sherlock Holmes really exists' I am not using 'Sherlock Holmes' to refer to the fictional character; under this interpretation the name does purport to refer to an existing entity. Nor am I using the sentence under the convention that what counts as true is what the story says.

Suppose I am using the sentence to express an alleged proposition about a detective, given to us by the story. Then I cannot say of a counterfactual situation that it is correctly describable as one in which 'Sherlock Holmes was fond of cricket', 'Sherlock Holmes was a detective', or 'Sherlock Holmes exists'. This is because when I think about them I cannot understand under what circumstances they would have been true—let alone any other propositions about Sherlock Holmes, like 'Sherlock Holmes was the best detective of all time'. Some of these statements are true and do express propositions when we are just reporting on what is said in the story, but, as I said, that is not the sort of usage in question here. (Similarly, sometimes one uses the statement just to say that the story says or implies that *p*, but that is a different sort of usage.) Nor am I talking about statements about fictional characters. These have truth-value in describing actual or counterfactual situations; in particular, such a fictional detective does in fact exist, but we can easily suppose counterfactual situations in which that detective wouldn't have existed, namely, situations where neither Doyle, nor (perhaps) anyone else, wrote or conceived such stories.[30]

---

[30] It would have been very tempting to fall back on the fictional character, so that the problem of 'Sherlock Holmes' as an empty name would disappear. Moreover, statements with 'Sherlock Holmes' have multiple ambiguities, on my view. They can be evaluated according to the story, or be about the fictional character (and such a character does exist); but, as we have seen, predicates applying to people can attach to that abstract entity in a derivative way.

Nevertheless, not all empty names are also used as names of fictional characters, nor am I sure that there is always an analogous class of entities. In any event, 'Sherlock Holmes does not exist' does look as if it has a usage under which it is true. Note, however, that this is a philosopher's tenseless usage. We are inclined really to say 'Sherlock Holmes never existed', similarly for 'Vulcan' (the planet). To me 'George Washington no longer exists, though he once did' seems to be a reasonably natural expression about a dead person, but I would be disinclined to put it as 'George Washington

Nevertheless, one may feel very strongly that one should truly say 'Unicorns don't exist'. I feel equally strongly, in fact, that one should say the same thing about bandersnatches, the animals Lewis Carroll mentions in 'Jabberwocky' (1872). Presumably, the bandersnatch is a fictional beast. According to the story, it is also a very dangerous one. Of course, there is no such animal as a bandersnatch; we can say 'There are no bandersnatches'. But surely no one would claim here that we can say that under certain circumstances bandersnatches would have existed—that we are just not told enough about them. They are just some dangerous sort of animal. Better get out of their way! They are also 'frumious'. But who knows what that means (though no doubt it is a dangerous or undesirable trait)? This does not prevent us from asserting 'bandersnatches don't exist and never did' or 'there are no bandersnatches'. Then the argument attempting to establish that 'unicorns exist' expresses a proposition on the basis of an intuition that the sentence is false surely cannot be conclusive. Just because we say 'unicorns don't exist', it does not follow that we can compare possible worlds with a concept of unicorns and declare that in it unicorns would have existed or not. In the case of bandersnatches, the situation is even more blatantly obvious.

Please do not say that bandersnatches would have existed if someone—even Lewis Carroll himself, say—had written this very poem about a real animal, for example, tigers, and so bandersnatches would have been tigers. This means that as language would have developed in that counterfactual situation, the sentence 'bandersnatches really existed' would have expressed something true. Of course that is the case, but that is talking about the language that Carroll *would* have used in that situation. It is not talking about Carroll's *actual* language as applied to that situation. Plainly, using 'bandersnatch' as it is used in the poem, one cannot say that this is a situation in which tigers would have been bandersnatches (or that the sentence 'tigers would have been bandersnatches' is true). Tigers would have been *called* 'bandersnatches', but one cannot say that they would have *been* bandersnatches. We cannot say when something would have been a bandersnatch any more than when some animal would have been 'frumious'.

Although we can say 'there are no bandersnatches' or 'bandersnatches don't exist', this plainly does not imply that we would know what it would be like for bandersnatches to have existed. Nor is an impossibility of the ordinary kind involved, such as the necessary nonexistence of round squares. We do say 'bandersnatches don't exist', and thus a certain sentence about bandersnatches seems to have a truth-value, but this does not mean that sentences containing 'bandersnatch' express ordinary propositions. And this I regard as a very substantial problem; perhaps the commentators will have something to say about it. They might just say that I'm wrong. David Kaplan, however, has expressed views

does not exist'. (I am taking it that here there isn't a problem of an empty name either.) I might have thought about this example after listening to a talk by Nathan Salmon.

very similar to mine at various points, and so it will be a problem for him, too. So I don't think he would be likely to say that I'm just wrong.

What can one say here? The same question arises for 'Sherlock Holmes'. We want to say, 'Sherlock Holmes doesn't exist'. One proposal might be to interpret it metalinguistically rather than as about a person. Thus, one might say that 'Sherlock Holmes does not exist' should be analyzed as meaning: 'The name "Sherlock Holmes" has no referent'. Then 'Sherlock Holmes does exist' should be analyzed as meaning 'The name "Sherlock Holmes" does have a referent'. And if one has a particular theory of reference, say a historical one, one might continue the analysis further and say 'Sherlock Holmes exists' means 'The chain goes somewhere' and 'Sherlock Holmes does not exist' means 'The chain goes nowhere'.

I reject this on a bunch of grounds, already stated in effect above. Let me say first what I accept. Although it may not be a priori, it is close enough to a priori for present purposes that Moses exists if and only if the name 'Moses' has a referent, and that Sherlock Holmes exists if and only if the name 'Sherlock Holmes' has a referent. That is the condition for the reference of the name. In general, relationships like these hold and the material equivalence of metalinguistic statements and corresponding statements in the 'material mode' is automatically accepted.

However, neither in the case of the name 'Moses' nor in the case of 'Sherlock Holmes' does this metalinguistic translation give an analysis that would apply to counterfactual situations also. Counterfactually speaking, Moses might have existed even though the name 'Moses' had no referent. This would be the case if neither he nor anyone else had ever been called 'Moses'. It is also true that the name 'Moses' might have had a referent, where that referent might not have been Moses.[31] However, my greatest emphasis, stated above, has been this. If we say, counterfactually, 'If Moses had not existed, then such and such . . .', or 'If his parents had never met, Moses would not have existed', or simply 'Moses might not have existed', we are speaking about *this man* and asking what might have happened to *him*.

Our problem, then, is this. If we use negative existentials, hypothetically, counterfactually, or whatever, we are normally supposing that we are talking about a referent and asking what would have happened if it had not existed. On the other hand, if we make the same statements categorically, we appear to be

---

[31] When I said these things, I was really ignoring many complications. First, many people may in fact be called 'Moses', and this is irrelevant. I would have to speak more carefully of 'the referent', and say something about the referent of the name as we use it in certain discourses, or in the King James translation, or whatever. I shouldn't be implying anything about whether he was, or anyone would have been, himself called 'Moses' in the ordinary sense of 'called'. The name appears to be ancient Egyptian, and is translated into Hebrew in the biblical original. It wasn't really 'Moses', and similar adjustments are needed for a literal description of the corresponding hypothetical situations. But none of this matters very much.

repudiating the object itself and saying that the name used only purports to be a name. Nor can we tell, simply by looking at a work, whether the Pentateuch or Doyle's stories, which strategy is appropriate. But don't we wish to give the statements in question a univocal analysis?

What I have said above about fictional characters gives us some respite. A name of a fictional character has a referent. One might then suppose that the name definitely has a referent (the fictional character). It will be a matter of empirical investigation, concerning a given work, whether it is about a fictional character or a real person.

However, I find myself uneasy about invoking this as a complete solution. There is an inclination to say 'Sherlock Holmes never existed'. Atheists have often been inclined to deny the existence of God, and perhaps sometimes they mean to use it as an empty name.[32] To use the example mentioned above, there is the denial of Moloch that I quoted from Eissfeldt, but if Eissfeldt is wrong, one could imagine two ancients arguing, with one saying that he believes in Jupiter but not in Moloch (and the usage of a follower of Eissfeldt must be explained, too, denying the existence of a particular mythical being). 'The bandersnatch' stands for a genuine fictional species or kind of beast, but we are inclined to say 'there are no bandersnatches', meaning in this instance to deny the existence of the kind (even though no one can say what a bandersnatch would have been).

What gives us any right to talk that way? I wish I knew exactly what to say. But the following is a stab at it. We can sometimes appear to reject a proposition, meaning that there is no true proposition of that form, without committing ourselves to mean that what we say expresses any proposition at all. Thus, without being sure of whether Sherlock Holmes was a person, or whether we can speak of hypothetical situations under which 'Sherlock Holmes did such and such' correctly describes the situation, we can say 'none of the people in this room is Sherlock Holmes, for all are born too late, and so on'; or 'whatever bandersnatches may be, certainly there are none in Dubuque'. Here we should, strictly speaking, be able to say that there is no true proposition to the effect that there are bandersnatches in Dubuque, without committing ourselves to the existence of such a proposition at all. Then 'Sherlock Holmes does not exist', 'there are no bandersnatches', and so on, are limiting cases of the same principle, really denying that there could be propositions of a certain kind at all.

In sum, I have stressed the following:

First, existence is a real predicate of individuals. Even though it may be trivial that everything exists, many things have only contingent existence and might not

---

[32] There might be some question about the term 'God' (see Kripke 1980:26–27). Here I am taking it to be a name. However, it might be taken to be a description, 'the unique divine being', and, if so, a Russellian analysis might be applied. (I am inclined to favor the first view, even if the reference is fixed by description.) There has traditionally been an uncontroversial proper name for God, but it is rarely found on the lips of ordinary speakers today.

have existed. Statements of this type should not be reduced to statements about the fulfillment of properties.

Second, whether a work is truth or fiction is not equivalent to whether existential statements asserting that some events occurring in the narrative did or did not happen (or whether some properties instantiated in the narrative did or did not get instantiated). The coincidence may be strange, but it is not impossible that things like these could have happened but had no connection with the work.

Third, when one evaluates what is true according to the story, existential statements have to be evaluated the same way as any others (not differently, as in Hintikka's case of 'Hamlet thinks' versus 'Hamlet exists' discussed above, Macbeth's dagger, etc.).

Fourth, questions of the existence of fictional characters, and other fictional objects, are empirical questions like any other, and sometimes have affirmative or negative answers. They depend on what fictional works exist. Thus, there certainly was a fictional detective, widely read about at the time he was described to exist, living on Baker Street, and so on. We have given examples, however, where the existence of various fictional or mythical objects can be dubious or controversial, and have remarked that the term 'fictional' can be iterated. We may mistakenly believe in the existence of a fictional character. Perhaps the most striking case (not mentioned above) would be a case where we took something to be a work of fiction when it was actually genuine history, written and so intended.

Finally, I had a residue of questions that appear to involve genuinely empty names and real assertions of nonexistence. These have just been discussed.[33]

REFERENCES

Beaney, M., ed. (1997). *The Frege Reader*. Oxford: Blackwell.
Carroll, L. [C. L. Dodgson]. (1872). *Through the Looking Glass, and What Alice Found There*. London: Macmillan.
Church, A. (1956). *Introduction to Mathematical Logic*. Princeton, NJ: Princeton University Press.
Davidson, D., and G. Harman, eds. (1972). *Semantics of Natural Language*. Dordrecht, the Netherlands: D. Reidel.

---

[33] I would like to thank Sam Wheeler and John Troyer for transcribing the original lecture. My thanks to Jeff Buechner, Gary Ostertag, and Harold Teichman for their editorial advice, and especially to Romina Padró for useful conversations and suggestions, and for her help in producing the present version. This paper has been completed with support from the Saul A. Kripke Center at the City University of New York, Graduate Center.

Eissfeldt, O. (1935). *Molk als Opferbegriff im Punischen und Hebräischen, und das Ende des Gottes Moloch.* Halle (Saale), Germany: M. Niemeyer.

Evans, G. (1982). *The Varieties of Reference.* Ed. John McDowell. Oxford: Oxford University Press.

Frege, G. (1897). 'Logic'. In *Posthumous Writings*, ed. and trans. Hans Hermes, Friedrich Kambartel, and Friedrich Kaulbach. Chicago: University of Chicago Press, 1979. Reprinted in part in Beaney (1997), 227–50; citations are to the reprint.

———. (1997). 'Function and Concept'. In M. Beaney (1997), 130–48. Translated by P. T. Geach. Originally published in 1891.

Gunderson, K. (1975). *Language, Mind, and Knowledge.* Minnesota Studies in the Philosophy of Science, Volume 7. Minneapolis: University of Minnesota Press.

Hintikka, J. (1962). '*Cogito, Ergo Sum*: Inference or Performance?' *Philosophical Review* 71:3–32.

Kripke, S. (1963). 'Semantical Considerations on Modal Logic'. *Acta Philosophica Fennica* 16:83–94. Reprinted in L. Linsky (1971); citations are to the reprint.

———. (1973). *Reference and Existence: The John Locke Lectures.* Unpublished.

———. (1980). *Naming and Necessity.* Cambridge, MA: Harvard University Press. First published in Davidson and Harman (1972), 253–355, 763–69.

Linsky, L., ed. (1971). *Reference and Modality.* Oxford: Oxford University Press.

Moore, G. E. (1933). 'Imaginary Objects', *Proceedings of the Aristotelian Society: Supplementary Volume XII*: 55–70. Reprinted in Moore (1959), 102–14.

———. (1936). 'Is Existence a Predicate?' *Proceedings of the Aristotelian Society, Supplementary Volume XV*: 175–88. Reprinted, with apparent changes, in Moore (1959), 115–26; citations are to the reprint.

———. (1959). *Philosophical Papers.* London: George Allen & Unwin.

Nabokov, V. (1955). *Lolita.* New York: Random House. 1st ed., Paris: Olympia, 1955.

Putnam, H. (1975a). 'The Meaning of "Meaning."' In Gunderson (1975). Reprinted in Putnam (1975b).

———. (1975b). *Mind, Language, and Reality: Philosophical Papers, Volume 2.* Cambridge: Cambridge University Press.

Quine, W. V. O. (1940). *Mathematical Logic.* Cambridge, MA: Harvard University Press.

———. (1960). *Word and Object.* Cambridge, MA: MIT Press.

Russell, B. (1905). 'On Denoting'. *Mind* 14:479–93.

———. (1918–19). 'The Philosophy of Logical Atomism'. *The Monist* 28: 495–527, and 29:33–63, 190–222, and 344–80. Reprinted in Russell (1988), 155–244.

———. (1988). *The Collected Papers of Bertrand Russell, Volume 8: The Philosophy of Logical Atomism and Other Essays, 1914–19.* Ed. John Slater. London: Routledge.

Salmon, N. (1998). 'Nonexistence'. *Noûs* 32:277–319. Reprinted in *Metaphysics, Mathematics, and Meaning: Philosophical Papers, Volume 1.* Oxford: Clarendon, 50–90.

Searle, J. R. (1958). 'Proper Names'. *Mind* 67:166–73.

Strawson, P. F. (1959). *Individuals.* London: Methuen.

van Inwagen, P. (1977). 'Creatures of Fiction'. *American Philosophical Quarterly* 14:299–308.

———. (1983). 'Fiction and Metaphysics'. *Philosophy and Literature* 7:67–77.

Whitehead, A. N., and Russell, B. (1910, 1912, 1913). *Principia Mathematica*. 3 Volumes. Cambridge: Cambridge University Press. 2nd ed., 1925 (Vol. 1), 1927 (Vols. 2, 3).

Wittgenstein, L. (1953). *Philosophical Investigations*. Trans. G. E. M. Anscombe. Oxford: Blackwell.

———. (1961). *Tractatus Logico-Philosophicus*. Trans. David Pears and Brian McGuinness. London: Routledge.

4
Outline of a Theory of Truth*

I. THE PROBLEM

Ever since Pilate asked, "What is truth?" (*John* XVIII, 38), the subsequent search for a correct answer has been inhibited by another problem, which, as is well known, also arises in a New Testament context. If, as the author of the Epistle to Titus supposes (*Titus* I, 12), a Cretan prophet, "even a prophet of their own," asserted that "the Cretans are always liars," and if "this testimony is true" of all other Cretan utterances, then it seems that the Cretan prophet's words are true if and only if they are false. And any treatment of the concept of truth must somehow circumvent this paradox.

The Cretan example illustrates one way of achieving self-reference. Let $P(x)$ and $Q(x)$ be predicates of sentences. Then in some cases empirical evidence establishes that the sentence '$(x)(P(x) \supset Q(x))$' [or '$(\exists x)(P(x) \wedge Q(x))$', or the like] itself satisfies the predicate $P(x)$; sometimes the empirical evidence shows that it is the *only* object satisfying $P(x)$. In this latter case, the sentence in question "says of itself" that it satisfies $Q(x)$. If $Q(x)$ is the predicate[1] 'is false', the Liar

---

* Presented in an APA symposium on Truth, December 28, 1975.
  Originally it was understood that I would present this paper orally without submitting a prepared text. At a relatively late date, the editors of *The Journal of Philosophy* (where this paper originally appeared) requested that I submit at least an "outline" of my paper. I agreed that this would be useful. I received the request while already committed to something else, and had to prepare the present version in tremendous haste, without even the opportunity to revise the first draft. Had I had the opportunity to revise, I might have expanded the presentation of the basic model in sec. III so as to make it clearer. The text shows that a great deal of the formal and philosophical material, and the proofs of results, had to be omitted.
  Abstracts of the present work were presented by title at the Spring, 1975, meeting of the Association for Symbolic Logic held in Chicago. A longer version was presented as three lectures at Princeton University, June, 1975. I hope to publish another more detailed version elsewhere. Such a longer version should contain technical claims made here without proof, and much technical and philosophical material unmentioned or condensed in this outline.

[1] I follow the usual convention of the "semantic" theory of truth in taking truth and falsity to be predicates true of sentences. If truth and falsity primarily apply to propositions or other nonlinguistic entities, read the predicate of sentences as "expresses a truth."
  I have chosen to take sentences as the primary truth vehicles *not* because I think that the objection that truth is primarily a property of propositions (or "statements") is irrelevant to serious work on

paradox results. As an example, let $P(x)$ abbreviate the predicate 'has tokens printed in copies of *Philosophical Troubles*, p. 76, line 4. Then the sentence:

$(x)(P(x) \supset Q(x))$

leads to paradox if $Q(x)$ is interpreted as falsehood.

The versions of the Liar paradox which use empirical predicates already point up one major aspect of the problem: *many, probably most, of our ordinary assertions about truth and falsity are liable, if the empirical facts are extremely unfavorable, to exhibit paradoxical features.* Consider the ordinary statement, made by Jones:

(1) Most (i.e., a majority) of Nixon's assertions about Watergate are false.

Clearly, nothing is intrinsically wrong with (1), nor is it ill-formed. Ordinarily the truth value of (1) will be ascertainable through an enumeration of Nixon's Watergate-related assertions, and an assessment of each for truth or falsity. Suppose, however, that Nixon's assertions about Watergate are evenly balanced between the true and the false, except for one problematic case,

(2) Everything Jones says about Watergate is true.

Suppose, in addition, that (1) is Jones's sole assertion about Watergate, or alternatively, that all his Watergate-related assertions except perhaps (1) are true. Then it requires little expertise to show that (1) and (2) are both paradoxical: they are true if and only if they are false.

The example of (1) points up an important lesson: it would be fruitless to look for an *intrinsic* criterion that will enable us to sieve out—as meaningless, or ill-formed—those sentences which lead to paradox. (1) is, indeed, the paradigm of an ordinary assertion involving the notion of falsity; just such assertions were characteristic of our recent political debate. Yet no syntactic or semantic feature of (1) guarantees that it is unparadoxical. Under the assumptions of the previous

---

truth or to the semantic paradoxes. On the contrary, I think that ultimately a careful treatment of the problem may well need to separate the "expresses" aspect (relating sentences to propositions) from the "truth" aspect (putatively applying to propositions). I have not investigated whether the semantic paradoxes present problems when directly applied to propositions. The main reason I apply the truth predicate directly to linguistic objects is that for such objects a mathematical theory of self-reference has been developed. (See also footnote 32.)

Further, a more developed version of the theory would allow languages with demonstratives and ambiguities and would speak of utterances, sentences under a reading, and the like, as having truth value. In the informal exposition this paper does not attempt to be precise about such matters. Sentences are the official truth vehicles, but informally we occasionally talk about utterances, statements, assertions, and so on. Occasionally we may speak as if every utterance of a sentence in the language makes a statement, although below we suggest that a sentence may fail to make a statement if it is paradoxical or ungrounded. We are precise about such issues only when we think that imprecision may create confusion or misunderstanding. Like remarks apply to conventions about quotation.

paragraph, (1) leads to paradox.² Whether such assumptions hold depends on the empirical facts about Nixon's (and other) utterances, not on anything intrinsic to the syntax and semantics of (1). (Even the subtlest experts may not be able to avoid utterances leading to paradox. It is said that Russell once asked Moore whether he always told the truth, and that he regarded Moore's negative reply as the sole falsehood Moore had ever produced. Surely no one had a keener nose for paradox than Russell. Yet he apparently failed to realize that if, as he thought, all Moore's *other* utterances were true, Moore's negative reply was not simply false but paradoxical.³) The moral: an adequate theory must allow our statements involving the notion of truth to be *risky*: they risk being paradoxical if the empirical facts are extremely (and unexpectedly) unfavorable. There can be no syntactic or semantic "sieve" that will winnow out the "bad" cases while preserving the "good" ones.

I have concentrated above on versions of the paradox using empirical properties of sentences, such as being uttered by particular people. Gödel showed essentially that such empirical properties are dispensable in favor of purely syntactic properties: he showed that, for each predicate $Q(x)$, a syntactic predicate $P(x)$ can be produced such that the sentence $(x)(P(x) \supset Q(x))$ is demonstrably the only object satisfying $P(x)$. Thus, in a sense, $(x)(P(x) \supset Q(x))$ "says of itself" that it satisfies $Q(x)$. He also showed that elementary syntax can be interpreted in number theory. In this way, Gödel put the issue of the legitimacy of self-referential sentences beyond doubt; he showed that they are as incontestably legitimate as arithmetic itself. But the examples using empirical predicates retain their importance: they point up the moral about riskiness.

A simpler, and more direct, form of self-reference uses demonstratives or proper names: Let 'Jack' be a name of the sentence 'Jack is short', and we have a sentence that says of itself that it is short. I can see nothing wrong with "direct" self-reference of this type. If 'Jack' is not already a name in the language,⁴ why can we not introduce it as a name of any entity we please? In particular, why can it not be a name of the (uninterpreted) finite sequence of marks 'Jack is short'? (Would it be permissible to call this sequence of marks "Harry," but not "Jack"? Surely prohibitions on naming are arbitrary here.) There is no vicious circle in our procedure, since we need not *interpret* the sequence of marks 'Jack is short' before we name it. Yet if we name it "Jack," it at once becomes meaningful and

---

² Both Nixon and Jones may have made their respective utterances without being aware that the empirical facts make them paradoxical.

³ On an ordinary understanding (as opposed to the conventions of those who state Liar paradoxes), the question lay in the sincerity, not the truth, of Moore's utterances. Paradoxes could probably be derived on this interpretation also.

⁴ We assume that 'is short' *is* already in the language.

true. (Note that I am speaking of self-referential sentences, not self-referential propositions.[5])

In a longer version, I would buttress the conclusion of the preceding paragraph not only by a more detailed philosophical exposition, but also by a mathematical demonstration that the simple kind of self-reference exemplified by the "Jack is short" example could actually be used to prove the Gödel incompleteness theorem itself (and also, the Gödel-Tarski theorem on the undefinability of truth). Such a presentation of the proof of the Gödel theorem might be more perspicuous to the beginner than is the usual one. It also dispels the impression that Gödel was forced to replace direct self-reference by a more circumlocutory device. The argument must be omitted from this outline.[6]

It has long been recognized that some of the intuitive trouble with Liar sentences is shared with such sentences as

(3) (3) is true.

which, though not paradoxical, yield no determinate truth conditions. More complicated examples include a pair of sentences each one of which says that the other is true, and an infinite sequence of sentences $\{P_i\}$, where P_i says that P_{i+1} is true. In general, if a sentence such as (1) asserts that (all, some, most, etc.) of the sentences of a certain class C are true, its truth value can be ascertained if the truth values of the sentences in the class C are ascertained. If some of these sentences themselves involve the notion of truth, their truth value in turn must be ascertained by looking at *other* sentences, and so on. If ultimately this process terminates in sentences not mentioning the concept of truth, so that the truth value of the original statement can be ascertained, we call the original sentence *grounded*; otherwise, ungrounded.[7] As the example of (1) indicates, whether a sentence is grounded is not in general an intrinsic (syntactic or semantic) property of a sentence, but usually depends on the empirical facts. We make utterances which we hope will turn out to be grounded. Sentences such as (3), though not paradoxical, are ungrounded. The preceding is a rough sketch of the usual notion of groundedness and is not meant to provide a formal definition: the fact that a formal definition can be provided will be a principal virtue of the formal theory suggested below.[8]

---

[5] It is *not* obviously possible to apply this technique to obtain "directly" self-referential *propositions*.
[6] There are several ways of doing it, using either a nonstandard Gödel numbering where statements can contain numerals designating their own Gödel numbers, or a standard Gödel numbering, plus added constants of the type of 'Jack'.
[7] If a sentence asserts, e.g., that all sentences in class C are true, we allow it to be false and grounded if one sentence in C is false, irrespective of the groundedness of the other sentences in C.
[8] Under that name, groundedness seems to have been first explicitly introduced into the literature in Hans Herzberger, "Paradoxes of Grounding in Semantics," *The Journal of Philosophy*, XVII, 6 (March 26, 1970): 145–167. Herzberger's paper is based on unpublished work on a "groundedness" approach to the semantic paradoxes undertaken jointly with Jerrold

II. PREVIOUS PROPOSALS

Thus far the only approach to the semantic paradoxes that has been worked out in any detail is what I will call the "orthodox approach," which leads to the celebrated hierarchy of languages of Tarski.[9] Let L_0 be a formal language, built up by the usual operations of the first-order predicate calculus from a stock of (completely defined) primitive predicates, and adequate to discuss its own syntax (perhaps using arithmetization). (I omit an exact characterization.) Such a language cannot contain its own truth predicate, so a meta-language L_1 contains a truth (really satisfaction) predicate $T_1(x)$ for L_0. (Indeed, Tarski shows how to define such a predicate in a higher-order language.) The process can be iterated, leading to a sequence $\{L_0, L_1, L_2, L_3, \ldots\}$ of languages, each with a truth predicate for the preceding.

Philosophers have been suspicious of the orthodox approach as an analysis of our intuitions. Surely our language contains just one word 'true', not a sequence of distinct phrases ⌜$true_n$⌝, applying to sentences of higher and higher levels. As against this objection, a defender of the orthodox view (if he does not dismiss natural language altogether, as Tarski inclined to do) may reply that the ordinary notion of truth is systematically ambiguous: its "level" in a particular occurrence is determined by the context of the utterance and the intentions of the speaker. The notion of differing truth predicates, each with its own level, seems to correspond to the following intuitive idea, implicit in the discussion of "groundedness" above. First, we make various utterances, such as 'snow is white', which do not involve the notion of truth. We then attribute truth values to these, using a predicate '$true_1$'. ('$True_1$' means—roughly—"is a true statement not itself involving truth or allied notions.") We can then form a predicate '$true_2$' applying to sentences involving '$true_1$', and so on. We may assume that, on each occasion of utterance, when a given speaker uses the word 'true', he attaches an implicit

---

J. Katz. The intuitive notion of groundedness in semantics surely was part of the folklore of the subject much earlier. As far as I know, the present work gives the first rigorous definition.

[9] By an "orthodox approach", I mean any approach that works within classical quantification theory and requires all predicates to be totally defined on the range of the variables. Various writers speak as if the "hierarchy of languages" or Tarskian approach *prohibited* one from forming, for example, languages with certain kinds of self-reference, or languages containing their own truth predicates. On my interpretation, there are no *prohibitions*; there are only *theorems* on what can and cannot be done within the framework of ordinary classical quantification theory. Thus Gödel *showed* that a classical language can talk about its own syntax; using restricted truth definitions and other devices, such a language can say a great deal about its own semantics. On the other hand, Tarski *proved* that a classical language cannot contain its own truth predicate, and that a higher-order language can define a truth predicate for a language of lower order. None of this came from any a priori restrictions on self-reference other than those deriving from the restriction to a classical language, all of whose predicates are totally defined.

subscript to it, which increases as, by further and further reflection, he goes higher and higher in his own Tarski hierarchy.[10]

Unfortunately this picture seems unfaithful to the facts. If someone makes such an utterance as (1), he does *not* attach a subscript, explicit or implicit, to his utterance of 'false', which determines the "level of language" on which he speaks. An implicit subscript would cause no trouble if we were sure of the "level" of *Nixon's* utterances; we could then cover them all, in the utterance of (1) or even of the stronger

(4) All of Nixon's utterances about Watergate are false.

simply by choosing a subscript higher than the levels of any involved in Nixon's Watergate-related utterances. Ordinarily, however, a speaker *has no way of knowing the "levels" of Nixon's relevant utterances.* Thus Nixon may have said, "Dean is a liar," or "Haldeman told the truth when he said that Dean lied," etc., and the "levels" of these may yet depend on the levels of Dean's utterances, and so on. If the speaker is forced to assign a "level" to (4) in advance [or to the word 'false' in (4)], he may be unsure how high a level to choose; if, in ignorance of the "level" of Nixon's utterances, he chooses too low, his utterance (4) will fail of its purpose. The idea that a statement such as (4) should, in its normal uses, have a "level" is intuitively convincing. It is, however, equally intuitively obvious that the "level" of (4) should not depend on the form of (4) alone (as would be the case if 'false'—or, perhaps, 'utterances'—were assigned explicit subscripts), nor should it be assigned in advance by the speaker, but rather its level should depend on the empirical facts about what Nixon has uttered. The higher the "levels" of Nixon's utterances happen to be, the higher the "level" of (4). This means that in some sense a statement should be allowed to seek its own level, high enough to say what it intends to say. It should not have an intrinsic level fixed in advance, as in the Tarski hierarchy.

Another situation is even harder to accommodate within the confines of the orthodox approach. Suppose Dean asserts (4), while Nixon in turn asserts

---

[10] Charles Parsons, "The Liar Paradox," *Journal of Philosophical Logic*, III, 4 (October 1974): 380–412, may perhaps be taken as giving an argument like the one sketched in this paragraph. Much of his paper, however, may be regarded as confirmed rather than refuted by the present approach. See in particular his fn 19, which hopes for a theory that avoids explicit subscripts. The minimal fixed point (see sec. III below) avoids explicit subscripts but nevertheless has a notion of level; in this respect it can be compared with standard set theory as opposed to the theory of types. The fact that the levels are not intrinsic to the sentences is peculiar to the present theory and is additional to the absence of explicit subscripting.

The orthodox assignment of intrinsic levels guarantees freedom from "riskiness" in the sense explained in sec. I above. For (4) and (5) below, the very assignment of intrinsic levels which would eliminate their riskiness would also prevent them from "seeking their own levels" (see pp. 695–697). *If we wish to allow sentences to seek their own levels apparently we must also allow risky sentences.* Then we must regard sentences as *attempting* to express propositions, and allow truth-value gaps. See sec. III below.

(5) Everything Dean says about Watergate is false.

Dean, in asserting the sweeping (4), wishes to include Nixon's assertion (5) within its scope (as one of the Nixonian assertions about Watergate which is said to be false); and Nixon, in asserting (5), wishes to do the same with Dean's (4). Now on any theory that assigns intrinsic "levels" to such statements, so that a statement of a given level can speak only of the truth or falsity of statements of lower levels, it is plainly impossible for both to succeed: if the two statements are on the same level, neither can talk about the truth or falsity of the other, while otherwise the higher can talk about the lower, but not conversely. Yet intuitively, we can often assign unambiguous truth values to (4) and (5). Suppose Dean has made at least one true statement about Watergate [other than (4)]. Then, independently of any assessment of (4), we can decide that Nixon's (5) is false. If all Nixon's other assertions about Watergate are false as well, Dean's (4) is true; if one of them is true, (4) is false. Note that in the latter case, we could have judged (4) to be false without assessing (5), but in the former case the assessment of (4) as true depended on a *prior* assessment of (5) as false. Under a different set of empirical assumptions about the veracity of Nixon and Dean, (5) would be true [and its assessment as true would depend on a prior assessment of (4) as false]. It seems difficult to accommodate these intuitions within the confines of the orthodox approach.

Other defects of the orthodox approach are more difficult to explain within a brief outline, though they have formed a substantial part of my research. One problem is that of transfinite levels. It is easy, within the confines of the orthodox approach, to assert

(6) Snow is white,

to assert that (6) is true, that '(6) is true' is true, that '"(6) is true" is true' is true, etc.; the various occurrences of 'is true' in the sequence are assigned increasing subscripts. It is much more difficult to assert that all the statements in the sequence just described are true. To do this, we need a metalanguage of transfinite level, above all the languages of finite level. To my surprise, I have found that the problem of defining the languages of transfinite level presents substantial technical difficulties which have never seriously been investigated.[11] (Hilary Putnam and his students essentially investigated—under the guise of a superficially completely different description and mathematical motivation—the problem for the special case where we start at the lowest level with the language of elementary number theory.) I have obtained various positive results on the problem, and there are also various negative results; they cannot be detailed here. But in the present state of the literature, it should be said that if the "theory

---

[11] The problem of transfinite levels is perhaps not too difficult to solve in a canonical way at level ω, but it becomes increasingly acute at higher ordinal levels.

of language levels" is meant to include an account of transfinite levels, then one of the principal defects of the theory is simply the *nonexistence* of the theory. The existing literature can be said to define "Tarski's hierarchy of languages" only for *finite* levels, which is hardly adequate. My own work includes an extension of the orthodox theory to transfinite levels, but it is as yet incomplete. Lack of space not only prevents me from describing the work; it prevents me from mentioning the mathematical difficulties that make the problem highly nontrivial.

Other problems can only be mentioned. One surprise to me was the fact that the orthodox approach by no means obviously guarantees groundedness in the intuitive sense mentioned above. The concept of truth for Σ_1 arithmetical statements is itself Σ_1, and this fact can be used to construct statements of the form of (3). Even if unrestricted truth definitions are in question, standard theorems easily allow us to construct a *descending* chain of first-order languages $L_0, L_1, L_2, \ldots$, such that L_i contains a truth predicate for L_{i+1}. I don't know whether such a chain can engender ungrounded sentences, or even quite how to state the problem here; some substantial technical questions in this area are yet to be solved.

Almost all the extensive recent literature seeking alternatives to the orthodox approach—I would mention especially the writings of Bas van Fraassen and Robert L. Martin[12]—agrees on a single basic idea: there is to be only one truth predicate, applicable to sentences containing the predicate itself; but paradox is to be avoided by allowing truth-value gaps and by declaring that paradoxical sentences in particular suffer from such a gap. These writings seem to me to suffer sometimes from a minor defect and almost always from a major defect. The minor defect is that some of these writings criticize a strawmannish version of the orthodox approach, not the genuine article.[13] The major defect is that these writings almost invariably are mere suggestions, not genuine theories. Almost never is there any precise semantical formulation of a language, at least rich

---

[12] See Martin, ed., *The Paradox of the Liar* (New Haven: Yale, 1970) and the references given there.

[13] See fn 9 above. Martin, for example, in his papers "Toward a Solution to the Liar Paradox," *Philosophical Review*, LXXVI, 3 (July 1967): 279–311, and "On Grelling's Paradox," *ibid.*, LXXVII, 3 (July 1968): 325–331, attributes to "the theory of language levels" all kinds of restrictions on self-reference which must be regarded as simply refuted, even for classical languages, by Gödel's work. Perhaps there are or have been some theorists who believed that *all* talk of an object language must take place in a distinct metalanguage. This hardly matters; the main issue is: what constructions can be carried out within a classical language, and what require truth-value gaps? Almost all the cases of self-reference Martin mentions can be carried out by orthodox Gödelian methods without any need to invoke partially defined predicates or truth-value gaps. In fn 5 of his second paper Martin takes some notice of Gödel's demonstration that sufficiently rich languages contain their own syntax, but he seems not to realize that this work makes most of his polemics against "language levels" irrelevant.

At the other extreme, some writers still seem to think that some kind of general ban on self-reference is helpful in treating the semantic paradoxes. In the case of self-referential *sentences*, such a position seems to me to be hopeless.

enough to speak of its own elementary syntax (either directly or via arithmetization) and containing its own truth predicate. Only if such a language were set up with formal precision could it be said that a theory of the semantic paradoxes has been presented. Ideally, a theory should show that the technique can be applied to arbitrarily rich languages, no matter what their "ordinary" predicates other than truth. And there is yet another sense in which the orthodox approach provides a theory while the alternative literature does not. Tarski shows how, for a classical first-order language whose quantifiers range over a set, he can give a *mathematical definition* of truth, using the predicates of the object language plus set theory (higher-order logic). The alternative literature abandons the attempt at a mathematical definition of truth, and is content to take it as an intuitive primitive. Only one paper in the "truth-gap" genre that I have read—a recent paper by Martin and Peter Woodruff[14]—comes close even to beginning an attempt to satisfy any of these desiderata for a theory. Nevertheless the influence of this literature on my own proposal will be obvious.[15]

III. THE PRESENT PROPOSAL

I do not regard any proposal, including the one to be advanced here, as definitive in the sense that it gives *the* interpretation of the ordinary use of 'true', or *the* solution to the semantic paradoxes. On the contrary, I have not at the moment thought through a careful philosophical justification of the proposal, nor am I sure of the exact areas and limitations of its applicability. I do hope that the model given here has two virtues: first, that it provides an area rich in formal structure and mathematical properties; second, that to a reasonable extent these properties capture important intuitions. The model, then, is to be tested by its technical fertility. It need not capture every intuition, but it is hoped that it will capture many.

Following the literature mentioned above, we propose to investigate languages allowing truth-value gaps. Under the influence of Strawson,[16] we can regard a

---

[14] "On Representing 'True-in-L' in L," *Philosophia*, 5, (1975): 217–221. In the terminology of the present paper, the paper by Martin and Woodruff proves the existence of *maximal* fixed points (not the minimal fixed point) in the context of the weak three-valued approach. It does not develop the theory much further. See Although it partially anticipates the present approach, it was unknown to me when I did the work.

[15] Actually I was familiar with relatively little of this literature when I began work on the approach given here. Even now I am unfamiliar with a great deal of it, so that tracing connections is difficult. Martin's work seems, in its formal consequences if not its philosophical basis, to be closest to the present approach.

There is also a considerable literature on three-valued or similar approaches to the set-theoretical paradoxes, with which I am not familiar in detail but which seems fairly closely related to the present approach. I should mention Gilmore, Fitch, Feferman.

[16] I am interpreting Strawson as holding that 'the present king of France is bald' fails to make a statement but is still meaningful, because it gives directions (conditions) for making a statement. I apply this to the paradoxical sentences, without committing myself on his original case of

sentence as an attempt to make a statement, express a proposition, or the like. The meaningfulness or well-formedness of the sentence lies in the fact that there are specifiable circumstances under which it has determinate truth conditions (expresses a proposition), not that it always does express a proposition. A sentence such as (1) is always *meaningful*, but under various circumstances it may not "make a statement" or "express a proposition." (I am not attempting to be philosophically completely precise here.)

To carry out these ideas, we need a semantical scheme to handle predicates that may be only partially defined. Given a nonempty domain D, a monadic predicate $P(x)$ is interpreted by a pair (S_1, S_2) of disjoint subsets of D. S_1 is the *extension* of $P(x)$ and S_2 is its *anti-extension*. $P(x)$ is to be true of the objects in S_1, false of those in S_2, undefined otherwise. The generalization to n-place predicates is obvious.

One appropriate scheme for handing connectives is Kleene's strong three-valued logic. Let us suppose that $\sim P$ is true (false) if P is false (true), and undefined if P is undefined. A disjunction is true if at least one disjunct is true regardless of whether the other disjunct is true, false, or undefined[17]; it is false if both disjuncts are false; undefined, otherwise. The other truth functions can be defined in terms of disjunction and negation in the usual way. (In particular, then, a conjunction will be true if both conjuncts are true, false if at least one conjunct is false, and undefined otherwise.) $(\exists x)A(x)$ is true if $A(x)$ is true for some assignment of an element of D to x, false if $A(x)$ is false for all assignments to x, and undefined otherwise. $(x)A(x)$ can be defined as $\sim(\exists x)\sim A(x)$. It therefore is true if $A(x)$ is true for all assignments to x, false if $A(x)$ is false for at least one such assignment, and undefined otherwise. We could convert the preceding into a more precise formal definition of satisfaction, but we won't bother.[18]

---

descriptions. It should be stated that Strawson's doctrine is somewhat ambiguous and that I have chosen a preferred interpretation, which I think Strawson also prefers today.

[17] Thus the disjunction of 'snow is white' with a Liar sentence will be true. If we had regarded a Liar sentence as *meaningless*, presumably we would have had to regard any compound containing it as meaningless also. Since we don't regard such a sentence as meaningless, we can adopt the approach taken in the text.

[18] The valuation rules are those of S. C. Kleene, *Introduction to Metamathematics* (New York: Van Nostrand, 1952), sec. 64, pp. 332–340. Kleene's notion of regular tables is equivalent (for the class of valuations he considers) to our requirement of the monotonicity of ϕ below.

I have been amazed to hear my use of the Kleene valuation compared occasionally to the proposals of those who favor abandoning standard logic "for quantum mechanics," or positing extra truth values beyond truth and falsity, etc. Such a reaction surprised me as much as it would presumably surprise Kleene, who intended (as I do here) to write a work of standard mathematical results, provable in conventional mathematics. "Undefined" is not an *extra* truth value, any more than—in Kleene's book—μ is an extra *number* in sec. 63. Nor should it be said that "classical logic" does not generally hold, any more than (in Kleene) the use of partially defined functions invalidates the commutative law of addition. *If* certain sentences express propostitions, any tautological truth function of them expresses a true proposition. Of course formulas, even with the forms of tautologies, which have components that do not express propositions may have truth functions

We wish to capture an intuition of somewhat the following kind. Suppose we are explaining the word 'true' to someone who does not yet understand it. We may say that we are entitled to assert (or deny) of any sentence that it is true precisely under the circumstances when we can assert (or deny) the sentence itself. Our interlocutor then can understand what it means, say, to attribute truth to (6) ('snow is white') but he will still be puzzled about attributions of truth to sentences containing the word 'true' itself. Since he did not understand these sentences initially, it will be equally nonexplanatory, initially, to explain to him that to call such a sentence "true" ("false") is tantamount to asserting (denying) the sentence itself.

Nevertheless, with more thought the notion of truth as applied even to various sentences themselves containing the word 'true' can gradually become clear. Suppose we consider the sentence,

(7) Some sentence printed in the *New York Daily News*, October 7, 1971, is true.

(7) is a typical example of a sentence involving the concept of truth itself. So if (7) is unclear, so still is

(8) (7) is true.

However, our subject, if he is willing to assert 'snow is white', will according to the rules be willing to assert '(6) is true'. But suppose that among the assertions printed in the *New York Daily News*, October 7, 1971, is (6) itself. Since our subject is willing to assert '(6) is true', and also to assert '(6) is printed in the *New York Daily News*, October 7, 1971', he will deduce (7) by existential generalization. Once he is willing to assert (7), he will also be willing to assert (8). In this manner, the subject will eventually be able to attribute truth to more and more statements involving the notion of truth itself. There is no reason to suppose that *all* statements involving 'true' will become decided in this way, but most will. Indeed, our suggestion is that the "grounded" sentences can be characterized as those which eventually get a truth value in this process.

A typically ungrounded sentence such as (3) will, of course, receive no truth value in the process just sketched. In particular, it will never be called "true." But the subject cannot express this fact by saying, "(3) is not true." Such an assertion would conflict directly with the stipulation that he should deny that a sentence is true precisely under the circumstances under which he would deny the sentence itself. In imposing this stipulation, we have made a deliberate choice (see below).

Let us see how we can give these ideas formal expression. Let L be an interpreted first-order language of the classical type, with a finite (or even

---

that do not express propositions either. (This happens under the Kleene valuation, but not under the van Fraassen.) Mere conventions for handling terms that do not designate numbers should not be called changes in arithmetic; conventions for handling sentences that do not express propositions are not in any philosophically significant sense "changes in logic." The term 'three-valued logic', occasionally used here, should not mislead. All our considerations can be formalized in a classical metalanguage.

denumerable) list of primitive predicates. It is assumed that the variables range over some nonempty domain D, and that the primitive n-ary predicates are interpreted by (totally defined) n-ary relations on D. The interpretation of the predicates of L is kept fixed throughout the following discussion. Let us also assume that the language L is rich enough so that the syntax of L (say, via arithmetization) can be expressed in L, and that some coding scheme codes finite sequences of elements of D into elements of D. We do not attempt to make these ideas rigorous; Y. N. Moschovakis's notion of an "acceptable" structure would do so.[19] I should emphasize that a great deal of what we do below goes through under much weaker hypotheses on L.[20]

Suppose we extend L to a language $\mathcal{L}$ by adding a monadic predicate $T(x)$ whose interpretation need only be partially defined. An interpretation of $T(x)$ is given by a "partial set" (S_1, S_2), where S_1, as we said above, is the *extension* of $T(x)$, S_2 is the *antiextension* of $T(x)$, and $T(x)$ is undefined for entities outside $S_1 \cup S_2$. Let $\mathcal{L}(S_1, S_2)$ be the interpretation of $\mathcal{L}$ which results from interpreting $T(x)$ by the pair (S_1, S_2), the interpretation of the other predicates of L remaining as before.[21] Let S_1' be the set of (codes of)[22] true sentences of $\mathcal{L}(S_1, S_2)$, and let S_2' be the set of all elements of D which either are not (codes of) sentences of $\mathcal{L}(S_1, S_2)$ or are (codes of) false sentences of $\mathcal{L}(S_1, S_2)$. S_1' and S_2' are uniquely determined by the choice of (S_1, S_2). Clearly, if $T(x)$ is to be interpreted as truth for the very language L containing $T(x)$ itself, we must have $S_1 = S_1'$ and $S_2 = S_2'$. [This means that if A is any sentence, A satisfies (falsifies) $T(x)$ iff A is true (false) by the evaluation rules.]

A pair (S_1, S_2) that satisfies this condition is called a *fixed point*. For a given choice of (S_1, S_2) to interpret $T(x)$, set $\phi((S_1, S_2)) = (S_1', S_2')$. ϕ then is a unary function defined on all pairs (S_1, S_2) of disjoint subsets of D, and the "fixed points" (S_1, S_2) are literally the fixed points of ϕ; i.e., they are those pairs (S_1, S_2) such that $\phi((S_1, S_2)) = (S_1, S_2)$. If (S_1, S_2) is a fixed point, we sometimes call $\mathcal{L}(S_1, S_2)$ a fixed point also. Our basic task is to prove the existence of fixed points, and to investigate their properties.

Let us first construct a fixed point. We do so by considering a certain "hierarchy of languages." We start by defining the interpreted language $\mathcal{L}_0$ as

---

[19] *Elementary Induction on Abstract Structures* (Amsterdam: North-Holland, 1974). The notion of an acceptable structure is developed in chap. 5.

[20] It is unnecessary to suppose, as we have for simplicity, that all the predicates in L are totally defined. The hypothesis that L contain a device for coding finite sequences is needed only if we are adding satisfaction rather than truth to L. Other hypotheses can be made much weaker for most of the work.

[21] $\mathcal{L}$ is thus a language with all predicates but the single predicate $T(x)$ interpreted, but $T(x)$ is uninterpreted. The languages $\mathcal{L}(S_1, S_2)$ and the languages $\mathcal{L}_\alpha$ defined below are languages obtained from $\mathcal{L}$ by specifying an interpretation of $T(x)$.

[22] I parenthetically write "codes of" or "Gödel numbers of" in various places to remind the reader that syntax may be represented in L by Gödel numbering or some other coding device. Sometimes I lazily drop the parenthetical qualification, identifying expressions with their codes.

$\mathcal{L}(\Lambda, \Lambda)$, where Λ is the empty set; i.e., $\mathcal{L}_0$ is the language where $T(x)$ is completely undefined. (It is never a fixed point.) For any integer α, suppose we have defined $\mathcal{L}_\alpha = \mathcal{L}(S_1, S_2)$. Then set $\mathcal{L}_{\alpha+1} = \mathcal{L}(S_1', S_2')$, where as before S_1' is the set of (codes of) true sentences of $\mathcal{L}_\alpha$, and S_2' is the set of all elements of D which either are not (codes of) sentences of $\mathcal{L}_\alpha$ or are (codes of) false sentences of $\mathcal{L}_\alpha$.

The hierarchy of languages just given is analogous to the Tarski hierarchy for the orthodox approach. $T(x)$ is interpreted in $\mathcal{L}_{\alpha+1}$ as the truth predicate for $\mathcal{L}_\alpha$. But an interesting phenomenon, detailed in the following paragraphs, arises on the present approach.

Let us say that $(S_1^\dagger, S_2^\dagger)$ *extends* (S_1, S_2) [symbolically, $(S_1^\dagger, S_2^\dagger) \geq (S_1, S_2)$ or $(S_1, S_2) \leq (S_1^\dagger, S_2^\dagger)$] iff $S_1 \subseteq S_1^\dagger$, $S_2 \subseteq S_2^\dagger$. Intuitively this means that if $T(x)$ is interpreted as $(S_1^\dagger, S_2^\dagger)$, the interpretation agrees with the interpretation by (S_1, S_2) in all cases where the latter is defined; the only difference is that an interpretation by $(S_1^\dagger, S_2^\dagger)$ may lead $T(x)$ to be defined for some cases where it was undefined when interpreted by (S_1, S_2). Now a basic property of our valuation rules is the following: ϕ is a monotone (order-preserving) operation on $\leq$: that is, if $(S_1, S_2) \leq (S_1^\dagger, S_2^\dagger)$, $\phi((S_1, S_2)) \leq \phi((S_1^\dagger, S_2^\dagger))$. In other words, *if* $(S_1, S_2) \leq (S_1^\dagger, S_2^\dagger)$, *then any sentence that is true (or false) in* $\mathcal{L}(S_1, S_2)$ *retains its truth value in* $\mathcal{L}(S_1^\dagger, S_2^\dagger)$. What this means is that *if the interpretation of $T(x)$ is extended by giving it a definite truth value for cases that were previously undefined, no truth value previously established changes or becomes undefined;* at most, certain previously undefined truth values become defined. This property—technically, the monotonicity of ϕ—is crucial for all our constructions.

Given the monotonicity of ϕ, we can deduce that for each α, *the interpretation of $T(x)$ in $\mathcal{L}_{\alpha+1}$ extends the interpretation* of $T(x)$ in $\mathcal{L}_\alpha$. The fact is obvious for $\alpha = 0$: since, in $\mathcal{L}_0$, $T(x)$ is undefined for all x, any interpretation of $T(x)$ automatically extends it. If the assertion holds for $\mathcal{L}_\beta$—that is, if the interpretation of $T(x)$ in $\mathcal{L}_{\beta+1}$ extends that of $T(x)$ in $\mathcal{L}_\beta$—then any sentence true or false in $\mathcal{L}_\beta$ remains true or false in $\mathcal{L}_{\beta+1}$. If we look at the definitions, *this says that the interpretation of $T(x)$ in $\mathcal{L}_{\beta+2}$ extends the interpretation of $T(x)$ in $L_{\beta+1}$. We have thus proved by induction that the interpretation of $T(x)$ in $\mathcal{L}_{\alpha+1}$ always extends the interpretation of $T(x)$ in $\mathcal{L}_\alpha$ for all finite α. It follows that the predicate $T(x)$ increases, in both its extension and its antiextension, as α increases. More and more sentences get declared true or false as α increases; but once a sentence is declared true or false, it retains its truth value at all higher levels.*

So far, we have defined only *finite* levels of our hierarchy. For finite α, let $(S_{1,\alpha}, S_{2,\alpha})$ be the interpretation of $T(x)$ in $\mathcal{L}_\alpha$. Both $S_{1,\alpha}$ and $S_{2,\alpha}$ increase (as sets) as α increases. Then there is an obvious way of defining the first "transfinite" level—call it "$\mathcal{L}_\omega$." Simply define $\mathcal{L}_\omega = \mathcal{L}(S_{1,\omega}, S_{2,\omega})$, where $S_{1,\omega}$ is the union of all $S_{1,\alpha}$ for finite α, and $S_{2,\omega}$ is similarly the union of $S_{2,\alpha}$ for finite α. Given $\mathcal{L}_\omega$, we can then define $\mathcal{L}_{\omega+1}, \mathcal{L}_{\omega+2}, \mathcal{L}_{\omega+3}$, etc., just as we did for the finite levels. When we get again to a "limit" level, we take a union as before.

Formally, we define the languages $\mathcal{L}_\alpha$ for each ordinal α. If α is a successor ordinal ($\alpha = \beta + 1$), let $\mathcal{L}_\alpha = \mathcal{L}(S_{1,\,\alpha}, S_{2,\,\alpha})$, where $S_{1,\,\alpha}$ is the set of (codes of) true sentences of $\mathcal{L}_\beta$, and $S_{2,\,\alpha}$ is the set consisting of all elements of D which either are (codes of) false sentences of $\mathcal{L}_\beta$ or are not (codes of) sentences of $\mathcal{L}_\beta$. If λ is a limit ordinal, $\mathcal{L}_\lambda = \mathcal{L}(S_{1,\,\lambda}, S_{2,\,\lambda})$, where $S_{1,\,\lambda} = \cup_{\beta < \lambda} S_{1,\,\beta}$, $S_{2,\,\lambda} = \cup_{\beta < \lambda} S_{2,\,\beta}$. So at "successor" levels we take the truth predicate over the previous level, and, at limit (transfinite) levels, we take the union of all sentences declared true or false at previous levels. *Even with the transfinite levels included, it remains true that the extension and the antiextension of $T(x)$ increase with increasing α.*

It should be noted that 'increase' does not mean "strictly increase"; we have asserted that $S_{i,\,\alpha} \subseteq S_{i,\,\alpha+1}$ ($i = 1,2$), which allows equality. Does the process go on forever with more and more statements being declared true or false, or does it eventually stop? That is to say, is there an ordinal level σ for which $S_{1,\,\sigma} = S_{1,\,\sigma+1}$ and $S_{2,\,\sigma} = S_{2,\,\sigma+1}$, so that no "new" statements are declared true or false at the next level? The answer must be affirmative. The sentences of $\mathcal{L}$ form a set. If new sentences of $\mathcal{L}$ were being decided at each level, we would eventually exhaust $\mathcal{L}$ at some level and be unable to decide any more. This can easily be converted to a formal proof (the technique is elementary and is well known to logicians) that there is an ordinal level σ such that $(S_{1,\,\sigma}, S_{2,\,\sigma}) = (S_{1,\,\sigma+1}, S_{2,\,\sigma+1})$. But since $(S_{1,\,\sigma+1}, S_{2,\,\sigma+1}) = \phi((S_{1,\,\sigma}, S_{2,\,\sigma}))$, *this means that $(S_{1,\,\sigma}, S_{2,\,\sigma})$ is a fixed point.* It can also be proved that it is a "minimal" or "smallest" fixed point: *any* fixed point extends $(S_{1,\,\sigma}, S_{2,\,\sigma})$. That is, if a sentence is valuated as true or false in $\mathcal{L}_\sigma$, it has the same truth value in *any* fixed point.

Let us relate the construction of a fixed point just given to our previous intuitive ideas. At the initial stage ($\mathcal{L}_0$), $T(x)$ is completely undefined. This corresponds to the initial stage at which the subject has no understanding of the notion of truth. Given a characterization of truth by the Kleene valuation rules, the subject can easily ascend to the level of $\mathcal{L}_1$. That is, he can evaluate various statements as true or false without knowing anything about $T(x)$—in particular, he can evaluate all those sentences not containing $T(x)$. Once he has made the evaluation, he extends $T(x)$, as in $\mathcal{L}_1$. Then he can use the new interpretation of $T(x)$ to evaluate more sentences as true or false and ascend to $\mathcal{L}_2$, etc. Eventually, when the process becomes "saturated," the subject reaches the fixed point $\mathcal{L}_\sigma$. (*Being a fixed point, $\mathcal{L}_\sigma$ is a language that contains its own truth predicate.*) So the formal definition just given directly parallels the intuitive constructions stated previously.[23]

---

[23] A comparison with the Tarski hierarchy:

The Tarski hierarchy uses a new truth predicate at each level, always changing. The limit levels of the Tarski hierarchy, which have not been defined in the literature, but have been to some extent in my own work, are cumbersome to characterize.

The present hierarchy uses a single truth predicate, ever increasing with increasing levels until the level of the minimal fixed point is reached. The limit levels are easily defined. The languages in the hierarchy are not the primary object of interest, but are better and better approximations to the minimal language with its own truth predicate.

We have been talking of a language that contains its own truth predicate. Really, however, it would be more interesting to extend an arbitrary language to a language containing its own *satisfaction* predicate. If L contains a name for each object in D, and a denotation relation is defined (if D is nondenumerable, this means that L contains nondenumerably many constants), the notion of satisfaction can (for most purposes) effectively be replaced by that of truth: e.g., instead of talking of $A(x)$ being satisfied by an object a, we can talk of $A(x)$ becoming true when the variable is replaced by a name of a. Then the previous construction suffices. Alternatively, if L does not contain a name for each object, we can extend L to $\mathcal{L}$ by adding a binary satisfaction predicate $Sat(s,x)$ where s ranges over finite sequences of elements of D and x ranges over formulas. We define a hierarchy of languages, parallel to the previous construction with truth, eventually reaching a fixed point—a language that contains its own satisfaction predicate. If L is denumerable but D is not, the construction with truth alone closes off at a countable ordinal, but the construction with satisfaction may close off at an uncountable ordinal. Below we will continue, for simplicity of exposition, to concentrate on the construction with truth, but the construction with satisfaction is more basic.[24]

The construction could be generalized so as to allow more notation in L than just first-order logic. For example, we could have a quantifier meaning "for uncountably many x," a "most" quantifier, a language with infinite conjunctions, etc. There is a fairly canonical way, in the Kleene style, to extend the semantics of such quantifiers and connectives so as to allow truth-value gaps, but we will not give details.

Let us check that our model satisfies some of the desiderata mentioned in the previous sections. It is clearly a theory in the required sense: any language, including those containing number theory or syntax, can be extended to a language with its own truth predicate, and the associated concept of truth is *mathematically* defined by set-theoretic techniques. There is no problem about the languages of transfinite level in the hierarchy.

---

[24] Consider the case where L has a canonical name for every element of D. We can then consider pairs $(A,\mathbf{T})$, $(A,\mathbf{F})$, where A is true, or false, respectively. The Kleene rules correspond to closure conditions on a set of such pairs: e.g., if $(A(a),\mathbf{F}) \in S$ for each name of a element of D, put $((\exists x)A(x), \mathbf{F})$ in S; if $(A(a),\mathbf{T}) \in S$, put $((\exists x)A(x), \mathbf{T})$ in S, etc. Consider the least set S of pairs closed under the analogues of the Kleene rules, containing $(A,\mathbf{T})$ $((A,\mathbf{F}))$ for each true (false) atomic A of L, and closed under the two conditions: (i) if $(A,\mathbf{T}) \in S$, $(T(k),\mathbf{T}) \in S$; (ii) if $(A,\mathbf{F}) \in S$, $(T(k),\mathbf{F}) \in S$, where 'k' abbreviates a name of A. It is easily shown that the set S corresponds (in the obvious sense) to the minimal fixed point [thus, it is closed under the converses of (i) and (ii).] I used this definition to show that the set of truths in the minimal fixed point (over an acceptable structure), is inductive in Moschovakis's sense. It is probably simpler than the definition given in the text. The definition given in the text has, among others, the advantages of giving a definition of 'level', facilitating a comparison with the Tarski hierarchy, and easy generalization to valuation schemes other than Kleene's.

Given a sentence A of $\mathcal{L}$, let us define A to be *grounded* if it has a truth value in the smallest fixed point $\mathcal{L}_\sigma$; otherwise, *ungrounded*. What hitherto has been, as far as I know, an intuitive concept with no formal definition, becomes a precisely defined concept in the present theory. If A is grounded, define the *level* of A to be the smallest ordinal α such that A has a truth value in $\mathcal{L}_\alpha$.

There is no problem, if $\mathcal{L}$ contains number theory or syntax, of constructing Gödelian sentences that "say of themselves" that they are false (Liar sentences) or true [as in (3)]; all these are easily shown to be ungrounded in the sense of the formal definition. If the Gödelian form of the Liar paradox is used, for example, the Liar sentence can get the form

(9) $(x)(P(x) \supset \sim T(x))$

where $P(x)$ is a syntactic (or arithmetical) predicate uniquely satisfied by (the Gödel number of) (9) itself. Similarly (3) gets the form

(10) $(x)(Q(x) \supset T(x))$

where $Q(x)$ is uniquely satisfied by (the Gödel number of) (10). It is easy to prove, under these hypotheses, by induction on α, that neither (9) nor (10) will have a truth value in any $\mathcal{L}_\alpha$, that is, that they are ungrounded. Other intuitive cases of ungroundedness come out similarly.

The feature I have stressed about ordinary statements, that there is no intrinsic guarantee of their safety (groundedness) and that their "level" depends on empirical facts, comes out clearly in the present model. Consider, for example, (9) again, except that now $P(x)$ is an empirical predicate whose extension depends on unknown empirical facts. If $P(x)$ turns out to be true only of (9) itself, (9) will be ungrounded as before. If the extension of $P(x)$ consists entirely of grounded sentences of levels, say, 2, 4, and 13, (9) will be grounded with level 14. If the extension of $P(x)$ consists of grounded sentences of arbitrary finite level, (9) will be grounded with level ω. And so on.

Now let us consider the cases of (4) and (5). We can formalize (4) by (9), interpreting $P(x)$ as "x is a sentence Nixon asserts about Watergate." [Forget for simplicity that 'about Watergate' introduces a semantic component into the interpretation of $P(x)$.] Formalize (5) as

(11) $(x)(Q(x) \supset \sim T(x))$

interpreting $Q(x)$ in the obvious way. To complete the parallel with (4) and (5), suppose that (9) is in the extension of $Q(x)$ and (11) is in the extension of $P(x)$. Now nothing guarantees that (9) and (11) will be grounded. Suppose, however, parallel to the intuitive discussion above, that some true grounded sentence satisfies $Q(x)$. If the lowest level of any such sentence is α, then (11) will be false and grounded of level $\alpha + 1$. If in addition all the sentences other than (11) satisfying $P(x)$ are false, (9) will then be grounded and true. The level of (9) will be at least $\alpha + 2$, because of the level of (11). On the other hand, if some sentence satisfying $P(x)$ is grounded and true, then (9) will be grounded and false with level $\beta + 1$, where β is the lowest level of any such sentence. It is crucial to the ability of the present model to assign levels to (4) and (5) [(9) and (11)] that the levels depend on empirical facts, rather than being assigned in advance.

We said that such statements as (3), though ungrounded, are not intuitively paradoxical either. Let us explore this in terms of the model. The smallest fixed point L is not the only fixed point. Let us formalize (3) by (10), where $Q(x)$ is a *syntactic* predicate (of L) true of (10) itself alone. Suppose that, instead of starting out our hierarchy of languages with $T(x)$ completely undefined, we had started out by letting $T(x)$ be true of (10), undefined otherwise. We then can continue the hierarchy of languages just as before. It is easy to see that if (10) is true at the language of a given level, it will remain true at the next level [using the fact that $Q(x)$ is true of (10) alone, false of everything else]. From this we can show as before that the interpretation of $T(x)$ at each level extends all previous levels, and that at some level the construction closes off to yield a fixed point. The difference is that (10), which lacked truth value in the smallest fixed point, is now *true*.

This suggests the following definition: a sentence is *paradoxical* if it has no truth value in *any* fixed point. That is, a paradoxical sentence A is such that if $\phi((S_1, S_2)) = (S_1, S_2)$, then A is neither an element of S_1 nor an element of S_2.

(3) [or its formal version (10)] is ungrounded, but not paradoxical. This means that we *could* consistently use the predicate 'true' so as to give (3) [or (10)] a truth value, though the minimal process for assigning truth values does not do so. Suppose, on the other hand, in (9), that $P(x)$ is true of (9) itself and false of everything else, so that (9) is a Liar sentence. Then the argument of the Liar paradox easily yields a proof that (9) cannot have a truth value in any fixed point. So (9) is paradoxical in our technical sense. Notice that, if it is merely an empirical fact that $P(x)$ is true of (9) and false of everything else, the fact that (9) is paradoxical will itself be empirical. (We could define notions of "intrinsically paradoxical", "intrinsically grounded", etc., but will not do so here.)

Intuitively, the situation seems to be as follows. Although the smallest fixed point is probably the most natural model for the intuitive concept of truth, and is the model *generated* by our instructions to the imaginary subject, the other fixed points never *conflict* with these instructions. We *could* consistently use the word 'true' so as to give a truth value to such a sentence as (3) without violating the idea that a sentence should be asserted to be true precisely when we would assert the sentence itself. The same does not hold for the paradoxical sentences.

Using Zorn's Lemma, we can prove that *every fixed point can be extended to a maximal fixed point*, where a maximal fixed point is a fixed point that has no proper extension that is also a fixed point. Maximal fixed points assign "as many truth values as possible"; one could not assign more consistently with the intuitive concept of truth. Sentences like (3), though ungrounded, have a truth value in every maximal fixed point. Ungrounded sentences exist, however, which have truth values in some but not all maximal fixed points.

It is as easy to construct fixed points which make (3) false as it is to construct fixed points which make it true. So the assignment of a truth value to (3) is *arbitrary*. Indeed any fixed point which assigns no truth value to (3) can be extended to fixed points which make it true and to fixed points which make it false. Grounded sentences have the same truth value in all fixed points. There are ungrounded and unparadoxical sentences, however, which have the same truth value in all the fixed points where they have a truth value. An example is:

(12) Either (12) or its negation is true.

It is easy to show that there are fixed points which make (12) true and none which make (12) false. Yet (12) is ungrounded (has no truth value in the minimal fixed point).

Call a fixed point *intrinsic* iff it assigns no sentence a truth value conflicting with its truth value in any other fixed point. That is, a fixed point (S_1, S_2) is intrinsic iff there is no other fixed point $(S_1^\dagger, S_2^\dagger)$ and sentence A of L' such that $A \in (S_1 \cap S_2^\dagger) \cup (S_2 \cap S_1^\dagger)$. We say that a sentence has *an intrinsic truth value* iff some intrinsic fixed point gives it a truth value; i.e., A has an intrinsic truth value iff there is an intrinsic fixed point (S_1, S_2) such that $A \in S_1 \cup S_2$. (12) is a good example.

There are unparadoxical sentences which have the same truth value in all fixed points where they have truth value but which nevertheless lack an intrinsic truth value. Consider $P \vee \sim P$, where P is any ungrounded unparadoxical sentence. Then $P \vee \sim P$ is true in some fixed points (namely, those where P has a truth value) and is false in none. Suppose, however, that there are fixed points that make P true and fixed points that make P false. [For example, say, P is (3).] Then $P \vee \sim P$ cannot have a truth value in any intrinsic fixed point, since, by our valuation rules, it cannot have a truth value unless some disjunct does.[25]

There is no "largest" fixed point that extends every other; indeed, any two fixed points that give different truth values to the same formula have no common extension. However, it is not hard to show that there is a largest intrinsic fixed point (and indeed that the intrinsic fixed points form a complete lattice under $\leq$). The largest intrinsic fixed point is the unique "largest" interpretation of $T(x)$ which is consistent with our intuitive idea of truth and makes no arbitrary choices in truth assignments. It is thus an object of special theoretical interest as a model.

It is interesting to compare "Tarski's hierarchy of languages" with the present model. Unfortunately, this can hardly be done in full generality without introducing the transfinite levels, a task omitted from this sketch. But we can say

---

[25] If we use the supervaluation technique instead of the Kleene rules, $P \vee \sim P$ will always be grounded and true, and we must change the example. See p. 94 below.

something about the finite levels. Intuitively, it would seem that Tarski predicates $\lceil \text{true}_n \rceil$ are all special cases of a single truth predicate. For example, we said above that 'true$_1$' means "is a true sentence not involving truth." Let us carry this idea out formally. Let $A_1(x)$ be a syntactic (arithmetical) predicate true of exactly the formulas of $\mathcal{L}$ not involving $T(x)$, i.e., of all formulas of L. $A_1(x)$, being syntactic, is itself a formula of L, as are all other syntactic formulas below. Define '$T_1(x)$' as '$T(x) \wedge A_1(x)$'. Let $A_2(x)$ be a syntactic predicate applying to all those formulas whose atomic predicates are those of L plus '$T_1(x)$'. [More precisely the class of such formulas can be defined as the least class including all formulas of L and $T(x_i) \wedge A_1(x_i)$, for any variable x_i, and closed under truth functions and quantification.] Then define $T_2(x)$ as $T(x) \wedge A_2(x)$. In general, we can define $A_{n+1}(x)$ as a syntactic predicate applying precisely to formulas built out of the predicates of L and $T_n(x)$, and $T_{n+1}(x)$ as $T(x) \wedge A_{n+1}(x)$. Assume that $T(x)$ is interpreted by the smallest fixed point (or any other). Then it is easy to prove by induction that each predicate $T_n(x)$ is totally defined, that the extension of $T_0(x)$ consists precisely of the true formulas of L, while that of $T_{n+1}(x)$ consists of the true formulas of the language obtained by adjoining $T_n(x)$ to L. This means that *all the truth predicates of the finite Tarski hierarchy are definable within L_σ, and all the languages of that hierarchy are sub-languages of $\mathcal{L}_\sigma$.*[26] This kind of result could be extended into the transfinite if we had defined the transfinite Tarski hierarchy.

There are converse results, harder to state in this sketch. It is characteristic of the sentences in the Tarski hierarchy that they are safe (intrinsically grounded) and that their level is intrinsic, given independently of the empirical facts. It is natural to conjecture that any grounded sentence with intrinsic level n is in some sense "equivalent" to a sentence of level n in the Tarski hierarchy. Given proper definitions of 'intrinsic level', 'equivalent', and the like, theorems of this kind can be stated and proved and even extended into the transfinite.

So far we have assumed that truth gaps are to be handled according to the methods of Kleene. It is by no means necessary to do so. Just about any scheme for handling truth-value gaps is usable, provided that the basic property of the monotonicity of ϕ is preserved; that is, provided that extending the interpretation of $T(x)$ never changes the truth value of any sentence of $\mathcal{L}$, but at most gives truth values to previously undefined cases. Given any such scheme, we can use the previous arguments to construct the minimal fixed point and other fixed points, define the levels of sentences and the notions of 'grounded', 'paradoxical', etc.

---

[26] We suppose that the Tarski hierarchy defines $L_0 = L$, $L_{n+1} = L + T_{n+1}(x)$ (truth, or satisfaction, for L_n). Alternatively, we might prefer the inductive construction $L_0 = L$, $L_{n+1} = L_n + T_{n+1}(x)$ where the language of each new level contains all the previous truth predicates. It is easy to modify the construction in the text so as to accord with the second definition. The two alternative hierarchies are equivalent in expressive power at each level.

One scheme usable in this way is van Fraassen's notion of *super-valuation*.[27] For the language $\mathcal{L}$, the definition is easy. Given an interpretation (S_1, S_2) of $T(x)$ in $\mathcal{L}$, call a formula A true (false) iff it comes out true (false) by the ordinary classical valuation under every interpretation $(S_1^\dagger, S_2^\dagger)$ which extends (S_1, S_2) and is *totally defined*, i.e., is such that $S_1^\dagger \cup S_2^\dagger = D$. We can then define the hierarchy $\{\mathcal{L}_\alpha\}$ and the minimal fixed point $\mathcal{L}_\sigma$ as before. Under the supervaluation interpretation, all formulas provable in classical quantification theory become true in $\mathcal{L}_\sigma$; under the Kleene valuation, one could say only that they were true whenever they were defined. Thanks to the fact that $\mathcal{L}_\sigma$ contains its own truth predicate, we need not express this fact by a schema, or by a statement of a meta-language. If $PQT(x)$ is a syntactic predicate true exactly of the sentences of $\mathcal{L}$ provable in quantification theory, we can assert:

(13) $(x)(PQT(x) \supset T(x))$

and (13) will be true in the minimal fixed point.

Here we have used supervaluations in which *all* total extensions of the interpretation of $T(x)$ are taken into account. It is natural to consider restrictions on the family of total extensions, motivated by intuitive properties of truth. For example, we could consider only *consistent* interpretations $(S_1^\dagger, S_2^\dagger)$, where $(S_1^\dagger, S_2^\dagger)$ is consistent iff S_1 contains no sentence together with its negation. Then we could define A to be true (false) with $T(x)$ interpreted by (S_1, S_2) iff A is true (false) classically when A is interpreted by any *consistent* totally defined extension of (S_1, S_2).

(14) $(x) \sim (T(x) \wedge T(\text{neg}(x)))$

will be true in the minimal fixed point. If we restricted the admissible total extensions to those defining *maximal* consistent sets of sentences, in the usual sense, not only (14) but even

$(x)(Sent(x). \supset . T(x) \vee T(\text{neg}(x)))$

will come out true in the minimal fixed point.[28] The last-mentioned formula, however, must be interpreted with caution, since it is still not the case, even on the supervaluation interpretation in question, that there is any fixed point that makes every formula or its negation true. (The paradoxical formulas still lack truth value in all fixed points.) The phenomenon is associated with the fact that, on the supervaluation interpretation, a disjunction can be true without it following that some disjunct is true.

---

[27] See his "Singular Terms, Truth-value Gaps, and Free Logic," *Journal of Philosophy*, LXIII, 17 (Sept. 15, 1966): 481–495.

[28] A version of the Liar paradox due to H. Friedman shows that there are limits to what can be done in this direction.

It is not the purpose of the present work to make any particular recommendation among the Kleene strong three-valued approach, the van Fraassen supervaluation approaches, or any other scheme (such as the Fregean weak three-valued logic, preferred by Martin and Woodruff, though I am in fact tentatively inclined to consider the latter excessively cumbersome). Nor is it even my present purpose to make any firm recommendation between the minimal fixed point of a particular valuation scheme and the various other fixed points.[29] Indeed, without the nonminimal fixed points we could not have defined the intuitive difference between 'grounded' and 'paradoxical'. My purpose is rather to provide a family of flexible instruments which can be explored simultaneously and whose fertility and consonance with intuition can be checked.

I am somewhat uncertain whether there is a definite factual question as to whether natural language handles truth-value gaps—at least those arising in connection with the semantic paradoxes—by the schemes of Frege, Kleene, van Fraassen, or perhaps some other. Nor am I even *quite* sure that there is a definite question of fact as to whether natural language should be evaluated by the minimal fixed point or another, given the choice of a scheme for handling gaps.[30] We are not at the moment searching for *the* correct scheme.

The present approach can be applied to languages containing modal operators. In this case, we do not merely consider truth, but we are given, in the usual style of modal model theory, a system of possible worlds, and evaluate truth and $T(x)$ in each possible world. The inductive definition of the languages $\mathcal{L}_\alpha$ approximating to the minimal fixed point must be modified accordingly. We cannot give details here.[31]

Ironically, the application of the present approach to languages with modal operators may be of some interest to those who dislike intensional operators and possible worlds and prefer to take modalities and propositional attitudes as predicates true of sentences (or sentence tokens). Montague and Kaplan have pointed out, using elementary applications of Gödelian techniques, that such approaches are likely to lead to semantic paradoxes, analogous to the Liar.[32]

---

[29] Though the minimal fixed point certainly is singled out as natural in many respects.

[30] I do not mean to *assert* that there are no definite questions of fact in these areas, or even that I myself may not favor some valuation schemes over others. But my personal views are less important than the variety of tools that are available, so for the purposes of this sketch I take an agnostic position. (I remark that if the viewpoint is taken that logic applies primarily to propositions, and that we are merely formulating conventions for how to handle sentences that do not express propositions, the attractiveness of the supervaluation approach over the Kleene approach is somewhat decreased. See fn 18.)

[31] Another application of the present techniques is to "impredicative" substitutional quantification, where the terms of the substitution class themselves contain substitutional quantifiers of the given type. (For example, a language containing substitutional quantifiers with arbitrary sentences of the language itself as substituends) It is impossible in general to introduce such quantifiers into classical languages without truth-value gaps.

[32] Richard Montague, "Syntactical Treatments of Modality, with Corollaries on Reflection Principles and Finite Axiomatizability," *Acta Philosophica Fennica, Proceedings of a Colloquium on*

Though the difficulty has been known for some time, the extensive literature advocating such treatments has usually simply ignored the problem rather than indicating how it is to be solved (say, by a hierarchy of languages?). Now, if a necessity operator and a truth predicate are allowed, we could define a necessity predicate $Nec(x)$ applied to sentences, either by $\Box T(x)$ or $T(nec(x))$ according to taste,[33] and treat it according to the possible-world scheme sketched in the preceding paragraph. (I do think that any necessity predicate of sentences should intuitively be regarded as derivative, defined in terms of an operator and a truth predicate. I also think the same holds for propositional attitudes.) We can even "kick away the ladder" and take $Nec(x)$ as primitive, treating it in a possible-world scheme *as if* it were defined by an operator plus a truth predicate. Like remarks apply to the propositional attitudes, if we are willing to treat them, using possible worlds, like modal operators. (I myself think that such a treatment involves considerable philosophical difficulties.) It is possible that the present approach can be applied to the supposed predicates of sentences in question without using either intensional operators or possible worlds, but at present I have no idea how to do so.

It seems likely that many who have worked on the truth-gap approach to the semantic paradoxes have hoped for a universal language, one in which everything that can be stated at all can be expressed. (The proof by Gödel and Tarski that a language cannot contain its own semantics applied only to languages without truth gaps.) Now the languages of the present approach contain their own truth predicates and even their own satisfaction predicates, and thus to this extent the hope has been realized. Nevertheless the present approach certainly does not claim to give a universal language, and I doubt that such a goal can be achieved. First, the induction defining the minimal fixed point is carried out in a set-theoretic meta-language, not in the object language itself. Second, there are assertions we can make about the object language which we cannot make in the object language. For example, Liar sentences are *not true* in the object

---

Model and Many Valued Logics, 1963: 153–167; David Kaplan and Montague, "A Paradox Regained," *Notre Dame Journal of Formal Logic*, I, 3 (July 1960): 79–90. See Chapter 2, this volume, Appendices 1 and 2.

At present the problems are *known* to arise only if modalities and attitudes are predicates applied to sentences or their tokens. The Montague-Kaplan arguments do not apply to standard formalizations taking modalities or propositional attitudes as intensional operators. Even if we wish to quantify over objects of belief, the arguments do not apply if the objects of belief are taken to be propositions and the latter are identified with sets of possible worlds.

However, if we quantify over propositions, paradoxes may arise in connection with propositional attitudes given appropriate empirical premises. [See, e.g., A. N. Prior, "On a Family of Paradoxes," *Notre Dame Journal of Formal Logic*, II 1 (January 1961): 16–32.] Also, we may wish (in connection with propositional attitudes but not modalities), to individuate propositions more finely than by sets of possible worlds, and it is possible that such a "fine structure" may permit the application of Gödelian arguments of the type used by Montague and Kaplan directly to propositions.

[33] As a formalization of the concept intended by those who speak of modalities and attitudes as predicates of sentences, the second version is generally better. This is true especially for the propositional attitudes.

language, in the sense that the inductive process never makes them true; but we are precluded from saying this in the object language by our interpretation of negation and the truth predicate. If we think of the minimal fixed point, say under the Kleene valuation, as giving a model of natural language, then the sense in which we can say, in natural language, that a Liar sentence is not true must be thought of as associated with some later stage in the development of natural language, one in which speakers reflect on the generation process leading to the minimal fixed point. It is not itself a part of that process. The necessity to ascend to a metalanguage may be one of the weaknesses of the present theory. The ghost of the Tarski hierarchy is still with us.[34]

The approach adopted here has presupposed the following version of Tarski's "Convention T", adapted to the three-valued approach: If '**k**' abbreviates a name of the sentence A, $T(\mathbf{k})$ is to be true, or false, respectively iff A is true, or false. This captures the intuition that $T(\mathbf{k})$ is to have the same truth conditions as A itself; it follows that $T(\mathbf{k})$ suffers a truth-value gap if A does. An alternate intuition[35] would assert that, if A is either false or undefined, then A is *not true* and $T(\mathbf{k})$ should be *false*, and its negation *true*. On this view, $T(x)$ will be a totally defined predicate and there are no truth-value gaps. Presumably Tarski's Convention T must be restricted in some way.

It is not difficult to modify the present approach so as to accommodate such an alternate intuition. Take any fixed point $L'(S_1, S_2)$. Modify the interpretation of $T(x)$ so as to make it false of any sentence outside S. [We call this "closing off" $T(x)$.] A modified version of Tarski's Convention T holds in the sense of the conditional $T(\mathbf{k}) \vee T(\text{neg}(\mathbf{k})) \bullet \supset \bullet A \equiv T(\mathbf{k})$. In particular, if A is a paradoxical sentence, we can now assert $\sim T(\mathbf{k})$. Equivalently, if A had a truth value before $T(x)$ was closed off, then $A \equiv T(\mathbf{k})$ is true.

Since the object language obtained by closing off $T(x)$ is a classical language with every predicate totally defined, it is possible to define a truth predicate for that language in the usual Tarskian manner. This predicate will *not* coincide in extension with the predicate $T(x)$ of the object language, and it is certainly reasonable to suppose that it is really the metalanguage predicate that expresses the "genuine" concept of truth for the closed-off object language; the $T(x)$ of the

---

[34] Note that the metalanguage in which we write this paper can be regarded as containing no truth gaps. A sentence either does or does not have a truth value in a given fixed point.
Such semantical notions as "grounded," "paradoxical," etc. belong to the metalanguage. This situation seems to me to be intuitively acceptable; in contrast to the notion of truth, none of these notions is to be found in natural language in its pristine purity, before philosophers reflect on its semantics (in particular, the semantic paradoxes). If we give up the goal of a universal language, models of the type presented in this paper are plausible as models of natural language at a stage before we reflect on the generation process associated with the concept of truth, the stage which continues in the daily life of nonphilosophical speakers.

[35] I think the primacy of the first intuition can be defended philosophically, and for this reason I have emphasized the approach based on this intuition. The alternate intuition arises only after we have reflected on the process embodying the first intuition. See above.

closed-off language defines truth for the fixed point *before* it was closed off. So we still cannot avoid the need for a metalanguage.

On the basis of the fact that the goal of a universal language seems elusive, some have concluded that truth-gap approaches, or any approaches that attempt to come closer to natural language than does the orthodox approach, are fruitless. I hope that the fertility of the present approach, and its agreement with intuitions about natural language in a large number of instances, cast doubt upon such negative attitudes.

There are mathematical applications and purely technical problems which I have not mentioned in this sketch; they would be beyond the scope of a paper for a philosophical journal. Thus there is the question, which can be answered in considerable generality, of characterizing the ordinal σ at which the construction of the minimal fixed point closes off. If L is the language of first-order arithmetic, it turns out that σ is ω_1, the first nonrecursive ordinal. A set is the extension of a formula with one free variable in $\mathcal{L}_\sigma$ iff it is Π^1_1, and it is the extension of a totally defined formula iff it is hyperarithmetical. The languages $\mathcal{L}_\alpha$ approximating to the minimal fixed point give an interesting "notation-free" version of the hyperarithmetical hierarchy. More generally, if L is the language of an acceptable structure in the sense of Moschovakis, and the Kleene valuation is used, a set is the extension of a monadic formula in the minimal fixed point iff it is inductive in the sense of Moschovakis.[36]

---

[36] Leo Harrington informs me that he has proved the conjecture that a set is the extension of a totally defined monadic formula iff it is hyperelementary. The special case of the Π^1_1 and hyperarithmetical sets if L is number theory is independent of whether the Kleene or the van Fraassen formulation is used. Not so for the general case, where the van Fraassen formulation leads to the Π^1_1 sets rather than the inductive sets.

5

Speaker's Reference and Semantic Reference*

I am going to discuss some issues inspired by a well-known paper of Keith Donnellan, "Reference and Definite Descriptions,"[1] but the interest—to me—of the contrast mentioned in my title goes beyond Donnellan's paper: I think it is of considerable constructive as well as critical importance to the philosophy of language. These applications, however, and even everything I might want to say relative to Donnellan's paper, cannot be discussed in full here because of problems of length.

Moreover, although I have a considerable interest in the substantive issues raised by Donnellan's paper, and by related literature, my own conclusions will be methodological, not substantive. I can put the matter this way: Donnellan's paper claims to give decisive objections both to Russell's theory of definite descriptions (taken as a theory about English) and to Strawson's. My concern is *not* primarily with the question: is Donnellan right, or is Russell (or Strawson)? Rather, it is with the question: do the considerations *in Donnellan's paper* refute Russell's theory (or Strawson's)? For definiteness, I will concentrate on Donnellan versus Russell, leaving Strawson aside. And about this issue I will draw a definite conclusion, one which I think will illuminate a few methodological

---

* Versions of this chapter—not read from the present manuscript—were given from 1971 onward to colloquia at New York University, M.I.T., the University of California (Los Angeles), and elsewhere. The present version was written on the basis of a transcript of the M.I.T. version. Donnellan himself heard the talk at U.C.L.A., and he has a paper, "Speaker Reference, Descriptions and Anaphora," (in Peter Cole, ed., *Syntax and Semantics 9: Pragmatics*. [New York: Academic Press, 1978] pp. 47–68), that to a large extent appears to be a comment on considerations of the type mentioned here. (He does not, however, specifically refer to the present paper.) I decided *not* to alter the paper I gave in talks to take Donnellan's later views into account: largely I think the earlier version stands on its own, and the issues Donnellan raises in the later paper can be discussed elsewhere. Something should be said here, however, about the pronominalization phenomena mentioned on p. 121 below. In his paper, Donnellan seems to think that these phenomena are incompatible with the suggestion that speaker's reference is a pragmatic notion. On the contrary, at the end of the present paper (and of the talk Donnellan heard), I emphasize these very phenomena and argue that they support this suggestion. See also footnote 31 below.

[1] *Philosophical Review* 75 (1966): 281–304. See also Keith S. Donnellan, "Putting Humpty Dumpty Together Again," *Philosophical Review* 77 (1968): 203–15.

maxims about language. Namely, I will conclude that the considerations in Donnellan's paper, *by themselves*, do *not* refute Russell's theory.

Any conclusions about Russell's views *per se*, or Donnellan's, must be tentative. If I were to be asked for a tentative stab about Russell, I would say that although his theory does a far better job of handling ordinary discourse than many have thought, and although many popular arguments against it are inconclusive, probably it ultimately fails. The considerations I have in mind have to do with the existence of "improper" definite descriptions, such as "the table," where uniquely specifying conditions are not contained in the description itself. Contrary to the Russellian picture, I doubt that such descriptions can always be regarded as elliptical with some uniquely specifying conditions added. And it may even be the case that a true picture will resemble various aspects of Donnellan's in important respects. But such questions will largely be left aside here.

I will state my preference for one substantive conclusion (although I do not feel completely confident of it either): that unitary theories, like Russell's, are preferable to theories that postulate an ambiguity. And much, though not all, of Donnellan's paper seems to postulate a (semantic) ambiguity between his "referential" and "attributive" uses. But—as we shall see—Donnellan is not entirely consistent on this point, and I therefore am not sure whether I am expressing disagreement with him even here.[2]

(1.) *Preliminary considerations.*

Donnellan claims that a certain linguistic phenomenon argues against Russell's theory. According to Russell, if someone says, "The x such that $\phi(x)$ ψ's," he means that there is an x which uniquely satisfies "$\phi(x)$" and that any such x satisfies "$\psi(x)$." (I.e., $(\exists x)\ (\phi!(x) \wedge \psi(x))$, where "$\phi!(x)$" abbreviates "$\phi(x) \wedge (y)\ (\phi(y) \supset y = x)$.") Donnellan argues that some phenomenon of the following kind tells against Russell: Suppose someone at a gathering, glancing in a certain direction, says to his companion,

(1) "The man over there drinking champagne is happy tonight."

Suppose both the speaker and hearer are under a false impression, and that the man to whom they refer is a teetotaler, drinking sparkling water. He may, nevertheless, be happy. Now, if there is no champagne drinker over there, Russell would regard (1) as false, and Frege and Strawson would give it a truth-value gap. Nevertheless, as Donnellan emphasizes, we have a substantial intuition that the speaker said something true of the man to whom he referred in spite of his misimpression.

Since no one is really drinking champagne, the case involves a definite description that is empty, or vacuous, according to both Russell and Frege. So as to avoid any unnecessary and irrelevant entanglements of the present question

---

[2] In his later paper mentioned above in footnote 1, Donnellan seems more clearly to advocate a semantic ambiguity; but he hedges a bit even in the later paper.

with the issues that arise when definite descriptions are vacuous, I shall modify this case (and all other cases where, in Donnellan's paper, the description was vacuous).[3] Suppose that "over there," exactly one man *is* drinking champagne, although his glass is not visible to the speaker (nor to his hearer). Suppose that he, unlike the teetotaler to whom the speaker refers, has been driven to drink precisely by his misery. Then *all* the classical theories (both Russellian and Fregean) would regard (1) as false (since exactly one man over there is drinking champagne, and he is *not* happy tonight). Now the speaker has spoken *truly* of the man to whom he refers (the teetotaler), yet this dimension is left out in all the classical analyses, which would assign falsehood to his assertion solely on the basis of the misery of *someone else* whom *no one* was talking about (the champagne drinker). Previously Linsky had given a similar example. He gave it as an empty case; once again I modify it to make the description non-vacuous. Someone sees a woman with a man. Taking the man to be her husband, and observing his attitude towards her, he says, "Her husband is kind to her," and someone else may nod, "Yes, he seems to be." Suppose the man in question is not her husband. Suppose he is her lover, to whom she has been driven precisely by her husband's cruelty. Once again both the Russellian analysis and the Fregean analysis would assess the statement as false, and both would do so on the basis of the cruelty of a man neither participant in the dialogues was talking about.

Again, an example suggested to me by a remark of L. Crocker: suppose a religious narrative (similar, say, to the Gospels) consistently refers to its main protagonist as "The Messiah." Suppose a historian wishes to assess the work for *historical accuracy*—that is, he wishes to determine whether it gives an accurate account of the life of its hero (whose identity we assume to be established). Does it matter to this question whether the hero really was the Messiah, as long as the author took him to be so, and addressed his work to a religious community that shared this belief? Surely not. And note that it is no mere "principle of charity" that is operating here. On the contrary, if someone other than the person intended were really the Messiah, and if, by a bizarre and unintended coincidence, the narrative gave a fairly true account of *his* life, we would not for that reason call it "historically true." On the contrary, we would regard the work as historically *false* if the events mentioned were false of its intended protagonist. Whether the story happened to fit the true Messiah—who may have been totally unknown to the author and even have lived after the time the work was composed—would be irrelevant. Once again, this fact seems inconsistent with the positions both of Frege and of Russell.

On the basis of such examples, Donnellan distinguishes two uses of definite descriptions. In the "attributive" use, a speaker "states something about whoever

---

[3] I will also avoid cases of "improper" descriptions, where the uniqueness condition fails. Such descriptions may or may not be important for an ultimate evaluation of Donnellan's position, but none of the arguments in his paper rest on them.

or whatever is the so-and-so." In the "referential" use, a speaker "uses the description to enable his audience to pick out whom or what he is talking about and states something about that person or thing. In the first [attributive] case, the definite description might be said to occur essentially, for the speaker wishes to assert something about whatever or whoever fits that description; but in the referential use the definite description is merely one tool for... calling attention to a person or thing... and... any other device for doing the same job, another description or name, would do as well."[4] For example, suppose I come upon Smith foully murdered. The condition of Smith's body moves me to say, "Smith's murderer is (must be) insane." Then we have an *attributive* use: we speak of the murderer, whoever he may be. On the other hand, suppose that Jones is on trial for Smith's murder and that I am among the spectators in the courtroom. Observing the wild behavior of the defendant at the dock, I may say, "Smith's murderer is insane." (I forgot the defendant's name, but am firmly convinced of his guilt.) Then my use is referential: whether or not Jones was the real murderer, and even if someone else was, if Jones accused me of libel, his failure to fit my description would give me no defense. All of the previous cases, (the teetotaling "champagne" drinker, the lover taken for a husband, the false Messiah), are all referential in Donnellan's sense.

An intuitive mark of the attributive use is the legitimacy of the parenthetical comment, "whoever he is." In the first case, we may say "Smith's murderer, whoever he is, is insane," but not in the second. But we should not be misled: a definite description may be used attributively even if the speaker believes that a certain person, say, Jones, fits it, provided that he is talking about *whoever* fits, and his belief that Jones in fact fits is not relevant. In the case where I deduce the murderer's insanity from the condition of Smith's body, I use the description attributively even if I suspect, or even am firmly convinced, that Jones is the culprit.

I have no doubt that the distinction Donnellan brings out exists and is of fundamental importance, though I do not regard it as exclusive or exhaustive. But Donnellan also believes that Russell's theory applies, if at all, only to attributive uses (p. 293), and that referential uses of definite descriptions are close to proper names, even to Russell's "logically proper" names (see p. 282 and Section IX). And he appears to believe that the examples of the referential uses mentioned above are inexplicable on Russell's theory. It is these views that I wish to examine.

(2.) *Some alleged applications of the distinction.*

Some alleged applications of Donnellan's distinction have entered the oral tradition, and even to an extent, the written tradition, that are not in Donnellan's

---

[4] "Reference and Definite Descriptions," p. 285. My discussion in this paragraph and the next is based on Donnellan's paper, pp. 285, 289–91.

paper. I will mention some that I find questionable. Unfortunately I will have to discuss these applications more briefly than the issues in question really deserve, since they are ancillary to the main theme.

(2a.) *De dicto-de re*

Many able people, in and out of print, have implied that Donnellan's distinction has something to do with, can be identified with, or can replace, the *de dicto-de re* distinction, or the small scope-large scope distinction in modal or intensional contexts.

"The number of planets is necessarily odd" can mean two things, depending on whether it is interpreted *de dicto* or *de re*. If it is interpreted *de dicto*, it asserts that the proposition that the number of planets is odd is a necessary truth—something I take to be false (there might have been eight planets). If it is interpreted *de re*, it asserts that the actual number of planets (nine) has the property of necessary oddness (essentialists like me take this to be true). Similarly, if we say, "Jones believes that the richest debutante in Dubuque will marry him," we may mean that Jones's belief has a certain content, viz., that the richest debutante in Dubuque will marry him; or we may mean that he believes, *of* a girl who is (in fact) the richest in Dubuque, that she will marry him. The view in question suggests that the *de dicto* case is to be identified with Donnellan's *attributive* use, the *de re* with the *referential*.

Any such assimilation, in my opinion, is confused. (I don't think Donnellan makes it.) There are many objections; I will mention a few. First, the *de dicto* use of the definite description cannot be identified with either the *referential* or the *attributive* use. Here the basic point was already noticed by Frege. If a description is embedded in a (*de dicto*) intensional context, we cannot be said to be talking *about* the thing described, either *qua* its satisfaction of the description or *qua* anything else. Taken *de dicto*, "Jones believes that the richest debutante in Dubuque will marry him," can be asserted by someone who thinks (let us suppose, wrongly) that there are *no* debutantes in Dubuque; certainly then, he is in no way talking about the richest debutante, even "attributively." Similarly, "It is possible that (France should have a monarchy in 1976, and that) the king of France in 1976 should have been bald" is true, if read *de dicto*; yet we are not using "the king of France in 1976" attributively to speak of the king of France in 1976, for there is none. Frege concluded that "the king of France in 1976" refers, in these contexts, to its ordinary sense; at any rate, if we wish to speak of "reference" here, it cannot be to the non-existent king. Even if there were such a king, the quoted assertion would say nothing about *him*, if read *de dicto*: to say that *he* might have been bald, would be *de re* (indeed, this *is* the distinction in question).

Second, and even more relevantly, Donnellan's referential use cannot be identified with the *de re* use. (I think Donnellan would agree.) Suppose I have no idea how many planets there are, but (for some reason) astronomical theory dictates that that number must be odd. If I say, "The number of planets (whatever it may be) is odd," my description is used attributively. If I am an essentialist, I will also say, "The number of planets (whatever it may be) is necessarily odd," on the grounds that all odd numbers are necessarily odd; and my usage is just as attributive as in the first case. In "Smith's murderer, whoever he may be, is known to the police, but they're not saying," or, more explicitly, "The police know concerning Smith's murderer, whoever he is, that he committed the murder; but they're not saying who he is," "Smith's murderer" is used attributively, but is *de re*.

Finally: Russell wished to handle the *de dicto-de re* distinction by his notion of the *scope* of a description. Some have suggested that Donnellan's referential-attributive distinction can replace Russell's distinction of scope. But *no* twofold distinction can do this job. Consider:

(2) The number of planets might have been necessarily even.

In a natural use, (2) can be interpreted as true: for example, there might have been exactly eight planets, in which case the number of planets would have been even, and hence necessarily even. (2), interpreted as true, is neither *de re* nor *de dicto*; that is, the definite description neither has the largest nor the smallest possible scope. Consider:

(2a) $\Diamond \Box (\exists x)$ (There are exactly x planets and x is even)
(2b) $(\exists x)$ (There are exactly x planets and $\Diamond \Box$ (x is even))
(2c) $\Diamond$ $(\exists x)$ (There are exactly x planets and $\Box$ (x is even)).

(2a)–(2c) give three alternative Russellian analyses of (2). (2a) gives the description the smallest possible scope (*de dicto*); it says, presumably falsely, that it might have been necessary that there was an even number of planets. (2b) gives the description the largest possible scope (*de re*); it says, still falsely, of the actual number of planets (viz., nine) that it might have been necessarily even. (2c) is the interpretation which makes (2) true. When intensional operators are iterated, intermediate scopes are possible. Three analogous interpretations are possible, say, for "Jones doubts that Holmes believes that Smith's murderer is insane"; or (using an indefinite description) for "Hoover charged that the Berrigans plotted to kidnap a high American official." (I actually read something like this last in a newspaper and wondered what was meant.)[5] This may mean: (a) there is a particular high official such that Hoover charged that the Berrigans plotted to kidnap him (largest scope, *de re*, this was the interpretation intended); or (b) Hoover charged that the Berrigans plotted as follows: let's kidnap a high official (smallest scope, *de dicto*); or (c) Hoover charged that there was a high official

---

[5] At the time, it had not yet been revealed that Kissinger was the official in question. (See also Chapter 8, p. 231.)

(whose identity may have been unknown to Hoover) whom the Berrigans planned to kidnap (intermediate scope).

As intensional (or other) constructions are iterated, there are more and more possible scopes for a definite description. No *twofold* distinction can replace Russell's notion of scope.[6] In particular, neither the *de dicto-de re* distinction nor the referential-attributive distinction can do so.

(2b.) *Rigid definite descriptions.*

If definite descriptions, $\iota x\phi(x)$, are taken as primitive and assigned reference, then the conventional non-rigid assignment assigns to such a description, with respect to each possible world, the unique object, if any, which would have ϕ'd in that world. (Forget the vacuous case, which requires a further convention.) For example, "the number of planets" denotes eight, speaking of a counterfactual situation where there would have been eight planets (and "the number of planets is even" is true of such a situation). Another type of definite description, $\iota x\phi x$, a "rigid" definite description, could be introduced semantically by the following stipulation: let $\iota x\phi x$ denote, with respect to all possible worlds, the unique object that (actually) ϕ's (then "the number of planets is odd," as interpreted, expresses a necessary truth). Both kinds of definite descriptions can obviously be introduced, theoretically, into a single formal language, perhaps by the notations just given. Some have suggested that definite descriptions, in English, are *ambiguous* between the two readings. It has further been suggested that the two types of definite descriptions, the nonrigid and the rigid, are the source of the *de dicto-de re* distinction and should replace Russell's notion of scope for the purpose. Further, it has been suggested that they amount to the same thing as Donnellan's attributive-referential distinction.[7]

My comments will be brief, so as to avoid too much excursus. Although I have an open mind on the subject, I am not yet convinced that there is any clear evidence for such an ambiguity. Being a twofold distinction, the ambiguity alleged cannot replace Russell's notion of scope, for the reasons given above. Once Russell's notion is available, it can be used to handle the *de dicto-de re* distinction; a further ambiguity seems unnecessary. More relevantly to the present context, the "rigid" sense of a definite description, if it exists, cannot be identified with Donnellan's "referential" use. I take it that the identification of the referential use with the rigid definite description was inspired by some line of

---

[6] In fact, no *n*-fold distinction can do so, for any fixed *n*. Independently of the present writer, L. Kartunnen has argued similarly that no dual or *n*-fold distinction can replace scope distinctions. I discussed the matter briefly in Chapter 1, p. 13, n. 10.

[7] See the papers of Stalnaker and Partee in *The Semantics of Natural Language*, eds. D. Davidson and G. Harman (Dordrecht: Reidel, 1972) for such suggestions and also for some of the views mentioned in the previous section. I should emphasize that most of the stimulating discussion in these papers can be made independent of any of the identifications of Donnellan's distinction with others which are rejected here.

reasoning like this: Donnellan holds that referential descriptions are those close to proper names, even to Russell's "logically proper names." But surely proper names, or, at least, Russellian "logically proper names," are rigid. Hence Donnellan's referential descriptions are just the rigid definite descriptions.

If we assume that Donnellan thinks of names as rigid, as I think of them, his referential definite descriptions *would* most plausibly be taken to refer rigidly to their referents. But it is not clear that he does agree with me on the rigidity of such reference.[8] More important, a rigid definite description, as defined above, still determines its referent via its unique satisfaction of the associated property—and this fact separates the notion of such a description from that of a referential description, as Donnellan defines it. David Kaplan has suggested that a demonstrative "that" can be used, in English, to make any definite description rigid. "That bastard—the man who killed Smith, whoever he may be—is surely insane!" The subject term rigidly designates Smith's murderer, but it is still attributive in Donnellan's sense.[9]

(2c.)

In *Naming and Necessity*,[10] one argument I presented against the description (or cluster-of-descriptions) theory of proper names concerned cases where the referent of a name, the person named by the name, did not satisfy the descriptions usually associated with it, and someone else did. For example, the name "Gödel" might be taken to mean "the man who proved the incompleteness of arithmetic"; but even if Gödel had been a fraud, who had proved nothing at all and had misappropriated his work from an unknown named "Schmidt," our term "Gödel" would refer to the fraud, not to the man who really satisfied the definite description. Against this it has been said that although the argument does succeed in its main purpose of refuting the description theory as a theory of reference (that is, it shows that the descriptive properties cited do not determine the referent), it does nothing to show that names are not abbreviated definite

---

[8] See his paper "The Contingent A *Priori* and Rigid Designators," *Midwest Studies in Philosophy Volume II: Studies in the Philosophy of Language*, Peter A. French, Theodore E. Uehling, Jr., and Howard K. Wettstein (eds.) (Morris, MN: University of Minnesota Press, 1977), pp. 12–27. In that paper, Donnellan asks whether I think proper names (in natural language) are *always* rigid: obviously, he thinks, proper names *could* be introduced to abbreviate nonrigid definite descriptions. My view is that proper names (except perhaps, for some quirky and derivative uses, that are not uses as *names*) *are* always rigid. In particular this applies to "Neptune." It would be logically possible to have single words that abbreviated nonrigid definite descriptions, but these would not be *names*. The point is not merely terminological: I mean that such abbreviated nonrigid definite descriptions would differ in an important semantical feature from (what we call) typical proper names in our actual speech. I merely state my position and do not argue it; nor can I digress to comment on the other points raised in Donnellan's paper.

[9] See Kaplan's paper "Dthat," *Syntax and Semantics*, Volume 9, P. Cole (ed.) (New York: Academic Press, 1978), pp. 221–43. In that paper, however, he also has some tendency to confuse rigidity with Donnellan's referentiality.

[10] Cambridge: Harvard University Press, 1980. (Originally published as "Naming and Necessity" in *Semantics of Natural Language, op. cit.*, pp. 253–355, 763–69; references will be to the reprint.)

descriptions, because we could take the descriptions in question to be referential in Donnellan's sense. Referential descriptions can easily refer to things that fail to satisfy the descriptions; nothing in my argument shows that names are not synonymous with such descriptions.[11]

My reaction to such an argument may become clearer later. For the moment, (too) briefly: In the case of "Her husband is kind to her," and similar cases, "her husband" can refer to her lover, as long as we are under the misapprehension that the man to whom we refer (the lover) *is* her husband. Once we are apprised of the true facts, we will no longer so refer to him (see, for example, pp. 300–301 of Donnellan's paper). Similarly, someone can use "the man who proved the incompleteness of arithmetic," as a referential definite description, to refer to Gödel; it might be so used, for example, by someone who had forgotten his name. If the hypothetical fraud were discovered, however, the description is no longer usable as a device to refer to Gödel; henceforth it can be used only to refer to Schmidt. We would withdraw any previous assertions using the description to refer to Gödel (unless they also were true of Schmidt). We would *not* similarly withdraw the *name* "Gödel," even after the fraud was discovered; "Gödel" would still be used to name Gödel, not Schmidt. The name and the description, therefore, are not synonymous. (See also footnote 26 below.)

(3.) *The main problem.*

(3a.) *A disagreement with Russell?*

Do Donnellan's observations provide an argument against Russell's theory? Do his *views* contradict Russell's? One might think that if Donnellan is right, Russell must be wrong, since Donnellan's truth conditions for statements containing referential definite descriptions differ from Russell's. Unfortunately, this is not so clear. Consider the case of "Her husband is kind to her," mistakenly said of the lover. If Donnellan had roundly asserted that the quoted statement is true if and only if the *lover* is kind to her, regardless of the kindness of the husband, the issue between him and Russell would be clearly joined. But Donnellan doesn't say this: rather he says that the speaker has referred to a certain person, the lover, and said *of him* that he is kind to her. But if we ask, "Yes, but was the statement he made true?", Donnellan would hedge. For if *we* are not under the misimpression that the man the speaker referred to was her husband, *we* would not express the same assertion by "Her husband is kind to her." "If it ['her husband'] is being used referentially, it is not clear what is meant by 'the statement.' . . . To say that the statement he made was that her husband is kind to her lands us in difficulties. For we [in so reporting what the speaker said must use the definite description] either

---

[11] For this view, see Jerrold J. Katz, "Logic and Language: An Examination of Recent Criticisms of Intensionalism," in *Minnesota Studies in the Philosophy of Science*, vol. VII (Minneapolis, 1975), pp. 36–130. See especially sections 5.1 and 5.2. As far as proper names are concerned, Katz thinks that *other* arguments tell against the description theory even as a theory of meaning.

attributively or referentially. If the former, then we misrepresent the linguistic performance of the speaker; if the latter, then we ourselves are referring to someone," and ordinarily we can refer to someone as "her husband" only if we take him to be her husband.[12]

Since Donnellan does not clearly assert that the statement "her husband is kind to her" ever has non-Russellian truth conditions, he has *not*, so far, clearly contradicted Russell's theory. His argument, as he presents it, that there is a problem in reporting "the statement," is questionable, in two ways.

First, it uses the premise that if we say, "Jones said that her husband is kind to her," we ourselves must use the description attributively or referentially; but, as we saw, a definite description in indirect discourse is *neither* referential nor attributive.[13]

Second, there is an important problem about the nature of the referential-attributive distinction. Donnellan says that his distinction is neither syntactic nor semantic:

> The grammatical structure of the sentence seems to me to be the same whether the description is used referentially or attributively: that is, it is not syntactically ambiguous. Nor does it seem at all attractive to suppose an ambiguity in the meaning of the words; it does not appear to be semantically ambiguous. (Perhaps we could say that the sentence is pragmatically ambiguous: the distinction between roles that the description plays is a function of the speaker's intentions.) These, of course, are intuitions; I do not have an argument for these conclusions. Nevertheless, the burden of proof is surely on the other side.[14]

Suppose for the moment that this is so. Then if the referential-attributive distinction is pragmatic, rather than syntactic or semantic, it is presumably a distinction about speech acts. There is no reason to suppose that in making an indirect discourse report on what someone else has said I myself must have similar intentions, or be engaged in the same kind of speech act; in fact, it is clear that I am not. If I say "Jones said the police were around the corner," Jones may have said it as a warning, but *I* need not say it as a warning. If the referential-attributive distinction is neither syntactic nor semantic, there is no reason, without further argument, to suppose that my usage, in indirect discourse, should match the man on whom I report, as referential or attributive. The case is quite different for a genuine semantic ambiguity. If Jones says, "I have never been at a bank," and I report this, saying, "Jones denied that he was ever at a bank," the sense I give to "bank" must match Jones's if my report is to be accurate.

---

[12] See Donnellan, "Reference and Definite Descriptions," p. 302.
[13] So I argued in the talks, and rightly, if Donnellan is taken literally. See footnote 24 below, however, for a more charitable reading, which probably corresponds to Donnellan's intent. We must, however, take descriptions to be *semantically* ambiguous if we are to maintain the reading in question: see the point raised immediately after this one.
[14] "Reference and Definite Descriptions," p. 297.

Indeed, the passage seems inconsistent with the whole trend of Donnellan's paper. Donnellan suggests that there is no syntactic or semantic ambiguity in the statement, "Her husband is kind to her." He also suggests that Russell may well give a correct analysis of the attributive use but not of the referential use. Surely this is not coherent. It is not "uses," in some pragmatic sense, but *senses* of a sentence which can be analyzed. If the sentence is *not* (syntactically or) semantically ambiguous, it has only *one* analysis; to say that it has two distinct analyses is to attribute a syntactic or semantic ambiguity to it.

Donnellan's arguments for his refusal to give a truth value to the speaker's assertion, "Her husband is kind to her," seem to be fallacious. My own suggested account of the matter below—in terms of a theory of speech acts—creates no problem about "the statement"; it is simply the statement that her husband is kind to her. But Donnellan's cautious refusal to say, under the circumstances mentioned, that "Her husband is kind to her" is true, seems nevertheless to be intuitively correct. The man to whom the speaker refers is—let us suppose—kind to her. But it seems hard for us to say that when he uttered, "Her husband is kind to her," it expressed a truth, if *we* believe that her husband is unkind to her.

Now Donnellan thinks that he has refuted Russell. But all he has clearly claimed, let alone established, is that a speaker can refer to the lover and say, of him, that he is kind to her by saying "Her husband is kind to her." So, first, we can ask: *If* this claim is correct, does it conflict with Russell's views?

Second, since Donnellan's denial that he advocates a semantic ambiguity in definite descriptions seems inconsistent with much of his paper, we can try ignoring the denial, and take his paper to be arguing for such an ambiguity. Then we may ask: has Donnellan established a (semantic) ambiguity inconsistent with Russell's theory?

(3b.) *General remarks: apparatus.*

We need a general apparatus to discuss these questions. Some of the apparatus is well known, but I review it for its intrinsic importance and interest. First, let us distinguish, following Grice,[15] between what *the speaker's words meant*, on a given occasion, and what *he meant*, in saying these words, on that occasion. For example, one burglar says to another, "The cops are around the corner." What *the words meant* is clear: the police were around the corner. But *the speaker may well have meant*, "We can't wait around collecting any more loot: Let's split!" That is not *the meaning of the words*, even on that occasion, though that is *what he meant in saying those words, on that occasion.* Suppose he had said, "The cops are

---

[15] For Grice, see the following papers, which I follow loosely in a good deal of the discussion at the beginning of this section: "The Causal Theory of Perception," *Proceedings of the Aristotelian Society*, supplementary vol. 35 (1961); "Logic and Conversation," Peter Cole and Jerry Morgan, eds., *Syntax and Semantics, Volume 3: Speech Acts* (New York: Academic Press, 1975), pp. 43–58; "Meaning," *Philosophical Review* 66 (1957): 377–88; "Utterer's Meaning, Sentence-Meaning and Word-Meaning," *Foundations of Language* 4 (1968): 225–42; "Utterer's Meaning and Intentions," *Philosophical Review* 78 (1969): 147–77.

inside the bank." Then on that occasion, "bank" meant a commercial bank, not a river bank, and this is relevant to what the *words* meant, on that occasion. (On other occasions, the same words might mean that the police were at a river bank.) But, if the speaker *meant* "Let's split," this is no part of the *meaning of his words*, even on that occasion.

Again (inspired by an example of Grice)[16]: A magician makes a handkerchief change color. Someone says, recalling the trick, "Then he put the red handkerchief on the side of the table"; and someone else interjects, cautiously, "It *looked* red." The words meant, on that occasion, that the object referred to (the handkerchief) looked red. What we speak of when we speak of the meaning of his words, on that occasion, includes a disambiguation of the utterance. (Perhaps, on some occasions, where "it" refers to a book, a phonetically identical utterance might mean, "it looked read"—well-thumbed and well-perused). But the speaker meant, on this occasion, to suggest that perhaps the handkerchief wasn't really red, that perhaps the trick relied on some kind of illusion. (Note that, on this occasion, not only do the *words* "it looked red" mean what they mean, but also the *speaker* means that it looked red, as well as that it may not have been red. On the other hand, the speaker has no intention of producing a belief in the hearer that the handkerchief looked red, or a belief in the hearer that he (the speaker) believed it looked red. Both facts are common knowledge. The same *could* hold for "The cops are around the corner."[17] Do these examples contradict Grice's analysis of "meaning"? Grice's theory has become very complex and I am not quite sure.)

The notion of what words can mean, in the language, is semantical: it is given by the conventions of our language. What they mean, on a given occasion, is determined, on a given occasion, by these conventions, together with the intentions of the speaker and various contextual features. Finally, what the speaker meant, on a given occasion, in saying certain words, derives from various further special intentions of the speaker, together with various general principles, applicable to all human languages regardless of their special conventions. (Cf. Grice's "conversational maxims.") For example, "It looks red" replaced a categorical affirmation of redness. A plausible general principle of human discourse would have it that if a second speaker insists that a stronger assertion should be replaced by a weaker one, he thereby wishes to cast doubt on the stronger assertion; whence, knowing the semantics of English, and the meaning of the speaker's words on this occasion, we can deduce what was meant (the Gricean "conversational implicature").[18]

---

[16] In "The Causal Theory of Perception."

[17] Suppose the second burglar is well aware of the proximity of the police, but procrastinates in his greed for more loot. Then the first burglar imparts no *information* by saying what he does, but simply urges the second burglar to "split."

[18] Although conversational principles are applicable to *all languages*, they may apply differently to *different societies*. In a society where blunt statement was considered rude, where "it looks red" replaced "it is red" just because of such a custom, "it looks red" might carry different conversational

Let us now speak of speaker's reference and semantic reference: these notions are special cases of the Gricean notions discussed above. If a speaker has a designator in his idiolect, certain conventions of his idiolect[19] (given various facts about the world) determine the referent in the idiolect: that I call the *semantic referent* of the designator. (If the designator is ambiguous, or contains indexicals, demonstratives, or the like, we must speak of the semantic referent on a given occasion. The referent will be determined by the conventions of the language plus the speaker's intentions and various contextual features.)

Speaker's reference is a more difficult notion. Consider, for example, the following case, which I have mentioned elsewhere.[20] Two people see Smith in the distance and mistake him for Jones. They have a brief colloquy: "What is Jones doing?" "Raking the leaves." "Jones," in the common language of both, is a name of Jones; it *never* names Smith. Yet, in some sense, on this occasion, clearly both participants in the dialogue have referred to Smith, and the second participant has said something true about the man he referred to if and only if Smith was raking the leaves (whether or not Jones was). How can we account for this? Suppose a speaker takes it that a certain object a fulfills the conditions for being the semantic referent of a designator, "d." Then, wishing to say something about a, he uses "d" to speak about a; say, he says "$\phi(d)$." Then, he said, of a, on that occasion, that it ϕ'd; in the appropriate Gricean sense (explicated above), he *meant* that a ϕ'd. This is true even if a is not really the semantic referent of "d." If it is not, then *that a ϕ's* is included in what he meant (on that occasion), but not in the meaning of his words (on that occasion).

So, we may tentatively define the speaker's referent of a designator to be that object which the speaker wishes to talk about, on a given occasion, and believes fulfills the conditions for being the semantic referent of the designator. He uses the designator with the intention of making an assertion about the object in question (which may not really be the semantic referent, if the speaker's belief that it fulfills the appropriate semantic conditions is in error). The speaker's

---

implicatures from our own. This might be the case even though the members of the society spoke *English*, just as we do. Conversational principles are matters for the psychology, sociology, and anthropology of linguistic communities; they are applicable to these communities no matter what language they may speak, though the applicable principles may vary somewhat with the communities (and may even, to some extent, be conditioned by the fact that they speak languages with certain structures.) Often, of course, we can state widely applicable, "cross-cultural," general conversational principles. Semantic and syntactic principles, on the other hand, are matters of the conventions of a language, in whatever cultural matrix it may be spoken. *Perhaps* sometimes it is difficult to draw the line, but it exists in general nonetheless.

[19] If the views about proper names I have advocated in *Naming and Necessity* are correct (Donnellan, in fact, holds similar views), the conventions regarding names in an idiolect usually involve the fact that the idiolect is no mere idiolect, but part of a common language, in which reference may be passed from link to link.

As the present chapter attests, my views on proper names in *Naming and Necessity* have no special connection with the referential-attributive distinction.

[20] *Naming and Necessity*, p. 25, n. 3.

referent is the thing the speaker referred to by the designator, though it may not be the referent of the designator, in his idiolect. In the example above, Jones, the man named by the name, is the semantic referent. Smith is the speaker's referent, the correct answer to the question, "To whom were you referring?"[21]

Below, the notion of speaker's reference will be extended to include more cases where existential quantification rather than designation is involved.

In a given idiolect, the semantic referent of a designator (without indexicals) is given by a *general* intention of the speaker to refer to a certain object whenever the designator is used. The speaker's referent is given by a *specific* intention, on a given occasion, to refer to a certain object. If the speaker believes that the object he wants to talk about, on a given occasion, fulfills the conditions for being the semantic referent, then he believes that there is no clash between his general intentions and his specific intentions. My hypothesis is that Donnellan's referential-attributive distinction should be generalized in this light. For the speaker, on a given occasion, may believe that his specific intention coincides with his general intention for one of two reasons. In one case (the "simple" case), his specific intention is simply to refer to the semantic referent: that is, his specific intention *is* simply his general semantic intention. (For example, he uses "Jones" as a name of Jones—elaborate this according to your favorite theory of proper names—and, on this occasion, simply wishes to use "Jones" to refer to Jones.) Alternatively—the "complex" case—he has a specific intention, which is distinct from his general intention, but which he believes, as a matter of fact, to determine the same object as the one determined by his general intention. (For example, he wishes to refer to the man "over there" but believes that he *is* Jones.) In the "simple" case, the speaker's referent is, *by definition*, the semantic referent.

---

[21] Donnellan shows in his paper that there are "referential" uses, of a somewhat exceptional kind, where the speaker, or even both the speaker and the hearer, are aware that the description used does not apply to the thing they are talking about. For example, they use "the king," knowing him to be a usurper, but fearing the secret police. Analogous cases can be given for proper names: if Smith is a lunatic who thinks he is Napoleon, they may humor him. Largely for the sake of simplicity of exposition, I have excluded such both from the notion of speaker's reference and from Donnellan's "referential" use (and the "D-languages" below). I do not think that the situation would be materially altered if both notions were revised so as to admit these cases, in a more refined analysis. In particular, it would probably *weaken* the case for a semantic ambiguity if these cases were allowed: for they shade into ironical and "inverted commas" cases. "He is a 'fine friend'," may be ironical (whether or not inverted commas are used in the transcription). "'The king' is still in power"; " 'Napoleon' has gone to bed" are similar, whether or not explicit inverted commas are used. It is fairly clear that "fine friend," "brilliant scholar," etc., do not have ironical and inverted commas *senses*: irony is a certain form of speech act, to be accounted for by pragmatic considerations. The case for a semantic ambiguity in definite descriptions is similarly *weakened* if we include such cases as referential uses.

In ordinary discourse, we say that the speaker was referring to someone under a wide variety of circumstances, including linguistic errors, verbal slips, and deliberate misuses of language. (If Mrs. Malaprop says, "The geography teacher said that equilateral triangles are equiangular," she *refers* to the geometry teacher.) The more such phenomena one includes in the notion of speaker's reference, the further one gets from any connection of the notion with semantical matters.

In the "complex" case, they may coincide, if the speaker's belief is correct, but they need not. (The man "over there" may be Smith and not Jones.) To anticipate, my hypothesis will be that Donnellan's "attributive" use is nothing but the "simple" case, specialized to definite descriptions, and that the "referential" use is, similarly, the "complex" case. If such a conjecture is correct, it would be wrong to take Donnellan's "referential" use, as he does, to be a use of a description as if it were a proper name. For the distinction of simple and complex cases will apply to proper names just as much as to definite descriptions.

(3c.) *Donnellan's argument against Russell: methodological and substantive considerations.*

In the light of the notions just developed, consider the argument Donnellan adduces against Russell. Donnellan points to a phenomenon which he alleges to be inexplicable on a Russellian account of English definite descriptions. He accounts for it by positing an ambiguity. Alternatively, we wish to account for the phenomenon on pragmatic grounds, encapsulated in the distinction between speaker's reference and semantic reference. How can we see whether Donnellan's phenomenon conflicts with a Russellian account?

I propose the following test for any alleged counterexample to a linguistic proposal: If someone alleges that a certain linguistic phenomenon in English is a counterexample to a given analysis, consider a hypothetical language which (as much as possible) is like English except that the analysis is *stipulated* to be correct. Imagine such a hypothetical language introduced into a community and spoken by it. *If the phenomenon in question would still arise in a community that spoke such a hypothetical language (which may not be English), then the fact that it arises in English cannot disprove the hypothesis that the analysis is correct for English.* An example removed from the present discussion: Some have alleged that identity cannot be the relation that holds between, and only between, each thing and itself, for if so, the nontriviality of identity statements would be inexplicable. If it is conceded, however, that such a relation makes sense, and if it can be shown that a hypothetical language involving such a relation would generate the same problems, it will follow that the existence of these problems does not refute the hypothesis that "identical to" stands for this same relation in English.[22]

By "the weak Russell language," I will mean a language similar to English except that the truth conditions of sentences with definite descriptions are *stipulated* to coincide with Russell's: for example, "The present King of France is bald" is to be true iff exactly one person is king of France, and that person is bald. On the weak Russell language, this effect can be achieved by assigning semantic reference to definite descriptions: the semantic referent of a definite description is the unique object that satisfies the description, if any; otherwise

---

[22] See the discussion of "schmidentity" in *Naming and Necessity*, p. 108.

there is no semantic referent. A sentence of the simple subject-predicate form will be true if the predicate is true of the (semantic) referent of its subject; false, if either the subject has no semantic referent or the predicate is not true of the semantic referent of the subject.

Since the weak Russell language takes definite descriptions to be primitive designators, it is not fully Russellian. By "the intermediate Russell language," I mean a language in which sentences containing definite descriptions are taken to be abbreviations or paraphrases of their Russellian analyses: for example, "The present king of France is bald" *means* (or has a "deep structure" like) "Exactly one person is at present king of France, and he is bald," or the like. Descriptions are not terms, and are not assigned reference or meaning in isolation. The "strong Russell language" goes further: definite descriptions are actually *banned* from the language and Russellian paraphrases are used in their place. Instead of saying "Her husband is kind to her," a speaker of this language must say "Exactly one man is married to her, and he is kind to her," or even (better), "There is a unique man who is married to her, and every man who is married to her is kind to her," or the like. If Russell is right, long-windedness is the only defect of these versions.

Would the phenomenon Donnellan adduces arise in communities that spoke these languages? Surely speakers of these languages are no more infallible than we. They too will find themselves at a party and mistakenly think someone is drinking champagne even though he is actually drinking sparkling water. If they are speakers of the weak or intermediate Russell languages, they will say, "The man in the corner drinking champagne is happy tonight." They will say this precisely because *they think, though erroneously, that the Russellian truth conditions are satisfied*. Wouldn't we say of these speakers that they are referring to the teetotaler, under the misimpression that he is drinking champagne? And, if he is happy, are they not saying of him, *truly*, that he is happy? Both answers seem obviously affirmative.

In the case of the weak Russell language, the general apparatus previously developed seems fully adequate to account for the phenomenon. The semantic referent of a definite description is given by the conditions laid down above: it is a matter of the specific conventions of the (weak) Russell language, in this case that the referent is the unique object satisfying the descriptive conditions. The speaker's referent, on the other hand, is determined by a general theory of speech acts, applicable to all languages: it is the object to which the speaker wishes to refer, and which he believes fulfills the Russellian conditions for being the semantic referent. Again, in asserting the sentence he does, the speaker means that the speaker's referent (the teetotaler) satisfied the predicate (is happy). Thus the rough theoretical apparatus above accounts fully for our intuitions about this case.

What about the other Russellian languages? Even in the strong Russell language, where explicit descriptions are outlawed, the same phenomena can occur. In fact, they occur in English in "arch" uses of existential quantification:

"Exactly *one person* (or: *some* person or other) is drinking champagne in that corner, and I hear he is romantically linked with Jane Smith." The circumlocution, in English, expresses the delicacy of the topic, but the speaker's reference (in quite an ordinary sense) may well be clear, even if he in fact is drinking sparkling water. In English such circumlocutions are common only when the speaker wishes to achieve a rather arch and prissy effect, but in the strong Russell language (which of course isn't English), they would be made more common because the definite article is prohibited.

This example leads to an extension of the notion of speaker's reference. When a speaker asserts an existential quantification, $(\exists x)(\phi x \wedge \psi x)$, it may be clear which thing he has in mind as satisfying "ϕx," and he may wish to convey to his hearers that that thing satisfies "ψx." In this case, the thing in question (which may or may not actually satisfy "ϕx") is called the "speaker's referent" when he makes the existential assertion. In English, as I have mentioned, such cases ("arch" uses) are rather rare; but they can be carried off even if the existential quantification is expressed in a highly roundabout and apparently nonreferring fashion. "Not *everyone* in this room is abstaining from champagne, and any such nonabstainer...."[23]

If the notion of speaker's reference applies to the strong Russell language, it can apply to the intermediate Russell language as well, since the speaker's referent of "$\psi(\iota x \phi(x))$" is then the thing he has in mind as uniquely instantiating "$\phi(x)$" and about which he wishes to convey that it ψ's.

Since the phenomenon Donnellan cites *would* arise in all the Russell languages, if they *were* spoken, the fact that they *do* arise in English, as *actually* spoken, can be no argument that English is not a Russell language.

We may contrast the Russell languages with what may be called the D-languages. In the D-languages the apparent ambiguity between referential and attributive definite descriptions is explicitly built into the semantics of the language and affects truth conditions. (The D-languages are meant to suggest "Donnellan," but are not called the "Donnellan languages," since Donnellan, as we have seen, is "ambiguous" as to whether he posits a semantic ambiguity.) The *unambiguous D-language* contains two distinct words, "the" and "ze" (rhymes with "the"). A statement of the form "...the *F*..." is true iff the predicate represented by the dots is true of the unique object fulfilling F (we need not specify what happens if there is no such thing; if we wish to follow Russell, take it to be false). A statement of the form "...ze F..." is to be true iff the predicate represented by the dots is true of the unique thing the speaker thinks F is true of. (Once again, we leave free what happens if there is no such thing.) *The ambiguous*

---

[23] Or, using variables explicitly, "There is a person *x* such that..." Notice that in an utterance of "$(\exists x)(\phi x \wedge \psi x)$," as long as it is clear *which* thing allegedly satisfying "ϕx" the speaker has in mind, there can be a speaker's referent, even if both the speaker and the hearer are aware that many things satisfy "ϕx."

D-language is like the unambiguous D-language except that "the," ambiguously, can be interpreted according to the semantics either of "the" *or* of "ze." The general impression conveyed by Donnellan's paper, in spite of his statement at one point to the contrary, is that English is the ambiguous D-language; only on such a hypothesis could we say that the "referential use" (really, referential *sense*) diverges from Russell's theory. The truth-conditions of statements containing "ze," and therefore of one sense of "the" in the ambiguous D-language, *are* incompatible with Russell's theory.[24]

We have two hypotheses: one says that English is a Russell language, while the other says that English is the ambiguous D-language. Which hypothesis is preferable? Since, as we have argued, the phenomena Donnellan adduces would arise in a hypothetical society that spoke any of the Russell languages, the existence in English of such phenomena provides no argument against the hypothesis that English is a Russell language. If Donnellan had possessed a clear intuition that "Her husband is kind to her," uttered in reference to the kind lover of a woman married to a cruel husband, expressed the literal truth, then he *would* have adduced a phenomenon that conforms to the ambiguous D-language but is incompatible with any Russell language. But Donnellan makes no such assertion: he cautiously, and correctly, confines himself to the weaker claim that the speaker spoke truly of the man to whom he referred. This weaker claim, we have seen, *would* hold for a speaker of a Russell language.

So Donnellan's examples provide, in themselves, no evidence that English is the ambiguous D-language rather than a Russell language. Granting that this is so, we can ask whether there is any reason to favor the Russell language hypothesis over the D-language hypothesis. I think there are several general methodological considerations that are relevant.

The Russell language theory, or any other unitary account (that is, any account that postulates no semantic ambiguity), accounts for Donnellan's referential-

---

[24] This description of the D-languages specifies nothing about semantical features more "intensional" than truth conditions. It is plausible to assume that "ze F" is a *rigid* designator of the thing believed to be uniquely F, but this is not explicitly included in the extensional truth conditions. Nor has anything been said about the behavior of "ze F" in belief and indirect discourse contexts. *If* we stipulate that "ze F," even in such contexts, designates the thing the speaker believes uniquely F's, then indeed "Jones said that ze man she married is kind to her," will not be a proper way of reporting Jones's utterance "Ze man she married is kind to her" (even if Jones and the speaker happen to have the same belief as to who her husband is; the difficulty is more obvious if they do not.) No doubt it is this fact that lies behind Donnellan's view that, in the referential case, it is hard to speak of "the statement," even though his exposition of the matter seems to be defective. Such implications, which are not present in the Russell language, lend only further implausibility to the supposition that English is the ambiguous D-language.

To repeat footnote 21, actually there are many other ways, other than taking something uniquely to satisfy "F," that might be included under referential uses of "the F." The best short way to specify the semantics of "ze F" would seem to be this: "ze F" refers, in the unambiguous D-language, to what would have been the speaker's referent of "the F" in the weak Russell language (under the same circumstances)! But this formulation makes it very implausible that the ambiguous D-language is anything but a chimerical model for English.

attributive phenomenon by a general pragmatic theory of speech acts, applicable to a very wide range of languages; the D-language hypothesis accounts for these same phenomena by positing a semantic ambiguity. The unitary account appeals to a general apparatus that applies to cases, such as the "Smith-Jones" case, where it is completely implausible that a semantic ambiguity exists. According to the unitary account, far from the referential use constituting a special namelike use of definite descriptions, the referential-attributive distinction is simply a special case of a general distinction, applicable to proper names as well as to definite descriptions, and illustrated in practice by the (leaf-raking) Smith-Jones case. And anyone who compares the Smith-Jones case, where presumably no one is tempted to posit a special semantic ambiguity, with Donnellan's cases of definite descriptions, must surely be impressed by the similarity of the phenomena.[25]

Under these circumstances, surely general methodological principles favor the existing account. The apparatus of speaker's reference and semantic reference, and of simple and complex uses of designators, is needed *anyway*, to explain the Smith-Jones case; it is applicable to all languages.[26] Why posit a semantic ambiguity when it is both insufficient in general and superfluous for the special case it seeks to explain?[27] And why are the phenomena regarding proper names so

---

[25] There is one significant difference between the case of proper names and that of definite descriptions. If someone uses "Jones" to refer to Smith, he has *misidentified* Smith as Jones, taken Smith for someone else. To some extent I *did* think that *Jones* was raking the leaves. (I assume that "Jones" is already in his idiolect as a name of Jones. If I am introduced to an impostor and am told, "This man is none other than Albert Einstein," if I am fooled I will have *taken* him, falsely, to be Einstein. Someone else, who has never heard of Einstein before, may merely be mistaken as to the impostor's name.) On the other hand, if I think that someone is "her husband" and so refer to him, I need not at all have confused two people. I merely think that one person possesses a property—that of being married to her—that in fact he lacks. The real husband is irrelevant.

[26] In terms of this apparatus, I can sharpen the reply to Katz, pp. 106–07, and footnote 11, above. If Schmidt had discovered the incompleteness of arithmetic but I had thought it was Gödel who did so, a complex ("referential") use of the description has a semantic reference to Schmidt but a speaker's reference to Gödel. Once I am apprised of the true facts, speaker's reference and semantic reference will coincide thereafter and I will no longer use the description to refer to Gödel. The name "Gödel," on the other hand, has Gödel as its *semantic* referent: the name will always be applied to Gödel in the presence of correct information. Whether a term would be withdrawn in the presence of correct information (without changing the language) is a good intuitive test for divergence of semantic reference and speaker's reference (disregarding the cases in footnote 21).

[27] There is another problem for any theory of semantic ambiguity. Donnellan says that if I say "Smith's murderer is insane," solely on the basis of the grizzly condition of Smith's body, my use of "Smith's murderer" is attributive (even if I in fact have a belief as to who the murderer is), but if I say it on the basis of the supposed murderer's behavior at the dock, my use is referential. Surely, however, my reasons can be mixed: perhaps neither consideration would have sufficed by itself, but they suffice jointly. What is my use then? A user of the unambiguous D-language would have to choose between "the" and "ze." It seems very implausible to suppose that the speaker is confused and uncertain about what sense he gives to his description; but what else can we say if we suppose that English is the ambiguous D-language? (This problem arises even if the man at the dock is guilty, so that in fact there is no conflict. It is more obvious if he is innocent.)

A pragmatic theory of the referential-attributive distinction can handle such cases much more easily. Clearly there can be borderline cases between the simple and the complex use—where, to some extent the speaker wishes to speak of the semantic referent and to some extent he wishes to

similar to those for definite descriptions, if the one case involves no semantic ambiguity while the other does?

It is very much the lazy man's approach in philosophy to posit ambiguities when in trouble. If we face a putative counterexample to our favorite philosophical thesis, it is always open to us to protest that some key term is being used in a special sense, different from its use in the thesis. We may be right, but the ease of the move should counsel a policy of caution: Do not posit an ambiguity unless you are really forced to, unless there are really compelling theoretical or intuitive grounds to suppose that an ambiguity really is present.

Let me say a bit more in defense of this. Many philosophers, for example, have advocated a "strong" account of knowledge according to which it is very hard to know anything; stiff requirements must be satisfied. When such philosophers have been confronted with intuitive counterexamples to such strong requirements for knowledge they either have condemned them as popular and loose usages or they have asserted that "know" is being used in a different "weak" sense. The latter move—distinguishing two or more "strong" and "weak" senses of "know"—strikes me as implausible. There *are* different senses of "know," distinguished in German as "kennen" and "wissen," and in French as "connaître" and "savoir"; a person is usually known in the one sense, a fact in the other. It is no surprise that other languages use distinct words for these various senses of "know"; there is no reason for the ambiguity to be preserved in languages unrelated to our own. But what about the uses of "know" that characteristically are followed by that-clauses, knowing that *p*? Are these ambiguous? I would be very surprised to be told that the Eskimos have two separate words, one for (say) Hintikka's "strong" sense of "know," another for his "weak" sense. Perhaps this indicates that we think of knowledge as a unitary concept, unlikely to be "disambiguated" by two separate words in any language. (See Chapter 2, pp. 40ff.)

We thus have two methodological considerations that can be used to test any alleged ambiguity. "Bank" is ambiguous; we would expect the ambiguity to be disambiguated by separate and unrelated words in some other languages. Why should the two separate senses be reproduced in languages unrelated to English? First, then, we can consult our linguistic intuitions, independently of any empirical investigation. Would we be surprised to find languages that used two separate words for the two alleged senses of a given word? If so, then, to that

---

speak of something he believes to be the semantic referent. He need not sort out his motives carefully, since he thinks these things are one and the same!

Given such mixed motives, the speaker's reference may be partially to one thing and partially to another, even when the semantic reference is unambiguous. This is especially likely in the case of proper names, since divergences between speaker's referent and semantic referent are characteristically *misidentifications* (see footnote 25). Even if the speaker's referent of "Jones" in "Jones is raking the leaves" is Smith, to some extent I have said *of Jones* that he is raking the leaves. There are gradations, depending on the speaker's interests and intentions, as to what extent the speaker's reference was to Jones and to what extent it was to Smith. The problem is less common in the case of descriptions, where misidentification need not have occurred.

extent our linguistic intuitions are really intuitions of a unitary concept, rather than of a word that expresses two distinct and unrelated senses. Second, we can ask empirically whether languages are in fact found that contain distinct words expressing the allegedly distinct senses. If no such language is found, once again this is evidence that a unitary account of the word or phrase in question should be sought.

As far as our main question is concerned, the first of these two tests, that of our intuitive expectation, seems to me overwhelmingly to favor a unitary account of descriptions, as opposed to the ambiguity postulated in the ambiguous D-language. If English really is the ambiguous D-language, we should expect to find other languages where the referential and attributive uses are expressed by two separate words, as in the *unambiguous* D-language. I at least would find it quite surprising to learn that say, the Eskimo, used two separate words "the" and "ze," for the attributive and referential uses. To the extent that I have this intuition, to that extent I think of "the" as a unitary concept. I should have liked to be able to report that I have reinforced this guess by an actual empirical examination of other languages—the second test—but as of now I haven't done so.[28]

Several general methodological considerations favor the Russell language (or some other unitary account) against the ambiguous D-language as a model for English. First, the unitary account conforms to considerations of economy in that it does not "multiply senses beyond necessity." Second, the metalinguistic apparatus invoked by the unitary account to explain the referential-attributive distinction is an apparatus that is needed in *any case* for other cases, such as proper names. The separate referential sense of descriptions postulated by the D-language hypothesis, is an idle wheel that does no work: if it were absent, we would be able to express everything we wished to express, in the same way. Further, the resemblance between the case of descriptions and that of proper names (where presumably no one would be tempted to postulate an ambiguity) is

---

[28] Of course these tests must be used with some caution. The mere fact that some language subdivides the extension of an English word into several subclasses, with their own separate words, and has no word for the whole extension, does not show that the English word was ambiguous (think of the story that the Eskimos have different words for different kinds of snow). If many unrelated languages preserve a single word, this in itself is evidence for a unitary concept. On the other hand, a word may have different senses that are obviously related. One sense may be metaphorical for another (though in that case, it may not really be a separate sense, but simply a common metaphor). "Statistics" can mean both statistical data and the science of evaluating such data. And the like. The more we can explain relations among senses, and the more "natural" and "inevitable" the relationship, the more we will expect the different senses to be preserved in a wide variety of other languages.

The test, therefore, needs further exploration and refinement. It is certainly wrong to postulate an ambiguity without any explanation of some connection between the "senses" that explains why they occur in a wide variety of languages. In the referential-attributive case, I feel that any attempt to explain the connection between the referential and the attributive uses will be so close to the kind of pragmatic account offered here as to render any assumptions of distinct senses inplausible and superfluous.

so close that any attempt to explain the cases differently is automatically suspect. Finally, we would not expect the alleged ambiguity to be disambiguated in other languages, and this means we probably regard ourselves as possessing a unitary concept.

Aside from methodological considerations, is there any direct evidence that would favor one of our two rival accounts? As I remarked above, if we had a direct intuition that "Her husband is kind to her" could be true even when her actual husband is cruel, then we would have decisive evidence for the D-language model; but Donnellan rightly disclaims any such intuition. On the other hand, I myself feel that such a sentence expresses a falsehood, even when "her husband" is used referentially to refer to a kind man; but the popularity of Donnellan's view has made me uncertain that this intuition should be pressed very far. In the absence of such direct intuitions that would settle the matter conclusively, it would seem that the actual practice of English speakers is compatible with either model, and that only general methodological considerations favor one hypothesis rather than another. Such a situation leaves me uneasy. If there really is no direct evidence to distinguish the two hypotheses, how are they different hypotheses? If two communities, one of whom spoke the ambiguous D-language and the other of whom spoke the (weak) Russell language, would be able to intermingle freely without detecting any linguistic difference, do they really speak two different languages? If so, wherein is the difference?

Two hypothetical communities, one of which was explicitly taught the ambiguous D-language and the other of which was taught the (weak) Russell language (say, in school), would have direct and differing intuitions about the truth-value of "Her husband was kind to her"; but it is uncertain whether English speakers have any such intuitions. If they have none, is this a respect in which English differs from both the Russell languages and the D-languages, and thus differentiates it from both? Or, on the contrary, is there a pragmatic consideration, deriving no doubt from the fact that the relevant rules of language are not explicitly taught, that will explain why we lack such intuitions (if we do) without showing that neither the D-language nor the Russell language is English?

Some commentators on the dispute between Russell and Frege and Strawson over sentences containing vacuous definite descriptions have held that no direct linguistic phenomena conclusively decide between the two views: we should therefore choose the most economical and theoretically satisfying model. But if this is so, are there really two views, and if there are, shouldn't we perhaps say that neither is correct? A hypothetical community that was explicitly taught Russellian or Frege-Strawsonian truth-conditions for sentences containing vacuous definite descriptions would have no difficulty producing direct intuitions that decide the Russell-Strawson dispute. If the commentators in question are correct, speakers of English have no such intuitions. Surely this fact, too, would be a significant fact about English, for which linguistic theory should give an account. Perhaps pragmatic considerations suffice for such an account; or, perhaps, the alleged lack of any such intuition must be accounted for by a feature built into the semantics of English itself. In the latter case, neither the Russellian nor the Frege-Strawsonian truth-conditions would be appropriate for English. Similar considerations would apply to the issue between Donnellan and Russell.[29]

I am uncertain about these questions. Certainly it would be best if there were directly observable phenomena that differentiated between the two hypotheses. Actually I can think of one rather special and localized phenomenon that may indeed favor the Russellian hypothesis, or some other unitary hypothesis. Consider the following two dialogues:

Dialogue I: A. "Her husband is kind to her."
             B. "No, he isn't. The man you're referring to isn't her husband."
Dialogue II: A. "Her husband is kind to her."
             B. "He is kind to her, but he isn't her husband."

In the first dialogue the respondent (B) uses "he" to refer to the semantic referent of "her husband" as used by the first speaker (A); in the second dialogue the respondent uses "he" to refer to the speaker's referent. My tendency is to think that both dialogues are proper. The unitary account can explain this fact, by saying that pronominalization can pick up *either* a previous semantic reference or a previous speaker's reference.[30, 31] In the case of the two contrasting dialogues, these diverge.

---

[29] That is, the *concept* of truth conditions is somehow inappropriate for the semantics of English. The vague uneasiness expressed in these paragraphs expresses my own rather confused occasional doubts and is ancillary to the main theme. Moore's "paradox of analysis" may be a related problem.

Quine's philosophy of language characteristically is based on a naturalistic doubt about building any "rules" or "conventions" into a language that are not recoverable from actual linguistic practices, even if such rules may be necessary to stipulate the language. In this sense, the uneasiness expressed is Quinean in spirit. I find Quine's emphasis on a naturalistic approach to some extent salutary. But I also feel that our intuitions of semantic rules as speakers should not be ignored cavalierly.

[30] Geach, in his book *Reference and Generality*, Emended edition (Ithaca, 1970), and elsewhere, has argued vigorously against speaking of pronominalization as picking up a previous reference. I do not wish to argue the extent to which he is right here. I use the terminology given in the text for convenience, but to the extent Geach's views are correct I think the example could presumably be reformulated to fit his scheme. I think the views expressed in this paper are very much in the spirit of Geach's remarks on definite descriptions and speaker's reference in the book just cited. See Geach's discussion, e.g., on p. 8.

[31] Donnellan, in "Speaker Reference, Descriptions and Anaphora" thinks that the fact that pronouns can pick up a previous semantic reference somehow casts doubt on a view that makes speaker's reference a nonsemantical notion. I don't see why: "he," "she," "that," etc., can, under various circumstances, refer to anything salient in an appropriate way. Being physically distinguished against its background is a property that may make an object salient; having been referred to by a previous speaker is another. In *Naming and Necessity*, footnote 3, I suggested tentatively that Donnellan's "remarks about reference have little to do with semantics or truth conditions." The point would be put more exactly if I had said that Donnellan's distinction is not itself a semantical one, though it is relevant to semantics through pronominalization, as many other non-semantical properties are.

If English were the ambiguous D-language, the second dialogue would be easy to explain. "He" refers to the object that is both the semantic referent and the speaker's referent of "her husband." (Recall that the notions of speaker's reference and semantic reference are general notions applicable to all languages, even to the D-languages.[32]) The first dialogue, however, would be much more difficult, perhaps impossible, to explain. When A said "her husband," according to the D-language hypothesis he was using "her husband" in the referential sense. Both the speaker's referent and the semantic referent would be the kind lover; only if B had misunderstood A's use as attributive could he have used "he" to refer to the husband, but such a misunderstanding is excluded by the second part of B's utterance. If the first dialogue is proper, it seems hard to fit it into the D-language model.[33]

(4.) *Conclusion.*

I said at the beginning that the main concern of this paper was methodological rather than substantive. I do think that the considerations in this paper make it overwhelmingly probable that an ultimate account of the phenomena behind Donnellan's distinction will make use of the pragmatic ambiguity between "simple" and "complex" uses, as I defined them above, rather than postulating an ambiguity of the D-language type. But any ultimate substantive conclusion on the issue requires a more extensive and thorough treatment than has been given here. First, I have not here examined theories that attempt to explain Donnellan's

---

Pronominalization phenomena are relevant to another point. Often one hears it argued against Russell's existential analysis of *indefinite* descriptions that an indefinite description may be anaphorically referred to by a pronoun that seems to preserve the reference of the indefinite description. I am not sure that these phenomena do conflict with the existential analysis. (I am not completely sure there are some that don't, either.) In any event, many cases can be accounted for (given a Russellian theory) by the facts that: (i) existential statements can carry a speaker's reference; (ii) pronouns can refer to the speaker's referent.

[32] The use of "ze" in the unambiguous D-language is such that the semantic reference automatically coincided with the speaker's reference, but nevertheless, the notions are applicable. So are the notions of simple and complex uses of designators. However, speakers of the unambiguous D-language might be less likely ever to use "the" in a complex case: for, one might be inclined to argue, if such are their intentions, why not use "ze"?

[33] Various moves might be tried, but none that I can think of seem to me to be plausible. It has been suggested to me that sometimes the respondent in a dialogue deliberately feigns to misunderstand an ambiguous phrase used by the first speaker, and that, given the supposed ambiguity of "her husband" in the ambiguous D-language, the first dialogue can be interpreted as such a case. For example, the following dialogue: "Jones put the money in a bank." "He put the money in one all right, but it wasn't a commercial bank; he was so much afraid it would be discovered that he hid it near the river." It seems implausible to me that the first dialogue in the text fits into such a very jocular model. But notice further that the joke consists in a mock *confirmation* of the first speaker's assertion. It would be rather bizarre to respond, "He didn't put the money in the bank, and it wasn't a commercial bank." The first dialogue would have to conform to such a bizarre pattern on the hypothesis in question.

Alternatively, it might be suggested that B uses "he" as a pronoun of laziness for A's "her husband," taken in the supposed referential sense. This move seems to be excluded, since B may well be in no position to use "her husband" referentially. He may merely have heard that she is married to a cruel man.

distinction as a *syntactic* ambiguity, either of scope or of restrictive and non-restrictive clauses in deep structure.[34] Both these views, like the line suggested in the present paper, are compatible with a unitary hypothesis such as the hypothesis that English is a Russell language. Although I am not inclined to accept either of these views, some others have found them plausible and unless they are rebutted, they too indicate that Donnellan's observations cannot be taken as providing a conclusive argument against Russell without further discussion.

Second, and most important, no treatment of definite descriptions can be complete unless it examines the complete range of uses of the definite article and related linguistic phenomena. Such a treatment should attempt, as I have argued above, to make it clear why the same construction with a definite article is used for a wide range of cases. It would be wrong for me not to mention the phenomena most favorable to Donnellan's intuitions. In a demonstrative use such as "that table," it seems plausible, as I have mentioned above,[35] that the term rigidly designates its referent. It also seems plausible that the reference of such a demonstrative construction can be an object to which the descriptive adjectives in the construction do not apply (for example, "that scoundrel" may be used to refer to someone who is not, in fact, a scoundrel) and it is not clear that the distinction between speaker's reference and semantic reference should be invoked to account for this. As I also said above, it seems to me to be likely that "indefinite" definite descriptions[36] such as "the table" present difficulties for a Russellian analysis. It is somewhat tempting to assimilate such descriptions to the corresponding demonstratives (for example, "that table") and to the extent that such a temptation turns out to be plausible, there may be new arguments in such cases for the intuitions of those who have advocated a rigid vs. non-rigid ambiguity in definite descriptions, or for Donnellan's intuitions concerning the referential case, or for both.[37]

---

[34] I believe that Kartunnen has advocated the view that the referential-attributive distinction arises from a scope ambiguity; I do not know whether this has been published. Since the referential-attributive "ambiguity" arises even in simple sentences such as "Smith's murderer is insane," where there appears to be no room for any scope ambiguity, such a view seems forced to rely on acceptance of Ross's suggestion that all English assertive utterances begin with an initial "I say that," which is suppressed in "surface structure" but present in "deep structure."

For the view that derives the referential-attributive "ambiguity" from a distinction of restrictive and non-restrictive clauses in "deep structure," see J. M. Bell, "What Is Referential Opacity?", *Journal of Philosophical Logic* 2 (1973): 155–180. See also the work of Emmon Bach on which Bell's paper is based, "Nouns and Noun Phrases," in *Universals in Linguistic Theory*, ed. E. Bach and R. T. Harms (New York, 1968), pp. 91–122. For reasons of space I have not treated these views here. But some of my arguments that Donnellan's distinction is pragmatic apply against them also.

[35] See p. 106 above; also see footnote 9 above.

[36] The term is Donnellan's. See "Putting Humpty Dumpty Together Again," p. 204, footnote 5.

[37] I believe that when Donnellan heard the present paper, he too mentioned considerations of this kind. The cases are mentioned briefly in Donnellan's paper, "Putting Humpty Dumpty Together Again," ibid. Donnellan's paper "Speaker Reference, Descriptions and Anaphora" also makes use of the existence of such incomplete descriptions but I do not find his arguments conclusive.

Because I have not yet worked out a complete account that satisfies me, and because I think it would be wrong to make any definitive claim on the basis of the restricted class of phenomena considered here, I regard the primary lessons of this paper as methodological. They illustrate some general methodological considerations and apparatus that I think should be applied to the problems discussed here and to other linguistic problems. They show in the present case that the argument Donnellan actually presents in his original paper shows nothing against a Russellian or other unitary account, and they make it highly probable to me that the problems Donnellan handles by semantic ambiguity should instead be treated by a general theory of speech acts. But at this time nothing more definitive can be said. I think that the distinction between semantic reference and speaker's reference will be of importance not only (as in the present paper) as a critical tool to block postulation of unwarranted ambiguities, but also will be of considerable constructive importance for a theory of language. In particular, I find it plausible that a diachronic account of the evolution of language is likely to suggest that what was originally a mere speaker's reference may, if it becomes habitual in a community, evolve into a semantic reference. And this consideration may be *one* of the factors needed to clear up some puzzles in the theory of reference.[38, 39, 40]

---

[38] See the Santa Claus and Madagascar cases in *Naming and Necessity*. See *Naming and Necessity*, pp. 93, 96–97 for the Santa Claus case and p. 163 for the Madagascar case.

[39] It seems likely that the considerations in this paper will also be relevant to the concept of a supposed "± Specific" distinction for indefinite descriptions, as advocated by many linguists.

[40] I should like to thank Margaret Gilbert and Howard Wettstein for their assistance in the preparation of this paper.

6

A Puzzle about Belief

In this chapter I will present a puzzle about names and belief. A moral or two will be drawn about some other arguments that have occasionally been advanced in this area, but my main thesis is a simple one: that the puzzle *is* a puzzle. And, as a corollary, that any account of belief must ultimately come to grips with it. Any speculation as to solutions can be deferred.

The first section of the chapter gives the theoretical background in previous discussion, and in my own earlier work, that led me to consider the puzzle. The background is by no means necessary to *state* the puzzle: As a philosophical puzzle, it stands on its own, and I think its fundamental interest for the problem of belief goes beyond the background that engendered it. As I indicate in the third section, the problem really goes beyond beliefs expressed using names, to a far wider class of beliefs. Nevertheless, I think that the background illuminates the genesis of the puzzle, and it will enable me to draw one moral in the concluding section.

The second section states some general principles which underlie our general practice of reporting beliefs. These principles are stated in much more detail than is needed to comprehend the puzzle; and there are variant formulations of the principles that would do as well. Neither this section nor the first is necessary for an intuitive grasp of the central problem, discussed in the third section, though they may help with fine points of the discussion. The reader who wishes rapid access to the central problem could skim the first two sections lightly on a first reading.

In one sense the problem may strike some as no puzzle at all. For, in the situation to be envisaged, all the relevant facts can be described in *one* terminology without difficulty. But, in *another* terminology, the situation seems to be impossible to describe in a consistent way. This will become clearer later.

I. PRELIMINARIES: SUBSTITUTIVITY

In other writings,[1] I developed a view of proper names closer in many ways to the old Millian paradigm of naming than to the Fregean tradition which probably

---

[1] "Naming and Necessity," in: *The Semantics of Natural Languages*, D. Davidson and G. Harman (eds.), Dordrecht, Reidel, 1971, pp. 253–355 and 763–769. (Subsequently published as *Naming and Necessity* [Cambridge: Harvard University Press, 1980]; references are to the reprint) "Identity and

was dominant until recently. According to Mill, a proper name is, so to speak, *simply* a name. It *simply* refers to its bearer, and has no other linguistic function. In particular, unlike a definite description, a name does not describe its bearer as possessing any special identifying properties.

The opposing Fregean view holds that to each proper name, a speaker of the language associates some property (or conjunction of properties) which determines its referent as the unique thing fulfilling the associated property (or properties). This property(ies) constitutes the 'sense' of the name. Presumably, if '...' is a proper name, the associated properties are those that the speaker would supply, if asked, "Who is '...'?" If he would answer "... is the man who ———," the properties filling the second blank are those that determine the reference of the name for the given speaker and constitute its 'sense.' Of course, given the name of a famous historical figure, individuals may give different, and equally correct, answers to the "Who is...?" question. Some may identify Aristotle as the philosopher who taught Alexander the Great, others as the Stagirite philosopher who studied with Plato. For these two speakers, the sense of 'Aristotle' will differ: in particular, speakers of the second kind, but not of the first kind, will regard "Aristotle, if he existed, was born in Stagira" as analytic.[2] Frege (and Russell)[3] concluded that, strictly speaking, different speakers of

---

Necessity" (Chapter 1, this volume). Acquaintance with this material is not a prerequisite for understanding the central puzzle of the present paper, but is helpful for understanding the theoretical background.

[2] Frege gives essentially this example as the second footnote of "On Sense and Reference." For the "Who is...?" to be applicable one must be careful to elicit from one's informant properties that he regards as defining the name and determining the referent, not mere well-known facts about the referent. (Of course this distinction may well seem fictitious, but it is central to the original Frege-Russell theory.)

[3] For convenience Russell's terminology is assimilated to Frege's. Actually, regarding genuine or 'logically proper' names, Russell is a strict Millian: 'logically proper names' *simply* refer (to immediate objects of acquaintance). But, according to Russell, what are ordinarily called 'names' are not genuine, logically proper names, but disguised definite descriptions. Since Russell also regards definite descriptions as in turn disguised notation, he does not associate any 'senses' with descriptions, since they are not genuine singular terms. When all disguised notation is eliminated, the only singular terms remaining are logically proper names, for which no notion of 'sense' is required. When we speak of Russell as assigning 'senses' to names, we mean ordinary names and for convenience we ignore his view that the descriptions abbreviating them ultimately disappear on analysis.

On the other hand, the explicit doctrine that names are abbreviated definite descriptions is due to Russell. Michael Dummett, in his recent *Frege* (Duckworth and Harper and Row, 1973, pp. 110–111) denies that Frege held a description theory of senses. Although as far as I know Frege indeed makes no explicit statement to that effect, his examples of names conform to the doctrine, as Dummett acknowledges. Especially his 'Aristotle' example is revealing. He defines 'Aristotle' just as Russell would; it seems clear that in the case of a famous historical figure, the 'name' is indeed to be given by answering, in a uniquely specifying way, the 'who is' question. Dummett himself characterizes a sense as a "criterion...such that the referent of the name, if any, is whatever object satisfies that criterion." Since presumably the satisfaction of the criterion must be unique (so a unique referent is determined), doesn't this amount to defining names by unique satisfaction of properties, *i.e.*, by descriptions? *Perhaps* the point is that the property in question need not be expressible by a usual predicate of English, as might be plausible if the referent is one of

English (or German!) ordinarily use a name such as 'Aristotle' in different senses (though with the same reference). Differences in properties associated with such names, strictly speaking, yield different idiolects.⁴

Some later theorists in the Frege-Russellian tradition have found this consequence unattractive. So they have tried to modify the view by 'clustering' the sense of the name (e.g., Aristotle is the thing having the following long list of properties, or at any rate most of them), or, better for the present purpose, socializing it (what determines the reference of 'Aristotle' is some roughly specified set of *community-wide* beliefs about Aristotle).

One way to point up the contrast between the strict Millian view and Fregean views involves—if we permit ourselves this jargon—the notion of propositional content. If a strict Millian view is correct, and the linguistic function of a proper name is completely exhausted by the fact that it names its bearer, it would appear that proper names of the same thing are everywhere interchangeable not only *salva veritate* but even *salva significatione*: the proposition expressed by a sentence should remain the same no matter what name of the object it uses. Of course this will not be true if the names are 'mentioned' rather than 'used': "'Cicero' has six letters" differs from "'Tully' has six letters" in truth value, let alone in content. (The example, of course, is Quine's.) Let us confine ourselves at this stage to *simple* sentences involving no connectives or other sources of intensionality. If Mill is completely right, not only should "Cicero was lazy" have the same *truth value* as "Tully was lazy," but the two sentences should express the same *proposition*, have the same content. Similarly "Cicero admired Tully," "Tully admired Cicero," "Cicero admired Cicero," and "Tully admired Tully," should be four ways of saying the same thing.⁵

---

the speaker's acquaintances rather than a historical figure. But I doubt that even Russell, father of the explicitly formulated description theory, ever meant to require that the description must always be expressible in (unsupplemented) English.

In any event, the philosophical community has generally understood Fregean senses in terms of descriptions, and we deal with it under this usual understanding. For present purposes this is more important than detailed historical issues. Dummett acknowledges (p. 111) that few substantive points are affected by his (allegedly) broader interpretation of Frege; and it would not seem to be relevant to the problems of the present paper.

⁴ See Frege's footnote in "On Sense and Reference" mentioned in note 2 above and especially his discussion of 'Dr. Gustav Lauben' in "*Der Gedanke.*" (In the recent Geach-Stoothoff translation, "Thoughts," *Logical Investigations*, Oxford, Blackwell, 1977, pp. 11–12). See also Chapter 9, this volume.

⁵ Russell, as a Millian with respect to genuine names, accepts this argument with respect to 'logically proper names.' For example—taking for the moment 'Cicero' and 'Tully' as 'logically proper names,' Russell would hold that if I judge that Cicero admired Tully, I am related to Cicero, Tully, and the admiration relation in a certain way: Since Cicero *is* Tully, I am related in exactly the same way to Tully, Cicero, and admiration; therefore I judge that Tully admired Cicero. Again, if Cicero *did* admire Tully, then according to Russell a single fact corresponds to all of 'Cicero admired Tully,' 'Cicero admired Cicero,' etc. Its constituent (in addition to admiration) is the man Cicero, taken, so to speak, twice.

Russell thought that 'Cicero admired Tully' and 'Tully admired Cicero' are in fact obviously not interchangeable. For him, this was one argument that 'Cicero' and 'Tully' are *not* genuine names, and that the Roman orator is no constituent of propositions (or 'facts,' or 'judgments') corresponding to sentences containing the name.

If such a consequence of Mill's view is accepted, it would seem to have further consequences regarding 'intensional' contexts. Whether a sentence expresses a necessary truth or a contingent one depends only on the proposition expressed and not on the words used to express it. So any simple sentence should retain its 'modal value' (necessary, impossible, contingently true, or contingently false) when 'Cicero' is replaced by 'Tully' in one or more places, since such a replacement leaves the content of the sentence unaltered. Of course this implies that coreferential names are substitutable in modal contexts *salva veritate*: "It is necessary (possible) that Cicero..." and "It is necessary (possible) that Tully..." must have the same truth value no matter how the dots are filled by a simple sentence.

The situation would seem to be similar with respect to contexts involving knowledge, belief, and epistemic modalities. Whether a given subject believes something is presumably true or false of such a subject no matter how that belief is expressed; so if proper name substitution does not change the content of a sentence expressing a belief, coreferential proper names should be interchangeable *salva veritate* in belief contexts. Similar reasoning would hold for epistemic contexts ("Jones knows that...") and contexts of epistemic necessity ("Jones knows *a priori* that...") and the like.

All this, of course, would contrast strongly with the case of definite descriptions. It is well known that substitution of coreferential descriptions in simple sentences (without operators), on any reasonable conception of 'content,' *can* alter the content of such a sentence. In particular, the modal value of a sentence is not invariant under changes of coreferential descriptions: "The smallest prime is even" expresses a necessary truth, but "Jones's favorite number is even" expresses a contingent one, even if Jones's favorite number happens to be the smallest prime. It follows that coreferential descriptions are *not* interchangeable *salva veritate* in modal contexts: "It is necessary that the smallest prime is even" is true while "It is necessary that Jones's favorite number is even" is false.

Of course there is a '*de re*' or 'large scope' reading under which the second sentence is true. Such a reading would be expressed more accurately by "Jones's favorite number is such that it is necessarily even" or, in rough Russellian transcription, as "One and only one number is admired by Jones above all others, and any such number is necessarily even (has the property of necessary evenness)." Such a *de re* reading, if it makes sense at all, by definition must be subject to a principle of substitution *salva veritate*, since necessary evenness is a property of the *number*, independently of how it is designated; in this respect there can be no contrast between names and descriptions. The contrast, according to the Millian view, must come in the *de dicto* or "small scope" reading, which is the *only* reading, for belief contexts as well as modal contexts, that will concern us in this paper. If we wish, we can emphasize that this is our reading in various ways. Say, "It is necessary that: Cicero was bald" or, more explicitly, "The following proposition is necessarily true: Cicero was bald," or even, in Carnap's 'formal' mode of speech,[6] "'Cicero was bald' expresses a necessary truth." Now the Millian asserts that all these formulations retain their truth value when 'Cicero' is replaced by 'Tully,' even though 'Jones's favorite Latin author' and 'the man who denounced Catiline' would *not* similarly be interchangeable in these contexts even if they are codesignative.

Similarly for belief contexts. Here too *de re* beliefs—as in "Jones believes, *of* Cicero (or: *of* his favorite Latin author) that he was bald"—do *not* concern us in this paper. Such contexts, if they make sense, are by definition subject to a substitutivity principle for both names and descriptions. Rather we are concerned with the *de dicto* locution expressed explicitly in such formulations as, "Jones believes that: Cicero was bald" (or: "Jones believes that: the man who denounced Catiline was bald"). The material after the colon expresses the *content* of Jones's belief. Other, more explicit, formulations are: "Jones believes the proposition—that—Cicero—was—bald," or even in the 'formal' mode, "The sentence 'Cicero was bald' gives the content of a belief of Jones." In all such contexts, the strict Millian seems to be committed to saying that codesignative names, but not codesignative descriptions, are interchangeable *salva veritate*.[7]

Now it has been widely assumed that these apparent consequences of the Millian view are plainly false. First, it seemed that sentences can alter their *modal* values by replacing a name by a codesignative one. "Hesperus is Hesperus" (or, more cautiously: "If Hesperus exists, Hesperus is Hesperus") expresses a necessary truth, while "Hesperus is Phosphorus" (or: "If Hesperus exists, Hesperus is Phosphorus"),

---

[6] Given the arguments of Church and others, I do not believe that the formal mode of speech is synonymous with other formulations. But it can be used as a rough way to convey the idea of scope.

[7] It may well be argued that the Millian view implies that proper names are *scopeless* and that for them the *de dicto–de re* distinction vanishes. This view has considerable plausibility (my own views on rigidity will imply something like this for *modal* contexts), but it need not be argued here either way: *de re* uses are simply not treated in the present paper.

Christopher Peacocke ("Proper Names, Reference, and Rigid Designation," in: *Meaning, Reference, and Necessity*, S. Blackburn (ed.), Cambridge, 1975; see Section I), uses what amounts to the equivalence of the *de dicto–de re* constructions in *all* contexts (or, put alternatively, the lack of such a distinction) to characterize the notion of rigid designation. I agree that for *modal* contexts, this is (roughly) equivalent to my own notion, also that for proper names Peacocke's equivalence holds for temporal contexts. (This is roughly equivalent to the 'temporal rigidity' of names.) I also agree that it is very plausible to extend the principle to all contexts. But, as Peacocke recognizes, this appears to imply a substitutivity principle for codesignative proper names in belief contexts, which is widely assumed to be false. Peacocke proposes to use Davidson's theory of intensional contexts to block this conclusion (the material in the 'that' clause is a separate sentence). I myself cannot accept Davidson's theory; but even if it were true, Peacocke in effect acknowledges that it does not really dispose of the difficulty (p. 127, first paragraph). (Incidentally, if Davidson's theory does block any inference to the transparency of belief contexts with respect to names, why does Peacocke assume without argument that it does not do so for modal contexts, which have a similar grammatical structure?) The problems are thus those of the present paper; until they are resolved I prefer at present to keep to my earlier more cautious formulation. Incidentally, Peacocke hints a recognition that the received platitude—that codesignative names are not interchangeable in belief contexts—may not be so clear as is generally supposed.

expresses an empirical discovery, and hence, it has been widely assumed, a contingent truth. (It might have turned out, and hence might have been, otherwise.)

It has seemed even more obvious that codesignative proper names are not interchangeable in belief contexts and epistemic contexts. Tom, a normal speaker of the language, may sincerely assent to "Tully denounced Catiline," but not to "Cicero denounced Catiline." He may even deny the latter. And his denial is compatible with his status as a normal English speaker who satisfies normal criteria for using both 'Cicero' and 'Tully' as names for the famed Roman (without knowing that 'Cicero' and 'Tully' name the same person). Given this, it seems obvious that Tom believes that: Tully denounced Catiline, but that he does not believe (lacks the belief) that: Cicero denounced Catiline.[8] So it seems clear that codesignative proper names are not interchangeable in belief contexts. It also seems clear that there must be two distinct propositions or contents expressed by 'Cicero denounced Catiline' and 'Tully denounced Catiline.' How else can Tom believe one and deny the other? And the difference in propositions thus expressed can only come from a difference in *sense* between 'Tully' and 'Cicero.' Such a conclusion agrees with a Fregean theory and seems to be incompatible with a purely Millian view.[9]

In the previous work mentioned above, I rejected one of these arguments against Mill, the modal argument. 'Hesperus is Phosphorus,' I maintained, expresses just as necessary a truth as 'Hesperus is Hesperus'; there are no counterfactual situations in which Hesperus and Phosphorus would have been different. Admittedly, the truth of 'Hesperus is Phosphorus' was not known *a priori*, and may even have been widely disbelieved before appropriate empirical evidence came in. But these epistemic questions should be separated, I have argued, from the metaphysical question of the necessity of 'Hesperus is Phosphorus.' And it is a consequence of my conception of names as 'rigid designators' that codesignative proper names are interchangeable *salva veritate* in all contexts

---

[8] The example comes from Quine, *Word and Object*, M.I.T. Press, 1960, p. 145. Quine's conclusion that 'believes that' construed *de dicto* is opaque has widely been taken for granted. In the formulation in the text I have used the colon to emphasize that I am speaking of belief *de dicto*. Since, as I have said, belief *de dicto* will be our *only* concern in this paper, in the future the colon will usually be suppressed, and all 'believes that' contexts should be read *de dicto* unless the contrary is indicated explicitly. For a discussion of Quine's views, see Chapter 11, this volume.

[9] In many writings Peter Geach has advocated a view that is non-Millian (he would say 'non-Lockean') in that to each name a sortal predicate is attached by definition ('Geach,' for example, by *definition* names a man). On the other hand, the theory is not completely Fregean either, since Geach denies that any definite description that would identify the referent of the name among things of the same sort is analytically tied to the name. (See, for example, his *Reference and Generality*, Cornell, 1962, pp. 43–45.) As far as the present issues are concerned, Geach's view can fairly be assimilated to *Mill*'s rather than Frege's. For such ordinary names as 'Cicero' and 'Tully' will have both the same reference and the same (Geachian) sense (namely, that they are names of a man). It would thus seem that they ought to be interchangeable everywhere. (In *Reference and Generality*, Geach appears not to accept this conclusion, but the *prima facie* argument for the conclusion will be the same as on a purely Millian view.)

of (metaphysical) necessity and possibility; further, that replacement of a proper name by a codesignative name leaves the modal value of any sentence unchanged.

But although my position confirmed the Millian account of names in modal contexts, it equally appears at first blush to imply a *non-Millian* account of epistemic and belief contexts (and other contexts of propositional attitude). For I presupposed a sharp contrast between epistemic and metaphysical possibility: Before appropriate empirical discoveries were made, men might well have failed to know that Hesperus was Phosphorus, or even to believe it, even though they of course knew and believed that Hesperus was Hesperus. Does not this support a Fregean position that 'Hesperus' and 'Phosphorus' have different 'modes of presentation' that determine their references? What else can account for the fact that, before astronomers identified the two heavenly bodies, a sentence using 'Hesperus' could express a common belief, while the same context involving 'Phosphorus' did not? In the case of 'Hesperus' and 'Phosphorus,' it is pretty clear what the different 'modes of presentation' would be: one mode determines a heavenly body by its typical position and appearance, in the appropriate season, in the evening; the other determines the same body by its position and appearance, in the appropriate season, in the morning. So it appears that even though, according to my view, proper names would be *modally* rigid—would have the same reference when we use them to speak of counterfactual situations as they do when used to describe the actual world—they would have a kind of Fregean 'sense' according to how that rigid reference is fixed. And the divergences of 'sense' (in this sense of 'sense') would lead to failures of interchangeability of co-designative names in contexts of propositional attitude, though not in modal contexts. Such a theory would agree with Mill regarding modal contexts but with Frege regarding belief contexts. The theory would not be *purely* Millian.[10]

---

[10] In an unpublished paper, Diana Ackerman urges the problem of substitutivity failures against the Millian view and, hence, against my own views. I believe that others may have done so as well. (I have the impression that the paper has undergone considerable revision, and I have not seen recent versions.) I agree that this problem is a considerable difficulty for the Millian view, and for the Millian *spirit* of my own views in *Naming and Necessity*. (See the discussion of this in the text) On the other hand I would emphasize that there need be no *contradiction* in maintaining that names are *modally* rigid, and satisfy a substitutivity principle for modal contexts, while denying the substitutivity principle for belief contexts. The entire apparatus elaborated in *Naming and Necessity* of the distinction between epistemic and metaphysical necessity, and of giving a meaning and fixing a reference, was meant to show, among other things, that a Millian substitutivity doctrine for modal contexts can be maintained even if such a doctrine for epistemic contexts is rejected. *Naming and Necessity* never asserted a substitutivity principle for epistemic contexts.

It is even consistent to suppose that differing modes of (rigidly) fixing the reference is responsible for the substitutivity failures, thus adopting a position intermediate between Frege and Mill, on the lines indicated in the text of the present paper. *Naming and Necessity* may even perhaps be taken as suggesting, for some contexts where a conventional description rigidly fixes the reference ('Hesperus–Phosphorus'), that the mode of reference fixing is relevant to epistemic questions. I knew when I wrote *Naming and Necessity* that substitutivity issues in epistemic contexts were really very delicate, due to the problems of the present paper, but I thought it best not to muddy the waters further. (See notes 43–44.)

After further thought, however, the Fregean conclusion appears less obvious. Just as people are said to have been unaware at one time of the fact that Hesperus is Phosphorus, so a normal speaker of English apparently may not know that Cicero is Tully, or that Holland is the Netherlands. For he may sincerely assent to 'Cicero was lazy,' while dissenting from 'Tully was lazy,' or he may sincerely assent to 'Holland is a beautiful country,' while dissenting from 'The Netherlands is a beautiful country.' In the case of 'Hesperus' and 'Phosphorus,' it seemed plausible to account for the parallel situation by supposing that 'Hesperus' and 'Phosphorus' fixed their (rigid) references to a single object in two conventionally different ways, one as the 'evening star' and one as the 'morning star.' But what corresponding *conventional* 'senses,' even taking 'senses' to be 'modes of fixing the reference rigidly,' can plausibly be supposed to exist for 'Cicero' and 'Tully' (or 'Holland' and 'the Netherlands')? Are not these just two names (in English) for the same man? Is there any special *conventional, community-wide* 'connotation' in the one lacking in the other?[11] I am unaware of any.[12]

Such considerations might seem to push us toward the extreme Frege-Russellian view that the senses of proper names vary, strictly speaking, from speaker to speaker, and that there is no community-wide sense but only a community-wide

---

After this paper was completed, I saw Alvin Plantinga's paper "The Boethian Compromise," *The American Philosophical Quarterly* 15 (April, 1978): 129–138. Plantinga adopts a view intermediate between Mill and Frege, and cites substitutivity failures as a principal argument for his position. He also refers to a forthcoming paper by Ackerman. I have not seen this paper, but it probably is a descendant of the paper referred to above.

[11] Here I use 'connotation' so as to imply that the associated properties have an *a priori* tie to the name, at least as rigid reference fixers, and therefore must be true of the referent (if it exists). There is another sense of 'connotation,' as in 'The Holy Roman Empire,' where the connotation need not be assumed or even believed to be true of the referent. In some sense akin to this, classicists and others with some classical learning may attach certain distinct 'connotations' to 'Cicero' and 'Tully.' Similarly, 'The Netherlands' may suggest low altitude to a thoughtful ear. Such 'connotations' can hardly be thought of as community-wide; many use the names unaware of such suggestions. Even a speaker aware of the suggestion of the name may not regard the suggested properties as true of the object; *cf.* 'The Holy Roman Empire.' A 'connotation' of this type neither gives a meaning nor fixes a reference.

[12] Some might attempt to find a difference in 'sense' between 'Cicero' and 'Tully' on the grounds that "Cicero is called 'Cicero' " is trivial, but "Tully is called 'Cicero' " may not be. Kneale, and in one place (probably at least implicitly) Church, have argued in this vein. (For Kneale, see *Naming and Necessity*, p. 68.) So, it may be argued, being called 'Cicero,' is part of the sense of the name 'Cicero,' but not part of that of 'Tully.'

I have discussed some issues related to this in *Naming and Necessity*, pp. 68–70. (See also the discussions of circularity conditions elsewhere in *Naming and Necessity*.) Much more could be said about and against this kind of argument; perhaps I will sometime do so elsewhere. Let me mention very briefly the following parallel situation (which may be best understood by reference to the discussion in *Naming and Necessity*). Anyone who understands the meaning of 'is called' and of quotation in English (and that 'alienists' is meaningful and grammatically appropriate), knows that "alienists are called 'alienists' "expresses a truth in English, even if he has no idea what 'alienists' means. He need *not* know that "psychiatrists are called 'alienists'" expresses a truth. None of this goes to show that 'alienists' and 'psychiatrists' are not synonymous, or that 'alienists' has *being called 'alienists'* as part of its meaning when 'psychiatrists' does not. Similarly for 'Cicero' and 'Tully.' There is no more reason to suppose that being so-called is part of the meaning of a name than of any other word.

reference.[13] According to such a view, the sense a given speaker attributes to such a name as 'Cicero' depends on which assertions beginning with 'Cicero' he accepts and which of these he regards as *defining*, for him, the name (as opposed to those he regards as mere factual beliefs 'about Cicero'). Similarly, for 'Tully.' For example, someone may define 'Cicero' as 'the Roman orator whose speech was Greek to Cassius,' and 'Tully' as 'the Roman orator who denounced Catiline.' Then such a speaker may well fail to accept 'Cicero is Tully' if he is unaware that a single orator satisfied both descriptions (if Shakespeare and history are both to be believed). He may well, in his ignorance, affirm 'Cicero was bald' while rejecting 'Tully was bald,' and the like. Is this not what actually occurs whenever someone's expressed beliefs fail to be indifferent to interchange of 'Tully' and 'Cicero'? Must not the source of such a failure lie in two distinct associated descriptions, or modes of determining the reference, of the two names? If a speaker does, as luck would have it, attach the same identifying properties both to 'Cicero' and to 'Tully,' he *will*, it would seem, use 'Cicero' and 'Tully' interchangeably. All this appears at first blush to be powerful support for the view of Frege and Russell that in general names are peculiar to idiolects, with 'senses' depending on the associated 'identifying descriptions.'

Note that, according to the view we are now entertaining, one *cannot* say, 'Some people are unaware that Cicero is Tully.' For, according to this view, there is no single proposition denoted by the 'that' clause, that the community of normal English speakers expresses by 'Cicero is Tully.' Some—for example, those who define both 'Cicero' and 'Tully' as 'the author of *De Fato*'—use it to express a trivial self-identity. Others use it to express the proposition that the man who satisfied one description (say, that he denounced Catiline) is one and the same as the man who satisfied another (say, that his speech was Greek to Cassius). There is no single fact, 'that Cicero is Tully,' known by some but not all members of the community.

If I were to assert, "Many are unaware that Cicero is Tully," *I* would use 'that Cicero is Tully' to denote the proposition that *I* understand by these words. If this, for example, is a trivial self-identity, I would assert falsely, and irrelevantly, that there is widespread ignorance in the community of a certain self-identity.[14] I *can*, of course, say, "Some English speakers use both 'Cicero' and 'Tully' with the usual referent (the famed Roman) yet do not assent to 'Cicero is Tully.'"

---

[13] A view follows Frege and Russell on this issue even if it allows each speaker to associate a cluster of descriptions with each name, provided that it holds that the cluster varies from speaker to speaker and that variations in the cluster are variations in idiolect. Searle's view thus is Frege-Russellian when he writes in the concluding paragraph of "Proper Names" (*Mind* 67 (1958): 166–173), "'Tully = Cicero' would, I suggest, be analytic for most people; the same descriptive presuppositions are associated with each name. But of course if the descriptive presuppositions were different it might be used to make a synthetic statement."

[14] Though here I use the jargon of propositions, the point is fairly insensitive to differences in theoretical standpoints. For example, on Davidson's analysis, I would be asserting (roughly) that many are unaware-of-the-content-of the following *utterance* of mine: Cicero is Tully. This would be subject to the same problem.

This aspect of the Frege-Russellian view can, as before, be combined with a concession that names are rigid designators and that hence the description used to fix the reference of a name is not synonymous with it. But there are considerable difficulties. There is the obvious intuitive unpalatability of the notion that we use such proper names as 'Cicero,' 'Venice,' 'Venus' (the planet) with differing 'senses' and for this reason do not 'strictly speaking' speak a single language. There are the many well-known and weighty objections to any description or cluster-of-descriptions theory of names. And is it definitely so clear that failure of interchangeability in belief contexts implies some difference of sense? After all, there is a considerable philosophical literature arguing that even word pairs that are straightforward synonyms if any pairs are—"doctor" and "physician," to give one example—are not interchangeable *salva veritate* in belief contexts, at least if the belief operators are iterated.[15]

A minor problem with this presentation of the argument for Frege and Russell will emerge in the next section: if Frege and Russell are right, it is not easy to state the very argument from belief contexts that appears to support them.

But the clearest objection, which shows that the others should be given their proper weight, is this: the view under consideration does not in fact account for the phenomena it seeks to explain. As I have said elsewhere,[16] individuals who "define 'Cicero' " by such phrases as "the Catiline denouncer," "the author of *De Fato*," etc., are relatively rare: their prevalence in the philosophical literature is the product of the excessive classical learning of some philosophers. Common men who clearly use 'Cicero' as a name for Cicero may be able to give no better answer to "Who was Cicero?" than "a famous Roman orator," and they probably would say the same (if anything!) for 'Tully.' (Actually, most people probably have never heard the name 'Tully.') Similarly, many people who have heard of both Feynman and Gell-Mann, would identify each as 'a leading contemporary theoretical physicist.' Such people do not assign 'senses' of the usual type to the

---

[15] Benson Mates, "Synonymity," *University of California Publications in Philosophy* 25 (1950): 201–226; reprinted in: *Semantics and the Philosophy of Language*, L. Linsky (ed.), University of Illinois Press, 1952. (There was a good deal of subsequent discussion. In Mates's original paper the point is made almost parenthetically.) Actually, I think that Mates's problem has relatively little force against the argument we are considering for the Fregean position. Mates's puzzle in no way militates against some such principle as: If one word is synonymous with another, then a sufficiently reflective speaker subject to no linguistic inadequacies or conceptual confusions who sincerely assents to a simple sentence containing the one will also (sincerely) assent to the corresponding sentence with the other in its place.

It is surely a crucial part of the present 'Fregean' argument that codesignative names may have distinct 'senses,' that a speaker may assent to a simple sentence containing one and deny the corresponding sentence containing the other, even though he is *guilty of no conceptual or linguistic confusion, and of no lapse in logical consistency.* In the case of two straightforward synonyms, this is not so.

I myself think that Mates's argument is of considerable interest, but that the issues are confusing and delicate and that, if the argument works, it probably leads to a paradox or puzzle rather than to a definite conclusion. (See also notes 23, 28, and 46.)

[16] *Naming and Necessity*, pp. 79–81.

names that uniquely identify the referent (even though they use the names with a determinate reference). But to the extent that the *indefinite* descriptions attached or associated can be called 'senses,' the 'senses' assigned to 'Cicero' and 'Tully,' or to 'Feynman' and 'Gell-Mann,' are *identical*.[17] Yet clearly speakers of this type can ask, "Were Cicero and Tully one Roman orator, or two different ones?" or "Are Feynman and Gell-Mann two different physicists, or one?" without knowing the answer to either question by inspecting 'senses' alone. Some such speaker might even conjecture, or be under the vague false impression, that, as he would say, 'Cicero was bald but Tully was not.' The premise of the argument we are considering for the classic position of Frege and Russell—that whenever two codesignative names fail to be interchangeable in the expression of a speaker's beliefs, failure of interchangeability arises from a difference in the 'defining' descriptions the speaker associates with these names—is, therefore, false. The case illustrated by 'Cicero' and 'Tully' is, in fact, quite usual and ordinary. So the apparent failure of codesignative names to be everywhere interchangeable in belief contexts is not to be explained by differences in the 'senses' of these names.

Since the extreme view of Frege and Russell does not in fact explain the apparent failure of the interchangeability of names in belief contexts, there seems to be no further reason—for present purposes—not to give the other overwhelming *prima facie* considerations against the Frege-Russell view their full weight. Names of famous cities, countries, persons, and planets are the common currency of our common language, not terms used homonymously in our separate idiolects.[18] The apparent failure of codesignative names to be interchangeable in belief contexts remains a mystery, but the mystery no longer seems so clearly to argue for a Fregean

---

[17] Recall also note 12.

[18] Some philosophers stress that names are not *words* of a language, or that names are not *translated* from one language to another. (The phrase 'common currency of our common language' was meant to be neutral with respect to any such alleged issue.) Someone may use 'Mao Tse-Tung,' for example, in English, though he knows not one word of Chinese. It seems hard to deny, however, that "*Deutschland*," "*Allemagne*," and "Germany," are the German, French, and English names of a single country, and that one translates a French sentence using "*Londres*" by an English sentence using "London." Learning these facts *is* part of learning German, French, and English.

It would appear that *some* names, especially names of countries, other famous localities, and some famous people *are* thought of as part of a language (whether they are called 'words' or not is of little importance). Many other names are not thought of as part of a language, especially if the referent is not famous (so the notation used is confined to a limited circle), or if the same name is used by speakers of all languages. As far as I can see, it makes little or no *semantic* difference whether a particular name is thought of as part of a language or not. Mathematical notation such as '<' is also ordinarily not thought of as part of English, or any other language, though it is used in combination with English words in sentences of mathematical treatises written in English. (A French mathematician can use the notation though he knows not one word of English.) 'Is less than,' on the other hand, *is* English. Does this difference have any semantic significance?

I will speak in most of the text as if the names I deal with are part of English, French, etc. But it matters little for what I say whether they are thought of as parts of the language or as adjuncts to it. And one need not say that a name such as '*Londres*' is 'translated' (if such a terminology suggested that names have 'senses,' I too would find it objectionable), as long as one acknowledges that *sentences* containing it are properly translated into English using 'London.'

view as against a Millian one. Neither differing public senses nor differing private senses peculiar to each speaker account for the phenomena to be explained. So the apparent existence of such phenomena no longer gives a *prima facie* argument for such differing senses.

One final remark to close this section. I have referred before to my own earlier views in *Naming and Necessity*. I said above that these views, inasmuch as they make proper names rigid and transparent[19] in modal contexts, favor Mill, but that the concession that proper names are not transparent in belief contexts appears to favor Frege. On a closer examination, however, the extent to which these opacity phenomena really support Frege against Mill becomes much more doubtful. And there are important theoretical reasons for viewing the *Naming and Necessity* approach in a Millian light. In that work I argued that ordinarily the real determinant of the reference of names of a former historical figure is a chain of communication, in which the reference of the name is passed from link to link. Now the legitimacy of such a chain accords much more with Millian views than with alternatives. For the view supposes that a learner acquires a name from the community by determining to use it with the same reference as does the community. We regard such a learner as using "Cicero is bald" to express the same thing the community expresses, regardless of variations in the properties different learners associate with 'Cicero,' as long as he determines that he will use the name with the referent current in the community. That a name can be transmitted in this way accords nicely with a Millian picture, according to which only the reference, not more specific properties associated with the name, is relevant to the semantics of sentences containing it. It has been suggested that the chain of communication, which on the present picture determines the reference, might thereby itself be called a 'sense.' Perhaps so—if we wish[20]—but we should not thereby forget that the legitimacy of such a chain suggests that it is just preservation of reference, as Mill thought, that we regard as necessary for correct language learning.[21] (This contrasts with such terms as 'renate' and 'cordate,' where more than learning the correct extension is needed.) Also, as suggested above, the doctrine of rigidity in modal contexts is dissonant, though not

---

[19] By saying that names are transparent in a context, I mean that codesignative names are interchangeable there. This is a deviation for brevity from the usual terminology, according to which the *context* is transparent. (I use the usual terminology in the paper also.)

[20] But we must use the term 'sense' here in the sense of 'that which fixes the reference,' not 'that which gives the meaning,' otherwise we shall run afoul of the rigidity of proper names. If the source of a chain for a certain name is in fact a given object, we use the name to designate that object even when speaking of counterfactual situations in which some *other* object originated the chain.

[21] The point is that, according to the doctrine of *Naming and Necessity*, when proper names are transmitted from link to link, even though the beliefs about the referent associated with the name change radically, the change is not to be considered a linguistic change, in the way it *was* a linguistic change when 'villain' changed its meaning from 'rustic' to 'wicked man.' As long as the reference of a name remains the same, the associated beliefs about the object may undergo a large number of changes without these changes constituting a change in the language. If Geach is right, an appropriate sortal must be passed on also. But see footnote 58 of *Naming and Necessity*.

necessarily inconsistent, with a view that invokes anti-Millian considerations to explain propositional attitude contexts.

The spirit of my earlier views, then, suggests that a Millian line should be maintained as far as is feasible.

II. PRELIMINARIES: SOME GENERAL PRINCIPLES

Where are we now? We seem to be in something of a quandary. On the one hand, we concluded that the failure of 'Cicero' and 'Tully' to be interchangeable *salva veritate* in contexts of propositional attitude was by no means explicable in terms of different 'senses' of the two names. On the other hand, let us not forget the initial argument against Mill: If reference is *all there is* to naming, what semantic difference can there be between 'Cicero' and 'Tully'? And if there is no semantic difference, do not 'Cicero was bald' and 'Tully was bald' express exactly the same proposition? How, then, can anyone believe that Cicero was bald, yet doubt or disbelieve that Tully was?

Let us take stock. Why do we think that anyone can believe that Cicero was bald, but fail to believe that Tully was? Or believe, without any logical inconsistency, that Yale is a fine university, but that Old Eli is an inferior one? Well, a normal English speaker, Jones, can sincerely assent to 'Cicero was bald' but not to 'Tully was bald.' And this even though Jones uses 'Cicero' and 'Tully' in standard ways—he uses 'Cicero' in this assertion as a name for the Roman, not, say, for his dog, or for a German spy.

Let us make explicit the *disquotational principle* presupposed here, connecting sincere assent and belief. It can be stated as follows, where '*p*' is to be replaced, inside and outside all quotation marks, by any appropriate standard English sentence: "*If a normal English speaker, on reflection, sincerely assents to '*p*', then he believes that p.*" The sentence replacing '*p*' is to lack indexical or pronominal devices or ambiguities, that would ruin the intuitive sense of the principle (e.g., if he assents to "You are wonderful," he need not believe that *you*—the reader—are wonderful).[22] When we suppose that we are dealing with a normal speaker of English, we mean that he uses all words in the sentence in a standard way, combines them according to the appropriate syntax, etc.: in short, he uses the

---

[22] Similar appropriate restrictions are assumed below for the strengthened disquotational principle and for the principle of translation. Ambiguities need not be excluded if it is tacitly assumed that the sentence is to be understood in one way in all its occurrences. (For the principle of translation it is similarly assumed that the translator matches the *intended* interpretation of the sentence.) I do not work out the restrictions on indexicals in detail, since the intent is clear.

Clearly, the disquotational principle applies only to *de dicto*, not *de re*, attributions of belief. If someone sincerely assents to the near triviality "The tallest foreign spy is a spy," it follows that he believes that: the tallest foreign spy, is a spy. It is well known that it does *not* follow that he believes, *of* the tallest foreign spy, that he is a spy. In the latter case, but not in the former, it would be his patriotic duty to make contact with the authorities. (Some have argued that this is not so obvious as I supposed. For discussion, see Chapter 11.)

sentence to mean what a normal speaker should mean by it. The 'words' of the sentence may include proper names, where these are part of the common discourse of the community, so that we can speak of using them in a standard way. For example, if the sentence is "London is pretty," then the speaker should satisfy normal criteria for using 'London' as a name of London, and for using 'is pretty' to attribute an appropriate degree of pulchritude. The qualification "on reflection" guards against the possibility that a speaker may, through careless inattention to the meaning of his words or other momentary conceptual or linguistic confusion, assert something he does not really mean, or assent to a sentence in linguistic error. "Sincerely" is meant to exclude mendacity, acting, irony, and the like. I fear that even with all this it is possible that some astute reader—such, after all, is the way of philosophy—may discover a qualification I have overlooked, without which the asserted principle is subject to counterexample. I doubt, however, that any such modification will affect any of the uses of the principle to be considered below. Taken in its obvious intent, after all, the principle appears to be a self-evident truth. (A similar principle holds for sincere affirmation or assertion in place of assent.)

There is also a strengthened 'biconditional' form of the disquotational principle, where once again any appropriate English sentence may replace 'p' throughout: *A normal English speaker who is not reticent will be disposed to sincere reflective assent to 'p' if and only if he believes that p.*[23] The biconditional form strengthens the simple one by adding that failure to assent indicates lack of belief, as assent indicates belief. The qualification about reticence is meant to take account of the fact that a speaker may fail to avow his beliefs because of shyness, a desire for secrecy, to avoid offense, etc. (An alternative formulation would give the speaker a sign to indicate lack of belief—not necessarily disbelief—in the assertion propounded, in addition to his sign of assent.) Maybe again the formulation needs further tightening, but the intent is clear.

Usually below the simple disquotational principle will be sufficient for our purposes, but once we will also invoke the strengthened form. The simple form can often be used as a test for disbelief, provided the subject is a speaker with the modicum of logicality needed so that, at least after appropriate reflection, he does

---

[23] What if a speaker assents to a sentence, but fails to assent to a synonymous assertion? Say, he assents to "Jones is a doctor," but not to "Jones is a physician." Such a speaker either does not understand one of the sentences normally, or he should be able to correct himself "on reflection." As long as he confusedly assents to 'Jones is a doctor' but not to 'Jones is a physician,' we *cannot* straightforwardly apply disquotational principles to conclude that he does or does not believe that Jones is a doctor, because his assent is not "reflective."

Similarly, if someone asserts, "Jones is a doctor but not a physician," he should be able to recognize his inconsistency without further information. We have formulated the disquotational principles so they need not lead us to attribute belief as long as we have grounds to suspect conceptual or linguistic confusion, as in the cases just mentioned.

Note that if someone says, "Cicero was bald but Tully was not," there need be *no* grounds to suppose that he is under *any* linguistic or conceptual confusion.

not hold simultaneously beliefs that are straightforward contradictions of each other—of the forms 'p' and '$\sim p$.'[24] (Nothing in such a requirement prevents him from holding simultaneous beliefs that jointly *entail* a contradiction.) In this case (where 'p' may be replaced by any appropriate English sentence), the speaker's assent to the negation of 'p' indicates not only his disbelief that p but also his failure to believe that p, using only the simple (unstrengthened) disquotational principle.

So far our principle applies only to speakers of English. It allows us to infer, from Peter's sincere reflective assent to "God exists," that he believes that God exists. But of course we ordinarily allow ourselves to draw conclusions, stated in English, about the beliefs of speakers of any language: we infer that Pierre believes that God exists from his sincere reflective assent to "*Dieu existe*." There are several ways to do this, given conventional translations of French into English. We choose the following route. We have stated the disquotational principle in English, for English sentences; an analogous principle, stated in French (German, etc.) will be assumed to hold for French (German, etc.) sentences. Finally, we assume the *principle of translation*: *If a sentence of one language expresses a truth in that language, then any translation of it into any other language also expresses a truth* (*in that other language*). Some of our ordinary practice of translation may violate this principle; this happens when the translator's aim is not to preserve the content of the sentence, but to serve—in some other sense—the same purposes in the home language as the original utterance served in the foreign language.[25] But if the translation of a sentence is to mean the same as the sentence translated, preservation of truth value is a minimal condition that must be observed.

Granted the disquotational principle expressed in each language, reasoning starting from Pierre's assent to '*Dieu existe*' continues thus. First, on the basis of his utterance and the French disquotational principle we infer (in French):

---

[24] This should not be confused with the question whether the speaker simultaneously believes *of* a given object, both that it has a certain property and that it does not have it. Our discussion concerns *de dicto* (notional) belief, not *de re* belief.

I have been shown a passage in Aristotle that appears to suggest that *no one* can really believe both of two explicit contradictories. If we wish to use the *simple* disquotational principle as a test for disbelief, it suffices that this be true of *some* individuals, after reflection, who are simultaneously aware of both beliefs, and have sufficient logical acumen and respect for logic. Such individuals, if they have contradictory beliefs, will be shaken in one or both beliefs after they note the contradiction. For such individuals, sincere reflective assent to the negation of a sentence implies disbelief in the proposition it expresses, so the test in the text applies.

[25] For example, in translating a historical report into another language, such as, "Patrick Henry said, 'Give me liberty or give me death!'" the translator may well translate the quoted material attributed to Henry. He translates a presumed truth into a falsehood, since Henry spoke English; but probably his reader is aware of this and is more interested in the content of Henry's utterance than in its exact words. Especially in translating fiction, where truth is irrelevant, this procedure is appropriate. But some objectors to Church's 'translation argument' have allowed themselves to be misled by the practice.

Pierre croit que Dieu existe.

From this we deduce,[26] using the principle of translation:

Pierre believes that God exists.

In this way we can apply the disquotational technique to all languages.

Even if I apply the disquotational technique to English alone, there is a sense in which I can be regarded as tacitly invoking a principle of translation. For presumably I apply it to speakers of the language other than myself. As Quine has pointed out, to regard others as speaking the same language as I is in a sense tacitly to assume a *homophonic* translation of their language into my own. So when I infer from Peter's sincere assent to or affirmation of "God exists" that he believes that God exists, it is arguable that, strictly speaking, I combine the disquotational principle (for Peter's idiolect) with the principle of (homophonic) translation (of Peter's idiolect into mine). But for most purposes, we can formulate the disquotational principle for a single language, English, tacitly supposed to be the common language of English speakers. Only when the possibility of individual differences of dialect is relevant need we view the matter more elaborately.

Let us return from these abstractions to our main theme. Since a normal speaker—normal even in his use of 'Cicero' and 'Tully' as names—can give sincere and reflective assent to "Cicero was bald" and simultaneously to "Tully was not bald," the disquotational principle implies that he believes that Cicero was bald and believes that Tully was not bald. Since it seems that he need not have contradictory beliefs (even if he is a brilliant logician, he need not be able to deduce that at least one of his beliefs must be in error), and since a substitutivity principle for coreferential proper names in belief contexts would imply that he does have contradictory beliefs, it would seem that such a substitutivity principle must be incorrect. Indeed, the argument appears to be a *reductio ad absurdum* of the substitutivity principle in question.

The relation of this argument against substitutivity to the classical position of Russell and Frege is a curious one. As we have seen, the argument can be used to give *prima facie* support for the Frege-Russell view, and I think many philosophers have regarded it as such support. But in fact this very argument, which has been used to support Frege and Russell, cannot be stated in a straightforward fashion if Frege and Russell are right. For suppose Jones asserts, "Cicero was bald, but Tully was not." If Frege and Russell are right, I cannot deduce, using the disquotational principle:

---

[26] To state the argument precisely, we need in addition a form of the Tarskian disquotation principle for truth: For each (French or English) replacement for 'p,' infer "'p' is true" from "p," and conversely. (Note that "'p' is true" becomes an English sentence even if 'p' is replaced by a French sentence.) In the text we leave the application of the Tarskian disquotational principle tacit.

(1) Jones believes that Cicero was bald but Tully was not,

since, in general, Jones and I will not, strictly speaking, share a common idiolect unless we assign the same 'senses' to all names. Nor can I combine disquotation and translation to the appropriate effect, since homophonic translation of Jones's sentence into mine will in general be incorrect for the same reason. Since in fact I make no special distinction in sense between 'Cicero' and 'Tully'—to me, and probably to you as well, these are interchangeable names for the same man—and since according to Frege and Russell, Jones's very affirmation of (1) shows that for him there *is* some distinction of sense, Jones must therefore, on Frege-Russellian views, use one of these names differently from me, and homophonic translation is illegitimate. Hence, if Frege and Russell are right, we *cannot* use this example in the usual straightforward way to conclude that proper names are not substitutable in belief contexts—even though the example, and the ensuing negative verdict on substitutivity, has often been thought to support Frege and Russell!

Even according to the Frege-Russellian view, however, *Jones* can conclude, using the disquotational principle, and expressing his conclusion in his own idiolect:

(2) I believe that Cicero was bald but Tully was not.

I cannot endorse this conclusion in Jones's own words, since I do not share Jones's idiolect. I *can* of course conclude, "(2) expresses a truth in Jones's idiolect." I can also, if I find out the two 'senses' Jones assigns to 'Cicero' and 'Tully,' introduce two names 'X' and 'Y' into my own language with these same two senses ('Cicero' and 'Tully' have already been preempted) and conclude:

(3) Jones believes that X was bald and Y was not.

All this is enough so that we can still conclude, on the Frege-Russellian view, that codesignative names are not interchangeable in belief contexts. Indeed this can be shown more simply on this view, since codesignative descriptions plainly are not interchangeable in these contexts and for Frege and Russell names, being essentially abbreviated descriptions, cannot differ in this respect. Nevertheless, the simple argument, apparently free of such special Frege-Russellian doctrinal premises (and often used to support these premises), in fact cannot go through if Frege and Russell are right.

However, if, *pace* Frege and Russell, widely used names are common currency of our language, then there no longer is any problem for the simple argument, using the disquotational principle, to (2). So, it appears, on pain of convicting Jones of inconsistent beliefs—surely an unjust verdict—we must not hold a substitutivity principle for names in belief contexts. If we used the *strengthened* disquotational principle, we could invoke Jones's presumed lack of any tendency to assent to 'Tully was bald' to conclude that he does not believe (lacks the belief) that Tully was bald. Now the refutation of the substitutivity principle is even stronger, for when applied to the conclusion that Jones believes that Cicero was bald but does not believe that Tully was bald, it would lead to a straightout contradiction. The contradiction would no longer be in Jones's beliefs but in our own.

This reasoning, I think, has been widely accepted as proof that codesignative proper names are not interchangeable in belief contexts. Usually the reasoning is left tacit, and it may well be thought that I have made heavy weather of an obvious conclusion. I wish, however, to question the reasoning. I shall do so without challenging any particular step of the argument. Rather I shall present—and this will form the core of the present paper—an argument for a paradox about names in belief contexts that invokes *no* principle of substitutivity. Instead it will be based on the principles—apparently so obvious that their use in these arguments is ordinarily tacit—of disquotation and translation.

Usually the argument will involve more than one language, so that the principle of translation and our conventional manual of translation must be invoked. We will also give an example, however, to show that a form of the paradox may result within English alone, so that the only principle invoked is that of disquotation (or, perhaps, disquotation plus *homophonic* translation). It will intuitively be fairly clear, in these cases, that the situation of the subject is 'essentially the same' as that of Jones with respect to 'Cicero' and 'Tully.' Moreover, the paradoxical conclusions about the subject will parallel those drawn about Jones on the basis of the substitutivity principle, and the arguments will parallel those regarding Jones. Only in these cases, no special substitutivity principle is invoked.

The usual use of Jones's case as a counterexample to the substitutivity principle is thus, I think, somewhat analogous to the following sort of procedure. Someone wishes to give a *reductio ad absurdum* argument against a hypothesis in topology. He does succeed in refuting this hypothesis, but his derivation of an absurdity from the hypothesis makes essential use of the unrestricted comprehension schema in set theory, which he regards as self-evident. (In particular, the class of all classes not members of themselves plays a key role in his argument.) Once we know that the unrestricted comprehension schema and the Russell class lead to contradiction by themselves, it is clear that it was an error to blame the earlier contradiction on the topological hypothesis.

The situation would have been the same if, after deducing a contradiction from the topological hypothesis plus the 'obvious' unrestricted comprehension schema, it was found that a similar contradiction followed if we replaced the topological hypothesis by an apparently 'obvious' premise. In both cases it would be clear that, even though we may still not be confident of any specific flaw in the argument against the topological hypothesis, blaming the contradiction on that hypothesis is illegitimate: rather we are in a 'paradoxical' area where it is unclear *what* has gone wrong.[27]

---

[27] I gather that Burali-Forti originally thought he had 'proved' that the ordinals are not linearly ordered, reasoning in a manner similar to our topologist. Someone who heard the present paper delivered told me that König made a similar error.

It is my suggestion, then, that the situation with respect to the interchangeability of codesignative names is similar. True, such a principle, when combined with our normal disquotational judgments of belief, leads to straightforward absurdities. But we will see that the 'same' absurdities can be derived by replacing the interchangeability principle by our normal practices of translation and disquotation, or even by disquotation alone.

The particular principle stated here gives just one particular way of 'formalizing' our normal inferences from explicit affirmation or assent to belief; other ways of doing it are possible. It is undeniable that we *do* infer, from a normal Englishman's sincere affirmation of 'God exists' or 'London is pretty,' that he believes, respectively, that God exists or that London is pretty; and that we would make the same inferences from a Frenchman's affirmation of '*Dieu existe*' or '*Londres est jolie.*' Any principles that would justify such inferences are sufficient for the next section. It will be clear that the particular principles stated in the present section are sufficient, but in the next section the problem will be presented informally in terms of our inferences from foreign or domestic assertion to belief.

III. THE PUZZLE

Here, finally(!), is the puzzle. Suppose Pierre is a normal French speaker who lives in France and speaks not a word of English or of any other language except French. Of course he has heard of that famous distant city, London (which he of course calls '*Londres*') though he himself has never left France. On the basis of what he has heard of London, he is inclined to think that it is pretty. So he says, in French, "*Londres est jolie.*"

On the basis of his sincere French utterance, we will conclude:

(4) Pierre believes that London is pretty.

I am supposing that Pierre satisfies all criteria for being a normal French speaker, in particular, that he satisfies whatever criteria we usually use to judge that a Frenchman (correctly) uses '*est jolie*' to attribute pulchritude and uses '*Londres*'— standardly—as a name of London.

Later, Pierre, through fortunate or unfortunate vicissitudes, moves to England, in fact to London itself, though to an unattractive part of the city with fairly uneducated inhabitants. He, like most of his neighbors, rarely ever leaves this part of the city. None of his neighbors know any French, so he must learn English by 'direct method,' without using any translation of English into French: by talking and mixing with the people he eventually begins to pick up English. In particular, everyone speaks of the city, 'London,' where they all live. Let us suppose for the moment—though we will see below that this is not crucial—that the local population are so uneducated that they know few of the facts that Pierre heard about London in France. Pierre learns from them everything they know about London, but there is little overlap with what he heard before. He learns, of course—speaking English—to call the city he lives in 'London.' Pierre's surroundings are, as I said, unattractive, and he is unimpressed with most of the rest of what he happens to see. So he is inclined to assent to the English sentence:

(5) London is not pretty.

He has *no* inclination to assent to:

(6) London is pretty.

Of course he does not for a moment withdraw his assent from the French sentence, "*Londres est jolie*"; he merely takes it for granted that the ugly city in which he is now stuck is distinct from the enchanting city he heard about in France. But he has no inclination to change his mind for a moment about the city he stills calls '*Londres.*'

This, then, is the puzzle. If we consider Pierre's past background as a French speaker, his entire linguistic behavior, on the same basis as we would draw such a conclusion about many of his countrymen, supports the conclusion ((4) above) that he believes that London is pretty. On the other hand, after Pierre lived in London for some time, he did not differ from his neighbors—his French background aside—either in his knowledge of English or in his command of the relevant facts of local geography. His English vocabulary differs little from that of his neighbors. He, like them, rarely ventures from the dismal quarter of the city in which they all live. He, like them, knows that the city he lives in is called 'London' and knows a few other facts. Now Pierre's neighbors would surely be said to use 'London' as a name for London and to speak English. Since, as an English speaker, he does not differ at all from them, we should say the same of him. But then, on the basis of his sincere assent to (5), we should conclude:

(7) Pierre believes that London is not pretty.

How can we describe this situation? It seems undeniable that Pierre *once* believed that London is pretty—at least before he learned English. For at that time, he differed not at all from countless numbers of his countrymen, and we would have exactly the same grounds to say of him as of any of them that he believes that London is pretty: if any Frenchman who was both ignorant of English and never visited London believed that London is pretty, Pierre did. Nor does it have any plausibility to suppose, because of his later situation *after* he learns English, that Pierre should *retroactively* be judged *never* to have believed that London is pretty. To allow such *ex post facto* legislation would, as long as the future is uncertain, endanger our attributions of belief to *all* monolingual Frenchmen. We would be forced to say that Marie, a monolingual who firmly and sincerely asserts, "*Londres est jolie,*" may or may not believe that London is pretty depending on the *later* vicissitudes of her career (if later she learns English and . . .). No: Pierre, like Marie, believed that London is pretty when he was monolingual.

Should we say that Pierre, now that he lives in London and speaks English, no longer believes that London is pretty? Well, unquestionably Pierre *once* believed that London is pretty. So we would be forced to say that Pierre has *changed his mind, has given up his previous belief.* But has he really done so? Pierre is very set in his ways. He reiterates, with vigor, every assertion he has ever made in French. He says he has not changed his mind about anything, has *not* given up any belief. Can we say he is wrong about this? If we did not have the story of his living in London and his English utterances, on the basis of his normal command of French we would be *forced* to conclude that he *still* believes that London is pretty. And it does seem that this is correct. Pierre has neither changed his mind nor given up any belief he had in France.

Similar difficulties beset any attempt to deny him his new belief. His French past aside, he is just like his friends in London. Anyone else, growing up in London with the same knowledge and beliefs that he expresses in England, we would undoubtedly judge to believe that London is not pretty. Can Pierre's French past nullify such a judgment? Can we say that Pierre, because of his French past, does not believe that (5)? Suppose an electric shock wiped out all his memories of the French language, what he learned in France, and his French past. He would then be *exactly* like his neighbors in London. He would have the *same* knowledge, beliefs, and linguistic capacities. We then presumably would be forced to say that Pierre believes that London is ugly if we say it of his neighbors. But surely no shock that *destroys* part of Pierre's memories and knowledge can *give* him a new belief. If Pierre believes (5) *after* the shock, he believed it before, despite his French language and background.

If we would deny Pierre, in his bilingual stage, his belief that London is pretty *and* his belief that London is not pretty, we combine the difficulties of both previous options. We still would be forced to judge that Pierre once believed that London is pretty but does no longer, in spite of Pierre's own sincere denial that he has lost any belief. We also must worry whether Pierre would *gain* the belief that London is not pretty if he totally forgot his French past. The option does not seem very satisfactory.

So now it seems that we must respect both Pierre's French utterances and their English counterparts. So we must say that Pierre has contradictory beliefs, that he believes that London is pretty *and* he believes that London is not pretty. But there seem to be insuperable difficulties with this alternative as well. We may suppose that Pierre, in spite of the unfortunate situation in which he now finds himself, is a leading philosopher and logician. He would *never* let contradictory beliefs pass. And surely anyone, leading logician or no, is in principle in a position to notice and correct contradictory beliefs if he has them. Precisely for this reason, we regard individuals who contradict themselves as subject to greater censure than those who merely have false beliefs. But it is clear that Pierre, as long as he is unaware that the cities he calls 'London' and '*Londres*' are one and the same, is in no position to see, by logic alone, that at least one of his beliefs must be false. He lacks information, not logical acumen. He cannot be convicted of inconsistency: to do so is incorrect.

We can shed more light on this if we change the case. Suppose that, in France, Pierre, instead of affirming "*Londres est jolie,*" had affirmed, more cautiously, "*Si New York est jolie, Londres est jolie aussi,*" so that he believed that *if* New York is pretty, so is London. Later Pierre moves to London, learns English as before, and says (in English) "London is not pretty." So he now believes, further, that London is *not* pretty. Now from the two premises, both of which appear to be among his beliefs (a) If New York is pretty, London is, and (b) London is not pretty, Pierre should be able to deduce by *modus tollens* that New York is not pretty. But no matter how great Pierre's logical acumen may be, *he cannot in fact make any such deduction, as long as he supposes that 'Londres' and 'London' may name two different cities.* If he *did* draw such a conclusion, he would be guilty of a fallacy.

Intuitively, he may well suspect that New York is pretty, and just this suspicion may lead him to suppose that '*Londres*' and 'London' probably name distinct cities. Yet, if we follow our normal practice of reporting the beliefs of French and English speakers, *Pierre has available to him (among his beliefs) both the premises of a modus tollens argument that New York is not pretty.*

Again, we may emphasize Pierre's *lack* of belief instead of his belief. Pierre, as I said, has no disposition to assent to (6). Let us concentrate on this, ignoring his disposition to assent to (5). In fact, if we wish we may change the case: Suppose Pierre's neighbors think that since they rarely venture outside their own ugly section, they have no right to any opinion as to the pulchritude of the whole city. Suppose Pierre shares their attitude. Then, judging by his failure to respond affirmatively to "London is pretty," we may judge, from Pierre's behavior as an *English* speaker, that he lacks the belief that London is pretty: never mind whether he disbelieves it, as before, or whether, as in the modified story, he insists that he has no firm opinion on the matter.

Now (using the *strengthened* disquotational principle), we can derive a contradiction, not merely in Pierre's judgments, but in our own. For on the basis of his behavior as an English speaker, we concluded that he does *not* believe that London is pretty (that is, that it is not the case that he believes that London is pretty). But on the basis of his behavior as a *French* speaker, we must conclude that he *does* believe that London is pretty. This is a contradiction.[28]

---

[28] It is not possible, in this case, as it is in the case of the man who assents to "Jones is a doctor" but not to "Jones is a physician," to refuse to apply the disquotational principle on the grounds that the subject must lack proper command of the language or be subject to some linguistic or conceptual confusion. As long as Pierre is unaware that 'London' and '*Londres*' are codesignative, he need not lack appropriate linguistic knowledge, nor need he be subject to any linguistic or conceptual confusion, when he affirms '*Londres est jolie*' but denies 'London is pretty.'

We have examined four possibilities for characterizing Pierre while he is in London: (a) that at that time we no longer respect his French utterance ('*Londres est jolie*'), that is, that we no longer ascribe to him the corresponding belief; (b) that we do not respect his English utterance (or lack of utterance); (c) that we respect neither; (d) that we respect both. Each possibility seems to lead us to say something either plainly false or even downright contradictory. Yet the possibilities appear to be logically exhaustive. This, then, is the paradox.

I have no firm belief as to how to solve it. But beware of one source of confusion. It is no solution in itself to observe that some *other* terminology, which evades the question whether Pierre believes that London is pretty, may be sufficient to state all the relevant facts. I am fully aware that complete and straightforward descriptions of the situation are possible and that in this sense there is no paradox. Pierre is disposed to sincere assent to '*Londres est jolie*' but not to 'London is pretty.' He uses French normally, English normally. Both with '*Londres*' and 'London' he associates properties sufficient to determine that famous city, but he does not realize that they determine a single city. (And his uses of '*Londres*' and 'London' are historically (causally) connected with the same single city, though he is unaware of that.) We may even give a rough statement of his beliefs. He believes that the city he calls '*Londres*' is pretty, that the city he calls 'London' is not. No doubt other straightforward descriptions are possible. No doubt some of these are, in a certain sense, *complete* descriptions of the situation.

But none of this answers the original question. Does Pierre, or does he not, believe that London is pretty? I know of no answer to *this* question that seems satisfactory. It is no answer to protest that, in some *other* terminology, one can state 'all the relevant facts.'

To reiterate, this is the puzzle: Does Pierre, or does he not, believe that London is pretty? It is clear that our normal criteria for the attribution of belief lead, when applied to *this* question, to paradoxes and contradictions. One set of principles adequate to many ordinary attributions of belief, but which leads to paradox in the present case, was stated in Section 2; and other formulations are possible. As in the case of the logical paradoxes, the present puzzle presents us with a problem for customarily accepted principles and a challenge to formulate an acceptable set of principles that does not lead to paradox, is intuitively sound, and supports the inferences we usually make. Such a challenge cannot be met simply by a description of Pierre's situation that evades the question whether he believes that London is pretty.

One aspect of the presentation may misleadingly suggest the applicability of Frege-Russellian ideas that each speaker associates his own description or properties to each name. For as I just set up the case Pierre learned one set of facts about the so-called '*Londres*' when he was in France, and *another* set of facts about 'London' in England. Thus it may appear that 'what's really going on' is that Pierre believes that *the city* satisfying *one* set of properties *is* pretty, while he believes that *the city* satisfying *another* set of properties *is not* pretty.

As we just emphasized, the phrase 'what's really going on' is a danger signal in discussions of the present paradox. The conditions stated may—let us concede for the moment—describe 'what's really going on.' But they do not resolve the problem with which we began, that of the behavior of names in belief contexts: Does Pierre, or does he not, believe that London (not the city satisfying such-and-such descriptions, but *London*) is pretty? No answer has yet been given.

Nevertheless, these considerations may appear to indicate that descriptions, or associated properties, are highly relevant somehow to an ultimate solution, since at this stage it appears that the entire puzzle arises from the fact that Pierre originally associated different identifying properties with 'London' and '*Londres*.' Such a reaction may have some force even in the face of the now fairly well-known arguments against 'identifying descriptions' as in any way 'defining,' or even 'fixing the reference' of names. But in fact the special features of the case, as I set it out, are misleading. The puzzle can arise even if Pierre associates exactly the same identifying properties with both names.

First, the considerations mentioned above in connection with 'Cicero' and 'Tully' establish this fact. For example, Pierre may well learn, in France, '*Platon*' as the name of a major Greek philosopher, and later, in England, learns 'Plato' with the same identification. Then the same puzzle can arise: Pierre may have believed, when he was in France and was monolingual in French, that Plato was bald (he would have said, "*Platon était chauve*"), and later conjecture, in English, "Plato was not bald," thus indicating that he believes or suspects that Plato was *not* bald. He need only suppose that, in spite of the similarity of their names, the man he calls '*Platon*' and the man he calls 'Plato' were two distinct major Greek philosophers. In principle, the same thing could happen with 'London' and '*Londres*.'

Of course, most of us learn a *definite* description about London, say 'the largest city in England.' Can the puzzle still arise? It is noteworthy that the puzzle can still arise even if Pierre associates to '*Londres*' and to 'London' *exactly* the same *uniquely identifying* properties. How can this be? Well, suppose that Pierre believes that London is the largest city in (and capital of) England, that it contains Buckingham Palace, the residence of the Queen of England, and he believes (correctly) that these properties, conjointly, uniquely identify the city. (In this case, it is best to suppose that he has never seen London, or even England, so that he uses *only* these properties to identify the city. Nevertheless, he has learned English by 'direct method.') These uniquely identifying properties he comes to associate with 'London' after he learned English, and he expresses the appropriate beliefs about 'London' in English. Earlier, when he spoke nothing but French, however, he associated *exactly* the same uniquely identifying properties with '*Londres*.' He believed that '*Londres*,' as he called it, could be uniquely identified as the capital of England, that it contained Buckingham Palace, that the Queen of England lived there, etc. Of course he expressed these beliefs, like most monolingual Frenchmen, in French. In particular, he used '*Angleterre*' for England, '*le Palais de Buckingham*' (pronounced '*Bookeengam*'!) for Buckingham

Palace, and '*la Reine d'Angleterre*' for the Queen of England. But if any Frenchman who speaks no English can ever be said to associate *exactly* the properties of being the capital of England etc., with the name '*Londres,*' Pierre in his monolingual period did so.

When Pierre becomes a bilingual, *must* he conclude that 'London' and '*Londres*' name the same city, because he defined each by the same uniquely identifying properties?

Surprisingly, no! Suppose Pierre had affirmed, '*Londres est jolie.*' If Pierre has any reason—even just a 'feeling in his bones,' or perhaps exposure to a photograph of a miserable area which he was told (in English) was part of 'London'—to maintain 'London is not pretty,' he need not contradict himself. He need only conclude that 'England' and '*Angleterre*' name two different countries, that 'Buckingham Palace' and '*le Palais de Buckingham*' (recall the pronunciation!), name two different palaces, and so on. Then he can maintain *both* views without contradiction, and regard *both* properties as uniquely identifying.

The fact is that the paradox reproduces itself on the level of the 'uniquely identifying properties' that description theorists have regarded as 'defining' proper names (and *a fortiori*, as fixing their references). Nothing is more reasonable than to suppose that if two names, A and B, and a single set of properties, S, are such that a certain speaker believes that the referent of A uniquely satisfies all of S and that the referent of B also uniquely satisfies all of S, then that speaker is committed to the belief that A and B have the same reference. In fact, the identity of the referents of A and B is an easy *logical consequence* of the speaker's beliefs.

From this fact description theorists concluded that names can be regarded as synonymous, and hence interchangeable *salva veritate* even in belief contexts, provided that they are 'defined' by the same uniquely identifying properties.

We have already seen that there is a difficulty in that the set S of properties need not in fact be uniquely identifying. But in the present paradoxical situation there is a surprising difficulty even if the supposition of the description theorist (that the speaker believes that S is uniquely fulfilled) in fact holds. For, as we have seen above, Pierre is in no position to draw ordinary logical consequences from the conjoint set of what, when we consider him separately as a speaker of English and as a speaker of French, we would call his beliefs. He cannot infer a contradiction from his separate beliefs that London is pretty and that London is not pretty. Nor, in the modified situation above, would Pierre make a normal *modus tollens* inference from his beliefs that London is not pretty and that London is pretty if New York is. Similarly here, if we pay attention only to Pierre's behavior as a French speaker (and at least in his monolingual days he was no different from any other Frenchmen), Pierre satisfies all the normal criteria for believing that '*Londres*' has a referent uniquely satisfying the properties of being the largest city in England, containing Buckingham Palace, and the like. (If Pierre did not hold such beliefs, no Frenchman *ever* did.) Similarly, on the basis of his (later) beliefs expressed in English, Pierre also believes that the referent of

'London' uniquely satisfies these same properties. But Pierre cannot combine the two beliefs into a single set of beliefs from which he can draw the normal conclusion that 'London' and '*Londres*' must have the same referent. (Here the trouble comes not from 'London' and '*Londres*' but from 'England' and '*Angleterre*' and the rest.) Indeed, if he *did* draw what would appear to be the normal conclusion in this case and any of the other cases, Pierre would in fact be guilty of a logical fallacy.

Of course the description theorist could hope to eliminate the problem by 'defining' '*Angleterre*,' 'England,' and so on by appropriate descriptions also. Since in principle the problem may rear its head at the next 'level' and at each subsequent level, the description theorist would have to believe that an 'ultimate' level can eventually be reached where the defining properties are 'pure' properties not involving proper names (nor natural kind terms or related terms, see below!). I know of no convincing reason to suppose that such a level can be reached in any plausible way, or that the properties can continue to be uniquely identifying if one attempts to eliminate all names and related devices.[29] Such speculation aside, the fact remains that Pierre, judged by the *ordinary* criteria for such judgments, *did* learn both '*Londres*' and 'London' by *exactly* the same set of identifying properties; yet the puzzle remains even in this case.

Well, then, is there any way out of the puzzle? Aside from the principles of disquotation and translation, only our normal practice of translation of French into English has been used. Since the principles of disquotation and translation

---

[29] The 'elimination' would be most plausible if we believed, according to a Russellian epistemology, that all my language, when written in unabbreviated notation, refers to constituents with which I am 'acquainted' in Russell's sense. Then no one speaks a language intelligible to anyone else; indeed, no one speaks the same language twice. Few today will accept this.

A basic consideration should be stressed here. Moderate Fregeans attempt to combine a roughly Fregean view with the view that names are part of our common language, and that our conventional practices of interlinguistic translation and interpretation are correct. The problems of the present paper indicate that it is very difficult to obtain a requisite socialized notion of sense that will enable such a program to succeed. Extreme Fregeans (such as Frege and Russell) believe that in general names are peculiar to idiolects. They therefore would accept no general rule translating '*Londres*' as 'London,' nor even translating one person's use of 'London' into another's. However, if they follow Frege in regarding senses as 'objective,' they must believe that in principle it makes sense to speak of two people using two names in their respective idiolects with the same sense, and that there must be (necessary and) sufficient conditions for this to be the case. If these conditions for sameness of sense are satisfied, translation of one name into the other is legitimate, otherwise not. The present considerations (and the extension of these below to natural kind and related terms), however, indicate that the notion of sameness of sense, if it is to be explicated in terms of sameness of identifying properties and if these properties are themselves expressed in the languages of the two respective idiolects, presents interpretation problems of the same type presented by the names themselves. Unless the Fregean can give a method for identifying sameness of sense that is free of such problems, he *has no sufficient conditions for sameness of sense, nor for translation to be legitimate.* He would therefore be forced to maintain, contrary to Frege's intent, that not only in practice do few people use proper names with the same sense but that *it is in principle meaningless to compare senses.* A view that the identifying properties used to define senses should always be expressible in a Russellian language of 'logically proper names' would be one solution to this difficulty but involves a doubtful philosophy of language and epistemology.

seem self-evident, we may be tempted to blame the trouble on the translation of '*Londres est jolie*' as 'London is pretty,' and ultimately, then, on the translation of '*Londres*' as 'London.'[30] Should we, perhaps, permit ourselves to conclude that '*Londres*' should not, 'strictly speaking' be translated as 'London'? Such an expedient is, of course, desperate: the translation in question is a standard one, learned by students together with other standard translations of French into English. Indeed, '*Londres*' is, in effect, introduced into French as the French version of 'London.'

Since our backs, however, are against the wall, let us consider this desperate and implausible expedient a bit further. If '*Londres*' is *not* a correct French version of the English 'London,' under what circumstances can proper names be translated from one language to another?

Classical description theories suggest the answer: Translation, strictly speaking, is between idiolects; a name in one idiolect can be translated into another when (and only when) the speakers of the two idiolects associate the same uniquely identifying properties with the two names. We have seen that any such proposed restriction, not only fails blatantly to fit our normal practices of translation and indirect discourse reportage, but does not even appear to block the paradox.[31]

So we still want a suitable restriction. Let us drop the references to idiolects and return to '*Londres*' and 'London' as names in French and English, respectively—the languages of two communities. If '*Londres*' is not a correct French translation of 'London,' could any other version do better? Suppose I introduced another word into French, with the stipulation that *it* should always be used to translate 'London.' Would not the same problem arise for this word as well? The only feasible solution in this direction is the most drastic: decree that no sentence containing a name can be translated except by a sentence containing the phonetically identical name. Thus when Pierre asserts '*Londres est jolie*,' we English speakers can at best conclude, if anything: Pierre believes that *Londres* is pretty. Such a conclusion is, of course, not expressed in English, but in a word salad of English and French; on the view now being entertained, we cannot state Pierre's belief in *English* at all.[32] Similarly, we would have to say: Pierre believes

---

[30] If any reader finds the term 'translation' objectionable with respect to names, let him be reminded that all I mean is that French sentences containing '*Londres*' are uniformly translated into English with 'London.'

[31] The paradox would be blocked if we required that they define the names by the same properties expressed in the same words. There is nothing in the motivation of the classical description theories that would justify this extra clause. In the present case of French and English, such a restriction would amount to a decree that neither '*Londres*,' nor any other conceivable French name, could be translated as 'London.' I deal with this view immediately below.

[32] Word salads of two languages (like ungrammatical 'semisentences' of a single language) need not be unintelligible, though they are makeshifts with no fixed syntax. "If God did not exist, Voltaire said, *il faudrait l'inventer*." The meaning is clear.

that *Angleterre* is a monarchy, Pierre believes that *Platon* wrote dialogues, and the like.³³

This 'solution' appears at first to be effective against the paradox, but it is drastic. What is it about sentences containing names that makes them—a substantial class—intrinsically untranslatable, express beliefs that cannot be reported in any other language? At best, to report them in the other language, one is forced to use a word salad in which names from the one language are imported into the other. Such a supposition is both contrary to our normal practice of translation and very implausible on its face.

Implausible though it is, there is at least this much excuse for the 'solution' at this point. Our normal practice with respect to some famous people and especially for geographical localities is to have different names for them in different languages, so that in translating sentences we translate the names. But for a large number of names, especially names of people, this is not so: the person's name is used in the sentences of all languages. At least the restriction in question merely urges us to mend our ways by doing *always* what we presently do *sometimes*.

But the really drastic character of the proposed restriction comes out when we see how far it may have to extend. In *Naming and Necessity* I suggested that there are important analogies between proper names and natural kind terms, and it seems to me that the present puzzle is one instance where the analogy will hold. Putnam, who has proposed views on natural kinds similar to my own in many respects, stressed this extension of the puzzle in his comments at the Conference. Not that the puzzle extends to all translations from English to French. At the moment, at least, it seems to me that Pierre, if he learns English and French separately, without learning any translation manual between them, *must* conclude, if he reflects enough, that 'doctor' and '*médecin*,' and '*heureux*' and 'happy,' are synonymous, or at any rate, coextensive;³⁴ any potential paradox of the present kind for these word pairs is thus blocked. But what about '*lapin*' and 'rabbit,' or 'beech' and '*hêtre*'? We may suppose that Pierre is himself neither a zoologist nor a botanist. He has learned each language in its own country and the examples he has been shown to illustrate '*les lapins*' and 'rabbits,' 'beeches'

---

³³ Had we said, "Pierre believes that the country he calls '*Angleterre*' is a monarchy," the sentence would be English, since the French word would be mentioned but not used. But for this very reason we would not have captured the sense of the French original.

³⁴ Under the influence of Quine's *Word and Object*, some may argue that such conclusions are not inevitable: perhaps he will translate '*médecin*' as 'doctor stage,' or 'undetached part of a doctor'! If a Quinean skeptic makes an empirical prediction that such reactions from bilinguals as a matter of fact can occur, I doubt that he will be proved correct. (I don't know what Quine would think. But see *Word and Object*, p. 74, first paragraph.) On the other hand, if the translation of '*médecin*' as 'doctor' rather than 'doctor part' in this situation *is*, empirically speaking, inevitable, then even the advocate of Quine's thesis will have to admit that there is something special about one particular translation. The issue is not crucial to our present concerns, so I leave it with these sketchy remarks. But see also note 36.

and '*les hêtres*' are distinct. It thus seems to be possible for him to suppose that '*lapin*' and 'rabbit,' or 'beech' and '*hêtre*,' denote distinct but superficially similar kinds or species, even though the differences may be indiscernible to the untrained eye. (This is especially plausible if, as Putnam supposes, an English speaker—for example, Putnam himself—who is not a botanist may use 'beech' and 'elm' with their normal (distinct) meanings, even though he cannot himself distinguish the two trees.[35] Pierre may quite plausibly be supposed to wonder whether the trees which in France he called '*les hêtres*' were beeches or elms, even though as a speaker of French he satisfies all usual criteria for using '*les hêtres*' normally. If beeches and elms will not serve, better pairs of ringers exist that cannot be told apart except by an expert.) Once Pierre is in such a situation, paradoxes analogous to the one about London obviously can arise for rabbits and beeches. Pierre could affirm a French statement with '*lapin*,' but deny its English translation with 'rabbit.' As above, we are hard-pressed to say what Pierre *believes*. We were considering a 'strict and philosophical' reform of translation procedures which proposed that foreign proper names should always be appropriated rather than translated. Now it seems that we will be forced to do the same with all words for natural kinds. (For example, on price of paradox, one must not translate '*lapin*' as 'rabbit'!) No longer can the extended proposal be defended, even weakly, as 'merely' universalizing what we already do sometimes. It is surely too drastic a change to retain any credibility.[36]

There is yet another consideration that makes the proposed restriction more implausible: Even this restriction does not really block the paradox. Even if we

---

[35] Putnam gives the example of elms and beeches in "The Meaning of 'Meaning'" (in: *Language, Mind, and Knowledge*, Minnesota Studies in the Philosophy of Science 7; also reprinted in Putnam's *Collected Papers*). See also Putnam's discussion of other examples on pp. 139–143; also my own remarks on 'fool's gold,' tigers, etc., in *Naming and Necessity*, pp. 118–28.

[36] It is unclear to me how far this can go. Suppose Pierre hears English spoken only in England, French in France, and learns both by direct method. (Suppose also that no one else in each country speaks the language of the other.) Must he be sure that 'hot' and '*chaud*' are coextensive? In practice he certainly would. But suppose somehow his experience is consistent with the following bizarre—and of course, false!—hypothesis: England and France differ atmospherically so that human bodies are affected very differently by their interaction with the surrounding atmosphere. (This would be more plausible if France were on another planet.) In particular, within reasonable limits, things that feel cold in one of the countries feel hot in the other, and *vice versa*. Things don't change their *temperature* when moved from England to France, they just *feel* different because of their effects on human physiology. Then '*chaud*,' in French, would be true of the things that are called 'cold' in English! (Of course the present discussion is, for space, terribly compressed. See also the discussion of 'heat' in *Naming and Necessity*. We are simply creating, for the physical property 'heat,' a situation analogous to the situation for natural kinds in the text.)

If Pierre's experiences were arranged somehow so as to be consistent with the bizarre hypothesis, and he somehow came to believe it, he might simultaneously assent to '*C'est chaud*' and 'This is cold' without contradiction, even though he speaks French and English normally in each country separately.

This case needs much more development to see if it can be set up in detail, but I cannot consider it further here. Was I right in assuming in the text that the difficulty could not arise for '*médecin*' and 'doctor'?

confine ourselves to a single language, say English, and to phonetically identical tokens of a single name, we can still generate the puzzle. Peter (as we may as well say now) may learn the name 'Paderewski' with an identification of the person named as a famous pianist. Naturally, having learned this, Peter will assent to "Paderewski had musical talent," and *we* can infer—using 'Paderewski,' as we usually do, to name the Polish musician and statesman:

(8) Peter believes that Paderewski had musical talent.

Only the disquotational principle is necessary for our inference; no translation is required. Later, in a different circle, Peter learns of someone called 'Paderewski' who was a Polish nationalist leader and Prime Minister. Peter is skeptical of the musical abilities of politicians. He concludes that probably two people, approximate contemporaries no doubt, were both named 'Paderewski.' Using 'Paderewski' as a name for the *statesman*, Peter assents to, "Paderewski had no musical talent." Should we infer, by the disquotational principle,

(9) Peter believes that Paderewski had no musical talent

or should we not? If Peter had not had the past history of learning the name 'Paderewski' in another way, we certainly would judge him to be using 'Paderewski' in a normal way, with the normal reference, and we would infer (9) by the disquotational principle. The situation is parallel to the problem with Pierre and London. Here, however, no restriction that names should not be translated, but should be phonetically repeated in the translation, can help us. Only a single language and a single name are involved. If any notion of translation is involved in this example, it is homophonic translation. Only the disquotational principle is used explicitly.[37] (On the other hand, the original 'two languages' case had the advantage that it would apply even if we spoke languages in which all names must denote uniquely and unambiguously.) The restriction that names must not be translated is thus ineffective, as well as implausible and drastic.

I close this section with some remarks on the relation of the present puzzle to Quine's doctrine of the 'indeterminacy of translation,' with its attendant repudiation of intensional idioms of 'propositional attitude' such as belief and even indirect quotation. To a sympathizer with these doctrines the present puzzle may

---

[37] One might argue that Peter and we do speak different dialects, since in Peter's idiolect 'Paderewski' is used ambiguously as a name for a musician and a statesman (even though these are in fact the same), while in our language it is used unambiguously for a musician-statesman. The problem then would be whether Peter's dialect can be translated homophonically into our own. Before he hears of 'Paderewski-the-statesman,' it would appear that the answer is affirmative for his (then unambiguous) use of 'Paderewski,' since he did not differ from anyone who happens to have heard of Paderewski's musical achievements but not of his statesmanship. Similarly for his later use of 'Paderewski,' if we ignore his earlier use. The problem is like Pierre's, and is essentially the same whether we describe it in terms of whether Peter satisfies the condition for the disquotational principle to be applicable, or whether homophonic translation of his dialect into our own is legitimate.

well seem to be just more grist for a familiar mill. The situation of the puzzle seems to lead to a breakdown of our normal practices of attributing belief and even of indirect quotation. No obvious paradox arises if we describe the same situation in terms of Pierre's sincere assent to various sentences, together with the conditions under which he has learned the name in question. Such a description, although it does not yet conform to Quine's strict behavioristic standards, fits in well with his view that in some sense direct quotation is a more 'objective' idiom than the propositional attitudes. Even those who, like the present writer, do not find Quine's negative attitude to the attitudes completely attractive must surely acknowledge this.

But although sympathizers with Quine's view can use the present examples to support it, the differences between these examples and the considerations Quine adduces for his own skepticism about belief and translation should not escape us. Here we make no use of hypothetical exotic systems of translation differing radically from the usual one, translating '*lapin*,' say, as 'rabbit stage' or 'undetached part of a rabbit.' The problem arises entirely within our usual and customary system of translation of French into English; in one case, the puzzle arose even within English alone, using at most 'homophonic' translation. Nor is the problem that many different interpretations or translations fit our usual criteria, that, in Davidson's phrase,[38] there is more than one 'way of getting it right.' The trouble here is not that many views as to Pierre's beliefs get it right, but that they all definitely get it *wrong*. A straightforward application of the principles of translation and disquotation to all Pierre's utterances, French and English, yields the result that Pierre holds inconsistent beliefs, that logic alone should teach him that one of his beliefs is false. Intuitively, this is plainly incorrect. If we refuse to apply the principles to his French utterances at all, we would conclude that Pierre never believed that London is pretty, even though, before his unpredictable move, he was like any other monolingual Frenchman. This is absurd. If we refuse to ascribe the belief in London's pulchritude only after Pierre's move to England, we get the counterintuitive result that Pierre has changed his mind, and so on. But we have surveyed the possibilities above: the point was not that they are 'equally good,' but that all are *obviously wrong*. If the puzzle is to be used as an argument for a Quinean position, it is an argument of a fundamentally different kind from those given before. And even Quine, if he wishes to incorporate the notion of belief even into a 'second level' of canonical notation,[39] must regard the puzzle as a real problem.

---

[38] D. Davidson, "On Saying That," in: *Words and Objections*, D. Davidson and J. Hintikka (eds.), Dordrecht, Reidel, 1969, p. 166.

[39] In *Word and Object*, p. 221, Quine advocates a second level of canonical notation, "to dissolve verbal perplexities or facilitate logical deductions," admitting the propositional attitudes, even though he thinks them "baseless" idioms that should be excluded from a notation "limning the true and ultimate structure of reality."

The alleged indeterminacy of translation and indirect quotation causes relatively little trouble for such a scheme for belief; the embarrassment it presents to such a scheme is, after all, one of riches. But the present puzzle indicates that the usual principles we use to ascribe beliefs are apt, in certain cases, to lead to contradiction, or at least, patent falsehoods. So it presents a problem for any project, Quinean or other, that wishes to deal with the 'logic' of belief on any level.[40]

IV. CONCLUSION

What morals can be drawn? The primary moral—quite independent of any of the discussion of the first two sections—is that the puzzle *is* a puzzle. As any theory of truth must deal with the Liar Paradox, so any theory of belief and names must deal with this puzzle.

But our theoretical starting point in the first two sections concerned proper names and belief. Let us return to Jones, who assents to "Cicero was bald" and to "Tully was not bald." Philosophers, using the disquotational principle, have concluded that Jones believes that Cicero was bald but that Tully was not. Hence, they have concluded, since Jones does not have contradictory beliefs, belief contexts are not 'Shakespearean' in Geach's sense: codesignative proper names are not interchangeable in these contexts *salva veritate*.[41]

I think the puzzle about Pierre shows that the simple conclusion was unwarranted. Jones's situation strikingly resembles Pierre's. A proposal that 'Cicero'

---

[40] In one respect the considerations mentioned above on natural kinds show that Quine's translation apparatus is insufficiently skeptical. Quine is sure that the native's *sentence* "Gavagai!" should be translated "Lo, a rabbit!", provided that its affirmative and negative stimulus meanings for the native match those of the English sentence for the Englishman; skepticism sets in only when the linguist proposes to translate the *general term* 'gavagai' as 'rabbit' rather than 'rabbit stage,' 'rabbit part,' and the like. But there is another possibility that is independent of (and less bizarre than) such skeptical alternatives. In the geographical area inhabited by the natives, there may be a species indistinguishable to the nonzoologist from rabbits but forming a distinct species. Then the 'stimulus meanings,' in Quine's sense, of 'Lo, a rabbit!' and 'Gavagai!' may well be identical (to nonzoologists), especially if the ocular irradiations in question do not include a specification of the geographical locality. ('Gavagais' produce the same ocular irradiation patterns as rabbits.) Yet 'Gavagai!' and 'Lo, a rabbit!' are hardly synonymous; on typical occasions they will have opposite truth values.

I believe that the considerations about names, let alone natural kinds, emphasized in *Naming and Necessity* go against any simple attempt to base interpretation solely on maximizing agreement with the affirmations attributed to the native, matching of stimulus meanings, etc. The 'Principle of Charity' on which such methodologies are based was first enunciated by Neil Wilson in the special case of proper names as a formulation of the cluster-of-descriptions theory. The argument of *Naming and Necessity* is thus directed against the simple 'Principle of Charity' for that case.

[41] Geach introduced the term 'Shakespearean' after the line, "a rose / By any other name, would smell as sweet."

Quine seems to define 'referentially transparent' contexts so as to imply that coreferential names and definite descriptions must be interchangeable *salva veritate*. Geach stresses that a context may be 'Shakespearean' but not 'referentially transparent' in this sense.

and 'Tully' *are* interchangeable amounts roughly to a homophonic 'translation' of English into itself in which 'Cicero' is mapped into 'Tully' and *vice versa*, while the rest is left fixed. Such a 'translation' can, indeed, be used to obtain a paradox. But should the problem be blamed on this step? Ordinarily we would suppose without question that sentences in French with '*Londres*' should be translated into English with 'London.' Yet the same paradox results when we apply this translation too. We have seen that the problem can even arise with a single name in a single language, and that it arises with natural kind terms in two languages (or one: see below).

Intuitively, Jones's assent to both 'Cicero was bald' and 'Tully was not bald' arises from sources of just the same kind as Pierre's assent to both '*Londres est jolie*' and 'London is not pretty.'

It is wrong to blame unpalatable conclusions about Jones on substitutivity. The reason does not lie in any specific fallacy in the argument but rather in the nature of the realm being entered. Jones's case is just like Pierre's: both are in an area where our normal practices of attributing belief, based on the principles of disquotation and translation or on similar principles, are questionable.

It should be noted in this connection that the principles of disquotation and translation can lead to 'proofs' as well as 'disproofs' of substitutivity in belief contexts. In Hebrew there are two names for Germany, transliteratable roughly as '*Ashkenaz*' and '*Germaniah*'—the first of these may be somewhat archaic. When Hebrew sentences are translated into English, both become 'Germany.' Plainly a normal Hebrew speaker analogous to Jones might assent to a Hebrew sentence involving '*Ashkenaz*' while dissenting from its counterpart with '*Germaniah*.' So far there is an argument *against* substitutivity. But there is also an argument *for* substitutivity, based on the principle of translation. Translate a Hebrew sentence involving '*Ashkenaz*' into English, so that '*Ashkenaz*' goes into 'Germany.' Then retranslate the result into Hebrew, this time translating 'Germany' as '*Germaniah*.' By the principle of translation, both translations preserve truth value. So: the truth value of any sentence of Hebrew involving '*Ashkenaz*' remains the same when '*Ashkenaz*' is replaced by '*Germaniah*'—a 'proof' of substitutivity! A similar 'proof' can be provided wherever there are two names in one language, and a normal practice of translating both indifferently into a single name of another language.[42] (If we combine the 'proof' and 'disproof' of

---

[42] Generally such cases may be slightly less watertight than the 'London'–'*Londres*' case. '*Londres*' just is the French version of 'London,' while one cannot quite say that the same relation holds between '*Ashkenaz*' and '*Germaniah*.' Nevertheless:

(a) Our standard practice in such cases is to translate both names of the first language into the single name of the second.

(b) Often no nuances of 'meaning' are discernible differentiating such names as '*Ashkenaz*' and '*Germaniah*,' such that we would not say either that Hebrew would have been impoverished had it lacked one of them (or that English is improverished because it has only one name for Germany), any more than a language is impoverished if it has only one word corresponding to

substitutivity in this paragraph, we could get yet another paradox analogous to Pierre's: our Hebrew speaker both believes, and disbelieves, that Germany is pretty. Yet no amount of pure logic or semantic introspection suffices for him to discover his error.)

Another consideration, regarding natural kinds: Previously we pointed out that a bilingual may learn '*lapin*' and 'rabbit' normally in each respective language yet wonder whether they are one species or two, and that this fact can be used to generate a paradox analogous to Pierre's. Similarly, a speaker of *English* alone may learn 'furze' and 'gorse' normally (separately), yet wonder whether these are the same, or resembling kinds. (What about 'rabbit' and 'hare'?) It would be easy for such a speaker to assent to an assertion formulated with 'furze' but withhold assent from the corresponding assertion involving 'gorse.' The situation is quite analogous to that of Jones with respect to 'Cicero' and 'Tully.' Yet 'furze' and 'gorse,' and other pairs of terms for the same natural kind, are normally thought of as *synonyms*.

The point is *not*, of course, that codesignative proper names *are* interchangeable in belief contexts *salva veritate*, or that they *are* interchangeable in simple contexts even *salva significatione*. The point is that the absurdities that disquotation plus substitutivity would generate are exactly paralleled by absurdities generated by disquotation plus translation, or even 'disquotation alone' (or: disquotation plus homophonic translation). Also, though our naive practice may lead to 'disproofs' of substitutivity in certain cases, it can also lead to 'proofs' of substitutivity in some of these same cases, as we saw two paragraphs back. When we enter into the area exemplified by Jones and Pierre, we enter into an area where our normal practices of interpretation and attribution of belief are subjected to the greatest possible strain, perhaps to the point of breakdown. So is the notion of the *content* of someone's assertion, the *proposition* it expresses. In the present state of our knowledge, I think it would be foolish to draw any conclusion, positive or negative, about substitutivity.[43]

'doctor' and 'physician.' Given this, it seems hard to condemn our practice of translating both names as 'Germany' as 'loose'; in fact, it would seem that Hebrew just has two names for the same country where English gets by with one.

(c) Any inclinations to avoid problems by declaring, say, the translation of '*Ashkenaz*' as 'Germany' to be loose should be considerably tempered by the discussion of analogous problems in the text.

[43] In spite of this official view, perhaps I will be more assertive elsewhere.
In the case of 'Hesperus' and 'Phosphorus' (in contrast to 'Cicero' and 'Tully'), where there is a case for the existence of conventional community-wide 'senses' differentiating the two—at least, two distinct modes of 'fixing the reference of two rigid designators'—it is more plausible to suppose that the two names are definitely not interchangeable in belief contexts. According to such a supposition, a belief that Hesperus is a planet is a belief that a certain heavenly body, rigidly picked out as seen in the evening in the appropriate season, is a planet; and similarly for Phosphorus. One may argue that translation problems like Pierre's will be blocked in this case, that '*Vesper*' must be translated as 'Hesperus,' not as 'Phosphorus.' As against this, however, two things:

Of course nothing in these considerations prevents us from observing that Jones can sincerely assert both "Cicero is bald" and "Tully is not bald," even though he is a normal speaker of English and uses 'Cicero' and 'Tully' in normal ways, and with the normal referent. Pierre and the other paradoxical cases can be described similarly. (For those interested in one of my own doctrines, we can still say that there was a time when men were in no epistemic position to assent to 'Hesperus is Phosphorus' for want of empirical information, but it nevertheless expressed a necessary truth.)[44] But it is no surprise that quoted contexts fail to satisfy a substitutivity principle within the quotation marks. And, in our *present* state of clarity about the problem, we are in no position to apply a disquotation principle to these cases, nor to judge when two such sentences do, or do not, express the same 'proposition.'

Nothing in the discussion impugns the conventional judgment that belief contexts are 'referentially opaque,' if 'referential opacity' is construed so that failure of coreferential *definite descriptions* to be interchangeable *salva veritate* is sufficient for referential opacity. No doubt Jones can believe that the number of planets is even, without believing that the square of three is even, if he is under a misapprehension about the astronomical, but not the arithmetical facts. The question at hand was whether belief contexts were 'Shakespearean,' not whether

---

(a) We should remember that sameness of properties used to fix the reference does *not* appear to guarantee in general that paradoxes will not arise. So one may be reluctant to adopt a solution in terms of reference-fixing properties for this case if it does not get to the heart of the general problem.

(b) The main issue seems to me here to be—how essential is a particular mode of fixing the reference to a correct learning of the name? If a parent, aware of the familiar identity, takes a child into the fields in the morning and says (pointing to the morning star) "That is called 'Hesperus,'" has the parent mistaught the language? (A parent who says, "Creatures with kidneys are called 'cordates,' definitely has mistaught the language, even though the statement is extensionally correct.) To the extent that it is *not* crucial for correct language learning that a particular mode of fixing the reference be used, to that extent there is no 'mode of presentation' differentiating the 'content' of a belief about 'Hesperus' from one about 'Phosphorus.' I am doubtful that the original method of fixing the reference *must* be preserved in transmission of the name.

If the mode of reference fixing *is* crucial, it can be maintained that otherwise identical beliefs expressed with 'Hesperus' and with 'Phosphorus' have definite differences of 'content,' at least in an epistemic sense. The conventional ruling against substitutivity could thus be maintained without qualms for some cases, though not as obviously for others, such as 'Cicero' and 'Tully.' But it is unclear to me whether even 'Hesperus' and 'Phosphorus' do have such conventional 'modes of presentation.' I need not take a definite stand, and the verdict may be different for different particular pairs of names. For a brief related discussion, see *Naming and Necessity*, p. 78.

[44] However, some earlier formulations expressed disquotationally such as "It was once unknown that Hesperus is Phosphorus" are questionable in the light of the present paper (but see the previous note for this case). I was aware of this question by the time *Naming and Necessity* was written, but I did not wish to muddy the waters further than necessary at that time. I regarded the distinction between epistemic and metaphysical necessity as valid in any case and adequate for the distinctions I wished to make. The considerations in this chapter are relevant to the earlier discussion of the 'contingent *a priori*' as well; perhaps I will discuss this elsewhere. (For discussion, see Chapter 10.)

they were 'referentially transparent.' (Modal contexts, in my opinion, are 'Shakespearean' but 'referentially opaque.')[45]

Even were we inclined to rule that belief contexts are not Shakespearean, it would be implausible at present to use the phenomenon to support a Frege-Russellian theory that names have descriptive 'senses' through 'uniquely identifying properties.' There are the well-known arguments against description theories, independent of the present discussion; there is the implausibility of the view that difference in names is difference in idiolect; and finally, there are the arguments of the present chapter that differences of associated properties do not explain the problems in any case. Given these considerations, and the cloud our paradox places over the notion of 'content' in this area, the relation of substitutivity to the dispute between Millian and Fregean conclusions is not very clear.

We repeat our conclusions: Philosophers have often, basing themselves on Jones's and similar cases, supposed that it goes virtually without saying that belief contexts are not 'Shakespearean.' I think that, at present, such a definite conclusion is unwarranted. Rather Jones's case, like Pierre's, lies in an area where our normal apparatus for the ascription of belief is placed under the greatest strain and may even break down. There is even less warrant at the present time, in the absence of a better understanding of the paradoxes of this paper, for the use of alleged failures of substitutivity in belief contexts to draw any significant theoretical conclusion about proper names. Hard cases make bad law.[46]

---

[45] According to Russell, definite descriptions are not genuine singular terms. He thus would have regarded any concept of 'referential opacity' that includes definite descriptions as profoundly misleading. He also maintained a substitutivity principle for 'logically proper names' in belief and other attitudinal contexts, so that for him belief contexts were as 'transparent,' in any philosophically decent sense, as truth-functional contexts.

Independently of Russell's views, there is much to be said for the opinion that the question whether a context is 'Shakespearean' is more important philosophically—even for many purposes for which Quine invokes his own concept—than whether it is 'referentially opaque.'

[46] I will make some brief remarks about the relation of Benson Mates's problem (see note 15) to the present one. Mates argued that such a sentence as (*)'Some doubt that all who believe that doctors are happy believe that physicians are happy,' may be true, even though 'doctors' and 'physicians' are synonymous, and even though it would have been false had 'physicians' been replaced in it by a second occurrence of 'doctors.' Church countered that (*) could not be true, since its translation into a language with only one word for doctors (which would translate both 'doctors' and 'physicians') would be false. If *both* Mates's and Church's intuitions were correct, we might get a paradox analogous to Pierre's.

Applying the principles of translation and disquotation to Mates's puzzle, however, involves many more complications than our present problem. First, if someone assents to 'Doctors are happy,' but refuses assent to 'Physicians are happy,' *prima facie* disquotation does not apply to him since he is under a linguistic or conceptual confusion. (See note 23.) So there are as yet no grounds, merely because this happened, to doubt that all who believe that doctors are happy believe that physicians are happy.

Now suppose someone assents to 'Not all who believe that doctors are happy believe that physicians are happy.' What is the source of his assent? If it is failure to realize that 'doctors' and 'physicians' are synonymous (this was the situation Mates originally envisaged), then he is under a linguistic or conceptual confusion, so disquotation does not clearly apply. Hence we have no reason to conclude from this case that (*) is true. Alternatively, he may realize that 'doctors' and 'physicians' are synonymous; but he applies disquotation to a man who assents to 'Doctors are happy' but not to 'Physicians are happy,' ignoring the caution of the previous paragraph. Here he is not under a simple linguistic confusion (such as failure to realize that 'doctors' and 'physicians' are synonymous), but he appears to be under a deep conceptual confusion (misapplication of the disquotational principle). Perhaps, it may be argued, he misunderstands the 'logic of belief.' Does his conceptual confusion mean that we cannot straightforwardly apply disquotation to his utterance, and that therefore we cannot conclude from his behavior that (*) is true? I think that, although the issues are delicate, and I am not at present completely sure what answers to give, there is a case for an affirmative answer. (Compare the more extreme case of someone who is so confused that he thinks that someone's *dissent* from 'Doctors are happy' implies that he believes that doctors are happy. If someone's utterance, 'Many believe that doctors are happy,' is based on such a misapplication of disquotation, surely we in turn should not apply disquotation to it. The utterer, at least in this context, does not really know what 'belief' means.)

I do *not* believe the discussion above ends the matter. Perhaps I can discuss Mates's problem at greater length elsewhere. Mates's problem is perplexing, and its relation to the present puzzle is interesting. But it should be clear from the preceding that Mates's argument involves issues even more delicate than those that arise with respect to Pierre. First, Mates's problem involves delicate issues regarding iteration of belief contexts, whereas the puzzle about Pierre involves the application of disquotation only to affirmations of (or assents to) *simple* sentences. More important, Mates's problem would not arise in a world where no one ever was under a linguistic or a conceptual confusion, no one ever thought anyone else was under such a confusion, no one ever thought anyone ever thought anyone was under such a confusion, and so on. It is important, both for the puzzle about Pierre and for the Fregean argument that 'Cicero' and 'Tully' differ in 'sense,' that they would still arise in such a world. They are entirely free of the delicate problem of applying disquotation to utterances directly or indirectly based on the existence of linguistic confusion. See notes 15 and 28, and the discussion in the text of Pierre's logical consistency.

Another problem discussed in the literature to which the present considerations may be relevant is that of 'self-consciousness,' or the peculiarity of 'I.' Discussions of this problem have emphasized that 'I,' even when Mary Smith uses it, is not interchangeable with 'Mary Smith,' nor with any other conventional singular term designating Mary Smith. If she is 'not aware that she is Mary Smith,' she may assent to a sentence with 'I,' but dissent from the corresponding sentence with 'Mary Smith.' It is quite possible that any attempt to clear up the logic of all this will involve itself in the problem of the present chapter. (For this purpose, the present discussion might be extended to demonstratives and indexicals.) (For discussion, see Chapter 10.)

The writing of this chapter had partial support from a grant from the National Science Foundation, a John Simon Guggenheim Foundation Fellowship, a Visiting Fellowship at All Souls College, Oxford, and a sabbatical leave from Princeton University. Various people at the Jerusalem Encounter and elsewhere, who will not be enumerated, influenced the paper through discussion.

7
Nozick on Knowledge*

1. A COUNTERFACTUAL ANALYSIS OF KNOWLEDGE

Like many other recent theorists, Robert Nozick advocates what has been called an "externalist," or "reliabilist," analysis of knowledge.[1] In his text Nozick states his indebtedness to those philosophers, such as Alvin Goldman, who give causal accounts of knowledge (Goldman 1967). His own contribution is to abandon causation in favor of a counterfactual analysis, which, he believes, will allow a uniform treatment of mathematical and ethical knowledge along with the straightforward empirical cases that seem to be more readily amenable to a causal analysis. However, as Nozick acknowledges in a footnote (689, note 53), actually he has rediscovered an approach that was in the published literature at least a decade before his book appeared. Among recent writers, Nozick mentions Fred Dretske, L. S. Carrier, David Armstrong, and Goldman himself; and there are others.[2] Carrier's formulation is a counterfactual theory very similar to Nozick's. Dretske's theory, which had already been developed in extensive detail, resembles Nozick

---

* This manuscript was prepared in 1986 for a review of Robert Nozick's *Philosophical Explanations* (Nozick 1981; page references without specification will always be to this book). I decided to concentrate on his treatment of knowledge, which was probably the most professionally influential part of the book. However, as is obvious, the result became very long for a conventional review. Many revisions and improvements have been made for the present version, although, except where I explicitly note otherwise, the basic ideas were in the original. The sheer detail and volume of the criticisms may actually make the points harder to grasp; I hope they don't create a problem of "background noise"! (689, note 53).

Throughout this paper I use ordinary quotation even when, according to Quine, technically I should use his corners. I do not think the reader will be confused.

Let me end this initial footnote with a tribute to Bob Nozick, and remark on the loss to philosophy that his early death meant to those of us who knew him. One had to experience his exceptional and extraordinary skills as a discussant and dialectician to realize exactly how great the loss was.

[1] The second characterization is qualified below.

[2] See 689, note 53, for the references. (Shatz, cited below, says that the ranks of theorists with views similar to Dretske "have swelled so greatly that a full listing would be impossible" [1981:406]; in addition to those already listed, he mentions A. J. Holland.) According to Nozick, Goldman's own paper using counterfactuals (Goldman 1976) appeared after Nozick's basic work had been completed.

even more closely. Two of its basic elements—an analysis of knowledge in terms of counterfactuals and a denial that knowledge is closed under known logical implication (as an answer to the skeptic)[3]—are identical to the basic elements of Nozick's theory. Moreover, some of Nozick's predecessors (Dretske and Goldman, in particular) have noted some significant problems that Nozick overlooks.[4]

Nozick gives four individually necessary and jointly sufficient conditions for a person S to know that p:

(1) p is true
(2) S believes that p
(3) If p weren't true, S wouldn't believe that p
(4) If p were true, S would believe that p

Condition 3 is supposed to be violated if S *might* have believed that p, (even) if p were false; it is not required for a violation to occur that S definitely *would* have believed that p. (This view agrees with David Lewis (1973), as against Robert Stalnaker (1968);[5] Nozick does not mention that he is taking sides on a question controversial in the literature, but here we will stipulatively assume that counterfactuals are to be interpreted in the manner suggested.) Condition 4 involves more problems of interpretation and will be discussed below. (Actually, to exclude contradictory beliefs about p, Nozick amends condition 4 so that its consequent reads "S would believe that p and would not believe that not p." Ordinarily, this amendment is irrelevant to the discussion, and I will follow Nozick and ignore it. Aside from the major modification involving "holding the method fixed" that I explain immediately below, Nozick mentions other tentative possible modifications later in the chapter. I will cite these only when they seem relevant.) When the third and fourth conditions hold, Nozick says that S's belief that p *tracks* the fact that p. This notion of "tracking" is the key to Nozick's analysis of knowledge, and is closely connected with ideas that Nozick applies elsewhere in the book, notably to his analysis of free will.

---

[3] I first heard this answer to the skeptic in question in a paper, or perhaps an informal presentation, given at Berkeley to a group of assistant professors there, by Thompson Clarke. My best guess for the time of the talk is the spring of 1965, but almost surely in the period 1963–66. As far as I know, the paper has never been published. This paper and the accompanying discussion gave as convincing support as I have heard for the idea that skepticism is to be overcome by denying that known logical implication preserves knowledge.

However, I myself certainly do not wish to endorse this strategy myself. The tangles Nozick gets into, and the way his intuitions actually conflict with his predecessor Dretske, in and of itself might indicate that this approach runs into trouble. Moreover, I am sympathetic to those philosophers who regard this idea as intrinsically implausible or even preposterous. But I am not going to presuppose such a strong rejection of the strategy in the discussion below.

[4] See Goldman (1976) and Dretske (1970, 1971). For Goldman, see, for example, my section 8 below.

[5] It might be noted that Stalnaker later proposed a supervaluationist interpretation of his view that might make it in effect closer to Lewis's, even though formally it would still differ in the way suggested in the text. See also the survey article in Harper (1981).

Nozick fails to note one amusing fact. Given his last two conditions, either one of the first two can be dropped. For, whatever else we believe about counterfactual logic, surely counterfactuals imply the corresponding material conditionals; in particular, (3) and (4) do. But then, obviously, (1) and (4) jointly entail (2); and (2) and (3) jointly entail (1).[6] Hence both (1), (3), (4), and (2), (3), (4) are equivalent to the original redundant set.[7] Nevertheless, we will normally follow Nozick and refer to the redundant formulation with four conditions.

Counterexamples lead Nozick to modify these beguilingly simple conditions, and to define a technical locution—*S* knows, via method M, that *p*—iff (1) holds[8] and:

(2′) *S* believes, via method M, that *p*.
(3′) If *p* weren't true and *S* were to use M to arrive at a belief whether (or not) *p*, then *S* wouldn't believe, via M, that *p*.
(4′) If *p* were true and *S* were to use M ... (as in 3′), then *S* would believe, via M, that *p*.

If *S* arrives at his belief that *p* using only one method M, then Nozick says that *S* knows that *p* iff *S* knows that *p* via M. Nozick's treatment of more complicated cases, where *S*'s belief is "overdetermined" by more than one method, will be discussed later; but usually it suffices to consider the simple case of only one method.

The revised account is meant to eliminate counterexamples like this: "A grandmother sees her grandson is well when he comes to visit; but if he were sick or dead, others would tell her he was well to spare her upset" (179). The original condition 3 is violated, but surely the grandmother knows that her grandson is well. The counterexample disappears if we "hold the method fixed": since the grandmother comes to believe her grandson is well by the method M of looking at him when he visits, the revised version 3′ would be violated only if her powers of observation were so poor that she would have believed, using that method, the he was well even if he were sick.

The problem was that although the grandmother actually used the method M of looking at her grandson to see whether he was well (*p*), if *p* had not been true, M would not have been used, and another method M′ would have been

---

[6] If there are any "relevance logicians" among the readers of the present paper, then one would have to note that the counterfactuals presumably imply the corresponding relevant conditionals.

[7] Michael Levin has called my attention to the fact that Luper (2004) also notes that (1) is redundant. I am relying on Levin for my information; I confess that, as of this time, I have not read Luper.

Nozick's way of putting the matter, in spite of the redundancies, is natural. It is an answer to the question: what conditions are needed to make a true belief into knowledge? Then the additional conditions are given in terms of counterfactuals. Probably this is why Nozick did not notice the redundancies.

[8] Actually, since (1) follows from (2′) and (3′), it can be dropped. Alternatively, given (1) and (4′), (2′) could be weakened to "*S* uses M to arrive at a belief whether *p*."

used in its place. Condition 3′ avoids the problem by stipulating in its antecedent that we are concerned with counterfactual situations where *p* is false but nevertheless M is used. (Carrier seems to give essentially the simple formulation that Nozick abandons here; Dretske seems to avoid such counterexamples by a different, though related, device.) I will follow Nozick (185) in mentioning the revised formulation only when it seems to cause confusion not to do so. Often the reader can simply verify for herself that the discussion does indeed "hold the method fixed."[9]

For future reference, I add two comments Nozick makes about method. First, Nozick writes that:

> [A]ny method experientially the same, the same "from the inside," will count as the same method. Basing our beliefs on experiences, you and I and the person floating in the tank are using, for these purposes, the same method. (184–85)

While Nozick's concept of knowledge is radically "externalist," his concept of method is "internalist." Second, under the influence of Wittgenstein (1969), Nozick thinks that some statements whose "centrality ensures that they will not escape notice" (185) regardless of the application of any particular methods, are best regarded as believed independently of any particular method(s). (Examples he gives are "I have two hands" and "the world has existed for many years already.") For these beliefs, Nozick recommends that we revert to the simple conditions 3 and 4.[10] Only for conclusions that would not have been drawn had I not applied some particular method or methods (even if the method were as simple as merely looking in front of me) do we need to use the more complicated 3′ and 4′. (Even in such cases, as we just said, in practice it often causes no confusion to replace 3′ and 4′ by 3 and 4.)

2. RELEVANT ALTERNATIVES AND NOZICK'S THIRD CONDITION

Condition 3 or 3′ (which has parallels in Dretske and Carrier) is Nozick's most important condition. Very early in his discussion, Nozick claims that condition 3 takes care of cases for which others have invoked the need to rule out "relevant alternatives." He quotes Gail Caldwell Stine's discussion, commenting principally

---

[9] But I am writing as if the idea of "holding the method fixed" is a clear one, when, in fact, as I remark below, I am not so sure it always is.

[10] However, Wittgenstein (1969) may be reluctant to call these basic framework propositions "knowledge," and, if so, Nozick may not be following him. On this possible difference between Wittgenstein and Nozick, my own sympathies are with Nozick.

Nozick should have mentioned that the two examples he gives come from Moore (1925) and (1939). These papers were important sources for Wittgenstein (1969).

on Goldman and Dretske, but also others, of an example she attributes to Carl Ginet:[11]

> [W]hat makes an alternative relevant in one context and not another? ... if on the basis of visual appearances obtained under optimum conditions while driving through the countryside Henry identifies an object as a barn, normally we say that Henry knows that it is a barn. Let us suppose, however, that unknown to Henry, the region is full of expertly made papier-mâché facsimiles of barns.[12] In that case, we would not say that Henry knows that the object is a barn, unless he has evidence against it being a papier-mâché facsimile, which is now a relevant alternative. So much is clear, but what if no such facsimiles exist in Henry's surroundings, although they [do in Sweden? What if they do not now exist in Sweden, but they] once did? Are either of these circumstances sufficient to make the hypothesis (that it's a papier-mâché object) relevant? Probably not, but the situation is not so clear. (Stine 1976:252)[13]

Nozick argues that condition 3 gives a precise formulation that handles this range of cases. For example, if, unknown to Henry, papier-mâché barns abound in the area, then even if there had been no (genuine) barn in the field, Henry might have believed that there was (owing to the presence of a counterfeit). So condition 3 is violated, and Henry does not know that there is a real barn in the field. On the other hand, if the area is a normal one without papier-mâché barns, then condition 3 is satisfied. If there had been no barn in the field, there would have been no counterfeit in its place, so Henry would not have judged that there

---

[11] Stine heard a version of Goldman's paper read in 1973 (see Stine 1976:252, and her note 1), which she says attributed the example to Carl Ginet. Goldman's paper later appeared in print (1976). Goldman calls the subject "Henry," and Stine follows him, as will I.

[12] Actually, Goldman (1976:773) emphasizes that "these facsimiles look from the road exactly like barns, but are really just façades, without back walls or interiors, quite incapable of being used as barns." They might just as well have been made of real wood, and they would have been equally deceptive. The material of which they are made is not really the main point. Nevertheless, both Goldman and, following him, Stine uses the term "papier-mâché facsimiles," and therefore I, too, use this terminology.

[13] Quoted by Nozick (174–75). Nozick's quotation inadvertently omits the words in square brackets, so that the passage has an apparent different sense and it is somewhat garbled. What are "either of these circumstances?" As quoted by Nozick, there is only one, viz., that the false barns used to be in Henry's surroundings, but are there no longer. Stine originally intended two other cases, that there are false barns in Sweden, though not in Henry's surroundings (probably in the United States), or that there used to be false barns in Sweden, but that they disappeared there. No doubt the case where there used to be false barns in Henry's surroundings, but they are there no longer, is also an interesting one; but Nozick's later discussion explicitly refers to "another country" where the papier-mâché barns are or were scattered.

One should add that the problem about the barns being in Sweden, not just the basic example, already appeared in Goldman (1976:775). Note also that Goldman, like Nozick, assumes that the presence of barn facsimiles in the area implies a counterfactual about the particular field Henry is looking at: "But if the object on that site were a facsimile, Henry would mistake it for a barn" (773). We will see immediately that the presence of counterfeit barns in the area does not imply that one might have been on this particular field. However, Goldman goes on to emphasize that the bearing of the facsimiles on the case is that they create a relevant alternative, and does not attempt to reduce this notion to counterfactuals (775). He makes quite different remarks about the case of Sweden (775–76), rather than attempting to define relevant alternatives in terms of counterfactuals.

was a barn in the field. Nozick claims that whether false barns are or were in another country (Sweden) is plainly irrelevant.[14] In those cases where Stine thinks that a "relevant alternatives" account gives unclear results, we supposedly have clear intuitions about condition 3. Nozick thinks condition 3 can replace "relevant alternatives" throughout; he writes:

Thus, condition 3 handles cases that befuddle the "relevant alternatives" account; though that account can adopt the above subjunctive criterion for when an alternative is relevant, it then becomes merely an alternate and longer way of stating condition 3. (175)[15]

It seems to me that Nozick is quite wrong about this; his third condition does not capture the idea of "relevant alternatives," even in the very case of the barn. It is not difficult to adapt counterexamples noted already by David Shatz (1981) and even Fred Dretske (1971)[16] (in his original paper on his own counterfactual account theory of knowledge) to show this. Let us suppose that papier-mâché barns are indeed prevalent in the area, but that they cannot be built on a few exceptional fields with unfavorable soil conditions. Suppose Henry knows nothing of the papier-mâché barns, nor of the soil conditions, nor of their relevance to the feasibility of building a counterfeit barn. He naively looks at a field with a real barn on it, whose soil conditions in fact would not have supported a

---

[14] In terms of Nozick's counterfactual formulation (condition 3), is it so clear what is relevant? Suppose that there are no counterfeit barns in the area, but that there are in a nearby area, and only by accident did Henry (driving around) arrive at this area rather than the neighboring one. Then again, what if Henry accidentally called off a trip to Sweden at the last minute? What if the farmers in this area were considering whether to follow the Swedish example, but decided at the last minute not to do so? I don't need to take a stand on all these questions, but Nozick is surely being too quick when he claims that his counterfactual formulation shows that the presence of facsimiles in another country is irrelevant. Nozick must show that in these cases, too, his counterfactual formulation captures our intuitions (of course, I think it doesn't anyway).

[15] If we agree with Nozick on this point, does this not show decisively that the relevant-alternatives account should be replaced by the account in terms of condition 3? Does this not "coerce" the relevant-alternatives theorist into abandoning his theory in favor of a counterfactual account? See Nozick's introduction (4–8) for his attack on "coercive philosophy." This, of course, is just one of many examples of Nozick's own argumentation that make it questionable that he is really following his own precepts.

There is a minor problem. Nozick, as quoted, says that condition 3 handles cases that "befuddle the 'relevant alternatives' account," and goes on to say that "that account can adopt the above subjunctive criterion" for when an alternative is relevant, and so on as quoted. Here he seems to regard the subjunctive condition as a novel replacement for the relevant-alternatives account, but elsewhere (689, note 53) he attributes to Dretske exactly the counterfactual definition of when an alternative is relevant. Since it is likely that Dretske's paper introduced the idea of relevant alternatives into the literature, this would mean that the counterfactual formulation is what "relevant alternatives" meant all along. I will not pursue this question, but the arguments below, following Shatz, seem to me to establish that the counterfactual formulation does not capture the intuitive idea of eliminating relevant alternatives.

[16] Although Shatz's paper appeared before Nozick's book was published, it appeared too late for Nozick to take it into account.

Both papers are well worth reading for the type of counterexample discussed here. Shatz's paper includes much interesting material that I do not reproduce in detail.

papier-mâché counterfeit, and judges that there is a barn in the field. Condition 3 is satisfied, since, had there been no real barn there, there would not have been a counterfeit in its place, and Henry would not have believed that there was a barn there. (Note that "the method is held fixed.") Yet the same intuitions that would lead someone to deny in the original case that Henry knows that there is a barn in the field also apply in this modified case; the soil conditions, which Henry has never heard about, can hardly help. Not only does condition 3 not handle this case, as Nozick thought, but condition 4 is also satisfied. I will discuss the interpretation of condition 4 below, but already at this point it should be clear that if it holds in a normal countryside (without papier-mâché barns), it holds here. So Nozick's conditions are satisfied; and, according to his analysis, Henry knows that there is a barn in the field.

David Lumsden and Mark Johnston have pointed out that unfavorable soil conditions are not really crucial to the example.[17] Even though imitation barns may be plentiful in the area, would we say of a particular field with a real barn that if the barn had not been there, there would (or even might) have been an imitation in its place? Normally, I think, not unless the owner of the field (or other responsible person) had potential plans possibly to erect an imitation barn. If the owner had been deciding, say, between a (genuine) barn and a silo, with no thought of a papier-mâché barn, then normally it simply does not matter that fairly nearby fields contain papier-mâché barns; if a real barn had not been built, a silo, not a counterfeit barn, would have been there in its place (and Henry would not have been deceived). In general, there is no particular reason to suppose that if there had not been a real barn there, what would, or might, be there is a counterfeit barn. Maybe the field would have been empty, maybe something else would have been built.

The stipulations in the previous paragraph, rendering it physically impossible to erect a papier-mâché barn on the field, are really just icing on the cake, making the point even more watertight. On the other hand, if the owner (who eventually opted for a real one) had been deciding between a real and a papier-mâché barn (and both were feasible), then if the real barn had not been built, there would have been a counterfeit there in its place, even if in fact there have never been any papier-mâché barns in the entire area.[18] Really, Nozick is wrongly trying to identify two distinct and largely independent issues, either of which might be thought to make papier-mâché barns into a relevant alternative[19]—whether in fact there are papier-mâché barns on *other* fields in the area, and whether a papier-mâché barn would or might have been erected on *this particular* field.

---

[17] Here I modify and add to their remarks in ways for which they are not responsible.

[18] And whether there are or were such barns in Sweden could be (indirectly) relevant to the counterfactual. Maybe the owner of the field comes from Sweden, and wonders whether to play the same trick they used to play in the old country!

[19] I am using the term "relevant alternative" intuitively. If Dretske defines it along the lines suggested in note 15, then I am not following his definition.

Someone might try to "defend" Nozick in a way that actually points to one of the greatest objections to his theory. Suppose Henry's belief were formulated as a belief that a real barn is on *the field in front of him*, where the definite description is taken to be non-rigid, in contrast to the demonstrative at the end of the previous paragraph. (One could even give an explicit Russellian analysis, say, that a real barn is on any field uniquely in front of him.) Then whether other fields in the area contain the fake barns (façades) is no longer irrelevant to the satisfaction of Nozick's condition 3. For Henry may be in front of this particular field by pure accident, and might just as well have stopped on another field. Then the other field might have contained one of the barn façades, and Henry's belief would indeed have been false. So Nozick's third condition is violated after all, for the newly stated belief.

But is this really a "defense" of Nozick? Surely intuitively, Henry knows that there is a real barn *on the field in front of him* if and only if he knows that there is a real barn on *this particular field.* For Henry knows that this particular field is the field in front of him, and hence for Henry the two conditions are epistemically equivalent. (Henry might even be familiar with the field in question under a proper name, say "Dracula Field," and therefore know that there is a real barn on the field in front of him if and only if there is a real barn on Dracula Field. But since the proper name is rigid, the counterfactual as to whether a counterfeit barn might have been on Dracula Field will give a different result from the one as to whether a counterfeit barn might have been on the field in front of him, if he might have been in front of a different field.) Thus Nozick's condition 3, involving a counterfactual, gives different results regarding formulations that are obviously epistemically equivalent for Henry, given what he knows. The counterfactual formulation is in plain conflict with obvious intuitions.

The reader will recognize the relation of this point to *Naming and Necessity* and its distinction between a priority and metaphysical necessity. Here, however, it is only a highly analogous point about the relation between garden-variety knowledge, that may well be empirical and a posteriori, and the truth of various ordinary counterfactuals. And, of course, the distinction between designators that are rigid or non-rigid with respect to counterfactual situations is explicitly invoked. This major objection to Nozick's theory should have been obvious from a consideration of my earlier work and very likely threatens many of the other related theories that attempt to define knowledge in terms of counterfactuals (and similar devices), though each particular one would have to be checked.[20]

---

[20] I only now (2009) realized how basic this objection to Nozick's theory is and how it is related to my earlier work. Although many other changes have been made to my original version, no addition is as important or improves the original nearly as much as this one, so I explicitly note it.

Actually, I find that I do anticipate this objection in a special case in section 9 (see especially the discussion of the blue barn and note 81, though some of the rest of the discussion is relevant, too). But I should have highlighted the problem much earlier and made the connection with the distinction between metaphysical and epistemological notions.

The artificial character of the situation in the preceding example—papier-mâché barns and their like abound only in philosophical discussions of knowledge[21]— obscures its full force. (Shatz used another standard artificial situation—two twins, one of whom is observed stealing a book.)[22] Actually, Nozick's analysis gives the accolade of "knowledge" to the fruits of much sloppy experimentation and research. It is inimical to the very idea of proper experimental controls. Consider a medical experimenter, testing the efficacy of a new drug on a certain disease. Suppose he neglects to apply proper experimental controls. To take an extreme case, suppose he neglects to give a placebo to a control group. If his patients in fact tend to have significantly above-average recovery rates, and he concludes that he

---

Moreover, in note 23 below, I explicitly distinguish between beliefs involving "this object," which is essentially a barn and could not be a barn façade, and beliefs about a non-rigidly designated object before me, but I note that I have kept the designation of the field rigid. Shouldn't I have thought there of the case where the designation of the field is *not* kept rigid?

[21] Actually, perhaps the examples need not be so artificial as I thought when I originally wrote this paper. In my 2009 spring seminar on epistemology, various people mentioned real examples. Harold Teichman mentioned a Hollywood set. Rohit Parikh mentioned situations where military camouflage or other decoys are involved; Jeff Buechner also suggested such examples. Nevertheless, it is important to Goldman's discussion of the example (1976) that, in the situation he is talking about, papier-mâché barn façades are unlikely to occur to anyone (since they are a wild and undreamt of speculation with no particular purpose), so that Henry is entirely reasonable in his conclusions, even with the weakest notion of relevant alternative. Later, I vary the example to a case where Henry has been warned and is plainly irrational.

Other counterfeits that actually take place might replace the papier-mâché barns, but depending on our purposes and the examples, we would have to check how much the features of the original example in Goldman's paper are preserved, given that his original example deliberately depended on the wild and exceptional nature of papier-mâché barns.

Counterfeit money might abound in a certain area, or counterfactually might have. (In World War II the Germans plotted to flood Britain with counterfeit money in pounds. The money was actually printed, but the plot was never realized. What about counterfeit government identification—false passports, green cards, social security cards, etc.?) I have just read (2009) a newspaper report about truly diabolical people who profit by the manufacture of false drugs against malaria, to be given to sufferers in Africa (remember Harry Lime in the film *The Third Man*). There is art forgery (as in the Vermeer–Van Meegeren case), false ancient artifacts, false gems, the Piltdown Man, false designer clothing, and many other examples. See note 43.

[22] Shatz derives the twin example, where one "Tom Grabit" is the thief, from Lehrer and Paxson (1969). Originally Lehrer and Paxson use the twin example to discuss the famous Gettier problem (see Gettier 1963), whereas Shatz uses it specifically in a discussion of reliabilism and relevant alternatives, which is directly relevant to Nozick's theory. For this reason I have cited Shatz now and before. (My thanks to Jonathan Adler for urging me to add a footnote about this.)

Similarly, Goldman (1976, 778) also mentions the case of two twins, Judy and Trudy. The subject, Sam, sees Judy but does not know that it is Judy in front of him since he cannot discriminate her from Trudy. (He may not even know about her). Goldman states a condition (influenced by Armstrong) that would give the intuitively proper result here, but goes on to state objections to it. However, the main point, stated by Goldman in his review of Nozick, is that Nozick's condition 3 is plainly insufficient for the case (Goldman 1983:84). It is not enough to require that if Judy had not been there, Trudy would (or even might) have. Maybe if Judy had not been there, no one would have. But this does not capture Sam's inability to distinguish the two twins. This case is really similar to some of the problems with Nozick's condition 3 in my main text. (My thanks to Michael Levin for calling my attention to Goldman's review in connection with something else.)

has tested a drug that is (chemically) effective against the disease,[23] the scientific community would judge that his research is worthless (or, at least, highly inconclusive). He has not ruled out the possibility that his favorable results are due to a placebo effect. If anything is a case of failure to rule out relevant alternatives, surely this one is.

Suppose, however, that in fact placebos are completely (or nearly completely) ineffective against this particular disease, although neither the experimenter nor anyone else in the medical community has any reason to suppose that this is so. Then, if the experimenter concludes that he has tested a drug that is chemically effective against the disease, his belief satisfies Nozick's conditions for knowledge. In particular, despite the fact that any medical scientist would say that the experimenter has not ruled out a relevant alternative,[24] Nozick's condition 3, or better, 3', is satisfied. For if the experimenter had tested a drug that was not chemically effective against the disease, little improvement in the patient would have resulted, since the disease is impervious to placebo effects. Therefore, using the same method M he actually used, he would not have concluded that he had tested a drug effective against the disease; so condition 3' is satisfied. Similarly, it seems clear that condition 4' is satisfied. But if this is a case of knowledge, knowledge is not what it is cracked up to be.[25]

Even this case is artificially dramatic—the experimenter is so very sloppy. But in many parallel cases, Nozick's conditions endorse an experimenter who ignores a relevant control. Condition 3, which should have been designed to guard against such failures, is often satisfied so long as the experiment would still have been successful, had the controls been applied (even though no one knows, or has any reason to believe, that this is so). It is unnecessary that the controls actually *be* applied.

My discussion of the experimenter could be applied to Henry and the barn, creating an even more blatant problem for the case. In the description above, Henry, who has never heard of the counterfeit barns (nor of their relation to

---

[23] Here I say "that he has tested a drug that is (chemically) effective against the disease," not "that this drug is (chemically) effective against the disease." Thus the proposition *p* in question would have been false if the experimenter had tested a different (ineffective) drug. Similarly, the belief of Henry that I have considered is that the field contains a real barn, not that this object in the field is real and not counterfeit. This allows us, in considering counterfactuals for the third condition, to suppose that the field contains a different (counterfeit) "barn." I adopt these formulations, which may appear cumbersome, so that I do not have to go into questions about the "essential properties" of the drug and the barn. For the latter case, about this barn and the like, see below. (But note that this field and this disease are supposed to be kept fixed, even when we consider condition 3.)

[24] In fact, a *known* relevant alternative, in the intuitive sense. The false barns are supposed to be a relevant alternative even if Henry has never heard of them. See the discussion of the difference immediately below. Moreover, though "relevant alternative" is a technical philosophical term, here it, or something like it, represents precisely the attitude of the appropriate scientific community, who would use some such phrase in complete ignorance of the philosophical literature.

[25] See my discussion below of "gnowledge," where the term is stipulatively defined as satisfaction of Nozick's conditions.

soil conditions), is perfectly rational in drawing his conclusion. Hence, his case is a counterexample, in the spirit of Gettier (1963), to the classical "justified true belief" analysis. (Shatz's [1981] and Dretske's [1971] original cases were similar.)[26] In contrast, the medical experimenter I have just described is by no means perfectly rational—most of us who know about proper experimental controls would say that his conclusion was neither justified nor rational. None of this irrationality prevents Nozick's conditions from being satisfied. It might be argued that much of the recent tradition that Nozick follows is content with just such a result—many of its advocates do not think that justification should be a necessary condition for knowledge. But it seems to me to be obvious that even the philosophers who follow this trend ought to acknowledge that cases of the present kind—where the believer really is irrational—go too far.

Let me modify Henry's case further. Suppose Henry is perfectly familiar with the papier-mâché barns in the area—they are known to everyone, and he himself has inspected a few counterfeits at close range. On the other hand, he has no idea that in some fields soil conditions render the erection of counterfeit barns impossible; perhaps he even assumes, wrongly, that a papier-mâché barn could be erected on any field in the vicinity. Suppose that, looking at a field with a real barn (where, unbeknownst to him, soil conditions would have precluded the erection of a counterfeit), Henry very stupidly and irrationally ignores the possibility that the barn might be a counterfeit and concludes that there is a genuine barn in the field. Even in this case, where Henry's irrationality is so blatant that it is hard to imagine how it could possibly arise in practice, Nozick's conditions are still satisfied. In particular, they are satisfied in the forms 3′ and 4′: Henry's "method M" is irrationally to follow the crude evidence of his eyes, ignoring the possibility that he is looking at a papier-mâché counterfeit. Similarly, unbeknownst to Henry, the owner of the field may have intended to build a silo, had he not built a barn, or to have left the field empty, or any number of things. As we said above, the unfavorable soil conditions are not necessary. The owner may not so much as have heard of the papier-mâché barns. Nevertheless, Nozick's conditions are still satisfied.

Similarly, we may modify the medical case so that the experimenter is even more irrational. Suppose that he has been told many times of the necessity for the use of control groups to exclude the placebo effect, that he has well understood the argument, and that he has acknowledged its cogency. If the experimenter, ignoring what he has learned before, nevertheless irrationally proceeds with his

---

[26] Shatz did, in fact, as I already mentioned in note 22, derive his case from Lehrer and Paxson (1969), who explicitly proposed the case in a discussion of Gettier (1963). Shatz explicitly gives his case as a counterexample to exactly Nozick's third condition, regarded as a replacement for, or analysis of, the relevant alternatives account. See his page 394, condition * (which is Nozick's third condition, though he writes in ignorance of Nozick and under the influence of Goldman and Dretske). Shatz's counterexample strengthens Dretske's earlier formulation of the counterexample (see Shatz 1981:408, note 14).

sloppy procedure, none of these additional stipulations prevents Nozick's conditions from being satisfied.

In a paper that Nozick cites, Laurence Bonjour[27] gives other cases where the subject's belief is irrational. Bonjour puts forth a large number of examples, but almost all concern a subject who irrationally regards himself as clairvoyant and believes, on the basis of his supposed powers, that the president is in New York.

Combining various features of Bonjour's cases, let us suppose that the subject has been presented with overwhelming evidence that the president is actually in Washington, that he knows that often he has definitely been wrong in the past when he drew conclusions on the basis of his supposed clairvoyance, and that scientific researchers have concluded that clairvoyance is impossible. Let us suppose that nevertheless the subject really is clairvoyant and the president is in fact in New York. (The evidence that the president is in Washington came from White House "disinformation" disseminated so that the public would be unaware of a secret presidential mission. Sometimes in the past, special interfering conditions, unknown to the subject, prevented his clairvoyance from operating; but these interferences are not present in the case at hand.) It should be clear that all of Nozick's conditions for knowledge are satisfied and that the method is "held fixed." Nevertheless, by ordinary standards of rationality the subject's belief is irrational, and Bonjour argues that he clearly does *not* know that the president is in New York. (Originally, Bonjour's argument was directed at Armstrong's [1973] analysis.)

Nozick suggests (196) that it might be appropriate to supplement his conditions with an added clause requiring that *S* not believe the negations of 3 and 4. He thinks that it would be too strong to require, positively, that the subject believe that 3 and 4 hold. His sole comment on Bonjour's paper is to say, in the footnote where he cites it: "It is along these lines that we should treat the examples in Laurence Bonjour...." This comment is puzzling, since clearly the extra conditions are irrelevant to Bonjour's example, whether or not Bonjour's intuitions are correct and whether or not some other argument refutes him.[28] Since Bonjour's subject believes in his own clairvoyance, he satisfies even the stronger condition that he believes that 3 and 4 hold, not to mention the weaker condition that he does not disbelieve them. The point is that his belief is irrational. Could we supplement the conditions with something like, "It would not be irrational for *S* to believe that 3 and 4 hold"? Indeed such a supplementary clause would exclude Bonjour's case, but it would reopen the problem of philosophical skepticism and would no longer be "externalist." A skeptic might

---

[27] Bonjour (1980), cited by Nozick (686, note 41). For those who are familiar with the events of June 2009, the whereabouts of the governor of South Carolina might be a more appropriate example.

[28] I am indebted to Christopher Peacocke for calling my attention to Bonjour's paper and to the irrelevance to it of Nozick's extra clause.

argue that our normal beliefs do not really satisfy the extra clause. A principal goal of externalist views of knowledge like Nozick's has been to exclude such questions by making knowledge solely a matter of whether the relevant counterfactuals hold in fact.

As I said, many "externalists" have explicitly held that knowledge need not imply justification. Others, like Goldman and, following him, Nozick, give an externalist analysis of justification as well as knowledge. However: (i) I trust that such philosophers do not really think that such highly irrational beliefs as the worst cases just given are knowledge, let alone justified. (ii) Even if they do—after all, we could stipulatively define a term "gnowledge" as satisfaction of Nozick's conditions—this would simply show that knowledge (or "gnowledge") is no great virtue. Similarly, we could invent a term "gustified" with the same result. A skeptic could concede *arguendo* that we may "know" (or "gnow") our customary beliefs (and be "gustified" in having them) but claim that we have no more business having them than do some of the subjects just mentioned. We have seen (i) that Nozick's externalized conditions do not rule out cases where the subject is highly irrational, and that (ii) even when the subject is rational and justified in the intuitive sense (and also when he is not) the third condition does not capture the idea of relevant alternatives. I should add (iii) that his conditions do not capture the idea of a "reliable method" either—not that he says that they do. Ignoring proper experimental controls and forgetting about counterfeit barns in an area where they abound are highly unreliable methods. True, in some sense Nozick's conditions guarantee that the method used is reliable for the case of the particular judgment *p* at hand. The trouble is that the intuitive concept of reliability seems to require reliability over a range of similar actual and hypothetical cases. In one paragraph Nozick realizes that his third condition may be "undercut" if it endorses a method that fails for cases similar enough to the case at hand (187). However, he drops the problem quickly, apparently failing to appreciate its full force. He explicitly realizes (abstractly, see 267) that there is a problem about the relation of his concept of "tracking" to that of a reliable method; but again he does not realize the problem created for his theory, and drops the matter quickly ("I prefer to leave this question unsettled"). All three problems mentioned in this paragraph seem to me to be related to each other, and to illustrate why Nozick's third condition seems not to achieve its intended effects.

Before (temporarily!) leaving Henry and his barn, let me mention another type of problem. Suppose the situation is as Nozick imagines it—because the area abounds in counterfeit barns, the owner of Henry's field would (or might) have erected a ringer there, too, had he not decided to build a real barn. (Henry knows nothing of all this.) But now suppose another oddity, unknown to Henry or anyone else, since the situation has not actually arisen. Had a papier-mâché barn been erected on the field, a subtle interaction of chemicals in the counterfeit with Henry's optic nerve would temporarily have disordered his perceptual apparatus.

He would not have seen a barn, but rather a mirage of a clear-water pond. Almost everyone else reacts to the counterfeit barn normally—only a unique defect in Henry's optic nerve produces the illusion. No one, including Henry, has the slightest awareness of the defect; the situation that would call it forth has never arisen. As usual, papier-mâché barns abound in the area. But now Henry clearly satisfies the third condition—had a real barn not been there, he would not have believed there was a real barn in the field.

Can we really believe that because of a bizarre *defect* in his perceptual apparatus, giving him an extraordinary *illusion* under certain circumstances that in fact may never be realized, Henry *knows* something that a normal percipient cannot know? Henry is not a person with a finely "discriminating" perceptual apparatus enabling him to distinguish counterfeit barns from genuine ones. Such a person is obviously conceivable, one with a fine visual acuity—sensitive to differences between counterfeit and real barns—that a normal person lacks. But Henry is not like this. He would be even more badly deceived in the presence of a papier-mâché barn than would a normal person. A papier-mâché barn really does resemble a real one very closely, and a normal percipient, unlike Henry, sees this. By accident, so to speak, Henry's very poor perception in this case would lead him not to make the erroneous judgment that a real barn is before him. Remember that he himself (like everyone else) is unaware of the defect and it has never in fact been realized. It would be very strange to describe his perceptual apparatus as one that enables him to discriminate counterfeit barns from real ones—and hence, when he looks at a real barn, thereby to know something he wouldn't have known had he not had this defect! The same problem arises if Henry's eyes simply would go dim in the presence of counterfeit barns, so that he would see nothing clearly (rather than having a hallucination). Not only Nozick, but others, even many of those who have restricted their theories to perceptual knowledge, seem to me to be vulnerable to this point.[29]

The situation would be different if Henry knew of the defect and could argue, "This barn must be real, since I am not seeing a pond." But we are supposing that neither Henry nor anyone else knows anything of his peculiarity. (We could even suppose that Henry has never confronted a papier-mâché barn, never experienced the mirage.) Then Nozick's theory (in common with other related theories) says that Henry knows that there is a barn there, even though no normal person would know this, just because of a bizarre defect in Henry's vision that has never in fact been realized!

The point seems to me to be of great importance for many current theories of perceptual knowledge. Too often the capacity of a perceptual apparatus to attain knowledge is equated with counterfactual conditions that allow knowledge to be a result of a defect in, rather than of a virtue of, the perceptual system. It is one

---

[29] See, e.g., Goldman (1976).

thing to say that if we know that a thermometer or an electric eye (or even a human eye) has the right kind of defect, under certain circumstance the thermometer (or other apparatus) is usable for certain purposes where a better device would fail. It is another thing to say, when everyone, including Henry, is totally unaware of the defect, that Henry himself has knowledge.

By suitably modifying the example, we can separate it from or combine it with our previous themes at will. If we suppose that Henry gets the mirage whenever he looks at a papier-mâché barn, then in some sense he has a "reliable method" for telling when something is a real barn—unlike other people, he never erroneously thinks he is looking at a real barn. Even so, it seems to me that this hardly can give him "knowledge" that others lack.[30] Moreover, we may suppose, if we wish, that Henry gets the mirage from papier-mâché barns only in conjunction with certain soil conditions peculiar to the field at hand—papier-mâché barns on other neighboring fields look the same to Henry as to anyone else.

Alternatively, some particular chemicals in the particular papier-mâché barn that the owner would have erected had he not decided to erect a real one would have produced the illusion in Henry, but these chemicals are not present in any actual counterfeit barns in the area. (He has often been fooled by the false barns in the past, though he does not know it.) Then Henry no longer has a "reliable" method for telling a real barn, even in the Pickwickian sense that held before. Nevertheless, Henry still "knows" there is a real barn, according to Nozick's conditions.

Return to the case we have mentioned before, where Henry has been warned many times of the presence of counterfeit barns in the area, but irrationally ignores it. That could be added to the present case where he has a perceptual defect, never realized and never known to anyone, himself included, making the case even worse because of Henry's irrationality. Actually, in the case where Henry has been warned in this way, I am inclined to worry about the knowledge claim even if Henry does have some special visual acuity (in the ordinary sense) that enables him to discriminate counterfeit from real barns. Suppose Henry has never been in the presence of a counterfeit barn; but if he had been, he would have said to his surprise that some subtle features of the barn make him sure that it is not genuine. However, neither he nor anyone else is aware of his powers. In that case, had he been warned of the danger of counterfeits, he would have been

---

[30] Nor can the existence of a "reliable method" in this sense give justification. Goldman (1979) equates justified belief with possession of a reliable method. Nozick accepts Goldman's proposal. The present case is not a counterexample to this equation, since intuitively Henry is justified here. (But see the case below where Henry is irrational.) So is a normal person, without Henry's defect; possibly Goldman would regard the general reliability of vision (regardless of subtleties about the reaction to counterfeit barns) as a reliable enough method. However, without working out the details, it seems to be all too obvious that the type of problem involved here signals trouble for Goldman's "externalist" account of justification as well. (Though I think there are more basic troubles.)

irrational to conclude that a real barn was in front of him. (Remember that in this case the barn is in fact real and that he has never looked at a counterfeit barn, even though he has been correctly warned that they abound in the area.) But then, unless blatant irrationality is compatible with knowledge, he wouldn't *know*. (And if they are compatible, then, as I argued above, "knowledge" is no great virtue, since the subject could "know" something he has no business believing.)

Given that counterfeit barns do abound in the area (and that he is making his judgment on the presupposition that they do not), should he be said to know even in the case where he hasn't been warned? Does the *absence* of a warning give him knowledge? Without going further into the problem here, these considerations suggest that in some cases knowledge obtained through the normal use of normal human senses is different from "knowledge" based on counterfactuals involving abnormal capacities peculiar to one subject, capacities that he has never exercised and of which he is unaware.

3. THE FOURTH CONDITION

Given that the first two conditions are satisfied, the fourth condition is a counterfactual whose antecedent and consequent are both true. Rarely do we knowingly assert such "factual counterfactuals"; my own intuitions about their truth conditions are shaky. Robert Stalnaker (1968) and David Lewis (1973) independently count them as automatically true. This stipulation, which Nozick explicitly rejects, would render the fourth condition completely superfluous.

I am much less confident than Nozick seems to be that we have a clear intuitive understanding of counterfactuals of this type, and I wish he had given much more elaborate discussion and defense of his views on this question than he does. It is hard to agree with Nozick (176) that the reader can rely on her "intuitive understanding" of these conditionals; and, as Nozick seems to recognize, his tentative technical remarks do not really fill the gap.[31] Nevertheless, he does give some indications of what he has in mind. For a counterfactual with true

---

[31] On 680–81, note 8, Nozick sketches a modified possible-world semantics. But he does not wish substantive philosophical points to depend on this tentative and sketchy discussion.

I can think of other possible ways to illuminate Nozick's intuitions on "factual counterfactuals." We might take one as true if it could reasonably be asserted by a speaker ignorant of the truth of the antecedent, or, perhaps, if it could be asserted without clairvoyance before the events in question had occurred. I will not elaborate on this here.

Nozick's confidence that we have an "intuitive understanding" of these counterfactuals strikes me as quite unfortunate, since I myself doubt this assertion and he invokes such counterfactuals often. (Notice that he implies that both Lewis and Stalnaker, the leading writers in this area, must lack such an intuitive understanding.) One aspect of our treatment, therefore, is lucky. We will show that the fourth condition is toothless, on any understanding, so we don't have to worry about the interpretation of it. See my section 4(a) below.

antecedent to be true, the consequent must be true, not only in the actual world but also in a range of "very near" possible worlds where the antecedent is true. (Lewis mentions a similar variant [1973: section 1.7].) Nozick seems to think that a counterfactual with a true antecedent can be true only if the consequent is in some sense inevitable, given the antecedent. After stating condition 4, Nozick mentions a case.

Compare: not only was the photon emitted and did it go to the left, but (it was then true that): if it were emitted it would go to the left. The truth of antecedent and consequent is not alone sufficient for the truth of a subjunctive; 4 says more than 1 and 2. (176)

In a footnote Nozick elaborates:

If it is truly a random matter which slit a photon goes through, then its going through (say) the right slit does not establish the subjunctive: if a photon were fired at that time from that source it would go through the right-hand slit. For when p equals A photon is fired at that time from that source, and q equals the photon goes through the right-hand slit, q is not true everywhere in the p neighborhood of the actual world. (680-61, note 8)

The discussion of the photon in note 8 is tentative only in its reference to the possible-world semantics tentatively proposed there. Nozick believes categorically in the photon example and is elaborating on the mention of it in the text.

We need not discuss whether Nozick is right about ordinary language. Rather, we can take his remarks as a partial indication of how he intends "factual counterfactuals" to be understood, and, in particular, how he understands the fourth condition.[32]

Given these remarks, I find it very hard to see how condition 4, or condition 4', can be a necessary condition for knowledge. Consider the photon case. Suppose that Mary is a physicist who places a detector plate so that it detects any photon that happens to go to the right. If the photon goes to the left, she will have no idea whether a photon has been emitted or not. Suppose a photon is emitted, that it does hit the detector plate (which is at the right), and that Mary concludes that a photon has been emitted. Intuitively, it seems clear that her conclusion indeed does constitute knowledge. But is Nozick's fourth condition satisfied? No, for it is not true, according to Nozick's conception of such counterfactuals, that if a photon had been emitted, Mary would have believed that a photon was emitted. The photon might well have gone to the left, in which case Mary would have had no beliefs about the matter. (Here the method is held fixed.)

Change Mary's belief (which she certainly will have) to the belief that a photon has been emitted and gone to the right. In that case, on Nozick's view, there is nothing wrong with condition 4. Indeed, if a photon had been emitted and gone

---

[32] Notice that Nozick in the two examples changes the actual path of the photon from the left in the first quotation to the right in the second one. In my own discussion, I have assumed the second case.

to the right, Mary would have believed it, even on Nozick's understanding of the condition. But hasn't failure of deductive closure[33] run amok here? Can we really suppose that Mary knows that a photon has been emitted and gone to the right,[34] but not that a photon has been emitted *simpliciter*? As I have said, it is the second part that I find counterintuitive by itself, but the failure of deductive closure is also counterintuitive. This case anticipates a theme that will be developed in the next section. (It also somewhat resembles, now in the context of condition 4, the red barn case discussed below.)

As I just formulated the case, Mary rightly is aware that the photon may be undetected if it goes to the left. Suppose, however, that Mary erroneously calculates that her detector will detect any photon emitted from the source. So she concludes that a photon has been emitted if the detector registers an emission and that none has been emitted if the detector registers no emission. Intuitively, her error does not affect the soundness of her conclusion that a photon has been emitted, or its status as knowledge, when a photon does hit the detector. That she would err in drawing a negative conclusion about the emission from the failure of the photon to hit the detector is intuitively irrelevant to her knowledge in the positive case. Nevertheless, Nozick's condition 4 and his condition 4' still fail, so we do not have knowledge in Nozick's sense.

Nozick mentions a case where someone knows that a bank robber is Jesse James after he sees a mask accidentally slip off his face, and Nozick claims that the case "causes no difficulty for condition 4, properly understood" (193, case (h)). He speaks of a method that can be used in some situations to draw the desired conclusion but is such that "some other situations might not allow that method to be used—these situations do not yield any belief." I find the statement that there is no difficulty here for condition 4 "properly understood" (?) doubtful even in the bank robber case, but I find it very hard to see how this comment could apply to the case of the photon. Perhaps Nozick means that the method M is looking at the

---

[33] Often I speak in connection with theories like Nozick's of failure of knowledge to be "deductively closed," or a failure of "deductive closure," as shorthand for what Nozick more properly calls "failure of knowledge to be closed under known logical implication" (the "known" here creates a problem, since Nozick must mean for his analysis of knowledge to apply to this case, too, but I do not go into it here, and let Nozick take the term "known" to be understood simply intuitively for this case). No one thinks that knowledge is literally deductively closed; mathematicians do add to our knowledge by their clever deductions. Perhaps occasionally even philosophers do.

[34] Of course, one must check that Nozick's first three conditions hold for the belief that a photon has been emitted and gone to the right. The first two are clearly verified since the statement in question is a true belief. For the third, what if it had not been the case that a photon was emitted and went to the right? Well, whatever the source of the failure may have been, either that a photon was not emitted or that it did not go to the right, Mary would not have believed the conjunction, and indeed would not have believed the first conjunct, since the detector plate would not have been hit (and this is the method to be held fixed). So the conjunctive statement will be knowledge in Nozick's sense, since on his interpretation the fourth condition holds too. See also section 4(a) in the text below, where the conditions are checked in this way in greater generality.

robber's unmasked face and that it is impossible to apply M if the mask has not slipped. But the method of looking at the detector plate is always applicable. We cannot say that it is inapplicable if the photon goes to the left, since Mary has no independent test, other than by the use of her detector plate, for whether a photon has been emitted or not, or where it went. (Recall that Nozick's concept of method requires that the subject should be able to tell, even "from the inside," whether he is applying a given method or not.) Further, it is irrelevant to the case whether Mary forms no belief about whether a photon has been emitted if no photon has registered on the detector, as we have just seen. If Nozick wishes to push the strategy of the Jesse James case far enough, and specify the method used in an ad hoc way, perhaps he can still avoid the counterexample. He could legislate that Mary applies two methods—a positive method that says that a photon has been emitted if one shows up on the detector plate, and a "separate," negative method that (erroneously) says that none has been emitted if it does not show up or, alternatively, gives no belief at all in that case. Then, if the positive method is applied at all, Mary must conclude that a photon has been emitted. It is equally obvious that if we stretch the specification of the method used this far, we could declare the fourth condition satisfied in every case, even those where Nozick wants it to fail. There is nothing to be gained from this kind of body English. (See my section 7 below.)

Hence, as far as I can see, Nozick's own paradigm of the photon emission shows that his fourth condition is not necessary. On the other hand, some of Nozick's own uses of the fourth condition to rule out various cases satisfying the other three strike me as dubious. For example:

As an effect of brain damage a person is led (irrationally) to believe he has brain damage, which he would not believe if he didn't have brain damage. However, condition 4 is not satisfied: if the brain damage had been slightly different, though using the same route to belief he would not believe he had it. (190)[35]

Is this really a satisfactory treatment of the case? Suppose the case had been just as Nozick describes, except that if the brain damage had been slightly different, it would still have caused him to have an irrational belief that he has brain damage. Does this modification really change our intuitions about the case? I find it hard to see that it does. Isn't it the irrationality of the belief that is crucial? Even the very first example Nozick uses to motivate the introduction of the fourth condition (two paragraphs) seems to me to be questionable in a similar way.

Nozick's third condition has a clear intuitive basis. "Even if p had been false, you'd still have believed it!" sounds like an objection to a knowledge claim. (Nevertheless, eventually I will argue that the third condition is very far from being a necessary condition for knowledge. See my section 5.)[36] But I find it hard

---

[35] He derives this case from Sosa (1969:39).
[36] Also, in the other direction, I will argue in section 4(b) that the third condition can very often be defanged by strengthening the knowledge claim.

to see why the fourth condition should have been thought to be necessary at all. Why should the method by which one comes to believe that p make it inevitable, or even make it merely highly probable, that one should have believed that p if p is true, as long as the method never can lead to an erroneous conclusion that p? The photon example is meant to bring this out, and any number of examples could be given in this vein. Because of the difficulty about the exact intuitive meaning of Nozick's condition 4, I have stuck to the rather special photon example, which corresponds to a case on which we have Nozick's explicit *ipse dixit*. But any case where the subject has a method that never leads to an erroneous conclusion that p, but will not inevitably yield a positive result given p, really goes against the fourth condition. Nozick says (682, note 12) that his fourth condition was chosen after experimenting among a large number of candidates for a supplement to the first three, but it seems to me to suffer from a lack of a definite intuitive motivation.

So far it looks as if we are arguing that the fourth condition is not a necessary condition for knowledge. In fact, I think it is not, but as we will see presently this is not the most important defect of the condition. Rather than ruling out too much, its real problem is that it does not effectively exclude even those cases that it apparently excludes. This remark will become clear in the next section.

4. LOGICAL PROPERTIES OF NOZICK'S THEORY: STRENGTHENED BELIEFS AND CONJUNCTIONS

4(a). The Fourth Condition: Strengthening the Belief

There is a more fundamental problem with the fourth condition, which ultimately affects the third condition as well. We can illustrate the problem with the fourth condition using an example Nozick (177) takes from Gilbert Harman. A dictator dies; the death is reported in the first edition of the official newspaper; but later an official denial is broadcast and printed everywhere. Almost everyone in the country is fooled by the denial, but one person, S, somehow misses all reports of the denial. S's belief that the dictator has died satisfies the first three conditions, but Nozick agrees with Harman's intuition that he does not know. Nozick thinks that the fourth condition fails. It is not true that had the dictator died, S would have believed that he died, since S's belief is the accidental result of his failure to hear the denial (otherwise he, too, would have been fooled).

However, S also believes the conjunction that the dictator has died and that he (S) has heard an uncontradicted newspaper report to this effect.[37] The method he uses to believe this conjunction is a combination of reading the undenied

---

[37] Here and elsewhere in this discussion I use "he (S)," or simply "he," in Castañeda's well-known sense (see Castañeda 1968, and many other publications); S would say, "I have heard an

newspaper report for the first conjunct and remembering what he has read and heard for the second. Then, on Nozick's understanding of the fourth condition, it does appear to be the case that if the conjunction had been true, then, using the method he actually uses, *S* would have believed it. (Note that the second conjunct guarantees that our attention is confined to counterfactual situations where *S* hears no denial.) There seems to be no problem with the first three conditions. So here, according to Nozick, *S does* know the conjunction!

As we shall discuss below, Nozick denies that knowledge is closed under known logical implication, and even holds that one can know a conjunction without knowing one of the conjuncts. However, from Nozick one would get the impression that these phenomena are normally confined to special cases related to philosophical skepticism; one would have no idea of their ubiquity in his theory. Is the present case really credible? Does it really capture Harman's intuition to say that although *S* does not know that the dictator died, he knows a simple conjunction with that death as the first conjunct?[38]

Here Harman's intuition was that *S* does not know, and the anomaly was that Nozick's theory restores knowledge by a simple strengthening of the belief. But as I already mentioned in the previous section, the problem applies to Mary the physicist as well. She did not satisfy Nozick's fourth condition for knowing that a photon was emitted, contrary to our intuition that she does know. But note that she certainly does know, even according to Nozick's theory, that a photon was emitted and that it went to the right. Really this problem was obvious from the previous discussion. Here strengthening the belief restores intuition rather than destroying it. Assuming that Harman's intuition about the dictator case is correct, the present case may be worse, but the real problem is that we can so easily restore the fourth condition in this trivial way.[39]

The crucial problem for the fourth condition is really one of great generality. Suppose *S* arrives at the belief *p* by a method M. Now consider *S*'s conjunctive belief (*q*), that *p* and that he (himself) believes that *p* via M, or, equivalently (in a form that is not a conjunction), that he correctly believes via M that *p*. Then *q* almost always satisfies the fourth condition, whether or not *S*'s original belief that *p* does. (If we are considering the simple conditions, without mention of method, then we are dealing simply with *S*'s belief that he correctly believes

uncontradicted newspaper report..." However, in most cases it would not matter if "I" were replaced by "*S*," since we can presume that *S* knows that he is *S*.

[38] The problem need not be put in terms of conjunctions, it is about strengthening the belief appropriately. In Harman's dictator case, it can be phrased as: "I have heard a correct uncontradicted newspaper report . . ."

[39] The general moral about the ineffectiveness of the fourth condition does not depend on agreement with Harman's intuition about this particular illustrative case. As we shall see, it applies virtually whenever the fourth condition is invoked to exclude a particular true belief as knowledge.

In fact, in my spring 2009 seminar on epistemology, several participants, especially Melvyn Nathanson and Romina Padró, gave serious reasons to doubt Harman's (and Nozick's) intuitions about this particular case.

that p.) The point is that normally (alleged special exceptions aside) belief is self-intimating: a subject who believes that p is aware that he believes p (and aware by what method M he came to believe it). Without thereby presupposing any particular philosophical doctrine, let us use "self-awareness" as a name for the method by which S comes to be aware of his own belief that p (and of the method M applied).[40] The method M′ by which S comes to believe the conjunction q is a combination of M plus self-awareness: M for the first conjunct, and self-awareness for the second. The second conjunct of q—that S does believe p via M—guarantees that application of M′ will lead to a belief that q. (The second conjunct says that S believes the first conjunct via M, and guarantees, given the self-intimating character of belief, that S will believe the second conjunct itself.) So for q, except in very exceptional cases, the fourth condition is trivially satisfied.

If the other three conditions held for S's belief that p, then normally they will still hold for his belief that q. What q says is that the first two conditions hold for p (i.e., that p is truly believed via M), so the old (1) and (2) imply that q is true, the new first condition. As was noted previously, the first and the fourth conditions (for q) jointly entail the second. So we need only consider the third condition. Suppose it held for p. Now if q had been false, either p would have been false or S would not have believed p via M. But if p had been false, then by hypothesis (since the third condition is supposed to have held for p), S would not have believed p via M and hence would not have believed q via M′. On the other hand, if S had not believed p via M, then, given normally reasonable assumptions about self-awareness, he would not have believed that he believed it (via M) either, and hence (normally) would not have believed that q. This shows that, normally,[41] if the third condition holds for p, it holds for q.

What we have shown is that prefixing "I correctly believe (via M) that . . ." or, if a method M is not involved, simply "I correctly believe that . . ." normally preserves the first three conditions if they held already and creates a new belief satisfying the fourth condition whether that condition held already or not. Below we will argue that there is also an interesting class of special cases for which the prefix generates a new belief satisfying not only the fourth condition but also the third, whether or not either one held already. But this class is relatively more special than the very general class of cases described above.

---

[40] Alternatively, we can suppose the original belief that p to have been formed without a method and modify the discussion accordingly. We would then have a case of a conjunction, one conjunct of which is believed by a particular method while the other conjunct is not. One defect of Nozick's discussion is that he does not consider such cases. (Recall that Nozick, under the influence of Wittgenstein 1969, regards certain basic cases of knowledge as so central that they are not formed by any particular method. See note 10.)

[41] Various exceptions are possible. The usual properties of self-awareness may fail. Or, perhaps, he somehow inconsistently would have believed q, but not its conjunct p. Or, perhaps, the hypothesis that p fails and S applies M′ has different counterfactual implications from the hypothesis that p fails and S applies M. And so on. Similar possibilities can arise for all the cases below, but in practice they will be very rare.

Nozick originally proposed the fourth condition because of various examples where the first three conditions hold but nevertheless (he thinks) S does not know. The preceding discussion shows that in every one of these examples S's belief that p will satisfy all four of Nozick's conditions if we change it to "I correctly believe that p (via M)." Doesn't this consideration show that the fourth condition is almost without force, a broken reed? What can be the point of a condition whose rigor can almost always be overcome by conjoining "and I believe (via M) that p," or equivalently, by prefixing "I correctly believe (via M) that..."? (A subject who wishes to be sure that he will satisfy the fourth condition can begin all his utterances with "I correctly believe....") And whatever we may think of deductive closure in general, surely there is something counterintuitive, almost silly, about the idea that although the subject does not know some proposition, he does know that he correctly believes it!

Harman's dictator case illustrates another relevant point. Usually the somewhat artificial conjunct "and I believe that p (via M)" can be replaced by another clause. This clause must state conditions that actually obtain and counterfactually imply that S would believe p; moreover, they must be self-intimating in the sense that, were they to obtain, S could not normally avoid being aware of them. (These counterfactuals are to be understood as Nozick understands counterfactuals with true antecedents.) In Harman's case, the added conjunct—that S learned his information from a newspaper report and has heard no denial—succeeds because it satisfies these requirements. Usually such a condition will exist; usually S's belief that p arises because of an independently specifiable source of which S himself is aware and which makes his belief nearly inevitable, given his predispositions. As we saw above, even for S's original belief that p these conditions often could be built into a narrower specification of the method M used. Except when, intuitively speaking, S's belief is overdetermined by multiple methods, Nozick's theory allows us to argue here over the "proper" description of "the" method M, and hence over whether condition 4' is "really" satisfied. No such leeway is allowed when we consider whether S believes the strengthened proposition q. Once again, Harman's case illustrates these general points.[42]

The problem with the fourth condition looks almost obvious once it is pointed out. After all, the consequent of the fourth condition says that S believes that p; and an obvious way to ensure that the consequent of a conditional is implied by the antecedent is to add either the consequent itself, or some condition causally implying it, to the antecedent. What needs to be checked is that the addition of this clause to the antecedent actually guarantees the fourth

---

[42] Aside from generating strengthened beliefs that may look somewhat more natural than beliefs of the form "I correctly believe that p," the possibility of adding conjuncts that causally or counterfactually imply that I believe that p shows that it would be pointless to try to remedy the situation by adding an ad hoc clause somehow exempting beliefs about the subject's own beliefs from the general theory and trying to handle these separately—not that such an ad hoc move would have much plausibility (or much chance of success) in any case.

condition for the entire conjunction, and that the other three conditions are preserved if they held before.

4(b). The Third Condition: Strengthening the Belief

Nozick praises his third condition as "powerful and intuitive, not so easy to satisfy" (173). The condition does seem to fit the characterization. "Even if p had not been the case, you still would have believed it" does sound like an objection to a knowledge claim, as I have already remarked. Moreover, Nozick seems right to claim that the condition places a strong constraint. The fourth condition, by contrast, seems to me to be more artificial, hard to understand, and added in an attempt to eliminate some residual counterexamples. The third condition is surely what is basic to Nozick's theory.

It is therefore somewhat surprising that in a large number of cases even the intuitively more plausible third condition is vulnerable to similar strengthening tricks like the fourth. Here we cannot simply add a conjunct implying the old consequent. The trouble is that p, the subject's belief, is negated in the antecedent of the third condition. Hence any added conjunct q changes p to $p \ \& \ q$ in the antecedent, and this weakens the antecedent rather than strengthens it. So we cannot use as simple a device as we did before. Nevertheless, very often there is a conjunct we can add that will ensure that the third condition holds for the conjunctive belief, even if it failed for the original belief that p. The construction will be such that the added conjunct is also a true belief, so that the first two conditions are preserved if they held for p. Ordinarily we can carry out the construction so that the fourth condition is also preserved if it held already. However, preservation of the fourth condition is of relatively little importance. We can almost always go through a second stage and fulfill the fourth condition by prefacing "I correctly believe that..." to the new belief. The other three conditions hold already and, as we argued above, are normally preserved when the preface is added. What we intend to show is that in a large class of cases, so long as p is a true belief, only two steps suffice to obtain a stronger belief satisfying all four of Nozick's conditions. Very often the construction can stop even at the first step with all four conditions satisfied, but this fact is of relatively less importance.

There are two major classes of these cases. We illustrate the first class with an example. Return to Henry and the barn. Suppose that the case really accords with Nozick's picture of it: that is, there is a real barn in the field Henry looks at, while unbeknownst to Henry counterfeit barns abound in the area, and but for the building of this real barn a counterfeit would surely have been built in its place. Henry naively judges that there is a real barn in the field, but the third condition is not satisfied (though the others are); had there been no genuine barn there, the counterfeit there in its place would have taken Henry in. So, according to Nozick's theory, Henry does *not* know that there is a barn in the field.

So far so good, but now let us suppose that the barn is red. Suppose further that any counterfeit erected in its place would have been green. (We can suppose, if we wish, that for some chemical reason the cardboard in the counterfeit barns cannot be painted red. Alternatively, those who erected counterfeit barns definitely preferred green ones, or even definitely preferred a green one in this particular location.) Now consider Henry's true belief (thus satisfying the first two conditions) that there is a (genuine) red barn in the field. Now the third condition is satisfied. If there had not been a red barn in the field, then there would have been a green counterfeit, and Henry would not have believed that there was a red barn in the field. There is no trouble with the fourth condition. So according to Nozick's criterion, although Henry may not know that there is a genuine *barn* in the field, he does know that there is a genuine *red barn* there!

Surely even someone who follows Nozick (and others mentioned before) in rejecting deductive closure in general cannot be very comfortable with this particular result. Notice that it is not essential that in the absence of a real barn a counterfeit definitely would have been erected—all that is required is that had any counterfeit been erected, it would not have been red. (If no object resembling a barn is in the field, clearly Henry will not believe that there is a red barn there.) Notice also that there would have been no problem with the result (and no failure of deductive closure) if Henry had been aware that redness is a distinguishing mark of real, as opposed to counterfeit, barns. The problem is that Nozick's theory says that Henry knows there is a red barn there even if he is entirely unaware of the connection of genuineness with color, or even of the danger that the barn might be counterfeit.[43]

It might be thought that the situation described is very special. After all, the strong connection we have postulated between color and genuineness is extremely unlikely in practice! In fact, the situation is by no means special. If, for any feature whose presence or absence is perceptible to Henry, the actual genuine

---

[43] The following is an actual case involving counterfeit money. (See note 21.) In 1998 the United States Bureau of Printing and Engraving issued special, new twenty-dollar bills that were much harder to counterfeit than the previous ones. There was a gross and perceptible difference between the new bills and their predecessors, though many of the changes made to deter counterfeiting were not perceptible to an ordinary user. Suppose these changes to be so successful that counterfeit bills never have the new appearance, only the old. Then, if Henry is holding a new twenty-dollar bill but is unaware that new, but not old, bills are never counterfeit, then analogously to the red barn, Nozick's theory (based on the third condition) dictates that although he does not know (just by looking at the bill) that he is holding a real twenty-dollar bill, he does know that he is holding a real *new* twenty-dollar bill. Here "new," or better, an actual description of the appearance of the new bills, plays the role of redness for the barn. Most people are aware of the existence of counterfeiting, but in practice when they handle small bills this does not occur to them, so that the case somewhat resembles Goldman's (1976) intentions with papier-mâché barns, as in note 21, though the bizarreness of the fake barns is not preserved. At a greater extreme, we might suppose the subject ignorant of counterfeiting altogether, making the case even more like that of Henry, though then it would be counterfactual or at least very rare. (My thanks to Romina Padró for suggesting this example.)

barn is distinguishable from the supposed counterfeit—the one that would have been erected in its place—then the argument goes through (with redness replaced by the appropriate feature). Once again, we suppose that Henry is entirely unaware of the connection of genuineness with the feature, and is even unaware of the danger of counterfeit barns. Such a feature might be, say, a somewhat different shape of the roof of the barn, or the exact position of some smokestack. Alternatively, suppose that it rained the previous night, leaving a visible smudge on the *real* barn. Unless the counterfeit would have exhibited exactly the same smudge (as far as Henry would have been able to see), then the presence of this smudge will serve as an appropriate perceptible feature.

Here we have spoken of "the" counterfeit barn that would have been erected in the absence of the real barn and "the" feature that distinguishes the two. But it is not necessary that these be unique. Suppose that the real barn has various perceptible features F_i, such that at least one would have failed in any counterfeit that might have been erected in its place. In other words, the real barn satisfies $F_1 \wedge \ldots \wedge F_n$; any counterfeit would have satisfied $\sim F_1 \vee \ldots \vee \sim F_n$. (A perceptible feature is one whose presence or absence Henry can detect.) Then the statement p that there is a real barn there with all the F_i's satisfies Nozick's conditions. In particular, for the third condition, had p been false, then the field would have contained either: nothing; or, some object or objects not resembling a barn; or, a counterfeit barn (or barn-like object) palpably lacking one of the F_i's. In any of these cases, Henry would not have believed that there is a real barn there with all the F_i's, which verifies the third condition. The argument can be avoided only if a counterfeit barn, indistinguishable in every perceptible respect from the particular genuine one that is actually there, might well have been erected had the genuine one been absent.[44] But counterfeiters are unlikely to be so extraordinarily skilled as to produce an object indistinguishable by every perceptible mark from a genuine one, nor are they likely to want to do so. (Even a counterfeit barn that would fool an expert, let alone Henry, need not satisfy such a strong condition.) But here even this skill is not sufficient—they would have to be able to duplicate this particular barn in every perceptible respect. And even if they had the ability to do so, why should they try? Remember that in the circumstances in question they would have to be duplicating a barn that would never have been built. Probably even plans for the genuine barn would never have existed. And an initial perfect duplication is not sufficient. Subsequently, the perceptible features of the counterfeit barn would have to be

---

[44] Suppose that Henry fails to notice the presence of some particular one of the F_i in the real barn that he sees or, alternatively, would have failed to notice its absence in the counterfeit barn that would have been erected. Then the argument in the text wouldn't go through. But could we really hold that Henry's failure to notice something, real or hypothetical, gives him knowledge that there is a real barn there, knowledge that he would otherwise lack? See my similar discussion of a defect in Henry's optic nerve above.

affected (e.g., by the rainstorm postulated above) in exactly the same way as those of the genuine one! This is highly unlikely.

Let us consider the problem in even greater generality. Let p be any true belief of a subject S. Suppose that the third condition fails. Suppose further, however, that there is some feature of S's experience that would have been absent had p not been true. Suppose that S is in general able to discern the presence or absence of the experiential feature in question but is unaware of its connection with p. Let q be S's true belief that the experiential feature in question is present. Then, normally, the conjunction p & q satisfies the first three of Nozick's conditions. This is obvious for the first two conditions. For the third condition, notice that, by hypothesis, if p & q had been false, no matter which conjunct was responsible for the falsity of the conjunction, the experiential feature in question would have been absent. Since S is supposed to be able to detect the absence of the feature, this means that he would not believe that q, and hence would not believe that p & q.[45]

Thus, unless p is a proposition whose falsity would have made no detectable difference to S's experiences, we can normally find a conjunct q such that p & q satisfies all of the first three conditions. It is easy to argue that, normally, if S's belief that p satisfied the fourth condition, so does the conjunction; this case is illustrated by the red barn. If p, and hence p & q, did not satisfy the fourth condition, normally little is lost. Simply prefix "I correctly believe (via M') that" to the new conjunction; normally, the result satisfies all four conditions. (An alternative trick that usually works is to reverse the order of the two procedures. Replace p by "I correctly believe that p" and then add the same q as before.)

Actually, the falsity of p need not necessarily affect S's experiences in the strict sense to make the argument work. Suppose that for some causal reason, had p been false, S's beliefs would have been affected even though his experiences in a narrow sense would have remained unchanged. Suppose in particular that had p failed, S would not have believed that q, even though he actually does believe q. Then the conjunction "p, and I believe that q" satisfies all the first three conditions, as before. (The situation with the fourth condition is as before.)

Another way of looking at the matter is this:[46] Suppose there is a method M_1 that would have served as a method for believing p satisfying Nozick's third

---

[45] Here we have omitted mention of the method M by which p is believed. Normally, adding mention of the method makes no essential change to the argument. The method M' for the conjunction is a combination of M for the first conjunct p and introspective awareness of one's own experiences for the second conjunct q. Then it is crucial that if p had been false, q would have been false in those near situations where the method M' is applied to p & q. Normally, the assumption that M' is applied will not interfere with the counterfactual if it holds otherwise, although in general, the counterfactual could become false if its antecedent is strengthened by mention of M. Similarly, other tacit steps in the argument normally pose no problem, though there may be exceptions.

[46] I believe that the ideas about methods in this and subsequent paragraphs may be connected with suggestions by John Collins.

condition, had S applied it. (That is, in fact, M_1 yields a belief that p but would not have done so had p been false.)[47] Suppose further that S knows nothing of M_1's reliability in this sense, but in fact he comes to believe that p by a method M_2 that does *not* satisfy the third condition. Nevertheless, normally there will be a conjunct q such that S believes that p *& q* by a method satisfying Nozick's first three conditions. (As before, if the fourth condition held for p, it is normally preserved under conjunction with q; otherwise prefix "I correctly believe that ... ") Ordinarily, the reason that M_1 would have been successful must consist in some fact q whose presence is discernible to S but would have been absent had p been false; take this q as the second conjunct. Thus, in the sense just explained, Nozick's theory is not really able to distinguish effectively between beliefs that p that the subject S *actually* obtains by a method "reliable" in the sense of condition 3, and beliefs that S merely *could have* so obtained. This situation is hardly satisfactory and is not alleviated by the denial of deductive closure.

Notice that, as the case of the red barn illustrates, the method M by which S believes p *& q* is in fact "reliable" (in the sense of Nozick's third condition), but for reasons completely different from what S supposes. (Henry does not know that redness guarantees the genuineness of his barn and naively ignores the danger of a counterfeit altogether.) In this sense, the cases considered here resemble Nozick's "hologram" case (case (c), 190), discussed below. The present discussion indicates that such cases are ubiquitous in the theory.

Even worse, notice that in one respect the red barn case, as described, need not be typical. Henry's conclusion that there is a barn there is at least rational, even if it is not knowledge. However, the rationality of the method M_2 by which S actually comes to believe that p is, in fact, completely irrelevant to the construction given above. S can use any "method" M_2, no matter how irrational—reading tea leaves, consulting a guru, succumbing to paranoia. It does not matter: as long as a method M_1 was available to S that *would have* satisfied Nozick's third condition, the construction allows us to find a conjunction p *& q* that S "knows" as far as Nozick's first three conditions are concerned. (If necessary, another conjunct can be added for Nozick's fourth condition.) The nature of the method M_2 by which S actually comes to believe that p is completely irrelevant, as far as Nozick's third condition is concerned, to the epistemic status of his belief that p *& q*.

Although I cannot make a survey here (and have not myself examined all the relevant proposals),[48] I think the red barn case is a major problem for many existing theories that analyze knowledge using counterfactual conditionals or similar ideas. Even if the account is restricted to perceptual ("noninferential," or

---

[47] In our paradigm case of the red barn, the method would be noting the color of the barn, and deducing that it must be real from its color. See also the discussion of the point attributed to Mark Johnston below.

[48] At the time when this paper was originally written, let alone now (in 2009).

"basic") knowledge—and I think such theories are much more plausible if so restricted—the red barn problem can still arise.[49] The problem also seems to affect theories that connect not only knowledge but also justification[50] with reliability. We have seen that Nozick's third condition, in itself, cannot really be equated with reliability of the method used. Nevertheless, it is obviously possible, in the situation described, that Henry should have invoked a totally reliable method for judging whether there is a red barn there, even though one of its components is a totally unreliable (or, in one of the cases above, even irrational) method for judging whether there is a barn there *simpliciter*. One could hardly hold that Henry is justified in thinking that the thing he sees is a red barn but not that it is a barn.[51]

Before we leave the case typified by the red barn, yet another feature of the case is worthy of note. Mark Johnston has pointed out that in this case Nozick's conditions for preservation of knowledge by deduction are satisfied. So far, we have assumed that Henry concludes that there is a barn in the field by simple observation. But suppose instead he deduces this conclusion from his belief that there is a red barn in the field. Nozick says (231) that deduction preserves knowledge, provided that the subject would not have believed the premise had the conclusion been false. But this condition is satisfied.[52] For if the conclusion had been false, that is, if there had not been a barn there, either there would have been no barn-like object there or, instead, a counterfeit barn that was not red. In either case, Henry would not have believed (the premise) that there was a red barn there—essentially this repeats what we said before.

In the case of any true belief p resembling the red barn situation, this observation threatens to give the subject a method, not only for "knowing"

---

[49] See, e.g., Armstrong (1973), Goldman (1976), and others. Goldman's article is formulated carefully to avoid some of the problems that do affect Nozick's (later) theory; but, although there are some ambiguities, it still seems to be affected by the red barn problem.

[50] See note 30 above.

[51] And note that, intuitively, in the case where Henry is irrational, the belief that it is a barn is not justified. Hence the situation cannot be saved by accepting deductive closure and declaring that logical consequences of beliefs obtained by reliable methods are justified. (Arguably, this follows from the equation of justifiability and reliability, since deduction from reliably obtained beliefs is itself reliable. But what would really follow is a paradox—if Henry concludes directly, from observation, that there is a barn there, he is not justified; but if he deduces the same thing from the belief that there is a *red barn* there, he is justified! See discussion of a remark by Mark Johnston in the text immediately below.)

Goldman does not simply equate justification and reliability, but proposes modifications (not completely worked out) to save the theory from counterexamples. To some extent the modifications are relevant here and would have to be discussed in a full treatment. Since the topic of justification is not our concern here, I shall not do this. (However, I doubt that in fact the modifications will dispel the problem.)

[52] See however, my discussion in section 5(a) of Nozick's condition for preservation of knowledge by deduction. There, I argue that some of Nozick's principal applications of the condition are fallacious. Further, I argue that though Nozick appears to have formulated an appropriate condition in terms of his own theory, in fact it makes no intuitive sense. I was not aware of these points in the original version of this paper.

some appropriate conjunction *p & q*, but also for "knowing" *p simpliciter* by deduction therefrom. However, there are some possible ways out and delicate considerations.[53]

I now move on to yet another type of case that creates logical trouble for Nozick's third condition, again by adding a conjunct to the original belief. Consider again a true belief *p* of *S* that may not satisfy condition 3. Previously, we looked for a true conjunct *q* that would have been false if *p* had been false. It follows that if *p & q* had been false, *q* would have been false. Now instead we look for a true conjunct *q* such that *p* is false in possible worlds (much) "farther from" or "less similar to" the real world than any world in which *q* is false. Then if *p & q* had been false, *q* would have been false, simply because the worlds in which *p* is false are too remote, compared to those in which *q* is false, to be relevant to the antecedent of the counterfactual. In David Lewis's terminology, not-*q* is "more possible" than not-*p*. The phenomenon is a familiar point of counterfactual logic,[54] validated by the systems of Lewis and Stalnaker; as we shall see, eventually Nozick himself explicitly accepts and invokes it. Given this, we can argue just as before that as long as *S*'s belief that *q* satisfies Nozick's first three conditions, so does *S*'s belief that *p & q*. Once again, this will be true even if the method by which *S* obtained his belief that *p* fails Nozick's third condition, and even if it is completely irrational. And once again, if the methods by which *p* and *q* were believed satisfy the fourth condition, so will the belief that *p & q*; otherwise, consider "I correctly believe that *p & q*," and the fourth condition will hold.

Let us give some examples. Suppose that Jones is an actress. If we evaluate a counterfactual such as "If Jones had not been an actress, Jones would have been a lawyer," generally we consider only those counterfactual situations in which Jones, still a woman, is not in the acting profession. Actually, the antecedent would also have been realized in counterfactual situations in which (at the relevant time) Jones is not a woman (say, because of a sex-change operation).[55] Apparently our intuition is that, when we evaluate counterfactuals with "If Jones had not been an actress" as antecedent, such situations are so much more remote from the actual situation than those in which Jones is a woman but not in the acting profession as to be irrelevant. That is, if Jones had not been an actress, that

---

[53] In the original version of this paper, I discussed delicate considerations about the individuation of methods that might affect this example (preservation of knowledge by deduction). See my section 7 on leeway below. Since I now think that Nozick's conditions for preservation of knowledge seem to be subject to much more fundamental objections, I omit this elaborate discussion in the present version.

[54] See Lewis (1973:52–56). Notice that the relation need not be defined in terms of possible-worlds semantics but can be defined in terms of the counterfactual itself. *q* is "more possible" than *p* if *q*, but not *p*, would have been true if at least one of *p* and *q* had been true. So we could make our discussion independent of any technical possible-worlds semantics for counterfactuals.

[55] I am supposing that a woman becomes a man if such an operation occurred. Perhaps in another sense, at the chromosomal level, being a woman is an essential property of Jones that could not have been different. In this case, what one is supposing in the counterfactual is hard to evaluate.

would have been because she did not go into acting, not because she was not a woman.

Suppose S truly believes that Jones is an actress, or equivalently, that Jones is a woman (p) and is in the acting profession (q). The third condition asks whether S would have believed this conjunction if Jones had not been an actress, that is, had not been both a woman and in the acting profession. Then the remarks in the previous paragraph indicate that the antecedent amounts to the supposition that Jones is not in the acting profession. It follows that (normally), if the third condition holds for the second component of p & q alone, it holds for the entire conjunction. For if the third condition holds for q, then, if p & q were false, q would be false, S would not have believed that q, and hence (normally) would not have believed that p & q. Notice that the third condition will hold for p & q no matter how irrational the method M that S uses to arrive at the belief that p may be, and no matter how much S's belief that p via M may violate Nozick's third condition. (In other words, S may believe that Jones is a woman for quite irrational reasons and would have believed this even if Jones had not been a woman.) Nevertheless, in the situation in question, S's belief that Jones is an actress (the conjunction) would satisfy Nozick's third condition, because of our remarks about the logical properties of the situation, as stated above.[56]

The logical situation parallels that in the red barn case, but for different reasons. In the former case (though Henry didn't know it), redness was connected to genuineness of the barn, but here acting is in no way connected to gender. It seems very likely—perhaps almost inevitable—that if S has a true belief that someone is a woman, that belief can be promoted to "knowledge" if a suitable conjunct is added. All we need is another true belief, satisfying the third condition, whose falsity would have changed the world less (in the sense relevant to counterfactuals) than a loss of the subject's sex (or humanity). The extra conjunct need not even be about the woman in question, though if some fact about her life is available—for example, that she was just elected to the Senate—it almost surely will do. If the conjunction satisfies the fourth condition, it will constitute "knowledge" in Nozick's sense; otherwise, the usual prefixing trick will get the fourth condition and make it into knowledge in Nozick's sense.

Another case: Suppose p is a (true) scientific law. Just as in the case of any other statement, S can believe p on irrational grounds that strongly violate Nozick's third condition. Nevertheless, regardless of the quality of the grounds, ordinarily we can find a statement q such that S satisfies Nozick's first three conditions in

---

[56] Notice, however, that if we replace "Jones" in the belief "Jones is an actress" by a definite description taken as non-rigid, such as "the star of such-and-such movie is an actress," then the situation about the counterfactual becomes quite different. Now, if the star had not been an actress, no doubt the star would still have been in the acting profession but would not have been a woman (i.e., there would have been a different star, a man). Yet the beliefs that Jones is an actress and that the star is an actress may intuitively be epistemically equivalent. This is another illustration of the situation emphasized above in my section 2, p. 169.

relation to p & q. For it is a familiar point about counterfactuals that normally we keep scientific laws fixed as much as possible when we evaluate them; if to imagine the antecedent of the counterfactual true we do not need to imagine the law violated, we do not do so.[57] Let q be any statement such that not-q, in this sense, does not require abandonment of the law p. Then normally we should suppose that not-p is "less possible" than not-q; in other words, that if p & q were false, q, rather than p, would be false. Suppose further that in relation to q, S satisfies all of Nozick's first three conditions. Then, by the familiar argument, p & q satisfies all three conditions also, regardless of how grossly S fails to satisfy the third condition in relation to p.

Notice that q need not have anything to do with p, as long as p is a law we would hold fixed in considering counterfactuals with not-q as antecedents. Nevertheless, the case may be more intuitively natural if p is a law that we would in fact invoke to support counterfactuals with not-q as antecedent. Usually it is easy to find a q with this feature as well.

As usual, if S satisfied the fourth condition in relation to p and to q, satisfaction will normally be preserved for the conjunction; otherwise, we just add an additional conjunct "and I believe that p & q." However, it is amusing that sometimes a simpler device may be possible. Suppose p is a scientific law that S believes by a method M satisfying neither the third nor the fourth condition. Let q be "I believe that p via M." Then very often p & q, or equivalently, "I correctly believe that p via M," satisfies all four conditions. That the fourth condition holds is by now familiar to us. As to the third condition, note that it probably is much "less possible" that the law p should fail than that S somehow should fail to conclude that p when he applies M (even though p holds). The fourth condition failed for p *simpliciter*. This means that there is no nomological necessity that application of M should lead to a conclusion that p. Hence, if either p must be false or application of M should fail to lead to the conclusion that p, a preference for the preservation of nomological necessity dictates that it is the second alternative, not the first, that should hold. In general, whether p is a scientific law or not, prefixing "I correctly believe (via M) that" to a true belief p violating both of the last two conditions will restore both these conditions in one fell swoop, provided that close worlds in which p holds, but where S's application of M fails to lead to the conclusion that p, are much closer to the real world than worlds in which p fails outright.

---

[57] This formulation is somewhat crude and inexact. The antecedent may entail not that a particular law is false but that at least one of several laws must be false. Also, the desire to "hold the past fixed" in counterfactuals may conflict with preservation of law, so that we are forced to choose between wholesale "backtracking" changes of the past and a slight local violation of the law. In this case, we may well choose the latter. (See Lewis 1973:72–77, for one discussion.) These complications do not materially affect the substantive point and are ignored to simplify the formulation.

How general is the second class of cases? Unlike the technique exemplified by the red barn case, this technique does not require even that there should be a method satisfying condition 3 *available* to S (if only he had known of it) that would have led him to conclude that p. Even if the failure of p would have made no difference to S's experiences, and even if no method is available in principle to S that would have enabled him to "know" (in Nozick's sense) that p, nevertheless, if the second technique is applicable, we can find a conjunct q such that S "knows" that p & q. We have seen that the technique applies whenever S truly believes a scientific law. The case of "Jones is a woman" shows that the phenomenon is not confined to laws. In general, to apply the technique to p, we need to find a q passing Nozick's first three tests, and such that not-q is "more possible" than not-p. But there are cases where the technique cannot be employed: clearly the technique is inapplicable when p, though (very accidentally) true, came to pass by such a slight freak accident that no change in the world is slighter than the change needed to make p false. Whether there are such p's, and how common they are, depends on one's views about the similarity relation used in evaluating counterfactuals. Moreover, even if a q satisfying the requisite comparative possibility condition exists, remember that it must satisfy the first three conditions in relation to S, and such a q may not be available.

In spite of these warnings, it would seem that the technique is very widely applicable. Consider Henry again and his belief, p, that there is a genuine barn there. Suppose Henry also notes the exact position of a pebble in the field, q. Intuitively, it would seem that a slight change in the position of the pebble would have made the world much less different than a failure to erect the barn. Whether this means that not-q is appropriately "more possible" than not-p depends upon how close our intuitive notion of the similarity of situations is to the "similarity relation" between worlds used in evaluating counterfactuals. It seems very likely that some appropriate q is available.

Notice that both techniques for restoring the third condition depend on the same phenomenon. Given p, we find a conjunct q such that if p & q had been false, q would have been false. Then the point is that the third condition for p & q depends only on q, the conjunct that would have been false; p is completely irrelevant. We can say that p is "absorbed" by q. The only difference lies in the reason for the absorption. In the one case, exemplified by the red barn, p is absorbed because it too would have been false if q had been false. In the other case, exemplified by the actress, this need not be so. (For example, it need not be true that had she not been a woman, she wouldn't have gone into acting.) Rather, p is absorbed because not-p is "less possible" than not-q. In the Lewis–Stalnaker counterfactual logics, it can be shown that absorption is exhausted by these two cases.

As I already mentioned, Nozick praises his third condition as "powerful and intuitive, not so easy to satisfy" (173). But in a vast class of cases, owing to absorption, it does not prevent these statements from being components of "known" conjunctions $p \& q$. Given the artificial way the absorption phenomenon allows the first conjunct to be ignored when we consider whether $p \& q$ passes the test, the third condition is much less intuitive than it may look at first sight. Further, in the large subclass of cases exemplified by the red barn (though not in the subclass exemplified by the actress), if someone goes on to deduce that p from $p \& q$, then on Nozick's analysis the third condition is satisfied even for p itself (even if it was not satisfied using the original method). Given these facts, it is unclear to me how much the third condition really accomplishes.

Ironically, it is not as if Nozick fails to notice the possibility of absorption. On the contrary, discussing an example with two special beliefs p and q, he writes:

> S's belief that $p \& q$ tracks the fact that $p \& q$; if it were true he would believe it, and if it were false he wouldn't believe it. It may be that if the conjunction $p \& q$ were false, it is the [second conjunct q] that would be false, and in that situation the person wouldn't believe q and so wouldn't believe $p \& q$. However, it does not follow that his belief in p tracks the fact that p; for if p were false (which is not what would or might be the case if the conjunction were false—q would then be the culprit) he might still believe p. We can satisfy condition 3 for a conjunction by satisfying it for its most vulnerable conjunct, the one that would be false if the conjunction were false; it does not follow that we satisfy condition 3 for the other conjuncts as well. (228)[58]

This is a very clear statement of the absorption phenomenon. Indeed, Nozick thinks that the absorption phenomenon is virtuous, in that it gives us an "intuitive understanding" (227) of how one can know a conjunction without knowing one conjunct.[59] I would protest that this "explanation" merely shows why the concept defined by Nozick's conditions is not closed under simplification. In no way does it give one an "intuitive understanding" of why *knowledge* is not closed in this way, unless we are already firmly convinced that Nozick has given the right analysis. Otherwise, the phenomenon might well be taken as an argument that Nozick *cannot* have gotten the concept right. We have already seen the very artificial way in which Nozick's analysis leads to a proliferation of cases where true beliefs get promoted to knowledge by adding a conjunct. Anyone aware of these cases could hardly believe that Nozick's analysis, in and of itself, gives one an "intuitive understanding" of the failure of knowledge to be closed under simplification. However, even aside from these cases, many (including me), will find it intuitively very hard to swallow any proposal that one can know a conjunction without knowing, or being thereby able to know, a conjunct. Even

---

[58] I have changed the quotation slightly so that it will be consistent with our previous usage, where p is the conjunct that is absorbed. In the original, it is q.

[59] Actually, the phrase occurs in connection with his view that knowledge is not closed under universal instantiation. It is clear from the context that Nozick thinks that the quoted paragraph gives an analogous understanding with respect to the failure of simplification (inference from a conjunction to a conjunct). (Michael Levin has commented that the connection Nozick draws is natural when UI is conceived as an infinitary generalization of simplification.)

Dretske, who, as we (and Nozick himself) have seen, proposed a counterfactual theory of knowledge and denied deductive closure long before Nozick, states, "It seems to me fairly obvious that if someone knows that P and Q, ... he thereby knows that Q" (1970:1009).[60]

In the paragraph just quoted from Nozick, p was "I am not floating in a tank in Alpha Centauri being stimulated to have my experiences," and q was "I am in Emerson Hall now." The conjunction in question (put now in Nozick's original

---

[60] As Nozick points out (692, note 63), however, if we deny the deductive closure of knowledge, we must also deny either closure under simplification or closure under known logical equivalence. For if S knows p entails q, then we can assume S knows p is logically equivalent to p & q, and hence, assuming closure under simplification and known logical equivalence, if S knows p, he knows p & q (equivalence) and hence knows q (simplification). Why, however, should one insist on closure under known logical equivalence, especially if one has already rejected deductive closure and is therefore forced to reject closure under simplification? Nozick seems to give no argument.

However, two arguments, one for the intuitive concept of knowledge, and one for "gnowledge," as formally defined by Nozick's conditions, favor closure under known logical equivalence. For knowledge, there is the intuitive argument that for S two statements known to be logically equivalent, especially when the equivalence is simple, "amount to the same thing" and hence ought to be epistemically interchangeable (see immediately below in the text; it is especially natural for the case Nozick considers).

Another argument can be given for "gnowledge," and really argues for closure when S truly believes (and notices) the logical equivalence (with qualifications noted below). Suppose S truly believes that p. Since q is logically equivalent to p, and S notices this, S truly believes that q. For the third counterfactual condition, notice that if S had not believed p, and S does believe p logically equivalent to q, S would not believe q either, so the third condition is preserved. Similarly for the fourth condition.

Really, the argument concerning the counterfactual conditions has a gap, and we need a more qualified statement. Take the third condition. If p had not been the case, then S would not have believed that p. Since p and q are supposed to be logically equivalent, the suppositions in the antecedent of the counterfactual are in effect the same. However, to conclude that under this condition S would not have believed that q, so that the third condition is preserved for q, one must assume that even if S had not believed that p, S would have retained the belief that p and q are logically equivalent (even if p had not been the case). Normally, this would be the case; but no doubt special counter-instances could be given. There is no corresponding problem for the fourth condition since its antecedent is supposed to be true.

The argument also must be made more precise when one has to mention the method used, though this does seem to lead to possible qualifications. If p had not been the case, then S would not have believed that p by method M. But then even if p and q are correctly believed to be logically equivalent, one must suppose that S would not have believed that q. But the method M' would have been subtly different (assuming that the complication in the previous paragraph had not arisen). Namely, the method M' would consist, say, of noting whether p by method M, and then noting the logical equivalence of p and q. It would seem that this would be satisfactory, and similarly for the fourth condition. Changing true belief of the logical equivalence of p and q to known logical equivalence does not seem to alter the slight complication mentioned in the previous paragraph.

One reason that one might ignore all complicated arguments is the idea mentioned above that at least statements that are obviously logically equivalent "amount to the same thing" and thus can be treated the same way both in counterfactuals, and intuitive cases of belief and knowledge.

Given Dretske's assertion, he must hold that it is closure under known logical equivalence, not simplification, that should be given up. I do not believe Dretske has taken a position on known logical equivalence (at least when I wrote the original version of this paper). I have not checked whether an argument analogous to the one I just gave for Nozick shows that Dretske's counterfactual theory too would ordinarily be committed to closure under known (or truly believed) logical equivalence (with the qualification discussed).

order) was "I am in Emerson Hall now and not floating in a tank in Alpha Centauri. . . ." This example has two special features that may have encouraged Nozick to think that he had given an intuitive justification for the absorption phenomenon and failure under simplification. First, the conjunction is analytically equivalent (or nearly so) to the conjunct "I am in Emerson Hall now." We all think, intuitively, that when Nozick is in Emerson Hall, he knows that he is, and so we may think that knowing the conjunction amounts to knowing the same thing.[61] This will be so, especially if we believe that assertions that are known to be (trivially) logically equivalent "amount to the same thing." Nozick has emphasized that, given this, failure of simplification goes hand-in-hand with failure of deductive closure (see my note 60 for a discussion). Second, and even more important, in this case p, the absorbed conjunct, is the denial of a skeptical hypothesis. Although according to Nozick we do not *know* that p, presumably we are rightly in no *doubt* about p. This is what makes not-p a skeptical hypothesis. This fact may make it seem less embarrassing that we know statements that entail p, or even contain p as a conjunct. The whole contemporaneous trend against deductive closure, well established for some time before Nozick, was based on the idea that only if knowledge is not deductively closed can we know ordinary beliefs that entail denials of skeptical hypotheses.

Hence I note that these special features of Nozick's example are completely irrelevant to the absorption phenomenon per se. As we have seen, in fact it is hard to find *any* true belief p that definitely cannot be absorbed by adding a suitable conjunct. Given his example, Nozick seems to be aware of absorption phenomena of the second (actress) type. In such cases, the falsity of p is so much farther from the actual world than that of q that p is absorbed in the third condition. However, in the red barn class of cases the falsity of p need not be farther from the real world than that of q. Even in the second class, exemplified by the actress, our examples show that the fact that not-p may be farther from the real world than not-q has nothing to do with any indubitability of p. In fact, p may be a statement that, intuitively, we have no business believing at all; perhaps almost all true beliefs p can be absorbed by an appropriate conjunct q. In neither class need the conjunction even approximately "amount to" its second conjunct; in fact, provided that the appropriate formal properties hold, the original proposition and the conjunct may have little intuitive or epistemic relation to each other.

---

[61] Since—at least in theory (for all the reader may know a priori)—Emerson Hall may be on Alpha Centauri, the conjunction, as formulated, might not be quite analytically equivalent to the statement about Emerson Hall. But Nozick plainly intends to ignore this possibility, as we do. A more exact discussion would reformulate the case.

Nozick's very text shows how the locutions involved are not really analytic or a priori. For the reader may be confused by Nozick's wide travels. An earlier discussion (207) of the same example uses "I am in Jerusalem" instead of "I am in Emerson Hall." Presumably the pages were written in different places. An ignorant reader might be tempted to conclude that Emerson Hall is in Jerusalem.

Nozick is simply unaware of the ubiquity of the absorption phenomenon (as he is unaware of the fact that in the first class of cases his criterion for preservation of knowledge under deduction is satisfied if one deduces p).[62]

I consider these results to be major objections to Nozick's theory, and, *mutatis mutandis*, to various related theories. In some sense it seems to me that Nozick's counterfactual conditions are reduced to triviality if someone who is convicted under them of failure to know can almost always defend himself by saying, "Though I didn't know that p, I knew that I correctly believed that p (or that p & q, for a simple q)." (Even worse, in some cases, he will satisfy the conditions for knowledge that p if he goes on to deduce p from the conjunction.) Given these results, I find it hard to see why the distinction between "knowledge" and true belief would be of any substantial interest, or indeed why we would have the former concept at all. Although Nozick's theory is not quite a theory that knowledge is true belief, in spite of appearances it comes closer to being one than any other recent proposal of which I am aware.

To summarize the main technical results of this section: (1) If p fails to be knowledge solely for lack of the fourth condition's being satisfied, the conjunction "p, and I believe that p (via M)" (or, equivalently, "I correctly believe that p (via M)") satisfies all four conditions. Usually the clause "and I believe that p (via M)" can be replaced by another clause if we like, one that gives causally sufficient conditions for the belief that p to occur. (2) If p fails the third condition (and perhaps even the fourth) but is a true belief, in a wide range of cases "p and q, and I believe that (p & q) (via M)" (or, equivalently, "I correctly believe (via M) that p & q") satisfies all four conditions for an appropriate choice of q. Here, too, the last clause can normally be replaced by one not mentioning belief. (Sometimes, particularly in cases where p satisfies the fourth condition, the construction can be simplified to p & q.) In particular this happens if: (2a) a method (not the one he actually uses) satisfying the third condition is in some sense "available" to S; or (2b) S has a true belief q satisfying the third condition such that not-q is "more possible" than not-p. In an interesting special case of (2b), exemplified by belief in scientific laws, prefixing "I correctly believe (via M) that" to p restores both of Nozick's two counterfactual conditions when they fail for p alone. In case (2a), deduction of p from p & q actually satisfies Nozick's conditions for preservation of knowledge under deduction.

---

[62] In the third condition, the counterfactual hypothesis that Jones is not an actress is equivalent to a disjunction that Jones is either not in the acting profession or not a woman. Some, especially and notably Donald Nute in one period (e.g., Nute 1975), thought that, analogously to other conditionals, a counterfactual with a disjunctive antecedent ought to be equivalent to the conjunction of the separate counterfactuals with the respective disjuncts as antecedents. Perhaps some might have heard some counterfactuals that way. This would not affect one's intuitions if the antecedent were expressed simply as "Jones is not an actress"—it would be substitutivity of logical equivalents in counterfactuals that would be given up—and therefore would not really affect our point. However, the failure of such a substitution is really rather implausible, and Nute did not maintain his position.

(Two marginal notes: First, the case of knowledge of necessary truths provides an especially simple and blatant instance of the phenomena just discussed. Second, we're not quite through with hapless Henry. We shall pick up both these threads below.)

5. LOGICAL PROPERTIES OF NOZICK'S THEORY: ADDING A DISJUNCT, WEAKENED CONCLUSIONS, AND NOZICK'S THIRD CONDITION

5(a). Nozick's Argument that Adding a Disjunct Must Preserve Knowledge

Surprisingly, Nozick seems to think that adding a disjunct is very different from simplification, and that failure of knowledge to be closed under such inferences would be counterintuitive (230, and 692, note 64). It is hard for me to see the intuitive difference. At any rate, it is obvious that an argument exactly parallel to the simplification case (see my note 60) shows that closure of knowledge under known logical equivalence and addition of a disjunct implies deductive closure. For if p entails q (and we know this), then assuming p, we deduce (p or q), which we know is logically equivalent to q, and all steps are knowledge preserving. Moreover, how can Nozick reject closure under simplification, given his just cited views? Suppose we know p *&* q. Adding a disjunct, we (almost always) know (p *&* q or p) but using closure under known logical equivalence, it follows that we know p. Nozick's supposition that there is a substantial intuitive difference between closure under universal instantiation and closure under existential generalization (230) is surprising and dubious on similar grounds.

So I wrote in the original version of the present paper, leaving the matter at that, though soon after I gave actual counterexamples to the supposition that Nozick's conditions for knowledge are closed under adding a disjunct (see below). However, Assaf Sharon and Levi Spectre sent me an unpublished paper on the very question of adding a disjunct in Nozick's theory that has led me to additional thoughts. First, Sharon and Spectre pointed out that Nozick himself is inconsistent on the point in question. As we saw in the previous section, Nozick emphasizes that knowledge is not closed under simplification. His key example is "I am in Emerson Hall now and not floating in a tank in Alpha Centauri being stimulated to have these experiences." According to Nozick, he knows the conjunction but not the second conjunct, which is the denial of a skeptical hypothesis. Immediately Nozick goes on to say:

Also, it is possible for me to know p yet not know the denial of a conjunction, one of whose conjuncts is not-p. I can know p yet not know (for I may not be tracking) not-(not-p & SK) ["SK" standing for a skeptical scenario in which p is false]. I know I am in

Emerson Hall now, yet I do not know that: it is not the case that (I am in the tank on Alpha Centauri now and not in Emerson Hall). (228)

However, clearly the denial of a conjunction is logically equivalent to the disjunction of the denials of the conjuncts. Given this, and Nozick's assertion of closure under known logical equivalence, he has plainly contradicted his commitment to closure under adding a disjunct. Yet Nozick may well be right that the same "intuitions" about skepticism that lead him to reject simplification would also justify the case in the paragraph in question.

More important, as we have already noted before, and as Sharon and Spectre emphasize in their paper, Nozick gives conditions for when a valid deduction preserves knowledge and argues that (almost always) adding a disjunct satisfies these conditions. It is incumbent on any author who rejects the deductive closure of knowledge to state such conditions, so Nozick should be commended for doing so. Without them, and with a mere rejection of the deductive closure of knowledge, anyone who proves anything from known premises could be criticized for the well-known fallacy of giving a valid argument for a conclusion![63]

In Nozick's theory a deductive argument itself can count as a method M for arriving at knowledge. Nozick applies his analysis to consider when this method satisfies his own conditions 3' and 4'.[64] Here, we omit consideration of the fourth condition. For the all-important third condition, Nozick arrives at the following (231) when S validly infers q from a known premise p. The inference yields knowledge that q provided that:

I: If q were false, S wouldn't believe p (or S wouldn't infer q from p).

The parenthetical part of the condition is a rare case and normally need not be considered. On page 232 (see the note), Nozick mentions some other rare exceptions.

Finally, Nozick goes on to claim that his condition will almost always be satisfied for proofs by existential generalization or adding a disjunct. Unfortunately for our present discussion, Nozick spells out his argument for the claim only for existential generalization and states merely that "similar remarks apply to inferring a disjunction from a disjunct" (236).[65] So we must reconstruct his

---

[63] Moreover, this consideration seems to me to show that the cases where knowledge fails to be closed under known logical implication ought to be rare exceptions. We have already seen that Nozick's theory runs into trouble on this point.

[64] See his section "Proof and the Transmission of Knowledge" (230–40).

[65] It might be remarked that, alternatively, Nozick could actually have deduced closure of knowledge under adding a disjunct from the supposed proof that knowledge is closed under existential generalization. Granting the latter principle, the following steps preserve knowledge. p, therefore $(p \land 0 = 0) \lor (q \land 0 = 1)$ (known logical equivalence, which Nozick accepts), therefore $(\exists x)((p \land x = 0) \lor (q \land x = 1))$ (*existential generalization*), therefore, $p \lor q$ (*known logical equivalence*).

However, as I remark in the main text, Nozick's explicitly stated proof that knowledge is closed under existential generalization makes the same fallacy in counterfactual logic as in our reconstruction of his direct (analogous) proof for the closure of knowledge under adding a disjunct.

argument ourselves. It appears (by analogy to his argument for existential generalization) to be as follows: Suppose S infers (p or r) from p, where the premise p by hypothesis satisfies Nozick's third and fourth conditions. Then taking (p or r) to be the conclusion q in the condition I above (and omitting the rare parenthetical part), what we need is that had (p or r) not been true, S wouldn't have believed p. But (*i*) if (p or r) had not been true, p would not have been true. But since Nozick's third condition is by hypothesis satisfied for S's belief that p, (*ii*) if p had not been true, S would not have believed that p. Therefore, (*iii*) if (p or r) had not been true, S would not have believed that p, which shows that the desired condition is satisfied.

The argument is fallacious. (The analogous argument stated for existential generalization commits a similar fallacy.) It takes the counterfactual conditional to be transitive, which is a well-known fallacy for counterfactual logic, even though transitivity holds for the material conditional, the strict conditional, and even the relevant conditional and entailment (if one is concerned with these). (One might also think that the indicative conditional in ordinary language ought to be transitive.)

David Lewis has enumerated a set of fallacies for counterfactual logic that are valid principles for other types of conditionals.[66] One is the fallacy of *strengthening the antecedent*. That this is a fallacy will follow immediately, given that a counterfactual "if p were the case, q would have been the case" can be true even though it is *possible* that p and not-q would have been the case (to say otherwise would be to say that true counterfactuals are always strict [necessary] conditionals). Hence, even though "if p were the case, q would have been the case" is true, it does not follow that "if p and not-q had been the case, q would have been the case" is true. That *transitivity* is also a fallacy is an immediate consequence. For otherwise we could argue that if p and not-q had been the case, p would have been the case. Also (by hypothesis), if p had been the case, q would have been the case. Hence, by transitivity, if p and not-q had been the case, q would have been the case, which we have seen to be absurd.[67]

Nozick's hypothesized argument for adding a disjunct (like his actually stated argument for existential generalization) commits precisely the fallacy of transitivity in counterfactual logic. Just because we have "if (p or r) had not been true, p would not have been true," and "if p had not been true, S would not have believed p," it does not follow that "if (p or r) had not been true, S would not have believed p."

---

[66] Lewis (1973: section 1.8 ["Counterfactual Fallacies"]). Lewis mentions some other authors who recognize these fallacies also. See his second footnote on page 31.

[67] Lewis also gives an extended discussion (in section 1.8) of why these arguments are fallacies in terms of his own possible-worlds semantics for counterfactuals. He also gives some concrete intuitive counterexamples to the fallacious patterns, but these discussions are not really necessary for the main point. It is part of the very nature of a counterfactual, if it is to be distinguished from the strict conditional, that neither strengthening of the antecedent nor transitivity should hold.

In fact, since not-(p or r) is logically equivalent to (not-p & not-r), the fallacy involved can simply be regarded as the one of strengthening the antecedent. Just because we have "if p had not been true, S would not have believed p," it does not follow that "if neither p nor r had been true, S would not have believed p."

It is certainly lucky that Nozick's argument for the preservation of knowledge by adding a disjunct is fallacious. I myself believe that for the intuitive concept of knowledge, adding a disjunct ought to preserve knowledge. But for "gnowledge" as defined by Nozick's conditions, the situation is otherwise. We have already seen in the opening paragraph of this section what tangles, problems, and even contradictions would arise for Nozick's theory if adding a disjunct really did preserve his conditions. Very soon, below, we will give concrete counterexamples, showing that adding a disjunct can lead Nozick's third condition to fail, even though it holds for an individual premise.

In addition, as far as I can see, there is a fundamental problem with Nozick's condition I, his formulation of how to get his condition $3'$ when a conclusion q is inferred from a premise p. This condition seems to have nothing to do with whether the premise p is known or even whether it is *true*. (An analogous remark applies to Nozick's version of condition $4'$.) The method M involved, with its tracking conditions, seems simply to be inferring a truly believed conclusion from a *believed* premise. The Gettier problem made the issue of conclusions derived from a justified but false premise famous. But Nozick's condition I does not even demand that the premise be justified (and allows it to be false). Nozick's condition I does seem to be the formulation of $3'$ appropriate to his theory when the method is inferring a conclusion from a premise. But this seems to me to be a crushing objection to the theory itself. It has nothing to do with obtaining knowledge from known premises, or even true ones, justifiably believed or not. Significantly, prior to his formulation of condition I, Nozick seems to discuss the situation concerning the formulation of 3 when the method M is making a deduction, which is in effect $3'$ (188–89), and to conclude that, in spite of apparent difficulties, the consequences are satisfactory. I am unable to see that he shows this. (In particular, contrary to what he suggests there, his formulation seems not to accord with Harman's requirement that "the lemmas be true.")

5(b). Logical Difficulties with the Supposed Necessity of the Third Condition

Given that Nozick's argument that his third condition must be preserved by adding a disjunct is fallacious, we can still consider the third condition in and of itself and what happens to it under such a weakening.

As I have already remarked, the third condition has a clear intuitive flavor. "Even if p had been false, you would have believed it anyway" does sound like an objection to someone's claim to know. So even if the preceding arguments show (among other things) that Nozick cannot have given *sufficient* conditions for knowledge, it may still seem plausible that the third condition is *necessary* (although it would hardly be a useful necessary condition, since it can almost invariably be satisfied by strengthening the belief). But, in fact, this is far from true. An argument entirely symmetrical to the one that shows how trivially we can restore the fourth condition by conjoining "and I believe that p (via M)" allows us, equally trivially, to falsify the third condition—only here we weaken the statement by adding a disjunct.

To be precise, let p be anything S knows, both intuitively and in the sense of Nozick's four conditions (by method M). Let q be the weaker statement "either p or I do not believe that p (via M)," or, equivalently, "I do not falsely believe that p (via M)." Here S believes that q via the method M' of using M to conclude that p and then deducing (by weakening) that q. But now the third condition is no longer satisfied. For if q had been false, S would have believed that p via M (though falsely). Hence if S had applied M', S would have deduced that q, violating the third condition for the belief that q.[68]

The argument holds equally for the case where we do not mention any method M at all. Here q is simply "p or I do not believe p" or equivalently "I do not believe falsely that p." The third condition (normally) fails for q. For if q had been false, S would have believed p, and hence (normally), would *a fortiori* have believed the simple logical consequence q.

The parallel with the previous discussion of the fourth condition is obvious. It is dual to that discussion. In the earlier case, we trivially *fulfilled* the fourth condition by adding a conjunct about true belief. Now we force the third condition to be false by adding a disjunct about failure to believe. And the argument is fatal in quite a parallel way to the idea that the third condition is a necessary condition for knowledge. That idea would entail that virtually every time S knows that p, he does not know that he does not falsely believe (via M) that p. So to one convinced of the necessity of the third condition, the remark "For all you know, you may falsely believe p" is virtually invariably correct. (Skepticism rides again?) Equivalently, he never knows the disjunction "p or I do not believe (via M) that p," even when he knows that p.[69]

The fallacy in Nozick's argument that his third condition is preserved by adding a disjunct should now be even more blatant. Cases where we have "if p were the case, q would have been the case" are precisely those where we cannot strengthen the antecedent of a counterfactual conditional with p by conjoining it with not-q. Here supposedly we have "if p had not been the case,

---

[68] Michael Levin has pointed out to me that a similar argument is given in Vogel (2000). At present, I have not read Vogel myself.
[69] Michael Levin has observed that this example is equivalent to the negation of the familiar Moore's paradoxical sentences for not-p, "not-p, but I do not believe that not-p." So, therefore, what I have pointed out is that the negations of Moore's paradoxical sentences never satisfy condition 3.

S would not have believed p (via M)," Nozick's third condition. However, we cannot strengthen counterfactuals with not-p in the antecedent by adding "S does believe that p (via M)" to the antecedent. But the antecedent thus strengthened is logically equivalent to "not (either p or S does not believe that p (via M))." No wonder then that the third condition fails to be preserved when the disjunct that S does not believe that p (via M) is added.

In special cases one can replace the mechanical formula "p or I do not believe p (via M)" by a formulation appropriate to the case involved by giving the source of the belief and/or by spelling out the method. For example, suppose S sees a tree and hence knows (p) that there is a tree in front of him. Now consider the weaker disjunction (q) that either there is a tree in front of S, or S is not having a visual impression of a tree. (Equivalently, consider the material conditional that if S is having a visual impression of a tree, there is a tree in front of him). S believes q because he deduces it from p, and he believes p because of his visual impressions. If q had been false, S would have had a visual impression of a tree. If he used the same method he actually applies, he would conclude on the basis of his visual impression that there is a tree in front of him. It therefore follows that, applying this method, he would deduce the disjunction q. So the third condition fails for q.

In the preceding discussion, we weakened the statement by adding a disjunct that is obviously false. In one case, we added the disjunct "S does not believe p," in another, the disjunct "S does not have a visual impression of a tree." However, there are variant formulations of the method of weakening a statement to destroy the third condition, ways to add a disjunct to a statement so that the disjunction violates the third condition, where both disjuncts are true. For example, "Either there is a tree there or I am not hallucinating a tree," or "Either there is a tree there or I do not have a false visual impression of a tree."

6. METHOD

I now turn to Nozick's condition that the "method be kept fixed."[70] I want to look at his basic concept, but I begin with his treatment of "multiple methods." Nozick says that, if two methods M_1 and M_2 are used, one might "outweigh" the other. Nozick has an elaborate discussion of several cases (180–84). Rather than go through all of these, let me discuss one case to make clear that I do not generally share Nozick's intuitions on two methods.

Nozick cites a case that Armstrong reports in the name of Gregory O'Hair:

A father believes his son innocent of committing a particular crime, both because of faith in his son and (now) because he has seen presented in the courtroom a conclusive

---

[70] See also my section 1, pp. 164–65.

demonstration of his son's innocence. His belief via the method of courtroom demonstration satisfies 1–4, let us suppose, but his faith-based belief does not. If his son were guilty, he would still believe him innocent, on the basis of faith in his son. (180)

Nozick's intuition, in agreement with what Armstrong (1973:208–10) at least conjectures,[71] is that the father does not know that his son is innocent. He thinks that the belief obtained by courtroom demonstration is clearly outweighed by the method of faith in the son. It would have prevailed if his son were guilty (and, Nozick presumably means, even if the son's guilt were apparently demonstrated in court). M_1, the method satisfying Nozick's conditions, is the method of courtroom demonstration, while M_2, the method that is not, is the "method" of faith. Then in the case stipulated, M_2 outweighs M_1, so that the father does not know that his son is innocent.[72]

I find Nozick's intuition highly dubious, certainly not one that can be presupposed, as Nozick does, without argument. If everyone else, lacking prior faith in the son, can know that he is innocent on the basis of a conclusive courtroom demonstration, is it really true that the father simply cannot know it? Religious philosophers who believed on faith that God exists have sought to transform their faith into knowledge by finding a proof, even though their faith would override an apparent disproof. (They would think there must be a mistake somewhere, e.g., in an argument from the problem of evil.) Does a proper analysis of knowledge really show they were doomed to failure in advance? Suppose one of them comes up with a valid proof. Was he really doomed to failure even though an erstwhile skeptic can know from his proof that God exists?

My doubts here are reinforced by the fact that once again failure of deductive closure runs amok here, along the lines of the previous sections. Suppose the son's defense lawyer proves conclusively in the courtroom that someone else, Smith, is the (sole) culprit. The father had no advance opinion as to the true culprit; courtroom demonstration is the only method by which he arrives at this belief. Then according to Nozick, the father does know that Smith is the sole

---

[71] Actually, Armstrong has much less of a firm intuition than Nozick. Originally, O'Hair's case (without a specification of what would have happened when M_1 and M_2 conflict) was supposed to be a case where the father clearly does know. Armstrong hopes (see 210) that if the father fails the extra test, he does not know, and that this result saves his analysis from the objection. Unlike Nozick, he does not use the intuition to motivate his analysis, nor does he seem to regard its truth as evident.

[72] Nozick actually gives a technical definition of outweighing (182), which we omit, taking the notion simply intuitively. As Nozick defines the idea, one method may outweigh another with respect to one belief p, but the situation may reverse in principle with respect to another belief.

Nozick also stresses that the father does not satisfy the original simple condition 3, mentioning no methods. In fairness to Nozick, he states: "Some may hold the father is made more sure in his belief by courtroom proof; and hold that the father knows because his degree of assurance (though not his belief) varies subjunctively with the truth" (683, note 17). This point of view differs from what Nozick seems to think categorically in his main text.

culprit. (Presumably he also knows that Smith is not his son.) Even if we deny the deductive closure of knowledge, is it really credible that the father knows that Smith is the sole culprit but not that his son is innocent—even though everyone else knows that the son is innocent on this basis? If the father really *does* know that Smith did it, what purpose can it serve to deny that he knows that his son is innocent? The situation here is almost inevitable. The defense has almost surely proved some more specific fact, not previously believed by the father on faith, that cleared the son.

Similarly, a religious philosopher may have produced a valid ontological argument, proving that it is analytic that God exists. He did not previously hold this technical doctrine as a matter of faith. Then according to Nozick, the religious philosopher knows that it is analytic that God exists, but does not know that God exists! One has to be a very fanatical opponent of deductive closure to swallow this particular case. The problem here is very general. Almost always, when a method is "outweighed," some stronger conclusion will have been reached by the outweighed method alone. I doubt that Nozick's intuition on "outweighing" can survive this problem.

Notice one other aspect of Nozick's account of the father. His criteria would seem to deny the father knowledge that his son is innocent on the basis of the courtroom demonstration even if he does not realize what his reaction would have been had the courtroom case gone the other way. As long as his faith in his son would have been dominant, he need not be aware of this hypothetical situation in order for one to deny him knowledge on the basis of his seeing his son cleared in court.

Let us reconsider Nozick's grandmother case (179, cited in my section 1). Surely a grandmother who clearly sees her grandson alive and well, talks to him, and so on, knows that he is alive and well. Yet if he were sick or dead, friends would assure her that he was alive and well, and she would believe them. Just this case led Nozick to introduce the requirement that the method (looking at the grandson and talking to him) be kept fixed. But does this really help? Let us look at the case in the light of Nozick's views about Armstrong's father case. Suppose that even if the grandmother had seen the grandson, she would have believed assurances from her friends that he was only pretending to be dead[73] (or sick) and was really alive and well. Then it seems that her method of looking at the grandson, and so on, is outweighed, according to Nozick, by the method of believing her friends.

Is this result really credible? Nozick's intuition, and mine, was that, of course, a grandmother who believes that her grandson is alive by looking and talking to

---

[73] Alternatively, she would have believed assurances that she had mistaken someone else for the grandson. The main point is that, analogously to Armstrong's father case, she is strongly motivated to accept assurances that her grandson is not dead (or sick).

him does know that he is alive. But whether his requirement of keeping the method fixed really saves the situation from falling to the third condition is no longer so clear to me.

Nozick mentions that in his cases of multiple methods (in particular the Armstrong father case) one might instead regard the subject as using a single complex method (684, note 20). For example, Armstrong's father might use the complex method: "believe about one's son whatever the method of faith tells one, and only if it yields no answer, believe the result of courtroom demonstration." Regarded this way, the father follows a single method that violates the third condition. Regarded similarly, the grandmother following a complex method—"give priority to favorable assurances from one's friends about one's grandson, and follow the evidence of one's own eyes and ears only if this yields no result"—does not know even if she has seen and talked to her grandson. Once again, the very intuition that Nozick wanted to preserve by his requirement that the method be kept fixed in fact appears to be violated.

Reconsider also Nozick's treatment of Harman's dictator (see my section 4 (a)). Nozick introduces this case (177) before he makes any consideration of the requirement that the method be kept fixed, illustrated by the grandmother, and states simply that the fourth condition handles the case, even though the other three conditions do not. Assume for the moment the Nozick–Harman intuition that the subject does not know that the dictator has died, and waive all our previous objections to Nozick's treatment of the case. Surely Nozick regards this case as involving a method also, like the grandmother case. It is not a case too central and obvious to invoke any particular method. I assumed as much in section 4(a).

What is the method used? If the case were analogous to Nozick's treatment of that of the grandmother, the method would simply be believing what one has read in the newspaper. But then there is no violation of the fourth condition. Let the method instead be believing what one has read in the newspaper as long as it is not contradicted by an official denial. Then on Nozick's lights, condition $4'$, mentioning the method, might be violated, even though the subject has not heard any official denial. But then, analogously, the grandmother's method should be believing the evidence of her own eyes and ears unless this is contradicted by assurances from friends. She has heard no such assurances, because they are not needed. Nevertheless, the new complex method violates the third condition. So Nozick has not saved his intuition after all.

Alternatively, one might view the Harman dictator case as involving two methods, believing the newspaper (M_1) and accepting official announcements (denials) (M_2). M_2 is supposed to outweigh M_1, and this fact is supposed to destroy the subject's knowledge, even though M_2 is not in fact used. But then the grandmother should have two methods also. M_1 is accepting the testimony of her own senses, and M_2 is believing assurances from friends. One can again suppose that M_2 outweighs M_1, even though M_2 is not in fact used, because it is not needed in this case. But M_2 is a method violating Nozick's condition $3'$, so again the grandmother's knowledge is lost.

So Nozick's treatments of Armstrong's father and Harman's dictator both appear to be in some tension with what he wants for the grandmother. The grandmother case is what motivated the introduction of "keeping the method fixed" in the first place. I do not say categorically that these are insurmountable problems. Perhaps a clarification will save the situation. However, one should not appeal to "leeway" to get around these problems. There should be some solution that can be stated in positive, precise language. See what immediately follows.

7. LEEWAY

The problem of multiple methods and complex methods above brings out the "leeway" that Nozick appeals to both in his use of counterfactuals and in his concept of method (193). Nozick seems to think that he can use the notion of method "loosely and intuitively" without a precise rule to choose between alternative descriptions of the method—or even between interpretations so that his conditions agree with intuition—provided that he does not "exploit the leeway or wobble inconsistently, first leaning in one direction and then in another." Unfortunately, he appears not to satisfy this desideratum, as our discussion in the preceding section would seem to show. Nor is it clear to me that his description of the method is always the "intuitive" one.

I think Nozick's four conditions (or any other theory) ought to be considered objectively, without prejudice as to whether they agree with our intuitive concept of knowledge. If the conditions are vague and indeterminate, or otherwise problematic, in some case where the question whether one knows is itself clear, that in and of itself is enough to show that the conditions do not define the concept of knowledge. No doubt the situation is not as bad as when they definitely disagree with the intuitive concept, but it would still be bad enough to show that the concepts are not the same. I agree with Nozick that if the answer is indeterminate for some cases, his theory (if unrefuted elsewhere) could still be a first step, compatible with something more precise. However, if the theory is highly confusing or problematic in some case where our intuitive concept about knowledge is clear, this seems to me to be a strong objection to it. Cases that I have in mind will become clear in section 12 below. Moreover, forcing the conditions so that they yield desired results is dangerous.

8. METHODS THAT DO NOT ALWAYS YIELD A CLEAR RESULT

Suppose I am introduced to someone at a party attended wholly by adults. If the situation is normal, surely I know that I have not been introduced to a four-year-old. But suppose I am not very good at estimating the exact ages of young children; often if I were introduced to a four-year-old, I might well guess his age as three or five. Hence Nozick's third condition is not satisfied: even if I had been introduced to a four-year-old, I might have believed that I had not been introduced to a four-year-old.

In this use of condition 3, did I "hold the method fixed"? Intuitively, I would say that the method M that I used was "sizing up the age of the person I met on the basis of her appearance," and this method is held fixed. But perhaps Nozick might try to save condition 3 by arguing that the method is, rather, "sizing up whether the person is an adult and, if the answer is affirmative, deducing that she is not four years old" (*leeway*). If that is the method used, then in the previous paragraph it was not held fixed. However, such a move strikes me as rather artificial; it seems to me that the situation would not be changed if no concept of adulthood were in my repertoire. Nor should I say that I have applied the method of deducing that she is not four years old from the proposition that she clearly is not four years old. In this situation, there is no independent proposition *that she clearly is not four years old* from which the proposition that she is not four years old could be deduced. The term "clearly" modifies the force or decisiveness with which the method of sizing up the person's age yields its result. It does not change the conclusion itself. (Note that, in this example, any vagueness of the term "four years old" is not at issue; we may suppose that the boundaries of the term are precisely fixed. The trouble is that I may have difficulty judging whether a given child fits into these boundaries.)

The problem illustrated by the example seems to be this: in some cases a method M may clearly and decisively lead S to believe that p, and do so properly. Yet if p had not been the case and S had attempted to apply M, the application of M would have been difficult or delicate, so that S might still have judged that p. Thus Nozick's third condition would be violated, but intuitively we would not deny that S knows that p, since the difficulties in applying M did not in fact arise.

Goldman, in a paper Nozick cites,[74] already gave another example that illustrates the problem. I look at a field and judge correctly that there is a dog there. Let this be the belief p in question. I can very easily distinguish the dog I saw (a dachshund) from a wolf. On the other hand, had there been no dog in the field, there might well have been a wolf in its place. There are other breeds of

---

[74] Goldman (1976:779).

dogs that I cannot easily distinguish from wolves (Goldman mentions malamutes and German shepherds). So, had there been a wolf there and not a dog, I might well still have thought there was a dog there (of the other breed, say, malamutes). So condition 3 is violated, since even had there not been a dog I might have thought there was. Intuitively, this does not appear to affect my knowledge claim, given that the particular dog in the field is of a breed that I never confuse with wolves. Note (perhaps Goldman does not stress this) that the conflict in this case of Nozick's condition 3 with intuition[75] does not require that I have any concepts of the breeds in question.

However, I wish to mention a possible way out that I did not consider in the original formulation of this section. It is a simple modification of the "clearly" formulation mentioned above. Nozick might consider the judgment that there is a dog there as deductively derived from the premise that there is a dog there that is in no way resembling (or confusable with) a wolf. From this premise, the subject deduces that there is a dog there. Nozick could then claim that his argument satisfies his conditions for preserving knowledge by deduction. To me, there are two difficulties with this. First, we have seen that Nozick's theory of when deduction preserves knowledge has considerable problems. But second, and waiving these difficulties, it is extremely implausible to suppose that the subject goes through such a deduction. The subject simply sees a dog and judges that there is one.

Such cases are troublesome for Nozick's condition 3' as it stands. Rather than try to force the description of the method used into a mold where condition 3' can be regarded as satisfied, I think it would probably be preferable to modify the statement of condition 3' so as to take into account the force or decisiveness of the way a method yields its conclusion. I will not investigate whether this can be done satisfactorily.[76]

9. KNOWLEDGE OF NECESSARY TRUTHS

Nozick emphasizes[77] that his analysis offers a unified account of knowledge, treating necessities such as mathematical and ethical truths in the same way it

---

[75] Obviously, Goldman, writing before Nozick's book appeared, did not direct his argument directly against Nozick's condition 3. But it obviously applies, and Goldman had a similar problem in mind. Michael Levin, who called my attention to Goldman's later review of Nozick's book (Goldman 1983), points out that there Goldman explicitly directs essentially the same counterexample to Nozick's condition 3 as formulated. Levin also seems to think that there is some conflict between Goldman's proposals for a way out of the difficulty in his paper and in his review, but I will not consider this question.

[76] Goldman's analyses ought to be considered in this connection, though he himself indicates in Goldman (1983) that it is unlikely that Nozick's condition 3 could plausibly be maintained as it stands.

[77] See page 186, first paragraph. This paragraph begins his section entitled "Knowledge of Necessities."

treats empirical truths. Indeed, the desire for a unified account was a major reason that Nozick replaced Goldman's earlier causal analysis (Goldman 1967) with a counterfactual formulation (see page 70). The point was that although causal notions do not apply to mathematical and ethical truths, counterfactual conditionals still make sense when applied to such truths. It is very plausible that a unified account is indeed desirable; prima facie it would seem that "*S* knows that *p*" expresses one and the same relation between *S* and *p*, regardless of what proposition *p* is, or, for that matter, who *S* is.

Nozick observes that if *p* is a mathematical truth, his third condition has an impossible antecedent, since it asks us to consider what would be the case if *p* were false. He writes:

Perhaps a theory of subjunctives can be constructed to cover such cases—none has yet been proposed that is remotely satisfactory—but we should try to avoid such a desperate expedient. (186)

He immediately concludes that "condition 3 does not come into play for necessary truths" and hence that the question whether a given belief in a necessary truth is knowledge reduces to the fourth condition.

Here I find Nozick's methodology very puzzling. First, if one of the conditions is unintelligible for mathematical truths, or at least one for which no remotely satisfactory account has been given, where after all is the greater generality and unity of a counterfactual account over a causal account? Even more important, if in a given case one clause of a conjunction is obscure, doesn't that make the entire conjunction obscure for that case? Clearly such a situation does not allow us simply to drop the conjunct.[78] Had Nozick believed, with Lewis and Stalnaker, that a counterfactual with an impossible antecedent is vacuously true, then indeed the third condition would drop out as vacuously satisfied; but Nozick's quoted remarks make it clear that this is not his opinion. He might have reformulated his theory disjunctively, with one disjunct applying to contingent truths, containing the third condition, and one applying to necessary truths, lacking it. But then knowledge of necessary truths is treated specially, not as the result of a unified theory treating necessary and contingent truths in the same way.

More important, it is hard to see how the third condition can simply be dropped here without replacement (as we would do if we followed the Lewis–Stalnaker condition for these counterfactuals). The third condition was meant to

---

[78] Suppose one has a mathematical condition on real numbers defined as a conjunction of several conjuncts. There could be just one variable, or more than one. Suppose that for certain value(s) of the variable(s), one of the conditions is ill-defined; say, it has a rational expression whose denominator comes out as zero. Then clearly the entire conjunction is ill-defined for that case; one cannot simply drop the ill-defined conjunct.

If one defined the condition disjunctively, dropping the ill-defined conjunct when it makes no sense, we would not have a "unified account."

rule out methods that conclude that p too readily—even had p been false, the third condition objects, the method would have concluded, or might well have concluded, that p. Don't we need some condition to rule out such methods even if p is necessary? The fourth condition, which, on the contrary, is meant to rule out methods that are insufficiently likely to conclude that p, is hardly likely to do the same job. (This is obvious even if we forget for the moment that we have shown above, in the section on strengthened conclusions, that the fourth condition is toothless, a broken reed.)

Let me give an example. Suppose S, unaware of the irrationality of $\sqrt{2}$ and of the Pythagorean theorem, assumes that all real numbers are rational. He then deduces that C is rational, where "C" abbreviates a definite description characterizing a particular real number either by contingent physical means or by a mathematical definition. Even if C is in fact rational, we should not think intuitively that S knows that it is—but why not? The fourth condition, intended to rule out methods that are too conservative in concluding that C is rational, seems irrelevant—the trouble is that the method draws this conclusion too hastily. In fact, the fourth condition seems to be satisfied—using this method, S would inevitably have concluded that C is rational whether it was rational or not. Suppose "C" abbreviates a physical definite description (e.g., the mass of some object, or a fundamental physical constant), where the value of "C" depends on contingent features of the world.[79] Then "C is rational" is only contingently true. Surely, then, Nozick would find the trouble in the third condition—even if C had been irrational, S would have believed, using this method, that C was rational.

If C is mathematically defined, and hence "C" abbreviates a rigid designator, then the third condition is a counterfactual with an impossible antecedent. Nozick tells us that the condition should be dropped, but doesn't it need a substitute if we are to deny that S knows that C is rational? We might try analyzing counterfactuals with impossible antecedents after all, or we might point out that the method is unreliable over a range of "similar" cases, or we might try something else, but we cannot just drop the third condition without replacement. Nozick's explanation (188, first two paragraphs) of why we "needn't worry" about the third condition when p is necessary seems to me to be quite wrong.

Further, Nozick seems to be unaware of the ubiquity of the problem of counterfactuals with impossible antecedents in his theory. He seems to suppose that it is confined to cases of mathematical and ethical truths, as if these exhausted the necessary truths. Since elsewhere I have argued to the contrary at length (Kripke 1980 and Chapter 1, this volume), may I be pardoned if I contest such a supposition here? Surely I know, if I know anything, that Ronald Reagan is not

[79] Some may argue that such examples are not so easy to find. But we will suppose for the argument that they are possible.

the Taj Mahal and that Jimmy Carter is not Cleopatra. These statements are not mathematical truths and may not seem to be "analytic" in any straightforward sense. But if I consider whether I know these things, must I ask what I would have believed if Ronald Reagan had been the Taj Mahal or if Jimmy Carter had been Cleopatra? What would such questions mean? Elsewhere, invoking the "closest continuer" theory of personal identity that he favors, Nozick doubts my view that true identities are necessary (656–69). Presumably, he also doubts the necessity of true negations of identities. I do not agree with Nozick about this, but even if he were right about the cases he has in mind, it would be hard to dream up cases to show that Reagan might have been the Taj Mahal or that Jimmy Carter might have been Cleopatra. Not that the third condition is irrelevant: once again, if it is dropped, it needs a substitute guaranteeing that the method used is not too hasty in drawing its conclusion.

Similarly, at least according to me, such straightforwardly empirical truths as that such-and-such a table was made from such-and-such a block of wood are necessary. So, according to me, are various truths about natural kinds and physical phenomena, such as that gold is the element with atomic number 79, that heat is molecular motion, that heat is not a caloric fluid, that whales are mammals, and so on; and in this view I have been ably supported by Hilary Putnam.[80] If any of these truths is necessary, and if we know any of them, then any time we try to verify that Nozick's condition 3 holds, we cannot avoid counterfactuals with impossible antecedents; there are no possible worlds, or counterfactual situations, in which they are false. Since our knowledge of these truths is straightforwardly empirical, it would appear that on Nozick's view something like the third condition is obviously needed to make sure that we have ruled out relevant alternatives, that we have not drawn our conclusion too hastily, and so on. (Of course, Nozick might reject some of these theses about necessity. But in fact he does not consider the issue at all.)

Perceptive readers may have noticed some awkwardness in my phraseology in previous discussions. Why did I speak of Henry believing that there is a genuine barn in the field or of the incautious experimenter as believing that he has tested a drug physically effective against the disease? I did so to make sure that the belief in question is contingent. Consider instead Henry's belief that *this object* (in the field) is a genuine barn. "This object" is a rigid designator. I can imagine that a papier-mâché barn, a different object from the one that is actually there, might have been erected on the field. However, it is impossible for me to imagine that

---

[80] See Kripke (1980), Lecture III; also Chapter 1, this volume. See also Putnam (1975), especially chapter 12 ("The Meaning of 'Meaning' "). In Putnam (1983), however, he criticizes my views on natural kind identities ("water is H_2O") as "far too strong," though he still endorses weaker versions. (These versions would be enough for the problems discussed here.)

Contrary to what some authors say, I did discuss the necessity of identity for natural kinds in Kripke (1980), not just proper names. In fact, Putnam (1983) attributes the view in question to me, and now accepts it only with considerable modification.

this very object, in fact a genuine barn, might have been a papier-mâché barn. If Nozick were to apply his explicit recipe to this case, and simply drop the third condition, then there would be no trouble about the remaining fourth condition. Henry, although he would not know that there is a genuine barn in the field, would know that this object is in the field and is a genuine barn, since being a genuine barn is an essential property of the object. What should we think of this failure of deductive closure? In a large number of cases, rigid designation presents a similar problem.[81]

Notice that the problem of rigid designation can arise even if the belief in question is straightforwardly contingent. Suppose Henry sees a (genuine) blue barn in the field. Suppose further that had the real barn not been there, a counterfeit of any color, blue included, might well have been erected in its place. As usual, Henry is ignorant of the presence of counterfeit barns in the area and would have been fooled had he seen a counterfeit. Everything is in place for us to conclude that Henry's belief that there is a blue barn in the field violates Nozick's third condition and hence is not knowledge according to Nozick's theory. But what of his belief that *this object* is a blue barn? The truth in question is contingent: this object might have been painted green. But now consider the third condition. If this object had not been a blue barn, that would have been because it would have been painted some other color, not because it was a papier-mâché counterfeit. (This very object could not have been a counterfeit.) But if the object had been of a different color, Henry would not have mistakenly believed that the object is a blue barn. So now the third condition is satisfied, and there is no trouble about the fourth. So Henry, ignorant as he is that there is *a* blue barn in the field, does know that *this object* is in the field and is a blue barn![82, 83]

I do not rule out a theory that allows nontrivial truth conditions for counterfactuals with impossible antecedents. We have strong inclinations to think that nontrivial counterfactuals with antecedents denying certain "empirical" necessary truths are possible. Even in the mathematical case, the counterfactual "if the consistency of set theory had been proved in a finitistic subsystem of set theory,

---

[81] Although I think that demonstratives and proper names are rigid, the problem does not depend on any such specific devices as long as: (a) in principle, rigid designators could be introduced into the language, and (b) objects can have essential properties that are known to be true of them. Indeed, as the next paragraph shows, the problem can arise even if the property attributed to the object is not essential.

[82] The present paragraph anticipates what I now regard as one of the most basic objections to Nozick's theory, and probably to similar theories using counterfactuals. See my discussion in section 2 and note 20.

[83] On page 219, Nozick shows some signs of accepting distinctions like these for some cases. See, for example, his discussion of the distinction between whether I know that I am having a dream according to his conditions, and whether I know that I am dreaming *this*. But, as in the case of the absorption phenomenon (see section 4(b)), he does not realize the great danger this type of problem presents for his counterfactual approach.

Hilbert would have been vindicated" looks true in a way that the corresponding counterfactual with "Hilbert would *not* have been vindicated" does not. On the other hand, it is quite true that it is hard to give a coherent theoretical account that yields such nontrivial truth conditions. Further, in many cases our intuitions do seem to go very dim when a counterfactual has an impossible antecedent. Can I really say, for condition 3, what I would have believed if Reagan had *been* the Taj Mahal, if 2×3 had *been* 7, or (to take an ethical case), if torturing children just for the fun of it had *been* a good thing? Do we have intuitions here?

Whether or not we try to revise the theory of the counterfactual to take care of impossible antecedents, or we attempt to adopt a different replacement for the third condition in the case of knowledge of necessary truths, the amendment would be pointless if it left the entire theory for contingent statements unchanged. For the trick of considering "p, and I believe that p (via M)" or, "I correctly believe that p (via M)," call it "q," works especially smoothly in the case of a necessary truth p. Note that even if p is necessary, the stronger statement q is contingent; so the ordinary theory would apply. If p is truly believed (via M), then the conjunction q obviously satisfies the first two conditions. Now the fourth condition is obviously trivialized, for reasons given above. For the third condition, to which we now are supposed to apply the usual theory for contingent statements, note that in considering situations where the conjunction is false, we need not worry about situations where p is false—by hypothesis, there are no such situations. Hence, if q had been false, I must not have believed that p (via M), and *a fortiori*, must not have correctly believed p, verifying the third condition for q. Hence the theory, for contingent truths alone, leads to the consequence that "I correctly believe that p" is known almost every time a necessary truth p is truly believed. This is hardly satisfactory.

10. THE FUTURE

If the sun were not to rise tomorrow, or if I were to release a book from my hands and it were to remain aloft in midair, I would be very surprised. I would maintain the same counterfactual retrospectively with respect to a date already past: if yesterday strange events such as these had happened, I would have been very surprised. The reason I would have been surprised is, of course, that under these circumstances I would have expected the opposite.

Assuming we know that the sun will not rise tomorrow, or that we did know it just before yesterday, these observations present a problem for Nozick's theory. The cases considered in the preceding paragraph go directly contrary to Nozick's third condition for the pieces of knowledge mentioned. For me to have known in advance that the sun would rise on a given date, the third condition demands that, if the sun had not risen then, I would not have expected the rising beforehand and hence would not have been surprised when it didn't rise. But it seems to me to be intuitively clear that, had the sun not risen, I would have been very surprised.

Nozick suggests the opposite intuition, that if "the sun were not going to arise tomorrow," we would "have seen that coming," because the event "would have been presaged" in antecedent events (222).[84] I think it is clear that things are not so obvious. I doubt that most readers would demur from the conditionals in the first paragraph of this section. Nevertheless, it is clear what idea motivates him. In a deterministic world, if the sun had not risen, how would that have happened? Only by some changes in the antecedent causes. In the literature on counterfactuals, this type of consideration is sometimes called "backtracking," and it has indeed been suggested that some counterfactuals do invoke backtracking. Does the third condition have at least an interpretation conforming to Nozick's backtracking ideas, so that "leeway" could be invoked here to rescue Nozick's third condition? Not to my ear, if the counterfactuals involved are to be understood "loosely and intuitively," as Nozick says. For me, it is unambiguously true that I would have been surprised had the sun not risen yesterday and that I would be surprised were it not to rise tomorrow. Even if I am wrong and this is not the only proper interpretation, surely Nozick should have taken this interpretation of the counterfactual into account and distinguished it (using "leeway"?) from the other one.[85]

Granted the backtracking interpretation, do Nozick's conclusions follow? I think they still do not. First, there could be quantum mechanical uncertainties, in principle unpredictable (or perhaps classical statistical mechanical uncertainties, unpredictable from a practical point of view) that caused an explosion, say, in the sun. Second, even in a fully deterministic world, if the sun had not risen this morning, would we obviously have seen that coming? For example, had the sun not risen, maybe it would have been because of some undetected problem in the interior of the earth that finally stopped its rotation, but which we would have been unaware of. Maybe it would have been as surprising to us as earthquakes are today.

Maybe these things are scientifically not the case, and indeed if the sun had ceased to rise, we could have seen that coming. But to me nothing is obvious here, it is a matter of delicate and very speculative scientific considerations. Intuitively, these issues have nothing to do with whether we know that the sun will rise tomorrow.

---

[84] Actually, Nozick phrases this as a rhetorical question, using a stylistic device that is frequent in his book. The context shows that he plainly intends an affirmative answer to be understood; he hardly intends to suggest without elaboration that his theory collapses at this point.

[85] In fairness to Nozick, in his note on page 223 he shows awareness of some of the problems with backtracking and even notes that David Lewis's discussion of the question does not agree with the tenor of his own footnote. Nevertheless, Nozick appears to me to be clearly wrong about this issue for the reasons stated in my main text.

Really, however, I should not let this discussion of "backtracking" issues detract from the clearly intuitive initial point in the first paragraph of this section. I think the reader, innocent of these discussions, would immediately agree that if the sun had not risen this morning, she would have been very surprised. Moreover, it is not an *objection* to a claim of knowledge (in advance of the rising) that the reader would have been surprised if it had not occurred. It is precisely because someone has adequate and rational grounds to have expected the rising that she would have been surprised had it not occurred. Nozick's third condition, requiring the exact opposite for a knowledge claim, seems to get matters reversed.

Like knowledge of necessities, knowledge of the future presents a problem for Goldman's old causal theory (1967)—the required causal relation would seem to run backward. Unfortunately, Nozick's form of the counterfactual theory appears to face similar difficulties. Even if the difficulties can be overcome, his own very brief and sketchy discussion hardly indicates how to solve the problems or even that his recognition of them is adequate.

11. SKEPTICAL HYPOTHESES

In agreement with many other recent theorists, Nozick thinks the skeptic argues successfully that we do not know that his skeptical hypotheses are false. Even though we *do* know various ordinary facts incompatible with a skeptical hypothesis, since knowledge is not deductively closed we can know the ordinary facts without knowing the skeptical hypothesis to be false.

We can discuss the intuitive and epistemological plausibility of this viewpoint later. Here I ask whether, as Nozick thinks, his counterfactual conditions really do yield this result. A favorite example is that none of us knows that he is not floating in a tank on Alpha Centauri (stimulated to have just the experiences that he actually has). The counterfactual situation described is "doxically identical for S to the actual situation," and "if S were in that situation, he would have exactly the beliefs (*doxa*) he actually does have" (202). In particular, he would still believe that he is *not* floating in a tank on Alpha Centauri, so that the third condition fails.

Actually, however, it is by no means clear that the situation described is "doxically identical" to the actual situation. Hilary Putnam's published work on skepticism and reference points out an essential problem, a problem that I discussed with John Dolan.[86] A tank floater on Alpha Centauri, stimulated with

---

[86] See Putnam (1981:1–25); also Putnam (1983). However, I do not necessarily endorse all of Putnam's conclusions. Surprisingly, Nozick mentions (168–69) Putnam's argument and criticizes it briefly, but does not notice its application to his own theory. As applied to Nozick's theory, Putnam's argument seems undoubtedly correct, whether or not it otherwise refutes skepticism. Nothing in Nozick's own discussion touches on this point.

exactly my experiences, will have a term "Alpha Centauri" and a term "Emerson Hall" in his vocabulary, but do these terms name the objects Alpha Centauri and Emerson Hall? They have none of the causal or historical connections with the star and the building that my terms do. The most typical definite descriptions the floater associates with "Alpha Centauri" will not be true of Alpha Centauri, for they will imply that "Alpha Centauri" names a star very distant from him. If the floater had been on earth, really living a life corresponding to his experiences, then "Alpha Centauri" would have referred to Alpha Centauri. But here there is no reason to think it refers to this star rather than to another one. Hence, there is no reason to ascribe to him a belief that he is in Emerson Hall and not floating in a vat on Alpha Centauri. This is entirely contrary to what Nozick says.

The problem is not confined to skeptical hypotheses containing proper names. As Putnam and I have emphasized, if I had lived in a world in which I had experiences qualitatively identical to the ones I actually have, my terms "gold" and "water" need not have referred to gold and water. They might have referred to substances other than gold and water, although similar to them in their surface qualitative effects. All the more so, wouldn't my terms "gold" and "water" have failed to refer to gold and water if I were a brain in a vat as described? What grounds could there be for assuming that they referred to these substances, rather than to various other hypothetical phenomenally similar substances? Problems of this kind arise also for terms purporting to refer to various physical phenomena.

Hence Nozick's claim that his third condition shows that we do not know the negations of various skeptical hypotheses is often vitiated, in particular for the hypothesis that I am on Alpha Centauri being stimulated to think that I am in Emerson Hall. If, following Nozick, we call the hypothesis in question SK (no pun on my name intended!), and the belief in question not-SK, then Nozick argues that since we do not have "if SK were the case, then I wouldn't believe SK," his third condition is violated for not-SK, and therefore SK is not known. Actually, Putnam's argument shows that, as Nozick puts matters, I am in no position to think or formulate the beliefs stated in SK, and therefore that the third condition does hold, at least in some vacuous manner.

It is not trivial to formulate skeptical hypotheses so "purified" of reference that no such problems arise. However, I have some inclination to think that this can be done (since I share Nozick's doubts that Putnam's argument really gets rid of skepticism). Perhaps there is a "narrow content" description of what the subject believes that is free of these problems. (Perhaps a "Ramsey sentence" version also would do.)

All we can say is that Nozick ought to have considered the problem, especially since he was aware of Putnam's argument, and that his picture does not seem to be true as stated. But perhaps the objection can be overcome in a revised version. Then there is yet another problem.

12. KNOWLEDGE OF THE CENTRAL AND OBVIOUS AND THE SUPERCREDULOUS PROBLEM

12(a). Central and Obvious Statements

Earlier I discussed whether I can know that someone I have met is not a four-year-old. Do I (Saul Kripke) know that I am no four-year-old? Prima facie, this proposition, just as much as the example "I have two hands" that Nozick gives explicitly (185) and for the same reasons, seems to be such a central and obvious proposition that it could not escape my notice and yet is not believed with the aid of any particular method or methods. For such propositions, Nozick recommends that we take his conditions in the simple form. But then condition 3 seems not to be satisfied. Presumably, a four-year-old might well be mistaken about his age: maybe he thinks he is three or five, and not four. Presumably I, too, had I been four years old, might have been liable to error and believed that I was not four years old. At least, the viability of condition 3 here seems to depend on the supposition that I, at least, were I fours years old, would be very reliable about my age. (Well, little children are fond of reciting their ages. But what about the proposition that I am not exactly four years, two months and sixteen days old? Would I have been reliable about that if I were exactly that age?) Here I ignore the complication that condition 3 may have an antecedent that is impossible or close to it. Might I really have been four years old now (in 1983)? Exactly how could that have happened?

Matters may be helped a bit if we take my belief that I am not four years old to be derived by a method after all, say, by inference from a more basic belief that I am an adult. The latter belief could then be a "central" one, that is, believed owing to no particular method. I am doubtful that this is a correct model, but even if it is, it doesn't seem clearly to help. Condition 3' would then require me to consider whether I would still believe via this method that I am not four years old even if I were a four-year-old. Well, might not a four-year-old fantasize that he is an adult and go on to deduce that he is not four years old? (Admittedly, this would be a worse mistake than getting his exact age wrong.) I think that this is a possibility, but it does not seem to me to give good grounds for a new form of philosophical skepticism—that I am merely a child fantasizing that I am an adult. Even granted the failure of the third condition, I do not see the appeal of this particular skeptical doubt (as long as I am not worried about some more fundamental form of skepticism).

Condition 3 is highly problematic for some of those statements that epistemologists since Descartes have regarded as expressing the firmest sort of knowledge: "I exist," "I am conscious," and the like. If I had not existed, how can I ask what I would have believed? Perhaps we could save condition 3 in this case by regarding it as vacuously satisfied: if I had not existed, I would not have been around to believe anything, including that I exist, so the third condition holds. Although this interpretation would save the third condition in this case, I am not sure whether it really captures the intuitive motivation of the third condition. I am not quite sure about the case of "I am conscious"—satisfaction of the third condition depends upon what my beliefs would be were I unconscious, a problematic notion that Nozick discusses very little, though he does refer to Freud (221).[87] Once again, one could protest that I wouldn't have any beliefs, vacuously satisfying the third condition.

What about my belief that the earth has existed for many years, one of those Nozick cites (185) as an example of a central belief? Well, what about my belief that it has existed for at least three years? Here, too, it is hard to understand the third condition. Had either of these beliefs been false, surely I would not have existed! It is (to say the least) unlikely that human beings would have evolved if the earth had existed for only a few years. Of course, we can save the third condition in the same somewhat artificial way we saved it for "I exist"—that is, count it as trivially true had I not existed.

But if we count condition 3 as true when its antecedent counterfactually implies my nonexistence or my lack of consciousness, we may not always avoid getting in trouble elsewhere. For example, in accordance with his general attitude about skeptical hypotheses, Nozick thinks (219) that I do not know that there are other people with genuine minds, rather than automata; and he thinks that the third condition fails. But, what would have been the case had all others, except perhaps me, been automata? Is it likely that I would have remained the one genuine human mind in the universe? It seems to me, on the contrary, that I would not have been conscious either, so that our rule would count condition 3 as trivially satisfied. Perhaps this case could be saved, either by subsuming it under condition 3', despite the centrality of the belief, or by a heavy invocation of leeway so as to count condition 3 as failing after all—maybe I would, or might, have been the only human mind in the universe.[88]

Nozick himself does actually discuss such statements as "I am alive" and "I am sentient," which are close to what I was just discussing (215, note). To my surprise, he regards them as known by a particular, though very basic, method, in contrast to the earlier statements (on 185) that are so basic and obvious that they are not known by any particular method. It is hard for me to see the difference between an example such as "there are eyes," which on page 215 (in the same

---

[87] Freud, however, really talked of unconscious beliefs, not of beliefs that someone has when he himself is unconscious.

[88] Of course, the situation is different for the belief that it is not the case that I alone in the universe have a mind and all others are automata. Then for the third condition, that I am the one exception is explicitly in the antecedent of the counterfactual. (Remember the fallacy of strengthening the antecedent.) However, is it really intuitively correct that the two beliefs (with or without the explicit condition about me) should be distinguished as known or not known in this way?

note) is supposed to be known by a particular method (apparently one that seems to require that one uses one's eyes), and "I have two hands," which is not supposed to be known by any particular method (185). He also seems to think we come to know that "looking," or some method using our eyes, is the method by which we come to believe that there are eyes. His basic problem, in the case of the "eyes" example (and also "I am alive" and "I am sentient") is that these statements are arrived at by a method that would not exist if they were false, creating a problem for the interpretation of condition 3'. Presumably, the method used to arrive at "I am alive" and "I am sentient" is Cartesian introspection, or some such thing. Also, in these cases, he does not regard the statements as so central and obvious that no particular method is used.

Although I do not really understand the reasons for this unexplained shift, nevertheless, given what Nozick says in the later passages, we ought to consider briefly what happens to some of our examples if we think of them as beliefs arrived at by a particular method M. Then condition 3' asks what I would have believed had I not existed but nevertheless went ahead and applied M. Plainly this becomes a counterfactual with a self-contradictory antecedent. In his discussion (which he also applies to other cases, such as my belief that I am not irrational or insane), he seems to be puzzled about the examples, and states, "I do not think this is simply incoherent, neither is it pellucidly clear" (216). In a footnote on the same page, he suggests that maybe he should apply the same methodology that he applied in the case of necessary truths, and drop the third condition because it becomes unintelligible. However, such a strategy is clearly methodologically unacceptable (see my discussion above, section 9). His puzzlement about the matter in the main text is methodologically far more appropriate. But then there is a problem. Consider, for example, "I am thinking" or "I am sentient." Epistemologists from Descartes onward have regarded these as among the most obvious and indubitable cases of knowledge, even if other things are doubted. Perhaps it took G. E. Moore (in philosophy, anyway) to add "there are eyes," as he explicitly added "there are hands," but to the common person, both are cases of very basic knowledge. It seems to me to be a considerable objection to Nozick's conditions, if they make such basic cases very problematic.

In the case of "the earth has existed for many years" (another example from Moore), if we applied condition 3', its antecedent would stipulate that even if the earth had existed for only a few years, I would nevertheless somehow have been around and able to apply method M. As I said above, I am not sure that this antecedent is really possible. Supposing, however, that this *is* possible, and that I were also in a position to apply the same method M that led me to believe that the earth has existed for many years (whatever M is supposed to be), what would I have concluded? Under such fantastic circumstances, and where M is difficult to specify, it is hard to say; perhaps condition 3' is satisfied, perhaps it is not.

As I said, Nozick discusses "I am sane and rational" (216–27) as a case in which I am not sure I am applying the method M that I think I am applying.

Nozick concludes that perhaps on his criteria we may not know that we are sane; the matter is difficult. If we were to treat the example "I am not four years old" similarly, we might run into similar difficulties—a four-year-old might think he was applying all the methods of an adult. So quite possibly, according to Nozick's criteria, I do not know that I am not four years old (even if we apply the primed conditions).

Remember what I said in section 7 about leeway. It seems to me that clear cases of knowledge, according to our intuitive concept, should not be difficult or unclear according to Nozick's theory. Thus the existence of such cases—clear cases of knowledge that are difficult or unclear according to his theory—is a basic objection to the theory.

One important case from Moore goes in another direction. One of Nozick's basic ideas is that, although ordinary beliefs may be known, the negations of skeptical hypotheses, even though they follow logically from these ordinary beliefs, are not known. But what of Moore's famous proof of an external world? (1939). Nozick accepts Moore's premise that I know that I have a hand (in fact, two). These are examples of basic knowledge. He also claims that existential generalization preserves knowledge, so that I also know that there is a hand (in fact, more than one). So it looks as if Moore's proof of an external world is valid and gives us knowledge.[89]

12(b). The Supercredulous Problem

Let me finish with the following case, a simple and obvious objection to anyone devoted to Nozick's third condition. Call someone *supercredulous* if he believes every proposition *p*. Of course, the concept of supercredulity is absurd: neither I, nor any other human being, has ever been supercredulous. Very well then, do I *know* that I am *not* supercredulous? This seems like the sort of central proposition that I do know, but not by any particular method.

Nevertheless, condition 3 fails. Since the belief in question is the belief that I am *not* supercredulous, the third condition states that even if I had *been* supercredulous, I would not have believed that I was not supercredulous. But then, of course, since a supercredulous person believes anything, I would have believed, along with everything else, that I was not supercredulous. So it would seem that, according to Nozick's theory, I do not know that I am not supercredulous, because the third condition is violated. This does not strike me as a very plausible form of skepticism. This argument against the third condition is

---

[89] Should one doubt that a hand is an external object? Of course, we have already seen that Nozick's argument that existential generalization preserves knowledge (as he defines it) is fallacious.

simple, almost silly,[90] but it shows very clearly how we cannot take Nozick's third condition as a "powerful and intuitive" test for whether I know.[91]

REFERENCES

Armstrong, D. M. (1973). *Belief, Truth and Knowledge*. London: Cambridge University Press.

Bonjour, L. (1980). "Externalist Theories of Empirical Knowledge." *Midwest Studies in Philosophy* 5:53–73.

Castañeda, H. N. (1968). "On the Logic of Attributions of Self-Knowledge to Others." *Journal of Philosophy* 65: 439–56.

Dretske, F. (1970). "Epistemic Operators." *Journal of Philosophy* 67:1007–23. Reprinted in Dretske (2000).

———. (1971). "Conclusive Reasons." *Australasian Journal of Philosophy* 49:1–22. Reprinted in Dretske (2000).

———. (2000). *Perception, Knowledge, and Belief: Selected Essays*. Cambridge: Cambridge University Press.

Gettier, E. (1963). "Is Justified True Belief Knowledge?" *Analysis* 23:121–23.

Goldman, A. (1967). "A Causal Theory of Knowing." *Journal of Philosophy* 64:357–72.

———. (1976). "Discrimination and Perceptual Knowledge." *Journal of Philosophy* 73:771–91. Reprinted in Pappas and Swain (1978).

———. (1979). "What is Justified Belief?" In Pappas (1979).

———. (1983). Review of *Philosophical Explanations*. *Philosophical Review* 92:81–88.

Harper, W. (1981). "A Sketch of Some Recent Developments in the Theory of Conditionals." In Harper, Stalnaker, and Pearce (1981).

Harper, W., R. Stalnaker, and G. Pearce, eds. (1981). *Ifs*. Dordrecht, Netherlands: D. Reidel.

Kripke, S. (1971). "Identity and Necessity." In *Identity and Individuation*, ed. M. Munitz. New York: New York University Press, 135–64. Reprinted in this volume, ch. 1.

———. (1980). *Naming and Necessity*. Cambridge, MA: Harvard University Press.

Lehrer, K., and T. Paxson. (1969). "Knowledge: Undefeated Justified True Belief." *Journal of Philosophy* 66:225–37.

---

[90] Indeed, Bertrand Russell would have rejected the argument as violating his ramified theory of types. In the notion of supercredulous as I have defined it, in the statement that someone believes every proposition p, p must be restricted as to type. Then the statement that he is supercredulous is also restricted as to type and is of higher type, not within the scope of the variable p in question. Hence the argument as given will fail. Someone could be supercredulous of a given type but not believe that he is not supercredulous (of that type).

Whatever we think of Russell's views, do we really think that such a technicality gets to the heart of the matter?

[91] My thanks to Jonathan Adler, Jeff Buechner, Harold Teichman, and Gary Ostertag for their helpful comments. Special thanks to Michael Levin for his very detailed comments and to Romina Padró for her help in producing the present version and for conversations about these issues and valuable suggestions. This paper has been completed with support from the Saul A. Kripke Center at the City University of New York, Graduate Center.

Lewis, D. (1973). *Counterfactuals*. Cambridge, MA: Harvard University Press.
Luper, S. (2004). "Indiscernibility Skepticism." In *Essential Knowledge*, ed. S. Luper. New York: Pearson.
Moore, G. E. (1925). "A Defense of Common Sense." In *Contemporary British Philosophy, 2nd Series*, ed. J. H. Muirhead. London: George Allen and Unwin. Reprinted in Moore (1959).
———. (1939). "Proof of an External World." *Proceedings of the British Academy* 25:273–300. Reprinted in Moore (1959).
———. (1959). *Philosophical Papers*. London: George Allen and Unwin.
Nozick, R. (1981). *Philosophical Explanations*. Cambridge, MA: Harvard University Press.
Nute, D. (1975). "Counterfactuals and the Similarity of Worlds." *Journal of Philosophy* 72:773–78.
Pappas, G., ed. (1979). *Justification and Knowledge*. Dordrecht, Netherlands: D. Reidel.
Pappas G., and M. Swain, eds. (1978). *Essays on Knowledge and Justification*. Ithaca, NY: Cornell University Press.
Putnam, H. (1975). *Mind, Language and Reality: Philosophical Papers, Volume 2*. Cambridge: Cambridge University Press.
———. (1981). *Reason, Truth and History*. Cambridge: Cambridge University Press.
———. (1983). "Possibility and Necessity." In *Realism and Reason: Philosophical Papers, Volume 3*. Cambridge: Cambridge University Press, 46–68.
Shatz, D. (1981). "Reliability and Relevant Alternatives." *Philosophical Studies* 39:393–408.
Sosa, E. (1969). "Propositional Knowledge." *Philosophical Studies* 20:33–43.
Stalnaker, R. (1968). "A Theory of Conditionals." In *Studies in Logical Theory*, ed. N. Rescher. Oxford: Basil Blackwell. Reprinted in *Causation and Conditionals*, ed. E. Sosa. Oxford: Oxford University Press, 1975; and in Harper, Stalnaker, and Pearce (1981).
Stine, G. C. (1976). "Skepticism, Relevant Alternatives and Deductive Closure." *Philosophical Studies* 29:249–61.
Vogel, J. (2000). "Reliabilism Leveled." *Journal of Philosophy* 97:602–23.
Wittgenstein, L. (1969). *On Certainty*. Ed. G. E. M. Anscombe and G. H. von Wright. Trans. G. E. M. Anscombe and D. Paul. Oxford: Blackwell.

8
Russell's Notion of Scope[1]

In analytic philosophy, contemporary Anglo-Saxon philosophy, Russell's 'On Denoting'[2] is surely the most famous paper written in the first half of the twentieth century. Quine's 'Two Dogmas of Empiricism' is no doubt the most famous paper written in the second half. (It probably has Russell's paper beat for the century as a whole.) I'm restricting this to analytic philosophy. The truth is I don't know (though maybe someone can tell me) whether famous papers—this shows my ignorance—as opposed to books, are in fact ever written in contemporary continental philosophy. I've heard of this or that famous book, but of no famous papers.[3] I also don't know when philosophical journals and philosophical papers as such began. Previously some essays had been written that might be called 'papers' today, but were chapters of books.[4]

Now, although 'On Denoting' was the most famous paper of the first half of the century, it seems basically to have gone unread or been ill-understood—people may have thought that they could be content with reading secondary accounts in the textbooks, or even in *Introduction to Mathematical Philosophy*. And of course the Theory of Descriptions as such can be stated (see formula (4) below) very simply.

---

[1] Those familiar with some of my previous writings, especially my first book, will recognize that this paper is based on a transcription from tape. It was delivered at Rutgers University through the good offices of Stephen Neale, editor of the issue of *Mind* where this paper originally appeared. References to 'the discussion', 'the tape' and the like are to the delivery at Rutgers.

[2] All references to this paper by page are to the reprint in Marsh (1956), pp. 41–56.

[3] In the discussion, I believe someone said that there were some.

[4] Since I said this, I have done some minimal research, though not enough to find out when the philosophical journal as such began.

As a chapter of a book, I had in mind, for example, Hume's famous essay 'Of Miracles', included (as far as I know) from the beginning in his *Enquiry Concerning Human Understanding*, but which could have been a separate journal article today. (It might later have been collected into a volume of the author's papers.) Addison and Steele, in their famous *Spectator*, had introduced the general intellectual magazine or journal; but Hume did not make use of such a publication for this paper or (as far as I know) for any philosophical paper. On the other hand, Kant's famous paper 'On a Supposed Right to Lie for Altruistic Reasons', appeared in an intellectual periodical in reply to a paper by Benjamin Constant in a similar publication. When the specialized philosophical journal began, I don't know.

In 'On Denoting', Russell defines a denoting phrase as

> ... a phrase such as any one of the following: a man, some man, any man, every man, all men, the present King of England, the present King of France,[5] the centre of mass of the solar system at the first instance of the twentieth century, the revolution of the earth round the sun, the revolution of the sun round the earth. Thus a phrase is denoting solely in virtue of its *form*. (Russell 1905, p. 41)

(Notice that some of these denoting phrases have denoting phrases as constituents: 'the twentieth century' is a constituent of 'the first instant of the twentieth century', which is itself a constituent of 'the centre of mass of the solar system at the first instant of the twentieth century'. This will be of some significance later.)

Russell's idea of a denoting phrase corresponds fairly well to the modern linguistic idea of a determiner followed by a predicate. I think this may be mentioned in Stephen Neale's book, *Descriptions*.[6] Anyway, one might find the implicit syntactic argument here, which is stressed in Neale's book, that although at first blush a definite description might appear to be a complex term designating a single object, it is parallel in form to the other denoting phrases. If it were natural to analyse the other 'denoting phrases', such as 'every man', 'some man', 'a man', and so on, as really quantifiers and quantifier phrases, so would it be to analyse corresponding phrases beginning with the word 'the'. It is important to realize that 'On Denoting' is not simply a theory of definite descriptions, though this is its most famous and lengthily argued part, but rather of all 'denoting phrases'. So a syntactic parallelism is an important part of 'On Denoting'. In his earlier discussions in the *Principles of Mathematics*, Russell has a complicated and obscure analysis of all these phrases as of the same kind, trying to give complex things to which they refer.[7]

---

[5] I myself am inclined to think that Russell should have written 'king' rather than 'King'. 'x is (now) king of y' expresses a relation between people and countries, and 'x is king of y at t' expresses a relation between people, countries, and times. If England *had* a king, his *title* was 'King of England' or, in this particular case, really 'King Edward VII', or 'King Edward VII of England'. Something of my worry can be given by the description 'the tallest living knight in England'. Maybe there are no knights in the United States or France, but what would it mean for there to be some? Is this a meaningful relation between a person and a country, or simply a title peculiar to England? The distinction is a subtle one, and I must quote Russell accurately.

[6] Neale (1990). Though Neale gives the syntactic argument that follows in *Descriptions*, he appears to believe that it is not in Russell. I think it *is*, and find it an important part of his motivation. I mentioned this in a seminar Neale gave in Oslo in 1991. In later work, Neale explicitly accepts my point: 'As Saul Kripke has pointed out to me, Russell himself seems to be aware of this in the first paragraph of "On Denoting"' (Neale 1993, p. 130, n. 17).

[7] The ghost of this theory survives in the first paragraph of 'On Denoting', where it is said that 'a man' denotes 'an ambiguous man'. However, in the terminology of 'On Denoting' a definite description does have a denotation, namely the unique object satisfying it. Nevertheless, it is not a complex term referring to its object. (David Kaplan, in his paper 'What is Russell's Theory of Descriptions?' (Kaplan 1972) does not properly follow Russell's terminology here, and says that according to Russell definite descriptions do not 'denote'. What Kaplan really means is correct, and has just been stated.)

Now, Russell's theory of *all* such phrases is the same: though they look, in terms of their superficial form, like terms, a true logical analysis (an analysis of some sort of underlying structure) will reveal them actually to be quantified. And in most cases the analysis is fairly simple. For example, 'every' is analysed as the universal quantifier, so 'every man is such-and-such' is analysed with a universal quantifier and a conditional:

(1) $(\forall x)$(if x is human then x is such-and-such).

(Russell's use of the predicate 'is human' shows that he uses the term 'man' in a sense that does not make a gender distinction.) The indefinite article 'a' is analysed as the existential quantifier—a pretty important case of Russell's analysis—so 'a man did such-and-such' is analysed with an existential quantifier and a conjunction:

(2) $(\exists x)($ x is human and x did such-and-such).

As he puts it, '"C (a man)" means "It is false that 'C(x) and x is human' is always false"' (Russell 1905, p. 44). The existential quantifier ($\exists x$) is really written '$\neg(\forall x)\neg$' for Russell. The resulting formulation leads to complex and stilted English when written in ordinary prose. This may simply be because of a preference for taking the universal quantifier as primitive. However, it also could contain an implicit reply to the 'objection', aren't you presupposing some notion of existence here, and thus some of the very philosophical problems

---

Notice that, contrary to what Joseph Almog claims (1986, pp. 210–42), Russell never *stipulated* as part of his concept of naming that names must be semantically simple (that is, cannot have parts whose semantics contribute to the meaning or reference of the whole). On the contrary, Russell requires particular and complicated arguments that definite descriptions are not names. Like Frege in his concept of *Eigennamen*, Russell allows names to be complex, but disagrees with Frege about definite descriptions on philosophical grounds. For Russell, at this stage of his thought, a clause such as 'that England is a monarchy' genuinely names a proposition. Later, when he abandoned propositions in favour of facts and the multiple relation theory of (pseudo-)propositional attitudes, he denied that such clauses were names, and, as a result, names did become semantically simple (eventually, only 'this' and 'that' in ordinary language).

Also, contrary to what Almog supposes, in Kripke (1980), I *am sympathetic* to the view that Almog attributes to Russell, although I do not make it a *criterion* for what a proper name is (see below). See my discussions of 'The United Nations', Voltaire's 'Holy Roman Empire', and Mill's 'Dartmouth', which may appear to have parts that contribute to the semantics of the whole, but do not. Perhaps the issue is really partly terminological, but in my book I actually stipulate that I simply take the concept of a name as given as it normally is intuitively used in ordinary language without proposing any further criterion. It is decidedly *not* my purpose to give a technical criterion for being a name. (See Kripke 1980, p. 24.) A view, such as Russell's ultimate view that ordinary names are not 'really' names, is ruled out by definition, and must be restated if in *some* sense what it really means is true (see Kripke 1980, p. 27, n. 4). Nor do I take rigidity to be an alternative criterion for naming to replace Russell's alleged opposed criterion. On the contrary, I state that definite descriptions can be rigid too, though typically they are not. In my discussion of 'π', as used in mathematics, I further state my belief that it is a name whose reference is given by description, rather than an abbreviated description, even though the term would be 'strongly rigid' in either case (see p. 60).

that you were trying to solve? Of course, if you write it this way, this objection is less likely to arise. But in any case, in *Principia* the universal quantifier, and not the existential quantifier, is taken as primitive.

Now, a definite description would be analysed as a complex binary quantifier. 'The ϕ ψ's', where ϕ is a predicate, would be analysed as

(3) [the x](ϕx, ψx)

with 'the x' a binary quantifier. However, it is also important to Russell that all quantifiers that he introduces be definable in terms of the universal quantifier, truth functions, and identity. Let's write this in a compact form, allowing ourselves to use the existential quantifier, as Russell does sometimes. His analysis of this binary quantification is (in effect)

(4) $(\exists x)((\forall y)(\phi y \equiv y = x) \wedge \psi x)$

which analyses everything in terms of quantification, truth functions, and identity.

Russell also takes 'some' to be synonymous with 'a', both being existential quantifiers. He has a footnote in 'On Denoting' in which he says, 'Psychologically "C (a man)" has a suggestion of *only one*, and "C (some men)" has a suggestion of *more than one*; but we may neglect these suggestions in a preliminary sketch' (Russell 1905, p. 43). But Russell never goes beyond the preliminary sketch (even, as far as I know, in later writings) and analyses these as the same. Now, actually, on the first page of 'On Denoting', in the passage I quoted earlier, Russell gives 'some man' as his example, while in the footnote he switches to 'some men'. One takes a singular complement, the other a plural. The singular, certainly, does not suggest more than one. Consider, 'Some burglar robbed us last night'. Does that suggest that there was more than one burglar? No, any suggestion is the opposite. Yet it is *compatible* with going on to say, 'Hey, look, I think maybe there were two burglars', without contradicting the first statement, which is more or less equivalent to 'A burglar robbed us last night'. On the other hand, 'Some burglars robbed us last night' does suggest more than one, and suggests a *class*—'Some Greeks were good philosophers' and so on—these are plural uses of 'some'. Russell doesn't note this distinction, though it appears in the paper itself. It could relate to later articles by Gareth Evans and George Boolos, if it had been gone into.[8] Now, I'm not even saying that the plural form is necessarily *false* if there is only one, but the singular and plural *are* different. In the traditional syllogistic, sometimes we see 'some *A*s are *B*s', sometimes 'some *A* is a *B*', but these are really different, and the second is probably more proper, given what the traditional syllogistic meant.

It will be clear that when a denoting phrase is analysed as a quantifier, the quantifier will have some determinate scope: it will govern a certain phrase. On

---

[8] Evans (1977). Boolos (1984).

the other hand, if it is looked at as a term and unpacked, and is embedded in some complex construction, of which the simplest might be a negation, '¬ some ϕ did ψ', it will have two readings, depending upon whether the negation or the quantifier has larger scope. Now, the point is a purely logical one: it arises directly from the theory. This is Russell's notion of scope. It is most interesting in the case of definite and indefinite descriptions, which he emphasizes a great deal. In *intensional* contexts, scope generally makes a difference to what is said, and often to truth-value. In a truth-functional context, scope *can* still make a difference. However, if the appropriate conditions are met, if there is a unique x such that ϕx—I'll use $\exists! x \phi x$ to abbreviate this—scope differences don't matter. By 'don't matter', I simply mean that the different scope interpretations lead to materially equivalent statements. The point is that for all allowable scopes (and we will give further details later), the following conditional is true:

(5) if $\exists!x\, \phi x$, then $A \equiv A^*$

where A and A^* are identical but for two different occurrences of the description with different scopes. (Actually, (5) as explained assumes that the description has no free variables in its predicate nor embeds any other descriptions. For the general case, see the appropriate discussion below.)

Now, I should say that these doctrines are well known *today*,[9] but they certainly weren't for a long time, even though 'On Denoting' was supposed to be a famous paper. Quine wrote a very well-known paper, 'Quantifiers and Propositional Attitudes' (Quine 1956)—one of his best known, in fact—treating many of the same subjects, even with surprising coincidences like the ambiguity of 'I want a sloop'. *Sloops* in one case and *yachts* in the other (see Russell's famous parallel example discussed below, p. 240)! 'Sloops' allows Quine to make the pun

---

[9] Even more recently, are they really well known enough? Could Davidson's 'slingshot' arguments—in particular the argument that if we believed in 'facts', there could be only one fact—have been so influential if people had realized that for Russell the problem would be a matter of scope, at least when statements about facts are embedded? It would have been natural for Russell to apply his scope distinctions in Davidson's (1980) examples of the form 'the fact that the ϕ is ψ caused it to be the case that the ζ is η'. These distinctions may be recognized by Stephen Neale in his discussion (Neale 2001, pp. 218–23), but they are not recognized by Davidson, who makes no mention of Russell, nor of the Russellian objections to the slingshot. To me the idea that 'facts' could be *repudiated* by arguments of this form is intuitively preposterous—any theory of descriptions, Russellian or other, should require the appropriate scope distinctions that dispel them. (There might be alternative formulations of the slingshot that do not turn on embedding, in which case the objection from Russell would be different.)

Gödel (1944) presents a Russellian objection but says '... I cannot help feeling that the problem raised... has only been evaded by Russell's theory of descriptions and that there is something behind it which is not yet completely understood' (1944, p. 130).) Russell, of course, became a strong believer in facts (in 'The Philosophy of Logical Atomism'). Quine's long-time hostility to modal logic gave rise to slingshot arguments, though finally he admitted he was wrong about Smullyan and scope—see my remarks in the text—and conceded that Smullyan's observations about substitution and scope cleared modal logic of 'any suspicion of inconsistency raised by my slingshot argument' (Quine 1999, p. 426).

that his sentence is ambiguous between wanting a particular sloop and mere 'relief from *sloop*lessness', a typical Quinean literary fillip, which could not be done with Russell's original, parallel example of the yacht. Now the two theories are probably different in that Quine suggests a syntactic distinction between *notional* belief and *relational* belief, belief *that p* and belief *of* something that it ψ's. Daniel Dennett, writing even later, in 'Beyond Belief',[10] pejoratively complains that people seem to think there might be two kinds of belief. Though it *does* look this way in Quine's account,[11] this is not Russell's view. In Russell there is only one kind of belief, always belief *that p*. What we would call *de re* belief is explained in terms of quantifying in from the outside, quantifying into a complex proposition. If we are on the inside of all the operators, this is what would usually be called *de dicto* belief. Russell has his own terms for all this, on p. 54 of 'On Denoting'. Where the descriptive operator governs the entire context it has a *primary* occurrence. A *secondary* occurrence is where it is within the context, on the inside. This strikes me as an unfortunate terminology. First, I would have preferred a reversal of the two terms. (If we have an operator applied to *p*, isn't the reading that unpacks *p* following the operator the 'primary' notion?) Second, and more important, it makes the distinction look like a *dual* distinction, and so does Quine's parallel discussion.[12] In any case, it is *not* a dual distinction, because there can be a pile up of operators. Then the question where to put the 'the' or the 'a', whether way on the outside or way on the inside, or in between, arises, and it is very important that Russell's theory allows for this. Quine's theory, too, allows for this, though he does not say so. I've given examples of this elsewhere myself.[13] Here's one with an indefinite description:

(6) Hoover charged that the Berrigans[14] planned to kidnap a high official.

I actually heard this on the radio once, long ago, and I wondered what was meant. In theory it could have been any of the following:

(6a) $(\exists x)(x$ is a high official and Hoover charged that the Berrigans planned to kidnap $x)$

(b) Hoover charged that $(\exists x)(x$ is a high official and the Berrigans planned to kidnap $x)$

---

[10] Dennett (1982).
[11] Strictly speaking Quine's theory might take belief to be a relation between finite sequences of length *n* and sentences with *n* free variables. *De dicto* (or 'notional' belief) might be the degenerate case of *n* = 0 (i.e., where the sequence is empty and there are no free variables). See the analogous relation between truth and satisfaction. But the impression that there are really two kinds of belief (where $n > 0$ and $n = 0$) persists, and their unification is an artificiality. It is also directly reflected in Quine's own terminology. See Chapter 11, this volume.
[12] Quine's theory also allows for more than a dual distinction, though his discussion does not bring this out.
[13] Kripke (1977). Reprinted here as Chapter 5.
[14] Here we have a plural definite description, or perhaps an unusual name for a pair of brothers. If this gives any worries, replace the example with 'Berrigan'.

(c) Hoover charged that the Berrigans planned $(\exists x)(x$ is a high official and they kidnap $x)$.[15]

If (b) was meant, Hoover's charge was that there was a particular high official the Berrigans planned to kidnap, and is *neutral* as to whether Hoover himself said who it was. If (a) is meant, Hoover identified the person. (c) allows, according to Hoover, that the Berrigans hadn't decided *which* high official to kidnap. I really heard this on the radio and didn't know what was meant. (In fact, it was Henry Kissinger whom Hoover had in mind.)

The following also has three readings (also from my previous paper):

(7) The number of planets might have been necessarily even.

We are taking it that there are nine planets and that every even (or odd) number is necessarily even (or odd). Now, the outer scope reading of this, which would mean it is true of the number of planets that it might have been necessarily even, is false because there are nine planets and it is false that the number might even have been even (pun?), let alone necessarily even. Nor is the inner scope reading true, because the inner scope reading would mean it is possible that it should have been necessary that there are exactly x planets and x is even. But that is false. That couldn't have been necessary, because it isn't even true.[16,17] So we reject that, but what *is* correct is the intermediate scope reading, which means it is possible that there exists an x such that there is/are exactly x planets, and necessarily x is even. The intermediate scope reading is not mentioned by Russell. (It is not mentioned by Quine either. It took a long time for Quine to see that you might do the same tricks he did in 'Quantifiers and Propositional Attitudes' with necessity also, and he wrote a paper on it. And, he said, not that he believes in necessity, that 'I am in the position of a Jewish chef preparing ham for a gentile clientele' (Quine 1977, p. 270). Why it took Quine a long time to realize this is a little obscure.) Quine's treatment of

---

[15] Alan Berger believes that there is yet another reading, a variant of (a): $(\exists x)(x$ is a person and Hoover charged that x was a high official and the Berrigans planned to kidnap $x)$. (Maybe, unbeknownst to Hoover, Kissinger had actually resigned.) If this is correct, we must read 'a high official' as 'a person who is a high official' and allow the definite description to be broken up so that 'high official' still goes inside the operator. Whether this agrees with intuition, or is a reading allowable in Russell's theory, are issues I won't discuss.

[16] That the number of planets is nine has long been a standard philosophical example, popularized by Quine. It is presupposed here, and its actual truth is irrelevant. While to claim that 'astronomers have changed their minds as to what the number of planets is' makes sense, to claim that 'mathematicians have changed their minds as to what the number nine is' seems barely intelligible, let alone possibly true. This seems to me to be one further reason for adopting a 'frankly inequalitarian attitude' towards two ways of supposedly designating the number nine. See my discussion of Malcolm's astronomical example in "On Two Paradoxes of Knowledge" (Chapter 2, this volume), especially footnote 15 (p. 41). Here, I guess, we do need to pay attention to what a committee of learned astronomers have said in correction of previous beliefs. (Footnote added in 2010.)

[17] Experts in modal logic will recognize that this argument presupposes the 'B' axiom—what is true could not have been necessarily false. Intuitively it certainly seems valid here.

this was regarded as completely new. There is no reference to Russell in Quine's paper in the mid-fifties. The linguists in the mid-sixties seemed to be rediscovering the same distinctions too. I do not know where I saw this, but I remember, particularly, reading a paper by Emmon Bach calling this a 'very recently noticed distinction'. But these distinctions and the theory of them, which may be different from the theories proposed by some of these later linguists and by Quine, were all in Russell's paper. Moreover, Quine criticized Arthur Smullyan, who simply applied Russell's scope distinctions to necessity, and stated that you don't necessarily get a paradox from universal substitutivity of identity and statements about the number of planets. The story is well told in a paper by Stephen Neale.[18] Now, the wide scope interpretation 'quantifies into' a modal context. So Quine could still object on the grounds that he regards this as 'essentialist'. Instead, he calls Smullyan's proposal a 'modification' of Russell's theory, which he erroneously thought allowed distinctions of scope only in the case of failure of existence and uniqueness (and this, he says, was indispensable for the idea that Russellian descriptions can serve as a surrogate for a theory that takes them as genuine terms). This is not true for intensional contexts, as is emphasized, surely, in 'On Denoting', though the case of a necessity operator is not treated (Russell's other writings showed that he regarded such an operator as illegitimate), and also in *Principia Mathematica*. At the very end of *14 of *Principia* in *14.3, but also in the special cases following, *14.31 *et al.*, it is asserted that in truth-functional contexts, if the existence and uniqueness conditions are fulfilled, then the scope of a single description included in that truth-functional context does not matter:

*14.3 $\{\forall p \forall q((p \equiv q) \supset f(p) \equiv f(q)) \wedge E!(\imath x)(\phi x)\} \supset$
        $f\{[(\imath x)(\phi x)] \chi(\imath x)(\phi x)) \equiv [(\imath x)(\phi x)] f(\chi(\imath x)(\phi x))\}$

*14.31 $E!(\imath x)(\phi x) \supset$
        $\{([(\imath x)(\phi x)] p \vee \chi(\imath x)(\phi x)) \equiv (p \vee [(\imath x)(\phi x)] \chi(\imath x)(\phi x))\}$

This is the content of *14.31 and subsequent theorems all the way down to the end of *14. Russell says on p. 186,

Propositions of the above type might be continued indefinitely but as they are proved on a uniform plan, it is unnecessary to go beyond the fundamental cases of $p \vee q$, $\sim p$, $p \supset q$, and $p \cdot q$. (*PM*, p. 186)

Thus he clearly asserts that we could continue this for more complex cases.[19]

A whole school of writers has emerged who state that *Principia* does not contain metatheorems, a school that includes Dreben, van Heijenoort and

---

[18] Quine (1953a), Smullyan (1948). Neale (1999).
[19] *14.3 is not an 'official' theorem of *Principia*, because quantification over propositions has not been introduced. Thus *14.31 et al. are proved independently, not deduced from *14.3.

Goldfarb.[20] The assertions following and preceding[21] *14.3 are an explicit counterexample to their claim, though there are many others, and this is not even the most important counterexample. It is an explicit *metatheorem* that in a truth-functional context the scope of a single description does not matter.

Russell may treat this as equivalent to a far more powerful metatheorem that scopes, even with multiple descriptions, and so on, never matter in an extensional context, if we assume an appropriate hypothesis that the existence and uniqueness conditions are fulfilled. Actually, as I have said, his result applies only to a truth-functional context with just one (occurrence of a) description without free variables and no descriptions embedded within the descriptions or quantified into. A statement of the more general case will be discussed later. At any rate, Quine originally said that Smullyan was modifying Russell's theory of descriptions because according to Russell scope never matters when the existence and uniqueness conditions are fulfilled, even in intensional contexts, contrary to Smullyan's treatment. In fact, Russell emphasizes just the opposite.

I pointed out the relevant passages of *Principia* to Quine. In the copy of his book *From a Logical Point of View* which Quine donated to the library at Bellagio he wrote in the margin, 'Kripke has convinced me that Russell shared Smullyan's position'. And in the 1980 edition, the criticism of Smullyan is finally deleted, and explicitly said to be deleted because it was wrong. (The story is well told by Stephen Neale in 'On a Milestone of Empiricism'.) But still Quine misses something here; because there isn't a *position* to be taken, there is simply an *analysis* of descriptions, and it either *follows* that scope matters in an intensional context, or it does not. There is nothing to *postulate*. Smullyan might propose a different analysis, but if he is following Russell's analysis, what he says either accords with Russell's analysis or it does not. And it *does*.

And eventually Quine applied his own and (at least at that time) more famous analysis to the same thing. Now whether Russell has taken care of all of these issues about ambiguities in, especially, the indefinite article 'a' and the definite article 'the', is a point of controversy, even in contemporary linguistic literature, and we need not discuss this, but the amazing thing is that Russell's discussion was completely ignored.

---

[20] Dreben and van Heijenoort (1986), in Feferman et al. (see pp. 44–5). Goldfarb (1979). See also Hylton (1990). Other writers could be mentioned. I hope to write on the general topic of metatheorems and metatheoretical ideas in *Principia* elsewhere.

[21] The assertion following has been quoted above. For the assertion preceding, see p. 184. 'This proposition [that is, that scope is irrelevant when the existence and uniqueness conditions are fulfilled—S.K.] cannot be proved generally [that is, for arbitrary contexts, including intensional contexts—S.K.], but it can be proved in each particular case [that is, in every context actually used in *Principia*, which supposedly are all truth-functional—S.K.]. The proposition can be proved generally when $(\imath x)(\phi x)$ occurs in the form $\chi(\imath x)(\phi x)$, and $\chi(\imath x)(\phi x)$ occurs in what we may call a 'truth-function', i.e. a function whose truth or falsehood depends only upon the truth or falsehood of its argument or arguments' (*Principia*, 184). The last sentence expresses the content of *14.3. The middle clause ('but it can be proved in each particular case') expresses the same metatheorem as the assertion on p. 186 quoted in the text above.

It must be mentioned also that, in the period when Russell's analysis of scope ambiguities was largely ignored, Alonzo Church did not ignore it, but actually stated that scope ambiguities were a *weakness* in Russell's approach.[22]

I state, hopefully, that this ignorance or misconception is no longer the case, and that now, everyone knows about the virtues of Russell's treatment of scope distinctions. Ramsey called this paper a 'paradigm of philosophy'. Paradigm of philosophy, famous paper indeed! It appears that few read it, or took it seriously, except for Russell and his own immediate circle. Nor did they read the relevant sections of *Principia*.[23]

Russell has two targets (contrasting philosophers) in his paper, Frege and Meinong. I also want to say a bit about the later famous criticisms of Strawson (whose views resemble Frege's in some respects, in spite of quite different motivations.) Of Meinong I know very little, outside of what Russell reports. According to Russell, he holds that non-existent entities, such as the king of France (and even the king of France who is not king) have some sort of weak existence, but all the properties attributed to them (so that, as Russell says, the law of contradiction can be violated). Sometimes I have wondered whether Meinong (at least the Meinong of 'On Denoting') was an imaginary figure invented by Russell, who was so upset that he did not really exist that he invented a doctrine that even beings like him have some weaker form of existence![24]

Now, I might mention something which also has a parallel in 'On Denoting', but is clear on p. 186 of *Principia*, in the discussion of 'the King of France is not bald'. Either interpretation, that is narrow or wide scope, might be meant by this: it is not the case that there is a unique king of France and that whoever is king of France is bald (narrow scope) or there is a unique king of France and he is not bald (wide scope), in effect. But *Principia* says that it is more natural to take the second, false interpretation, as the meaning of the words. And we have here the germ of a reply to Strawson's much later criticisms. If you are asked, 'So, look, is the king of France bald or isn't he?' you feel reluctant to answer either yes or no. One's reluctance could be explained by the simple remark that the second reply naturally abbreviates, 'No, the present king of France is not bald'. Given the remark in *Principia*, that the wide scope interpretation is the more natural one, we get an explanation of the reluctance that it is purely Russellian.[25]

---

[22] Church (1950) p. 63.

[23] Smullyan (1948), Prior (1963), Fitch (1949), and, in agreement with him, his student Ruth Marcus (then Ruth Barcan; see Barcan 1948), were shining exceptions in their grasp of the intensional aspects of Russellian scope distinctions. (Fitch and Marcus are not totally free of criticism in this regard.)

[24] Actually, of course, in previous writings Russell took the actual Meinong seriously and discussed him with respect. My own ignorance remains.

[25] Russell's own late reply to Strawson, 'Mr. Strawson on Referring' (Russell 1957) emphasizes that Strawson's discussion relies on contextual matters (such as 'present' in 'the present King of France') that are not highly relevant to the issue. On the level Strawson presents the matter, Russell seems to me to be basically right about this point, but on a deeper analysis, Strawson's problem can

Actually, I consider Strawson's 'On Referring' a marvellous paper, but it's too strong in claiming to be a refutation of Russell's theory, that's for sure.[26]

Why the somewhat impolite phrase 'is bald' in Russell's example? (Strawson decorously changes it to 'is wise' without even saying that he has altered Russell's example.) Here's what Russell says:

> If we say "the King of England is bald", that is, it would seem, not a statement about the complex *meaning* "the King of England", but about the actual man denoted by the meaning. (1905, p. 46)

Edward VII was king of England at that time, and bald he was, I am told. Russell goes on:

> But now consider "the King of France is bald". By parity of form, this also ought to be about the denotation of the phrase "the King of France". But this phrase, though it has a *meaning* provided "the King of England" has a meaning, has certainly no denotation, at least in any obvious sense. (ibid, p. 46)

Probably this is all Russell means, the analogy. (It would be just possible that he had in mind the sort of mischaracterization or misdescription of the speaker's referent made famous in Donnellan's paper: 'Hey, no, stupid, it's the King of *England* you're thinking of, not the King of *France*'.[27] But, there's no indication here of that.) Russell continues:

> Hence one would suppose that "the King of France is bald" ought to be nonsense; but it is not nonsense, since it is plainly false. (ibid, p. 46)

Both Frege and Strawson would rightly complain that this begs the question against them, that the dichotomy is not correct, true-or-false or otherwise meaningless; it might be meaningful but lacking in truth-value.[28, 29] However,

---

still be upheld, and his distinction between sentence and statement is certainly important. Furthermore, aside from all this, the question what to do with empty descriptions survives, but this is not the whole of the problem. Moreover, in one passage he comes a bit too close to stressing the syntactic ambiguities of ordinary language, perhaps giving the misleading impression that he agrees with the view of Quine discussed below that he was not attempting to analyse ordinary language. But then his reply to Strawson, and the entire debate, would be superfluous. I hope to discuss all this elsewhere.

[26] Stephen Neale reports to me that Grice once quipped that 'On Referring' was a wonderful paper marred only by a discussion of Russell's theory of descriptions!

[27] Donnellan (1966).

[28] Actually Strawson is ambiguous as to whether there are truth-gaps here; or no 'statement' has been made (even though the *sentence* is meaningful), and 'statements' must be true-or-false, that is, have no truth-gaps. I once asked Strawson about this question. If I understood him correctly, he acknowledged the ambiguity but said that the *second* position was really the intended one. Stephen Neale, who also asked Strawson, reports the same reply in Neale (1990).

[29] Perhaps this is the place to discuss the view given the authority of W. V. Quine in his famous *Word and Object* (Quine 1960, see especially p. 259): for ordinary language Strawson is right about the truth-gaps, but for a symbolic language they are an engineer's 'don't care' cases, fillable arbitrarily for technical convenience:

Strawson (who was criticizing Russell's paper) overlooks other examples Russell already gives that refute the view that whenever you have an empty definite description there is no truth-value:

> Or again consider such a proposition as the following: "If u is a class which has only one member, then that one member is a member of u," or, as we may state it, "If u is a unit class, *the u* is a u". (ibid, p. 46)

This is definitely true. We can assume the quantifier u ranges over classes. Two points are ignored by Strawson here. First, that descriptions can be quantified into, they need not be phrases without variables like 'the present King of France', but might contain variables that are bound by outside quantifiers. Second, that conditionals of this type can be true even though, according to Frege and to Strawson, some of the instances of the quantification lack truth-value. So this would be a refutation of both Frege and Strawson.[30] It's also, it seems to me, a refutation of what is later stated by Hilbert and Bernays, who say that in both ordinary language and mathematics, we require that a description containing variables be everywhere defined, when it is used.[31] Hilbert and Bernays's

---

(1) In 'On Denoting', p. 47, Russell criticizes Frege for doing *exactly* such artificial gap filling (of empty denotations): 'But this procedure, though it may not lead to actual logical error, is plainly artificial, and does not give an exact analysis of the matter'. 'On Denoting' is intended to be a contribution to the philosophy of natural language and of thought.

(2) Other 'friends' of Russell—including occasionally, the later Russell himself—have 'defended' him as merely proposing an artificial symbolic convention. But they are surely wrong about 'On Denoting' and unjust to Russell's true contribution.

(3) Taken as such a convention, it is a poor one. Why not use '$(\exists x)(Ax \wedge Fx)$' for 'the A F's', or alternatively, '$(\forall x)(Ax \supset Fx)$'? These are simpler, fill the 'don't care' cases arbitrarily, and don't invoke identity. When I and other logicians have given courses on formalized elementary number theory, we have used precisely the first convention. (Normally the appropriate uniqueness condition is fulfilled.) I have even heard someone attribute a view to some linguist that this is the correct analysis for *natural* language!

(4) Intuitively, Strawson and Frege are not always right about the gaps. Russell already gave *true* cases (e.g. 'my only son', as discussed below). Further, a con-man who says, 'My company owns the largest of the many corn farms in Kansas', when he owns no company and ('South Pacific' notwithstanding—'I feel as corny as Kansas in August') Kansas grows wheat (and little or no 'corn' in the American sense) and he has no such farm, would be normally considered a *liar*, uttering a *falsehood*. (My thanks to S. B. Coots for the information about the crops and Kansas.)

(5) Strawson eventually conceded such cases (in Strawson (1964)). In assuming as late as 1960 that Strawson is always right about the gaps, Quine is being 'more Catholic than the Pope' and ignores Russell's own counterexamples!

[30] Actually Frege wouldn't allow this because it's not a genuine function unless it's everywhere defined, but *intuitively* Frege is wrong, and he has to provide artificial denotations for empty terms.

Now, of course, there are other theories of presupposition that are not refuted by this example. I am well aware of various theories and have discussed the so-called projection problem myself (Chapter 12, this volume). My point is that the theories actually propounded by Frege and Strawson are refuted. In terms of the modern discussion of the projection problem they reflect the so-called cumulative hypothesis of Langendoen and Savin (1971).

[31] Hilbert and Bernays (1934).

statement about ordinary language and mathematics is false in connection with Russell's conditional and similar cases.[32]

Even for the singular case, without variables in the description, Russell gives an example of a conditional truth that contains vacuous descriptions:

The King in "The Tempest" might say, "If Ferdinand is not drowned, Ferdinand is my only son". Now 'my only son' is a denoting phrase, which, on the face of it, has a denotation when, and only when, I have exactly one son. But the above statement would nevertheless have remained true if Ferdinand had been in fact drowned. (1905, p. 47)[33]

A better case, perhaps, would be if there were two children, Ferdinand and Sue, and the King had said, 'if Ferdinand is drowned, then Sue is my only remaining child'. This is still a true statement, even if 'my only remaining child' might be vacuous. It might even be the case that at least one description would *have* to be vacuous. Consider the following disjunction (forget about the incomplete descriptions here, another problem, perhaps, but they could be filled out): You are to imagine that a last minute peace conference has taken place, and the deadline is over, but the speaker has not heard news of the result.

(8) Either the peace treaty has been drawn up and signed or the war has broken out.[34]

One of the two descriptions is vacuous, but we don't know which, and nevertheless may assert the disjunction.

So, Russell has an interesting range of counterexamples to both Frege and Strawson here. I do not discuss another, more complicated argument Russell uses against Frege in 'On Denoting', the famous and obscure 'Gray's Elegy' argument.[35] But anyway, as we have just seen, there are much simpler arguments against Frege that are in Russell's paper.

Now in an earlier correspondence between Russell and Frege, which has been made famous in papers by Joseph Almog and by Nathan Salmon, Frege says that surely Mont Blanc with all its snowfields is not a constituent of the proposition, of the thought, that Mont Blanc is over 1000 metres high. And Russell replies (roughly), 'Yes, that's what I think, Mont Blanc with all its snowfields is a

---

[32] Parallel instances are given later by Benson Mates (Mates 1973) in refutation of Strawson, but Russell already mentions such a case. Mates appears not to notice this. Mates does give mathematical examples in addition to Russell's that are quite natural, refuting Hilbert and Bernays.

[33] Mates *does* notice this example from 'On Denoting'.

[34] Those linguists engaged in the projection problem no doubt recognize cases like these (and Russell's 'Ferdinand' case). However, I myself recall giving the example (8) to G. H. von Wright as early as 1962, presumably long before this literature, or at least most of it. All the more so, the same holds for Russell and his original examples! My thanks to Stephen Neale for a correction of the example.

[35] Salmon (2005) discusses this argument.

constituent of the proposition'. This correspondence is mentioned in a footnote in 'On Denoting':

> In the proposition "Mont Blanc is over 1000 metres high", it is, according to him, the *meaning* of "Mont Blanc", not the actual mountain, that is the constituent of the *meaning* of the proposition. (Russell 1905, p. 46)

And Russell here is surprised, I guess, and disagrees. I had the good fortune of a trip to Switzerland recently where I saw Mont Blanc from my own hotel window 'with all its snowfields'. I looked very hard but could not see whether it itself or only its *Sinn* was a constituent of the relevant proposition. But at least I knew what they were talking about anyway. Frege seemed to think that the snowfields made Russell's view implausible. If so, maybe global warming will eventually help Russell.

Now let's take Russell's arguments for his theory otherwise.

> I shall therefore state three puzzles which a theory as to denoting ought to be able to solve; and I shall show later that my theory solves them.
>
> (I) If *a* is identical with *b*, whatever is true of the one is true of the other.... Now George IV wished to know whether Scott was the author of *Waverley*, and in fact Scott *was* the author of *Waverley*. Hence we may substitute *Scott* for *the author of "Waverley,"* and thereby prove that George IV wished to know whether Scott was Scott. Yet an interest in the law of identity can hardly be attributed to the first gentleman of Europe. (1905, p. 47)

Now, first, in this example I would replace 'wished to know' with 'wished that he should know'—not only does it involve the famous newer problem of the *de se*, it is a double embedding (and involves intermediate scope problems), whereas Russell is considering this as a single embedding. Therefore I change it to 'George IV wondered whether Scott was the author of *Waverley*' or 'George IV asked whether Scott was the author of *Waverley*', which was in fact the case at the famous banquet.[36]

The last sentence is a bit of an insult. Most regard the law of identity as obvious, though a few philosophers have questioned it. George IV appears in almost all places to have been a rather bad man, though not all bad,[37] but he was one of the most intelligent and educated kings in the history of the British

---

[36] There is supposed to have been a famous dinner where George IV asked Scott whether he wrote *Waverley*, and Scott falsely denied having written it. (Actually, George IV, then only 'Prince Regent' not 'King', prepared a toast to 'the author of *Waverley*', implicitly asking Scott to acknowledge authorship.) Scott wrote a series of novels anonymously. The first one was *Waverley*. A derogator of Scott wrote recently in the *New York Times* that all of these novels, famous in their own days, are far from classics, and every single one of them is out of print except for *Ivanhoe*, which has to be read in American high schools. (Later, after I said this in this very talk, a professional writer told me that the novels *are* in print.)

[37] His secret marriage and devotion to his Catholic wife, when British law then forbade marriage between royalty and Catholics, strikes me as exemplary. He also struck an alliance with Charles Fox, the leading British progressive of his time, though this may have been for opportunistic reasons.

monarchy. He is more likely to have been interested in this than any other English king I can think of, if I understand the relevant history correctly. So he might well have known what is meant by the phrase, 'law of identity'. (An interesting figure actually. If you've seen the play or the film, *The Madness of King George*—the madness is that of his predecessor, George III—his character is fairly well delineated.)

I will skip for the moment the next two puzzles, which are simpler. This one involves an intensional context. Russell says, 'The puzzle about George IV's curiosity is now seen to have a very simple solution' (Russell 1905, p. 51).

When we say George IV wished to know whether so-and-so—and I replace this by wondered whether so-and-so or asked whether so-and-so—or when we say that so-and-so is surprising, so-and-so must be a proposition.

Now here's where the distinction between primary and secondary occurrences is first made, and used, in the paragraph:

When we say... "So-and-so is surprising" or "So-and-so is true," etc., the "so-and-so" must be a proposition. Suppose now that "so-and-so" contains a denoting phrase. We may either eliminate this denoting phrase from the subordinate proposition "so-and-so," or from the whole proposition in which 'so-and-so' is a mere constituent. Different propositions result according to which we do. I have heard of a touchy owner of yacht to whom a guest, on first seeing it, remarked, "I thought your yacht was larger than it is"; and the owner replied, "No, my yacht is not larger than it is". (1905, p. 52)

I have always enjoyed this witty joke and myself use a simpler version, which I have actually tried out in practice.

A: Hello. Oh, sorry, I thought you were someone else.
B: No, I am not someone else.

This is an ambiguity involving an indefinite description. Is person *A* saying 'There is an x such that x is not you and I thought you were x'? If so, the existential quantifier has outer scope. But taking it with the inner scope, what *A* is saying is 'I thought that there is an x such that: x is *not* you and x *is* you. This joke actually works—a bit anyway.

Russell's old example may be a good joke too. I have done some research on yachts in order to figure it out.[38] Surprisingly enough, though the size of a yacht might be thought to be measured in cubic measure—since, after all it's a three dimensional object—it is in fact measured in linear measure. And it doesn't mean the length of the yacht or the length of the keel on the bottom or any such thing, but is given by a complex formula using various factors

---

Otherwise, he was foppish, corrupt, and a schemer. And his relations with a later wife were much less admirable.

[38] From 'Yachting' in my edition of *The Encyclopedia Britannica* (1953). In 1905, the formula for yacht size was actually different in different countries. The next year (1906), there was a new formula adopted throughout Europe.

involving the yacht, but comes out linear, so a yacht could be 30 metres or 30 yards, but that doesn't mean its length, but its *size*. Russell speaks not of its length but rather of its *size*: it is thirty metres in *size*. Russell's analysis of these things, I said, was ignored too much; now, perhaps, it is ignored too much the other way: the joke is wrong. The meaning attributed to the guest by the owner is that of:

(9) I thought that the size of your yacht was greater than the size of your yacht.

That's impossible, and that's what the owner is complaining about. But what the guest actually meant was:

(10) The size that I thought your yacht was is greater than the size that your yacht is.

That implies that there was a unique size that the guest thought the yacht was. Say, if the yacht was 30 metres in size, he thought it was 35 metres in size. But that plainly need not be true: who said that he previously had any exact idea of the size of the yacht? He doesn't have to, and he still can be surprised and say 'I thought your yacht was larger than it is'. The point is stronger when one realizes that yacht size, rather than length, is in question, though the point holds for the weaker notion.[39] So Russell's analysis in terms of his theory of descriptions, as stated, is incorrect. I believe my own example is correct. That is an advantage.

(However, since I said the preceding paragraph, Nathan Salmon, with whom I discussed the problem some time ago—probably a year or more—has recently come up with a purely Russellian analysis. His initial reaction had been to use the apparatus he set up in his book *Frege's Puzzle*. Now Salmon points out that the sentence 'I thought that: your yacht was larger than it is' must be analysed as 'I thought that: the size of your yacht was greater than the size of your yacht', which simply does not contain the description 'the size I thought your yacht was', but rather simply 'the size of your yacht'. Give all occurrences of descriptions inner scope and you get the yacht owner's jocular (or 'touchy') reply. Give the second occurrence of the description outer scope and the first inner scope and you get a plausible analysis of the guest's remark.)

How to fix up Russell's example is a little complicated, and not clear.[40] As far as I know, no one has noted that his famous example is, in fact, wrong. There need be no such size as the size the guest thought the yacht was.[41]

---

[39] It would be very difficult to establish the exact size of a yacht, or even get a close estimate, at a glance since the formula for calculating it is complicated. The question of yacht size should not be confused with the question of yacht length.

[40] Remember I said this before Salmon talked to me about his new proposal. I was unconvinced by his earlier proposal.

[41] If one took Russell's example as given, with 'the size I thought your yacht was', an obvious proposal is to replace sizes by size intervals, a proposal I had thought of myself. It is not devoid of problems, and to make it plausible the intervals must be vague in their boundaries. (In the

Now back to the George IV example, modified in the way I have suggested so as to disallow intermediate scope: 'George IV asked whether the author of *Waverley* was Scott'. The inner scope (or secondary) analysis will be:

(11) George IV asked whether there is an x such that x and only x wrote *Waverley*, and x = Scott.

Now, intuitively one trouble with this, which has been largely overlooked in the literature, is that it does look from Russell's analysis as if one thing George IV wanted to know is whether exactly one person wrote *Waverley*.[42] Perhaps it was written in collaboration (a possibility Russell mentions elsewhere, in connection with another book that was written in collaboration). But probably, in fact, George IV *presupposed* it was not the product of a collaboration. On the other hand, Scott could perhaps be allowed to reply, 'Actually it was written in collaboration'. And though George IV would be surprised, it is not ruled out. Nevertheless, there is a bit of a question about the orthodox Russellian analysis here.

But now consider, worse, the large scope analysis. (In the first part of the talk it looked as if I came to praise Russell; perhaps now it looks as if I came to bury him. But I think this a *marvellous* piece of work.) So the other analysis is:

(12) There is an x such that x and x alone wrote *Waverley*, and George IV asked whether x = Scott.

Now, Russell comments, 'This would be true, for example, if George IV had seen Scott at a distance, and had asked "Is that Scott?"' (Russell 1905, p. 52). Common sense suggests this would be a reasonable interpretation. However, we are not just dealing with common sense here, but with Russell's theory. Russell's characterization is a good common sense interpretation of the large scope analysis. However, this is an existential quantifier and the variable takes a unique value. What can that value be? Scott himself! But then the first gentleman of Europe *is* interested in an instance of the law of identity, after all! Since the value of the propositional function here is Scott = Scott, the question *would* express an interest in the law of identity. Now, in the paper, Russell introduces his famous distinction between knowledge by acquaintance and knowledge by description and says we often use definite descriptions to denote objects we know only by description and are not acquainted with. In particular, we're not acquainted with the centre of the mass of the sun. We are also not acquainted

---

discussion Jason Stanley mentioned a paper on comparatives in linguistics published in 1976 that had noticed the problem and made such a proposal, but at the time of this writing I have not received the reference.)

[42] I am indebted to Christopher Peacocke for pointing out to me that this possible problem for Russell's theory was in fact already discussed by Peter Geach (though the example is no longer George IV and *Waverley*, it is in fact quite similar; see Geach (1967: 631). A similar problem, involving indefinite descriptions and 'wishes that' is attributed to Geach by Prior (1968: 105–6).

with *other minds*, he says at the end of the paper. However, there is no suggestion that Scott is to be identified with his *mind* here, nor that 'Scott' is anything other than a genuine proper name. If so, to repeat, an interest in the law of identity *has* been attributed to the first gentleman of Europe! This despite the fact that his interpretation of the large scope analysis is a very commonsensical one. (That is, intuitively it might seem to be quite reasonable.)[43]

As time went on, Russell's doctrine of acquaintance grew narrower and narrower. By the time of his Lectures on Logical Atomism, we are not acquainted with Scott himself, nor even with a time-slice of Scott. I would have liked to have thought that we were acquainted only with the things in our minds, but that never appears to have been Russell's view. Perhaps we are acquainted only with things in our own *brain*. (I don't really get it.) When I said something about our own *mind*, a Russell scholar (Gideon Makin) referred to the relevant references. Either way, we're not acquainted with Scott anymore, and 'Scott' will be a disguised definite description and this particular problem is solved.

Some later writers have concluded from this type of example—Nathan Salmon is the most elaborate one—that one can wonder whether $a = a$, but not whether a is self-identical, and set up an apparatus allowing the distinction.[44] I do not think that this distinction is available to Russell in his apparatus, either in *Principia* or in 'On Denoting'. So I don't think that this will go for Russell,[45] and the doctrine of

---

[43] For a parallel discussion, see Soames (2003) Ch. 5. (I thank Stephen Neale for this reference.) Soames correctly observes that Russell would be saved by his later views about acquaintance, which allows acquaintance with very few things; certainly not Scott (and of 'Scott' as therefore a disguised description). But then, as he says, Russell's example and analysis would be destroyed. To suggest that Russell *already* denied that George IV was 'acquainted' with Scott seems therefore, to be quite impossible. In 1905, he even still seems to suppose, as we have seen above, that Mont Blanc is a genuine component of a proposition, so that we must be genuinely acquainted with the mountain (at least if we have seen it).

[44] See Salmon (1986), and Salmon and Soames (1988) (see especially their introduction to the collection and Salmon (1986a). Salmon and Soames are the principal advocates of the approach mentioned.

[45] In a personal communication Salmon assures me that at least he (I'm not so sure about Soames) never thought that he was in agreement with Russell in this respect, even though I can attest that intelligent readers sympathetic with Salmon's position took him that way, and I did too. However, Salmon makes no explicit claim either way, as far as I know, and those readers have simply read it in. An explicit denial that he is purely Russellian here would have been highly desirable. The Salmon–Soames apparatus depends on a distinction between $\lambda x \phi x(a)$ and $\phi(a)$, which supposedly are different propositions. Then 'a is self-identical' is expressed by '$\lambda x(x = x)(a)$', while '$a = a$' expresses a different proposition. One can doubt or even disbelieve the latter, but not the former (unless one is an exceptional and bad philosopher). Russell has his own more cumbersome notation in *Principia* for $\lambda x \phi x$. Though the Salmon–Soames apparatus may seem to give a reasonably plausible solution to the philosophical problem of 'reflexivity', it seems to me to be plainly unavailable to Russell for the following reasons:

(a) The very term 'propositional function' clearly suggests that Russell did not intend any distinction between $\lambda x \phi x(a)$ and $\phi(a)$. Nor does a mathematician analogously intend any distinction between $\lambda x(x!)(3)$ and the number 6. Nor did Church, inventor of the lambda notation, intend any such distinction.

acquaintance better be narrowed as much as possible to get rid of these examples, even though they seem like common sense.

So, two things have been ignored. First, up to a certain late point, Russell's important treatment of scope distinctions of descriptions in intensional contexts, and even in extensional contexts, was unduly neglected. Second, every single example Russell actually gives for intensional contexts is either questionable or definitely wrong according to Russell's own philosophy, or to the truth. The first has finally come through;[46] the second, as far as I know, has been largely unnoticed and unknown.[47] Nevertheless, Russell is right. Scope does matter in intensional contexts. Too bad his own examples have these problems. The Smullyan example, involving modality, is much more straightforward than the examples as Russell gives them, involving propositional attitudes.

About definite descriptions in extensional contexts, surely Russell's beautiful joke foreshadows his later comments on the tendency to construe 'the present King of France is not bald' with the widest possible scope.

> By the law of excluded middle, either "*A* is *B*" or "*A* is not *B*" must be true. Hence either "the present King of France is bald" or "the present King of France is not bald" must be true. Yet if we enumerated the things that are bald, and the things that are not bald, we should not find the present King of France in either list. Hegelians, who love a synthesis, will conclude that he wears a wig. (Russell 1905, p. 48)

The late Gareth Evans once mentioned to me in conversation that Russell's theory predicts more ambiguities than actually occur, and this remark was meant to be an objection to Russell. Now, first, it can be some credit to Russell's theory that it predicts the existence of scope ambiguities that actually do occur, and predicts them from the very nature of the theory, not as some sort of *ad hoc*

(b) Russell obviously intends to use the existence of scope distinctions in intensional and even extensional contexts as an important argument that definite descriptions are not genuine names or terms, but rather require his quantificational analysis. But given Salmon's ideas about the lambda notation this argument is lost. For example one could distinguish between λx George IV believes ϕx (the author of *Waverley*) and George IV believes ϕ(the author of *Waverley*). This solution resembles Quine's, and I believe something close to it (using the lambda notation) is made explicitly by Robert Stalnaker and Richmond Thomason (1968).

Moreover, I myself am disinclined to accept Salmon's idea for the following reasons:

(a′) Consideration (a) above strikes me as correct in terms of the truth, not just for Russell.
(b′) If Salmon is right, there are distinct propositions $\phi(a)$, $\lambda x \phi x(a)$, $\lambda y \lambda x \phi \, x(y)(a)$, and so on *ad infinitum*, all closely related but distinct. If *n*-place relations are involved, the situation comes to involve complicated infinite trees. Is all this really plausible?
(c′) Someone might argue against the necessity of identity by claiming that only the self-identity of *x* is necessary, while the identity of *x* and *x* is contingent. Similarly, he or she might 'refute' Salmon's own argument against vague identity by a parallel argument. Surely Salmon should be wary of this. I am.

[46] But see note 9 on Davidson above.
[47] With the shining exception of Scott Soames's discussion of the large scope reading of Russell's George IV-Walter Scott example, as mentioned above.

solution to a problem. But second, I think, however, that any defender of Russell must concede that in ordinary language the predicted scope ambiguities don't all occur and are subject to some restrictive conditions. There are various restrictions, expressions such as 'a certain' that often call for a wider scope, and perhaps 'scope islands'. Already in *Principia* Russell mentions that in 'the King of France is not bald', the wide scope interpretation is to be preferred. Moreover, Russell himself, as we have seen, regards 'If Ferdinand has not drowned, then Ferdinand is my only son' uttered by King Alonso in *The Tempest*, as true even if Ferdinand *has* drowned, and there is no son. He does *not* say that the statement is ambiguous, and on a wide scope interpretation is false if Ferdinand drowned. Perhaps Russell is inconsistent. If we wish to be charitable, we must commit him to the view that not all scopes are allowed in English.

Now Delia Graff Fara[48]—and maybe this is even in an earlier paper by George Wilson[49]—observes that we cannot construe 'Aristotle was not a philosopher' as having a true interpretation, namely:

(13) There exists an x such that x is a philosopher and $x \neq$ Aristotle.

(13) is true, but no one would take 'Aristotle was not a philosopher' in this way. The corresponding case for definite descriptions is more delicate, but Graff Fara and Wilson are surely right in the *indefinite* description case. Graff Fara uses this example as part of an argument, which surely has independent intuitive appeal, as mentioned already by Strawson and Geach,[50] that sometimes when you use the word 'the' in the predicate after 'is' we are predicating something of the object rather than identifying it, that this is an 'is' of predication rather than of identity. In 'Gödel was the greatest logician of the twentieth century', we seem to be *predicating* something of Gödel rather than *identifying* him with the greatest logician of the twentieth century.[51] Russell says, in *Introduction to Mathematical Philosophy*, that in 'Socrates is a man' the 'is' used is the 'is' of identity:

(14) There is an x such that x is human and Socrates = x.

---

[48] Graff Fara (2001). Graff Fara gives a long list of references concerned with her main issue, predicative vs. objectual interpretations of definite descriptions, including Wilson's paper mentioned next, but as we shall see, seems ignorant of the earliest and most basic one.

[49] Wilson (1978).

[50] See Graff Fara (2001) for the references.

[51] Probably the example is better if it is false, with the qualification below. (I think the statement about Gödel is true.) But (with all due respect to him), 'Quine is the greatest logician of the twentieth century' is a false statement about Quine (I don't think he would have disputed my assertion), but does not erroneously equate Quine with Gödel. (Graff Fara already mentions the importance of false examples.)

The example could be improved further if the somewhat artificial tenseless 'is' beloved of philosophers were replaced by the more common tensed use of 'was', 'Gödel *was* the greatest logician of the twentieth century'. The 'was' certainly does not suggest that maybe Gödel became someone else later. Nor does 'Bill Clinton *was* the president of the US, but he is no longer'. (Grice and Myro, who believed that such changes of identity are possible—I don't—are *not* supported by such examples.)

On the other hand, in 'Socrates is human', the 'is' simply predicates 'human' of Socrates. Richard Montague, apparently in ignorance of Russell (at least, he doesn't cite him, as far as I can remember), tries to treat 'Socrates is human' as simply an abbreviated form of 'Socrates is a man', and accepts Russell's interpretation of the latter, thus eliminating the 'is' of predication altogether.[52] (Russell, in contrast, regards it as scandalous that 'is' is used ambiguously between predication and identity.) But intuitively one might feel the exact opposite, namely, that it's 'is a man' which is the predicate, that the 'is' here is the 'is' of predication. The negative instance mentioned by Graff Fara (maybe something similar is already in Wilson) could support this: 'Socrates is not a man' does not have a true interpretation either, whereas if all scopes were allowed it certainly would. Of course, this can be gotten rid of by making a restriction on what scopes are allowed rather than by abandoning the interpretation using the identity sign.

Really the basic argument for the predicative nature of 'the' in predicative form is already in a very old example by Leonard Linsky.[53] If someone says 'De Gaulle is not the King of France' that would be a natural expression by an opponent of de Gaulle who thinks he's getting too big for his britches, and too dictatorial. (Linsky himself imagines a parent instructing a child.) It would not appear to presuppose the existence of any king of France, let alone to assert it, and the wide scope interpretation is implausible. The statement seems to deny the predication of something to de Gaulle. However, 'The King of France is not de Gaulle' sounds a little weird, and seems more likely to have been asserted by a monarchist, who regards de Gaulle as a pretender occupying the throne, which should be occupied by a true Bourbon (or, more simply, someone who erroneously thinks that France is still a monarchy). Linsky's example, much earlier than Graff Fara (and even Wilson's) has the germ of all the arguments given by Graff Fara. The first form, with 'de Gaulle' as subject is, Linsky argues, predicative, and not the 'is' of identity. After all, Linsky points out, $a \neq b$ should be equivalent to $b \neq a$! (As President Clinton once said, it all depends on what 'is' is!) Yet Graff Fara, careful to list all her predecessors, seems unaware of the Linsky paper. Really, the Linsky paper foreshadows the later arguments. Take Fara's central case with indefinites — that 'Aristotle was not a philosopher' has no true reading. But now put 'a philosopher' in a subject position. (I invent an expanded dialogue to make this more plausible.) 'A [or: some] philosopher was not Aristotle himself, but held that he faithfully followed all his positions'. 'Who is it you have in mind?' 'Averroes'. Then, with the indefinite article in subject position, the wide scope *is* the preferred interpretation, just as Linsky would have predicted.[54]

---

[52] Thomason (1974).   [53] Linsky (1960).

[54] But I must admit 'the greatest living logician is Ernest Nagel', which I once heard seriously affirmed at a sister institution of Nagel's own Columbia, strikes me as a false assertion about Nagel, not about Gödel (who I think was alive). The same point is true of other assertions, the ϕ is ψ in x, which are 'about' x, so I suppose subject vs. predicate position is not the whole of the story.

However, there is trouble here. 'Yvonne de Gaulle did not marry the King of France', 'Dora Black never married a philosopher', and the like appear not to have wide scope readings either, but 'the King of France', 'a philosopher' and so on, do appear to be substantive *objects* of their verbs. (And Linsky's argument about $a \neq b$ and $b \neq a$ applies to 'married' also, since 'married' is a symmetric relation.) Maybe the *reason* someone might make the statement about Yvonne is sarcastically to deny that de Gaulle is king of France, but the statement appears to be an assertion about the relation between two objects.[55] (Graff Fara proposes a theory that definite descriptions are really *always* predicative, but at this time I have not studied her paper enough to comment, nor have I studied Wilson's; but I am relying on naive intuition, which is just as compelling here as in the apparent predicative uses with the copula.)

Many times scope in a complicated case can be indicated by the form of the words, and is unlikely to be interpreted otherwise:

(15) I mistakenly took it to be the case that the President of Harvard was a teaching fellow

might be most naturally interpreted with inner scopes and as attributing a dual role to the President of Harvard. Graff Fara predicative interpretation, at least of the indefinite, *may* also seem to be natural. Well, maybe. In fact, in Princeton, the President at least at one time did teach sections of a course, but that's not the most likely interpretation of the displayed formula about Harvard. More likely, someone ran into the President and he was so youthful looking that he was mistaken to be a teaching fellow, not the President. Now, if you say, 'I mistook the President of Harvard for a teaching fellow' then it is probably interpreted as 'The President is such that I mistook him for a teaching fellow', wide scope for 'the President', narrow for 'a teaching fellow'. If you say, in spite of the symmetry of the relationship involved, 'I mistook a teaching fellow for the President of Harvard', it is likely that 'a teaching fellow' has the wider scope and 'the President of Harvard' the inner scope (that is, some teaching fellow one encountered was so old and distinguished looking that I thought he was President of Harvard).[56] Here language may contain its own scope indicators.

---

[55] It should also be noted in this connection that Russell states his analysis in a way that brings out the predication in 'On Denoting' (p. 55) when he says that 'Scott is the author of *Waverley*' can be paraphrased as what amounts to 'Scott and only Scott authored *Waverley*,' though the predication itself still involves identity. (As Stephen Neale has reminded me, Russell does this again in 'Knowledge by Acquaintance and Knowledge by Description', p. 217.) The sentences 'Scott and the author of *Waverley* are one' and 'Scott and the author of *Waverley* are one and the same man' both appear to be statements about the identity of objects and are highly relevant in the historical situation, since many books were published under the by-line 'by the author of *Waverley*'.

[56] Yet another question, relevant to the predicative versus the object uses of definite and indefinite articles is the issue of whether I have actually confused two people with each other, the teaching fellow in question, if that's whom I encountered, or the president. See my remarks on this in Kripke (1977), and also Ludlow and Neale (1991).

As I already said, in *Principia* Russell proves a metatheorem to the effect that a single description (or, strictly speaking, a single occurrence of a description) can be moved in or out if the existence and uniqueness conditions are fulfilled. He may think he has settled the scope question for extensional formal languages, but it is hardly so. First, there may be more than one description, or even more than one occurrence of the same description. Second, as he, himself, mentions in 'On Denoting'—see the first paragraph, quoted above—a description can occur within a description, which gives more possibilities for scope ambiguities but is not treated. Third, a description can be quantified into, as when it stands for a function, as he himself emphasizes in *Principia*. Now, one needs a fixed set of rules for what is allowed in *all* these cases, and it's not that the treatment will be essentially different, but that Russell himself omits these cases. (In fact, *14.242 and its two subservient theorems underlies the special case.) A description operator may bind a description within its scope and so may an ordinary quantifier. A general theorem will assert that under general conditions, a description can indifferently be moved to any appropriate scope and you get something equivalent. However, if it is bound by a quantifier or another description, it cannot be moved outside of what binds it. Also, suppose a description occurs within another description, but is not bound by the variable in the first description, then you can move in either of the following orders. Move the inner description out first; or move the whole thing. But the orders of moving around and so on have a rather complicated structure only very partially treated by *Principia*, though the authors certainly have the basic idea.

The various ways of moving a description around can be represented in the form of a tree. In underlying structure, all the descriptions are quantifiers already and there is no moving around. If you look at it from the bottom up, that is, consider the 'true logical form' first and then use descriptions as abbreviations, everything has been decided at the bottom. The problem arises when the descriptions appear to be terms, and there are no scope operators. A general metatheorem will have the form of a tree of disambiguations depending on how we give a scope to this or that description. When we do want disambiguation, the result may still be ambiguous, and we disambiguate it further until we get, hopefully, to the end. Now we need sufficient conditions for a 'scope indifference' theorem, asserting that it follows from certain hypotheses, that once we get to the ultimate logical forms postulated by Russell's theory, the resulting forms are materially equivalent, regardless of the choices of scope. This theorem will hold for extensional first-order logic. Formula (5) is a special case, with a weak hypothesis that does not work in general. The Hilbert–Bernays conditions mentioned above, though not correct for English or mathematics (see above), are nevertheless *sufficient* for a scope indifference theorem. The exact formulation of such a theorem need not be given here, but is illustrated by the cases discussed above. Descriptions may be moved around freely, and need not be given explicit scope indicators. But of course, as is clear, descriptions containing a variable bound by a description operator of a quantifier must remain inside the operator or quantifier. The problem of finding weaker sufficient conditions than those of Hilbert–Bernays has been given little real attention in the standard literature—perhaps the literature on free logic pays some such attention, but I am ignorant. (And 'little real attention' is itself a 'scholarly hedge'!)

Whereas in the first edition of *Principia* Russell takes negation and alternation as primitive, in the second edition, he proposes to replace them by the Sheffer stroke, or alternatively, it could be the dual notion ('joint denial'). The Sheffer stroke $p|q$ means 'not-p or not-q'. (The Sheffer stroke was, in fact, already known to Peirce, but forgotten. And presumably Peirce knew the dual notion, which is used by Quine in his *Mathematical Logic*.[57] Russell thinks that this is the most 'definite improvement' of *Principia* if it were to be rewritten—that is, one that uncontroversially should be made (see exact quotation below).

If we're granted that every truth function can be defined in term of negation and alternation, then these terms can be defined in terms of the stroke, as on page xvi of the introduction to the second edition:

$\neg p =_{df} p|p$
$p \vee q =_{df} \neg p | \neg q$

Now, here is the problem. Eliminating descriptions means taking them as terms and then translating them into quantifiers, but regardless of scope, under the hypothesis for a 'scope indifference theorem', and subject to the restrictions that I have mentioned. So, what is Russell's definition of

$\psi(\imath x)(\phi x)$?

We wrote it before as:

$(\exists x)((\forall y)(y = x \equiv \Phi y) \wedge \psi x))$

Now, assuming for the moment that the material biconditional and conjunction are both primitive, and granting the 'scope indifference theorem' sketched above, it should be clear that an iteration of the procedure will terminate. But rarely is the biconditional taken as primitive, it is usually defined. Suppose the Sheffer stroke is taken as primitive. Then negation is:

$\neg A =_{df} A | A$
$A \vee B =_{df} \neg A | \neg B =_{df} (A|A)|(B|B)$
$A \wedge B =_{df} \neg (A|B) =_{df} (A|B)|(A|B)$
$A \equiv B =_{df} (A \wedge B) \vee (\neg A \wedge \neg B),$

where I leave the last expansion into primitive notation to the reader. Alternatively, try defining the material biconditional as $(\neg A \vee B) \wedge (\neg B \vee A)$.

---

[57] Quine (1940).

At any rate, what looks like only *one* occurrence of ϕ and ψ in the conventional Russellian analysis of $\psi\,(\imath x\,\phi(x))$ is obviously becoming many, many occurrences of ϕ and ψ in the analysis. Now, suppose either ϕ or ψ itself, or worse, both, contain a description, or one or both contain many (occurrences of) descriptions. With an unfavourable choice of scopes there will be more (occurrences of) descriptions in the analysis than there were originally in the analysand! The dangers involved in this situation I call the dangers of a *hydra*; that is where you are trying to unpack things you always have more occurrences of descriptions than you had before. That's what I call the 'hydra problem'.[58]

Now, Russell says in the introduction to the second edition of *Principia*:

The most definite improvement resulting from work in mathematical logic during the past fourteen years is the substitution, in Part I, Section A, of the one indefinable 'p and q are incompatible', (or, alternatively, 'p and q are both false') for the two indefinables 'not-p' and 'p or q'. This is due to Dr. H. M. Sheffer. (Whitehead and Russell 1927, p. xiii)

Now, Russell does not say, contrary to what is attributed to him by Warren Goldfarb,[59] that this is the most important work done in mathematical logic since the first edition of *Principia*. The 'most definite improvement': Russell is talking about the ways the book should be rewritten if he had the time, and, in fact that's all he means. 'The most definite improvement' means the improvement least open to controversy or doubt. It shows that propositional logic needs only a single primitive, and moreover Nicod has shown that you can get by with only one axiom for propositional logic that way. In deference to Goldfarb, I should add, though he has lost the battle perhaps he could have won the war.[60]

---

[58] Nathan Salmon once emailed me. He couldn't see the problem, because he had learned logic from the textbook by Kalish and Montague (1964) which takes all the connectives, including the material biconditional, as primitive. This is unusual. Later, Salmon wrote he doubted they were trying to avoid hydras.

[59] Warren Goldfarb, in the paper cited in note 20 above.

[60] Nicod (1917). Though Goldfarb has lost this battle, in a way his basic point is right. Russell probably did not properly follow later work on logic. Russell may or may not have known of such developments as the work of Löwenheim or Skolem, but, in any event, he would have regarded them as irrelevant to the *Principia* project. However, he is very concerned with the problem of developing mathematics purely predicatively, dropping the axiom of reducibility and adding axioms of extensionality. He believes, what is now known to be in error, that he has managed to prove mathematical induction without postulating it. However, in the introduction to the second edition, he still sees a problem in the Dedekind ordering of the continuum, and hence presumably in the developments of real analysis. But one of the books he cites at the end of his paper as a further development of mathematical logic—this bibliography of further developments also gives the lie to Goldfarb's assertion that he thought the Sheffer stroke the most significant later development in mathematical logic—is Hermann Weyl's *Das Kontinuum*. This book, which postulates mathematical induction and deals precisely with the problem about developing analysis predicatively, assuming induction, and hence with the problem he is concerned with about the continuum, is a work he probably, despite his excellent German, has not read. The proper conclusion is that although he *is* aware (probably contrary to the impression Goldfarb has) that significant other developments in logic have taken place, he probably has not kept up with them, even when they are highly relevant to his project in *Principia*.

Now to state a theorem: In the second edition Russell favours taking the Sheffer stroke as the sole primitive of propositional logic. One theorem that I recall I proved is that with a bad choice of scopes, using a Sheffer stroke or its dual will allow for a hydra. Some paths of the tree will go on infinitely and never come to an end. It is intuitively obvious, although syntactically much more difficult to prove, that all terminating paths are equivalent. But non-terminating paths are equivalent to nothing in particular because they don't lead to any analysis. The general thing to do to try to get a path *not* to terminate is to choose the scopes so they have as many occurrences of descriptions embedded in them as possible. That will improve the chances for an increase in the number of occurrences of descriptions. The opposite strategy, making the scopes as narrow as possible, is what would lead to a termination. Now, even for alternation and negation as primitive, or dually for conjunction and negation, the problem still exists. Temporarily, if everything is in primitive notation, an elimination of descriptions may lead to an analysis with more occurrences of descriptions than there were before. In these cases, however, I recall proving—though it really takes proving!—that there are no real hydras. Every path eventually terminates, and all are equivalent.

Hilbert and Bernays give an analysis in their book, not with the Sheffer stroke as primitive, that a certain particular procedure terminates and eliminates descriptions. Other treatments of the problem are given by Joseph Shoenfield[61] and Edward Nelson.[62] A model-theoretic treatment of the problem, which is much easier, has been given by Elliot Mendelson.[63] All these treatments show that specific procedures can be given to eliminate descriptions.

As Quine wrote in his original criticism of Smullyan, for a formal language (without intensional contexts and not in natural language—in other words, we eliminate Quine's original errors), under reasonable hypotheses (actually, Quine ignores the case of descriptions with variables, where the Hilbert–Bernays hypotheses we have been using are rather strong), if descriptions are thought of as terms it is unnatural to have scope distinctions in the language. So a 'scope indifference theorem' is important to Russell's theory as a surrogate for one in which definite descriptions are definite terms. Such a theorem does exist in the case of all terminating paths, and this is not brought out in the specific elimination procedures cited in the preceding paragraph. However, as I have said, in the case of the Sheffer stroke and its dual, not all paths terminate, while with disjunction and negation (or its dual, conjunction and negation), all paths do terminate, but the result is not trivial.

In sum, it is hardly so incontestable as Russell thought, that the Sheffer stroke should be taken as primitive. If we want scope to make no difference at all in the case of non-empty descriptions and totally defined functions, perhaps we want *all*

---

[61] Shoenfield (1967).   [62] Nelson (1986).   [63] Mendelson.

paths to terminate and be equivalent—which does not happen (no hydras). If ∨ and ¬ are primitive, as in the first edition, the desiderata are achieved, but the proof is nontrivial. As far as I can see, only a choice of connectives with redundancies (not all independent) can avoid hydras trivially.

Guess what? I guess I'm through![64, 65]

REFERENCES

Almog, J. (1986). "Naming without Necessity." *Journal of Philosophy* 83: 210–42.
Barcan, R. (1948). Review of Smullyan, "Modality and Description." *Journal of Symbolic Logic* 13: 149–50.
Boolos, G. (1984). "To be is to be the Value of a Variable (or to be Some Value of Some Variables)." *Journal of Philosophy* 81: 430–49.
Caton, C. (ed.) (1963). *Philosophy and Ordinary Language.* Urbana: University of Illinois Press.
Church, A. (1950). Review of Fitch "The Problem of the Morning Star and the Evening Star." *Journal of Symbolic Logic* 15: 63.
Davidson, D. (1980). *Essays on Actions and Events.* Oxford: Clarendon Press.
Dennett, D. (1982). "Beyond Belief." In Woodfield (1982), pp. 1–96.
Donnellan, K. (1966). "Reference and Definite Descriptions." *Philosophical Review* 75: 281–304.
Dreben, B., and J. van Heijenoort. (1986). "Introductory Note to 1929, 1930, and 1930a." In Feferman et al. (1986), pp. 44–59.
Evans, G. (1977). "Pronouns, Quantifiers and Relative Clauses (I)." *Canadian Journal of Philosophy* 7: 467–536.
Fara, D. Graff (2001). "Descriptions as Predicates." *Philosophical Studies* 102: 1–42.
Feferman, S. et al. (1986). *Kurt Gödel: Collected Works*, Vol. I. Oxford: Oxford University Press.
Fitch, F. (1949). "The Problem of the Morning Star and the Evening Star." *Philosophy of Science* 16: 137–41.
Frege, G. (1892). "Uber Sinn und Bedeutung." *Zeitschrift für Philosophie und philosophische Kritik* 100: 25–50.
French, P. A., T. E. Uehling, Jr., and H. K. Wettstein. (1989). *Contemporary Perspectives in the Philosophy of Language.* Minneapolis: University of Minnesota Press.
Geach, P. (1967). "Intentional Identity." *Journal of Philosophy* 74: 626–32.
Gödel, K. (1944). "Russell's Mathematical Logic." In Schilpp (1944), pp. 125–53.
Goldfarb, W. (1979). "Logic in the Twenties: The Nature of the Quantifier." *Journal of Symbolic Logic* 44: 351–68.

---

[64] My thanks to the transcriber, whose identity I don't know. Special thanks go to Stephen Neale and Romina Padró for their invaluable help in the editing of this paper. Since they took such an active part in the editing, clearly any philosophical or technical errors that remain are due to them!

[65] A technical investigation of the hydra problem raised in this paper has been made by Visser, Gramayer, Leo and Oostrom (2009). I haven't studied their paper in detail, except to note its basic claims, but my respect for the authors is such that I assume that their results are correct.

Hilbert, D. and Bernays, P. (1934). *Grundlagen der Mathematik*, Vol. I. Berlin: Springer. 2nd ed., 1968.

Hylton, P. (1990). *Russell, Idealism and the Emergence of Analytic Philosophy*. New York: Oxford University Press.

Irvine, A. D. and G. A. Wedeking (eds.) (1993). *Russell and Analytic Philosophy*. Toronto: University of Toronto Press.

Kalish, D. and R. Montague. (1964). *Logic: Techniques of Formal Reasoning*. New York: Harcourt Brace Jovanovich.

Kaplan, D. (1972). "What is Russell's Theory of Descriptions?" In Pears (1972), pp. 227–44.

Kripke, S. (1977). "Speaker's Reference and Semantic Reference." In French, Uehling and Wettstein (1977), pp. 6–27. Reprinted in this volume as Chapter 5.

——— (1980). *Naming and Necessity*. Cambridge: Harvard University Press.

——— (2009). "Presupposition and Anaphora." *Linguistic Inquiry* 40: 367–86. Reprinted in this volume as Chapter 12.

Linsky, L. (1960). "Reference and Referents." In Caton (1963), pp. 74–89.

Ludlow, P. and Neale, S. (1991). "Indefinite Descriptions: In Defense of Russell." *Linguistics and Philosophy* 14: 171–202.

Mates, B. (1973). "Reference and Description." *Foundations of Language* 10: 409–18.

Mendelson, E. (1960). "A Semantic Proof of the Eliminability of Descriptions." *Mathematical Logic Quarterly* 6: 199–200.

Neale, S. (1990). *Descriptions*. Cambridge: MIT Press.

——— (1993). "Grammatical Form, Logical Form, and Incomplete Symbols." In Irvine and Wedeking (1993), pp. 97–139. Reprinted in Ostertag (1998), pp. 79–121.

——— (1999). "On a Milestone of Empiricism." In Orenstein and Kotatko (1999), pp. 237–346.

——— (2001). *Facing Facts*. Oxford: Oxford University Press.

Nelson, E. (1986). *Predicative Arithmetic*. Princeton: Princeton University Press.

Nicod, J. G. (1917). "A Reduction in the Number of Primitive Propositions of Logic." *Proceedings of the Cambridge Philosophical Society* 19: 32–41.

Orenstein, A. and P. Kotatko (eds.) (1999). *Knowledge, Language and Logic*. Dordrecht: Kluwer.

Ostertag, G. (ed.) (1998). *Definite Descriptions: A Reader*. Cambridge: MIT Press.

Pears, D. F. (ed.) (1972). *Bertrand Russell: A Collection of Critical Essays*. Garden City, New York: Doubleday Anchor.

Prior, A. N. (1963). "Is the Concept of Referential Opacity Really Necessary?" *Acta Philosophica Fennica* 16: 189–200.

——— (1968). "Intentionality and Intensionality." *Proceedings of the Aristotelian Society, Supplementary Volume* 42: 91–106.

Quine, W. V. O. (1940). *Mathematical Logic*. Cambridge: Harvard University Press.

——— (1953). *From a Logical Point of View*. Cambridge: Harvard University Press. Reprinted 1961, 1980.

——— (1953a). "Reference and Modality." In Quine (1953), pp. 139–59 (revised in 1961 and 1980 editions).

——— (1956). "Quantifiers and Propositional Attitudes." *Journal of Philosophy* 53: 177–87. Reprinted in Quine (1966), pp. 183–94.

——— (1960). *Word and Object*. Cambridge: MIT Press.
——— (1966). *The Ways of Paradox and Other Essays*. New York: Random House.
——— (1977). "Intensions Revisited." In Quine (1981), pp. 113–23.
——— (1981). *Theories and Things*. Cambridge: Harvard University Press.
——— (1999). "Reply to Neale." In Orenstein and Kotatko (1999), pp. 426–27.
Rosser, B. (1939). "On the Consistency of Quine's New Foundations for Mathematical Logic." *Journal of Symbolic Logic* 4: 15–24.
Russell, B. (1905). "On Denoting." *Mind* 14: 479–93. Reprinted in Ostertag (1998) pp. 35–49.
——— (1957). "Mr Strawson on Referring." *Mind* 66: 385–9.
——— (1918, 1919). "The Philosophy of Logical Atomism." *The Monist* 28: 495–527; 29: 32–63, 190–222, 345–380. Reprinted in Russell (1988), pp. 155–244.
——— (1988). *The Collected Papers of Bertrand Russell*, Vol. 10, *The Philosophy of Logical Atomism And Other Essays, 1914–19*, John Slater (ed.). London: Routledge.
Salmon, N. (1986). *Frege's Puzzle*. Cambridge: MIT Press.
——— (1986a). "Reflexivity." *Notre Dame Journal of Formal Logic*, 27, pp. 401–29. Reprinted in Salmon and Soames (1988), pp. 24–74.
——— (2005). "On Designating." *Mind* 114: 1069–133.
Salmon, N. and S. Soames (eds.)(1988). *Propositions and Attitudes*. Oxford: Oxford University Press.
Schilpp, P. A. (ed.) (1944). *The Philosophy of Bertrand Russell*. Evanston, Illinois: Northwestern University Press.
Shoenfield, J. (1967). *Mathematical Logic*. Reading, Mass.: Addison-Wesley.
Smullyan, A. (1948). "Modality and Description." *Journal of Symbolic Logic* 13: 31–7.
Soames, S. (2003). *Philosophical Analysis in the Twentieth Century, Volume 1: The Dawn of Analysis*. Princeton: Princeton University Press.
Stalnaker, R. and R. Thomason. (1968). "Modality and Reference." *Noûs* 2: 359–72.
Strawson, P. (1964). "Identifying Reference and Truth-Values." *Theoria* 30: 96–118.
——— (1950). "On Referring." *Mind* 59: 320–44.
Thomason, R. (ed.) (1947). *Formal Philosophy: Selected Papers of Richard Montague*. New Haven: Yale University Press.
Visser, A., C. Grabmayer, J. Leo, and V. van Oostrom (2009). "On the Termination of Russell's Description Elimination Algorithm." Utrecht, The Netherlands: Logic Group Preprint Series.: http://www.phil.uu.nl/preprints/lgps/list.html (accessed, October 2010).
Weyl, H. (1918). *Das Kontinuum*. Leipzig: Veit.
Whitehead, A. N., and B. Russell. (1910, 1912, 1913). *Principia Mathematica, 3 Vols*, Cambridge, Cambridge University Press. Second edition, 1925 (Vol. 1), 1927 (Vols. 2, 3).
Wilson, G. (1978). "On Definite and Indefinite Descriptions." *Philosophical Review* 87: 48–76.
Woodfield, A. (ed.) (1982). *Thought and Object: Essays on Intentionality*. Oxford: Clarendon Press.

9
Frege's Theory of Sense and Reference: Some Exegetical Notes[1]

In translating Frege's terms "*Sinn*" and "*Bedeutung*", I follow Max Black's translation as "sense" and "reference", or "referent". For a long time this was standard, although other translations have been proposed, and later some have thought that standard German usage should be followed in the translation of "*Bedeutung*". However unusual Frege's usage may be, there should not be any doubt that for Frege "*Bedeutung*" is what a term stands for.[2]

---

[1] The present chapter is based on a transcript of a lecture given in Stockholm, Sweden, on 24 October 2001, on the occasion of the award of the Schock Prize in Logic and Philosophy. There are occasional references to works postdating the original lecture, obviously added to the present version. There has been considerable rewriting and editing of the transcript, but the essence of the lecture remains unchanged, except in a few places that are explicitly noted.

[2] In standard German "*Bedeutung*" should be translated as "meaning" and recent translators have advocated that this be done. See Beaney (1997, pp. 36–46), for some of the controversy over this issue; he himself leaves "*Bedeutung*" untranslated.

The argument for translating "*Bedeutung*" as "meaning" is a principle of "exegetical neutrality"; that one should not deviate from standard German for exegetical reasons. However, I assume that there would be no such issue had Frege used "*das Bezeichnete*" and "*bezeichnen*", and he does explain that by "*bedeuten*" he means "*bezeichnen*", and uses "*das Bezeichnete*" for the designatum (see Künne, 2010, footnote 15, who corrects my original statement). Already in "Über Sinn und Bedeutung" Frege says: "Ein Eigenname ... drückt aus seinen Sinn, bedeutet oder bezeichnet seine Bedeutung. Wir drücken mit einem Zeichen dessen Sinn aus und bezeichnen mit ihm dessen Bedeutung" (Frege, 1892, p. 31 in the original; p. 156 in Beaney, 1997). Beaney's edition translates "*bedeutet*" as "stands for" and "*bezeichnet*" as "designates". Whatever ambiguity there might be in the first verb, I assume that there is no such ambiguity in the second one. (My thanks to Dagfinn Føllesdal for this reference.) I have seen other passages where "*bedeuten*" and "*bezeichnen*" are used interchangeably.

I should mention that Church (1995, p. 69) objects to the use of "reference" as violating proper *English* usage. (His point appears to be that it is speakers who refer to things, and that they can do so without using any term designating the object.) Maybe so, but since Black introduced "reference", it has become too standard to give up. Perhaps "referent" is somewhat better. Church himself favors Russell's "denotation", which is also used by Montgomery Furth and David Kaplan, and no doubt others. (However, Russell himself also uses "denoting" in another way of his own.) One might have favored "designation"; Feigl's "nominatum", which Feigl followed, clearly failed to gain wide currency because it was too awkward.

Subsequently all references to "Über Sinn und Bedeutung" come from Beaney (1997) with pagination accordingly, unless otherwise specified. Beaney himself gives the original pagination.

Frege introduced the notion of sense to explain how there can be non-trivial but true identity statements. In such a case, there are two terms with the same reference but different senses. For example, the phrase "the president of the US when I am giving this lecture" designates the same thing as "the president of the US in 2001",[3] which also has the same *Bedeutung* as the proper name "George W. Bush". So there can be many different senses with one referent. This leads to Russell's famous slogan: "There is no backward road from denotations to meanings",[4] or as we would put it, from referents to senses. There could be many senses determining the same reference.

The phrase "there is no backward road", however, should not mislead: one does not, when using an expression or introducing an expression, have to specify two things, its reference and its sense. Once one specifies the reference one has specified the sense. How can that be? It is because the sense is the way the reference or *Bedeutung* is specified. So, for example, in *Grundgesetze* (Frege, 1893, sections 31 and 32, pp. 87–90), Frege gives[5] the truth-conditions for all the sentences of his language. Then he concludes that every sentence of his language expresses a thought, namely that these given truth-conditions hold. In that way there *is* a backward road in every particular case of an explanation of a given phrase.[6]

So far, perhaps, so easy. Complications come in with Frege's doctrine of so-called "indirect" or *ungerade* reference. If someone says (this is Frege's own example; Frege, 1892, p. 160):

Although I have used "reference" and "referent" in this chapter, when quotations from Frege derive from Beaney's edition they perforce follow his practice of leaving "*Bedeutung*" untranslated.

[3] Or most of 2001 anyway. He took office on 20 January. In an article like this we need not discuss whether he was "really" elected.

[4] Russell writes:

And C must not be a constituent of this complex (as it is of "the meaning of C"); for if C occurs in the complex, it will be its denotation, not its meaning, that will occur, and there is no backward road from denotations to meanings, because every object can be denoted by an infinite number of different denoting phrases. (1905, p. 487)

[5] It does not matter for present purposes that Frege's attempt to do this is fallaciously circular, and therefore fails.

[6] Dummett says:

... when Frege is purporting to give the sense of a word or symbol, what he actually *states* is what the reference is ... in saying what the referent is, we have to choose a particular way of saying this, a particular means of determining something as the referent.... we *say* what the referent of a word is, and thereby *show* what its sense is. (This is the correct answer to Russell's objection ... that there is "no backward road" from reference to sense.) (1973, p. 227; original emphasis)

There are qualifications and other remarks in Dummett's text that I do not necessarily endorse. Dummett seems to imply that the point he is making can be found in many places in Frege, but the main case I am aware of is the one cited above from the *Grundgesetze* (1893). Many who write on Frege give insufficient recognition to this point, perhaps to an extent even Dummett himself. That there is a "backward road" in the sense in question already states the main moral of the present paper in advance.

Copernicus believed that the planetary orbits are circles this is an example of indirect discourse. Frege's doctrine was that in a case like this, the referent of "the planetary orbits" is not the orbits themselves, but the *Sinn* or meaning[7] of the phrase "the planetary orbits". Some commentary on Frege would be needed as to why he says this, but the arguments will be familiar to the present readership.

Frege believed that the referent of a sentence is its truth-value, the True or the False. The *Gedanke* or thought expressed is its *Sinn*. The referent of "that the planetary orbits are circles" is the *Gedanke*; that is what is believed. But since the *Gedanke* is the *Sinn* of the sentence, its components are themselves *Sinne*, and hence must be the references of the component parts of the sentence following the "that" clause.[8]

So there is a reference shift in indirect contexts. Since the reference must be determined in some way, there has to be therefore not only an indirect reference but also apparently an indirect sense. As far as I know Frege does not ever explicitly consider iterations of "that" clauses, such as, for example, "We should remember that Copernicus believed that the planetary orbits are circles", and so on for arbitrary iterations.[9] If we do consider such iterations, the familiar consequence is that Frege is committed to a hierarchy of doubly oblique indirect referents and senses, triply oblique, and so on.

Another way of generating a hierarchy ought to be mentioned also. If an expression has a *Sinn*, presumably another expression could designate that *Sinn*. But then the second expression presumably has a *Sinn* also, which can be designated by yet another expression, and so on. Given Frege's doctrine that an expression in indirect contexts designates its *Sinn*, the two ways of generating a hierarchy are of course related.

There are papers on the hierarchical question by Terry Parsons (1981) and Tyler Burge (1979b).[10] There is a famous objection to Frege, made by Donald Davidson (1965) in a well-known paper that precedes the papers by Parsons and Burge. Davidson argues that if there were such an infinite hierarchy, then, say, for a Swede to learn English as a foreign language, the Swede would have to learn

---

[7] Later Tyler Burge's claim (in 1979b) that *Sinn* and meaning have been wrongly equated will be discussed (and his argument rejected). The issue is probably not crucial at this point, but may affect some of my own argument below.

[8] The general compositional principles involved will be stated below.

[9] Künne (2010) and Burge (in personal communication) have pointed out that a particular double iteration is considered in the letter to Russell dated 28-12-1902 (Frege, 1980) that I myself cite below.

[10] I agree with Burge (see especially his postscript in Burge, 2004) that the hierarchy is an actual consequence of Frege's theory. (Qualifications of this will emerge from the present chapter.)

Various writers have tried to avoid this consequence. Carnap (1947) abolishes it by *fiat*, replacing Frege's "method of the name relation" by his "method of extension and intension". Dummett (1973, pp. 267–268) proposes to emend Frege's theory to avoid this consequence. Without going into the matter, I do not find his proposal to be successful, but nevertheless I have found his discussion helpful and influential for my own interpretation.

infinitely many things. That is, not just the sense—if that is the meaning of the English phrase—but also its indirect sense, its doubly indirect sense, and so on. He similarly objects to Church's (1951) well-known formalization of Frege's theory in "A Formulation of the Logic of Sense and Denotation", where the infinity of primitives is very clear.[11]

How could that be? How could we learn such a language, either a natural language under the Fregean hierarchical view, or the corresponding formal language given by Church? It cannot be that we have to learn infinitely many independent things. I actually think this objection is valid, but I also think it is not so much needed as people seem to believe. A simpler version, indeed inspired by Davidson's remarks, can take its place.

Let us forget about any iterations either of operators such as "believes that", or of referring to a sense. Let us just consider the original simple case:

Copernicus believes that the planetary orbits are circles.

There are two problems here. Ordinarily, we should think that to teach English to a foreigner one simply teaches some grammar, the vocabulary, and what all the words mean, and then we are through. But not according to this: she will not understand this sentence because she has not learned the indirect senses of these words, if these are independent entities from the ordinary senses.

To know what the sense of a sentence is to understand it, to know what thought it expresses. Normally, we would think that that is enough, that the foreigner has learned English. But apparently this is not so according to Frege's theory of indirect senses. According to this theory, it appears that the foreigner cannot understand belief and other indirect discourse sentences, such as the one about Copernicus. The foreigner should say to the teacher: "Unfortunately you have not taught me how to understand these 'belief-sentences', or 'said that-sentences', or other indirect discourse sentences. For these I need not only to know the senses of the English words, as I have just been taught, but also their indirect senses." And the teacher might then reply "Oh yes! Next year we will get out Volume II, the dictionary of indirect senses. Then you will learn indirect English, and will be able to understand these belief sentences. But I cannot go so fast as to teach this in the first year." Clearly the teacher's speech is absurd, as is the student's puzzlement, and no infinite hierarchy is needed to see this.[12]

---

[11] This paper, and the issue of its fidelity to Frege's intent, will be discussed in a little more detail below.

[12] See Davidson (1968, p. 214). He remarks that in our "semantic innocence", we never would have imagined that expressions mean something different in indirect discourse from what they mean in ordinary contexts. This in effect expresses the objection to Frege's theory that I have just given in a stronger and simpler way. See Kaplan (1968), who emphasizes that Frege's theory is an ambiguity theory. It should be noted that Russell's theory of descriptions is semantically innocent in Davidson's sense, and that he could have claimed this as an advantage of his view. I am not sure that I can really get Frege out of the "innocence objection", but I will try to come close. See footnote 46 below.

English, if the issue stopped there, might be a learnable language in Davidson's sense, but it takes an implausible amount of work to learn it.

A related objection which has been raised against Frege is: what *are* these indirect senses? He does not give us any idea what they are.[13] Given Russell's slogan, "there is no backward road from denotations to meanings",[14] assuming it applies at every level, there could be words with the same senses but different indirect senses. And expressions could actually be synonymous, in the sense of having the same *Sinn*, but nevertheless have different *ungerade Sinne* (indirect senses). Then we have a very strange situation for language learning.

Frege does say the following:

In order to speak of the sense of an expression "*A*" one may simply use the phrase "the sense of the expression '*A*'". (Frege, 1892, p. 154)

That certainly has the same reference—namely, the ordinary sense—as the indirect sense, whatever entity this may be. Could this be what Frege thinks is the indirect sense? The suggestion that this is what an indirect sense is, is rejected by Dummett as implausible in *Frege: Philosophy of Language* (1973, pp. 267–268); but then in his later book, *The Interpretation of Frege's Philosophy* (1981, pp. 89ff.),[15] he says that he does not know why he regarded this suggestion (which he attributes to Heidelberger) as so obviously implausible and gives a more elaborate discussion.

Whatever an indirect sense is, it is not plausible to me that it is this. To understand any English sentence, it is (necessary and) sufficient to understand the senses of all its components. In particular, to understand an indirect discourse context, it is sufficient to understand the indirect senses of its components. Now someone who knows virtually no English can perfectly well understand the phrase "the sense of 'the planetary orbits are circular'" if all he knows are the English words "the sense of", but has no idea what "the planetary orbits are circular" means. Then, if the analysis in question were true, he will understand

---

[13] I have in mind Carnap (1947). He writes:

And since he [Frege] assumes that nominatum and sense must always be different, he had thus to introduce a third entity as the oblique sense. Incidentally, it seems that Frege nowhere explains in more customary terms what this third entity is. (Carnap, 1947, p. 129)

Since Carnap actually studied with Frege (and the direction of his entire career was changed by the experience), it is too bad that he apparently found Frege to be an intimidating teacher. He might simply have asked him.

[14] There are those who believe that here Russell has anticipated Davidson's learnability argument, or perhaps has the germ of a beginning of his argument. See Salmon (2005) (who sees an anticipation both of Davidson's learnability argument and Carnap's question) and earlier writers, some of whom he cites. Dummett (1973, pp. 267–268) thinks that Russell has anticipated Carnap's question in the following form: since there is no "backward road", which of the infinitely many candidates for an indirect sense is the right one?

[15] I have not checked Heidelberger's original, which, as Dummett remarks, would obviously be inconsistent since he accepts Church's translation argument.

"Copernicus believed that the planetary orbits are circular" as long as he understands "Copernicus believed that" and the phrase "the sense of 'the planetary orbits are circular'" without having any idea what "the planetary orbits are circular" means. But this consequence is plainly absurd.[16,17]

This suggestion about indirect senses would make them a metalinguistic notion. On the other hand, Casimir Lewy in his "Critical Notice" (1949)—actually, *very* critical notice—of Carnap's book denies that Frege gives no explanation in "more customary terms" of what an indirect sense might be. He points out that Frege says explicitly that the sense of a sentence in an indirect context is the sense of the words "the thought that...", where the dots are supposed to be filled in with the sentence in question (see Frege, 1892, p. 160). Well, *of course* this is Frege's view; but it says nothing as to what the indirect senses of the significant parts of the sentence are, nor how they combine to give the sense of the whole. Lewy's remarks do avoid the unfortunate ascent to a metalinguistic notion in indirect contexts, as in the theory discussed in the previous paragraph; but they really leave the matter as mysterious as Carnap says it is.

The discussion of the metalinguistic interpretation of indirect senses suggests a further requirement on indirect senses. An indirect sense must be *revelatory*. First let me say what I mean by a sense being revelatory: a sense is revelatory of its referent if one can figure out from the sense alone what the referent is. For example, one can understand the description "the prime minister of England on 1 January 1970" perfectly well without knowing the relevant historical fact: not knowing who was the prime minister of England at that time, one fails to know the referent even though one knows the sense.[18] Similarly, for the famous

---

[16] Fussy details: on this account one really needs simply the concept (Fregean *Sinn*) expressed by the English phrase "the sense of 'the planetary orbits are circular'" (including, therefore, quotation), and that this is what "the planetary orbits are circular" means in English indirect discourse. One need not have learned this by learning even the *English* phrase "the sense of". What one does need to know about English is how to recognize indirect quotation contexts ("that clauses") and that in them words have indirect senses.
Another delicate point: should one really have written "the sense in *English* of 'the planetary orbits are circular'", as most writers on the subject probably assume? Or should one understand quote conventions in such a way that the expression referred to carries its language with it, even if a phonetically identical expression might appear in another language? See Geach (1957, pp. 86–87) (on "ja"), and pp. 97–98 ("jam dies"). Kaplan (1990), in his rejection of the conventional type/token analysis of expressions (the "orthographic conception"), might well agree with Geach.

[17] In his second discussion of the matter, Dummett says that he hopes he was not misled by the Church translation argument (or something similar), which he rejects. (See Dummett, 1981, pp. 89ff.) I myself am a believer in the argument, but I also think, as Church does (see Church, 1950, p. 98 (the objection to (6) and the translation argument following), and 1956, p. 62, footnote 136), that the translation argument only brings out the arbitrariness of the connection of a given phonetic or written sequence and what it stands for or means. Normally this can be brought out in another way.

[18] In other contexts (not this one), I have heard some people object to an example on the grounds that "it depends on the analytic–synthetic distinction" (really the *a priori–a posteriori distinction*), which Quine supposedly refuted. If someone really worries about this, replace it with the notion of what could have been known to someone, say in the year 1000, even in principle. The date could

Quinean example of "the number of planets".[19] In each case, one can understand the sense without knowing the referent. Further information is required for the latter. So the senses of these phrases are *not* revelatory. On the other hand, both "nine" and perhaps even "the square of three" do have revelatory senses. Given that one can understand them, one can tell what the referent is. The same holds for "George W. Bush" and almost for "the father of George W. Bush's (biological) children" (though in the latter case, strictly speaking, one has to know that George W. Bush is male and has children).

Now, these "knowing what" phrases or "knowing who" phrases have had a curious history in recent philosophy. Some have declared them to be entirely unscientific and context-dependent or even interest-relative.[20] And under the influence of Quine and others this view has been widespread.[21] Sometimes the extreme position is taken that any definite description determining the object tells us what it is given some appropriate interest, but I do not see that the examples of interest-relativity that have been given would support such an extreme position.[22] Quine's longstanding remarks against "frankly inequalitarian" attitudes towards different ways of designating the same object have been a big influence here.[23]

---

vary with the example, and other things could vary. Anyone who says that Quine or anyone else showed that such distinctions make no sense is simply incredible.

Of course Quinean objections to the analytic–synthetic distinction and to the notion of meaning are out of place in a discussion of Fregean *Sinne* anyway. Surely these objections would go against Frege's entire apparatus, except on a very unusual interpretation of Frege that I can only speculate about.

[19] That the number of planets is nine has long been a standard philosophical example, popularized by Quine. It is presupposed here, and its actual truth is irrelevant. While to claim that 'astronomers have changed their minds as to what the number of planets is' makes sense, to claim that 'mathematicians have changed their mind as to what the number nine is' seems barely intelligible, let alone possibley true. This seems to me to be one further reason for adopting a "frankly inequalitarian attitude" towards two ways of supposedly designating the number nine. See my discussion of Malcolm's astronomical example in "On Two Paradoxes of Knowledge" (Chapter 2, this volume), especially footnote 15 (p. 41). Here, I guess, we do need to pay attention to what a committee of learned astronomers have said in correction of previous beliefs. (Footnote added in 2010.)

[20] In my own opinion the latter two notions should carefully be distinguished, but I will not go into the matter here.

[21] See Quine (1979, p. 273); see also Sosa (1970) (which strictly speaking is about *de re* propositional attitudes, not "knowing who", and as far as I know remains the classic exposition of its point of view), and Boër and Lycan (1986) (with which I am only partly familiar). In his book *Knowledge and Belief* (1962), Hintikka emphasizes "knowing who" as the condition for a transition from *de dicto* to *de re* knowledge. Not every author accepts the connection, but some do. Many regard "knowing who" and related notions as hopelessly interest-relative, even taking the extreme view mentioned in my text. I regard the interest-relativity of these notions as exaggerated, though not entirely nonexistent.

[22] Most or many of these examples simply do not work, to repeat my opinion, though perhaps there are special cases where they do. One thing that helps create an exaggerated impression of context or interest relativity is an overemphasis on the case of persons. Also, even in the case of people, philosophers pay insufficient attention to the variety of "knowing wh-" notions available in ordinary language.

[23] See his famous example of "the number of planets" and "nine", alluded to before.

I have a lot more to say about this issue and I have done so in lectures on the natural numbers (Kripke, unpublished).[24] It is *not* true, as I have heard some say, that whatever may be the case for ordinary language and day-to-day thought, no serious science is based on such notions. I assume that recursion theory or computability theory is a serious science. A computable function is a function f such that for each given n, if you put in a particular number, the value $f(n)$ can be computed. And what does that mean? That given the definition of the function and an argument n, you can know, by computation, what the value $f(n)$ is. This would hardly make sense if all ways, even all mathematical ways, of designating a number, were on a par. For then every function[25] would be computable, since the value of f for a given n could simply be "computed" as $f(n)$! To say otherwise would be to adopt an "inequalitarian" attitude towards different ways of designating a number, supposedly a sin. Similarly, complexity theory is another such inequalitarian science.[26]

In the light of this discussion, one might say that a sense is *immediately revelatory* if no calculation is required to figure out its referent. If f is a non-computable mathematical function, then the sense of "$f(n)$" might be revelatory in the weak sense that no empirical information is required to find the referent, though perhaps a mathematical argument is required to do so. More important, even a computable function may not yield an immediately revelatory sense. For example, even "the square of three" does not have an immediately revelatory sense, since a computation, in this case a very easy one, is required to obtain its value. In the general case, the computation could be much more difficult. "Nine", however, is immediately revelatory.[27] We can now strengthen the requirement on indirect senses to say that they must be immediately revelatory: anyone who understands an indirect sense must immediately know its referent (the direct sense).

Frege thought that the *Bedeutung* of a sentence is its truth-value, T or F. One might understand the sense of a sentence but not know what its truth-value is. Will George W. Bush run in 2004 and win? Or, who will be the president at the end of the century (or whatever)? We do not know.[28] Now, suppose you take the sentence "George W. Bush will run and be elected in 2004". We do not know the outcome of the 2004 election, and so we do not know the truth-value

---

[24] The argument given here is excerpted from these lectures, which go into the matter in greater detail. Other versions of the material have been given as lectures elsewhere, sometimes with the last part of the title changed ("The identification of numbers", or something like that).

[25] Or if one restricts the view to mathematically defined functions, every mathematically defined function. (Though one should watch out about such a restriction, in view of the Richard paradox.)

[26] Strictly speaking, the formal theorems of these theories would still exist, even given the "equalitarian" view, but their motivation (as, say, in Turing's analysis) would not.

[27] In the case of the natural numbers, there are subtleties involved that are discussed in my aforementioned lectures on the natural numbers, where numerical terms with immediately revelatory senses are called "buck stoppers".

[28] Remember, for some of the examples, that these lectures were given in 2001.

(*Bedeutung*) of the sentence, though we understand it and therefore grasp its *Sinn*. But if all ways of designating an object were equally good, we *would* know the truth-value of the sentence about George W. Bush, namely the truth-value that Bush will run and be elected in 2004. Similarly for any other sentence. But in fact, only an omniscient being could know the Fregean referent of every sentence. This could be true of God but of no one else. To favor equalitarianism of ways of designating truth-values is to obliterate this important distinction between God and His creatures.[29]

Let me turn to another aspect of Frege's theory. In his well-known paper "Quantifying In", David Kaplan says that one should not let the complications of Frege's theory obscure the basic idea. According to Kaplan, Frege's theories of indirect and direct quotation are simply instances of the familiar fact that some words have a usual denotation (reference), but in some secondary contexts have a less usual one. He gives the following example: "F.D.R." is the name of a president of the United States (and that is its usual reference). Apparently it was also the name of some television show, an unusual reference (the truth is I have never heard of this show, and there is some joke here, but I am not sure exactly what it is) (Kaplan, 1968, p. 183).[30] And of course though "London" primarily refers to a great city in England, it is also the name of a city in Ontario (Canada), and for all I know of other cities. No doubt many other examples could be given.

According to Kaplan, Frege's theory of direct and indirect quotation (and, he suggests, of other contexts that are unspecified) is that the ambiguity in these contexts is similar. In direct and indirect quotation contexts phrases do not have their usual denotation. So far so good, and no doubt this *is* Frege's theory.[31]

However, Frege surely believed that a formal logical language should avoid ambiguities, even if they exist in natural language. Frege actually confirms this in a letter to Russell, where he says:

---

[29] I owe this point to Nathan Salmon, who has in print otherwise advocated the interest-relative view of "knowing which", but he gave me this example.

[30] Kaplan's example of a confusing sentence is:

Although F.D.R. ran for office many times, F.D.R. ran on television only once.

His example actually (without explicit acknowledgment) trades not only on the ambiguity (really homonymy) of "F.D.R.", but also of "ran". (Prominent philosophers have denied that the "F.D.R." case is any sort of homonymy, because names are not in the language. I will not go into the issue here; but "F.D.R.", especially the second usage, is surely grist for their mill. I myself disagree with these philosophers, and I have been criticized by them; but no one will dispute the "ran" case.) See footnote 79, below.

[31] But it is significant that these are not ordinary ambiguities or unusual references, unlike the F.D.R. case Kaplan cites, or the "London" example. For in Frege's theory of indirect quotation and the like, the unusual references are determined entirely by the context. In the other examples the unusual reference can often be *guessed* from the context, but it is not determined by any semantic rule. Kaplan's discussion does not make this distinction clear.

To avoid ambiguity, we ought really to have special signs in indirect speech, though their connection with the corresponding signs in direct speech should be easy to recognize. (Frege, 1980, p. 153)[32]

But there is something a bit evasive about the assertion that the connection should be "easy to recognize". Are they independent symbolic expressions or are they not?

It is significant that Frege says that, because in Church's famous paper, "A Formulation of the Logic of Sense and Denotation" (1951), he does in fact use distinct symbols for each expression and its counterpart in indirect speech. Since indirect contexts can be iterated, there is an infinity of separate and independent symbols, giving rise to Davidson's unlearnability objection. Dummett criticizes Church for doing so, and states that he has abandoned Frege's doctrine of indirect references and senses, that is, the contextually determined ambiguity doctrine. ("Most striking, perhaps, is the fact that the doctrine of indirect reference is abandoned".)[33] In fact, in this respect it is Church, and not Dummett, who is faithful to Frege's explicit *ipse dixit*. Not only that, but Frege's declaration, as we have seen, is an obvious consequence of his general attitude that a proper formal language should avoid such ambiguities.[34]

In spite of my criticism of Dummett on the question of fidelity to Frege, Dummett's approach (taking the contextual ambiguities to be an essential part of the theory) seems to me to be highly suggestive and to have a good deal to recommend it, but that is for later in this discussion.[35]

---

[32] My thanks to Eva Picardi for helping me to relocate the passage in the correspondence with Russell.

Perhaps Frege's remark in "Über Sinn und Bedeutung" itself could also be cited in this connection: "To every expression belonging to a complete totality of signs, there should certainly correspond a definite sense; but natural languages often do not satisfy this condition, and one must be content if the same word has the same sense in the same context" (Frege, 1892, p. 153). As I remarked in the previous footnote, the ambiguity created by indirect discourse is completely determined by context. But Frege seems clearly to be saying that such an ambiguity is a defect of natural language, and therefore that it should be avoided in a scientific *Begriffsschrift*.

[33] See Dummett (1973, pp. 292-293, top). The quoted sentence is on p. 292. In contrast, Kaplan recognizes that Church's system is the natural result of an attempt to avoid ambiguities. See Kaplan (1968, p. 184). Kaplan does not quote Frege's explicit assertion (which may not have been available to him at the time).

[34] Dummett makes several doubtful criticisms of Church's paper, but he is strangely unaware of the main problem with it, viz. that all three systems proposed collapse for purely formal reasons, even formal inconsistency in at least one case.

Church later published revised versions of his original formal systems, which in general lead to even more complicated hierarchies. At least one of his revisions was inconsistent, and yet another version was proposed by C. Anthony Anderson. We do not need to go into these complications here, and we will stick to the original formulation.

[35] When Dummett says that the doctrine of indirect reference has been abandoned, he is motivated by the fact that a person who began with Church's system alone would no longer think of indirect or "oblique" contexts as special problematic cases of "intensional" contexts, generating a special problem for substitutivity that Frege needs to solve. Such a person would think of belief contexts, etc., as just as obviously extensional as any others. For Dummett, the double (and iterated) uses of terms in indirect contexts are an essential part of the theory. As we have seen,

Now Church has a category o_0 of truth-values T and F, which are the referents of the sentences. Then there is a category o_1 of senses of sentences, that is, Fregean thoughts, *Gedanken*. And then there is a category o_2 of what Church calls "propositional concepts", that is, senses of "that clauses" or of names of Fregean thoughts, and so on. Each category consists of senses determining elements of the previous category as referents. There is a similar sequence starting out with the individuals (or objects). One way Church does deviate from Frege is that the truth-values are not assumed to be among the individuals, but are assigned a separate logical type of their own.[36]

Then various particular notions also come in a hierarchy. For example, and here I simplify Church's own notation, consider the (material) conditional. $\supset_0$ is the function on the truth-values {T, F}, given by the familiar truth-table. $\supset_1$ is supposed to be a sense determining $\supset_0$ as a referent, and so on. However, not only does this automatically lead to Davidson's unlearnability objection, there is something else. $\supset_1$ is supposed to be a sense determining $\supset_0$ as a referent, but which one? Plainly many such senses determine the same referent ("no backward road"). Church gives no explanation whatsoever. Thus, it is not merely a problem of an infinite sequence: as early as the second level we are not told what a symbol is supposed to mean.

If Church had a doctrine of "privileged" senses, then perhaps the system might be intelligible. But this was not Church's view. In very late writings his attitudes are close to Quine's on this point. In fact, on this type of issue he comes in this very paper to the extreme conclusion that the problem of different ways of designating the same thing makes a problem even for modal propositional logic, a conclusion that Quine never drew.[37]

Church's paper is faithful to Frege in this disputed respect. However, Dummett's contrary point of view is close in spirit to my final conclusions.

As I have mentioned (footnote 10 above), Dummett himself proposes a modification of Frege's notion of sense (and of indirect sense), giving rise to a two-level theory similar to that of Carnap, but with another justification. I myself am not inclined to accept Dummett's modification. The present article will show why I think such a modification unnecessary. Without going into details, I also think that Dummett's modified definition of 'sense' probably suffers from a problem of circular definition.

[36] Dummett (1973, pp. 182–184) favors just such a revision of Frege, but in his very critical discussion of Church's system, he fails to note that Church makes exactly the same revision. Nor does he note in the pages just cited that he is echoing Church (no doubt with more philosophical discussion of the desirability of the revision, which Church makes without argument and without even noting that it is a revision).

[37] Discussing the characteristic axiom of S4–that necessity implies double necessity–Church says:

According to the present theory, the answer to this question depends on what concept of the proposition is employed. For example, *that it is necessary that everything has some property or other* is no doubt itself necessary; but that *the proposition mentioned on lines 27–28 of page 272 of Lewis and Langford's Symbolic Logic is necessary* is true but not necessary. (Church, 1951, footnote 23; original emphasis)

Some of the rest of us would take the first way of determining the proposition in question to be privileged over the second. In my own terminology above, the first way of determining the

Leaving Church, we return to Kaplan. He believes that Frege's treatment of indirect quotation is a special case of a more general principle governing all "oblique" contexts, that is, contexts in which words cannot have their ordinary referents.[38] He also thinks that Frege in "Über Sinn und Bedeutung" applies the theory to direct quotation, taking him to advocate the theory that in direct quotation the whole of an expression, and each of its component parts, refers to itself. In other words, just as the prefixes "believes that", "says that", and the like create contexts in which terms refer to their senses, so the "says" of direct quotation (followed by quotation marks in the written language) creates a context in which words are used autonomously, i.e., referring to themselves.

Now what Frege actually says is:

If words are used in the ordinary way, what one intends to speak of is their *Bedeutung*. It can also happen, however, that one wishes to talk about the words themselves or their sense. This happens, for instance, when the words of another are quoted. One's own words then first designate words of the other speaker, and only the latter have their usual *Bedeutung*. We then have signs of signs. In writing, the words are in this case enclosed in quotation marks. Accordingly, a word standing between quotation marks must not be taken as having its ordinary *Bedeutung*. (Frege, 1892, pp. 153–154)

In the very next paragraph he goes on to give his well-known theory of indirect quotation and indirect reference (to the ordinary sense), the dominant theme of this paper, already alluded to in the paragraph just quoted.

---

proposition is immediately revelatory, whereas the second is not revelatory at all. So, if Church regards this example as typical, he ought to be a believer in S4. But clearly Church accepts no such distinctions. There is more that I would have to say here, even from the point of view of Church's system, but the matter would call for an extensive digression. For a later writing, see Church (1973) p. 27, and the accompanying footnote 2. See also Church (1988). But see also footnote 90 below.

[38] Kaplan says:

Frege's treatment of oblique contexts is often described as one according to which expressions in such contexts denote their ordinary sense or meaning or intension (I here use these terms interchangeably). But this is a bad way of putting the matter for three reasons. (1) It is, I believe, historically inaccurate. It ignores Frege's remarks about quotation marks (see below) and other special contexts. (2) It conflates two separate principles: (a) expressions in oblique contexts don't have their ordinary denotation (which is true), and (b) expressions in oblique contexts denote their ordinary sense (which is not, in general, true). And (3) in focusing attention too rapidly on the special and separate problems of intensional logic, we lose sight of the beauty and power of Frege's general method of treating oblique contexts... My own view is that Frege's explanation, by way of ambiguity, of what appears to be the logically deviant behavior of terms in intermediate contexts is so theoretically satisfying that if we have not yet discovered or satisfactorily grasped the peculiar intermediate objects in question, then we should simply continue looking.

...Look for something denoted by a compound, say, a sentence, in the oblique context. (In ordinary contexts sentences are taken to denote their own truth values and to be intersubstitutable on that basis.) And then using the fundamental principle: the denotation of the compound is a function of the denotation of the parts, look for something denoted by the parts. It was the use of this principle which, I believe, led to Carnap's discovery of individual concepts, and also led Frege to the view that quotation marks produce an oblique context within which each component expression denotes itself (it is clear in quotation contexts what the whole compound denotes). (1968, p. 185)

So far one might think that everything supports Kaplan's interpretation, but there is an oddity. If types, not tokens, are in question, then the theory amounts to what Kaplan says; but if so, why not state things as Kaplan does, that the words designate themselves, rather than the words of the other speaker?

When I gave the present talk I left the matter there, but assumed that Kaplan was correct, in spite of the oddity. However, a few pages later Frege says:

In direct quotation, a sentence designates *another* sentence, and in indirect speech a thought. (Frege, 1892, p. 159; emphasis added)

So there are two possibilities. One is that here "sentence" means a token, since otherwise one should not speak of "another" sentence. To me, to use "sentence" in English to mean a token, so that two people that say exactly the same thing are uttering different sentences, is very odd. The same thing would seem to apply to the German "*Satz*"; I would like to know if "*Satz*" ever means a token elsewhere in Frege's writings. Moreover, even stipulating that tokens are meant, the proposed Fregean theory in terms of tokens seems to me to have considerable substantive difficulties.[39] If such a theory cannot be defended, one seems forced to conclude that Frege was confused in the passages in question.

As is well known, Frege does use quotation in his own writings to designate signs, without their necessarily being used by another particular speaker or writer.[40] I have been hard pressed for an explicit statement of his convention. Such a statement might give his general theory of direct quotation. Perhaps the following helps:

As such proper names of the sentences of the object-language I use these very sentences, but enclosed in quotation marks. (Frege, 1979, p. 261; original emphasis)

Read very carefully, this does indeed seem to say that quotation simply creates a context in which the sentences are used autonomously. (One can presume them to be composed out of their component parts, also used autonomously, in agreement with Kaplan's attribution.) But I must say that this is a great deal to be squeezed out of a single sentence.

---

[39] See, however, Picardi (1992), pp. 284–290. She defends a token interpretation and even thinks that it is required for the case in question, if I understand her communication to me correctly. The book, written in Italian and published in Italy, was for these reasons unknown to me then and now. Obviously she deserves considerable credit for noticing that the autonymous interpretation of Fregean quotation marks, as stated by Kaplan, does not seem to accord with the text. Notice that the putative Fregean theory in terms of tokens should not be confused with Davidson (1979).

Picardi has also called my attention to the discussion in Mendelsohn (2005), ch. 10, section 1. He thinks that Frege was simply mistaken in regarding quotation of another speaker as a case of reference at all; as opposed to the usual use of quotation marks discussed in philosophy, and indeed introduced by Frege himself.

However, Künne (2010) regards the use of "another sentence" as due to Black and translates the original as "again a sentence" (see p. 537 and his note 15). But to me there is still a residual puzzle: why not "the same sentence"?

[40] This is Mendelsohn's "philosopher's quotation", much discussed in the literature, especially since Davidson (1965) emphasized the theoretical problems involved in earlier accounts.

One should add (or repeat) that the analogy between direct and indirect quotation stated by Frege in "Über Sinn und Bedeutung", as quoted above, certainly would go best with Kaplan's interpretation, even though the rest of the text does not seem to mean that. I will go on, as I originally did, assuming that Frege does hold the theory of direct quotation that Kaplan attributes to him.[41]

Strangely enough no one, to my knowledge, has raised the hierarchy problem regarding the theory of direct quotation. After all, direct quotation can be iterated any number of times. Would Frege's theory lead to a hierarchy problem, analogous to the problem people see for indirect quotation?

Now, analogously to Frege's "indirect reference", we could naturally use the term "direct reference" for the reference of a term to itself in direct quotation. But in recent philosophy "direct reference" has come to mean something else, so instead we shall introduce the cumbersome phrase "the direct quotation reference". Let me abbreviate this as the "quote-reference". Then there will be a quote-sense, and then won't there also be a whole hierarchy of a quote-quote reference, a quote-quote sense, and so on? Yet no one has thought that there was such a mystery here, or at least no one has argued for there being such a mystery, given Frege's theory of direct quotation. Nor have the issues that I raised about indirect quotation (the second German course and so on) been raised about direct quotation. So let us take another look at this.

Let me first mention some analogues to what I want to say. Suppose we make a very general statement:

(1) When someone uses the word "here" the speaker (or writer) refers to the place of utterance (or writing).

David Kaplan has made clauses like (1) prominent in his theory of demonstratives (statement (1) is not entirely accurate, and I think Kaplan (1989) realizes that fact, but to simplify matters let us retain it).[42] Is there anything else about the sense of "here" that you need to know? Doesn't (1) determine the reference for all cases? And similarly for other indexicals. For example, "now" refers to the time of utterance, and "I" (a case that we will return to later) refers to the speaker or source of the utterance. These are general directions for the referents in the language, no matter when and by whom they are uttered. One does not, it would

---

[41] Corey Washington (1992) advocates the theory in question and attributes it to Frege and to Searle (1989, p. 76) (presumably independently; I have not read Searle on this question). Peter Geach, a great admirer of Frege, advocates the same theory but attributes it to no one else. See Geach (1963; also in 1972, section 5.8) (in the preface to Geach (1972) he expresses some hesitation as to whether this theory of quotation is true). Mendelsohn (2005, p. 173) quotes Reichenbach (1947) as advocating a similar theory. Already Church (1956, p. 61) interprets Frege in the same way as Kaplan does later.

[42] Theories such as those of Davidson and Montague would have similar clauses.

seem, need anything more. However, in any particular case, to determine the reference one needs a specification of the speaker, the time, or both (or alternatively, of the particular utterance token, which might determine both).[43]

In other cases, however, general directions like (1) can be given that will determine the reference for any sentence, or perhaps discourse, without the supplementation of anything external to the sentence or discourse in question. I am thinking of anaphora, pronominalization, and the like. In such cases as "the latter", "the former", "the aforementioned person", and various pronominal cases such as "him", where the reference is determined by the sentence itself, as opposed to demonstrative pronouns, the general rule determines the reference for each sentence or discourse, without the supplementation of anything else such as speaker, time, or whatever. The general rule given may be syntactically complicated, but it should determine the reference in any particular case. Hence, as applied to any particular case, it must be, on a Fregean theory, a Fregean sense, since anything that determines a reference is a sense.

Let us apply these ideas to Frege's apparent theory of direct quotation, and to his theory of indirect quotation.

There are two relevant principles. For direct quotation we have:

(α) When words appear in direct quotes, they refer autonomously, that is, to themselves.

As Kaplan emphasizes, the corresponding principle for indirect quotation is completely analogous:

(β) When words appear in indirect contexts, that is, "says that", "believes that", and so on, they refer to their senses in the clause following the "that".

Both (α) and (β) are intended to be understood iteratively, so that when there are iterative direct quotations, or "that clauses", the reference is determined recursively from the clause within the quote or following "that".[44]

Certainly in the case of (α), one is unlikely to feel any mystery about the iteration, since the rule that expressions refer autonomously is very clear. One would feel no more mystery than in the case of anaphoric usages such as "the latter", and the syntactic rule involved is actually more straightforward. What about the case of (β)? Well, consider first the simple uniterated case. Words in an indirect context refer to their ordinary senses. But what is the sense in the indirect context? Here we should surely say that the rule (β) itself, applied to each indirect case, gives the indirect sense. For we have conceded that it determines the

---

[43] This case, and some qualifications of the apparent drift of this paragraph, will be discussed again below.

[44] Actually, (α) and (β) should be understood together, since a direct quotation may appear inside an indirect quotation, and vice versa, producing a more complex pattern of iterations.

reference in each particular case, and whatever determines a reference is a Fregean sense. This consideration can then be applied iteratively, and we appear to have a theory of the entire hierarchy.

Something very strange has gone on here, because these are entirely general directions that ought to determine the reference in every case. How could there be any mystery here? In the case of (β), one aspect of the mystery has come from such feelings as that the ambiguity involved in indirect senses is an ordinary ambiguity, as in Kaplan's exposition, without emphasizing the contextual determination of the ambiguity. This leads to the feeling that in a real *Begriffsschrift* the ambiguity ought to be removed, as Frege says (with some fudging) in the letter to Russell quoted before, and hence to Church's system. In Church's system, as I have said, there is in effect a similar fudge, since the different symbols in the infinite sequence do systematically resemble each other in the subscripting system, but in fact are completely independent, as Davidson rightly emphasizes. I doubt that this aspect of the mystery would have arisen if case (α), as brought out by Kaplan, had been the primary case considered.

However, even more crucial for the feeling of mystery in case (β) has been the feeling that we have little real idea what the indirect senses, doubly indirect senses, and so on, are. When this is combined with the aspect mentioned in the previous paragraph, one feels that one not only has an unlearnable infinite hierarchy, but that one has scarcely any idea what this hierarchy might be. My reply here is that the rule (β), every time it (recursively) specifies a reference, also implicitly gives a sense, since Frege's theory is that to determine a reference is to give a sense. Hence, (β) itself gives the indirect sense, and when recursively applied gives the doubly indirect sense, and so on. (What I say here will be expanded, and in a sense qualified, later.) Here I am in agreement with Dummett (as I anticipated above) that the contextual ambiguity of phrases in indirect contexts (both for reference and for sense) is an essential, not an accidental, part of the theory,[45] in spite of Frege's own *ipse dixit*.

Important to this presentation of Frege is that he has given general directions for the reference of terms in all contexts and that this cannot possibly be incomplete. There are indeed infinite hierarchies generated by both (α) and (β), but these are given by a recursive rule.

Two compositional principles are generally attributed to Frege, rightly I should think, though he himself used them rather than stating them. The first is that the referent of a whole is a function of (or is determined by) the referents of its parts. The second principle analogously replaces "reference" by "sense". What these principles mean is that if in any piece of language one

---

[45] I am not in agreement with his attempt to revise the sense-reference theory, so as to appear to avoid any hierarchy problem, in parallel with the earlier attempt by Carnap. See footnote 35.

replaces some significant part by one with the same referent (sense), the referent (sense) of the whole is unchanged.[46]

A converse principle about senses seems less widely stated: the relation of senses of a whole to the senses of its significant parts is not only that of a function, but that of a *one-to-one* function. This is because to understand the whole one must understand its constituent parts, and hence the sense of the whole breaks down into the senses of its constituent parts. As Dummett puts the matter:

The sense of a complex is compounded out of the senses of its constituents. (Dummett, 1973, p. 152; original emphasis)[47]

But this means that we not only have a functional relationship from the parts to the whole, but a converse functional relationship, in effect a one-to-one relation.[48] (Clearly no such principle holds for reference.) For Frege's own enunciation of this principle, see a passage from his letter to Russell of 13 November 1904:

...Mont Blanc with its snowfields is not itself a component part of the thought that Mont Blanc is more than 4000 metres high... The sense of the word "moon" is a component part of the thought that the moon is smaller than the earth. The moon itself... is not part of the sense of the word "moon"; for then it would also be a component part of that thought. (Frege, 1980, p. 163)

---

[46] For senses (if they are identified with meanings of the constituent parts of a whole sentence and hence constituent parts of the thought they express) the principle should be obvious. But is the principle so obvious for reference (*Bedeutung*)? Why shouldn't the reference of the whole be allowed to depend on other features of the parts? Indeed, why not just say that exceptions to this principle obviously exist, e.g., in indirect contexts and possibly in quotation? (In fact just this appears to be Quine's position. See Quine (1960), p. 151, where he says that Frege "nominally rectified" exceptions to the principle by inventing his doctrine of oblique reference, whereas Quine himself says that such contexts are not purely referential.) Then the entire complicated doctrine of oblique and, in particular, indirect contexts that has been my main topic would not exist. (See also Davidson's remarks quoted in footnote 12.)

Looking over the transcript of my lecture, I see that I raised this question in passing, but did not give an answer that I had previously proposed in classes on Frege. It could be argued that for Frege the principle is analytic. The context shows what we are talking about, and that is what the referent is. See for example Frege (1892), p. 153:

If words are used in the ordinary way, what one intends to speak of is their *Bedeutung*. It can also happen, however, that one wishes to talk about the words themselves or their sense. (Full quotation given above.)

I think that what I am saying here is in agreement with Kaplan's exposition in his (1968).

[47] That Dummett has in effect stated the relevant principle, though not perhaps in terms of one-to-oneness, is new to the present version of this lecture.

[48] As is well known, there are late passages where Frege appears to go back on this. See his letter to Husserl of 9 December 1906 (Beaney, 1997, pp. 305–306), which comes close to identifying the thoughts expressed by logically equivalent sentences, though it has a qualification that only adds perplexity (at least to the present writer).

Since according to Frege arithmetic reduces by appropriate definitions to logic, a sentence containing "738" will retain the same sense with "643 + 95" in its place. This is a radical alteration of Frege's earlier remarks on sense and reference. See also Frege (1918–1919), p. 331, on the active–passive transformation, or the corresponding interchange of "give" and "receive", which are said not to affect the thought; but perhaps allowing these transformations is compatible with the principle.

Russell himself, in "On Denoting", says:

In the proposition "Mont Blanc is over 1,000 meters high", it is, according to him [Frege], the *meaning* of "Mont Blanc", not the actual mountain, that is the constituent of the *meaning* of the proposition. (Russell, 1905, p. 483, footnote 2; original emphasis)[49]

The general principle is enunciated in Frege's late *Introduction to Logic*, in the section on sense and reference:

As the thought is the sense of the whole sentence, so a part of the thought is the sense of part of the sentence. (Frege, 1979, p. 192)

The same passage also mentions the "Mont Blanc" example again.

One does not grasp the sense of the whole, without grasping the sense of the parts. And to understand something is to grasp its sense.

As I said, Frege has given general directions for a theory of the references of words in quotation-context in (α) and for indirect contexts in (β), and no one has ever suggested that there is a mystery about the theory in (α).[50]

Why is (α) not mysterious? What (α) says is clear enough. But for it to be of any use speakers or writers must be able to apply it in particular cases. For example:

Abraham Lincoln said "Four score and seven years ago..."

(α) says that the quoted words refer autonymously to themselves. How do we know what these words are? Well, in a particular case of writing or utterance we see or hear the entire sentence, and *a fortiori* hear or see any parts, including the autonymously referential part. Here what we hear or see are tokens, and thereby are aware of the corresponding types. So there should be no mystery as to how to apply the theory in a particular case. Even if we are only contemplating the sentence type in our mind, to fully comprehend it is to comprehend the type as a part. It is like Russellian acquaintance.

Similarly for case (β). Once we see that any time a referent is given it must be given by a sense, we have seen that (β), just like (α), really does give general (recursive) directions for the entire hierarchy of senses and indirect senses. However, there is the question of how an individual speaker will apply (β). My suggestion, once again, is that Frege, like Russell, has a doctrine of direct acquaintance. Every time we determine a referent, we are introspectively acquainted with how the referent is determined, and that is the corresponding sense. And our introspective acquaintance with this sense gives us a way of determining it, and of referring to it, and this is the indirect sense. Thus the

---

[49] Note Russell's terminology: he uses "meaning" for Frege's "*Sinn*". He himself thought (at the time of the relevant correspondence with Frege) that the mountain itself was a constituent or component part of the proposition, and takes this position in the correspondence.

[50] Although I must admit that it is unfair to stress this fact too much; perhaps no one thought that there was a mystery about (α) because almost all the discussion of Frege and the mysterious hierarchy has concentrated on (β), and (α) has received much less attention.

Fregean hierarchy of indirect senses, doubly indirect senses, and the like is given this way. Each level of the hierarchy is the acquaintance-sense of the previous level. So Frege, although the doctrine may be less explicit, depends on a theory of acquaintance very much like that of Russell.[51]

I already talked about a revelatory sense, and more strongly, about an immediately revelatory sense. One could now use the term *acquaintance-revelatory*. An indirect sense, since it determines its referent by acquaintance, is such that one needs no information, or even calculation, to realize what the referent is. On this interpretation, not only does Frege, at least implicitly, have a doctrine of acquaintance; but also, the list of objects of acquaintance that he would accept is not so vastly different from Russell's final position. In "On Denoting", as is well known, he says, in contrast to Frege, "there is no *meaning* [that is, there is no *Sinn*], and only sometimes a *denotation*" (Russell, 1905, p. 483, footnote 3; original emphasis) as he puts it. He also ends the paper with his well-known conclusion that "in every proposition that we can apprehend...all the constituents are really entities with which we have immediate acquaintance" (ibid., p. 492). Under the pressures of the requirements of his semantical theory, the list of such entities becomes progressively narrower. One's own sense-data, perhaps one's own self, and abstract entities such as universals, are the objects of acquaintance and the constituents of propositions.[52] One could never be acquainted with Mont Blanc, with all its snowfields, nor could it be a constituent of a proposition. There is an unconditional surrender to Frege on this point.

That Russell's ultimate list of propositional constituents would be acceptable to Frege, or close to it, is in large part already clear. Some of the rest might become clearer if we consider Frege's relatively late paper "Der Gedanke" (1918–1919).[53] This paper contains Frege's first extensive explicit discussion, as far as I know, of indexicals, demonstratives, the first person, one's own private inner states, and so on.[54]

Three distinguished and well-known writers have based important claims about the interpretation of Frege on a crucial passage in this paper. Tyler

---

[51] The order of presentation here is not the order in which I thought about these problems. Some years before this lecture I had concluded that Frege must have an implicit doctrine of direct acquaintance with senses, in order to make sense of the Fregean hierarchy of indirect senses and so on. I had stated this view in various seminars. That the matter should be put in terms of how individual speakers apply general directions, as in the case (β), and the analogy with the case (α) was much more recent. Nor did I think of the analogy between (α) and (β) and general linguistic rules for anaphora. Also the relation to cases with indexicals (some of which will be discussed in Fregean terms later in the lecture). It was probably presented this way in the present lecture for the first time.

[52] In saying this we ignore his later rejection of propositions altogether.

[53] The title is translated by Beaney as "Thought", by Geach and Stoothoff as "Thoughts", and by A. M. and M. Quinton as "The Thought". (Otherwise Beaney follows the Geach–Stoothoff translation in the text of the paper.) I will follow the Beaney pagination as usual.

[54] On my view, anyway. Tyler Burge, as will be discussed below, interprets "Über Sinn und Bedeutung" as already involved in a theory of indexicals. (However, see footnote 60 below for a possible anticipation of one aspect of "*Der Gedanke*" already in the *Grundlagen* in 1884.)

Burge, in his marvelously titled paper, "Sinning Against Frege" (Burge, 1979a),[55] argues that "the basic misunderstanding is the identification of Frege's notion of *Sinn* (sense) with the notion of linguistic meaning" (Burge, 2004, p. 213) (surely the "misunderstanding", if there is one, is indeed a common one). Burge's argument is simple. What about tensed senses, or sentences containing indexicals? Consider, for example, "Today it is raining in Stockholm".[56] The meaning of this sentence does not vary from day to day. Obviously its truth-value does vary, and the variation in truth-value is due to a variation in the reference of "today". But sense determines reference, and the reference of the whole sentence is its truth-value. Hence, "today" must have different senses on different days (otherwise sense would not determine reference). Similarly, the whole sentence must have different senses on different days, since it has different truth-values (references, and sense here determines truth-value).

John Perry, in his influential article "Frege on Demonstratives" (1977), first states (correctly) that, where *S* and *S′* are two sentences, "*If S is true and S′ is not, S and S′ express different thoughts*" (ibid., p. 476).[57] Perry then argues that there is a problem for Frege here: "Russia and Canada quarreled today" can be true on 1 August but false on 2 August (ibid., pp. 478–479):

So, if "today" provides a completing sense on both days, its sense must change just at midnight. But what we know when we understand how to use "today" doesn't seem to change from day to day. (ibid., p. 479)

The main difference between Perry's argument (which Burge cited) and Burge's is that Perry presents the argument simply as a problem for Frege, where Burge draws the conclusion that for Frege sense and meaning are two different things. Burge does not note the odd omission in Frege, if *Sinn* is *not* meaning, of any technical term for the ordinary notion of meaning.[58] It is as if David Kaplan, in his well-known distinction in "Demonstratives" (1987), had introduced his term "content" but no term for "Character". (If Burge were right, Frege's use of *Sinn* would be closely analogous to Kaplan's "content", and "meaning", in the ordinary sense, to Kaplan's "character".) Kaplan, by the way,

---

[55] All references are to the 2004 reprint. Burge gives some credit for the pun in the title to Paul Benacerraf.

[56] The example is my own, obviously influenced by the place where the lecture was given. That I am giving a fair representation of Burge's argument should be clear to any reader of the first few pages of his chapter. Frege himself discusses "today", and the passage containing this discussion is the basis of Burge's interpretation.

[57] Perry refers to some opening passages in "Der Gedanke" to support his claim. Actually, Frege says there: "And when we call a sentence true we really mean [meinen] that its sense is true" (Frege, 1918–1919, p. 327). But without going into fussy terminological questions (and Perry himself quotes the passage as saying that it is thoughts for which the question of truth-value arises) it is easy to see that, carefully phrased, Perry's claim would obviously be correct.

[58] Frege, of course, has preempted "*Bedeutung*" for denotation or reference, whatever the translators may decide to do, and therefore, on Burge's account, still owes us a technical term for meaning in the ordinary sense.

is deeply influenced in his discussion of the relevant issues in Frege by Perry's paper, and is the third distinguished author to whom I have alluded.[59]

But all this goes directly contrary to what I understand to be the plain meaning of Frege's explicit *ipse dixit* in the very passage quoted and emphasized by Burge:

> If a time-indication is conveyed by the present tense one must know when the sentence was uttered in order to grasp the thought correctly. Therefore the time of utterance is part of the expression of the thought. (Frege, 1918–1919, p. 332)

What does this mean? "Today it is raining in Stockholm", or even better, "Now it is raining in Stockholm", or more simply, "It is raining in Stockholm", is not the expression of a complete thought. Also included in the expression of the thought, and hence in the sentence (*Satz*), is not merely the verbiage, but also a time. The real *Satz* or expression of a thought (*Gedankenausdruck*) is therefore an ordered pair:

$$\langle L, t \rangle$$

Here t is the time of utterance, where L is the piece of language, such as "It is raining now in Stockholm". But really, since it is part of the expression of the thought, the time of utterance is, for Frege, an unrecognized piece of language.

To what does t refer? That is, what is its *Bedeutung*? To make any sense of the passage, it must refer autonomously, that is, to itself. Thus, "It is raining in Stockholm" is incomplete—what it expresses must be filled out.[60] Take it to be "It is raining in Stockholm at—". If this were read with a tenseless "is" (not really much to be found in ordinary language in connection with times and dates; it is really philosophers' jargon)[61] it could be filled out with various completions such as "noon", "15 April 2005", or "the same moment when Kennedy was shot", and the like. But if uttered with the ordinary present-tense "is", the completion is the time of utterance used autonomously. It therefore stands in place of a specific date and time, or definite description, as in the examples above, which are conventional pieces of language.

---

[59] See Kaplan (1989). Kaplan gives no sign of agreement with Burge on the point in question, and I do not intend to give the opposite impression. Perry's influence on him will come out below.

[60] See already in the *Grundlagen* where he says:

> The concept "inhabitant of Germany" contains, in fact, a time-reference as a variable element in it, or, to put it mathematically, is a function of the time. Instead of "*a* is an inhabitant of Germany" we can say "*a* inhabits Germany", and this refers to the current date at the time. (Frege, 1884, pp. 59–60)

Perhaps the last sentence is a bit vaguely stated, but the whole is an anticipation of the later doctrine of "*Der Gedanke*"—that present-tensed verbal expressions are incomplete.

[61] In his discussion of the matter, Frege explicitly recognizes the use of "is" in the laws of mathematics as tenseless. This we may accept, and there may be other cases, but I do not think that a tenseless "is" is involved in ordinary language very often in connection with ordinary things. In particular, ordinary language giving the time when an event occurred (occurs or will occur) is invariably tensed. If a speaker does not know whether a given date is past, present or future, she/he will use a disjunction of tensed clauses, not a tenseless "is".

The *Sinn* of the time of utterance in the corresponding *Gedanke* is therefore that of autonymous designation via acquaintance with the referent, just as in the case of quotation.[62] The speaker (or writer or thinker) is acquainted both with the time of utterance (or writing or thought), and he must be acquainted with the *Sinn* as well, a *Sinn* of autonymous designation. Everything could be put in terms of general truth-conditions analogous to (a) above, but to apply these general conditions the subject must be acquainted with the time of utterance, as in the quotation case and the application of (a). As general conditions, we have conditions for when a present-tense expression of a thought is true, even though no token needs to be uttered, written, or thought. What expresses the thought is an ordered pair of a sentence and a time.[63] But in particular applications, there is a token, and the speaker (writer, thinker) is acquainted with the time it is uttered. The speaker is also acquainted with the autonymous *Sinn* involved.[64, 65]

---

[62] Thus Burge is right to deny that the referent is a part of the thought, or that in this case sense is to be identified with referent. See Burge (2004, p. 216). Rather the sense is that of autonymous designation. Nevertheless, Burge does recognize that Frege says that the time of utterance is part of the expression of the thought. How after all can something be part of the expression of a thought and not have a *Sinn* that is part of the thought? Burge simply seems to ignore this question in his argument against the identification of *Sinn* and meaning, and does not recognize that it threatens his argument, regardless of what the *Sinn* of the time may be. For there is no longer a *Sinn* that changes while the meaning is constant, once one realizes that the *Sinn* of a time is part of the thought too.

If my exegesis is correct, the situation is very close to what Burge wants to deny, even though sense and referent cannot literally be identified.

Dagfinn Føllesdal has called my attention to the writings of Wolfgang Künne of which Künne (1992) is a representative example. Like the present account, Künne stresses that for Frege times, persons, etc., can be part of the expression of the thought. However, his reading is certainly not mine in significant respects. For example, he agrees with Burge that Frege's *Sinn* is not meaning, and concludes that Frege has no term for linguistic meaning (see p. 723). Nor, at least here, does he say anything about my doctrine of acquaintance with *Sinne* for autonymous designation. I should add, where demonstration is involved, as in pointing, to me it is clearly that act of demonstration, not the object designated (as in Künne), which is part of the expression of the *Gedanke*. The object itself is the *Bedeutung*, and the *Sinn* is the rule connecting a demonstration such as pointing to its object.

[63] The ordered pair representation is of course my own mathematical transcription of Frege's informal idea that the time is part of the representation of the thought. Nothing hangs on it if someone prefers something else. Frege himself would no doubt think of this as a simple expression F(t), where F is the unsaturated linguistic part and t is the time of utterance.

[64] Perry writes:

By breaking the connection between senses and thoughts, we give up any reason not to take the options closed to Frege. We can take the sense of a sentence containing a demonstrative to be a role, rather than a Fregean complete sense, and thoughts to be the new sort, individuated by object and incomplete sense, rather than Fregean thoughts. (1977, p. 493)

Actually, the theory Perry is suggesting (which I have not entirely tried to grasp) seems to be related to Frege's actual theory. The real Frege holds that the senses of statements containing demonstratives and indexicals are incomplete. They are completed by senses given by objects that autonymously designate themselves, or sometimes by gestures such as pointing, whose senses are that the object pointed to is what is designated.

[65] Gareth Evans, in his important paper "Understanding Demonstratives" (1981; all references are to the 1985 reprint), also discusses the question of whether Perry's position is "just a notational variant of Frege's [real] theory" (1985, p. 314; and see also the subsequent pages through 317). See

Frege reiterates his view towards the end of the paper:

> The thought that we express by the Pythagorean theorem is surely timeless, eternal, unvarying. But are there not thoughts which are true today but false in six months' time? The thought, for example, that the tree there is covered with green leaves, will surely be false in six months' time. No, for it is not the same thought at all. The words "This tree is covered with green leaves" are not sufficient by themselves to constitute the expression of a thought, for the time of utterance is involved as well. Without the time specification thus given we have not a complete thought, i.e. we have no thought at all. Only a sentence with the time-specification filled out, a sentence complete in every respect, expresses a thought. But this thought, if it is true, is true not only today or tomorrow but timelessly. (Frege, 1918-1919, p. 343)[66]

On this theory, then, tensed sentences are on Frege's view incomplete. What is their *Bedeutung*? Plainly concepts, that is concepts applying to times, or functions from times to truth-values. On this theory "now" designates an identity function mapping each time to itself. "Today" denotes a function mapping each time into the day containing it (it could be explicitly defined as "the day it is now").[67]

However, the way Frege continues the earlier passage, where he asserts that the time is part of the expression of the thought, does create some confusion:

> If someone wants to say today what he expressed yesterday using the word "today", he will replace this word with "yesterday". Although the thought is the same its verbal expression must be different in order that the change of sense which would otherwise be effected by the differing times of utterance may be cancelled out. (Frege, 1918-1919, p. 332)

Burge instead translates the end of the passage as:

> ... the verbal expression must be different, to compensate for the change of sense which would otherwise be brought about by the different time of utterance. (Burge, 2004, p. 214)

---

also his representations by ordered triples, etc., of various Fregean thoughts in reply to Perry. It is clear that Evans's views have some strong relation to my own, though I have not attempted a detailed comparison.

I regret that when I gave the present lectures I was apparently unaware of Evans's discussions of the relevant issues about time, the first person, demonstratives, and his reply to Perry. Perhaps I did not know this paper at the time (though I have discussed Evans's views in some later presentations of the material). Alternatively, I may have remembered it primarily for its controversial and, as stated, I think unacceptably strong claim (under some influence of John McDowell) that "I know of no passage in which Frege can be construed as insisting that singular terms *must* have an existence-independent sense", even in natural language. I may have mistakenly thought of the paper as entirely *resting* on this claim. (Evans seems to have softened his position on the issue later, and he is right to call attention to Frege's emphasis in some passages on fiction and lapses into fiction.)

[66] I am indebted to Evans's "Understanding Demonstratives" (1981) for emphasizing this passage.

[67] Frege thinks that in a *Begriffsschrift* functions should be defined for all arguments, and artificially extends the definitions of functions with restricted domains. But here we are concerned with ordinary language.

If Frege really means that we have expressed literally the same thought again, it is very hard for me to see how to reconcile this assertion with his other doctrines. On my own exegesis, there are two times of utterance t_0 and t_1 and the two utterances are ordered pairs, $\langle S_0, t_0 \rangle$ and $\langle S_1, t_1 \rangle$, where S_0 is the earlier utterance with "today", and S_1 is the later utterance with "yesterday". "Today" denotes a function which when applied to t_0 (used autonymously) gives the day containing t_0, and "yesterday" similarly denotes a function that gives the previous day to the day containing t_1. Although these are indeed the same day, they plainly pick it out in different ways, paradigmatic cases of difference in sense. Moreover, it is hard to see how *any* exegesis compatible with Frege's general principles could yield a different result. If times of utterance are indeed part of the expression of a thought, and designate autonymously, it is clear that different times (considered as bits of language) have different senses. Also, the sense of "the previous day to the day containing" is part of the sense of the second sentence.

How could anyone argue that the two sentences in question have the same sense? The basic principle that would have to be violated is that the sense of a sentence (the thought) is composed of the senses of its parts. In this case the principle would have to be replaced by Frege's talk of "canceling out" or "compensation". But such a move would be a highly specialized violation of Frege's own general principles.

My own view is that a present-tense thought expressed at a time t_0 (and perhaps using "now" or "today") cannot be recaptured at any later time, if Frege's account of how these thoughts are expressed is correct.[68] This is simply because the earlier time is never with us again, and it is supposed to be part of the expression of the thought. We can indeed remember having had such a thought, and describe it, including the time at which it occurred, but it can never be repeated in exactly the same way.[69]

These considerations are reinforced when one considers longer passages of time. In English we have to say "the day before yesterday". But in Frege's own language we could say "*vorgestern*".[70] In principle we could imagine expressions for arbitrarily long time lapses. Or we could consider expressions frankly involving a number, for example, "*n* days ago", "524 days ago". How could anyone imagine that they preserve the sense of the original? One could doubt them, or make mistakes about them, not because of any change of mind, or forgetting the original situation, but rather because of a miscalculation of the number of days. It

---

[68] Thus I do not agree with Evans's attempt to rescue Frege on this point, even though his paper should certainly be consulted, as an attempt to argue the contrary. I will not go into his arguments against the "atomistic" nature of my conception.

[69] What about modern "four-dimensionalist" views? Perhaps in some sense the earlier time is still with us. First, there is little evidence that Frege is involved in these all-too-modern views. Second, in any case the time t_0 was the time of utterance; this indeed happened only once.

[70] I mentioned Hebrew in the lectures, but as people pointed out, why not emphasize Frege's own language?

would be very un-Fregean to say that the thought is the same as long as the number of days involved is reasonably short. What would be the boundary for "reasonably short"?[71]

However, there are some important problems to be considered here. We can pick up an old newspaper and read, "Russia and France are now at war". How can we understand this if the thought expressed can never be entertained at any later time, as I have claimed must be the Fregean view? We understand this because we understand the general rule, discussed above, as to how to understand sentences containing "now". They are incomplete and are to be completed by the time of utterance considered as part of the expression of the thought, and so on, as we have seen. A general rule was given, and we know how the rule is to be applied by a writer, speaker, or reader, at any time. This involves the fact that the writer was acquainted with the time of writing when he wrote the sentence, just as we are acquainted with the present time when we are reading the old report. And so on.

What if we report on what the newspaper said? We express this by something like, "At the time of its appearance, the newspaper said that Russia and France were then at war". This does not mean that "Russia and France were then at war" expresses the same thought at the present time as "Russia and France are now at war" expressed at that time in the newspaper. Rather, the change from "now" to "then" expresses at the present time a conventional way of describing a thought expressed with "now" at the earlier time. The very same convention would be followed by the journalist who wrote the report at the earlier time.[72]

The case of reporting on the next day is similar. If someone says, "today it is raining in Stockholm", the next day we can report "yesterday John said that it was raining in Stockholm". Perhaps more relevantly, someone can tell me today "yesterday it was raining in Stockholm", and I can report "John told me that yesterday it was raining in Stockholm". The same will hold for an individual

---

[71] See Frege's remarks on Kant in Frege (1884), p. 6 (last paragraph). Even if only one day's lapse in time appears to be involved, one can be confused about the time period. See Kaplan (1989), p. 538, who mentions Rip van Winkle (in spite of his admiration for Frege's remarks on "yesterday" and "today" as anticipating the modern theory of demonstratives).

[72] Gareth Evans mentions the problem of an old newspaper (yesterday's in his case), using it to argue that of course we understand yesterday's newspaper, that we would report on it using "yesterday", and that these facts must support Frege's statements that we still understand the old *Gedanke* and can report on it using "yesterday". He quotes some other philosophers as taking Frege to hold that we (nearly enough) can reproduce a thought provided that the reference of the subject is preserved even with a change of sense.

Evans rejects these philosophers' interpretation of Frege as totally "antagonistic...to the theory...of sense and reference" (Evans, 1985, p. 307). He asks whether Frege might just as well have used "my birthday" instead of "yesterday". In view of Frege's notorious footnote on "Aristotle" as quoted in *Naming and Necessity* and this chapter, there is some opening for the philosophers he opposes to be right. (See also Kaplan on the pseudo *de re*, (1989), p. 555.) However, I think Evans is right that Frege is supposing a more intimate relation between the "yesterday" and "today" statements, leading him to suppose that they express the same thought. In the "Aristotle" case, he plainly does not think that the same thought is literally expressed by different speakers, as I have argued.

recalling his own past beliefs. These reporting conventions should not give rise to the illusion (in a *Fregean* analysis)[73] that "yesterday it was raining in Stockholm" expresses the same thought on one day that "today it was raining in Stockholm" expresses on the previous day. The point is that we know what it is like to express beliefs involving "now", both because of the general principles enunciated involving the content of these beliefs and what it is like for a believer to be acquainted with a given moment. We apply conventional transformations in indirect discourse reports on these beliefs, even though such reports describe thoughts that are no longer, strictly speaking, available to us.[74] And we can read the old newspaper and understand it, though the thought it expresses is no longer available.[75]

Frege's treatment of the analogous case of first person statements will be described below. My revision of Frege's remarks on "today" and "yesterday" is meant to make Frege's treatment of the temporal case consistent with his treatment of the interpersonal case. The later discussion of that case may make my remarks on the temporal case clearer.

Let me return to Burge's views on the nature of *Sinn*. Burge argued that Frege's treatment of (temporal and other) indexicals shows that *Sinn* cannot be identified with meaning. My own analysis is that Frege's treatment of the phenomena in question, properly understood, creates no objection against such an identification. Burge uses his analysis to criticize some of my remarks in *Naming and Necessity* (Kripke, 1980) on Frege's view of ordinary proper names. Since I have rejected Burge's view, it will give me no reason to retract the remarks in question. However, in my own self-defense, I will take the opportunity to elaborate a bit further on the issue.[76]

---

[73] I am not saying what one should think in a non-Fregean analysis. See footnote 80, 81 below.

[74] In a discussion session after my lecture, Gunnar Björnsson asked how I would handle "you promised (yesterday) that you were coming today". At the time I took this question under advisement. John Perry also thinks, in his "Afterword" to the reprinted version of "Frege on Demonstratives" in Perry (1993), that indirect discourse reports, both in the temporal and the interpersonal cases, form a crucial objection to Evans's defense of Frege. In the discussion above, I have tried to reply to these objections. The indirect discourse reports, and other reports on thoughts we cannot express or even think, give our own conventional descriptions of the nature of these thoughts.

I should add that although Perry is not sure he is interpreting Evans rightly on the issue (and I have not looked into the matter), he takes Evans to be defending Frege by proposing that days (times, subjects) actually are components of thoughts. To this notion of thoughts he objects that "if objects, rather than modes of presentation of them, figure in Evans's thoughts, then they represent the same sort of departure from Frege's theory as . . . I proposed . . . It is a departure, for Frege disavowed such hybrids" (Perry, 1993, p. 23). As I have said, I have not tried to figure out the relation to Evans's proposal, but on my interpretation, it is not the time of utterance itself that figures as a *Sinn* in the "now" thought, but the type of autonymous designation of a time by itself given by the speaker's acquaintance with the time. "Today" is analysed as "the day containing now", etc.

[75] I am indebted here to conversations with Romina Padró.

[76] Burge also has things to say about rigid designation and the like. I confine my remarks here to what he says about one issue, the issue raised by Frege's "Aristotle" footnote in "Über Sinn und Bedeutung."

Consider the following well-known footnote in "Über Sinn und Bedeutung", which I quote from Burge's own translation:

> In the case of an actual proper name such as "Aristotle" opinions as to the sense may differ. It might for instance be taken to be the following: the pupil of Plato and teacher of Alexander the Great. Anybody who does this will attach another sense to the sentence "Aristotle was born in Stagira" than will a man who takes as sense of the name: the teacher of Alexander the Great who was born in Stagira. So long as the reference remains the same, such variations of sense may be tolerated, although they are to be avoided in the theoretical structure of a demonstrative science and ought not to occur in a perfect language. (Burge, 2004, p. 217)

Since Burge makes a point of giving his own translations of all quotations from Frege, and seems to be suggesting that previous translators are unreliable, I must add that in this instance his translation is virtually identical with that of Max Black, as anyone who compares the two will see. I myself took Frege to be saying that given the first definition, "Aristotle was born in Stagira" would be non-trivial, whereas someone who used the second definition would regard the same sentence as trivial. I also took him to be supposing that the definition of proper names by definite descriptions was typical, and attacked the description theory of ordinary proper names as a view to be found in Frege and Russell.

Whether I was right in ascribing a description theory of proper names to Frege (which certainly agrees with his examples) would not be the main issue here. Gareth Evans, in a piece of writing that as far as I know was not published, remarked that certainly Frege, like Russell, had generally been understood in this way. This made it important for me to rebut the theory, whether historically it was Frege's theory or not.

More important for present purposes is the following: I certainly had understood Frege as saying that many proper names mean one thing to one speaker and another to another; that there is a divergence of idiolect, and that this result is counterintuitive. Burge thinks that his own understanding of Frege on the distinction between "sense" and "meaning", and its relation to Frege's theory of indexicals, will give rise to an entirely different interpretation of the passage.

Burge points out that Feigl's translation, though it usually renders "*Sinn*" as "sense", translates one sentence in the footnote just quoted as: "Whoever accepts this sense will *interpret the meaning* [my italics] of the statement 'Aristotle was born in Stagira' differently from one who interpreted the sense of 'Aristotle' as the Stagirite teacher of Alexander the Great".[77] According to Burge, this "slip" reads the identification of sense and meaning into the passage, and was "probably influential, as we shall see" (Burge, 2004, p. 220).

---

[77] "On Sense and Nominatum", trans. H. Feigl, in H. Feigl and W. Sellars (eds.), *Readings in Philosophical Analysis* (New York, Appleton-Century-Crofts, 1949).

The influence turns out to be on me. I did indeed quote the Feigl translation in *Naming and Necessity* (Kripke, 1980, p. 30). Burge seems to suggest (Burge, 2004, p. 203) that if I had only been aware of the Black translation, I would not have been misled into thinking that, strictly speaking, different speakers have different idiolects in which "Aristotle" and other names mean different things. And I guess my readers must have been unaware of Black's translation also, or at least they failed to look it up.

As against all this let me say the following: I do not remember why I quoted this particular translation. I may simply have grabbed it before the lecture, which was orally delivered, or *perhaps* I thought that it makes the point more explicit. However, I doubt that the point would appear to be any different had I quoted Black's translation (which, as I said, is substantially the same as Burge's). I submit that if the translation I read had been "will attach a different sense", as in Black and Burge, a reader understanding this as ordinary English, and innocent of Burge's special exegesis, would understand the passage in exactly the same way as I intended, that is, that different speakers use the name "Aristotle" differently, though preserving the reference. I myself had taught the Geach–Black collection (Frege, 1952) in classes on Frege, including other papers, especially "Function and Concept" (Frege, 1891). As against any serious suggestion that I was unaware of the Black translation, note that I follow Black in my book in using "reference" rather than Feigl's "nominatum" or Russell's "denotation" (in contrast to Carnap, Russell, and Church. See footnote 2).

To get to the really substantive issue: Burge suggests that "the senses associated with proper names and other indexical constructions shift with context… In this respect Frege treats names and indexicals in the same way" (Burge, 2004, p. 217). However, we have seen that Frege does *not* hold that tensed sentences (and senses involving demonstratives and indexicals) shift their senses from time to time (context to context). Rather their senses are constant but incomplete, and must be completed by the time of utterance (or other relevant contextual factors). It is strange in any case that one must rely on "Der Gedanke", which was written more than a quarter of a century later than "Über Sinn und Bedeutung", to understand the former paper. Readers must have been greatly misled for a long time![78]

---

[78] Really, an even longer time. Long after "Über Sinn und Bedeutung" was well known to philosophers, the importance of "*Der Gedanke*" was not recognized. It was not included in the Geach–Black collection (Frege, 1952). The first translation of it into English was that of the Quintons, appearing only in 1956. The Geach–Stoothoff translation dates from 1977. My impression is that the contemporary philosophical community only gradually recognized the fundamental importance of this paper.

Burge does quote a sentence from "Über Sinn und Bedeutung" itself: "To every expression belonging to a complete totality of signs, there should certainly correspond a definite sense; but natural languages often do not satisfy this condition, and one must be content if the same word has the same sense in the same context" (Burge, 2004, p. 217). Without Burge's special exegetical apparatus, I would have understood the passage as saying that in natural language, unlike in a scientific *Begriffsschrift*, ambiguities occur and one must be content that an ambiguous term has a fixed sense in a given context. (And see my reference to this remark in footnote 32 above.)

Having made this joke, I myself wish to cite a passage from "Der Gedanke" that conclusively shows that Frege thinks that different speakers, attaching different descriptions to the same name, strictly speaking have different idiolects.

Now if both Leo Peter and Rudolph Lingens understand by "Dr Gustav Lauben" the doctor who is the only doctor living in a house known to both of them, then they both understand the sentence "Dr Lauben was wounded" in the same way; they associate the same thought with it . . .

Suppose further that Herbert Garner knows that Dr Gustav Lauben was born on 13 September 1875 in N.N. and this is not true of anyone else; suppose, however, that he does not know where Dr Lauben now lives nor indeed anything else about him. On the other hand, suppose Leo Peter does not know that Dr Lauben was born on 13 September 1875 in N.N. Then as far as the proper name "Dr Gustav Lauben" is concerned, Herbert Garner and Leo Peter do not speak the same language, although they do in fact designate the same man with this name; for they do not know that they are doing so. (Frege, 1918–1919, pp. 332–333)

The relevant original German, which I cite because of the suggestions that readers are relying on erroneous translations, is "*sprechen . . . nicht dieselbe Sprache*" (ibid., p. 65 in the original German). I cannot imagine a more explicit statement—in the very paper that Burge is relying on—of the view that Burge says that Frege has been misunderstood to hold; namely, that common natural languages are really unions of idiolects or dialects that differ from person to person according to what sense they associate with a given name, even when the reference is the same.

This is exactly in accordance with the usual and orthodox exegesis of the "Über Sinn und Bedeutung" footnote on different senses of "Aristotle".[79] There is no

---

[79] It is unlikely that Frege is basing his point about "Dr Lauben" on the view, pressed by some philosophers, that proper names are not part of the language (German, English, etc.). Whatever plausibility this view may have with respect to "Dr Lauben", plainly some proper names are parts of natural languages. I may wonder what Aristotle is called in Hebrew or Greek. A German may wonder what word we English speakers use for his country, and an English speaker may ask the converse question about the German word for "Germany". In the case, for example, of the last question my knowledge of German has a gap if I do not know the answer. Yet the point that different descriptions might be associated with a name remains the same. If Frege thought "Dr Lauben" was a special case, he might have said so.

The issue raised in the previous paragraph is a brief and only partial treatment of views about proper names expressed by some philosophers. It deserves a fuller treatment elsewhere.

One must also admit that the situation supposed regarding Dr Lauben is rather peculiar. When Frege supposes that someone associates with the name "Aristotle" the sense "the pupil of Plato and teacher of Alexander the Great" (who may or may not have any idea where Aristotle was born), while someone else associates with the name "the teacher of Alexander the Great who was born in Stagira", the situation is completely analogous to that of Dr Lauben. But would Frege have actually written that the two different speakers "do not know" that they are designating the same man? Surely this would be an embarrassment. His statement that such variations of sense are tolerable in natural language seems to go in a different direction. Perhaps the difference in attitude does indeed have something to do with the fact that "Aristotle" is the name of a well-known man, part of the common language. But theoretically the cases are the same.

reason to doubt the exegesis on the basis of suspicions of bad translation, or unfamiliarity with Frege's theory of indexicals, or anything else.[80]

Let me go back to our current topic, indexicals. What about Frege's theory of the first person singular, of "I"? There is of course much current and past discussion of the first person point of view—Descartes, Wittgenstein, Castañeda, and many others.

"Now", Frege says, "everyone is presented to himself in a special and primitive way, in which he is presented to no one else" (Frege, 1918–1919, p. 333). Perry and, following him, Kaplan (who in one place calls the passage beginning with this sentence "tortured", while he commends Frege's remarks on "yesterday" and "today" criticized above),[81] seems to take Frege to be saying that each person must be presented to himself in a special, unique qualitative way, statable in the common language. It is easy to doubt, or indeed to reject, such a view. And, as Perry says, the analogue would be to interpret "now" in such a way that each instant must have its own qualitative character. We have seen that Frege's treatment of "now" involves no such thing. Let me continue the passage where Frege discusses tense, passing over some of the discussion (such as the remarks on "yesterday" and "today"):

If Frege's view of names like "Aristotle" in natural language makes his view problematic, as I think it does, then, modifying a suggestion of Devitt and Sterelny (1999), I would call it "the problem of unwanted idiolects".

[80] Burge claims (2004, p. 217) that "Der Gedanke" confirms his theory that for Frege names are like indexicals, and so on. But I do not see how.

It might be mentioned that Burge himself (in Burge, 1973) holds that names are demonstratives followed by special predicates. But presumably he is not reading his view back into Frege.

I must admit that some passages in Burge's paper make me wonder whether he is consistently disputing the point I am reiterating here. For example, in (2004), p. 232, he acknowledges that the Aristotle footnote implies that what may be a near logical truth in one speaker's mouth will be a factual assertion in that of another. On p. 218, first paragraph, perhaps Burge might be read as after all agreeing that according to Frege different speakers speak different idiolects in connection with names. These and other passages make me wonder sometimes whether on the points in question he really disputes my interpretation or rather disputes my claim that Frege's view, so interpreted, is implausible. But then the emphasis on indexicals and the dispute over the nature of *Sinn* would have little relevance.

[81] Kaplan (1989), p. 501. Probably Kaplan is thinking of "yesterday" and "today" as directly referential demonstratives, picking out the same date in two different ways, and yielding the same "content", in Kaplan's terminology (see also my own distinction between fixing a reference and giving a meaning). However, I am discussing the passage from Frege's point of view, not alternative later points of view. It is possible that some of the remarks I have made against the view in Frege could be maintained against the later points of view, but we need not discuss the issue here.

Kaplan's emphatic rejection, under the influence of Perry, of the passage beginning with what I have quoted, seems to me simply to be wrong. (In fairness to Kaplan, I should add that in later communications with me about this issue, he could see my point and described his earlier writing as influenced by "irrational exuberance". See also Kaplan's later discussion of the passage from Frege on pp. 533–535, which is more nuanced than the earlier characterization, though, in my opinion, still not free of serious objections.)

In all such cases the mere wording, as it can be preserved in writing, is not the complete expression of the thought; the knowledge of certain conditions accompanying the utterance, which are used as means of expressing the thought, is needed for us to grasp the thought correctly. Pointing the finger, hand gestures, glances may belong here too. The same utterance containing the word "I" in the mouths of different men will express different thoughts of which some may be true, others false. (Frege, 1918–1919, p. 332)

We recall that Frege's theory is that the present tense and "now" involve an autonymous use of a time as a piece of language. In general, Frege thinks that such wording leaves an incomplete sense. Pointing, for example, is part of the expression of the thought. Its sense determines the referent as the object pointed to.

If one looks at the last sentence about "I" in isolation it might appear to suggest that first person sentences express complete thoughts, with different interpretations in the mouths of different people. But if the analogy with tense is to be strict, just as the time used autonymously completes the expression of the thought, so the subject, also taken as an autonymous designator of himself, completes the expression of the first person thought. Thus, by analogy to what has been said before, a first person sentence (with the word "I") can be represented as an ordered pair of the wording and the subject. The subject (not a name of the subject, but the subject him-or herself) is part of the sentence. The wording is an incomplete predicate, standing for a concept applying to people. "I" must denote a function, mapping each person to herself (himself), just as "now" functions for times. And the sense in the complete thought is one given by autonymous designation, just as in the tensed case. Only here it is the subject who is an autonymous designator.[82]

It should be clear what the role in this is for the remark that "everyone is presented to himself in a special and primitive way, in which he is presented to no one else". In this, as in other cases of autonymous designation, the use requires that the speaker or thinker be acquainted with the object. Just as the speaker is acquainted with the present time, so following the familiar Cartesian idea, each speaker or thinker is acquainted with him- or herself. The role of this acquaintance is strictly analogous to its role in the temporal case. And notice that here Frege *does not* think that the very same thought can be expressed by anyone

---

[82] Since most first person statements will be tensed, they should really be triples, in the obvious way, of verbal wording, speakers, and times. If they contain demonstratives (with pointing, gestures, etc.) the representation is even more complicated. In a portion of the passage that I have not quoted Frege also mentions "here" and "there".

I should add that the important point about first person statements just stated in my text is not in the original transcript of my lecture. It is new to the present version. For more discussion of this issue see also Chapter 10, section I.

else. The cases are analogous, and so should the corresponding doctrines be analogous.[83, 84]

Before discussing this further, let me make some remarks on Perry's discussion, which influenced Kaplan. Perry (more or less followed by Kaplan) argues that "what is needed is a primitive aspect of me, which is not simply one that only I am aware of myself as having, but that I alone have" (Perry, 1977, p. 490).[85] If we did assume that "I" must be defined by a definite description in the common language, Perry's conclusion would indeed follow. But it is not in Frege's text at all, nor will it turn out to be needed. Certainly this plays little part in the philosophical tradition about the first person to which Perry himself alludes.[86]

Second, Perry writes at the very beginning of his paper that "nothing could be more out of the spirit of Frege's account of sense and thought than an incommunicable, private thought" (Perry, 1977, p. 474). He thinks that Frege was driven to a doctrine of private, incommunicable thoughts by the pressures of his linguistic theory. Peter Geach goes further:

> ... certain ideas he [Frege] plays with in the essay [*"Der Gedanke"*]—private sensations with incommunicable qualities, a Cartesian *I* given in an incommunicable way—are really bogus ideas... For Frege affirms (1) that any thought is by its nature communicable, (2) that thoughts about private sensations and sense-qualities, and about the Cartesian *I*, are by their nature incommunicable. It is an immediate consequence that there can be no such thoughts. Frege never drew this conclusion, of course... But... Wittgenstein was to draw it. (Geach, preface to Frege, 1977, p. viii)

Would that the notoriously difficult and controversial "private language argument" of the later Wittgenstein were so easy! Frege would really have to be censured for his failure to see the obvious contradiction in his own remarks. In fact, although Frege distinguishes between thoughts, abstract entities, and ideas, events in particular minds, so that different people could have the same thought, and thoughts could be (and usually were) communicable, this in no way

---

[83] Many contemporaries who think in terms of person-stages might think that there is really only one acquaintance here, with "I-now". There would not be an analogy, but perhaps a single case. But there is little reason to ascribe this doctrine to Frege.

Of course Descartes would have granted that one can doubt whether one existed in the past or will exist in the future. But this is not the same thing as saying that the enduring self is simply a union of temporal stages.

I should add that one need not ascribe to Frege a doctrine that the object of acquaintance is some special evanescent entity, a "Cartesian ego". What Frege says is that everyone is acquainted with himself in a special way, not that the entity with which one is acquainted in this way is different from the ordinary person.

[84] I am indebted here to conversations with Romina Padró.

[85] He also argues (p. 491) that analogous considerations would place the same requirement on "now", making each time separately specifiable in a unique way associated with that word.

[86] Little part, but perhaps it goes too far to say "no part". Perhaps some have argued that "I" denotes "the metaphysical subject", or even that these two phrases have the same sense. But if anyone really held this, his conclusion was surely some sort of metaphysical solipsism.

precludes the existence of thoughts that for special reasons might be intelligible to only one person.[87]

The fact is that Frege always held that certain thoughts were incommunicable. See his example already in the *Grundlagen der Arithmetik* about two people whose inner perceptual spaces were of three-dimensional projective spaces, but one means by "point" what the other means by "plane", and vice versa. He concludes that the two persons could not detect the difference: "What is purely intuitable is not communicable" (Frege, 1884, p. 35).[88] A simpler geometric example would be that of two people whose inner spaces were three-dimensional Euclidean mirror images of each other. On the next page Frege says that "the word 'white' ordinarily makes us think of a certain sensation, which is, of course, entirely subjective; but even in ordinary every day speech it often bears, I think, an objective sense. When we call snow white, we mean to refer to an objective quality..." (ibid., p. 36). It is easy to conclude that the subjective usage is incommunicable. This, in fact, is Frege's view in "Der Gedanke" itself:

> My companion and I are convinced that we both see the same field; but each of us has a particular sense impression of green... For when the word "red" is meant not to state a property of things but to characterize sense impressions belonging to my consciousness, it is only applicable within the realm of my consciousness. For it is impossible to compare my sense impression with someone else's. (Frege, 1918-1919, p. 334)[89]

Here the view is adopted, not because of any semantic pressures, but simply because this is the way Frege himself sees things. Presumably any one of us can entertain thoughts about our color impressions.

These issues having been cleared away, what is the role of the special first person use of "I"? Simply as before, in the cases of direct quotation, indirect quotation, the present tense, and so on, a competent user of the language must be acquainted with the appropriate sense.[90] One need not be a rigid follower of

---

[87] Gareth Evans elaborates on this point (1981, p. 313). I find myself in complete agreement with him here.

[88] My thanks to Eva Picardi for calling my attention to this passage. The point is that in three-dimensional projective geometry any statement about "points" and "planes" retains its truth-value if the terms are interchanged.

[89] The switch from "green" to "red" becomes clear when the omitted material, also involving color blindness, is read.

[90] Here I will take the opportunity to say something about how Church's system, criticized above for its unexplained hierarchies (say of material conditionals), each of which denotes the sense of the previous one, should be recast. We saw that Church has no doctrine of "privileged" senses. But on our interpretation of Frege, there are such privileged senses. Every term in the infinite sequence of conditionals, etc., ought to be given by our introspective awareness of the way the previous one determines its referent (the "backward road").

Each level might be called the sense given by acquaintance of the previous one, and indicated by an explicit operator. One might even suppose that this is what Church really had in mind, even though it is not part of his official doctrine. See also footnote 16 above, where I cite Church's remarks that his translation argument is only a way of bringing out the arbitrariness of the connection of a given piece of language and what it means. The point must be that the "that

Descartes to see that indeed each of us is acquainted with her/himself in a special first person way. There is nothing mysterious about this. I have taken longer about the matter than necessary, simply because I have had to deal with statements made by other writers.

Frege writes:

So, when Dr Lauben [the character who was mentioned before] has the thought that he was wounded, he will probably be basing it on this primitive way in which he is presented to himself. And only Dr Lauben himself can grasp thoughts specified in this way. (ibid., p. 333)

Here, Dr (Gustav) Lauben has said to himself "I was wounded", or he can just be thinking this. In either case, he is using an acquaintance-sense, given by the first person view point.

However, Frege goes on to say that:

...he [Dr Lauben] may want to communicate with others. He cannot communicate a thought he alone can grasp. Therefore, if he now says "I was wounded", he must use "I" in a sense which can be grasped by others, perhaps in the sense of "he who is speaking to you at this moment"... (ibid., p. 333)

It is easy to see why this remark might encourage others to think that Frege has gone wrong in his analysis of "I". Is it really plausible that everyone uses "I" in two senses, one when he is speaking to himself, and one when he is speaking to others? The tentative proposal Frege makes is beset by difficulties. Perhaps more than one person is speaking to the other at the moment, so the description is not uniquely specified. Or perhaps Dr Lauben suffers from a temporary attack of hoarseness or muteness, so that the description in question is vacuous, or if at the same time exactly one other person is speaking to Dr Lauben's intended hearer, the description denotes someone else. But even if Dr Lauben cannot speak, there was an intended referent of his use of "I", though he failed to produce the sound, and this must be Dr Lauben himself. David Kaplan, both in "Demonstratives" (1989) and in "What is Meaning? Explorations in the Theory of *Meaning as Use*" (unpublished), wittily ridicules various analyses of "I" of this kind. If we ask for a volunteer to do something, and someone in the crowd raises her hand and says, "I volunteer", just imagine it replaced by "The person who is speaking volunteers". Maybe the point would still come across, but it would be oddly put.

Frege's implausible moves are quite unnecessary. A speaker who uses the word "I" is part of the expression of the thought, autonomously designating himself. The sense of this designation is given by acquaintance. Everyone knows what this type of acquaintance is by analogy with his own case. So the hearer who hears Dr Lauben

---

clause" designates the proposition meant more directly than any metalinguistic paraphrase. (Church also uses the argument to show that propositions are not dispensable in favor of sentences.) And see also the accompanying example in my text. C. Anthony Anderson tells me he has a transcript of a lecture where Church does say that terms have preferred senses. So there seems to be some ambiguity and tension in Church on this point.

knows what type of thought is being expressed, even though, strictly speaking, he cannot have the thought. It is like the case of the reader of the old newspaper.[91]

In indirect discourse we use the type of expression emphasized by Castañeda and others. Dr Lauben said (thought) that he himself was wounded. Here what follows the that clause is plainly not a literal repetition of Dr Lauben's thought, but rather our own description of it.[92]

Let me restate our main points. First, there is in a sense a "backward road" from references to senses. For everyone who specifies a reference must do so in some way. Then, by her awareness of how she has specified the reference, she is aware of the way the reference is fixed, and hence is aware of the sense. Frege's most explicit use of this known to me is in the beginning of the *Grundgesetze* (1893), where, after concluding that every term has a unique referent, and every sentence a truth-value, he concludes that every sentence of the system expresses a thought given by the way the truth-conditions are specified.[93] Linguistic rules, and the Fregean thoughts involved, can normally be given by general directions exemplified by (α) and (β). [(β) makes sense as a recursive specification of indirect senses because of the backward road, and the requirements about being revelatory are satisfied.]

But to apply these rules, and indeed to understand them, a user of the language or a thinker must have something very like Russellian acquaintance with directly or indirectly quoted material, senses, times, subjects, and inner mental states. Despite their differences over the analysis of descriptions, Frege and Russell are basically more similar than is usually thought.[94] The doctrine of acquaintance is much less explicit in Frege than in Russell, but I have long believed that it is needed for a proper understanding of him. Let me hope that I am right.*

---

[91] The late Wittgenstein might object to the suggestion that hearers can grasp the subjective first person use of "I" by analogy to their own case, but there is no reason to suppose that Frege would have so objected.

[92] I have made several corrections of Frege's formulations, trying to make his view consistent according to his own lights. Naturally it is something in favor of an exegesis that it makes the author studied correct in terms of his own system, but people do make mistakes even in terms of their own view. I have not been forced to go nearly as far as Perry in claiming that various pressures have led Frege to abandon some of his own fundamental beliefs.

[93] Frege, 1893, sections 31 and 32, pp. 87–90.

[94] One might think that my doctrine of acquaintance implies that phrases with the same sense will automatically have the same indirect sense. In a later seminar on Frege, I came to think that this may not necessarily follow, but a discussion would be beyond the scope of the present paper.

* I would like to thank Sama Agahi and Peter Pagin for transcribing the original lecture. My thanks to Harold Teichman and especially to Romina Padró for their help in producing the present version. Also thanks to Dagfinn Føllesdal and Eva Picardi for the references attributed to them above. In relatively late correspondence, having seen a draft of this paper C. Anthony Anderson, Dagfinn Føllesdal, and Nathan Salmon added helpful comments that have been imperfectly taken into account. This paper has been completed with support from the Saul A. Kripke Center at The City University of New York, Graduate Center.

REFERENCES

Beaney, M. (1997) *The Frege Reader*. Oxford: Blackwell.
Boër, S. E. and Lycan, W. G. (1986) *Knowing Who*. Cambridge, MA: MIT Press.
Burge, T. (1973) "Reference and Proper Names." *Journal of Philosophy*, 70: 425–439.
——— (1979a) "Sinning Against Frege." *Philosophical Review*, 88: 398–492. Reprinted with a postscript in Burge (2004), pp. 213–242.
——— (1979b) "Frege and the Hierarchy." *Synthese*, 40: 265–281. Reprinted with a postscript in Burge (2004), pp. 153–210.
——— (2004) *Truth, Thought, Reason: Essays on Frege*. Oxford: Oxford University Press.
Carnap, R. (1947) *Meaning and Necessity. A Study in Semantics and Modal Logic*. Chicago: University of Chicago Press.
Castañeda, H. N. (1967) "The Logic of Self-Knowledge." *Noûs*, 1: 9–22.
——— (1968) "On the Logic of Attributions of Self-Knowledge to Others." *Journal of Philosophy*, 65: 439–456.
Church, A. (1950) "On Carnap's Analysis of Statements of Assertion and Belief." *Analysis*, 10(5): 97–99.
——— (1951) "A Formulation of the Logic of Sense and Denotation." In P. Henle, H. M. Kallen and S. K. Langer (eds.), *Structure, Method, and Meaning, Essays in Honor of H. M. Scheffer*, pp. 3–24. New York: The Liberal Arts Press.
——— (1956) *Introduction to Mathematical Logic*. Princeton: Princeton University Press.
——— (1973) "Outline of a Revised Formulation of the Logic of Sense and Denotation (Part I)." *Noûs*, 7(1): 24–33.
——— (1988) "A Remark Concerning Quine's Paradox about Modality." Reprinted in Salmon and Soames (1988), pp. 58–65. Originally published in Spanish in *Análisis Filosófico*, 2(1982): 25–32.
——— (1995) "A Theory of the Meaning of Names." In V. F. Sinisi and J. Woleski (eds.), *The Heritage of Kazimierz Ajdukiewicz*, pp. 69–74. Amsterdam and Atlanta: Rodopi.
Davidson, D. (1965) "Theories of Meaning and Learnable Languages." In Y. Bar-Hillel (ed.), *Proceedings of the 1964 International Congress for Logic, Methodology, and Philosophy of Science*, pp. 383–393. Amsterdam: North Holland. Reprinted in Davidson (1984).
——— (1968) "On Saying That." *Synthese*, 19(1/2): 178–214. Reprinted in Davidson (1984).
——— (1979) "Quotation." *Theory and Decision*, 11: 27–40. Reprinted in Davidson (1984).
——— (1984) *Inquiries into Truth and Interpretation*. Oxford: Oxford University Press.
Devitt, M. and Sterelny, K. (1999) *Language and Reality: an Introduction to the Philosophy of Language*. Oxford: Blackwell.
Dummett, M. (1973) *Frege: Philosophy of Language*. London: Duckworth.
——— (1981) *The Interpretation of Frege's Philosophy*. Cambridge, MA: Harvard University Press.

Evans, G. (1981) "Understanding Demonstratives." In H. Parret and J. Bouveresse (eds.), *Meaning and Understanding*. Berlin: W. de Gruyter. Reprinted in Evans (1985), pp. 291–321.

——— (1985) *Collected Papers*. Oxford: Oxford University Press.

Frege, G. (1884) *Die Grundlagen der Arithmetik*. Breslau: Verlag von Wilhelm Koebner. Trans. by J. L. Austin as *The Foundations of Arithmetic*. Oxford: Blackwell, 1950.

——— (1891) "Function and Concept." In Beaney (1997), pp. 130–148.

——— (1892) "Über Sinn und Bedeutung." *Zeitschrift für Philosophie und philosophische Kritik*, 100: 25–50. Trans. by Max Black, in Beaney (1997), pp. 151–171.

——— (1893) *Grundgesetze der Arithmetik, begriffsschriftlich abgeleitet*, Vol. I. Jena: Pohle. Trans. in part by M. Furth as *The Basic Laws of Arithmetic*. University of California, Berkeley and Los Angeles, 1967.

——— (1918–1919) "Der Gedanke." In *Beiträge zur Philosophie des deutschen Idealismus* I, pp. 58–77. Trans. as "Thought" by P. Geach and R. H. Stoothoff, in Beaney (1997), pp. 325–345. Also translated by A. M. and M. Quinton (1956), "The Thought: A Logical Inquiry", *Mind*, 65(259): 289–311.

——— (1952) *Translations from the Philosophical Writings of Gottlob Frege*, edited by P. T. Geach and M. Black. New York: Philosophical Library.

——— (1977) *Logical Investigations*, ed. with a preface by P. T. Geach, trans. by P. T. Geach and R. H. Stoothoff. New Haven: Yale University Press.

——— (1979) *Posthumous Writings*, ed. by H. Hermes, F. Kambartel and F. Kaulbach. Chicago: University of Chicago Press.

——— (1980) *Gottlob Frege: Philosophical and Mathematical Correspondence*, ed. by G. Gabriel, H. Hermes, F. Kambartel, C. Thiel, A. Veraart, B. McGuinness and H. Kaal, trans. by Hans Kaal. Chicago: University of Chicago Press.

Geach, P. T. (1957) *Mental Acts. Their Content and Their Objects*. London: Routledge and Kegan Paul.

——— (1963) "Quantification Theory and the Problems of Identifying Objects of Reference." *Acta Philosophica Fennica*, 16: 41–52. Also included in Geach (1972), section 4.3 and 5.8.

——— (1972) *Logic Matters*. Oxford: Blackwell.

Hintikka, J. (1962) *Knowledge and Belief: An Introduction to the Logic of the Two Notions*. Ithaca, NY: Cornell University Press.

Kaplan, D. (1968) "Quantifying in." *Synthese*, 19(1/2): 178–214.

——— (1989) "Demonstratives." In J. Almog, J. Perry and H. Wettstein (eds.), *Themes from Kaplan*, pp. 481–563. New York, Oxford University Press.

——— (1990) "Words." *Proceedings of the Aristotelian Society, Supplementary Volumes*, 64: 93–119.

——— (unpublished) "What is Meaning? Explorations in the Theory of *Meaning as Use*."

Kripke, S. (1980) *Naming and Necessity*. Cambridge, MA: Harvard University Press.

——— (unpublished) *Whitehead Lectures: Logicism, Wittgenstein, and De Re Beliefs about Numbers*.

Künne, W. (1992) "Hybrid Proper Names." *Mind*, 101(404): 721–731.

Künne, W. (2010) "Sense, Reference and Hybridity: Reflections on Kripke's Recent Reading of Frege." *Dialectica*, 64: 529–551.

Lewy, C. (1949) "Review of Carnap's *Meaning and Necessity.*" *Mind*, 58: 228–238.
Mendelsohn, R. (2005) *The Philosophy of Gottlob Frege.* Cambridge: Cambridge University Press.
Parsons, T. (1981) "Frege's Hierarchies of Indirect Sense and the Paradox of Analysis." *Midwest Studies in Philosophy*, 6: 37–57.
Perry, J. (1977) "Frege on Demonstratives." *Philosophical Review*, 86(4): 474–497. Reprinted with a postscript in Perry (1993).
——— (1993) *The Problem of the Essential Indexical and Other Essays.* Oxford: Oxford University Press.
Picardi, E. (1992) *Elementi di Filosofia del Linguaggio.* Bologna: Patron.
Quine, W. V. O. (1960) *Word and Object.* Cambridge, MA: MIT Press.
——— (1979) "Intensions Revisited." In P. French, T. Uehling, Jr. and H. K. Wettstein (eds.), *Contemporary Perspectives in the Philosophy of Language*, pp. 268–274. Minneapolis: University of Minnesota Press.
Reichenbach, H. (1947) *Elements of Symbolic Logic.* New York: Macmillan.
Russell, B. (1905) "On Denoting." *Mind*, 14(56): 479–493.
Salmon, N. (2005) "On Designating." *Mind*, 114(456): 1069–1133.
——— and Soames, S. (1988) *Propositions and Attitudes.* Oxford: Oxford University Press.
Searle, J. (1989) *Speech Acts.* New York: Cambridge University Press.
Sosa, E. (1970) "Propositional Attitudes *De Dicto* and *De Re.*" *Journal of Philosophy*, 67 (21): 883–896.
Washington, C. (1992) "The Identity Theory of Quotation." *Journal of Philosophy*, 89 (11): 582–605.

10

The First Person*

I

I will concentrate here on the perplexities some philosophers have felt concerning the simple first person pronoun 'I'. The genesis of these reflections is a fairly recent invitation to Barcelona[1] to give a talk about my views on David Kaplan's manuscript 'What Is Meaning? Explorations in the Theory of *Meaning as Use*' (n.d.),[2] as well as on his classic publication, 'Demonstratives' (1989).

Were I to be making a general discussion of Kaplan's recent material, I would emphasize my enthusiasm for his general approach.[3] There is one aspect of his

---

* The present paper was delivered at the conference 'Saul Kripke: Philosophy, Language, and Logic' held at the City University of New York, Graduate Center on January 25, 2006. There has been substantial revision of the original talk, which was delivered without a written text, but I have not entirely eliminated the conversational tone. I give special thanks to Gilbert Harman and Robert Stalnaker for showing me that one of my criticisms of David Lewis in the original version was too strong.

My paper 'Frege's Theory of Sense and Reference: Some Exegetical Notes' (chapter 9) was unpublished and unknown to the audience when I gave the present talk—thus my presentation included much overlapping material, since it was highly relevant to the topic. In the current version I have cut down on the overlap but certainly not eliminated it. There are some significant considerations raising problems for Frege that should have been in Kripke (2008) (included here as chapter 9), but were not known to me when I wrote its final version; nor were they known when I gave the original presentation of this talk. See pp. 303–04.

[1] I was invited by the Logos Group to give three lectures at the University of Barcelona, Spain, in December 2005. Joseph Macià suggested Kaplan's papers as a possible topic for one of the lectures. For further remarks on the background of this topic in the philosophy of language, especially due to the influence of Castañeda, see note 12 below.

[2] From now on I will call this manuscript 'Meaning as Use'. The version that I have is subtitled 'Brief Version—Draft #1'. Of course, the slogan 'meaning is use' is derived from Wittgenstein, and certainly Kaplan's manuscript to some extent is influenced by Wittgenstein's later work and even some of his most famous examples, but the manuscript should probably not be regarded (nor was it so regarded by its author) as adopting a 'Wittgensteinian' approach.

[3] In particular, I share (and have always shared) his broad conception, as I understand it, of what should be included in semantics (and not relegated to pragmatics). Anything that a language teacher should regard as part of the teaching of the meanings of a particular language, as opposed to customs and sociological facts about speakers of the language at a particular time, should be included in semantics. I have never understood why some people wish to restrict semantics so as to include only what is clearly to be given by truth-conditions, excluding, among other things, the study of indexical expressions. One may think that the issue is purely terminological, but I have a strong feeling that

approach that I would also applaud in general terms, but that I would warn may lead one astray in its particular application to the main theme of this talk. One should not, he argues, think of the task of the linguist or the semanticist—as, for example, Quine does in some of his writings—as analogous to that of translating utterances into one's own language. That presupposes the semantics of one's own language and doesn't get us very far. Rather, the linguist or the semanticist gives a description 'from above' of the uses in the community.

Kaplan refers to what some philosophers have called 'scientific language',[4] and assumes that the description 'from above' is formulated in such a language. The

---

this is not entirely so, that the opposite conception will lead one astray. For example, Ludlow and Segal (2004) think that on Gricean principles 'but' and 'and' 'literally mean the same thing' (424), though they differ in conventional implicature. Similarly, they think that 'a' and 'the' are synonyms in English (424), even though they state how they are used differently in English (in this view, they have surprised many philosophers who might have followed them thus far). Following Kaplan, as I understand him, '*tu*' and '*vous*' (as the polite second person singular) are not synonymous in French. In contrast, changes in French attitudes as to when it is appropriate to use '*tu*' are matters of the changing sociology of the French, not of changes in the language. (Perhaps one can imagine cases where the distinction is not sharp.) Distinctions of Gricean 'conversational implicature', as in my own suggested treatment in Kripke (1977) of the referential-attributive distinction for definites, are not distinctions in the language. (At the end of Kripke 1977, I suggested that the same strategy might apply to indefinites, as was carried out by Ludlow and Neale 1991.) Ludlow and Segal (2004) should not have considered their own strategy to be a case of the same one that was used in the two papers just mentioned. Note that the issue has nothing to do with whether Ludlow and Segal are correct in their views about 'a' and 'the'. However, they are not entitled to say that, on their view 'a' and 'the' 'are two expressions with different spellings, but the same meanings—synonyms, rather like "gray" and "grizzled" or "grisly" and "gruesome"' (424). In contrast, 'and' and 'but', on my view, though not theirs, are not differently spelled expressions with the same meanings.

I hope I understand Kaplan correctly when I express agreement with him about this. He has a great deal of illuminating material, in particular, about a novel conception of logical validity that accords with this conception of semantics. His remarks about 'oops' and 'goodbye', and about pejoratives, looked at in terms of a use theory of meaning, are also very illuminating.

[4] Kaplan mentions Quine as an originator of the conception that scientific language should not contain indexicals, tense, and the like, even though Kaplan himself disagrees with the view (which he states Strawson got from Quine) that such devices are not susceptible to logical study. I believe that in conversation he also mentioned Russell in connection with this conception of 'scientific language'. Even though he also (see below) clearly would recognize that this conception has little to do with what is allowed in actual scientific papers, it nevertheless influences his idea of how to describe a language 'from above'.

Quine is a philosopher who might be described as 'pro-scientific' (by an admirer of the orientation), or 'scientistic' (by a detractor). On the other hand, the later Wittgenstein was probably 'anti-scientistic'. However, he has a similar conception of 'scientific language'. In *Philosophical Investigations* he writes: '"I" is not the name of a person, nor "here" of a place, and "this" is not a name. But they are connected with names. Names are explained by means of them. It is also true that physics is characterized by the fact that it does not use these words' (Wittgenstein 1953: §410) (I have altered the translation of the last sentence, which is weaker and less puzzling in the printed version: '. . . it is characteristic of physics not to use these words'.) What does he mean here? Certainly, as I have said, not that such indexical terminology never appears in physics papers. It might be claimed that such terminology never appears in physical laws, but once it is granted that many terms are explained by them, this strikes me as dubious. Moreover, physics may say that such-and-such a physical quantity has a certain value now, but it is decreasing. Even more puzzling to me (if my translation is right) is the claim that this restriction (the absence of indexicals and demonstratives) tells us what physics is.

so-called scientific language itself would contain neither indexicals nor tense, but be generally stated as applicable to arbitrary speakers, places, times, and the like; if modality is involved, to arbitrary possible worlds as well. Moreover, all this must be done coolly. For example, as Kaplan says, one must be able to describe words expressing anger without getting angry at the same time. This is relevant to what others have written on historiography. We have at one extreme the view of, for example, C. G. Hempel (1942), which takes historical writing to be little different in principle from writing in physics, involving general laws, confirmations, refutations, and so on. The other extreme says that history employs a particular method of *Verstehen*. I think the second view certainly has something to it: the historian is trying to put himself in the position of his subjects to see what they themselves might have thought. Some have given a strong formulation: if you write about any historical character, you should literally try to *become* that character.[5] Whatever one might say about history, surely the 'coolness' requirement as Kaplan states it is correct for the description of a language 'from above'.[6]

What is description 'from above'? (I perhaps add something here to Kaplan's formulation.) The description, first and foremost, is a description of how the language is used, but it also has an instructional aspect. If language can be described completely and correctly 'from above', in a neutral indexical-free language, the description (of, say, English) should be usable as an *instruction* manual, a set of imperatives for a foreigner wishing to learn English. The instructions themselves should, if given for this purpose, be stated in the foreign language. Thus they will tell the foreigner that 'goodbye' is conventionally used in English when taking leave. Even when only truth-conditional semantics is in question (or truth-conditions with respect to indices—such as speaker, time, possible world described, and the like), the description from above should be usable not just as a description but also as an instruction manual for a language learner.

Now, in 'Meaning as Use' (in the section 'Meaning vs. Uses'), Kaplan writes:

Consider the indexical 'I'. What does it mean? An initial answer might be that it is the first person pronoun. But this is a kind of functional description. What does the first person pronoun *mean*?

As I said, I was invited to speak on Kaplan, and under such circumstances one naturally emphasizes those points where one disagrees. (Having been invited to

---

[5] When I was in college, I wrote a paper on this topic called 'History and Idealism: The Theory of R. G. Collingwood', which I never published, though an expert in the field did recommend that I do so. In the paper, I remarked that if you write about Hitler, you should not try to become Hitler; this would be a very dangerous idea. Some of you have probably heard of the writer David Irving—he originally started with very respectable publishers, and he is at any rate *something* of an embodiment of this approach (see, e.g., Irving 1977, where he explicitly says that he will attempt to describe the war through Hitler's eyes). Unfortunately, from this book onward he became increasingly successful at fulfilling my youthful fear that it was a dangerous idea.

[6] However, even in that case there is something to be said for the method of *Verstehen*. One might have to experience anger to understand descriptions of words expressing anger.

give a paper on Kaplan's material, my audience would not have been so enthusiastic if I could only remark, 'Yes, I agree, and this says it all'.) So here I will comment on one point on which I have some agreement but on which I ultimately diverge significantly from Kaplan—namely, his views on the proper treatment of the first person pronoun. And I will talk about some other authors as well.

Kaplan gives the following example to show that in the case of 'I' a proper semantical treatment is not provided by a definition but rather by an account of how the term is used:

> For example, my *Webster's Third* provides, 'the one who is speaking or writing' and they quote the Psalm 'I shall not want' in order to drive the point home. (This caused me to imagine sitting in the back of the auditorium at a lottery award ceremony, and whispering to the psalmist, 'which of the people here won the ten million dollars?', and he whispers back 'the one who is speaking' or, equivalently, according to *Webster's Third*, 'I did; I shall not want'.) (Ibid.)

Two or three comments here. I, of course, am in agreement[7] with the semantical point Kaplan is trying to make about how to explain the word 'I'. But does '*the psalmist*' say 'I shall not want'? Many educated Americans appear to think that the psalmist (like other biblical authors) wrote, or completed his work, in 1611.[8] In fact, 'the psalmist' who 'wrote' the 23rd Psalm must have consulted the published standard Hebrew *Urtext*. It does not contain a Hebrew equivalent of the separate word 'I' at all: as in many languages, 'I' is used only for emphasis and is, in most cases, simply a suffix or prefix to the verb.[9])

Now, in some respects this observation may even support Kaplan, because his point is that you should not look for the meaning of 'I'. Kaplan's basic thought is that the search, as in Frege, for what the word 'I' means, or the *sense* of 'I', is obviously a mistake. The correct semantical account of 'I' is wholly given by the 'scientific language' in which its truth-conditions are neutrally expressed from above: when a speaker S says 'I...' what he says is true (or true of the possible world he is thinking of at the time, if that is relevant) if and only if S... This is a purely general statement, and it wholly determines the semantics of 'I'.[10] The point (that a definition of 'I' as a term denoting the speaker is not really in

---

[7] However, Kaplan is not completely right. If I were writing a paper I could say 'the present writer thinks there is a mistake'. 'The present writer' may or may not be synonymous with 'I', but it is standard in some academic writing to use it to replace 'I', perhaps to be a little more formal or impersonal. 'The present speaker' in the same sense is rarer, certainly not a stock phrase like 'the present writer', but maybe on some occasions it can be used in that way.

Or suppose someone has written, 'all Americans support such-and-such'. One could object, 'not *this* American', meaning *not me*. One could no doubt imagine many other such cases.

[8] I believe, if my memory is correct, that I read in the *New York Times* something like this: 'The Bible says... [or 'the Old Testament says'], as opposed to the more recent Bible versions.' My father heard a Christian fundamentalist radio preacher say 'until, or rather 'til, as scripture says,...'

[9] In the perfect and imperfect respectively (in Biblical Hebrew).

[10] This point is independent of Kaplan's emphasis on meaning as use, as in the later Wittgenstein. It would be compatible with a truth-conditional (or truth-conditional with

question) can only be strengthened when we consider the existence of languages in which the first person is expressed exclusively by a prefix or suffix (or where this is usual and 'I' or its equivalent occurs only in cases of special emphasis).[11]

Kaplan notes that *Webster's* itself realizes that its attempt to define 'I' 'won't do' and that it goes on to say 'used... by one speaking or writing to refer to himself.' He comments 'Now here they have finally given us what we need to know, how the expression is *used*'.

Consider Kaplan's distinction between character and content. The character gives a general rule for the use of 'I', and the content will depend on one's view of content. If one takes the simple propositional view, it will be about the speaker; or, as Kaplan states, it doesn't have to be a speaker, it could just as well be a writer, or a thinker, thinking to herself. We will return to this.

Kaplan's treatment of the first person in 'Demonstratives' (1989) is rather strongly influenced by Perry's criticisms of Frege (Perry 1977) on first person statements (and other demonstratives).[12] I myself have dealt with Frege's views on these issues, including the problems Perry raises for Frege, and their relation to Frege's much-discussed views on indirect quotation and his less-discussed views on direct quotation (see chapter 9). But here I not only want to talk about what is *true according to Frege* but also about what is *true according to the truth*, or, that is—to use a predicate that I should like to think is coextensive—true according to *me*.

In conversation, Kaplan has acknowledged that 'scientific language', in the sense that he has used the term, is obviously not satisfied by the language of scientists in a lab, who use tenses and indexicals all the time. It is not satisfied in

---

respect to various indices, such as speaker, time, possible world described, etc.) conception of semantics.

At the end of Anscombe (1975), discussed below at some length, she attributes to J. Altham the remark that such a rule about 'I', viewed truth-conditionally, has a problem of sufficiency: 'How is one to extract the *predicate* for purposes of this rule in "I think John loves me"? The rule needs supplementation: where "I" or "me" occurs within an oblique context, the predicate is to be specified by replacing "I" or "me" by the indirect reflexive pronoun' (65). The grammatical notion 'indirect reflexive' is explicated in Anscombe's paper.

In Kaplan (1989:505) the two main rules are that '"I" refers to the speaker or writer' and that 'I' directly refers. Perhaps Kaplan thinks that a direct reference account of 'I' and 'me' gives an adequate treatment of examples such as Altham's. I am sympathetic to such a viewpoint myself. It would have been good if this had been spelled out.

[11] I spoke with Kaplan about this, and he said he was familiar with the example of Latin.

[12] One should mention, whenever one talks of the first person as a special subject in contemporary philosophy, the papers of Hector Neri Castañeda (1966, 1968, and others), who more than anyone else made this a special topic for the philosophy of language (both first person sentences and their relation to the indirect discourse locution exemplified by 'Betty believes that she herself...'). See also Geach (1957a) and Prior (1967), cited by Lewis (1983:139). I think also of Wittgenstein (1953), as mentioned below.

There is a mutual influence between Kaplan and Perry. Perry himself mentions an earlier version of Kaplan (1989) in Perry (1977).

Of course, contemporary philosophy of mind, as well as philosophy of language, has emphasized the difference between first and third person points of view, and this is also related.

scientific papers either. No scientific journal would reject a paper for failing to use exclusively 'scientific language', especially tense. I think it is relatively hard to give genuine examples of tenseless sentences about particular ordinary objects (though not about mathematical objects or the like) in natural language. Some examples that I have seen in the literature are not really tenseless.[13] Scientific language in the sense in question is a philosophers' invention, spoken by no one. In spite of Kaplan's recognition of these facts, this conception of what can be stated in a 'scientific language' is important to his own account.

Now, Kaplan calls some statements Frege makes about the first person 'tortured' (1989:501), though later (533) he says that reinterpreted in the light of his own theory, Frege could be thought of as talking about the character of 'I', and that under such an interpretation this passage (which supposedly 'has provoked few endorsements and much skepticism') could be defended as essentially correct. Kaplan goes on to say how 'a sloppy thinker' might misinterpret the situation. Given his earlier characterization of the passage, and taking into consideration the influence of Perry (1977), I think that Kaplan really thinks that the sloppy thinker is Frege himself.[14]

Frege writes:

Now everyone is presented to himself in a special and primitive way, in which he is presented to no one else. So, when Dr Lauben has the thought that he was wounded, he will probably be basing it on this primitive way in which he is presented to himself. And only Dr Lauben himself can grasp thoughts specified in this way. But now he may want to communicate with others. He cannot communicate a thought he alone can grasp. Therefore, if he now says 'I was wounded', he must use 'I' in a sense which can be grasped

---

[13] For example, Sider's impressive book (2001) gives as examples 'World War I occurred after the American Civil War' and 'There existed dinosaurs before the appearance of this book'. Neither of these sentences can change their truth values if uttered at different times, but to me it is obvious that both are past tense; I don't know exactly what someone would have in mind imagining them uttered before World War I or before the appearance of 'this book'.

Another example Sider gives, 'It is raining on 28 June 2000', is dubious English, unless uttered on 28 June 2000, in which case 'It is raining today, 28 June 2000' is much better. After 28 June 2000 one must say 'It was raining on 28 June 2000', and before that date 'will be'. (Obviously, a particular place in which the raining occurs is presupposed.) Someone might of course be sure of the rain on the date in question, but not be sure of the date now, or not wish to commit herself. But in that case she should say, 'It either was, is, or will be raining on June 28 2000'. This is not a tenseless statement, but amounts to a disjunction of tensed statements (or, alternatively, applies a disjunction of tensed predicates). Probably something amounting to this disjunction is what Sider has in mind as the interpretation for his 'tenseless' statement, but his attempt at expressing it in English seems defective. His example was supposed to contrast with 'It is *now* raining,' which he gives earlier as an example of a tensed statement but which does not appear to be a proper English sentence. While genuine examples of such tenseless statements may exist in English, they do not occur nearly as much as has been suggested.

In spite of these remarks, I am *not* suggesting that we have no conception of a language giving the entire history of the world tenselessly. I think that we can imagine such a language. However, most of it will be a philosophical invention. It is an intelligible language but does not overlap with natural language to any significant degree.

[14] See chapter 9 (page 284).

by others, perhaps in the sense of 'he who is speaking to you at this moment'; by doing this he makes the conditions accompanying his utterance serve towards the expression of a thought. (1918–19:333, note omitted)[15]

Not only has the passage been discussed critically by Perry and by Kaplan (under Perry's influence), it has also been defended against Perry's criticisms in Evans (1981). What Frege is saying about the way everyone is presented to himself seems to me not to be at all unfamiliar. It is the familiar view, going back at least to Descartes, that I am aware of myself in a special first person way. However, Perry, and following him, Kaplan, both argue that for his view of the first person to go through, 'what is needed is a primitive aspect of me, which is not simply one that only I am aware of myself as having, but that I alone have' (Perry 1977:490).

Why does Perry think that this is needed? Well, the special first person Cartesian sense would have to be something like *the subject*, or *the thinker*. But who is that? Is there only one thinker, only one subject? If one reformulates it as *the subject for me, the subject that I am aware of, by being aware of my own thinking*, the formulation obviously runs into a circle. How can one avoid the circle? Only by there being a special quality, a primitive aspect of me, that I alone have. This is Perry's argument for his conclusion, and Kaplan follows him.

Following Perry, Kaplan makes two objections to Frege. First, he says:

I sincerely doubt that there is, for each of us on each occasion of the use of 'I', a particular, primitive, and incommunicable Fregean self-concept which we tacitly express to ourselves. (1989:534)

So far, Kaplan might just seem to be doubting the neo-Cartesian doctrine of a particular first person perspective (except to the extent that it is given by his theory of the 'character' of 'I'). However, he immediately goes on to assume that the theory must involve Perry's stronger conclusion that the self-concept in question would have to characterize its subject uniquely in a neutral language, and objects:

[E]ven if Castor were sufficiently narcissistic to associate such self-concepts[16] with his every use of 'I', his twin, Pollux, whose mental life is qualitatively identical with Castor's, would associate the *same* self-concept with *his* every (matching) use of 'I'. (Kaplan 1989:534; italics in the original)

One of Kaplan's basic points in 'Demonstratives' is the distinction between demonstratives and indexicals. Demonstratives (such as 'this') require some gesture or something else (such as pointing) to determine their reference, whereas

---

[15] All references to 'Der Gedanke' (Frege 1918–19) are to the Geach and Stoothoff translation, titled 'Thoughts', as reprinted in Beaney (1997) with the title 'Thought'. Note that the translation of the passage that Kaplan himself uses (1989:533) is the earlier Quinton and Quinton translation. As far as I can see, the differences do not affect the discussion.

[16] Kaplan plainly means to write 'such a self-concept'.

indexicals (such as 'I' and 'now') require only a general linguistic rule to determine their reference.[17] For example, 'I', when used by a given speaker, always refers to the speaker (or thinker, or writer, etc.); 'now', when said at a given time, refers to that time; and so on.[18]

Kaplan accuses 'the sloppy thinker' (Frege in the naïve interpretation) of holding a 'demonstrative theory of indexicals'. It is as if one needed something other than the semantical rule for 'I', a subject somehow pointing to himself in a special inner way, to determine the reference of 'I', and similarly for 'now' and 'here' (Kaplan 1989:534–35). Descartes, and many who have followed him, might be accused of this mistake, except that it is hard to see that Descartes's point was particularly semantical.[19]

Returning to the earlier view that Frege requires some unique qualitative description of the subject that the subject alone is uniquely aware of and that, in fact, uniquely characterizes 'the subject', it may be tempting to conclude that there can be only one subject in existence. Indeed, there may be some philosophers who have drawn such a conclusion, a special form of solipsism about minds, but I am not sure who.[20, 21]

---

[17] Perry later called them 'automatic indexicals' (1997). The speaker need not indicate specific demonstrative intentions on the occasion of utterance.

[18] Kaplan (1989:491) attributes to Michael Bennett the point that 'here' is usually an indexical, but sometimes is a demonstrative, as when one says 'she lives here' and points to a location on a map, and so on. Similarly, in a footnote on the same page, Kaplan concedes that the rule given for 'now' is too simple. If someone leaves a message on the answering machine 'I am not at home now', 'now' refers to the time when the message was heard, not the time when it was recorded. The opposite can be true: 'I am in Italy now but will be in Belgium by the time you get this letter' makes good sense. (My own example; I also changed the answering machine example a bit.)
As far as I can see, no such problems arise for 'I', as, indeed, in the first clause of this very sentence.

[19] Perry does in fact concede that some philosophers 'have come to hold somewhat similar views about the self, beliefs about oneself, and "I"' without being motivated by any semantical problems (1977:489). He thinks it is possible that Frege was simply writing under the influence of these views, but he thinks it more likely that it was the pressures of an attempt to find a theory of demonstratives compatible with his overall semantical framework that is responsible for Frege's views.

[20] In the talk I suggested, though I wasn't sure, that perhaps the early Wittgenstein (1961) could be an example. Since then it has been suggested that L. E. J. Brouwer might be an example; once again this is uncertain (see, e.g., Brouwer 1948).

[21] Let me here make the following digression concerning 'other minds'. People argue that there *have* to be other minds: after all, everyone behaves similarly to me and since I have a mind they must, too. But some other people say one shouldn't generalize from only one case. A reply to this objection might perhaps be that minds form a natural kind, so that an examination of one instance is sufficient to determine the basic features of the entire natural kind. But what's really the trouble here is this: there's lots of evidence that we are *not* members of the same kind, because various philosophers—or so-called philosophers—of mind state theories that would seem to me to imply that they *themselves* have no inner states (or if they do use expressions that purport to say that they have inner states, they give analyses which I know perfectly well are *not* compatible with genuine inner states). So, what explanation of their behavior can there be? Otherwise, they seem to satisfy criteria of sincerity, honesty, and intelligence (if one assumes that they have minds). So, they are obviously just what they themselves claim to be, that is, very cleverly programmed robots similar to a genuine human subject like *me*. In philosophy departments, at least, there seem to be many more of them than there are genuine human subjects. So, when I look at a random person who is not even a

So what's wrong with the argument that *either* each subject must be psychologically unique or, otherwise, any definite description of the subject must itself use an egocentric term, and thus run into a circle? Well, again, the people who argue this way are thinking of a language spoken by no one, the so-called scientific language. Since Dr. Lauben is the one speaking the language, by 'the subject' he of course means himself. If Rudolph Lingens[22] speaks of 'the subject', he means himself. There is no difficulty for Frege (nor indeed for Descartes), once we rid ourselves of the idea of a 'scientific language' spoken by no one, in supposing that the reference is determined in this way. Nor do we have to worry about the supposed problem of Castor and Pollux. None of these people speaks an impersonal 'scientific language' where the problem would arise. So each of them could determine the referent in the Cartesian–Fregean way, by his own acquaintance with himself.

But perhaps this is not the whole answer. Aren't all these people speaking German, a language in which 'I' (actually '*ich*') should mean the same thing for *anyone*? And isn't Kaplan right to say that the whole use of the word 'I' can be captured in a neutral way by saying that a sentence containing 'I' expresses a truth if and only if the rest is actually true of the subject—the thinker, or the speaker? Or if one doesn't wish to restrict oneself to truth-conditional utterances, even with respect to indices,[23] at least that 'I' in any sentence refers to the speaker (writer, thinker)? So, doesn't Kaplan's characterization (that is, the description of the 'character' in his technical sense) suffice for everything? And doesn't it give the 'content' in each particular case, which indeed is different depending on whom is being referred to by 'I'?

At first this may seem quite conclusive. Doesn't Kaplan's rule give a complete description of the matter? What else could be needed? Well, recall my remarks that the 'description from above' ought to be usable as an instruction manual for someone wishing to learn the language. Though Kaplan's explanation is all very well for some sort of descriptive anthropologist who may in fact have the concept of 'I', it would be very difficult to get it across to Frege (or anyone else who is presumed to lack this concept). So, for example, let Kaplan say to Frege or to anyone else (but if it is Frege, one should use German): 'If any person *S* speaking German attributes a property using the word "*ich*," then what *S* says or thinks is

---

philosopher, the chances seem much greater that that person is one of these cleverly programmed robots, since from the only sample I have I can be sure of only one genuine human subject (with a mind). So, the robots are right in saying that most of the humanlike people are robots—and I must be a very rare case with genuine inner states!

[22] In Frege's paper 'Der Gedanke', some characters with various interrelations are discussed. In addition to Dr. Gustav Lauben, one person discussed is Rudolph Lingens. Frege considers alternative cases in which Lingens knows Dr. Lauben personally or has only heard of him.

[23] Such philosophers as Donald Davidson and David Lewis have attempted to reduce the semantics of non-indicative utterances (or sentences) to cases where truth-conditional semantics do apply. In stark contrast to this picture, see Wittgenstein (1953: §23). In his later paper 'Meaning as Use', Kaplan intends no particular reduction.

true if and only if *S* has that property.' But how can Frege use the word '*ich*' on the basis of these instructions? Should he think, '*Hmm*, so how am *I* going to use the word "*ich*" on the basis of this general statement? Well, any German should attribute, say, being in pain or being a logician to *himself* if and only if the German is in pain or is a logician, as Kaplan says. So *I* should do this.' Alternatively, Frege might remark, 'So Frege, or Dr. Gustav Lauben, should attribute a property to Frege, or respectively to Dr. Lauben, using "*ich*" if and only if Frege (or Dr. Lauben) has the property. But *I* am Frege, so I suppose that I should use the word "*ich*" if and only if Frege has the property.' Either formulation would presuppose that Frege already has the concept of *himself*, the concept he expresses using '*ich*,' so here we really are going in a circle.

The point is that each one of us speaks a language that he himself has learned. Each one of us can fix the reference of the word 'I' by means of acquaintance with oneself, self-acquaintance. There is no requirement that this type of acquaintance is given to us by a qualitative description expressible in a 'scientific language' spoken by no one. This is so even if the language each of us uses is a common one—English, German, and so on. No one can grasp the rule for 'I' stated in the common language except by means of one's own self-acquaintance. Otherwise, there would be no way of learning how that rule tells us to refer. This is what Frege means when he says that Dr. Lauben uses the word 'I', thinking to himself, 'he will probably be basing it on this primitive way in which he is presented to himself' (Frege 1918–19:333). Frege also says, a bit before that, 'The same utterance containing the word "I" in the mouths of different men will express different thoughts of which some may be true, others false' (332). To put this matter in Kaplanian terms, the utterance[24] has the same character in the mouths of all speakers of the language but has different contents in the mouths of different speakers. I have explained in some detail in my paper on Frege how to put the matter in Frege's own terms (chapter 9, pages 284ff). Put either way, this is possible because of one's own self-awareness when one is speaking.

However, Frege's discussion, as quoted above (298–99), of how Dr. Lauben communicates to others using 'I' (or '*ich*') does confuse the issue. Frege says that when he wishes to communicate, he can hardly use 'I' in a sense he alone can grasp. But if that is so, it is easy to see how someone would respond that this alleged special and incommunicable sense of 'I' must be a chimera. Why should the primary sense of 'I' be something that one never uses in interpersonal communication? One might after all doubt that ordinary language is used in thought at all. Surely, its primary purpose is for communication.

Matters become even more problematic when Frege discusses what Dr. Lauben means by 'I' when he wishes to communicate with others. He conjectures that it is in the sense of 'he who is speaking to you at this moment'

---

[24] Notice that by 'utterance' Frege here means a type, not a token. He is not following current technical philosophical terminology.

(Frege 1918–19:333). This can be understood by the hearer in a way that the primary sense of 'I' cannot. Kaplan, as I have already quoted him, wittily ridicules those (such as the writers of the definition in *Webster's Third*) who wish to analyze the ordinary use of 'I' in such a way. Moreover, as I wrote in chapter 9 (pp. 288–98), the proffered definition of 'I' may not work. For example, perhaps the person I am addressing is at the same time being addressed by someone else. Then the description will not uniquely determine its object. In the same chapter I gave other objections of a similar kind. I add some objections that I had not thought of in the earlier paper (nor in the original version of this talk).

Suppose that the definition does correctly determine its object, and we don't entertain Kaplan's worries about its artificiality. There is yet another problem. What, after all, is the Fregean sense of 'you' in the proffered definition? Shouldn't it be 'the person I am addressing at the present moment'? But then the proffered sense of 'I' plainly goes in a circle.

Moreover, Dr. Lauben may think to himself, 'Leo Peter realizes that I am wounded', or, alternatively, 'Is Leo Peter aware that I am wounded?'[25] Since Dr. Lauben is thinking to himself, surely (following Frege) he uses 'I' in the special sense that only he can understand. But how can he wonder whether Leo Peter has a thought that Peter cannot understand? Something is going wrong here.[26]

Surely, one must give an analysis of first person sentences where 'I' is univocal, whether used in talking to oneself (discouraged in our society, anyway), or in

---

[25] Remember that, for Frege, asking a question is a paradigmatic way of entertaining a thought without asserting it.

[26] See also my discussion soon below of Frege's remarks on 'yesterday' and 'today', and my more elaborate discussion in chapter 9 (pages 277ff), and especially my remarks in note 74 on the objection of Gunnar Björnsson, and related objections by John Perry, concerning indirect discourse. Björnsson phrased his objection in terms of tense, but it could just as well have been phrased in terms of persons, as indeed has been emphasized by Castañeda (and others, see below). (Perry does mention the interpersonal case.)

The present problem is a sort of converse form of the same problem. Someone can use 'I' in an indirect discourse attribution to someone else's thought about herself, even though the other person would not use 'I' or an equivalent expression, nor could she understand the expression as used by the subject in question—in this case Dr. Lauben. The paragraph following in the present paper is only a partial answer to the problem. Applying the principles of that paragraph to the present version, one must recognize that it is legitimate for the subject (say, Dr. Lauben) to attribute a thought using 'I' to someone else (say, Leo Peter), provided that the other person has the appropriate belief *about the subject*.

However, there is a reason specific to Frege that makes me say that for him these principles give only a partial answer to the problem. Frege's theories, with or without the 'I' problem form of them, are in danger of running into a problem related to my own problem about exportation (chapter 11, this volume). The problem is with Frege's apparent view that it is sufficient for a name (or pronoun) to designate a given person (and for its user to have a thought about that person) that it be defined for its user by a definite description designating the person (similarly for entities that are not persons). Frege (1892:153) appears to express this view in his well-known footnote on Aristotle and in his later discussion of the way various people may think of Dr Lauben (1918–19). Something must be done to fix the matter up, and if this can be done, the objection raised here could also be addressed.

diary entries (not so discouraged), or in communicating with others. If it is the sense determined by its subject's first person acquaintance with herself, how can it be used to communicate to someone else? Here is one possibility. The hearer is aware that each person, including the hearer herself, uses 'I' to refer to herself by direct self-acquaintance. Hence, knowing what this is in one's own case and taking it to be the same way for others, one understands what the first person statement is, even though it has a sense that is, strictly speaking, incommunicable to the hearer.[27]

Similarly, according to my own understanding of Frege, at no later time can I have the thought I expressed with 'now', and at no later date can I have the thought that I express with 'today'. Nevertheless, I can understand a piece of writing written in the past using 'now' or 'today', similarly to the way I can understand someone else's utterance of 'I'.[28] Therefore, on my view, Frege was wrong on his own theory to say that one could express the same thought using 'yesterday' as one previously expressed using 'today'. Ironically, Kaplan, who is critical of Frege's discussion of 'I', commends his remarks on 'yesterday' and 'today'. My own view is that, from a Fregean standpoint, Frege's remarks on 'yesterday' and 'today' cannot be defended, while his remarks on the first person and the present are correct from a Fregean standpoint (with the exception of his discussion of the ambiguity of 'I', which I have criticized above).

In fact, however, when I discussed these issues with Kaplan, he said that he had come to accept my point that someone must have a concept of the self to follow the general direction for the use of 'I', and attributes his stronger original statements to 'irrational exuberance'. And probably Kaplan did not really

---

[27] The reader should be warned that I have not given a full presentation of my exegesis of Frege's view, in particular, of the fact that the verbal expression does not express a complete thought. For a more complete account, see my discussion in chapter 9. An important conclusion from the Fregean point of view not mentioned in the present discussion is that 'I', 'now', 'today', and the like have to be viewed as unsaturated expressions according to Frege, strictly speaking standing for functions. This has been omitted, and perhaps even distorted, in the present version, where one would think, as Kaplan says, of 'I' as a singular term denoting its user. The reason is, as I said, that I am only marginally concerned with Frege and Fregean exegesis in this sense in the present paper.

As I mentioned in chapter 9, the later Wittgenstein, and those following him, might object to any idea that one understands 'I' in the mouth of someone else by analogy to one's own case, but I am scouting this issue here (actually, in the earlier paper I had the excuse that Frege was unlikely to have been worried about such an objection; here I don't have it).

[28] Perry (1977:491) in fact objects that Frege would have to be committed by analogy to what he says about 'I' to the view that a thought containing 'now' is inexpressible at any later time. I think that this is indeed the correct consequence of Frege's theory, and say so in chapter 9. However, in my more complete Fregean exegesis, I take the verbally expressed part (in English) to be the same at all times. However, this does not express a complete thought. What does so in the case of 'now' is the verbally expressed part together with the supplementation whose sense is given by autonomous reference and acquaintance with time of utterance. It is this that is unrepeatable, since the acquaintance is preserved at no later time. See chapter 9 for the details.

mean, when he commended Frege for his treatment of 'yesterday' and 'today', that this treatment is correct on a Fregean approach.[29]

II

Enough about Frege—what about according to me? Well, according to me, the first person use of 'I' of course does *not* have a Fregean sense, at least if this means that it has a definition. But it might be a paradigmatic case, one that I did not mention in *Naming and Necessity* (1980), of fixing a reference by means of a description: it is a rule of the common language that each of us fixes the reference of 'I' by the description 'the subject'. However, since each of us speaks a natural language, and not an imaginary 'scientific language' spoken by no one, for each of us the referent can be different. This is the moral that I wish to stress.

A long time ago, in conversation, Harry Frankfurt suggested to me that the Cartesian cogito might be an example of the contingent a priori.[30] At the time I thought that whatever may be said about this case, it has a very different flavor from the examples in *Naming and Necessity*. It is certainly contingent because I (or whichever subject is involved in the relevant cogito) might never have been born, and it is a priori at least in the sense of not requiring any specific experience for its verification. But it now seems to me that it does indeed have some of the flavor of my own examples, and perhaps lacks some of their more problematic features. For it follows from the way I fix the reference, as the subject of my own thought, that I must exist. (I will discuss the famous Humean objection to this conclusion later, but here I am assuming that Descartes is right.) In both the cases of the meter stick ('stick S') and Neptune, I must grant that the object might not exist. In the meter stick case, the stick I think I am looking at might be illusory (I was tacitly assuming in *Naming and Necessity* that the reference is being fixed

---

[29] See chapter 9 (page 284, note 81). Kaplan himself mentions one of the objections to the 'yesterday' and 'today' case from a Fregean point of view, and as I said, probably thinks of them as directly referential demonstratives, yielding a single 'content' (in Kaplan's terminology). See also my own distinction between fixing a reference and giving a meaning, as spelled out immediately below. In fairness to Kaplan, I should add that his original theory in Kaplan (1989) was not simply that 'I' is a term that, when used by any speaker, directly refers to that speaker, but also that it is directly referential.

I might mention that Buber's *Ich und Du* (1923) (translated as *I and Thou*, or *I and You*) may be thought of, as among other things, giving an alternative account of the semantics of 'you' to the one I have, in my discussion above, claimed that Frege must give. I am familiar with this work only in part.

[30] I don't remember when I had this conversation with Frankfurt. I am now uncertain about the history of my own thoughts on this matter. Such examples of the contingent a priori have been widely accepted even by those who doubt my own examples of Neptune and the meter stick. Kaplan's example 'I am here now', with 'I exist' as an obvious corollary, is well known as an example of the contingent *a priori* (see Kaplan 1989, pp. 508-509). Even 'I exist' (or strictly speaking, its negation) is explicitly mentioned by Kaplan on p. 495. Plantinga also suggests that 'I exist' is contingent *a priori* (see Plantinga 1974, p. 8).

by someone who has the stick in front of her), and in the Neptune case the astronomical deduction might have been wrong, with no such planet existing, as turned out to be the case with Vulcan. Thus, if I wish to express a priori truths, I must say 'if there is a stick before me as I see it, then . . . ' (In the Neptune case I must say 'if some planet causes the perturbations in Uranus in the appropriate way, then . . .).[31] The whole point of the cogito is that no such existence problem arises, epistemically speaking. Yet another difference with the meter stick and Neptune cases is this: in both cases there is a closely related statement that is necessary and trivial given the way the reference is fixed, such as 'the planet, if any, that causes this perturbations, does cause them', and 'stick S, if there is such a stick, has as its length the length of stick S'. Thus someone might argue (but see my accompanying note here) that these examples of the contingent a priori are really cases where one has no information beyond that provided by the related and trivially analytic necessary truth.[32] The cogito does not seem to be involved in this problem.

I remember when I was very young, about twelve or thirteen, reading Descartes and finding the cogito very convincing. Some time later, reading Hume, I found this:

There are some philosophers, who imagine we are every moment intimately conscious of what we call our SELF; that we feel its existence and its continuance in existence; and are certain, beyond the evidence of a demonstration, both of its perfect identity and simplicity. The strongest sensation, the most violent passion, say they, instead of distracting us from this view, only fix it the more intensely, and make us consider their influence on *self* either by their pain or pleasure. To attempt a farther proof of this were to weaken its evidence; since no proof can be deriv'd from any fact, of which we are so intimately conscious; nor is there any thing, of which we can be certain, if we doubt of this.

Unluckily all these positive assertions are contrary to that very experience, which is pleaded for them, nor have we any idea of *self*, after the manner it is here explain'd. . . .

For my part, when I enter most intimately into what I call *myself*, I always stumble on some particular impression or other, of heat or cold, light or shade, love or hatred, pain or pleasure. I never can catch *myself* at any time without a perception. . . . If any one, upon serious and unprejudic'd reflexion, thinks he has a different notion of *himself*, I must confess I can reason no longer with him.[33] All I can allow him is, that he may be in the right as well as I, and that we are essentially different in this particular. He may, perhaps,

---

[31] I discuss these cases from *Naming and Necessity* in an unpublished manuscript 'Rigid Designation and the Contingent *A Priori*: The Meter Stick Revisited' (Kripke 1986). For the examples in question see Kripke (1980:54–57; 79, note 33; 96, note 42).

[32] See my note on this matter in Kripke (1980:63, note 26). I now have more to say about the issue and think that some such stipulations may significantly affect the way one thinks about the world, in particular, in the case of the meter. I have discussed these issues in two unpublished manuscripts, the one mentioned in the previous note, and 'Logicism, Wittgenstein, and *De Re* Beliefs about Natural Numbers' (Kripke 1992).

[33] That's just how I feel about the robot philosophers. See note 21.

perceive something simple and continu'd, which he calls *himself,* tho' I am certain there is no such principle in me. (2000:164-65 [Book I, Part IV, Section VI])

The concluding sentences are, of course, a sarcasm. Now, after I had read this passage with shock, I thought that philosophy was a very confusing subject. One philosopher is very convincing, and then another one comes along and gives a very decisive refutation. Who knows what will happen if I read a third one?

Some years later, when I was in my twenties, I talked about it to a non-philosopher, a friend of mine at the time (my attempt when I first read it to talk about it to a classmate was completely unsuccessful). She said, 'Well, Hume must never have looked in a mirror'. At that time I probably thought that her remark simply showed how uncomprehending non-philosophers could be. For of course Hume was objecting to the notion of a Cartesian ego, a pure mind that is the subject of thoughts and impressions. But at the present time I see some justice in her remark, since the idea of a subject, one that I am aware of through self-awareness, as described above, need not in itself imply that the reference is sometimes other than a person, the same person one is aware of, with or without the help of a mirror, or even a sense of sight.[34]

Moreover, the last sentences of the quoted paragraph, witty and effective as they may be, are strangely near to contradictory: 'If any one, upon serious and unprejudic'd reflexion, thinks he has a different notion of *himself,* I must confess I can reason no longer with him. All I can allow him is, that he may well be in the right as well as I, and we are essentially different in this particular. He may, perhaps, perceive something simple and continu'd, which he calls *himself,* tho' I am certain there is no such principle in me'. *Me? He? I?* The beginning of the paragraph is similarly confusing. It appears to presuppose entirely the very notions it attempts to deny.

As is well known, Hume regarded the self as a notion constructed by relating various impressions through resemblance, contiguity, or causation.[35] All we really have is a bundle of perceptions, unified by these relations. Many problems beset this idea. Why should my own impression not equally resemble that of someone else, or be equally contiguous with that of someone else?[36] And similarly, couldn't an impression of mine have a causal relation to that of

---

[34] Of course, recognizing yourself in a mirror presupposes some concept of self-awareness already. Also, I have been warned that my reference to a mirror in the conversation I reported might suggest something about the use by psychologists of mirror self-recognition tests to see whether a subject has a concept of her/himself. Nothing like that was in my interlocutor's mind (nor mine), and the example could have been given without a mirror (though Hume would have seen less of himself). I believe the test had not yet been developed when the conversation took place.

[35] Since he is in this section relating the notion of the self to that of a pure Cartesian ego, completely independent of a body, the question of bodily identity is not discussed. But what Hume has to say about physical bodies elsewhere shows that he thought that, for similar reasons, they would be of no help.

[36] By 'contiguity' Hume is referring to the succession of impressions in time, rapidly after each other.

someone else? In fact, all these things do happen.[37] It is not fair to say that only the impressions that *I* am aware of count. And, as I have already emphasized, Hume says that we confusedly form the notion of a single, persisting entity because of the close relations between the various impressions. But who is this 'we' who do this?[38] (The discussion here and following might be compared with my discussion of the issues in the last chapter of my book on Wittgenstein, Kripke 1982).

A more basic problem for Hume is that he seems to think that there could be impressions, mental acts, and so on with no bearer.[39] They can simply 'float'— that is, each impression could simply exist in and of itself, and it is only an accident that they are connected by the relations that he mentions. I myself find the notion of an impression or idea without any subject who has it hard to understand. I must admit that even more recently there are those who seem to agree with the Humean picture. In Kripke (1982:123), I quote Moore's account of Wittgenstein's Cambridge lectures in 1930–33:

[Wittgenstein said that] 'a [physical] eye doesn't enter into the description of what is seen . . . ;'[40] and he said that similarly 'the idea of a person' doesn't enter into the description of 'having [a] toothache'. . . . And he quoted, with apparent approval, Lichtenberg's saying 'Instead of "I think" we ought to say "It thinks"' ('it' being used, as he said, as 'Es' is used in 'Es blitzet').[41]

As I've indicated, there are others, even more recently, who appear to agree. For example, Peter Geach argues that if Descartes is merely solipsistically thinking to himself, instead of saying 'I am getting into a muddle', he might as well simply

---

[37] Given Hume's well-known skepticism concerning the notion of causation, it is interesting how he invokes it here and elsewhere. But this is probably no inconsistency and is rather a statement of how one dubious notion depends on another.

[38] I find that Chisholm (1976:39–41) has a discussion of Hume closely related to this one. He himself mentions some similar comments by Price.

[39] I emphasize this problem in Kripke (1982:130–31, note 12).

[40] Probably Moore's quotation is somewhat inaccurate here. Of course an eye is involved in seeing, but what Wittgenstein points out is that it is not part of the visual field, that we do not see the eye. See *Tractatus* 5.633, which also states the analogy to the nonexistence of the subject. See also *Tractatus* 5.631: 'There is no such thing as the subject that thinks or entertains ideas.' He adds that no such subject could be found if I wrote a report on 'the world as I found it'. The remainder of the paragraph elaborates on the point. Moore's quotation shows that Wittgenstein still holds this view in his lectures in the 30s.

Apropos of my friend's comment on Hume: if Wittgenstein looked in a mirror, wouldn't he see his eye? Or should one argue that all he sees is a mirror image? If so, the same would apply to Hume in a mirror, even if the self in question were not some pure Cartesian ego, but rather a person with a body. However, Hume can look at some of himself without a mirror. One thing he cannot see without one is his own eye, so perhaps the issue of the eye is directly related.

[41] Moore(1954/1955). The quotation is on page 309 in the (1959) reprint. As to Lichtenberg, 'Es regnet' in German would mean 'It is raining' in English. 'Es blitzt' correspondingly would mean 'It is lightning,' used in an analogous sense to 'It is raining'. But for lightning there is no analogous usage in English. The point is that the 'It' (or 'Es') in the subject does not refer to any entity.

have said 'that is a muddle'.⁴² But what would a muddle be with no one to be in the muddle?⁴³

In spite of Wittgenstein (in the periods in question, anyway), Lichtenberg, and so on, Hume's view, for the reasons that I have given, seems to me to be quite unintelligible. He must have gone wrong somewhere. (Though Descartes might have gone wrong somewhere, too.) I mean, what would a floating impression not belonging to anyone be? Yet, according to Hume, the supposed self is simply constructed from a bundle of such impressions that in principle could each 'float' independently of any other impressions, let alone a bearer.

So, basically, I think my friend had a point. So far there is nothing in the notion of a subject, as I have defended it above and as Frege presupposed it, that in and of itself excludes the first person pronoun as referring to the whole person in the ordinary sense.⁴⁴

Thomas Nagel once delivered a paper, unpublished as far as I know,⁴⁵ in which he proposed that a person be identified with her brain. Rogers Albritton was the commentator, and remarked that if that were so, he shouldn't have been so worried about his weight—it is much less than he had thought.⁴⁶

What did Nagel have in mind when he proposed to identify each of us with her or his brain? What he meant was that if I lose my arm, this is very unfortunate, but I have remained. As a matter of practical medicine, not too much could be stripped away if I am to remain alive, but assuming medicine to have conquered the problem, I could survive the loss of a great deal more. But my brain, from a point of view that is not immaterialist in this respect, is essential as the seat of my thought. As long as it is still functioning, I have not disappeared; but if it goes, I have gone. While this is so, Albritton's comment means that it is still true that my arm is a part of me, as long as it is there. And if I lose it, I have lost one of my parts.

---

⁴² Geach (1957b:117–21, §26 ['The Fallacy of "Cogito Ergo Sum"']).

⁴³ In fairness to Geach, what he is arguing is that the cogito does not directly give us the idea of an immaterial subject. Perhaps not, but not because there might be no subject at all. There is also, in the passage in question, some discussion of how 'I' is used in ordinary communication, supposedly distinct from the Cartesian case.

⁴⁴ I don't know why John Perry, in talking about this, wanted to emphasize someone who erroneously thought he was Hume, rather than a more standard example like Napoleon or Christ. A while ago, I was having dinner, and someone who wanted to criticize philosophers said: 'Philosophers think one is not certain of anything, that you are not certain whether you are Napoleon or not'. I replied: 'Napoleon must have been the greatest philosopher of all time, because only *he* was right when he thought he was Napoleon'.

⁴⁵ Someone looked it up and reported that it was not in his bibliography, so maybe it hasn't seen the light of day, though I'm pretty sure it was read before an audience.

⁴⁶ I was not present at the exchange between Nagel and Albritton, but when I delivered this talk someone who heard the exchange told me afterward that he remembered it vividly.

Nagel has, of course, written important material on the nature of the self, which I do not discuss here.

Descartes held that my essence is thinking. The only thing that is really indubitable, and therefore constitutes me, is the thinker—what I am aware of whenever I think and feel. It is easy to conclude that he holds that I really am simply the Cartesian ego that Hume (and others following him) have found hard to comprehend, or to locate in their own self-consciousness. And perhaps he is usually read in this way. But, of course, there is a well-known passage that appears to be to the contrary. Once Descartes has proved to his own satisfaction (what initially he doubted) that his own body is real, he states:

> Now there is no more explicit lesson of nature than that I have a body; that it is being injured when I feel pain; that it needs food, or drink, when I suffer from hunger, or thirst, and so on. So I must not doubt that there is some truth in this. Nature also teaches by these sensations of pain, hunger, thirst, etc., that I am not present in my body merely as a pilot is present in a ship; I am most tightly bound to it, and as it were mixed up with it, so that I and it form a unit. (1971:117, translated by Anscombe and Geach)[47]

Descartes goes on to argue in the same vein that the way I feel sensation shows that I am a unity, including my body. The case involved in the Nagel–Albritton exchange is similar, though more materialistically expressed. Am I my brain alone, directing my body like a pilot in a vessel? Or am I a unity, including all of my physical body, even though the brain could be the only part that remains, and as long as it is functioning, I have not disappeared? For Descartes, although I may still exist if my body were stripped away and I were still thinking, as long as that has not occurred, I am a unity including my whole body.

It would be very far from my competence or intent to be giving a historical talk on Cartesian exegesis, though I am drawing attention to a suggestive and well-known passage from Descartes. But the philosophical point is that though I might believe that I can doubt the existence of my left hand (and it might be only a contingent fact that I have it), that does not mean that the left hand is not, in fact, a part of me. The commonsense view (and there is no reason to think that Frege, for one, is opposed to it) is that when Lauben says 'I', he means to refer to the person himself, including all bodily parts as genuine parts of himself. Yet he could also think that such parts are subject to Cartesian doubt, that they are only perceived by him as subject, and so on. One could certainly agree with Frege that each of us is aware of himself in a special way. And we have seen that even Descartes ultimately concludes that he is an entity including his own body, even if he believes that he might survive without a body, as long as there is a subject for the cogito.

One notable instance of those who refuse to identify Descartes with the reference of 'I' is Elizabeth Anscombe. In the following passage I am her direct target:

---

[47] Though Cottingham may have become the standard translation (Descartes 1996), the Anscombe and Geach translation was better suited to my purposes—namely, discussing Anscombe's interpretation of Descartes (see below).

Saul Kripke has tried to reinstate Descartes' argument for his dualism. But he neglects its essentially first-person character, making it an argument about the nonidentity of *Descartes* with his own body. Whatever else is said, it seems clear that the argument in Descartes depends on results of applying the method of doubt. (Anscombe 1975:45; emphasis in text)

I certainly don't think Descartes is identical to his body. This point in itself I don't regard as particularly deep, or even incompatible with views that are, broadly speaking, materialist. For Descartes, I say, was not his body when the body was a corpse. 'Descartes had a serious accident, did he survive?' 'Yes, of course—take a look in this coffin.' The response is absurd; rather, we have to say, 'I am afraid Descartes is no longer with us'.[48] But in and of itself that simply might mean that mere nonidentity is not so important. Perhaps a person is nothing 'over and above' her body, even if they are, strictly speaking, not identical.[49]

However, this hardly touches the main points that Anscombe wishes to make, either substantively or as criticism of my own version of the Cartesian argument in *Naming and Necessity*, that it neglected the first person character of what Descartes says. She mentions Castañeda's well-known discussion (Castañeda 1967; see also his 1966 and 1968) as noting the existence of the indirect reflexive in English, which is grammatically a special form in Greek (the form is exemplified by 'Betty believes that she herself...'; see my note 12 above). However, she regards Castañeda's discussion as excessively complicated, a point that Castañeda himself appears to concede. Castañeda does not, as far as I know, mention the technical grammatical term from Greek, but the very simple and clear presentation in Geach (1957b), cited in Lewis (1983:139), does so (see my note 12 again). One would think she would have been aware of this particular author.

Although Castañeda's papers are indeed complicated, Anscombe's is itself none too easy. (I wish I had had the opportunity to talk with her about the paper.) She makes various claims. One is that 'I am not Descartes' follows from the logic of Descartes's argument. She also even argues, from a historical perspective, that Descartes would have accepted this conclusion (see 1975: 55–56). In so arguing, she holds that Descartes uses 'I' to designate the pure Cartesian ego whose nature Hume and others claim not to understand. The idea is supposed to be that, by his very nature, Descartes is a human being, a member

---

[48] But don't we say, when asked 'Who is that?' (pointing to a tomb), 'That's Napoleon'? Isn't it even better if the corpse is embalmed? For example, 'That's Lenin'. But we could say the same kind of thing at Madame Tussauds, pointing to a wax figure. I have something to say about related examples (see my discussion of the toy duck fallacy in chapter 11, this volume), but no more detail need be given here.

I am aware that some people will reject the simple argument for nonidentity on various grounds. I don't wish to deal with them, but feel obligated to mention such things when I am writing about Anscombe, since, after all, there is Peter Geach and the notion of relative identity.

[49] See my discussion of this point in Kripke (1980:145, note 74).

of an animal species, with a body, and so on, whereas 'I' as used in the *Meditations* does not designate such an entity.[50]

Now, we have seen that Descartes's ultimate conclusion—'I' and my body form a unit—is not so simple. There is nothing here to distinguish 'I' from 'Descartes' in the sense Anscombe is talking about. (Of the several translations of Descartes, I have used the one she is most likely to endorse; but everyone agrees that Descartes makes this point.) However, perhaps Descartes believes in an incorporeal entity whose essence is thinking and is the most indubitable part of this unity, one that would remain if everything else were stripped away. But even granting that this is so, I do not see that he would say that such an entity would not be Descartes—nothing I am aware of supports such a dramatic and paradoxical conclusion.[51] Had he accepted it, I would have expected some explicit assertion of such a claim.

Anscombe believes, however, that 'if "I" is a "referring expression", then Descartes was right about what the referent was' (59). And this is her Descartes, where the relevant use of 'I' refers to a Cartesian ego that must be distinct from the man, *Descartes*. She performs certain thought experiments, involving a person being anesthetized, to support her conclusion. Although I am not exactly certain what the argument from these thought experiments is, the conclusion is at least clear: ' "I" is neither a name nor another kind of expression whose logical role is to make a reference, *at all*' (60).[52] She also states, ' "I am E. A." is not an identity proposition'(63).

Very likely Anscombe is writing under the influence of passages in the *Investigations*,[53] where Wittgenstein says that 'I' is not the name of a person, and distinguishes between 'I' and 'L. W.' The influence goes down to the use of initials to make the contrast—'E. A.' in the one case and 'L. W.' in the other.[54]

---

[50] Very likely she is also influenced by the view, advocated by both Peter Geach and Noam Chomsky, that a proper name such as 'Descartes' has a semantical requirement that it name a human being. This might or might not already imply the possession of a body, depending on other views. For my own discussion of Geach's view (in Geach 1957a: §16), see Kripke (1980:115, note 58).

[51] Part of Anscombe's argument, also to be found in other authors (see below), is that the indirect reflexive allows someone to be mistaken about who he is, so the conclusion is not self-contradictory. But Descartes is not in this sense mistaken about who he is.

[52] Her discussion has an elaborate contrast of the use in an imaginary society of some name that everyone uses for him/herself ('A'-users) with our use of the first person pronoun, which is not entirely clear to me. She also remarks that calling it a personal pronoun, and the like, is simply a trivial restatement of first person usage and, in and of itself, gives no information.

However, her general conclusion is clearly stated in what I have just quoted.

I confess that in both the sentence I am footnoting and the present note, I would be willing to replace 'I' by 'Saul Kripke'—only the resulting awkwardness and pomposity would stand in the way. And I have noted the usage of 'the present writer' above (see note 7). Surely 'the present writer' does make a reference, or at any rate, is a definite description.

[53] Wittgenstein (1953: §§405–6).

[54] Geach (1957a: §26), in the anti-Cartesian passage referred to above, similarly contrasts the Cartesian 'I' with 'P. T. G.', probably under the same influence. At least, so I conjecture. In my own discussion, I probably would not be inclined to use initials. See note 52.

No doubt when Wittgenstein makes the relevant distinction in the *Investigations*, his thought is continuous with his earlier worries about the metaphysical subject, as quoted above (see note 40 and related discussion). The *Investigations* passages are about many things, most of which can't be discussed here, such as the difference between first and third person attributions of sensations, the alleged connection of first person 'avowals' of sensations with more primitive expressions such as groaning or crying, and so on. Obviously, we can't talk about all these things here (they are to some extent in Anscombe's paper too).[55]

I won't attempt to give an exegesis of Wittgenstein on these topics. But one should note the following. Remember that in §410 he says: ' "I" is not the name of a person, nor "here" of a place, and "this" is not a name' (see note 4). In one sense this is obvious, because 'I' is not a name at all, but maybe something deeper is meant. See §405, where he says:

'But at any rate when you say "I am in pain", you want to draw the attention of others to a particular person.'—The answer might be: No, I want to draw their attention to *myself*.— (§405; emphasis in original)

It is unfortunate that in §405 and the following paragraphs there is a concentration on the case of 'I am in pain'. Perhaps one might wish to be thinking of a 'Cartesian' case of describing one's own inner states. Obviously, however, this is not the general case of first person usage (see what I say in note 55).

A common criticism of Anscombe's position is that if 'I' is not a referring expression, why should we be confident in the inference pattern from, say, 'I live in North Carolina' to 'Someone lives in North Carolina' (in other words, existential generalization), or in the fact that any inference pattern where 'I' is treated as if it refers is valid. Indeed, such an objection is only a technical expression of one's natural reaction that Anscombe's thesis is in and of itself incredible, difficult to understand at all.[56]

As I said, I was never able to talk to Anscombe about these matters, but I do recall a report from someone else as to what she said when queried as to why 'I' behaves as if it refers in inference patterns. Her answer as reported was 'I don't know'.

---

[55] See Wittgenstein (1953), §398, passim. In §406 there is Wittgenstein's well-known derivation of 'avowals' from more primitive expressions. He says: ' "But surely what you want to do with the words 'I am . . . .' is to distinguish between *yourself* and *other* people."—Can this be said in every case? Even when I merely groan?' Of course, the one who groans does not use the word 'I' or any equivalent at all; and even if one somehow regards 'I am in pain' as simply derived from a groan, this is hardly an obvious illumination of the general case of all first person usage. But I don't say that Wittgenstein thinks that it is.

[56] See, for example, Peacocke (2008:80). He calls Anscombe's conclusion 'barely credible', and makes the criticism about inference patterns. He also uses the argument about inference patterns to show that 'I' cannot be compared with 'it' in 'it is raining', where the grammatical pattern superficially suggests a subject of reference but there is none. (There are plenty of such cases; 'nobody' is a famous one.) Peacocke's comments are a common reaction to Anscombe's view.

One might here remark that Anscombe is a very special case, coming from a special background, that of Wittgenstein. And though, clearly, some of the argumentation is her own, as is the formulation of her thesis, and though Castañeda's well-known discussions of the matter are plainly an influence, the predominant influence may be the special background.

III

Let me turn to a philosopher with quite a different background and orientation. David Lewis was worried about the problem of belief *de se* (Lewis 1979). According to Lewis, there is general agreement that the objects of all the so-called propositional attitudes are propositions, though he acknowledges that not all authors agree as to what propositions are. For him, propositions are sets of possible worlds. But though sometimes I have heard Lewis say that here he simply is giving a stipulative definition—and remember, in addition, that Lewis has his own very special sense of the term 'possible worlds'—presumably, in one sense, it is supposed to represent a thesis or discovery having something to do with traditional uses of the term 'proposition'. I myself am one of the originators of this proposal (in connection with modal logic, anyway), though I wasn't thinking of possible worlds in Lewis's sense, and now might modify it. Today, I even feel some reservations about the idea that *all* the phrases traditionally called propositional attitude constructions have the same sort of entities as objects, though this issue is not for the present paper.[57] Lewis also correctly remarks that the general agreement that the objects are propositions is "to some extent phony" (1983:134), since some authors take propositions to be more highly structured entities, more like an abstract, nonlinguistic, analogue of sentences.

In any event, Lewis proposes a theory that was formulated independently by Roderick Chisholm (1981),[58] and actually was anticipated by Quine (1968).[59]

---

[57] In the first section of Lewis (1979), he gives some reasons for hoping for uniform objects. As far as the arguments of this section go, I agree.

[58] I am familiar with Chisholm's version only superficially. Like Lewis, he proposes that self-ascription be taken as primitive. However, he doesn't put matters in terms of Lewis's special apparatus of possible worlds. In fact, at the end of his book, he states his own view on the nature of possible worlds, which he thinks is the traditional one.

[59] My thanks to Gilbert Harman for emphasizing that Quine's paper anticipates Lewis's theory. However, as Lewis says, Quine uses a different notion of possible world. Other than that, the theories, though in my own opinion somewhat differently motivated, can be interpreted as the same. Perhaps I should add that Quine's paper somewhat surprised the present writer, given what he had said about possible worlds elsewhere. There is even a paper entitled 'Worlds Away' (Quine 1976) expressing his repudiation of the notion, and not mentioning that he had written his own version of a kind of possible world semantics earlier. One might also add that the original journal version in Quine (1976) and the one printed in Quine (1981) are significantly different, representing an unacknowledged change of argument.

Also, Lewis acknowledges Brian Loar (1976) as making the same proposal (Lewis 1983:519, note 4).[60] He also makes a comparison of his views with a proposal by John Perry (1977) (Lewis 1983:150),[61] and plainly Lewis is considerably influenced by Perry's paper, as Lewis himself says (139).

Neither Lewis nor Chisholm actually gives an analysis of statements with 'I'. Rather, as Chisholm says explicitly (1979), what is explained is the indirect reflexive. For example, one takes as primitive '*A* self-ascribes such and such a property', where self-ascription is a primitive notion, corresponding to '*A* believes that he himself has such and such a property'. Since self-ascription, like any reflexive property $\lambda x\ (xRx)$, is derived from a relation R, Lewis rightly concludes his paper (sections XIII and XIV) with a brief discussion of belief *de re*. He regards beliefs *de re* as beliefs based on acquaintance, and adds that belief *de se* is a par excellence case of belief *de re*, based on the highest form of acquaintance, namely, one's acquaintance with oneself.[62]

I should mention that Lewis also wishes to account for 'now' and the present tense, and for this reason regards it as a person stage that has an attitude *de se*. But this is a separable part of the view, drawn from the rest of Lewis's philosophy. As far as the present issue is concerned, he could just as well say that a person (not a stage, but an enduring object) self-ascribes not a property (corresponding to a set of worlds), but a two-place relation between a person (himself) and a time (the time of the ascription, corresponding to the same set).

Note also that Lewis, in contrast with some of those to whom he compares himself, regards all attitudes as *de se*, even those that seem to make no reference to the subject (say, 'lightning is an electrical discharge', or 'Australia is a large island', etc.). For this Lewis cites the advantages of uniformity, so that there

---

Lewis himself (1983:147–48) discusses some of the differences in motivation that he sees between himself and Quine. He remarks (147) that Quine differs from him in considering a divided theory: the objects of some primitive attitudes may be stimulation patterns rather than sets of worlds, making his theory highly nonuniform, something Lewis wishes to avoid. Moreover, Quine is concerned with attitudes and desires of animals too, an issue that Lewis does not consider (nor shall I). Lewis mentions other differences in motivation, and Quine does not share Lewis's modal realism (as Lewis calls it).

I myself would treat possible worlds differently, even given Quine's project. In particular, I do not agree that either classical or relativistic physics has shown the notion of a (physical) geometrical point to be absurd, as Quine thinks, even though he informally uses this notion to motivate his definitions. The important thing for the present purposes is that to explain *de se* attitudes, Quine introduces the notion of 'centered possible worlds', where the centering is on the subject (or its physical location). In and of itself a possible world is not centered, so that a centered possible world might be thought of as an ordered pair of a world and a center.

[60] Lewis states that Loar formulates his view for 'certain exceptional beliefs'.
[61] I have discussed Perry's paper above and in chapter 9.
[62] Elsewhere, Chisholm advocates the theory, rightly (in my opinion) rejected by Lewis in his paper, that one has a belief *de re* about an object as long as one has any description designating the object under which one has the appropriate belief (what I have called 'universal exportation', chapter 11, this volume). So he cannot regard belief *de se* as a special case of belief *de re*. I have not researched whether Chisholm says anything about the issue.

are not two kinds of objects of beliefs, and so on, sometimes propositions, and sometimes properties, but only one. But really, other reasons can be given in Lewis's own framework. First, in the old theory, the object of a propositional attitude is the same for logically equivalent sentences, so that, for any p, 'p' and 'p and David Lewis is self-identical' express the same attitudinal object (set of possible worlds), even where p makes no reference to David Lewis. It would be natural to preserve this feature with 'I' in place of 'David Lewis'.[63] Second, and most important, for Lewis the actual world is distinguished as the one the subject inhabits, and hence any ordinary belief is really a belief that I inhabit a world with certain properties; the uniformity is not really artificial at all, given Lewis's view of the nature of possible worlds as vast concrete worlds and his theory of actuality. For example, my belief that *actually* Australia has kangaroos is a belief that *I* inhabit a world where Australia has kangaroos.

All this, however, seems to me to be an odd reversal of matters.[64] As I say in *Naming and Necessity*, 'a possible world is *given by the descriptive conditions we associate with it*' (1980:44; emphasis in original). By this I did not mean to identify possible worlds with sets of descriptive conditions, for example, as Carnapian state descriptions (probably impossible in a countable language anyway). But I wish to emphasize the legitimacy of setting up possible worlds by any description we understand, and in particular that it need not be purely qualitative. For example, I emphasize, as against those who worry about a problem of 'transworld identification', that a counterfactual possibility could be stipulated as being about Nixon, using the name 'Nixon', and not worrying about any reduction to a qualitative description.

Now, what language does a person use when describing counterfactual possibilities? Not a 'scientific', indexical-free language—one that none of us speaks. Each of us has a notion of the self and often a word for it (in English, 'I'). Why can we not use such a language to describe a counterfactual situation, and hence a possible world (even if we normally do so only in part)? I use the word 'I' to designate myself, and to designate myself in a particular way, as has been

---

[63] Pardon the abuse of quotation here. I suppose I should have used Quine's corners. Everyone knows what I mean, and I wish to be excused.

[64] Evans (1977) suggests that perhaps the indirect reflexive could be thought of as deriving from the *oratio recta* construction with the first person pronoun (98). For example, he sees 'John thinks that he is under suspicion' as 'somehow derived from' 'John thinks "I am under suspicion"' in *oratio recta*, and refers to Anscombe's paper. I am sympathetic with something Evans is trying to say, namely, that the form with the first person pronoun is primary. However, one cannot make this point by deriving the indirect reflexive from an *oratio recta* construction. Nothing in the indirect reflexive form implies that John is speaking or thinking in English. The trouble is that if we wish to ascribe to John an 'I'-thought using a 'that-clause', we use the indirect reflexive itself, and thus get into a tangle expressing the derivation, which I do think goes in the direction indicated by Evans.

I confess that I have not taken Evans's other writings on *de se* attitudes into account.

discussed above. Quine speaks of 'centered possible worlds'.[65] I would rather speak of possible worlds *simpliciter*; the 'centering' comes when a particular person describes a counterfactual situation.

Lewis himself rightly (as I have said) describes *de se* belief as a special case of *de re* belief, and bases the latter on a notion of acquaintance. Self-acquaintance is such acquaintance in the highest degree. Why then can someone not use such acquaintance to formulate a word 'I', and use it to designate an object in a special way? It will follow from this means of designation that it is rigid, or more strongly, as Kaplan puts it, 'directly referential' (if we are putting the matter that way, 'directly referential in a special way').

One should not think that any situation, actual or counterfactual, really should be described in a 'scientific' language (see note 4), one free of person and tense, and so on, and then tack on an identification of the people and times in it, as 'I', 'now', and so on. Lewis makes much of a situation with two gods (1983:139), one of whom does one thing and one of whom does another. The gods, he says, could be omniscient, as far as propositional knowledge is concerned, without either one knowing which one of the gods he is. Robert Stalnaker has observed that it is difficult to imagine such a situation as intelligible. How can someone be doing something without realizing that it is he himself that is doing it? (Stalnaker 2008:56ff).[66]

My own view is that to describe a possible world is to give a 'possible history of the world' (Kripke 1980:48, note 15). Such a history, or a portion of it, might well be describable in an indexical free (or 'scientific') language, but nothing says that it need be so described. In particular, when I am speaking the language, I am entitled to use the first person singular in describing such a history. Thus, both in an informal, intuitive sense, as well as in the technical sense of determining a set of possible worlds, statements about myself do express propositions, only they determine them in a special way.

Let me speak of possibilities in the way that I spoke of 'metaphysical possibility' in *Naming and Necessity*. I can wonder what will happen to me, and how things might have come out otherwise, even in the past, had only I done such-and-such. Here the picture should not be as if I might be thinking about possible

---

[65] See note 59 above. Stalnaker (2008:49) ascribes the notion of 'centered possible worlds' to David Lewis. In fact, the terminology, and the associated picture, is due to Quine, even though Lewis's view can be considered equivalent.

[66] Can two people get into an argument without each participant knowing which side she is taking? I won't discuss Stalnaker's analysis, and some of his other objections to Lewis's version, further. It appeared subsequent to the original version of this paper. Nor do I discuss some possibilities for reinstating Lewis's example.

worlds and then 'tacking on' which person is me. The situation is the opposite; I am determining possibilities by reference to myself.[67, 68]

One might also consider Lewis's earlier paper 'Anselm and Actuality' (1970) in relation to this one (i.e., Lewis 1979). In one sense, which both Lewis and I would acknowledge, each world is the unique one that is actual with respect to itself. However, we think of one world as the actual one. For me, that is the unique world w such that a proposition p is true with respect to w if and only if p, for all p.[69] For Lewis, it is the unique world that I inhabit. Then for Lewis the proponent of the ontological argument has little plausibility in arguing that God must have actuality in this sense in order to have every perfection. Why is this a

---

[67] Lewis (see his 1983:135), aside from other differences in the conception of possible worlds, is not concerned with metaphysical necessity and possibility in my sense, but rather in connection with propositional attitudes, predominantly doxastic attitudes. He discusses the problem of whether attitudes can be attitudes toward sets of possible worlds, since one can apparently have different attitudes toward propositions that hold in the same sets. He says that 'believing that 2+2=4 is clearly not the same as believing that 123+456=579', because the latter calculation is not as trivial as the first. He goes on, 'I know perfectly well that there is such a thing as ignorance of noncontingent matters'. Wishing to leave this issue aside, he says that, if one wishes, one could imagine that we are talking about 'the attitudes of imaginary hyper-rational creatures'. So, clearly, examples of metaphysical but not epistemic necessity that I have advocated, such as 'water is H_2O', are not contemplated. One can suppose that another notion of epistemically possible worlds, or of what I called 'epistemic counterparts' of metaphysically possible worlds, is involved. However, from my own perspective, as stated in this very paragraph, real metaphysical possibilities are an important notion when considering 'I'-sentences, and indeed this is an important reason that they should be considered in and of themselves, not simply in terms of indirect reflexive constructions. And it is what I call metaphysical possibility that is relevant to counterfactuals as Lewis and Stalnaker analyze them (see Lewis 1973).

[68] In fairness to Lewis, he certainly considers that situation (by reference to an amnesiac, Rudolph Lingens, lost in the Stanford Library, an example discussed by Perry). (For Lingens, see note 22. Evidently, Perry has transported Frege's character from Germany to the Stanford Library. No wonder he has become confused. He is supposed to be reading things in the library, but no matter how much he reads, he won't know where he is. I hope his English is good. Otherwise, it is not surprising the library is not so helpful.)

But the real points are these. First, of course my conception of possibility is different from Lewis's. Second, I don't see why Lingens isn't expressing definite propositional knowledge using the word '*ich*', or fails to be contemplating genuine possibilities using it. This is true even in the unusual case of amnesia, where although in some sense the subject doesn't know who he is, there would appear to be another sense in which even he could be said to know this, and in which it would be impossible not to.

Suppose someone wonders what time it is now (a case Lewis considers [1983:143–44]). So, in some sense, he is wondering what time it is, and the answer is given by the clock. Or he may be wondering when it will be noon, and the answer may be 'now', or 'two minutes from now'. 'When did she die?' 'Just now'. Both forms of question are legitimate, and equally so. In the first case, the very same situation is regarded in two ways. In my own opinion, the relativity and indeterminacy of '*wh*-questions' like this is exaggerated in the philosophical literature, but it exists and the present instance is a strong case.

[69] And p is true with respect to w could be defined as: if w were the case, then p (where in spite of the linguistic form we might as well interpret the conditional as strict). (I won't go into complications for someone who doesn't believe in S5 or even S4.)

perfection, inhabiting the same world that I do?[70] Here, of course, much depends on our different conceptions of what a world is. I don't think of myself as inhabiting a world in Lewis's sense, nor do I think much of his answer as a solution to the 'problem' of how we know that we are inhabiting the actual world, rather than a merely possible one. But note that, given Lewis's later view, to say that the world is actual is not to state any proposition about it, it is to attribute a special sort of property to the speaker.

What then are the differences between me and Lewis? First, there is the well-known difference in our conception of possible worlds. For Lewis, if I wonder what possible world I am in, it is as if I am wondering whether I am in Pennsylvania or West Virginia, as if I were traveling by car (though, of course, according to Lewis, at least in his ultimate view, such a trip between worlds is impossible). But second, I do not think that genuine propositions must be described in some neutral scientific language. Anyone can describe them in any language he himself speaks. In some sense, one might call this a merely terminological difference, since (and in spite of the considerable influence on him of Perry's paper) Lewis agrees with me that everyone has a special *de se* acquaintanceship with himself. And, of course, he does not deny that special contents using the first person and involving tense are asserted, entertained, and the like. But he does think that these are not genuine propositions, in some intuitive sense. How can a proposition depend on who expresses it? The room around me (and this would be valid for worlds even if one had Lewis's conception of them) is not dependent on who looks at it, but everyone is permitted to describe it using person and tense.[71, 72]

---

[70] Doesn't this depend on what I think of myself? The argument could have a plausible premise for Anselm, and not for me.

[71] In the original version of this talk, I was worried that Lewis might face the same difficulty as Anscombe about logical inferences containing the word 'I'. In the sense of classical logical inference, I still think this might be true, since in this classical sense such an inference is valid simply in virtue of its form. (The Quinean notion of a logical truth has a similar motivation.) It is indeed true that an inference involving 'I' in the premise does not, for Lewis, even express a genuine premise (proposition), let alone one involving 'I' as a singular term. But Gilbert Harman and Robert Stalnaker have pointed out to me that Lewis can easily explain in his apparatus why we can validly infer from a self-ascription p to a self-ascription entailed by it: it is simply a matter that one who self-ascribes the property of being in a set of possible worlds is thereby committed to self-ascribing to himself the property of being in any larger set of possible worlds. I haven't really thought about whether such problems arise on Chisholm's version. Note that in the crudest sense the Lewis–Chisholm theory could be regarded as one that solves the supposed self-ascription problem simply by taking self-ascription as a special primitive; then, questions as to the logic of this predicate would obviously arise.

[72] From this point of view, 'I am Saul Kripke' is little different in principle from 'Hesperus is Phosphorus', or 'Cicero is Tully', and the like, though 'I' determines its referent in a very special way. Similarly, 'I am Jesus Christ', said falsely, misdescribes an actual or possible situation, as would 'Hesperus is Mars'. A better analogy might be 'that man is Jesus Christ', which could be uttered by a believer, or denied by a disbeliever (and might even be expressed by a proper name for 'that man'), but it is no longer first person. On my view, the statement would also misdescribe every possible world.

Well, what I have been arguing? Not anything really so special, on a topic that has a considerable literature. But each of us does have a special acquaintanceship with himself or herself, as philosophers from Descartes to Frege have held. This self-acquaintance is more fundamental than anything purely linguistic, and is the basis of our use of first person locutions. And each of us can use them to make genuine claims, to express genuine propositions.[73]

REFERENCES

Almog, J., J. Perry, and H. Wettstein, eds. (1989). *Themes from Kaplan*. New York: Oxford University Press.

Anscombe, G. E. M. (1975). 'The First Person'. In *Mind and Language*, ed. S. Guttenplan. Oxford: Clarendon, 45–65.

Beaney, M. (1997). *The Frege Reader*. Malden, MA: Blackwell.

Brouwer, L. E. J. (1948). 'Consciousness, Philosophy and Mathematics'. In Brouwer (1975), 480–94.

———. (1975). *L. E. J. Brouwer, Collected Works. Volume 1*. Ed. A. Heyting. Amsterdam: North-Holland.

Buber, M. (1923). *Ich und Du*. Leipzig, Germany: Insel-Verlag.

Castañeda, H. N. (1966). '"He": A Study in the Logic of Self-Consciousness'. *Ratio* 8:130–57.

———. (1967). 'The Logic of Self-Knowledge'. *Noûs* 1:9–22.

———. (1968). 'On the Logic of Attributions of Self-Knowledge to Others'. *Journal of Philosophy* 65:439–56.

Chisholm, R. M. (1976). *Person and Object*. London: George Allen & Unwin.

———. (1979). 'The Indirect Reflexive'. In Diamond and Teichman (1979).

———. (1981). *The First Person: An Essay on Reference and Intentionality*. Minneapolis: University of Minnesota Press.

Descartes, R. (1971). *Descartes: Philosophical Writings*. 2nd ed.. Ed. and trans. G. E. M. Anscombe and P. T. Geach. Indianapolis: Bobbs-Merrill.

———. (1996). *Meditations on First Philosophy, with Selections from the Objections and Replies*. Ed. and trans. J. Cottingham. Cambridge: Cambridge University Press.

Diamond, C., and J. Teichman, eds. (1979). *Intention and Intentionality*. Sussex, UK: Harvester.

One could also use tense in describing counterfactual as well as actual situations. However, there could be special problems in using 'now' in the description of a hypothetical total world history. For one thing, the description would necessarily be very fleeting. For another, there could be relativistic histories for which its referent is problematic. Also, one might be accused of smuggling in views about 'A-series/B-series' problems, if these are problems. A tenseless version of such a total world description could be thought of as not taking a stand on these issues.

[73] I would like to thank Romina Padró for transcribing the original lecture and for helpful suggestions and discussions. I also want to thank Jeff Buechner, Gary Ostertag, and Harold Teichman for editorial assistance. This paper has been completed with support from the Saul A. Kripke Center at the City University of New York, Graduate Center.

Evans, G. (1985). 'Pronouns, Quantifiers, and Relative Clauses (I)'. In Evans (1985), pp. 76–152.

———. (1981). 'Understanding Demonstratives'. In *Meaning and Understanding*, ed. H. Parret and J. Bouveresse. Berlin: W. de Gruyter. Reprinted in Evans (1985), pp. 291–321.

———. (1985). *Collected Papers*. Oxford: Oxford University Press.

Frege, G. (1892). 'Über Sinn und Bedeutung'. *Zeitschrift für Philosophie und philosophische Kritik*. 100:25–50. Translated by Max Black, in Beaney (1997), pp. 151–71.

———. (1918–19). 'Der Gedanke'. *Beiträge zur Philosophie des deutschen Idealismus* I:58–77. Translated as 'Thoughts' by Peter Geach and R. H. Stoothoff, in Gottlob Frege, *Logical Investigations* (New Haven, CT: Yale University Press, 1977), and included in Beaney (1997), pp. 325–45, under the title 'Thought'. Also translated by A. M. and M. Quinton, as 'The Thought: A Logical Inquiry,' in *Mind* 65 (1956):289–311.

Geach, P. (1957a). *Mental Acts: Their Content and Their Objects*. London: Routledge & Kegan Paul.

———. (1957b). 'On Beliefs about Oneself'. *Analysis* 18:23–24.

Hempel, C. G. (1942). 'The Function of General Laws in History'. *Journal of Philosophy* 39:35–48.

Hume, D. (2000). *A Treatise of Human Nature*. Eds. David Fate Norton and Mary Norton. Oxford: Oxford University Press.

Irving, D. J. C. (1977). *Hitler's War*. New York: Viking.

Kaplan, D. (1968). 'Quantifying In'. *Synthese* 19:178–214.

———. (1989). 'Demonstratives'. In *Themes from Kaplan*, ed. Joseph Almog, John Perry, and Howard Wettstein. New York: Oxford University Press.

———. (n.d.). 'What Is Meaning? Explorations in the Theory of *Meaning as Use*'. Unpublished manuscript.

Kripke, S. (1961). 'History and Idealism: The Theory of R. G. Collingwood'. Unpublished manuscript.

———. (1977). 'Speaker's Reference and Semantic Reference'. *Midwest Studies in Philosophy* 2:255–76. Reprinted in this volume as Chapter 5.

———. (1979). 'A Puzzle about Belief'. In *Meaning and Use*, ed. A. Margalit. Dordrecht, Netherlands: D. Reidel. Reprinted in this volume as Chapter 6.

———. (1980). *Naming and Necessity*. Cambridge, MA: Harvard University Press. First published in *Semantics of Natural Language*, ed. D. Davidson and G. Harman. Dordrecht, Netherlands: D. Reidel, 1972, 253–355, 763–69.

———. (1982). *Wittgenstein on Rules and Private Language*. Cambridge, MA: Harvard University Press.

———. (1986). 'Rigid Designation and the Contingent *A Priori*: The Meter Stick Revisited.' Unpublished manuscript.

———. (1992). 'Logicism, Wittgenstein, and *De Re* Beliefs about Natural Numbers'. Unpublished manuscript.

———. (2008). 'Frege's Theory of Sense and Reference: Some Exegetical Notes'. *Theoria* 74:181–218. Reprinted in this volume as Chapter 9.

———. (2010). 'Unrestricted Exportation and Some Morals for the Philosophy of Language'. Reprinted in this volume as Chapter 11.

Lewis, D. (1970). 'Anselm and Actuality'. *Noûs* 4:175–88. Reprinted in Lewis (1983).
———. (1973). *Counterfactuals.* Cambridge, MA: Harvard University Press.
———. (1979). 'Attitudes *De Dicto* and *De Se*'. *Philosophical Review* 88:513–43. Reprinted in Lewis (1983); page references are to the reprint.
———. (1983). *Philosophical Papers, Volume I.* Oxford: Oxford University Press.
Loar, B. (1976). 'The Semantics of Singular Terms'. *Philosophical Studies* 30:353–77.
Ludlow, P., and S. Neale (1991). 'Indefinite Descriptions: In Defense of Russell', *Linguistics and Philosophy* 14:171–202.
Ludlow, P., and G. Segal (2004). 'On a Unitary Semantical Analysis for Definite and Indefinite Descriptions'. In *Descriptions and Beyond*, ed. M. Reimer and A. Bezuidenhout. Oxford: Oxford University Press.
Moore, G. E. (1954/1955). 'Wittgenstein's Lectures in 1930–33'. *Mind* 63 (1954), and 64 (1955). Reprinted in Moore (1959), 252–324.
———. (1959). *Philosophical Papers.* London: George Allen & Unwin.
Peacocke, C. (2008). *Truly Understood.* Oxford: Oxford University Press.
Perry, J. (1977). 'Frege on Demonstratives', *Philosophical Review* 86:474–97. Reprinted with a postscript in Perry (1993).
———. (1993). *The Problem of the Essential Indexical and Other Essays.* Oxford: Oxford University Press.
———. (1997). 'Indexicals and Demonstratives'. In *A Companion to the Philosophy of Language,* ed. Bob Hale and Crispin Wright. Oxford: Blackwell.
Plantinga, A. (1974). *The Nature of Necessity,* Oxford: Oxford University Press.
Prior, A. N. (1967). 'On Spurious Egocentricity'. *Philosophy* 42:326–35.
Quine, W. V. O. (1968). 'Propositional Objects'. *Crítica: Revista Latinoamericana de Filosofía* 2:3–29. Reprinted in Quine (1969).
———. (1969). *Ontological Relativity and Other Essays.* New York: Columbia University Press.
———. (1976). 'Worlds Away'. *Journal of Philosophy* 73:859–63. Reprinted in Quine (1981).
———. (1981). *Theories and Things.* Cambridge, MA: Harvard University Press.
Sider, T. (2001). *Four Dimensionalism.* Oxford: Oxford University Press.
Stalnaker, R. (2008). *Our Knowledge of the Internal World.* Oxford: Oxford University Press.
Wittgenstein, L. (1953). *Philosophical Investigations.* Ed. and trans. G. E. M. Anscombe. Oxford: Blackwell.
———. (1961). *Tractatus Logico-Philosophicus.* Trans. David Pears and Brian McGuinness. London: Routledge & Kegan Paul.

11

Unrestricted Exportation and Some Morals for the Philosophy of Language*

I am going to discuss a distinction that has a fairly long history in philosophy.[1] In the contemporary discussion of intensional discourse it really should be attributed to Bertrand Russell in "On Denoting," (1905) but got much more attention when it was revived by Quine in his paper "Quantifiers and Propositional Attitudes" (1956) and in his book *Word and Object* (1960). Russell and Quine gave different accounts of the matter. But the problem was the same.[2] As Quine pointed out, there appears to be an important distinction between (1) and the weaker (2):

(1) There is someone I believe to be a spy.
(2) I believe that there are spies.

While (2) expresses a triviality, (1) expresses important information that might be communicated to, say, the CIA. Now, (1) is, of course, a quantified sentence. A semiformal version is obtained by prefixing an existential quantifier to (3):

(3) I believe of *y* that he is a spy.

Or, in conformity with (1), prefixing an existential quantifier to (3a):

(3a) I believe *y* to be a spy.

Using standard terminology, (1) and (3) are examples of *de re* belief and (2) of *de dicto* belief. On Russell's theory, it is not really as if there are two kinds of belief; but the way Quine puts the matter suggests that there are ("notional" and "relational" belief), and his version seems to carry over to the discussions given by others. (However, most of these authors attempt to reduce the *de re* sense to

---

* The present paper was delivered at the opening conference of the Saul Kripke Center, held at the City University of New York, Graduate Center on May 21–23, 2008.
[1] For this history, see the brief remarks at the beginning of Sosa (1970) and references given there.
[2] For more on my view of Russell's account, and on the relation of his views to Quine's, see Chapter 8, especially 228ff (229ff 228ff.).

the *de dicto* sense somehow, or at least to relate them; we shall discuss this momentarily.) One thing that made Dan Dennett incredulous about the theory is this feature of it (Dennett 1987). Are there really two kinds of belief?

When does the *de dicto* formulation imply the *de re* formulation? Suppose α is a term (though proper names could be included here, the main case is that of a definite description).[3] Then suppose we have:

(4) E(α)

to be read as "α exists," which in the case of a definite description simply means that the relevant existence and uniqueness conditions are satisfied. And suppose we have:

(5) *S* believes that α is *F*

(where we assume that (5) reports *S*'s *de dicto* belief).

When can we deduce the existential statement that "there exists a *y* which *S* believes to have *F*"? Or, to use the example under discussion, when—taking *F* to be the predicate "is a spy"—can we deduce "there is someone *S* believes to be a spy"? This, in turn, depends on when we can deduce (6) from (4) and (5):

(6) *S* believes of α that it is *F*

Unrestricted exportation is the doctrine that the implication always holds. And, in fact, if things are so simple, one is on the way to a very straightforward analysis of *de re* belief in terms of *de dicto* belief.[4]

This doctrine has a very strange history. When Quine originally discussed the distinction in his paper (1956), as its title indicates, he applied it to propositional attitudes in general. One particularly amusing example he gave shows the systematic ambiguities generated by combining notional or relational attitudes with existential quantification. For example, "I want a sloop" is ambiguous: it may mean that there is a particular sloop that I want, or simply that I seek "mere relief from slooplessness" (Quine 1956:177).[5] The notional, and more likely sense, where there is no particular sloop that I want, is expressed as:

---

[3] For Russell, of course, definite descriptions, like other "denoting phrases," are not really terms at all, but rather quantifiers. See Chapter 8 for my own discussion. (But for the purposes of the formulation of the problem of exportation, we must pretend, anyway, that definite descriptions are terms.)

[4] To get such an analysis one must assume that, conversely, whenever one has a *de re* belief, one must have a *de dicto* belief referring to the object of the *de re* belief. Then the analysis will be that (6) holds if and only if there are some true statements (4′) and (5′) that hold when α is replaced by some term β coreferential with α. See also the discussion of the matter in connection with Sosa below.

[5] I once heard a story (from a third party) about a man who reported that he was spending the summer in Germany because he wanted to marry a German woman. The person relating the story had assumed that there was a particular German woman he wanted to marry (Quine's relational sense). Actually, my informant came to realize that what he meant was that he was so enamored of Germany and Germans that he was trying to find an appropriate German woman to marry (Quine's notional sense). True story.

(7) I want it to be the case that $(\exists x)(x$ is a sloop and I have $x)$

whereas the relational sense, where there is a particular sloop that I want, is expressed as:

(8) $(\exists x)(x$ is a sloop and I want that I have $x)$

Similarly, he mentions a corresponding ambiguity for "hunts." For belief, the two forms would be symbolically expressed as:

(9) $(\exists x)$(I believe that x is a spy)

and

(10) I believe that $(\exists x)(x$ is a spy)

Quine stresses that, for most of us, (2) and its representation (10), are true, while (1) and equivalently (9), are false.[6]

In his initial formulation, Quine did assume the principle of unrestricted exportation (1956:182, first sentence).[7] Various people[8] pointed out that this threatens to trivialize the difference between (1) and (2) (and the corresponding symbolic expressions, (9) and (10)), because if someone believes (2)—that there are spies—then the same person will presumably believe (11):

(11) The tallest spy is a spy.

(Here one assumes that no two spies are of exactly equal height, and that they are finite in number, so that the description is not vacuous.)[9] This will imply by exportation and existential generalization that there is someone S believes to be a spy. So, the distinction will, in effect, be obliterated.

The same argument clearly would apply if belief were replaced by knowledge. For anyone who knows that there are spies, together with a few other obvious things,

---

[6] For Quine's views as of this period, Quine (1956) seems to me to be far superior to the parallel discussion in his famous philosophical work *Word and Object* (1960:145–51). The latter discussion seems to favor a treatment similar to what is briefly stated at the end of section 1 of Quine (1956) and rejected in favor of a "more suggestive treatment" (Quine 1956:180). The difference leads me to conjecture that in spite of the publication dates, Quine had finished the *Word and Object* treatment before Quine (1956) was written, and did not revise it afterward. (The last two pages of the *Word and Object* discussion get closer to Quine 1956.)

Incidentally, it always seemed to me to be obvious that if Quine (1956) and the idea of "notional belief" were formally correct, then there would be a parallel way of treating quantified modal logic, free of formal objection, regardless of whether the latter is philosophically objectionable. I regarded Quine's apparent failure to see this in *Word and Object* as odd. Kaplan (1968) made the point in a footnote, and it was recognized by Quine himself in Quine (1981:116).

[7] See Quine (1956:82, first paragraph). Russell (1905) would never have been tempted to postulate unrestricted exportation for definite descriptions, since it amounts to saying that a small scope formulation always implies the corresponding large scope formulation, which he clearly does not believe.

[8] For references, see Sosa (1970:887, note 11).

[9] See also note 23 below.

there is someone she knows to be a spy. The same holds for certainty and many other propositional attitudes.[10] However, the trivialization would not as clearly follow for "wants," as in the amusing example quoted from Quine.[11] Even if unrestricted exportation held for "wants that," it would not follow quite so obviously that anyone who wants a sloop wants a particular one, nor would it follow that anyone who wants to marry a German woman already has one picked out, and so on.[12]

One might think that the objection would simply have been accepted for the cases where it works, and otherwise sent people back to the drawing board. Quine himself initially accepted the objection (Quine 1968). Ernest Sosa was one of the people who made the criticism of Quine (Sosa 1969). Yet he later wrote a contrasting classic and influential paper on the subject (Sosa 1970).[13] In this later paper, it would appear at first that Sosa accepts the objection, and indeed states an alternative formulation of the reduction of *de re* to *de dicto*, using a restriction on exportability. However, he thinks—citing examples where the apparent restrictions on exportation depend on either context or the interest of the discussants—that arguments using the Gricean distinction between what is literally true and what it is appropriate to say can be given to show that Quine's original unrestricted exportation principle is the correct account of literal English and can be used to give a simple account of *de re* belief.[14]

Quine himself, apparently writing independently of Sosa, has an even more dialectical approach in a later paper (Quine 1981). But although in the later

---

[10] I should add that in this talk I am treating all propositional attitudes as if they were on a par as to their object, though, in fact, I am not sure that this is so. I do so because nothing turns on such an assumption here.

[11] Although the example is expressed with "wants that" or "wants it to be the case that," and Quine expresses another with "strives to find," his main concern is with belief.

[12] See note 5. Though anyone who believes that there are sloops may believe that there is a longest sloop, a sloop more expensive than any other, etc., it does not follow that he wants the longest sloop, or the most expensive sloop, etc., so there is nothing to export. One might try a suggestion such as "the best sloop his budget will allow." However, such a description may not pick out a unique sloop, and even if it does, it is not necessarily the case that he wants that.

[13] Since I will necessarily be highly critical of much of Sosa's paper in my discussion, I wish to emphasize my view of it as a classic. To my knowledge, after all these years it remains the best formulation of its point of view and an enduring influence.

[14] In one sense, I have not reported Sosa carefully. Sosa bases his entire discussion on a special locution, using Quine's corners, "S believes $\ulcorner\alpha$ is $F\urcorner$" defined as "S has a belief (in a proposition) that, given normal circumstances, he could correctly express in our language by asserting the sentence composed of 'α' followed by 'is' followed by 'F'" (Sosa 1970: 885). At the end of his paper, Sosa says, "Note that I have never supposed that 'S believes $\ulcorner\alpha$ is $F\urcorner$' is equivalent to 'S believes that α is F.' This is a separate question that cannot be treated here" (896, note 20). In the same footnote he adds that regardless of this question, his formulation in either of its forms I or III (for an explanation, see below) gives a reduction of *de re* to *de dicto* belief.

I wish I had a better idea why Sosa formulates the problems in terms of his special notion rather than in terms of "believes that" (a notion whose meaningfulness he does not deny). Quine and Dennett, and some of the speakers in Sosa's examples, simply use "believes that" and related locutions, and I am following them. However, if I am being careless about Sosa here, and should have used the notion he emphasizes, as far as I can see my discussion of his paper would not be materially affected.

paper he initially writes "evidently we must find against exportation" (120), using the same "tallest spy" argument given above,[15] he, like Sosa, later reverses himself, but this time the reversal takes place in a single paper, retracting the categorical statement just quoted. Much more quickly than Sosa and with fewer examples,[16] he concludes that a restriction on exportability must depend wholly on contextual features. From this he concludes (though I find the conclusion far from obvious myself, even given the premises) that the only true rule for exportability must be his original unrestricted one, obliterating the distinction between (1) and (2), the very distinction he has himself emphasized. He says, "At first this seems intolerable, but it grows on one" (121).[17]

Although both Quine (writing, as we have seen, apparently independently of Sosa) and Daniel Dennett (1987) (writing later in agreement with both) really agree with Sosa, they express themselves very differently. While Sosa, defending unrestricted exportation, says "a simpler reduction of *de re* to *de dicto* attitudes is hard to imagine" (1970:896), both Quine (briefly) and Dennett (very vigorously), state that they *reject* the notion of *de re* belief. Quine writes, "We end up rejecting *de re* or quantified propositional attitudes generally, on a par with *de re* or quantified modal logic" (1981:122). Yet it is Quine himself, who in his earlier (1956) paper, sparked the contemporary interest in the notion!

Dennett, too, states in many places in his paper that there is no such thing as *de re* belief.[18] However, his actual position is not really a rejection of *de re* belief

---

[15] Actually, in Quine it is "the shortest spy." There appear to be two different sources. If some philosopher finds a subtle difference depending on which is used, that person will deserve some extraordinary praise.

[16] Using Kaplan's term "vivid designator" for the restriction on exportability, he assumes that the condition on exportability is given by the "knowing who the *F* is" restriction in Hintikka (1962). He then states that this is obviously context relative, and concludes that restrictions on exportation must be dropped.

[17] Igal Kvart wrote that this collapse "did not grow on" him (1982:298). Me neither.

In fact, Kvart shows that Hintikka's conditions for exportation (Hintikka 1962) are not intuitively correct as stated. For belief, Hintikka apparently thinks that "having a belief who α is," or its supposed symbolic expression in his system, is sufficient for exportation in belief contexts. However, Gail Stine already showed that the condition is not sufficient, given that the subject's belief who α is may be false (Stine 1969, 1972). Kvart (1982) rediscovers the objection. My own example (12) in the present paper could be used for the same purpose.

For knowledge, Kvart correctly remarks that for a definite description α, "knowing who α is" has both a *de dicto* reading (the more probable one) and a *de re* reading (for Russell this would be a scope ambiguity). He also shows that "knowing who she/he is" is not always satisfied, even when a subject has a *de re* belief about her/him. For example, one may know of a man in a lineup, or actually seen committing a crime, that he committed the crime, but when asked "who is he?" properly reply "I don't know who he is." (Dennett's example, quoted below, also shows this, though that was not his primary intention.) However, I should add that even in such a case, I know who robbed me (the *de dicto* reading), namely, that man over there. I also know *which man in the lineup* robbed me, and I can *identify* the robber.

Kvart has told me that, in correspondence, Quine conceded that "knowing who he is" is not always the relevant premise, even in context. However, to my knowledge he never retracted the point in print.

[18] Dennett seems to have various things in mind when he states that he rejects the notion. Sometimes he is rejecting theories of causal connections to the object a belief is about, or "direct" as

but rather a defense of unrestricted exportation. This is at most a trivialization, in some sense, of *de re* belief, but not really a rejection of the notion.[19] Really, Dennett in no way disagrees with Sosa, whose formulation (that he has a simple theory of *de re* belief) I would myself use if I accepted their views. Dennett even implicitly admits that some terms of ordinary language involve the notion of belief about an object. When he says he rejects *de re* belief, it appears that he means that he rejects various views that make it a less trivial notion.

His position is stated as follows ("Hoover" is J. Edgar Hoover, who is investigating Smith's murder):

> One is a (minimal) suspect if one satisfies *any* definite description Hoover takes to pick out Smith's murderer. It follows trivially that Smith's murderer is a minimal suspect (because he satisfies the description "Smith's murderer") even in the situation when Hoover is utterly baffled, but merely believes the crime has been committed by a single culprit. This would be an objectionable consequence only if there were some principled way of distinguishing minimal suspects from genuine, or true or *de re* suspects, but there is not. Thus, as Quine suggests, the apparently sharp psychological distinction between
>
> (48) Hoover believes that someone (some *one*) murdered Smith
>
> and
>
> (49) Someone is believed by Hoover to have murdered Smith
>
> collapses (the logical difference in the ontological commitment of the speaker remains). It remains true that in the case in which Hoover is baffled he would naturally deny to the press that there was anyone he believed to be the murderer. What he would actually be denying is that he knows more than anyone who knows only that the crime has been committed. (Dennett 1987:197–98)

Why do I say that Dennett actually acknowledges that *de re* notions appear in ordinary language? This follows from his use of the term "suspect" and his statement that the murderer is a minimal suspect. The term "suspect," of course, is a *de re* notion, having to do with the relation of the police's beliefs to various people. The term "*de re*" simply means that it is a belief (or whatever other attitude) of or about a particular person or object. Dennett does not reject such a

---

opposed to indirect (i.e., merely descriptive) reference to it. But these are theories of *de re* belief, and if one wishes to formulate one's rejection of these theories as a rejection of *de re* belief, one can do so. But, in my opinion, for the reasons given in my text, this would be a misleading way to express oneself.

[19] In contrast to Dennett, perhaps Quine really does intend to reject the notion of *de re* belief. Apparently, he wishes to exclude it even from the level of canonical notation that allows doxastic and epistemic notions. (See Quine 1960:221 for the two levels of canonical notation.) But at the end of his paper he talks about some problems even in the notion of belief *de dicto*. Presumably, however, he does not deny that ordinary language has the locutions that gave rise to his original discussion in Quine (1956). But they are of relatively little concern to him. Quine states that in context, notions like these may be helpful, but everything depends on what one wishes to know.

concept; he simply claims that in the case of "suspect," the term must really always apply to the real murderer.[20]

Let me briefly state my own position. First, the doctrine of unrestricted exportation, for belief and even for knowledge, has far more sweeping consequences than its advocates have ever hinted. These consequences are the main point of this talk.

Second, along the way, some of the advocates of the doctrine presuppose or even state various supposed Gricean principles, allegedly based on the distinction between the literal truth and when it can be misleading to say it (owing to conversational implicature). These principles were never defended by Grice or anyone else, and in fact are devoid of plausibility. They are not similar to the more plausible examples given by Grice himself. Furthermore, some of the examples that supposedly support the context relativity of when a term is exportable seem to me to be mistaken.

Finally, and most importantly for the philosophy of language, the advocates of unrestricted exportation commit what I shall call "the pragmatic wastebasket fallacy," assuming that one can ignore intuitive distinctions simply by calling them "pragmatic" and giving them a Gricean explanation. This fallacy ignores important semantic considerations for the projectability of predicates in all sentences of the language. Moreover, it dismisses as "merely psychological" or "merely pragmatic" distinctions that are important for mathematics and for the criminal law.

Another fallacy I shall mention is the "toy duck fallacy." It is an important case of citing features, supposedly of ordinary language, that, looked at carefully, may not be real.

1. UNNOTICED CONSEQUENCES OF UNRESTRICTED EXPORTATION

Let me get to the first and main point. For the case of belief, the unrestricted exportation view has a rather sweeping consequence. Everyone, except perhaps the Deity, has a false belief. For S, let the false belief in question be p. Consider the following:

---

[20] I am not sure that his linguistic intuitions about "suspect" are right. I might have thought that someone is a suspect if the police have reason to think he committed the crime (or think that they have such reasons) but are not certain. However, if the police are certain that there was a murder committed by one person, then surely they are certain that the murderer committed it. But then the murderer would not be a suspect!

Another linguistic criterion would be: someone is a suspect if the police have reasons (possibly even reasons they regard as conclusive) to believe he committed the crime, and so on. Nothing really hangs on this question, so I will not dwell on it. In fact, I will accept the broader use of the term "suspect." But the term actually has legal definitions in relevant jurisdictions. My impression is that they tend to agree with the narrower usage.

(12) *S* believes that the *y* that is Philby if *p*, and is the Eiffel Tower if not *p*, is a spy.

(12) can be written symbolically as follows:

(13) *S* believes that: Is-a-spy($\imath y$ [(y = Philby $\wedge$ p) $\vee$ (y = the Eiffel Tower $\vee \neg p$)])

(Note that in the verbal form I found it natural to use a conjunction of conditionals, though in the symbolic form I used a disjunction of conjunctions.)[21]

Now, we know that (12) and (13) are true because *S* believes that *p* and believes that Philby is a spy. From the doctrine of unrestricted exportation, we get:

(14) *S* believes of *the Eiffel Tower* that it is a spy

because that is what is denoted by the definite description in question!

On the views that I have been discussing, we are unable to say what we would say intuitively. Intuitively, because of *S*'s misconception that *p* is true, the belief ascribed in (12) is actually a belief about Philby, not a belief about the Eiffel Tower. For it is Philby whom *S* thinks satisfies the description in (12). This, however, is precisely what we cannot say on the views we have been considering. We cannot say that a subject's belief using a description α is about the object he *thinks* satisfies the description, since such a criterion uses the very notion we are trying to define (and to undermine). Instead, it is supposed to be the object that *actually* satisfies the description.[22]

Moreover, we need not suppose that *S* knows about any particular spy, such as Philby. As long as *S* believes that there are spies, the term "Philby" can be replaced by "the tallest spy."[23]

What about the Eiffel Tower? Plainly this object can be replaced by any object that *S* can identify, such that there is some term, name, or definite description denoting it in *S*'s language. This, in turn, can be any object that occupies space and time. Material objects of an ordinary kind are included, as are persons (where we need not be materialists to say this as long as persons have bodies). For we can enumerate all the rational points of space-time. For any ordinary object, there will be a first rational point in the enumeration that is occupied by that object.

---

[21] Actually, I could have used the conditional form, since: $\imath y$ (($p \supset y$ = Philby) $\wedge$ ($\neg p \supset y$ = Eiffel Tower)) = $\imath y$ ((y = Philby $\wedge$ p) $\vee$ (y = Eiffel Tower $\wedge \neg p$)).

[22] Sosa states his theory at the end of his paper: "Indeed, in general, to believe about *x* that it is *F* is to have a belief that is about *x*, one to the effect that it is *F*; which is to believe a proposition that is about *x*, and according to which *x* is *F*. A simpler reduction of *de re* to *de dicto* attitudes is hard to imagine" (1970: 896). But this makes Sosa's account closer to intuition than it is (though still not close enough to intuition). Is the belief in question in the present case about Philby or about the Eiffel Tower? Intuitively, I would say "about Philby." (Then Sosa's general declaration would not in this instance have any conflict with intuition.) Presumably, however, on Sosa's account it is about the Eiffel Tower. For a more detailed discussion of Sosa's views, see below.

[23] On my view, if there is no one *S* believes to be the tallest spy, then the resulting new belief is not clearly a belief of or about a particular person. This is not the view of the authors I am criticizing, but nothing hangs on it in this case.

Then, assuming that we can specify a kind K (in S's vocabulary), such that there is only one object of that kind that includes the region occupied by it, we can then specify the object as the one of kind K occupying a region containing the first rational point in the enumeration.[24]

The mention of rational coordinates leads to another remarkable consequence of unrestricted exportation. The subject S will believe of each natural number, each rational number, and each real number specifiable in S's vocabulary that it is a spy.

Thus, for a normal subject S, a normal predicate F, and a normal object y:

(15) S believes of y that it is F

reduces to:

(16) S believes that there are F's.

Note that here the object y drops out of the picture altogether. The apparent logical form of (15) is tremendously misleading. Even without the argument about rational points, (15) reduces to:

(17) S believes that there are Fs, and y is identifiable by S.

Even in version (17), let alone version (16), the statement only apparently expresses a relation between S, F, and y. In version (17) there are really two independent conjuncts and no relation between F and y at all. And, as I mentioned, in version (16) the object y drops out of the picture altogether. It is strange that our language should contain locutions of such misleading surface form and of such a trivial character.

I do not know whether the defenders of unrestricted exportation would accept even this awful consequence.[25] I would hope not. From reading them one might

---

[24] I am not going to worry about elementary particles, or other such exotica, about which we normally would not be thought to have *de re* beliefs. I am also not going to worry about whether restrictions should be placed in the enumeration on whether entities can be located arbitrarily in the future, past, and so on.

Occasionally, someone has objected to the tallest spy example because of the assumption that no two spies are of exactly the same height. Maybe the two tallest spies are exactly tied (identical twins?)! If one is really worried about this problem, one can use the same device, about occupying the first rational point, to pick out a unique spy. In any case, I doubt that any serious issue could hang on such an objection. One who maintains unrestricted exportation would be very lucky indeed if "the tallest spy" were actually a vacuous description.

David Kaplan (1968) proposed a similar device somewhere and called it "the least spy."

[25] One philosopher I admire, who was an advocate (in part) of the view I am criticizing, reportedly reacted as follows: only a few people will be clever enough to think of the tricky sort of definite description in (12) and (13). So, for most people, unrestricted exportation will not imply that they have the weird *de re* beliefs I am mentioning, though a few very clever ones will. Were one to take such a reply seriously, it might even have been used against the "shortest spy" example (Dennett does express somewhat similar reservations even for this example; see his 1987:202). I am not sure what standard of cleverness is involved, especially since a belief need not be explicitly expressed or thought of to be properly ascribed to a person. For example, don't most of my readers

think that only a few extra cases, like the tallest spy, or the shortest, need be accepted, though a little thought even about these examples would add quite a bit to the list. But the present case shows the list is much longer still. Even just the one example about the Eiffel Tower is rather weird.

Others have advocated this view as well. I have discussed this consequence of the view in seminars and have wanted to make it public for some time. In the case of knowledge, we could not draw such a strikingly awful consequence, because the argument depends on there being a false belief in the definite description. And, of course, if it is knowledge, we can't do it that way, since false knowledge, unlike false belief, is impossible.[26] So, the consequence won't be quite so awful. Igal Kvart, who heard me talk about this once, remarked—rightly, it seems to me: "Well, even if your argument doesn't go through for knowledge, one's confidence in unrestricted exportation will be greatly weakened even for the case of knowledge because of the consequence about belief."

However, it is interesting to see what follows if we assume that unrestricted exportation holds for knowledge. The appropriate consequence in this case will be:

(18) The CIA knows, of y, that y is a spy iff y is a spy.

We assume that the CIA knows that there are spies. Otherwise, no assumption need be made about the CIA, so that the argument follows with "the CIA" replaced by any term that refers to one of us. The CIA certainly will know that the tallest spy is a spy, and therefore, according to the unrestricted exportation principle, will know of the tallest spy that he or she is a spy. However, the CIA will also know of the second-tallest spy that he or she is a spy, and so on down the rank. To avoid running into a vacuous description, we should add a clause: "or if there is none that short, back to the tallest spy." In this way one always gets a definite description denoting a spy, and every spy will be denoted by some appropriate description.[27] So, the CIA will know precisely of all and only the spies, that they are spies. I don't know why they have so much work to do. In fact, all of us are in the same position. Any subject S who knows that there are spies will do.

---

believe that Paris is not in China, even though they may have never thought of the question before? Similarly, S may not have to be so clever to respond properly to (12) and (13) if they are put to her or him, and then the belief may properly be ascribed to S all along. (The distinction in question has been discussed in the literature.)

In any event, which of the following sounds truer to the reader?
(a) Anyone who is sufficiently intelligent believes of each tree in this forest that it is a spy.
(b) Only a psychotic person believes of any tree in this forest that it is a spy.

[26] Or so almost all philosophers agree, though perhaps not absolutely all.

[27] This is given the usual assumptions mentioned before, that no two spies are of the same height, and that there are only finitely many. We have seen above how such assumptions could be avoided if one wished. (See note 24.)

Moreover, the predicate "is a spy" could be replaced by a wide variety of predicates "is F." The assumptions needed are that the subject S knows that there is an F, and that an appropriate definite description will denote each F for S. We have seen already what assumptions about F may guarantee this. We need not repeat them. They apply to a wide variety of predicates.[28]

However, there do appear to be predicates where unrestricted exportation for belief will not lead to any kind of striking collapse, not even the type of problem of which all our authors are aware (the tallest/shortest spy). We have seen above that the assumption of unrestricted exportation does not obviously collapse Quine's distinction between the two readings of "I want a sloop" (see note 12). This propositional attitude ("wants that") is not belief. However, there is a related, though not equivalent, attitude involving belief, namely, "I believe that I should have a sloop."[29, 30] As before in the case of "wants that," nothing follows to the effect that "I believe that I should have the longest sloop that I should have." Nor do the other ideas mentioned in note 12 work here either. So even unrestricted exportation will not collapse the relevant distinction in this case.

2. SOME REMARKS, METHODOLOGICAL AND OTHERWISE

I have said that I wish to draw a few morals in the philosophy of language. Let me mention some summarily, though all of them have applications other than the problem at hand and deserve further discussion elsewhere.[31] These are, first, the overuse (*misuse*) of Gricean methodology and the related "pragmatic wastebasket fallacy" and, second, what I call the "toy duck fallacy."

But before reaching the methodological morals, I must return to some of the authors I have been discussing. Sosa and Dennett, especially, give a wide variety of cases and arguments, and I hope I may be pardoned if I don't discuss them all. I should first mention Sosa, since he states and considers various theories of reductions of *de re* to *de dicto* belief (and presumably applying to analogous propositional attitudes as well). After first stating the unrestricted exportation idea, and stating the "tallest spy" objection to it, he then considers alternative

---

[28] Once again, (18) and analogous cases show that the apparent logical form of *de re* knowledge, like *de re* belief, is highly misleading. Typically, both knowledge and the subject of the knowledge drop out on the right-hand side.

[29] The special case discussed in this paragraph is one that I had not noticed when I gave the original version of this talk.

[30] I could want to have a cigarette, even though I don't believe that I should have one. Conversely, I could believe that I should have something without wanting to have it. When one considers other forms in the same family, the difference is even more pronounced.

[31] In fact, even if someone were to doubt a particular application of the morals in question to one of the arguments I give below, they ought to be recognized as being of general significance for the philosophy of language.

theories. One is that of Kaplan (1968), which he regards as requiring for exportability that a, the term to be exported, be a name (or "vivid" name) of the object it refers to. Little else is said in Sosa's statement of the principle, but in side remarks he states that Kaplan requires that a be at the end of a causal chain leading up to it. He then rejects Kaplan's view on intuitive grounds, since it does not allow *de re* beliefs about anything existing only in the future, which Sosa thinks is contrary to the intuitive data.[32]

Sosa's own first approach to an appropriate account, stated as "my own view," is:

III. *S* believes about *x* that it is *F* (believes *x* to be *F*) if and only if there is a singular term a such that *S* believes ⌜a is *F*⌝, where a both denotes *x* and is a distinguished term. (1970:890)

This account is a theory only because Sosa states the problem in terms of possible reductions of *de re* to *de dicto* beliefs. Conceivably, these might not be conditions on exportability. However, as I have presented the matter, assuming we are asking when a term is exportable (and all the alternatives Sosa discusses fit this pattern), III no longer becomes a theory of exportability but simply a restatement of the issue. Since, as is clear from Sosa's discussion, there is nothing in III that precludes a term's being distinguished for one sentence and not another, or even for a given sentence in one context and not in another, it is hard to see how III even counts as a "theory" or "view" regarding exportability. "Distinguished" is little more than a synonym for "exportable," so that I certainly believe III, at least in the direction of the sufficiency of the condition, which is simply a tautology. Perhaps the converse, essentially that a *de re* belief requires a *de dicto* belief with an exportable term, is not tautological, but it is assumed by many writers on the subject.[33] Sosa's "view" III is not really an alternative to Kaplan's, but subsumes it as a special case. The real point is simply that Sosa rejects Kaplan's views on when a term is exportable.

In fairness to Sosa, I should add that he does present intuitively plausible special cases that he regards as always distinguished (exportable). One important example is the first person (he also introduces his subject with an interesting discussion of Castañeda's problem of self-knowledge). Moreover, he uses the same principle to *deny* that certain other terms, which would otherwise be exportable, are in fact exportable when the subject is unaware that the term is describing him. Much of Sosa's discussion, shorn of his references to cases that

---

[32] Kaplan appears to be writing under the influence of discussions with me—prior to *Naming and Necessity*—of my views on proper names, discussions with Charles Chastain, and of course ideas of his own. See Kaplan (1968:211, note 1, and 213, note 24).

It is somewhat surprising to me that Sosa should argue against another theory on the basis of intuitive data, when his own ultimate conclusion is that intuitive data should be thrown to the wind, at least in regard to what is literally true.

[33] Sosa commends Kaplan (1968) for giving "an excellent case in favor of such reduction" (Sosa 1970:884, note 6).

are alleged to show that exportation is an entirely pragmatic matter, is in fact an illuminating treatment of our intuitions regarding exportability.[34] I am not going to do any better than Sosa at stating a criterion for exportability (at least here). But, intuitively, when a speaker's use of a term makes him sufficiently *en rapport* with its object, it is exportable; this, however, does not say all that much.[35]

Sosa then argues that whether a term is distinguished depends entirely on very arbitrary contextual factors: "This, I fear, is a wholly pragmatic matter which can change radically from one occasion to the next" (890). He gives examples to convince us of this. It seems to me that some have more apparent force than others. Quine, without Sosa's detailed consideration of examples, draws a similar conclusion, basing it on Hintikka's "knowing who" criterion for exportability, which he regards as highly contextual and pragmatic.

I think the significance of contextual factors here is greatly exaggerated. But assume for the moment that Sosa's examples given to support it are all correct. To make his argument (where I somewhat feel I have to fill in the gaps), one must argue that cases like these, where exportation is a "pragmatic" matter, are quite typical, and Sosa does, in fact, seem to think that this is the case (894).

By the end of the paper Sosa reinstates what he calls "account I" (what I have called "unrestricted exportation"), which he had apparently rejected previously on the basis of the "tallest spy" objection.[36] He writes:

An attractive reduction of *de re* belief to *de dicto* belief is the following:

I. S believes about x that it is F (or believes x to be F) if and only if there is a singular term α such that S believes ⌜α is F⌝, where α denotes x.

His analysis of account III leads him to think that the simpler account I will do, provided that in those cases in which account III would prohibit exportation, account I would declare the exportation to be, although rhetorically misleading, logically correct (Sosa 1970:896, note 20). As we have seen, Sosa says that "a

---

[34] For example, Sosa carefully discusses when a "subjective curtain" (1970: 893) (that is, when I am, perhaps unknowingly, talking about myself) is or is not a block to exportation. Regardless of whether one entirely agrees with his intuitions, it is once again hard for me to reconcile his careful, intuitive discussion here, including cases where exportation is blocked, with his ultimate advocacy of universal exportation as the literal truth.

[35] Kvart (1982) relies on the notion of the "intended reference" of a term and refers in this connection to my own paper, Kripke (1977) (Chapter 5 of this volume). Thus, in my own example (12), it is Philby, not the Eiffel Tower, that is the intended reference. Surely, this conclusion agrees with intuition, as I have said. However, as I also remarked above (see the discussion immediately after (14)), my opponents would think that this intuitive characterization appeals to the ideas that they are questioning. But in my view this gets things the wrong way around. However, Kvart gives an elaborate counterfactual causal analysis, meant to free the notion of intended referent from any such objections. It would require much more work than I have done to evaluate his theory.

[36] Not just "apparently" in Quine (1981). Recall, as we noted above, that he says categorically "evidently we must find against exportation" (1981:20), only to reinstate exportation later on.

simpler reduction of *de re* to *de dicto* attitudes is hard to imagine" (896). But why does this move have any particular plausibility?

In the first place, Sosa's conclusion that exportation is always allowed (although sometimes rhetorically misleading) would be more plausible if *every* term were exportable in *some* appropriate context. The more terms there are for which there is no appropriate context that would license the exportation, the less plausibility Sosa's defense of unrestricted exportation, as stated immediately below, has. (Much less does it follow [as Quine suggests] from the supposed context relativity of "knowing who.")[37]

In the second place, even if every term, or at least a significant number of terms, were exportable in some context, why depart from the general strategy stated in account III to embrace account I? Sosa acknowledges that his own paradigmatic example of a pragmatic explanation of "logically correct but rhetorically incorrect (misleading)"—namely, that the statement made is too weak (so that an impression is given that the stronger statement may not be true)—is inapplicable here. We must glean an explanation from his discussion of particular cases (such as the "Metropolis Pyromaniac" case, discussed below), which are supposed to illuminate the principle, and from his statement of general principles.

Sosa says:

If my train of thought has been right, then "S believes about x that it is F" has much in common with, say, "Jupiter is too far away," or "The end of the century is sufficiently far

---

[37] In the earlier part of the paper, I tried to point out that there is a wealth of such terms, and the relevant *de re* notions are surprisingly trivialized.

In a rather surprising footnote, Sosa writes that the context-sensitivity of exportation is no greater than that of demonstrative reference or ambiguities of predication (1970:895, note 19). But surely various authors have proposed quite formal analyses of these. What Sosa is alleging appears to me to be quite worse (and no one ever proposed any analogue of Sosa's account I, unrestricted exportation, for these).

Also puzzling is Quine's dismissal of restrictions on exportation, which he assumes to be based on a "knowing who he is" restriction (but see my note 17). He says that this notion "is utterly dependent on context," and adds, "Sometimes, when we ask who someone is, we see the face and want the name; sometimes the reverse. Sometimes we want to know his role in the community. Of itself the notion is empty" (Quine 1981:121). Strictly speaking, the argument as stated, even assuming its premises, might be taken as compatible with completely determinate context-free conditions for "knowing who" (maybe we need to know all three conditions, even if this is not in fact the case). But presumably Quine means that one might say that one knows who someone is but then, apprised of his role in the community or asking about it, say that one didn't really know who he was.

I am not sure how ubiquitous this contextuality is, but assume it to be so. Why does contextuality imply that a notion is empty? Perhaps that the notion pretends not to be contextual when it is? Or that contextuality makes it not amenable to formal treatment? (For the latter idea, see Kaplan's introduction to "What is Meaning?," where he reports Strawson as telling him that he assumed on the authority of Quine that even such context-sensitive phenomena as demonstratives were not amenable to treatment on the basis of modern logic. Kaplan cites his own work, and could have cited others, as contesting this claim.) The parameters of contextuality can be imagined to be kept fixed, for a given treatment, which is what Hintikka (1962) seems to imagine.

in the future." Whether Jupiter is too far away depends on the context, and not just because it depends on the physical position of the speaker or thinker, but also because it depends on the question under consideration. (1970:894)

Now, I am not so sure that the examples Sosa gives for *de re* belief support this comparison. But assume the comparison to be valid, and the conclusions about the context-sensitivity of the expression cited to be correct. I assume that this is not a special question about Jupiter (that in most ordinary contexts it happens to be far away, and probably even too far away),[38] but about the predicate "too far away," which is indeed highly relative not only to the resources and position of the speaker, but also to the purposes envisaged. (Is London too far away? Greenwich Village? Suppose the speaker is in upper mid-Manhattan.) But, why should it follow that we can simplify the conclusion to "every entity is too far away," and delete the reference to context? The idea would be that whenever we apply the expression "too far way," we are logically correct though perhaps rhetorically misleading. I am not even sure what that would mean. It does appear to be the natural analogue of Sosa's reversion to account I.[39]

It appears to me that the argument proceeds by leaps and bounds, and that the conclusions drawn are hardly justified or plausible, even given the premises. But I wonder whether Sosa or Dennett would have maintained their argument if they knew what their position really entailed. Is it plausible that, strictly speaking, though it may be rhetorically misleading, we all believe of the Eiffel Tower that it is a spy? Or take the contextual account III that Sosa imagines can be simplified to the unrestricted exportation theory: Are there really contexts in which any of us believes of the Eiffel Tower that it is a spy? What are these contexts? Remember that these examples, even on the basis of the weaker contextual theory, would have to show that for any object identifiable by a speaker (and that means almost every ordinary object), she believes of it that it is a spy in some context or other.

But for the moment let's set examples of this kind aside. There is another point to be made. As we have seen, Sosa distinguishes what is true from what it is rhetorically appropriate to say and thinks that this will remove the intuitive objection to unrestricted exportation. "Just as," he says, "strictly speaking, those who know also believe" (Sosa 1970:896).

---

[38] Sosa does envisage special contexts in which Jupiter might or might not be too far away for the purposes mentioned.

[39] David Lewis proposed that whether one knows something can depend on the context in which one is considering a question, and others have followed him with similar theories (see Lewis 1983:247, second paragraph, and Lewis 1996). If one is in an ordinary context, one knows a lot of things that one would not know if a skeptical hypothesis had been raised. In the latter context, one knows neither the negation of the skeptical hypothesis nor the usual cases of knowledge that entail it. Suppose for the moment that Lewis was right. Should he have drawn the consequence, or suggested the theory that really we know very little (or nothing subject to skeptical doubt), even though it would be rhetorically misleading to say this? It would be very unlike Lewis to have drawn such a conclusion, but it seems to me to be the analogous move to Sosa's transition from his theory III to theory I (unrestricted exportation).

There may indeed be cases where it is rhetorically misleading to make a statement even when it is true. In the quoted example, Sosa has in mind cases where what is asserted is too weak. Maybe a natural example can be found where saying that someone believes something is misleading when the person in question actually knows it. Another somewhat different case, known because Grice used it in the paper in which he originally set up his well-known methodology of conventional meaning (including conventional implicature) versus conversational implicature (Grice 1961), is that of "looks red." Although in appropriate circumstances (though not really all) a speaker may imply that she doubts or denies that an object really is red when she says that it looks red, nevertheless this is a mere matter of "conversational implicature," and really (of course) an object that is red often, indeed usually, looks red too.[40]

However, as Dennett rightly notes (in the above quotation), the present case is not merely one where it is rhetorically misleading to say something literally true. When J. Edgar Hoover knows that a murder has been committed by just one person, according to Dennett (and other unrestricted exporters), he actually has a suspect, namely, the murderer.[41] Nevertheless, Dennett rightly goes on to observe, it isn't just that J. Edgar Hoover would be *misleading* were he to assert that he has a suspect; under these circumstances, "he would naturally *deny* to the press that there was anyone he believed to be the murderer" (198, my emphasis).

This is very different from the type of situation noted by Sosa. Maybe at some point it might be rhetorically misleading for someone who knows something merely to say that he believes it, even though, strictly speaking, it is true, and similarly for other cases.[42] It is something quite different to say that it is

---

[40] It would seem from Grice's paper that some "ordinary language" philosophers held that "looks red" cannot be used except in the presence of the appropriate doubt or denial conditions. But I don't know who these people were. I know of nothing in print. I may have missed something. Arguments of that type certainly were common in the era of "ordinary language" philosophy.

[41] See the quotation from Dennett above and note 20 for the term "suspect." Actually, the main argument of the present paper, *modulo* any reservations about the term "suspect," shows that countless entities are suspects (or "minimal suspects") if Dennett's unrestricted exportation is right. But the point remains even if we leave this aside (though I do not know how Dennett would have reacted had he been aware of this consequence of his views.).

[42] Actually, I am somewhat worried that Sosa chose a rather difficult example. No doubt, as he says, strictly speaking, those who know also believe. Nevertheless, the use of "I believe" presents special problems. I have some inclination to think, for example, that if someone says "I believe she has gone to the movies," the speaker is sometimes not simply reporting a mental state but explicitly expressing some degree of caution or hesitation, as opposed to the categorical statement without the prefix. Moreover, as Quine notes, "x does not believe that p" usually means "x believes that not p," rather than "it is not the case that x believes that p" (1960:145–46). Such complications make comparison of this case with others difficult.

However, no doubt this does not affect the general point that a statement can be rhetorically misleading, though logically true, for being too weak, though semantically true, as I have acknowledged in the main text. Also, Sosa maintains that this explanation does not apply to the *de re* case he is considering.

appropriate actually to *deny* the statement.⁴³ For example, to use Grice's original case, is there any inclination to *deny* that a red object looks red (unless, of course, there really is some special reason for such a denial)? So, though it may sometimes be rhetorically misleading, though correct, to say that something "looks red," suggesting a reservation about its real color that is not there, that does not mean that it would be appropriate in these circumstances to deny that it does look red. And indeed the whole point of Grice's example is that this is not the case.⁴⁴

Let me make a few additional remarks about Dennett's characterization of Hoover's denial "that there was anyone he believed to be the murderer." First, Dennett says, "What he would actually be denying is that he knows more than anyone knows who knows only that the crime has been committed" (198).⁴⁵ Actually, Hoover may know much more than that and have many clues but still have no belief as to the murderer. Let us amend Dennett's statement: what Hoover is denying is that he has nontrivial reasons to believe of anyone that he committed the murder. Such a reformulation would be closer to what Dennett is imagining but hardly expresses a genuine pragmatic principle. Someone might as well say that her blood is not circulating, because she thinks that the only reasons her blood is circulating are the usual trivial reasons, not some special pacemaker or the like. Plainly, there is no such principle.⁴⁶

Dennett goes on to say:

---

⁴³ Actually, the very hypothetical case in connection with which Sosa cites the notion of what is true but rhetorically misleading (that of a secret pyromaniac, as described in Sosa's paper; see also below) is one in which Sosa, too, recognizes that the pyromaniac would *deny* that he is suspected. Sosa's later, weaker characterization of the case is very misleading.

⁴⁴ It is reasonably well known that what looks like a negation can sometimes be used to reject a statement as too weak (the phenomenon was first called to my attention by David Lewis). For example, someone says, "The Iraq war has gone on at least a little bit longer than when Bush pronounced it was over" (his "mission accomplished" statement in 2003). And then someone else says, "Come on, it didn't go on *at least a little bit longer*, it's been going on for years" (this is sometimes called metalinguistic negation).

A similar example derives from a Gricean example of "generalized conversational implicature." He writes, "Anyone who uses a sentence of the form '*X* is meeting a woman this evening' would normally implicate that the person to be met was someone other than X's wife, mother, sister, or perhaps even close platonic friend" (Grice 1989:37). The old jocular routine— "'Who was that lady I saw you with last night?'—'That was no lady, that was my wife'"—trades on the ambiguity of a genuine denial and a mere denial of the Gricean conversational implicature (as well as old-fashioned connotations, ambiguous here, of "lady").

But it is clear that the present cases are not like either of these; Hoover actually *denies* that there was anyone he believed to be the murderer. Sosa's pyromaniac *denies* that he is suspected.

⁴⁵ Presumably, Dennett really intends an extra clause "that the crime has been committed *by a single culprit*," as he himself has said previously.

⁴⁶ This is so even though it would be rhetorically odd for someone to say, "out of the blue" and with no special context, that her blood *is* circulating. Why does she say that? Is something wrong or something special going on? For it to be rhetorically odd or misleading for someone to say something does not mean we have a license to deny it.

He is certainly not denying that he has a *de re* belief directly about some individual to the effect that he is the murderer, a belief he has acquired by some intimate cognitive rapport with that individual, for suppose Hoover wrestled with the murderer at the scene of the crime, in broad daylight, but has no idea who the person was with whom he wrestled; surely on anyone's causal theory of *de re* belief, that person is believed by him to be the murderer, but it would be most disingenuous for Hoover to claim to have a suspect. (1987:198)

Two comments are relevant here. First, how can it be "most disingenuous for Hoover to claim to have a suspect," when according to Dennett he does have one? I suppose Dennett means that it would be rhetorically misleading, for the dubious reasons discussed above. More important for the present case concerns why it is that writers so concerned with the hidden contextuality of a family of statements ignore the most blatant contextual parameters. Statements about a subject having or not having a belief (whether *de re* or *de dicto*) plainly vary over time. All that is needed to handle Dennett's case is to suppose that Hoover *did* believe of his wrestling partner, *at the time of the wrestling*, that he was the murderer but has not retained the *de re* belief later. (Maybe *someone's* "causal" theory is refuted by Dennett's example, but I don't know whose.)[47]

Let us mention another case emphasized by Sosa. He writes:

[A] spy and his accomplice see through a window how an investigator finds some incriminating evidence in the spy's footlocker. The accomplice could very naturally say "He knows that you are a spy now."[48] You must escape." In fact, and so far as the accomplice knows, the investigator does not know the spy, and knows practically nothing about him: the footlocker had been searched only as part of a general investigation of the base. What the investigator knows is ⌜the owner of the footlocker is a spy⌝. Since the accomplice is right to export, 'the owner of the footlocker' is a distinguished term in the circumstances. (1970:891)

---

[47] Kvart (1982:300) gives a related example where someone *S* has a purse snatched, and where the thief immediately disappears into the crowd. Kvart thinks that *S* has no opinion (either in the *de dicto* or the *de re* sense) as to whom the purse snatcher is, but still, surely, has a *de re* belief about the thief. Presumably Kvart thinks that the *de re* belief has been retained because the time is short and the memory vivid. But then, there is no reason to suppose that the *de dicto* knowledge "who snatched the purse," namely, "that tall man over there," should be lost either. However one rules in either case, there is no reason to suppose that the *de re* belief and the *de dicto* "knowing-*who*" locutions do not go together.
 More elaborate treatments of Dennett's case and Kvart's might involve more than the vividness of the memory, the time elapsed, and so on. Even when the police have identified the culprit in the ordinary sense, the culprit may have disguised himself, and the police may have no idea how to find him. We need not go into all these subtleties here.

[48] Here Sosa assumes that "knows you are a spy," where a pronoun is used, implies that the subject of knowledge has *de re* knowledge that the person referred to is a spy. I am not going to contest this assumption, and indeed I am inclined to think it correct. In some sense, the assumption is Russellian in character. Sosa does mention Russell's views in his paper (1970:884) but does not emphasize them. (In the present instance, the assumption would not be consistent with Russell's later very narrow characterization of acquaintance, which Sosa also mentions.)

Dennett echoes Sosa's example, citing him as well (197). Suppose Hoover knows many bits of evidence that will put him close on the trail of the murderer (George). These are uniquely identifying. According to Dennett:

> [S]ince George is the lone satisfier of Hoover's description, Hoover believes of George that he did it. "No, Gracie," George says, "Hoover knows only that *whoever* fits this description is Smith's murderer. He doesn't know that *I* fit this description, so he doesn't know that I am Smith's murderer. Wake me up when you learn that *I* am suspected. (1987:197)

Dennett clearly thinks George is being absurd. He gives what he regards as a parallel case where Poirot gathers a number of people in a room and states that he does not have a suspect but will know who the culprit is when he finds the person with the pantry key on his person (197).

Sosa's and Dennett's intuitions are strange to me, because clearly there are two distinct questions. One is whether a criminal has been identified; the other is whether the criminal is in danger of being identified soon. To me, Sosa's accomplice obviously would *not* say, "he knows that you are a spy now," though he might say, "watch out, they may soon find out that you are a spy, once they find out who owns the footlocker." Similarly, maybe George *should* wake up. It depends on how long Hoover has to pore over the evidence before he identifies George. If this might take some time and George will have some time to escape even after he has been identified, his remarks will have been correct. Poirot's suspects are indeed in very imminent danger, but there is no reason to think that Poirot's remark that he does not yet have a suspect is literally incorrect. Dennett immediately follows his remarks on Poirot with his material on a "minimal suspect," apparently drawing it as a moral of the examples just discussed.[49] Recall what he says:

> It is not true that George is safe so long as Hoover's beliefs are of the form *whoever fits description D is Smith's murderer,* for if description D is something like "the only person in Clancy's bar with yellow mud on his shoes," the jig may soon be up. One is a (minimal) suspect if one satisfies *any* definite description Hoover takes to pick out Smith's murderer. It follows trivially that Smith's murderer is a minimal suspect (because he satisfies the description "Smith's murderer") even in the situation when Hoover is utterly baffled, but merely believes the crime has been committed by a single culprit. This would be an objectionable consequence only if there were some principled way of distinguishing minimal suspects from genuine, or true or *de re* suspects, but there is not. (Dennett 1987:198)

---

[49] I should add, since it is unclear that these things are distinguished by Quine, Sosa, or Dennett, that whether a criminal has been identified and whether he has been caught are two different things. Escapes even of known culprits obviously occur. But this is not the main point.

Moreover, the remarks by Sosa and especially by Dennett on Poirot give the impression that they realize that one might be inclined to deny, under the circumstances they consider, that the respective culprits have been identified. Precisely this inclination seems to motivate the idea that these relevant idioms are "interest relative" or "context dependent."

Grice brought about a general attitude that one should try to keep the semantics of the language simple and ascribe pragmatic explanations for various semantic phenomena if at all possible.[50] The view that this strategy should be followed in this case is fairly explicit in Sosa, even though Grice is not mentioned by name. It is not as clear in Dennett. However, both authors mistakenly take descriptions that denote a culprit and make his capture imminent to be exportable descriptions. Dennett goes further, concluding that the second half of the condition—that the relevant term be "distinguished"—can be dropped, though he gives no argument. He concludes that there is no "principled way of distinguishing" among various descriptions Hoover may have to denote the suspect, including the minimal one, even though the latter hardly puts the culprit in any danger of ultimate identification. (Maybe sometimes the line is vague or difficult to draw.)

It is unclear whether Dennett's attitude is also Gricean (though this might be used to make his position more plausible). His attitude can also depend on various arguments that there cannot be such a principled distinction or that it is difficult for a theorist to see her way as to what it would be.[51] There is also the Quinean attitude of rejecting intuitive distinctions when certain theories exclude them or find them hard to explain.

Here, I am concerned with the attitude stemming from Grice. It seems to me that this principle can be overused. As I've mentioned, an important moral I want to talk about in the philosophy of language is that we should not think of pragmatics as a wastebasket. This is well illustrated by Dennett's "minimal suspect" example, regardless of Dennett's own motivations.

Suppose, as in Dennett's example, that a crime has been committed by a unique culprit. Such terms as "suspects" are predicates and there are corresponding verbs.[52] Consider, for example:

---

[50] This is echoed, for example, by myself in Kripke (1977). (However, neither Kripke 1977 nor Donnellan 1966 is compatible with unrestricted exportation since both acknowledge that descriptions admit of a use in which the object spoken of by means of the description may not satisfy it.)

[51] Dennett gives his own reasons for doubting the distinction, some of which have been mentioned above. I have said that it would be impossible to deal with all his numerous cases. But I will mention briefly as an example his case about people sitting around a table (1987:196–97). According to Dennett, there appears to be a sharp contrast between thinking about "the youngest person present," and about "Bill." If one has no idea as to the ages of the people present, the description generates no *de re* belief, whereas it appears that "Bill" does so. But "Bill" generates no *de re* belief either, if his twin brother has appeared in disguise, so the probably difference is only psychological. The case is somewhat underdescribed as presented. Probably Dennett assumes the subject knows Bill. In this case, he has *de re* beliefs both about Bill and about "that man," who may or may not really be Bill. If, at another extreme, the subject has never heard of Bill, then the belief is only about "that man," who may or may not be Bill. Dennett's earlier bizarre fantasy about the two places called "Shakey's Pizza Parlor" (167ff), which he acknowledges might be considered too anomalous a case to destroy a theory, should be handled similarly, insofar as it is clear.

[52] Logically, a transitive verb is a two-place predicate. "Suspect" is a verb, and can be reduced to the one-place predicate, "a suspect." (Actually, of course, there are other parameters in "*a* suspects *b*," namely, what *b* is suspected of, tense, etc.)

(19) For every two people the Chicago police suspect of the crime, the New York police suspect three.

This is a ratio—it might be that there are four suspects that the Chicago police have, and six that the New York police have. Since the police believe that there is a unique culprit, they are well aware that many of the suspects are in fact innocent.

Suppose that in fact all the suspects are innocent. Then, according to Dennett, in the true semantics of the language, the ratio given in (19) will be wrong. The true culprit must always be included in the extension of "suspect." In fact, according to the argument I gave in the previous section, the supposed "true" extension of "suspect" (by the police force of any city) will be much larger—it will include even the Eiffel Tower. However, even if what Dennett imagines is correct and only the true culprit need be included, such a statement as (19) will be wrong.

The point is this: such terms as "suspect" are predicates. They interact with quantifiers and cardinality and such like, in the language, and we have to project them to a wide variety of sentences. How can these predications and interactions be explained? Ultimately, they depend on the notion of (15) ("S believes of y that it is F"). They can only be explained by saying that, in addition to literal English, in which statements such as (19) are trivially false and should not be made, there is something else—"pragmatic English"—which confused speakers, not aware of the literal extension of "suspect" that follows from universal exportation, do accept and do use.[53] In pragmatic English, "suspect" interacts with quantifiers and cardinality in a way that matches the intuitions of ordinary, "confused" speakers. There must be some principles of projection that will enable one to evaluate the statements of confused English, or pragmatic English, over the entire language. But then why shouldn't pragmatic English simply be called "English"? Its semantics, like that of other languages, must be given recursively, starting from the extensions of terms like "suspect," and their interactions with cardinality, and so on.[54]

That is the first moral I want to draw from this discussion: under the influence of Grice we have sometimes gone too far. Let's make the semantics as simple as possible, the rest is all pragmatics and we don't have to think about it. But,

---

[53] Presumably, Sosa would agree with Dennett about the term "suspect." Indeed, in his "pyromaniac" case, the question is whether anyone suspects the pyromaniac of the murder.

[54] Compare the "suspect" case with the "woman" case as mentioned (see note 44). In spite of the Gricean implicatures of "woman" (or "lady") in the special contexts he mentions, the extension of "woman" is not affected. Consider: "How many women are there on the board of directors?," "...in this room?," and so on. The extension of "woman" can be projected in the natural way throughout the language, as spoken by ordinary speakers. Hence, the special implicatures mentioned by Grice need not be brought into the semantics of the language.

This ought to be true of "suspect," if only Gricean conversational implicature were contaminating its apparent extension in some special cases; but it is not.

sometimes we do have to think about it, and then maybe the phenomenon should be treated as part of the semantics of the language. Pragmatics is not a wastebasket. Ordinary speakers seem to be able to handle these distinctions that supposedly can't be made or "shouldn't" be made. Perhaps we should just take a better look at what they are, and, if they are too hard, we may just have to admit that they are too hard. If we cannot make out the distinctions, it is our fault and not that of ordinary speakers, and in that respect our semantics is incomplete.

Perhaps these distinctions are indeed built into the language, as we have it, but are not important from a genuine, truly philosophical point of view. Dennett says,

[T]hus, as Quine suggests, the apparently sharp psychological distinction between

(48) Hoover believes that someone (some *one*) murdered Smith

and

(49) Someone is believed by Hoover to have murdered Smith,

collapses. (198)

Psychological? *Psychological?*[55] I do not think that the criminal law, the very area emphasized by Dennett and Sosa, regards the relevant *de re* notions as merely psychological. I know less about the significance of these things than I ought to, but I know enough to believe that real legal issues are involved. First, the police often make official announcements as to whether so-and-so is indeed a suspect.[56] A grand jury, in this country, often will send someone a warning letter—and this is *de re*: it is about the particular person; it is to a particular person—that he or she is a target of the investigation, a so-called target letter. Of course, there is no philosophical issue here about the recipient of the letter. But what raises the *de re* belief question is the legal assumption that a person whom the grand jury strongly suspects committed the crime, and whom it is investigating accordingly, should receive such a letter. In appropriate jurisdictions, that someone is a target of an investigation can have legal consequences.

A related claim, which I have sometimes heard made, is the following: whatever may be the case for ordinary language, scientific language should not admit such expressions as "there is someone I believe to be a spy," and presumably related ones such as "the object has been identified," "we know which F it

---

[55] Dennett's paper shows that he is quite serious in saying that psychology, once it is worked out, will eliminate many of these notions about belief and reference and dissolve the associated puzzles. See the concluding sentences of his paper (1987:200).

[56] Apparently, in many jurisdictions, the term "suspect" has an official legal definition. Because of the negative connotations of "suspect," nowadays the police sometimes use the term "person of interest," but it appears not to have an official legal definition. In either case, the police are generally cautious in accusing someone of being the perpetrator. Eventually, the police may be prepared categorically to identify someone as the perpetrator or culprit.

is," and so on. This comes, of course, from the Quinean view that all ways of identifying an object are on a par, that "frankly inequalitarian" theories about different ways of identifying an object are plainly unscientific. Just this idea underlies the feeling for unrestricted exportation. Quine most famously applied it to modal logic, and only later to belief and knowledge contexts. But this seems to me to be plainly untenable. On this view, computability theory—that is, recursion theory—would not be a serious science. What question does it seek to answer? It seeks to answer the question, when is a function f such that, given an argument n, we can eventually tell its value $f(n)$ (with no limits on how long the computation takes). But, on the strict Quinean idea, any number theoretic function, once it is defined, is automatically computable. For given any n, the value is simply $f(n)$. To suppose otherwise is to adopt, as Quine would put it, a "frankly inequalitarian" attitude toward two ways of designating the same number. But, I am afraid, that is just what computability theory *does* do. We suppose the natural numbers given in a canonical notation (the simplest, for the purposes of computability theory, is 0 followed by a finite number of successor symbols), and ask that the computation be given in that notation. A computable function is one where you always, by applying an appropriate process, can get the answer. This does *not* hold for an arbitrary function.[57] Complexity theory also serves as an example.[58]

Anyone who says that these notions are not serious, either from the point of view of science or from the point of view the law, is, I think, wrong. No one, just to make philosophy of language simpler and avoid drawing too many distinctions, should think otherwise.

This is not the place to discuss all the special problems and ambiguities that in unusual cases may arise for the "knowing who" locution. The concentration on this locution, and thus on the case of people, seems to stem from its emphasis in Hintikka (1962). In this case, not only might there be ambiguities in the locution, there may in special cases be divergences from related locutions such as "knowing which person" and "identifying the person," and there is a *de dicto–de re* ambiguity. The conventional "interest relative" or "context

---

[57] Of course, independently of any idea of intuitive computability, one can state the formal definitions of the theory. (There were several, which were shown to be equivalent.) However, without the idea of such intuitive computability, the entire motivation of the theory would be lost. In this notion of computability, one ideally supposes that one who is performing the computation has no limitations of time or space. (Strictly speaking, of course, the notion of computability is best seen as one of having a procedure for knowing which number is the value of the function, and the relation of this to knowing *de re* of a number that it is the value might be complex. In this instance, I am inclined to think that the notions do coincide. In any event, in both cases hostility toward the distinction stems from a Quinean opposition to "frankly inequalitarian" preferences for one way of designating a number over another.) (I discuss this in Kripke 1992.)

[58] Complexity theory adds a formal limitation on the length of the computation, which is supposed to codify the idea that computations that go beyond a certain length cannot be carried out in practice.

dependent" formulation does not seem to me always to bring out the essential problems.[59] The ambiguities are much more rare in the case of "knowing which" as applied to objects in general, not necessarily people (as in the example of numbers above).

Indeed, the ambiguities are rather unusual even when involving people and do not in themselves generate a problem about whether or not a person has a *de re* belief about a subject. I am speaking somewhat dogmatically, but I ask the reader to think about her or his own reaction to a television report that the perpetrator of a crime has now been identified, or that there is someone the police now believe to be the culprit. Does someone who hears such a report, even knowing little or nothing about the crime, think "What is the context? What interests are involved?," or anything related? I think one finds the report perfectly clear, and should not listen to philosophers who tell one otherwise. (Indeed, they themselves do not think otherwise, except when they write on the problem.)

The second general problem in the philosophy of language is what I call the "toy duck fallacy." Let me give an example of this, because, on the one hand, the people I've been criticizing have been talking about all kinds of examples that they must take to be literally false or incorrect; but, on the other hand, there can be a tendency to give examples as if they were correct that have got to be literally false. Suppose a parent takes a child to a toy store. The toys are plastic models of various animals. The child asks, "Is that a goose?" The parent says, "No, that's a duck."

Some morals plainly should not be drawn from this type of example. First, that there are two kinds of duck: some are living organisms, others are made of plastic. (Wasn't the parent correct to answer, "That's a duck"?) Or, that the term "duck" is ambiguous. It has a narrow sense in which the duck has to be an organism, and a broader one in which it could be made of plastic. Nor could we argue, for example, that the term "duck" has a unitary broad sense, including both the plastic toys and the water fowl, but that in certain contexts there is a pragmatic implication that the duck must be a biological animal. Nor should we say that the example shows that the term "duck" is highly contextual or even "interest relative," so that if someone is primarily interested in biology, or eating meat, or just seeing an animal moving gracefully in the water or at a zoo, ducks

---

[59] For example, when I saw the classic film "Charade," I eventually realized (before it was revealed in the film) that a mysterious killer was really Carson Dyle, erroneously reported earlier in the film to have been killed long ago. But I did not realize that Dyle had pretended to be a CIA agent, who was a character in the movie under another name. Did I realize who the killer was? Possibly the answer is ambiguous. (However, "interest relative" or "context dependent" does not seem to me to be the happiest characterization of the ambiguity.) Unambiguously, I did have a correct belief about Dyle that he committed the murders. (But if asked to choose, I confess that probably I would prefer to admit that I had not figured out "whodunit.")

It would be beyond the scope of this paper to discuss all the issues involved in the "knowing who" locution, or the issues raised by Boër and Lycan (1986).

have to be animals; but if one is interested in having a toy, then a duck can be made of plastic. None of these conclusions is correct. No dictionary should include an entry under "duck" with a sense in which ducks may be made of plastic and not be living creatures at all.

The point here, independently of the correctness of the application I will suggest in connection with the issues in the present paper, is that when giving any example in the philosophy of language, one has to be careful that it is not a toy duck example. One should not conclude that something is a legitimate use of language, something that ought to be recognized by a dictionary or semantic theory, even though there are appropriate circumstances in which one would say it.

One sign of a toy duck example would be, in this kind of case, that the child might ask, "But is this a real duck?," and the parent might reply, "No, this is not a real duck." Or, as we would say, "A toy duck is not really a duck." Unfortunately, for the dialogue in the toy store, possibly situations can be set up in which the "real" duck test won't work. But, in general, it can help, and for us surely a toy duck is not really a duck.

I should add that the problem in semantics I am mentioning here was originally suggested to me by an example of John Austin. He mentions someone who points to a picture and says, "That is a lion" (Austin 1962:91).[60] However, in this example, or a corresponding one, in which pointing to a picture one says, "that is my grandfather," it is not clear that one has not said something intended to be literally true. For example, in the grandfather case, one is pointing out *the man in the picture*, and in the case of the lion, *the animal in the picture*.[61] I propose to replace Austin's example of a picture with my own example of the plastic toy duck as achieving the purpose that Austin intended.

One thing I don't know quite how to explain is why usages like this are allowed to arise, even though they do not accord with a proper dictionary of the language. Austin says, in connection with his own example, that one is cutting down on verbiage. But that does not seem to be the right explanation. Why should it be so annoyingly prolix to say "that is a toy duck," or "that is a plastic duck"? I do not know a proper explanation of the contexts in which these locutions are allowed.[62] In the absence of such an explanation, until we figure one out, one must simply recognize that these contexts occur. No doubt an explanation would help us recognize when these locutions occur, but the point is

---

[60] He writes, "Does this show that the word 'lion' has *two senses*—one meaning an animal, the other a picture of an animal? Plainly not. In order (in this case) to cut down verbiage, I may use in one situation words primarily appropriate to the other. No problem arises provided the circumstances are known."

[61] I discuss this example in my John Locke Lectures (Kripke 1973). I think this applies even if there isn't a real lion depicted, though I don't elaborate here.

[62] Romina Padró has suggested to me that some such locutions might be viewed as introducing special fictional contexts or games, allowing the omission of "toy" or "plastic."

that the philosopher of language must be careful to avoid drawing the wrong conclusions from them.[63]

Some of the examples Sosa gives to show the extreme contextuality or interest relativity of exportability seem to me to be toy duck examples. In fact, Sosa's argument for the extreme contextuality of exportability seems to me to indicate that these are toy duck examples. In one case, Sosa mentions a multiple-choice test asking "Which of these is a spy?," where the correct answer is "the tallest spy." Most children taking the test get the right answer, and the tester says to the tallest spy, whom he happens to know (and whom he also knows to be the tallest spy)—yes, this is a tall story in more than one sense—"most of the children realized that you are the spy on the list." But, of course, the children have never heard of the spy in question, let alone of the relevant facts about him. So do they really have a belief about him? The correct analysis, I suggest, is that the tester is plainly being somewhat humorous when he reports this to the spy. Hence, this is a toy duck case.

Consider Sosa's final example, which he clearly takes to confirm his main point (1970 894–96). An apparently solid citizen of the city of Metropolis, well known in the community, and in particular to the chief of police, has a secret propensity for setting fires. The police call the person who has set the fires, perhaps with some characteristic modus operandi, and so on, the "Metropolis Pyromaniac." Another fire has just occurred and the police announce that they believe, on the basis of the usual clues, that the Metropolis Pyromaniac did this one, too. Then Sosa points out that the citizen can rightly assure his wife (who does know about his crimes) that no one suspects him of setting any fires. On the other hand, the police chief is represented as announcing that he has a suspect on the basis of their knowledge of the characteristic modus operandi of the Metropolis Pyromaniac. As Sosa puts it, "The chief... is pleased that they are not completely in the dark, and he emphasizes this by reporting that someone is suspected of having set the fire. (They don't just suspect that someone set the fire; at least they know ⌜The Pyromaniac, and not any of his fellow arsonists, did it.⌝)" (895).

According to Sosa, this apparently paradoxical case is to be resolved by appealing to the extreme context-sensitivity of the notion of a suspect. In one sense (described as the "solid citizen"), he is not, and in the other sense (called the "Metropolis Pyromaniac"), he is. Sosa initially describes this apparently paradoxical case using his account III, but quickly uses the case to support his

---

[63] I should add that Austin, too, regards a philosophically significant case as being based at least in part on a toy duck usage, namely, Ayer's suggestion that there are two conflicting senses of "see" (see Ayer 1940).

I admit that in the absence of a clear criterion, not only is there the danger of a philosopher drawing the wrong conclusion from a toy duck usage, but there is also the opposite danger of dismissing a valid example as a toy duck usage. In the text I mention the question of whether it is a "real" duck as one criterion, but I do not have a general criterion.

reversion to account I (permitting universal exportation). The citizen, who is also the Metropolis Pyromaniac, is suspected, but it may be rhetorically misleading to say so. However, as we have already seen, to put it that way is to misdescribe the situation. For, as Sosa explicitly says, the solid citizen, who is also the Metropolis Pyromaniac, rightly *denies* that anyone suspects him (Sosa 1970:894–95).

It is hard for me to share Sosa's intuitions about this case. Could the London police really announce, "We have a suspect; it is Jack the Ripper"? Both Sosa's police chief and the London police are speaking very strangely to my ear. Yes, they may know or believe more than merely nothing as to who did it, but a suspect they don't have. I wonder whether Sosa's intuitions are influenced by the fact that the police had given both criminals a name (or a "name"). What if the police had said, "We think that the same person committed this crime as previous similar ones"? Would we have any inclination to think of them as having a suspect?

Even if we shared Sosa's intuitions, the police chief's claim to have a suspect would clearly be a toy duck case. Perhaps the case would be stronger if the Pyromaniac's wife, after hearing the police's announcement, said, "They think you did this one, too." (The case would be more poignant if, in this instance, he was innocent, and someone else had imitated his methods.) In this version, her statement has a greater genuine air of being *de re*. Even so, I think it is plainly a toy duck case. Once again, one should remember that "suspect" is a predicate, interacting with quantifiers, cardinality, and the like, and one should bear in mind how it would normally be projected. The Pyromaniac could appropriately reply to his wife: "Oh, come on, I am not a suspect at all." Only the husband's reassurances that he is not a suspect fit the way we normally project the predicate. The reply is correct, I think, and amounts to a rejection of this case as a toy duck case.[64]

Independently of the particular application I have been discussing, I hope to have convinced my readers that what I have called the "pragmatic wastebasket fallacy" and the "toy duck fallacy" are indeed temptations to be avoided in the philosophy of language. As to the specific issue under discussion, I hope to have eliminated any temptation to fall back on unrestricted exportation.[65]

---

[64] If one thinks of a genuine proper name as always licensing exportation, then one must deny that the "Metropolis Pyromaniac" is a genuine proper name. One need not elaborate on the issue here, but undoubtedly a toy duck–type feeling that the "Metropolis Pyromaniac" must license exportation contributes to any illusion created by the example.

[65] I would like to thank Monique Whitaker for her original transcription of the talk. My thanks to Jeff Buechner and Gary Ostertag for their editorial help, and especially to Romina Padró for her help in revising the original transcription as well as helpful suggestions and conversations. This paper has been completed with support from the Saul A. Kripke Center at the City University of New York, Graduate Center.

REFERENCES

Austin, J. L. (1962). *Sense and Sensibilia.* Oxford: Clarendon.
Ayer, A. J. (1940). *The Foundations of Empirical Knowledge.* London: Macmillan.
Boër, S. E., and W. G. Lycan (1986). *Knowing Who.* Cambridge, MA: MIT Press.
Dennett, D. (1982). "Beyond Belief." In *Thought and Object.* Ed. A. Woodfield. Oxford: Clarendon. Reprinted in Dennett (1987); citations are to the reprint.
———. (1987). *The Intentional Stance.* Cambridge, MA: MIT Press.
Donnellan, K. (1966). "Reference and Definite Descriptions." *Philosophical Review* 75:281–304.
Grice, H. P. (1961). "The Causal Theory of Perception." *Proceedings of the Aristotelian Society* 35:121–53.
———. (1989). *Studies in the Way of Words.* Cambridge, MA: Harvard University Press.
Hahn, L. E., and P. A. Schilpp, eds. (1986). *The Philosophy of W. V. O. Quine.* LaSalle, IL: Open Court.
Hintikka, J. (1962). *Knowledge and Belief: An Introduction to the Logic of the Two Notions.* Ithaca, NY: Cornell University Press.
Kaplan, D. (1968). "Quantifying In." *Synthese* 19:178–214.
———. (1986). "Opacity." In Hahn and Schilpp (1986).
———. (n.d.) "What Is Meaning? Explorations in the Theory of *Meaning as Use.*" Unpublished manuscript.
Kripke, S. (1973). *The John Locke Lectures: Reference and Existence.* Unpublished manuscript.
———. (1977). "Speaker's Reference and Semantic Reference." *Midwest Studies in Philosophy* 2:255–76. Reprinted in this volume as Chapter 5.
———. (1980). *Naming and Necessity.* Cambridge, MA: Harvard University Press.
———. (1992). "Logicism, Wittgenstein, and *De Re* Beliefs about Natural Numbers." Unpublished manuscript.
———. (2005). "Russell's Notion of Scope." *Mind* 114:1005–37. Reprinted in this volume as Chapter 8.
Kvart, I. (1982). "Quine and Modalities De Re: A Way Out?" *Journal of Philosophy* 79:295–328.
Lewis, D. (1979). "Scorekeeping in a Language Game." *Journal of Philosophical Logic* 8:339–59. Reprinted in Lewis (1983); citations are to the reprint.
———. (1983). *Philosophical Papers Volume I.* New York: Oxford University Press.
———. (1996). "Elusive Knowledge." *Australasian Journal of Philosophy* 74:549–67.
Quine, W. V. O. (1956). "Quantifiers and Propositional Attitudes." *Journal of Philosophy* 53:177–87. Reprinted in Quine (1966), 185–96; citations are to the reprint.
———. (1960). *Word and Object.* Cambridge, MA: MIT Press.
———. (1961). "Reply to Professor Marcus." *Synthese* 13:323–30. Reprinted in Quine (1966).
———. (1966). *The Ways of Paradox and Other Essays.* New York: Random House.
———. (1968). "Replies." *Synthese* 19:264–322.
———. (1979). "Intensions Revisited." In *Contemporary Perspectives in the Philosophy of Language,* ed. Peter French, Theodore Uehling Jr., and Howard K. Wettstein.

Minneapolis: University of Minnesota Press. Reprinted in Quine (1981); citations are to the reprint.
———. (1981). *Theories and Things.* Cambridge, MA: Harvard University Press.
———. (1986). "Reply to Kaplan." In Hahn and Schlipp (1986), 290–94.
Russell, B. (1905). "On Denoting." *Mind* 14:479–93.
Sosa, E. (1969). "Quantifiers, Beliefs, and Sellars." In *Philosophical Logic*, ed. W. Davis, D. J. Hockney, and W. K. Wilson. New York: Humanities Press, 1969.
———. (1970). "Propositional Attitudes *De Dicto* and *De Re.*" *Journal of Philosophy* 67:883–96.
Stine, G. (1969). *Quantification in Knowledge and Belief Contexts.* Unpublished doctoral dissertation, Harvard University.
———. (1972). "Two Women." *Philosophical Studies* 23:84–90.

12

Presupposition and Anaphora: Remarks on the Formulation of the Projection Problem*

From the stock example "Have you stopped beating your wife?" we are all familiar with the intuitive concept of presupposition. Though there have been many conflicting attempts in the literature to capture what this concept means, to some degree Justice Stewart's comment about pornography holds here: we all recognize it when we see it, even if we can't say exactly what it is. In this paper, I will be concerned with what is called in the linguistics literature "the projection problem for presuppositions." That problem is simply this: if we have a logically complex sentence whose clauses bear certain presuppositions, how do we compute the presuppositions of the whole? The main thesis of this paper is

---

* This paper is an edited transcript of a talk delivered at the conference "Linguistic and Philosophical Approaches to the Study of Anaphora," held at Princeton University in October 1990. Thanks to Scott Soames and Stephen Neale for urging me to present this material. Also, in another way, to Scott and to the tenure system since it was reading his papers on these matters as part of his tenure review that got me interested in these issues in 1984. Had I not read Soames's papers, I might never have gotten interested in the problem.

I would like to thank Richard Holton, Michaelis Michaels, and Scott Soames for transcribing the original lecture and for helpful comments. My thanks to Harold Teichman and especially to Romina Padró for their help in producing the present version. This paper has been completed with support from the Saul Kripke Center at The City University of New York, Graduate Center.

The fact that this is a transcript of a paper delivered orally (with a handout), rather than written, accounts for a certain amount of conversational tone.

In a later seminar given at Princeton in the fall of 1994, I gave a more elaborate presentation of the material in which some particular cases discussed were modified. However, I do not incorporate these modifications in the present text, which is basically correct. The basic main points about anaphora, active and passive context, and the like, were unaffected by any modifications.

The contents of this paper and/or its basic ideas have been in professional circulation for some time. Nevertheless, I felt (and have been urged) that it ought finally to see formal print.

Some cases where the reference carried by a presuppositional word is to an unspoken element of the active context (or called into the active context from the passive context) might best be thought of as deixis rather than anaphora. Because of the title of the symposium, and the relation between deixis and anaphora, I have used the term *anaphora* throughout, and do not worry about the question.

that the usual literature on the projection problem for presupposition ignores an anaphoric element that ought to have been taken into account. When this element is put in, there is a considerable change in the formulation of the problem.

Since I do not consider myself an expert in this area, I will begin by giving a brief review of the portion of the literature that I know. Soames (1982:488) gives a fairly standard list of different kinds of presupposition.

(1) Bill regrets lying to his parents. (Factive)
    P: Bill has lied to his parents.

(2) Ivan has stopped beating his wife. (Aspectual)
    P: Ivan has beaten his wife.

(3) Andy met with the PLO again today. (Iterative)
    P: Andy met with the PLO before.

(4) It was in August that we left Connecticut. (Cleft)
    P: We left Connecticut.

(5) What John destroyed was his typewriter. (Pseudocleft)
    P: John destroyed something.

(6) *Billy* is guilty, too.[1] (*Too*)
    P: Someone other than Billy is guilty.

(7) All of John's children are asleep. (Certain quantifiers)
    P: John has children.

(8) The king of France is in hiding. (Referential)
    P: There is a king of France.

Frege, who was perhaps the first philosopher to introduce the notion of presupposition, described it in such a way that the last of these examples is the paradigmatic case. It is not clear whether he thought that presuppositions went beyond this sort of example. His theory was that the presupposition fails precisely when there is a truth-value gap. For him, all such failure came from failure of reference. This might be made to extend to some of the other cases as well. Strawson, rather famously, reintroduced this notion into the philosophical literature (see Strawson 1950, 1952). In Strawson's case, there are two strains. One is a Fregean strain, but the more important strain is that nothing has been said—that is, no statement has been made—when the presupposition fails.[2]

---

[1] Throughout this paper, I have italicized the focus element in the *too* cases.
[2] Evans (1982:12) has argued with some limited success that there is a Strawsonian strain in Frege's later manuscripts, though it is not in "Über Sinn und Bedeutung" (Frege 1892) to my knowledge.

In addition to the Fregean and Strawsonian conceptions of presupposition, there is the broader characterization of the presuppositions of a speaker, or of the participants in a conversation, introduced by Stalnaker (1973, 1974) and discussed by Lewis (1979). The idea, roughly speaking, is that you shouldn't make an utterance involving a presupposition unless it is in the background assumptions of the participants in the conversation that the presupposition holds. Stalnaker and Lewis recognize that there are cases in which this rule seems to be violated. They recognize that you can introduce a presupposition into the conversation even though it was not a prior background assumption, without having to state the introduced presupposition explicitly. For example, you can say that you are going to meet your sister, and the presupposition that you have a sister is thereby introduced (Stalnaker calls this "accommodation"). It is argued that in such cases, conversational participants recognize that the existing conversational context does not satisfy the presuppositional requirements of the utterance, but accommodate the speaker by adding the required information to bring the context into harmony with the presuppositional rule. It is suggested that speakers exploit this process when they think the required information will be agreed upon as uncontroversial by all hands, or something like that.[3]

Another feature of presupposition that people have often noticed is that, unlike the asserted contents of sentences, presuppositions survive when sentences are embedded under negation, or as the antecedents of conditionals. The simplest hypothesis about the projection problem is the cumulative one: if you have a presupposition to a clause, it is also a presupposition to the whole complex sentence.[4] Although this is similar to certain aspects of Frege's theory, even he did not hold the cumulative hypothesis in its most general form. What would follow from his theory is that truth functions[5] have the cumulative property, but

---

[3] I haven't thought that this formulation as it is stated in print always works. A problem for me is that a French monarchist might belligerently say to a republican, "No matter what you Republicans say, I met the king of France last week." Here it isn't taken to be uncontroversial or expected to be uncontroversial that there is a king of France. There are various things that can be said about such a case; I don't know if any are quite satisfactory. But I'm going to assume the general satisfactoriness of this roughly sketched picture. It is pretty good; possibly it can be stretched to cover a case like this. That's enough for the present discussion.

Nevertheless, I think Richmond Thomason had a point when he said in the discussion of this paper at the 1990 symposium that Stalnaker states conditions for the conversational notion of presupposition that, even according to him, hold except insofar as they don't. The dangers are already present in the *sister* case mentioned by Stalnaker himself; they are more obvious in the monarchist-republican exchange just given. Nothing in the present discussion really depends on Stalnaker's characterization of presupposition, which was mentioned because of its prominence in Soames (1982). In fact, it is not so crucial even to Soames's paper.

[4] The cumulative hypothesis was introduced to the linguistic literature by Langendoen and Savin (1971).

[5] Karttunen and Peters (1979) seem willing to accept the truth functions as formalizations of *and*, *or*, *not* (at least in its primary use), and *if. . . then* in English. Not too much hangs on the issue as far as the present discussion is concerned. Probably it could be modified to fit another account of some or all of these particles in English.

indirect discourse, propositional attitudes, and so on, do not. The latter are what are called *plugs* by Karttunen and Peters (1979): sentences that do not inherit the presuppositions of their clauses.[6] However, even for the truth functions, Russell (1905) gave an example for the conditional that he thought refuted Frege's presupposition theory. He pointed out that in the case of a conditional sentence where the presupposition of the consequent is asserted in the antecedent, the participants need not assume that the presupposition is true.[7] Russell's point is reflected in the algorithm proposed by Karttunen and Peters for computing the presupposition of both a conditional sentence *If A then B* and a conjunction *A and B*.

(9) $(A_p \;\&\; (A_\alpha \supset B_p))$

In this notation, S_α stands for the assertive content of a sentence S and S_p stands for the presupposed content of S. So, according to Karttunen and Peters, conditionals and conjunctions presuppose both the presupposition of A and the claim that if the assertive content of A is true, then the presupposed content of B is true. It follows that if the assertive content of the antecedent, plus perhaps certain background assumptions, entails B_p, then any necessity to assume or presuppose B_p disappears, or is filtered out. This is the feature they wanted to capture.

I don't want to suggest that this account of the presuppositions of conditionals and conjunctions is a perfect theory. In fact, I don't know of any account that is free from descriptive problems or apparent counterexamples.[8] For present purposes, however, the Karttunen and Peters algorithm will do. Similar remarks apply to the algorithm for disjunction proposed by Karttunen and Peters, and modified by Soames (1979) in the last clause.

(10) $(\neg A_\alpha \supset B_p) \;\&\; (\neg B_\alpha \supset A_p) \;\&\; (A_p \vee B_p)$

Although Soames has shown that there are cases in which even this definitely doesn't work, it will be good enough for the moment. Only two examples, (49) and (50), not crucial to the main discussion, involve disjunction. I do not discuss

---

[6] This is not to say that Frege's theory necessarily makes the correct predictions about what the plugs should be. Frege also does not discuss the related Russellian question of scope ambiguities. [One could now consult my own discussion of this topic in Kripke 2005, included here as Chapter 8.]

[7] Russell's example is this:

The King in "The Tempest" might say, "If Ferdinand is not drowned, Ferdinand is my only son."... But the above statement would nevertheless have remained true if Ferdinand had been in fact drowned. (Russell 1905:484)

Russell also gives a set-theoretic example involving a universally quantified conditional. (His example strikes me as a bit artificial, but reasonable mathematical examples can be given.) [Once again, one could now consult my own discussion of this topic in Chapter 8, pp. 237–38.]

[8] I am familiar with only a small subset of the proposals in the literature covering such cases.

cases involving *believes that*, *wants that*, and the like, nor how my approach might affect them.

An assumption underlying this whole project, as standardly conceived, is that we assign presuppositions to separate clauses, independently of the environments in which they occur, and then compute the presupposition of the whole. This is very natural, for example, from Frege's formulation of the problem, but it survives outside the Fregean background as well. Certainly it is recognized that if there is *explicit* pronominal anaphora or cross-reference in any of the clauses, then the clauses will have to be interpreted in the light of this. More importantly, if quantifiers are interacting with presuppositions, this simple picture clearly doesn't hold (Heim 1983). But in the absence of such elements, this seems to be the picture that is presented in the literature.

The argument of this paper is that an important anaphoric element that is carried by the presuppositional terms themselves is left out of the standard picture. As a result, the appropriate presuppositions are misdescribed, for example, in the list quoted from Soames 1982 above.[9] I feel in retrospect that this list doesn't get our intuitions about the relevant presuppositions as we would naturally think of them, and is even highly counterintuitive in many cases. Although I will try to establish this point, I will not present an explicit countertheory, partly because of the small amount of time I have had to devote to this problem, and partly because of a feeling that some people will be more expert in relevant considerations than I am at the moment (without having read up in particular on a lot of the literature on standard anaphora in syntax).[10] But I will sketch considerations relevant to the development of a theory of presuppositional anaphora, and I will say some things about the form such a theory should take.

Consider the following relatively complex case (more blatant and simpler counterexamples to the usual picture will follow soon):

(11) If Herb comes to the party, *the boss* will come, too.

---

[9] The only place I know of where this approach is questioned is the final section of Soames (1989). That section contains a footnote reporting a conversation with me about some of the material in this paper. Also, some of the text of the relevant section appears to be influenced by my approach, as I reported it to him.

[Since I gave this paper, I saw a circulated draft of Heim (1992) (not the final version). Though recognizing that the existential (nonanaphoric) accounts of presuppositions cited at the beginning of this paper from Soames (1982) have been dominant, Heim cites Karttunen (1974:184) as mentioning an analysis of *too*, said to be based on Green (1968), similar to that proposed here. Indeed, Karttunen (incidentally) does appear to give such an analysis, but seems to follow it immediately with the purely existential analysis that it is my main point to criticize, and moreover maintains the existential analysis of *too* in Karttunen and Peters (1979) (see, e.g., page 35). I couldn't find the point in Green (1968), though I may have missed something. The points made about inclusions and converse inclusions are indeed illustrated there. See, for example, Green's sentences (12) and (19), pages 24–25.]

[10] There is probably material for the syntactician here as well as for the semanticist.

According to the usual view, the presupposition of the consequent is that someone other than the boss will come to the party.[11] In my own view, the presupposition of the consequent is that Herb is not the boss. The important thing to note here is that my own view gives a presupposition to the consequent that cannot be understood in isolation from the antecedent.

It seems to me incontestable that we would normally think that this is what is presupposed. However, there is an appropriate pragmatic explanation of why we would think this, which is related to an explanation that Karttunen and Peters have already given. Recall the Karttunen and Peters algorithm for the presupposition of conditionals.

(9) $(A_p \,\&\, (A_a \supset B_p))$

How can the standard algorithm explain the presuppositions here? Given the Karttunen and Peters theory, the presupposition of the consequent in (11) is "someone other than the boss will come" and the presupposition of the entire conditional is "if Herb comes, someone other than the boss will come." Then one can try a "conversational implicature" explanation in the style of Grice (see Grice 1961, 1975, 1989) for any feeling that at least the entire conditional presupposes that Herb is not the boss. For how would someone know the conditional "if Herb comes to the party, someone other than the boss will come"? A natural explanation would be that the speaker takes for granted that Herb is not the boss. This might be a reasonable explanation for the "illusion" of the stronger presupposition that Herb is not the boss.

However, this explanation would not work for cases like (12).

(12) If Herb and his wife both come to the party, *the boss* will come, too.

The presupposition of the consequent according to the standard account is that someone other than the boss will come to the party. But on my view the presupposition of the consequent is that neither Herb nor his wife is the boss. Notice that on the standard view the presupposition of the whole conditional is

(13) If Herb and his wife both come to the party, then there exists an x not equal to the boss such that x comes to the party.

This conditional is trivial, and we need no extra information to assume it other than that Herb and his wife are two people. Therefore, no feeling of its being either implied or presupposed that neither Herb nor his wife is the boss can be

---

[11] The inheritance condition for the conditional as a whole was given by Karttunen and Peters (1979) as a primitive semantic notion (involving conventional implicature). Stalnaker (1974), and following him Soames (1982), tried to give a pragmatic explanation of the inheritance conditions that is sensitive to context. Heim (1983) offers a more semantical account that also involves changes in the context associated with the clauses and predicts the inherited presuppositions in an algorithmic way.

accounted for by a theory that assigns (13) as the presupposition of (12).[12] The simple suggestion is that in general, if I say so-and-so and so-and-so are coming, and he's coming too, the presupposition is that "he" is an extra person. This presupposition is not in addition to, but actually replaces, the existential presupposition given by the usual account.[13] How to extend this to other cases is complicated but will emerge from later examples.

The general idea is that the presupposition arises from the anaphoric requirement that when one says *too*, one refers to some parallel information that is either in another clause (that's the interesting case for the projection problem) or in the context. (Actually, in what I will later call the "active context" rather than the "passive context." One might wish to subsume the clause case under the context case in some form of theory, but I won't commit myself either way here.) When the focused element is a singular term, it is presupposed to be noncoreferential with the other corresponding elements in the parallel clauses or other bits of information in the (active) context. Since what we have is a species of anaphora, what we need is a theory, parallel to that for pronominal anaphora, of what types of anaphora are permitted, and of how these new types of presuppositional anaphora are related to other, more familiar types of anaphora, including ordinary anaphoric pronouns.

The following example is simpler and very striking:

(14) *Sam* is having dinner in New York tonight, too.

Imagine (14) as uttered out of the blue; no context is being presupposed in which we are concerned with anyone else having dinner in New York.[14] On the usual

---

[12] This could even be true of (11) if we assume a background in which no one comes to the party unless accompanied by his or her spouse.
  Even more so, it would probably be part of the background assumptions that many people are expected to be coming to the party. It would hardly be a party otherwise. So *of course* someone other than the boss is coming. Then the case would be closer to (14) below.

[13] Since I think that even the consequent of (11) presupposes that Herb is not the boss, and of (12) that neither Herb nor his wife is the boss, if one otherwise accepts the Karttunen and Peters algorithm, the presupposition of (11) becomes "if Herb comes to the party, then Herb is not the boss," read as a material conditional, and analogously for (12). Soames (1979) and Gazdar (1979) see a problem with cases where the consequent of a conditional seems to be presupposed. However, one could give a Gricean reply as proposed by Karttunen and Peters and argue that since there is already a unique boss (of the company or group), the only grounds for asserting the material conditional can be truth-functional knowledge of the consequent. There is no connection between Herb's coming to the party and whether or not he is the boss. See Soames (1982) for a discussion of the contrast between the earlier Soames and Gazdar approaches and the Karttunen and Peters approach. For my own reason for thinking that the consequent of the conditional, rather than the conditional as a whole, presupposes that Herb is not the boss, and that pragmatic Gricean reasons must be used to explain the intuition attaching the same presupposition to the entire conditional (assuming the Karttunen and Peters algorithm), see my discussion of (20) further on.

[14] There is a related discussion of this example in the last section of Soames (1989). Very likely, as I said in footnote 9, he was influenced by the discussion and examples he ascribes to me in a footnote.

view, the presupposition of (14) is that someone other than Sam is having dinner in New York tonight. But this is wrong. Since a sentence is appropriate as long as its presuppositions are fulfilled, the usual view predicts that (14) is virtually invariably appropriate without any special context. Surely many people are having dinner in New York on a given night. But, contrary to the usual prediction, it is obvious that the *too* here is particularly bizarre. The hearer will say, "'Too'? What do you mean, 'too'? What person or persons do you have in mind?"

Example (15) is similar.

(15) Priscilla is eating supper, again.

On the usual view, the presupposition is that Priscilla has eaten supper before. Since if she is a grown woman this can easily be assumed, an utterance of (15) should invariably be perfectly appropriate. But in the absence of any special background, the natural reaction to such an utterance is "What do you mean, 'again'? Maybe she had supper an hour ago, also? Are you suggesting that she is bulimic? Or is she on a diet where she is supposed to skip supper and she has broken it recently and now has broken it again? What is going on here?" It is obvious that the usual prediction is not correct.

To take care of examples like (14) and (15), I propose a distinction between two types of context.[15] Let us call material that has been explicitly mentioned in the conversation, or is on people's minds and is known to be on people's minds, or is highly salient in some way, the *salient* or *active* context. The active context could include a set of questions or topics as well as assertions. The active context might be a complex sort of entity, but it will be the kind of thing that makes uses of *again* and *too* appropriate. There is also a *passive* context, which consists of general background information available to the speakers that is not taken as relevant or on their minds. *Too* or *again* should refer to parallel elements, that is, to something parallel to Priscilla's eating supper, or Sam's having dinner in New York, or the boss's coming to the party. These parallel elements must come from the active context or from other clauses in the assertion in question. They cannot come merely from the passive context: that they are merely very well known is not sufficient.[16]

Something is introduced into the active context merely by mentioning it. Consider this example:

---

[15] This can be seen as relevant to a couple of considerations mentioned in the last section of Soames 1989.

[16] Notice, as opposed to the impression given by Soames (1989), that this is not merely a matter of whether we know various particular people who are having dinner in New York or that Priscilla has had supper at various particular times. We may very well know many particular people who are having dinner in New York, or particular times when Priscilla has had supper before, that are not relevant here.

(16) Tonight many other people are having dinner in New York, and *Sam* is having dinner there, too.

This is a pretty strange performance still. Why is the speaker putting things that way? But once the speaker has done so—for example, in reply to a worried mother who is saying, "Should Sam really be going out to New York in the evening? Isn't that a dangerous place?"—the *too* is entirely appropriate.[17] The content of the sentence obtained by dropping *too* from (16) is the same as the content of (17).

(17) Like many others, Sam is having dinner in New York tonight.

Except for those people whose information state is very poor, for whom a very broad range of possible worlds are not excluded, (17) simply conveys the same information as (18), since it is well known that many people are having dinner in New York tonight.

(18) Sam is having dinner in New York tonight.

But as far as the appropriateness of adding *too* is concerned, (17) is not equivalent to (18). If someone just says (14),

(14) *Sam* is having dinner in New York tonight, too,

without any suitable background, then the *too* is inappropriate and should not be said, even to the worried mother. However, (19) is acceptable.

(19) Like many others, *Sam* is having dinner in New York tonight, too.

The presupposition (tautologous here) is that Sam is not one of the many others.

On the other hand, if the appropriate material is, for whatever reason, in the active context, then (14) becomes all right. The active context need not consist of a clause or even an immediately preceding discourse element. Examples have already been suggested. The participants in the conversation may actively have in mind particular people who are having dinner in New York. Similarly, as in some of the suggestions about Priscilla mentioned in the discussion, (15) can be appropriate if people have such suggestions in mind.

So the idea is that there is a back-reference to parallel information either in the active context or in other clauses or discourse elements. Something gets into the active context if it has been explicitly mentioned or if it is very much in mind. The passive context, however, is sufficient for the nonidentities; people do not have to be desperately thinking or saying that Herb is not the boss as long as they

---

[17] Although (16) is a conjunction, I could equally well have given two separate sentences and still gotten the information that many people are having dinner in New York into the active context. Nevertheless, *too* could be regarded as anaphoric in these cases. An explicit mention is a special way of bringing something into the active context.

are aware of this. The required presupposition of nonidentity can be satisfied by either the active or the passive context. Heim (1983), I believe, rolls the whole context into one grand proposition that is a set of possible worlds. On my account, it seems likely that not only will there have to be two contexts, the active and the passive, but also the nature of the active context, at least, will have to be more complicated than simply a set of worlds. First, the active context will be a set containing propositions, which might better be thought of as structured. Moreover, the set might be divided into questions and topics as well as assertions and so on. Alternatively, we might even just have interpreted sentences instead of propositions in the context. (Since they are already there, we may as well use them.) None of these speculations are crucial. I certainly do not want the paper to depend on any particular formal semantics.

At this point, an important question arises. In discussing (11), I identified the presupposition that Herb is not the boss. Should this presupposition be attached to the consequent clause—that is, to the clause that contains the presuppositional element *too*—or should it be attached to the whole conditional, as we would intuitively think in many of these cases? If we attach it merely to the consequent clause, then we have to invoke the type of explanation given by Karttunen and Peters for why it is that we intuitively think something stronger. I do, indeed, favor attaching it to the consequent clause. The need for this is seen from example (20).

(20) If Nancy does not win the contest and the winner comes to our party, *Nancy* will come, too.

The presupposition according to my proposal is that Nancy will not be the winner. According to Karttunen and Peters, if the presupposition is attached to the consequent, it is "filtered out" and need not be presupposed by the speaker who utters the entire conditional. This result seems to me to be intuitively correct. The entire conditional in no way presupposes that Nancy will not win. Since this presupposition is explicitly stated in the antecedent, it need not be presupposed by the speaker who utters the entire conditional. Thus, (20) is acceptable without any presupposition in advance that Nancy will not be the winner, and indeed is explicitly compatible with the idea that Nancy may well win.

The corresponding case for *again* is introduced by example (21).

(21) If Kasparov defeats Karpov in the game in Tokyo, probably he will defeat him again in the game in Berlin.

On the conventional account, the presupposition attached to the consequent is that Kasparov has previously defeated Karpov. This may in fact be well known. By contrast, I take the presupposition normally to be that the game in Berlin will be played after the game in Tokyo. Once more, that the presupposition should be attached to the consequent rather than to the entire conditional should be argued for on the basis of the parallel example.

(22) If the game in Tokyo precedes the game in Berlin and Kasparov defeats Karpov in Tokyo, probably he will defeat him again in the game in Berlin.

As before, (22) need not presuppose (in the entire conditional) that the game in Tokyo will precede the game in Berlin, since this is explicitly stated in the antecedent and is "filtered out" in the entire conditional.

Now let us consider the case of *stop* (perhaps the most famous one).

(23) If Sam watches the opera, he will stop watching it when the Redskins game comes on.

According to my view, a presupposition attached to *stop* is that the Redskins game comes on during the opera, but not at the very beginning of it. The traditional presupposition in the consequent, that Sam has watched the opera before, is also, of course, valid, but in (23) it is filtered out in the entire sentence by being explicitly included in the antecedent. However, it can only be filtered out because of the presupposition that the Redskins game begins after the opera does (and in fact, during the opera, though this is not needed for the filtering).

However, there does appear to be a significant difference between the *stop* case, on the one hand, and the *again* and *too* cases, on the other. Whereas *again* and *too* have obligatory anaphora to parallel statements in the active context or in other clauses, that is not always true for *stop*. Consider:

(24) Jill has stopped smoking.

(24) is something that can be said even if there is no particular concern about Jill smoking, so long as her smoking is well known to the conversational participants. The assumption is not required to be in the active context or in other clauses. Thus, in this respect *stop* contrasts with what I have said regarding *too* and *again*.

In the case where (24) is uttered out of the blue, as just envisaged, normally the presupposition would not merely be that Jill has smoked before; it would also be that she smoked until relatively recently. There may be other cases where the presupposition is weaker, but I do not intend to go into detail here.[18] But in some cases in which there is another clause or an element of the active context that gives a time or date, as in (23), there is an intended anaphoric reference to that clause or element. In such a case, the presupposition is that the stopping takes place after that time, or after a continuous period starting with that time, or after a period ending when the stopping occurs and the thing mentioned in the clause containing the anaphoric element takes place.

---

[18] Since I gave the original paper, some such cases have been suggested to me by Romina Padró.

Thus, in many cases the presupposition carried by *stop* refers to a time or time period. In the case of (24) uttered out of the blue, the reference is simply to the time of utterance, whereas in other cases such as (23), the reference is carried by other clauses or elements of the passive context. The usual account of the presupposition, perhaps influenced by the stock interrogative example with which this paper begins (and where the weak presupposition may indeed be all that is carried by *stop*), has been too influential and it is not the general case.[19]

Consider a case that is unlike *stop*.

(25) It was John who solved the projection problem.

Here there is a compulsory reference, I think, to another clause or to the active context. Or at least, usually there is; sometimes there is some accommodation (in Stalnaker's sense) that occurs when the sentence is introduced.

Soames (1989:605) mentions something relevant to this. Suppose someone says, out of the blue, "It was Mary who broke the typewriter," where there is no background knowledge that the typewriter was broken. The presupposition is that someone broke the typewriter (very soon I will argue that this account of the presupposition is too weak; let us accept it for the moment). Accommodation might take place; but there is, Soames suggests, something odd about this—there is a kind of pretense that a topic of conversation prior to the remark was that of determining who broke the typewriter. I agree with that.

In some contexts, however, it is not so bad. It is a fairly familiar rhetorical trope in academic writing, and so should be very familiar to us (that is, to academics). I have frequently seen sentences like "It was Mary Smith who should be given the credit for first observing that _____," where the information that _____ is really supposed to be unknown to the reader. The writer is trying to give the information that _____ and at the same time give Mary Smith the credit. But the main thing is to convey the information that _____. The writer might just as well have said, "That _____ is true is an important observation. Mary Smith gets the credit for noting it first," using straight assertions. (Possibly the trope is most common when the supposed fact Smith discovered is reasonably well known, but not necessarily to the reader.)

However, something is really very bad, in fact quite terrible, about the usual picture of what is presupposed. It is illustrated by this example:

(26) If John Smith walked on the beach last night, then it was Betty Smith who walked on the beach last night.

The usual presupposition for the consequent is this:

(27) Someone walked on the beach last night.

---

[19] Richard Holton and Michaelis Michael found my original discussion of *stop* unclear in certain respects. I hope my revisions answer their queries about my intent.

According to the Karttunen and Peters filtering rule, the presupposition for the whole conditional is (28).

(28) If John Smith walked on the beach last night, then someone walked on the beach last night.

Since (28) is incontestably true, (26) should always be okay. But (26) is obviously very bizarre. Similarly with the following cases:

(29) a. If Sally opposed his tenure, it was Susan who opposed it.
b. Sally opposed his tenure, and it was Susan who opposed it.

These are also pretty bizarre. Like (26), (29a) and (29b) should be perfectly acceptable on the usual account, but out of the blue they are very bizarre indeed. The Karttunen and Peters filtering rule, taken with the usual account of the presupposition carried by clefts, gives as the presupposition carried by both (29a) and (29b) the conditional "if Sally opposed his tenure, someone opposed it," which is trivially true. So nothing should be wrong with (29a) and (29b).

In fact, (29b) especially provokes the reaction, "Wait a minute! You said it was Sally who opposed his tenure! Why do you continue by saying it was Susan?" You could try to modify the standard proposal in light of these examples by saying that the real presupposition involves a uniqueness condition. According to this proposal, the real presupposition of (26) is that someone uniquely walked on the beach last night, and of (29a–b) that someone uniquely opposed tenure. That would account for the bizarreness of the two statements. The presupposition of (26) would then be that if John Smith walked on the beach last night, then someone uniquely walked on the beach last night, directly contradicting the claim of the consequent. Similarly for (29a–b). But this proposal does not work because such a uniqueness presupposition does not always hold, as the usual proposal correctly asserts. For example, in the tenure case the statement "If anyone opposed his tenure, I bet it was Sally and Susan who did so" is fine, contrary to any uniqueness presupposition in the cleft.

What seems to me to be going on is this: a cleft requires an explicit reference to the active context or to another clause (sometimes the presupposition can be introduced into the active context by a rhetorical trope with accommodation, as mentioned above). The active context or another clause does indeed entail that someone has some property P or did something. It must also suggest a question, "Who has the property?" or "Who did it?" The answer given in the cleft, as is suggested by its surface form *It was so and so who did it*, is supposed to be a *complete* answer to the relevant question, "Who did it?"

On this account, (26) is normally bizarre because, if the antecedent is assumed, then the consequent does not give a complete answer to the relevant question, "Who walked on the beach last night?" Similarly, (29a) and (29b) are bizarre. For example, (29b) suggests that a complete answer to the question "Who opposed his tenure?" is given by *it was Susan who opposed it*, even though the previous clause says that Sally opposed the tenure.

However, sometimes the complete answer will not be a complete list of all the satisfiers of the condition. The list can be restricted by a relevant condition in the active context. For example, someone may have asked, "Which *woman* walked on the beach last night?" Someone might suggest that John Smith is always accompanied by his wife, and that there is reason to suppose that he walked on the beach last night. In such a situation, (26) is unobjectionable, though in a normal context it would be bizarre.

In all these cases, I am assuming the nonidentity of the people referred to—as, for example, John Smith and Betty Smith, Sally and Susan, and so on. This is a cause of the bizarreness of the examples. When we have two ways of referring to the same person, then a similar cleft construction can be perfectly appropriate. I could use the stock case of Cicero and Tully, but let me try some other examples.

(30) If Viscount Amberley is giving the lecture, it is Bertrand Russell who is giving the lecture.

In (30), the question in the active context might be "Who is giving the lecture?," as before, but it could also be "Who is Viscount Amberley?" or "Should I go to this lecture which is being given by one Viscount Amberley? Who is that?" Someone might answer, "Yes, you should go," and continue with (30).[20]

Similarly, in appropriate contexts we could have these sentences:

(31) If the author of "On Denoting" is giving the lecture, it is Bertrand Russell who is giving the lecture.
(32) If Bertrand Russell is giving the lecture, it is the author of "On Denoting" who is giving the lecture.[21]

It should be clear without running through the examples again that the case of pseudoclefts is like that of clefts.

Next consider (33).

(33) If Kasparov doesn't defeat Karpov in the next game, probably he won't defeat him *in the Berlin game*, either.

Either behaves like *too* except that it goes with a negative element. In (33), the presupposition is that the Berlin game is not the next game. Similarly:

---

[20] Russell's father was Viscount Amberley (as was his grandfather). Russell eventually inherited the title himself (and later inherited the title "Earl Russell"). One might imagine (30) uttered at a time when Russell had inherited the Amberley title but not yet the other one. (Actually, Bertrand Russell's father used "Amberley" as a surname and made use of the title "Viscount Amberley," but I don't know of any instance where Russell himself did—say, when giving a lecture. In that sense, the example is probably somewhat fictive.)

[21] Examples (30)–(32) were added in response to a question by Scott Soames.

(34) *Sam* is not having dinner in New York tonight, either.

The presupposition is not merely that someone other than Sam is not having dinner in New York tonight, which as in (14) is trivial. Rather, something in the active context must mention some particular person, persons, class of people, or the like, who are not having dinner in New York tonight.

An example similar to (33) is (35).

(35) If Karpov checkmates Kasparov in the next game, probably the challenger will defeat the champion *in the Berlin game,* too.

In such cases, the focused element is supposed to be different from the corresponding element in the anaphoric parallel. Thus, the first presupposition of the conditional is that the next game is not the game in Berlin. But here some identities and one inclusion are presupposed that have been left tacit in previous examples because they have been exhibited by mere repetition of the terms, or by pronouns. Here they became explicit. The presuppositions are that Kasparov is the champion, that Karpov is the challenger, and that anyone who checkmates an opponent defeats him or her (the last case is an inclusion).[22] So, in addition to presupposed nonidentities, there are also presupposed identities and inclusions. These are needed to support the back-reference to parallel information and can come from either the passive or the active context. They can also be filtered out by appropriate information in other clauses. Similar remarks apply to *again*, as illustrated by (36).

(36) If Kasparov checkmates Karpov in the next game, probably the champion will defeat the challenger in the Berlin game, again.

The presuppositions are as follows:

The next game will be before the one to be held in Berlin.
Kasparov is the champion.
Karpov is the challenger.
Anyone who checkmates a player defeats him or her.

Example (37) illustrates another point about this.

(37) The Republicans supported the bill, and *Senator Blank* supported it, too.

---

[22] The examples about chess have been modified in the light of comments by Richard Holton and Michaelis Michael. One of their remarks about *checkmates* was politely understated; they said, "Resignations are common." In fact, resignations are the norm in tournaments; playing to explicit checkmate is very rare. Strictly, nothing is wrong with (35) as now stated, but there is some sort of implicature that games are played to checkmate, which is fictive (perhaps there is also some suggestion that this is a championship series, which in my impression is rarely played in a number of different places). Rather than changing the example, I suggest that the reader just assume the appropriate things, even if they are contrary to normal fact.

The relevant presupposition here is not a nonidentity between singular terms, but a nonmembership statement: Senator Blank is not a Republican. In (37), *all* the Republicans are supposed to have supported the bill, but this does not seem to be necessary. This is illustrated by (38).

(38) A few Republicans supported the bill, and *Senator Blank* supported it, too.

Here again, the relevant presupposition is that Senator Blank is not a Republican.
Consider now the following pair of examples:

(39) The chemists are coming to the party, and *Harry* will come, too.
(40) If some other chemists come to the party, *Harry* will come, too.

The presupposition in (39) is that Harry is not one of the chemists. The presupposition in (40) is directly opposite. Here, it is obviously presupposed that Harry is a chemist, and the presupposition is carried by *other* rather than by *too*. There is no more obvious case of presuppositional anaphora than the presupposition carried by *other*. The presupposition attached to *too*, that Harry is not one of the chemists other than Harry, is tautologous.

Clearly, a converse to (40) is also acceptable, as in (41).

(41) If Harry comes to the party, *some other chemists* will come, too.

The presupposition carried by *other* is the same, though the anaphoric order has been reversed. Also, though it is natural to include *too*, the sentences (40) and (41) would be acceptable without it.

So clear it is that *other* is a presuppositional element, that I cannot imagine that it has not been mentioned in the linguistic literature on presupposition. However, it doesn't appear to have been, although I haven't made a systematic search.[23]

Another case arises where *other* refers to the active context, or previous discourse elements—for example, in (42).

(42) Smith will come. Some other chemists are coming, too.

Then the presupposition carried by *other* is clearly that Smith is a chemist. A more complicated case is (43).

(43) Smith will come. Harry doesn't like Smith. Nevertheless, if some other chemists come, Harry will come, too.

Depending on what is known, the presupposition in (43) carried by *other* can be either that Smith is a chemist or that Harry is (or possibly that both are). Suppose

---

[23] At least, I had not seen *other* as an example in the linguistics literature on presupposition I had read in 1990. In 1957, I had heard the example given by Max Black (in another context), in comments, unpublished as far as I know, on a paper by Arthur Pap. However, I now find that a later version of Pap's paper was posthumously published and mentions Black's example. See Pap (1960:50).

it is just the first of these cases. Then in that case the presuppositions in the last sentence of (43) are that Smith is a chemist, carried by *other*, while the presuppositions carried by *too* are that Harry is not Smith (perhaps vacuous because it is implied by the preceding sentence) and that Harry is not one of the *some other chemists* (i.e., other than Smith) hypothesized in the antecedent. In this instance, Harry himself may or may not be a chemist. In (40), I had of course supposed it uttered with no previous context, or at least that it is clear that *other* is meant to refer to Harry, and to no one else.[24]

The *other* case can be used to illustrate what may be a source of the usual view that *too* has the weak presupposition given in the list initially quoted from Soames 1982. This can be seen by considering the following example:

(44) If someone other than Harry volunteers, *Harry* will volunteer, too.

What is the presupposition carried by *too* on the present model? It is that Harry is not someone other than Harry. No doubt that is (very trivially) true. However, one might be tempted to look at the situation in (44) in the following way: In (44), the presupposition carried by *too* is filtered out in the conditional; (44) itself carries no presupposition. But this can only mean that the presupposition carried by *too* in the consequent is entailed by the antecedent. This antecedent is that someone other than Harry volunteers. Applying this argument uniformly, the standard account of the presuppositions of *too* cited at the beginning of this paper from Soames 1982 would appear to follow. However, although this argument might seem very convincing, it does not in fact follow. The present model handles it in a very different way. And I hope I have convinced the reader that the standard account cannot be correct.[25]

There are certainly idiolects, dialects, and contexts in which *other* is not explicitly said but nevertheless is meant. We were told in school not to leave *other* implicit in this way—for example, not to say "I can lick any man in the house" if we do not mean to include ourselves. Similarly, "In his country, Harry

---

[24] Richard Holton and Michaelis Michael have influenced this discussion. The examples in (42) and (43) respond to a query of theirs. Also, some material in the original talk was deleted, since their queries made me unsure of the correct position.

[25] Actually, the *other* case was unknown to the literature on presupposition of which I was aware (see footnote 23), but similar filtering arguments can be given for many of the other presuppositions in Soames (1982), and they are fallacious in every case.

(i) If Priscilla has had supper before, then she is having supper again (now).
(ii) Priscilla has had supper before, and she is having supper again (now).
(iii) If someone voted against his tenure, it is Susan who voted against his tenure.

In every case, the antecedent states the presupposition in Soames (1982). Since it is filtered out in the conditionals (or conjunctions), it might seem to follow that the antecedent must state the entire presupposition required. Such filtering arguments, however, are never correct. In the tenure case, the antecedent raises the question "If so, who voted against his tenure?," which requires a complete answer. In the supper case, vague and obvious (in the case of a normal grown woman) as the antecedent or the first conjunct may be, it gives enough context for *again* to have a proper anaphora.

is better than any chemist around" might mean any other chemist around. Perhaps there are even dialects in which *some chemist* can be used in this way. The school insistence on *any other* can be ascribed to the devotion of schoolteachers to standard quantification theory. In fact, if we follow the school prohibition, our language is certainly more precise and unambiguous.

Another issue is illustrated by (45) and (46).[26]

(45) If the Nebraskans come to dinner, the Cornhuskers will *stay for drinks*, too.
(46) If the Poles defeat the Russians, (then) the *Hungarians* will defeat the Russians, too.

Obviously, general terms and verbs can be involved as the focused elements and also as the identity elements. This is illustrated in (45), where coming to dinner is contrasted with staying for drinks. I have chosen a case where *Nebraskans* and *Cornhuskers* are synonyms. Sentence (46) is an example from Soames (1982:497). Here, *Russians* is repeated but according to me, the presupposition is that the Poles and the Hungarians are different groups.

More important are the following examples:

(47) The people from the Midwest are coming to dinner, and the Nebraskans will *stay for drinks*, too.
(48) All of John's friends are from Nebraska, and Bill's friends are all from the Midwest, too.

Apart from the distinction between coming to dinner and staying for drinks, the important presupposition in (47) is that Nebraskans are people from the Midwest. *Nebraskans* is the element figuring in an identity or inclusion statement as a result of anaphoric reference by *too* to parallel information. Of course, the Nebraskans are not identical with the people in the Midwest; rather, they are included in that set. So the sentence means that a bunch of people from the Midwest are coming to dinner, and a certain subset of them—namely, the Nebraskans—are going to stay for drinks. (There is also a supposition that the group of people from the Midwest includes some Nebraskans—in other words, that the subset is nonempty.) We know, of course, that if the people from the Midwest are coming, they include the Nebraskans, because the Nebraskans are from the Midwest. However, the inclusion can go the other way, as in (48). Here, the element from *the Midwest* in the second conjunct, which carries the presupposition, has an extension that contains (rather than is contained in) the extension of the parallel element *from Nebraska*. In (48), then, we have the same inclusion as in (47), but the order of the terms, and their association with the presuppositional word, are reversed. An inclusion was already mentioned above

---

[26] This issue partly was introduced above in the examples from chess.

in connection with the chess matches, where there was a presupposition that checkmating implies defeating.

Barbara Partee mentioned a similar example,[27] which people who worked on the syntax of *too* were concerned with years ago. It was something like *If John will leave at ten o'clock, Jill will leave the party early, too.* The presupposition in this case is that those who leave at ten o'clock will leave the party early. The relation here and in (48) is what I call a *converse inclusion* or *superset.*

There doesn't always have to be a strict inclusion or converse inclusion. Sometimes the sets that are presupposed to stand in the inclusion relation do not come directly from the antecedent and the consequent, but from the antecedent and the consequent together with other relevant background information.[28] Semantically, though, the general picture ought to be clear. The inclusions and converse inclusions are calculated from the requirement that anaphoric elements like *too, again,* and so on, refer to parallel information. It remains a project to characterize syntactically when we have inclusions and when converse inclusions. In the examples above, antecedents with a predicate or group characterization in subject position require inclusions in the consequents, while predicates correspondingly require converse inclusions.[29]

With *or* there is yet another consideration. Take the following example:

(49) Either the Waring number is odd, or *the Waring number plus six* is even, too.[30]

The predicate *is odd* can be regarded as parallel to *is even.* In this case, it is presupposed that the Waring number, like all whole numbers, is even if it is not odd. The focused element is *the Waring number plus six,* which is supposed to be distinct from the Waring number, to justify the *too.*

---

[27] In a previous paper in the symposium where the present paper was given.

[28] In fact, the background information (probably in the active context) may be such that no inclusions are required. Suppose we know that the people from New York have been coming to events only when accompanied by their friends from California. Then one might say this:

(i) If the people from New York come, *their friends from California* will stay for drinks, too.

The presupposition is that if the people from New York come, their friends from California will come. But this is plainly no inclusion—say, that the friends from California are from New York.

[29] If the relevant antecedent is put in the form *all As are Bs,* and the latter is expressed as a universally quantified conditional, then the subject will be logically in negative position, while the consequent is in positive position. I tentatively conjecture that this has something to do with the phenomenon and might lead to a generalization. (In quantification theory, every atomic formula is in positive position as a part of itself. In the antecedent of a conditional, positive and negative positions are reversed as part of the whole conditional, while they are retained in the consequent. Negation reverses positive and negative positions. Conjunction, disjunction, and universal and existential quantification leave positive and negative occurrences unreversed.)

[30] The Waring number of a given number q is the least number such that every positive integer can be represented as the sum of that many qth powers. (For example, every positive integer is the sum of four squares.) Here I am supposing that the parameter q was mentioned in the previous explicit context.

A parallel example is (50).

(50) Either the boss will not come to the party, or *John* will come, too.

I assume that this is acceptable, with the presupposition that John is not the boss.

Another issue concerns the rules for when this type of anaphora is allowed. This parallels the corresponding questions for explicit pronominal and quantificational anaphora. Let me give a couple of examples.

(51) Perhaps Sam will come to the party. If there isn't a board meeting, *the boss* will come, too.

Obviously, the anaphora doesn't have to be within the same sentence, but can refer back to a previous sentence, at least if the sentence is at a reasonable distance back in the discourse in question. In (51), the presupposition carried by *too* is that Sam is not the boss. Examples for *other* were already given above, and the general point has really already been made in this paper. In fact, the presupposition may be unspoken in the immediately preceding discourse, as long as it is in the active context.

Look now at (52), based on examples from Soames (1982:525–526).

(52) a. If Haldeman is guilty, (then) *Nixon* is (guilty), too.
    b. *Nixon* is guilty, too, if Haldeman is (guilty).
    c. If *Haldeman* is guilty, too, (then) Nixon is (guilty).
    d. Nixon is guilty, if *Haldeman* is (guilty), too.

In (52b), the parallel element occurs in the antecedent of the conditional, but after the consequent clause has been uttered. For me, this is a problem of anaphora that is analogous to one for pronominalization. Notice the obvious analogy of this problem to the stock elementary pronominal examples.

(53) a. If John is free, he will come to the party.
    b. He will come to the party, if John is free.
    c. If he is free, John will come to the party.
    d. John will come to the party, if he is free.

In (53a-d), *he* is analogous to *too* in (52a–d). Moreover, in each of (52a–d), *too* is in a position in the conditional analogous to the position of *he* in each of (53a–d), respectively. However, the restrictions on anaphora are different. In (53), as is well known, *he* and *John* can be anaphorically related in all cases except (53b). In that case, *he* must be anaphoric to some (fairly immediately) previously mentioned person in the discourse, or must be deictic to some person in the context of utterance, not anaphoric to John.

In (52a–d), the anaphoric rules are different. Here, it is (52c) rather than (52b) where *too* cannot carry anaphora, in this case from *Nixon* to *Haldeman*. In (52c), as in (53b), there must be an anaphora or deixis to some previously mentioned or contextual figure (say, John Mitchell).[31]

An important question on the present account is this: what are the rules of anaphora for presuppositions, analogously to those for pronominalization? I discussed the case of *too* in part just now. The rules need not be the same for all the presuppositional elements discussed in this paper.

Normally the presuppositions are the ones predicted by my theory. There may well be cases that appear to be counterexamples and that may even require weakening of the presuppositions predicted, but every such case I have considered seems to require a corresponding weakening of the standard view, too. Such cases often seem to involve some special kind of trope and should not be seen as typical.[32]

REFERENCES

Evans, Gareth. 1982. *The varieties of reference.* Oxford: Clarendon Press.
Frege, Gottlob. 1892. Über Sinn und Bedeutung. *Zeitschrift für Philosophie und philosophische Kritik* 100: 25–50. Trans. by Max Black, reprinted in *The Frege reader*, ed. by Michael Beaney, 151–171. Oxford: Blackwell (1997).
Gazdar, Gerald. 1979. A solution to the projection problem. In *Syntax and semantics 11: Presupposition*, ed. by Choon-Kyu Oh and David Dineen, 57–89. New York: Academic Press.
Green, Georgia. 1968. On *too* and *either*, and not just on *too* and *either*, either. In *Papers from the Fourth Regional Meeting of the Chicago Linguistic Society*, ed. by Bill J. Darden, Charles-James N. Bailey, and Alice Davison, 22–39. Chicago: University of Chicago, Chicago Linguistic Society.
Grice, H. P. 1961. The causal theory of perception. *Proceedings of the Aristotelian Society, Supplementary Volume* 35:121–152. Reprinted in part in Grice 1989, 224–247.
——— 1975. Logic and conversation. In *The logic of grammar*, ed. by Donald Davidson and Gilbert Harman, 64–75. Encino, CA: Dickenson.
——— 1989. *Studies in the way of words.* Cambridge, MA: Harvard University Press.

---

[31] In the original version of this paper, I expressed some hesitation about the acceptability of (52d), which was endorsed by Soames, and said that sometimes I hear it his way, but not always. At the present time, I don't see why I was hesitant. Also in the original version, there was some contrast with Soames's own discussion of the Haldeman-Nixon examples. Soames pointed out that without *too*, the statements are all equivalent, since conditionals are equivalent whether the antecedent is stated before or after the consequent. He then concluded that neither semantics nor Gricean conversational implicature can be used to explain the exceptional status of (52c). My own explanation is in terms of anaphoric rules for *too* analogous to the well-known rules for *he* in (53). The interested reader can compare it with Soames's discussion in (1982:525–526). At the end of my original remarks on Soames's discussion, I raised and did not answer the question of whether the morals he draws disappear in the present analysis or can be supported by some examples other than the one he gave.

[32] See the opening footnote, where I mention a later seminar in which I indeed discussed such cases.

Heim, Irene. 1983. On the projection problem for presuppositions. In *Proceedings of the Second West Coast Conference on Formal Linguistics*, ed. by Michael Barlow, Daniel P. Flickinger, and Michael T. Wescoat, 114–125. Stanford, CA: Stanford University, Stanford Linguistics Association.

——— 1992. Presupposition projection and the semantics of attitude verbs. *Journal of Semantics* 9:183–221.

Karttunen, Lauri. 1974. Presupposition and linguistic context. *Theoretical Linguistics* 1:181–194.

———, and Stanley Peters. 1979. Conventional implicature. In *Syntax and semantics 11: Presupposition*, ed. by Choon-Kyu Oh and David Dineen, 1–56. New York: Academic Press.

Kripke, Saul. 2005. Russell's notion of scope. *Mind* 114:1005–1037. Reprinted in this volume as Chapter 8.

Langendoen, D. Terence, and Harris B. Savin. 1971. The projection problem for presupposition. In *Studies in linguistic semantics*, ed. by Charles J. Fillmore and D. Terence Langendoen, 55–60. New York: Holt, Rinehart and Winston.

Lewis, David. 1979. Scorekeeping in a language game. *Journal of Philosophical Logic* 8:339–359. Reprinted in *Philosophical papers, vol. 1*, 233–249. Oxford: Oxford University Press (1983).

Pap, Arthur. 1960. Types and meaninglessness. *Mind* 69:41–54.

Russell, Bertrand. 1905. On denoting. *Mind* 14:479–493.

Soames, Scott. 1979. A projection problem for speaker presupposition. *Linguistic Inquiry* 10:623–666.

——— 1982. How presuppositions are inherited: A solution to the projection problem. *Linguistic Inquiry* 13:483–545.

——— 1989. Presupposition. In *Handbook of philosophical logic, vol. 4*, ed. by Dov Gabbay and Franz Guenthner, 553–616. Dordrecht: Reidel.

Stalnaker, Robert. 1973. Presuppositions. *Journal of Philosophical Logic* 2:447–457.

——— 1974. Pragmatic presuppositions. In *Semantics and philosophy*, ed. by Milton K. Munitz and Peter K. Unger, 197–214. New York: New York University Press.

Strawson, P. F. 1950. On referring. *Mind* 59:320–344.

——— 1952. *Introduction to logical theory*. London: Methuen.

13

A Puzzle about Time and Thought

Suppose at a given moment I think of a set S of instants of time (call these instants "times"). For example, I may think of the set of all times when television was unknown, the set of all times when interplanetary travel will be routine, and the like. Notice that I need not know whether the set in question is empty or not—I can think of it by a defining property.

However, there is a problem: suppose I think, at a certain time t_0, of the set S_0, where S_0 contains all times t at which I'm thinking of a given set S_t of times, and S_t does not include t itself. In conventional notation:

$S_0 = \{t | S_t \text{ exists } \& t \notin S_t\}$

Now, I am thinking of S_0 at a certain time t_0. Is t_0 a member of S_0 or not? The reader can fill in the resulting paradox for herself.

The problem, quite similar to Russell's paradox, is clear. But in contrast to Russell's paradox, given that the predicate "I think of a set S (of times)" is meaningful, there is nothing in it incompatible with conventional Zermelo set theory, or stronger theories such as ZF. We are simply dealing with a subset of the set of all times, defined by the axiom of separation.[1]

I originally thought of this problem some time in the '60s. Like many other of my works, publication has been long delayed. However, I always thought that it was an interesting problem that deserved to be published.

David Kaplan subsequently discovered another puzzle. His puzzle questions the notions of possible world and of proposition (identified with sets of worlds) as follows: if the set of all worlds has a cardinality κ, the set of all propositions, taken to be sets of worlds, must have cardinality 2^κ. Kaplan adds the additional

---

[1] In the usual axiomatic formulation of Zermelo set theory, the axiom of separation is a schema restricted to properties that are first-order definable in the language of set theory. Zermelo himself intended separation to say that any "definite property" can be used to define a subset of a given set. Hence, if the language is extended so that the predicates involved in the argument are meaningful, we can formalize the problem in a separation axiom for the extended language. (Incidentally, the set of times could be identified with the real numbers—and these with one of their conventional set theoretic definitions—reducing the need for one extra primitive, though this is not necessary.)

assumption that for each proposition p and fixed time t_0, there is a world in which I entertain precisely that proposition p at t_0. But this gives a one-to-one mapping of the power set of a set into the set itself, contrary to Cantor's well-known theorem. (Note that if someone has a more fine-grained notion of proposition than a set of possible worlds, this only makes the problem worse.)

After a long period in which Kaplan was content to have the problem remain in the oral tradition and be quoted by others—though he presented the puzzle at meetings—he eventually published it.[2] He has also formalized the argument and, in particular, posited the following axiom:

(A) $(\forall p) \Diamond (\forall q)(Q q \leftrightarrow p = q)$

Here Q could be interpreted as saying that a certain person entertains a proposition at a certain time.[3] Kaplan argues that even if one has one's doubts about (A) for some philosophical reason or other, surely modal logic should not exclude (A) in its very formulation. It should be as neutral as possible in its metaphysical/philosophical assumptions.[4] Over the years, I have heard the view expressed that the cardinality considerations in question give real trouble for the notion of possible worlds, and for "possible world semantics." Now that I am finally writing about this issue, I find that other papers have appeared on Kaplan's problem, and these may not be the last.[5]

In this note I wish to say that whatever the issue raised by Kaplan's argument may be, it is not really a cardinality problem for the notion of a set of all possible worlds,[6] nor need it depend on any assumption like (A). Of course, Kaplan's argument, as he presented it, appeared to involve all these things. However, my own puzzle is given for the case of time. The analogy between time and modality, tense logic and modal logic, and the role of times and possible worlds in each is

---

[2] Lewis (1986:104) says he heard the paradox directly from Kaplan in 1975. I also heard it directly from him; I don't remember the date. It is published in Kaplan (1995). Kaplan says that he has been thinking about the problem for about fifteen years (41). I'm not sure exactly or even approximately what date is implied by this remark, since I don't know when Kaplan's paper was written as opposed to the publication date of the book (1995). However, Kaplan's first footnote says that the "first airing" of the argument was in the mid-'70s, which nearly enough agrees with David Lewis's date.

[3] Syntactically, Kaplan takes Q to be an intensional propositional operator on a par with $\Diamond$.

[4] This particular question aside, I agree with Kaplan on the general principle he advocates. I say this because other people have seemed to think that modal logic, at least as based on the possible worlds idea, involves rich and controversial metaphysical assumptions and classical logic does not. See explicitly Lewis, who, writing on the issue of Kaplan's (A), says: "I am not a logician, and metaphysical neutrality is not among my aims" (1986:105, note 2). It is clear that Lewis's entire book is in fact a work of metaphysics. But I think that the attitude that modal logic is a deeply metaphysical subject is not confined to Lewis.

[5] See, e.g., Anderson (2009) and Lindström (2009).

[6] I actually have my doubts, if we can speak of all possible worlds, that they do form a set, let alone that one can speak of their power set. But not for the reasons being discussed here. See "Concluding Unscientific Postscript," below.

well known.[7] Nor is there any cardinality problem; the cardinality of the set of all instants of time is simply that of the continuum. Therefore, no one is likely to question the meaningfulness of the notion of a set of all instants of time. Nor do I make an assumption like Kaplan's (A). The only assumption made is that I am free to think of the set S_0 at a chosen time t_0. Not only does this assumption seem quite unexceptionable, I have in fact fulfilled it; for in presenting the paradox, I have in fact thought of this set at some particular time.[8] When I told my own paradox to David Lewis, he pointed out (correctly, in my opinion) that I could also have formulated the problem in terms of sets of people rather than of instants of time. Presumably he was thinking of egocentric logic, where people, in analogy to instants or worlds, are the appropriate indices.[9] For the same reasons, it is also unexceptionable to assume that I am free to think at a designated time about the property of being a world w where I am thinking at that time about a set S_w of possible worlds w such that S_w does not have w as a member. In fact, as before, have I not done this simply by stating the problem?

Even though when we discussed the matter Lewis seemed to agree with me that my paradox showed that there was no special problem about possible worlds that wouldn't be a problem about times or people, there is no trace of our discussion in his well-known book on possible worlds (1986:104ff). There he simply rejects Kaplan's assumption (A) and argues in terms of Cantorian cardinalities that "most sets of worlds, in fact all but an infinitesimal minority of them, are not eligible contents of thought" (Lewis 1986:105). He adds that there is no place for "neutrality" as an argument that assumption (A) cannot be excluded.

If we think of the problem simply in terms of cardinalities, then there does not seem to be anything paradoxical about the result in terms of instants of times. It would just happen to be the case that most sets of times are not objects of my thought at any particular time. The result might seem worse if presented in terms of possible worlds as Lewis does, since it might mean (nearly enough) that there are propositions whose essence is such that no possible mind can entertain them.

---

[7] But nothing in the argument depends on a commitment to tense logic, as opposed to a four-dimensional treatment that simply takes time as another index.

[8] Perhaps there is also another vague analogy with Russell. Thinking of the paradox of the greatest cardinal, he came to realize that the problem was that of the existence of a certain set, the set of all sets not members of themselves, and thus, as Gödel remarked (1983:452), freed the problem from unnecessary technicalities. However, in the present case, the order is in a way reversed. The present writer, thinking of Russell's paradox, discovered the paradox presented here directly, without thinking at all about cardinality problems. In contrast, it was Kaplan's formulation of his own paradox that put the matter in terms of a cardinality paradox.

[9] As I recall, when this conversation took place, Kaplan's problem had been floating around in the oral tradition. As I said (note 2), I recall having heard it from Kaplan himself, and telling him my own paradox in response (see the text below). For Lewis, see also note 2.

Kaplan (1995:48–49, note 1) lists many earlier places where he gave the argument, including one abstract in print (1983). He also has an extensive list of earlier authors, including Lewis, who mentioned or discussed his argument. I do not intend to go into all of these.

In his discussion, Lewis goes on to argue in terms of his own psychological views that this result is not implausible.[10]

I also discussed my own problem about time with Kaplan himself and argued that it meant that a special paradox about possible worlds and cardinalities did not get to the essence of the matter. However, once again, my conversation did not affect his subsequent talks and writings on the subject. I don't know what he thought, or whether I got my point of view across well. In any case, it may not have made a lasting impression.

Kaplan eventually came to conclude that his assumption (A) leads directly to a form of the Cretan liar paradox (1995:45–46). In this sense, his argument might support my view that cardinalities of the set of all possible worlds and its power set are not the essence of the problem.[11]

It is only natural that the first thing to occur to each of us (that is, Kaplan and me) as a solution to our respective problems was to follow Russell in his ramified theory of types. This is what Russell explicitly does in his treatment of the Cretan form of the liar paradox. When the Cretan says, "every proposition asserted by a Cretan is false," or, alternatively, "for all p, if a Cretan says that p, then not p," the Cretan's assertion must be of higher type, and therefore does not come within the scope of the quantifier "for all p." In my case, the property by which one defines a set of instants must vary in type, as must the predicate "thinking of a set of instants." One must think of a set of instants by virtue of thinking of it through a defining property, and hence there would be a type-theoretic hierarchy of different predicates "thinking of." Once one has observed the appropriate restrictions, the predicate S_0, as defined above, must be of a higher type than the properties defining the sets S_t and the relation "thinking of" involved in them.

Kaplan and I have long agreed that Russell's motivation for ramifying his theory of types was based on important philosophical arguments, misunderstood and underestimated by any number of logicians and philosophers. Russell's primary motivations for the ramification were problems of intensional logic, illustrated by the liar paradox. Viewed with this motivation in mind, he did not wipe away the ramification by proposing an axiom of reducibility.[12]

---

[10] Moreover, not to accept Kaplan's (A) does not seem to me necessarily to commit oneself to the idea that there are propositions no possible being can entertain. I might mention that in addition to his intuitive motivation for (A), Kaplan also abstractly motivates it by analogy to a corresponding assumption about a predicate of individuals (see his 43). However, any analogy with the plausibility of an assumption about individuals strikes me as somewhat dubious, since in (A) we are concerned with an assumption about arbitrary sets of worlds, and thus about entities of higher type than the worlds themselves, whereas in the case of individuals we are not.

[11] Actually, such a conclusion is not emphasized in Kaplan's paper, and he says explicitly (1995:46) that (A) is not to be blamed for the paradox. However, this is in a context where he says that ramified type theory should be a solution to the problem, and that many other empirically true assumptions would produce a liar paradox.

[12] Russell's motivation seems to be understood better today by many philosophers, whether or not they advocate ramified type theory as an appropriate solution (as indeed the papers by Anderson

One illustration of how the axiom of reducibility does not wipe away the intensional logic motivation for ramified type theory is the paradox presented here. Nothing in the solution of the problem by intensional ramified type theory is in conflict with accepting Zermelo's complete axiom of separation for sets of instants of time, even though this axiom allows sets to be defined impredicatively. The point is that, as in Russell's axiom of reducibility, one can maintain in effect an impredicative point of view for extensions, while maintaining the predicative (ramified) point of view for intensions.[13]

However, I do not wish to commit myself to ramified type theory as the proper solution to my problem or to Kaplan's. If one thinks of paradoxes in intensional logic as in some way analogues of semantic paradoxes—and Kaplan even mentions such an analogy in his own case—then ramified type theory might be an analogue of the finite Tarski hierarchy.[14] An alternative might be an intensional logic analogue of my own approach in Kripke (1975) (reprinted here as Chapter 4), and the many papers extending it or giving alternatives. Different views and alternatives to a ramified approach are presented in the papers by Anderson and Lindström (and Anderson especially criticizes the ramified approach). I do not propose as of this writing to investigate the matter any further and "frame no hypotheses."

Concluding Unscientific Postscript. When I did my own work on the semantics of modal logic, I posited a set **K** of worlds with an accessibility relation **R**, a

---

and Lindström show), and was understood by some all along (probably, e.g., by Prior 1958, even though he rejects ramified type theory).

There is another motivation for the ramification, also coming out of Russell's work (and some others, such as Poincare and Weyl). This motivation is to give a treatment of mathematics, especially analysis, that does not use impredicative definitions. Once one proposes an axiom of reducibility, one does indeed wipe away this motivation. (Russell does discuss in the introduction to the second edition of *Principia*, with inconclusive results and little knowledge of what was already done by Weyl, how far mathematics can get without the axiom of reducibility (see Chapter 8, note 61). In conversation with me, and in print, well-known logicians and philosophers have held that Russell did indeed wipe away all motivation for the ramification when he proposed the axiom of reducibility. For instance, in conversation Kreisel expressed the view to me that ramified type theory was a major achievement of Russell, but that combining it with the axiom of reducibility was foolish. I said in reply that ramified type theory with reducibility still had a motivation in terms of intensional logic, but I doubt that I got the point across.

[13] One paradox that certainly is a cardinality problem and that is somewhat analogous to Kaplan's is Russell's problem about sets of propositions. Russell assumed that for every set of propositions there is a unique proposition that is its conjunction. But then we get a one-to-one mapping of arbitrary sets of propositions into propositions, contrary to Cantor's theorem that there can never be a one-to-one mapping of the power set of a set into the set itself. Russell would have greatly clarified his motivations for ramified type theory, and why the axiom of reducibility does not eliminate the need for it, if in *Principia* he had discussed this paradox and how it is solved by ramified type theory, even with the axiom of reducibility. For an exposition of this point, see Church (1984) and Klement (2005).

Myhill (1958) rediscovered essentially the same paradox, showing that it arises formally in Church's most intensionally refined alternative for a formalization of the logic of sense and denotation in Church (1951).

[14] See also Church (1976).

distinguished actual world, and a domain function. My main point was to find a definition, set theoretically meaningful, of validity, satisfiability, and other model-theoretic notions, and to be able to raise completeness problems, and so on. But the set **K** was arbitrary and, in a definition of validity, was allowed to vary. There was no concern with *the* unique set (or class) of possible worlds.

Thus, I was not particularly concerned with questions of truth in all possible worlds *simpliciter*. (The distinction might be analogous to that of "truth" and "truth in a model" in standard quantificational logic.) Much less was I concerned, as David Lewis certainly was, with giving a reductive analysis of modal notions. However, given possible-worlds semantics, the development was inevitable that one consider absolute truth in the unique collection of all possible worlds. I myself would have considerable doubts that they form a set, let alone that they have a power set (see note 6). In particular, it seems to me to be reasonable to suppose (and certainly not in conflict with my view of modal logic) that for every cardinality κ it is possible that there are exactly κ individuals. But then it would immediately follow that the possible worlds cannot form a set.[15] This is not related to Kaplan's paradox, nor to my own. And whatever one thinks of Kaplan's problem, I think it ought to be considered in the light of the present one.[16]

REFERENCES

Almog, J., and P. Leonardi, eds. (2009). *The Philosophy of David Kaplan*. New York: Oxford University Press.

Anderson, C. A. (2009). "The Lesson of Kaplan's Paradox about Possible Worlds Semantics." In Almog and Leonardi (2009), 85–92.

Benacerraf, P., and H. Putnam (1983). *Readings in the Philosophy of Mathematics*. 2nd ed. Cambridge: Cambridge University Press.

Church, A. (1951). "A Formulation of the Logic of Sense and Denotation." In *Structure, Method, and Meaning: Essays in Honor of Henry M. Sheffer*, ed. P. Henle et al. New York: Liberal Arts.

———. (1976). "Comparison of Russell's Resolution of the Semantical Antinomies with that of Tarski." *Journal of Symbolic Logic* 41:747–60.

---

[15] As I recall Jubien (1988) (which I have not reread for the present paper), his doubts about possible worlds do not affect my original semantics for modal logic but might affect "possible worlds semantics" if these require arbitrary higher types of sets of possible worlds in a way that would be violated if these do not form a set. There may be something to be done with this, but I do not go into the matter here.

[16] I would like to thank Jeff Buechner, Gary Ostertag, and especially Romina Padró for their help in producing this paper. My editors at the Kripke Center have rightly complained that this paper alludes too briefly to complicated topics that really need more treatment and explanation in the paper. I have done a bit to comply, but properly to fulfill their desires would turn this paper not into one that presents a paradox of my own, but into a monograph on all these other topics, such as ramified type theory. This paper has been completed with support from the Saul A. Kripke Center at the City University of New York, Graduate Center.

———. (1984). "Russell's Theory of Identity of Propositions." *Philosophia Naturalis* 21:513–22.
Gödel, K. (1944). "Russell's Mathematical Logic." In *The Philosophy of Bertrand Russell*, ed. P. A. Schlipp. Evanston, IL: Northwestern University Press. Reprinted in Benacerraf and Putnam (1983), 447–69; references are to the reprint.
Jubien, M. (1988). "Problems with Possible Worlds." In *Philosophical Analysis: A Defense by Example*, ed. D. F. Austin. Norwell, MA: Kluwer, 299–322.
Kaplan, D. (1983). "Abstracts of Sections 5 and 12." In *7th International Congress of Logic Methodology and Philosophy of Science*. Salzburg, Austria: Hutteger.
———. (1995). "A Problem in Possible-Worlds Semantics." In *Modality, Morality and Belief*, ed. W. Sinnott-Armstrong, D. Raffman, and N. Asher. Cambridge: Cambridge University Press.
Klement, K. C. (2005). "Russell-Myhill Paradox." *Internet Encyclopedia of Philosophy*. http://www.iep.utm.edu/par-rusm
Kripke, S. (1975). "Outline of a Theory of Truth." *Journal of Philosophy* 72:690–716. Reprinted in this volume as Chapter 4.
———. (2005). "Russell's Notion of Scope." *Mind* 114:1005–37. Reprinted in this volume as Chapter 8.
Lewis, D. K. (1986). *On the Plurality of Worlds*. Oxford: Blackwell.
Lindström, S. (2009). "Possible World Semantics and the Liar. Reflections on a Problem Posed by Kaplan." In Almog and Leonardi (2009), 93–108.
Myhill, J. (1958). "Problems Arising in the Formalization of Intensional Logic." *Logique et Analyse* 1:78–83.
Prior, A. (1958). "Epimenides the Cretan." *Journal of Symbolic Logic* 23:261–66.
Russell, B. (1903). *Principles of Mathematics*. Cambridge: Cambridge University Press.
Whitehead, A. N., and B. Russell. (1910, 1912, 1913). *Principia Mathematica*. 3 Volumes. Cambridge: Cambridge University Press. 2nd ed., 1925 (Vol. 1), 1927 (Vols. 2, 3).

Index

Absorption, 194–98, 214n83
accommodation, 353, 362–64
Ackerman, Diana, 131n10
acquaintance. *See also* self-acquaintance
    Frege on, 275, 285n83
    reference and direct, 271–72
    Russell on, 241–42
acquaintance-revelatory senses, 271
Albritton, R., 26n19, 308
Almog, Joseph, 227n7, 237
anaphora, 268, 351–71
Anscombe, Elizabeth, 296, 309–13, 315, 318
a posteriori truth, 16–17, 21
a priori truth
    contingent, 304–5
    essentialism distinguished from, 16–17
    necessary statements and, 14–15, 18n14
attributive definite description, 101–9
Austin, John, 346, 347n63
autonymous designators, 267–68, 271, 274–75, 277, 284–85

Bach, Emmon, 232
backtracking, Nozick's analysis of knowledge and, 216–17, 216n85
Bedeutung
    Frege on, 261–62
    tensed senses and, 276
    translation of, 254, 254n2
belief. *See also de dicto* belief; *de re* belief
    assent and, 137–38, 143
    contradictory, 145–46
    disquotational principle and, 137–38, 137n22
    Lewis on possible worlds and, 317n67
    proper names and, 128, 142–43, 148, 156–57
    referential opacity of, 159–60
    consciousness of, 183
    substitutivity principle and, 130, 141–42
    translation and, 139, 148–49, 157
    two kinds of, 230, 314–15, 322–23
    unrestricted exportation and, 322–48
Berger, Alan, 231n15
Bernays, P., 236–37, 248, 250
Black, Max, 255, 366n23
Bonjour, Laurence, 173, 173n27
Boolos, George, 228
Buechner, Jeff, 170n21

Burge, Tyler, 256, 256n9, 273
    on *Sinn*, 279–81
Butler, Joseph, 23

Carroll, Lewis, 69
Cartesian argument, 26n19
centered possible worlds, 315–16, 316n65
Chisholm, Roderick, 313–14, 313n58
Church, Alonzo, 257, 259n15, 377n13
    on fictional entities, 58n11
    on indirect speech, 263–64, 263n35, 264n36
    on privileged senses, 286n90
    on scope ambiguities, 234
clefts, 352, 363
    pseudoclefts and, 364–65
complexity theory, 261, 344, 344n58
computability theory, 344, 344n57
connotation, proper names and, 132, 132n11
contingent *a priori*, 304–5
contingent identity statements, 1–3, 8–9, 18–20, 21–23
    mind-body problem and, 8–9, 23–26
    proper names and, 6–8
    scientific discoveries and, 8–9
    Wiggins on, 2–3
contradictory beliefs, 138–40, 145–46
conversational principles, 110n18, 111, 328, 337
counterfactual analysis of knowledge, 162–223
counterfactual statements
    fictional entities and, 53–55, 69
    impossible antecedents and, 212–13, 215
    knowledge and, 162–223
    Lewis on, 163, 163n5, 211
    Stalnaker and, 163, 163n5, 211
    tense and, 318, 318n72
    transitivity of, 201–2
    vacuous names and, 57
counterparts, 11
    contingent identity statements and, 20n15
Crocker, L., 101
cumulative hypothesis, projection problem for presuppositions, 353–54

Davidson, Donald, 256–58, 257n12, 300n23
de dicto belief, 322–23
    de re belief implied by, 323, 323n4
    Sosa on, 332–33

deductive closure of knowledge, 31, 31n7, 37, 43, 46n23
  challenges to, 196–197, 206
  Nozick on, 179, 179n33, 185–86, 196n60
definite description, 99. *See also* attributive definite description; referential definite description
  belief puzzle and, 148
  de dicto-de re distinction and, 103–5
  definite article and, 115, 123
  Donnellan on, 101–5
  "knowing wh-" phrases and, 260–61, 260n22
  as predicative, 246
  proper names and, 106–7, 117–18, 117n25
  referential opacity and, 160n45
  rigid, 105–6
  scope and, 225–51
  semantically ambiguous, 108
  speaker's reference and, 107–8
  translation and, 148–49
  vacuous, 100–101
deixis, 371
  anaphora and, 352
demonstratives
  indexicals compared to, 298–99, 299n18
  Kaplan on, 106, 281n81
Dennett, Daniel, 230, 337–39
  on *de re* belief, 326–27, 326n18, 341, 341n51
  on unrestricted exportation, 327
denoting phrases
  analysis of, 226–28
de re belief, 322–23
  de dicto belief implying, 323, 323n4
  Dennett on, 326–27, 326n18, 341, 341n51
  in ordinary language, 327–28
  Quine on, 328n19
  Sosa on, 332–33, 336
  unrestricted exportation and, 325–26, 326n14, 330n25
Descartes, R., 26n19, 287
  self-consciousness and, 308–10
descriptions. *See* definite description; indefinite description
direct acquaintance, reference and, 271–72
direct quotation, 268
  Frege's theory of, 268–69
  Kaplan on, 262
disquotational principle
  belief and, 137–38, 137n22, 154
  biconditional form of, 138
  homophonic translation and, 142
  simple form of, 138–39
  strengthened, 141–42, 146
  substitutivity principle and, 140–41
  Tarskian, 140n26
  translation and, 139–40

dogmatism paradox, 48–49
Dolan, John, 217
Donnellan, Keith, 13, 99–124, 235, 341
double-K principle, 33–35
Dretske, Fred, 31n7, 162–63, 162n2, 167
dualism, 26n19, 310
Dummett, Michael, 63n18, 255n6, 258, 270
  on indirect reference, 263, 263n35

egocentric logic, 375
Eissfeldt, Otto, 63n20
Ekbom, Lennart, 27n1
empty names. *See* vacuous names
epistemic modalities, 128
essentialism, 15–16
  a priori truth and, 16–17
  existence and, 15n11
  necessity and, 16–17
essential property, equivalent definitions of, 15n12
Evans, Gareth, 228, 243, 278n72
  on indirect reflexive, 315n64
existence. *See also* necessary existence
  essentialism and, 15n11
  fictional entities and, 54–55, 55n6, 63–65, 71–72
  as predicate, 57
  sense-data and, 60–61
existential generalization, Nozick's analysis of knowledge and, 200–201
existential quantification
  speaker's reference and, 115
  in strong Russell language, 114–15

faith, knowledge and, 206. *See also* belief
Fara, Delia Graff, 244–46
fictional entities
  free logic and, 62, 62n17
  Frege on, 58n11
  Kaplan on, 69–70
  metalinguistic analysis of, 70
  mythical entities compared to, 67–72
  necessary existence and, 55–56
  pretended propositions and, 59
  pretense principle and, 58–60
  a priori truth and, 70
  proper names and, 53
  properties of, 65
  quantification over, 63–64
  reference and, 59, 61–63, 71
  truth and, 65–66
  vacuous names as, 68–69, 68n30
  vacuous names differing from, 62–63
first person statements. *See also* 'I' pronoun
  autonymous designators and, 284–85
  Frege on, 279

incommunicable thoughts and, 287–88
indexicals and, 283–84
other minds and, 299n21
Perry on, 285
senses and, 286–87
Fitch, Frederic B., 46–47, 46n23, 83n15, 234n23
letter to, 47–48
fixed points
hierarchy of languages and, 86–87
intrinsic, 92
maximal, 91–92
minimal, 91, 94–95
truth and construction of, 88
truth-value gaps and, 93–94
Frankfurt, Harry, 64n22, 305
free logic, 62, 62n17
Frege, Friedrich Ludwig Gottlob
on acquaintance, 285n83
on *Bedeutung*, 261–62
on direct quotation, 268–69
on fictional entities, 58n11
on first person statements, 278
on incommunicable thoughts, 285–87
on indirect reference, 255–56
on indirect senses, 258
on 'I' pronoun, 297–98, 302–3, 303n27
Kaplan on indirect quotation and, 265–67, 265n38
Mill's views on proper names compared to, 126–37
Perry's criticisms of, 296
on presupposition, 352–53
on proper names, 52–56, 126
on propositions, 273–74
Russell's correspondence with, 238
Russell's similarity to, 288
on scope, 5n5
on 'yesterday' and 'today,' 303, 304n29
Freud, Sigmund, 220, 220n87
future evidence, 40–41, 43–45
Harman on, 49
surprise examination paradox and, 45n17

Geach, Peter, 121n30, 130n9, 241n42, 285
Gedanke, 256, 264, 275, 278n72
Gettier problem, 202
Ginet, Carl, 166
Gödel, Kurt
Liar paradox and, 90
second incompleteness theorem of, 47–48, 78
Gödel-Tarski theorem, 78
Goldbach conjecture, 14–15
Goldfarb, Warren, 233, 250
Goldman, Alvin, 162–3, 166, 170n21, 209–11, 210n75, 217

Greene, Graham, 28
Grice, H. P., 342, 343
analysis of meaning, 109–111
conversational principles of, 293n3, 328, 337, 338n44, 356

Harman, Gilbert, 48, 181–84, 207, 318n71
on future evidence, 49
Harrington, Leo, 98n36
heap paradox
surprise examination paradox and, 29–30
Hempel, C. G., 294
Hertzberger, Hans, 78n8
"Hesperus is Phosphorus" statement, 6–8, 17–19
hierarchy of languages
fixed points and, 86–87
modal operators and, 95–96
Tarski and, 79, 79n9, 82, 88n23, 93, 377
translation and, 256–57
truth predicates in, 88–89
Hilbert, D., 215, 236–37, 248, 250
Hintikka, Jaakko, 5n5, 34–35, 39–40, 61–62, 72, 118, 260n21, 326n16, 326n17, 334, 335n37, 344
Holton, Richard, 365n22, 367n24
homophonic translation, 140–41, 142, 154
Hume, D., 41n15, 225n4, 305–10
hydra problem, 249–50, 249n58

identity. *See also* self-identity
of mental state and physical state, 8–9
across possible worlds, 16
identity statements. *See also* contingent identity statements
illusion of contingency of, 25
as metalinguistic, 18
as necessary, 9, 17
identity theory and, 8–9, 24n17, 26n19
idiolect
proper names and, 111, 111n19, 127, 133, 149n29, 150, 150n31, 280, 282
sharing common, 141
incommunicable thoughts
first person statements and, 287–88
Frege on, 285–87
indefinite description, 122n31, 123, 230, 244–6
ambiguity of, 239
Russell's analysis of, 228–9, 233
scope and, 230–31, 239
indeterminacy of translation, Quine, 154–56
indexicals, 281
demonstratives compared to, 298–99, 299n18
first person statements and, 283–84
proper names compared to, 283n81

indirect quotation, 262
  Kaplan on Frege's treatment of, 265–67, 265n38
indirect reference
  ambiguity and, 262–63
  Dummett on, 263, 263n35
  Frege on, 255–56
indirect reflexive, 314
indirect senses, 257–58, 262–63, 269, 272
indirect speech
  ambiguities and, 262–63
  Church on, 263–64, 263n35, 264n36
  'I' pronoun and, 302n26
intensional context, 128–29, 129n7
  puzzle with, 239–41
  scope and, 243
intermediate scope, 13n10, 231
'I' pronoun. *See also* self-consciousness
  Anscombe on, 309–12
  Cartesian ego and, 311
  character and content of, 296
  Frege on, 297–98
  indirect speech and, 302n26
  interpersonal communication and, 301–2
  Kaplan on, 295, 295n10, 296n7, 300–1
  Lewis on, 314–18
  logical inference and, 318n71
  possible worlds and, 316–18
  self-acquaintance and, 301, 303, 316
  self-consciousness and, 308–9
  Wittgenstein on, 311–12
Irving, David, 294n5

Johnston, Mark, 168, 190

Kant, Immanuel, 1, 55n6, 225n4
Kaplan, David
  on content and character, 273–74
  on demonstratives, 106, 283n81
  on direct quotation, 262
  on fictional entities, 69–70
  on Frege's treatment of indirect quotation, 265–67, 265n38
  on 'I' pronoun, 295, 295n7, 295n10, 300–1
  on knowledge, 46n23
  possible worlds and proposition puzzle of, 373–76
  scientific language and, 293–94, 296–97
Kleene, S. C., 84, 84n18, 88, 89n24
Klement, Kevin, 377n13
"the Knower" paradox, 46n23
"knowing wh-" phrases
  ambiguities with, 344–45, 345n59
  definite description and, 261–62, 260n22
knowledge. *See also* Nozick's analysis of knowledge
  counterfactual analysis of, 162–223
  deductive closure of, 31, 31n7, 37, 43, 46n23, 179, 179n33, 185–86, 196n60, 197, 206
  faith and, 206
  future evidence and, 40–45
  justification and, 174
  linguistic differences of, 42–43
  logic of, 34–35
  Malcolm on truth and, 40–41, 40n12
  Montague on, 46n23
  perceptual, 175–76
  reliability and, 190
  strong requirements for, 118
  surprise examination paradox and, 33–34
  truth and, 34
  unrestricted exportation and, 331–32
  Wittgenstein on, 165, 165n10
Kvart, Igal, 326n17, 331, 334n35, 339n47

Levin, Michael, 164n7, 195n59, 203n68, 203n69, 210n75
Lewis, David K., 177, 191, 191n54, 201, 201n67, 300n23, 374n2
  on belief and possible worlds, 313–14, 316n67
  contextualist theory of, 49n23, 336n39
  on counterfactual statements, 163, 163n5, 211
  on egocentric logic, 375
  on 'I' pronoun, 314–18
  on possible worlds, 11–12
  on presupposition, 353
  Quine and, 313n59
Lewy, Casimir, 260
Liar paradox, 46n23
  belief puzzle and, 156
  empirical predicates in, 76
  Gödelian form of, 90
  truth and, 75–76
  universal language and, 96–97
  utterances and, 76–77
Linsky, Leonard, 101, 245–46
Löb's theorem, 47
logically proper names, 52n2, 102, 149n29
Lumsden, David, 168

Makin, Gideon, 60n14, 242
Malcolm, N., 45n17, 232n16, 260n19
  on knowledge and truth, 40–41, 40n12, 43
Marcus, Ruth Barcan, 6–7, 234n23
Martin, Robert L., 82–83, 83n14, 95
Mates, Benson, 134n15, 160n46, 237n32
mathematical truths, 211–13
meaning.
  Grice on, 110
  senses and, 273–74

speaker's reference and, 109–10
  time of utterance and, 274
Meinong, Alexius, 64, 234
metalinguistic negation, 338n44
metalinguistic statements
  fictional entities and, 70
  identity statements as, 18
  indirect senses and, 259–60
metatheorem of scope, 232–33, 246
Michael, Fred, 45
Michael, Michaelis, 365n22, 367n24
Mill, John Stuart, 52–53, 59
  Frege's views on proper names compared to, 126–37
  on proper names, 125–26
mind-body problem, 1n1
  contingent identity statements and, 8–9, 23–26
  rigid designators and, 24–25, 25n18
modality *de re*, 3–4, 103–5
monotone operations, 87
Montague, Richard, 95, 95n32, 267n42
  on knowledge, 46n23
  on scope, 245
Moore, G. E., 221
  on necessary existence, 55n6
Moore's paradox, 33n9
Moschovakis, Y. N., 86

Nagel, Thomas, 308
names. *See* codesignative names; fictional entities; proper names; vacuous names
natural kind terms,
  fictional entities and, 65–9
  proper names and, 152
  semantics of, 52
  translation of, 152–53, 156n40, 158
Neale, Stephen, 225n1, 226–27, 233, 235n28, 246n55, 246n56, 293n3
  scope distinctions of, 229n9, 232
necessary truths
  a priori truth and, 14–15, 18n14
  essentialism and, 16–17
  identity statements and, 17
  Mathematical statements and, 211–13
  Nozick's analysis of knowledge, and, 211–15
Nicod, J. G., 250, 250n60
Noth, Martin, 56n9
Nozick, Robert, 49n31
  backtracking, 216–17, 216n85
  conjunction, 181–99
  deductive closure, 179, 179n33, 196n60
  factual counterfactuals, 177–78, 177n31
  "gnowledge" and, 196n60
  knowledge of truths, 219–22
  necessary truths, 210–15
  relevant alternatives, 167, 167n15, 171, 171n24
  skepticism, 217–18
  supercredulous problem and, 222–23
Nute, Donald, 198n62

'On Denoting,' by Russell, 225–27, 227n7, 237, 271
other minds, 299n21

Pap, Arthur, 366n23
paradoxes. *See specific paradoxes*
Parikh, Rohit, 170n21
Parsons, Charles, 80n10
Parsons, Terry, 256
Peacocke, Christopher, 241n42
  on inference patterns, 312n56
  on rigid designators, 129n7
Peano Arithmetic, 46n23
perceptual knowledge, 175–76
Perry, John, 273–74, 275n65, 279n74, 308n44
  on first person statements, 284–85
  Frege criticized by, 296
Philosophical Explanations (Nozick), 162–223
Picardi, Eva, 266n39
possible worlds
  cardinality problem and, 374–75
  centered, 315–16, 316n65
  contingent identity statements and, 10–12
  counterfactual statements and, 12
  descriptive conditions and, 315
  fictional entities and, 59
  identity across, 16
  instants of time and, 374–75
  'I' pronoun and, 316–18
  Kaplan on, 95, 95n32
  Kaplan's puzzle of proposition and, 373–76
  Lewis on, 11–12, 313–14, 316n67
"pragmatic wastebasket fallacy," 328, 332, 341–43
presupposition. *See also* projection problem for presuppositions
  accommodation and, 353
  active context and, 357, 361, 366–67
  again cases and, 360–61, 365
  anaphora, 355–56, 366, 370–71
  clauses and, 355
  clefts and, 363
  conflicting accounts of, 351
  converse inclusion and, 369
  Frege on, 352–53
  identity elements and, 368–69
  other cases and, 366–68
  plugs and, 354
  presupposed nonidentities and, 365–66
  Russell on, 354, 354n7
  Stalnaker and Lewis on, 353
  stop cases and, 361–63
  Strawson on, 352–53

Index

presupposition (*Continued*)
  time of utterance and, 361–62
  too cases in, 357–61, 367
  types of, 352
pretended propositions, fictional entities and, 59
pretense principle, fictional entities and, 58–60
primary occurrences, scope and, 239–41
Principia Mathematica (Whitehead and Russell), 232–33, 234, 248–49
privileged senses, 264
  Church on, 286n90
projection problem for presuppositions, 352
  cumulative hypothesis for, 353–54
pronominalization phenomena, 99, 121n31
  anaphora and, 370–71
pronouns, semantic reference and, 121n31.
  See also 'I' pronoun
proper names
  belief and, 128, 130, 141–42, 148, 156–57
  belief and substitutivity principle with, 141–42
  chain of communication and, 136, 136n21
  connotation and, 132, 132n11
  contingent identity statements and, 6–8
  definite descriptions and, 6–7, 106–7, 117–18, 117n25
  Donnellan on, 106, 106n8
  fictional entities and, 53
  Frege's analysis of, 52–56, 126–37
  function of, 5–6
  idiolect and, 111, 111n19, 127, 133, 149n29, 150, 150n31, 280, 282
  indexicals compared to, 283n80
  interchangability of, 133–34
  in language, 150n29
  logically, 52n2, 102, 149n29
  Mill's analysis of, 125–37
  natural kind terms and, 152
  paradox of belief and, 142–43
  propositions and, 127–28
  reference and, 126–27, 126n2
  reference-fixing and, 106–7
  referential definite description and, 107
  rigidity of, 17, 20, 131–32, 131n10, 134, 136
  Russell's analysis of, 52–56, 126n3
  self-reference and, 77–78
  senses and, 134–35, 134n15, 281
  skepticism and, 218
  speaker's reference and, 117n25
  as tags, 7–8
  technical criterion for, 227n7
  translation of, 135n18, 150–51, 150n30, 282
  transparency of, 136, 136n19
  unrestricted exportation and, 322–48
propositional attitudes, 96, 125–61

propositional function, 242n45
propositions
  Frege on, 272–73
  Kaplan's puzzle of possible worlds and, 373–76
  self-referential, 78n5
  senses and, 272
pseudoclefts, 364–65
Putnam, Hilary, 65, 81, 152, 153n35, 213, 213n80
  on skepticism, 217, 217n86
puzzle. *See specific puzzles*

Quine, Willard Van Orman, 5–7, 11, 13, 16–17, 27n1, 140, 229–35, 242n45, 248, 250, 259n18, 260, 270n41, 313, 315, 316n65
  indeterminacy of translation of, 152n34, 154–56
  philosophy of language and, 121n29
  scientific language and, 294n4
  on surprise examination paradox, 32, 32n8, 39
  opacity of *de dicto* belief, 130n8
  'Two Dogmas of Empiricism' by, 225
  unrestricted exportation and, 322–48
quotation. *See* direct quotation; indirect quotation
quote-reference, 267

reference. *See also* indirect reference; self-reference; semantic reference; speaker's reference
  direct, 267
  fictional entities and, 59, 61–63, 71
  intended, 334n35
  of 'I' pronoun fixed by subject, 304
  proper names and, 126–27, 126n2
  senses determining, 269–70, 284, 288
  specifying, 255
  vacuous names and, 60
referentially-used definite description, 102–8
referential opacity, 159–60
reflexivity, 242n45
relevant alternatives
  Nozick's analysis of knowledge and, 167, 167n15, 171, 171n24
reliability
  justification and, 190, 190n51
  knowledge and, 190
rigid definite description, 105–6
rigid designators
  intuitive test for, 13
  mind-body problem and, 24–25, 25n18
  nonrigid designator compared to, 9–10

Nozick's analysis of knowledge, third
  condition and, 214
 Peacocke on, 129n7
 proper names as, 17, 20, 134
Russell, Bertrand, 52n2, 223n90, 255
 on acquaintance, 241–42
 Cretan liar paradox and, 376
 definite descriptions and, 99–124, 225–251
 on denoting phrases, 226–28
 Donnellan's distinction and, 99–124
 Frege's correspondence with, 238
 Frege's similarity to, 288
 modal paradoxes eliminated by, 5n5
 'On Denoting' by, 225–27, 226n7, 238, 272
 on presupposition, 354, 354n7
 on proper names, 52–56, 126n3
 on scope, 3–4, 5n5, 104–5, 225–251
 type theory of, 376–77
 on vacuous names, 60–61, 60n14

Salmon, Nathan, 237, 242, 249n58, 262n29
 on scope, 240
scientific discoveries, contingent identity
  statements and, 8–9
scientific language
 Kaplan and, 293–94, 296–97
 object identification in, 343–44
 propositions and, 318
 Quine and, 293n4
 subject in, 300
 tensed senses and, 297, 297n13
scope
 ambiguities, 233, 243
 definite description and, 4–6, 13n10, 104–5, 229
 Frege on, 5n5
 indefinite descriptions and, 230–31
 indifference theorem and, 248–49, 250
 intensional context and, 243
 intermediate, 13n10, 231, 238
 interpreting, 246
 islands, 244
 metatheorem of, 233–33, 246
 Montague on, 245
 Neale on, 229n9, 232
 path termination and, 250–51
 primary occurrences and, 239–41
 Russell on, 3–4, 5n5, 104–5, 225–251
 Salmon on, 240
 secondary occurrences and, 239–41
Searle, J. R., 20–21, 133n13, 268n41
self-consciousness. *See also* 'I' pronoun
 belief and, 183
 body and, 308–9
 Descartes and, 308–10
 'I' pronoun and, 308–9

logic of, 160n46
 mirrors and, 306, 306n34
 Wittgenstein and, 306–8
sense. *See also* indirect senses; tensed senses
 compositionality and, 269–70, 270n45
 first person statements and, 286–87
 meaning and, 273–74
 privileged, 264, 286n89
 proper names and, 134–35, 134n15, 281
 propositions and, 272
 reference determined by, 268–69, 284, 288
 revelatory, 259–60
 of sentences, 264
 specifying, 255
 time of utterance and, 277
 translation and understanding, 257–59, 282–83
 understanding and, 271
Shatz, David, 162n2, 167, 172n26
 twin example of, 170n22
Sinn, 254, 256
 autonymous, 275, 275n64
 Burge's view on, 279–82
 Frege's theory of, 254–88
 synonymy and, 258
Slote, M., 15n11, 26n19
Smullyan, Arthur, 5n5, 47n26, 229n9, 232, 233, 250
Soames, Scott, 242n43, 242n44, 243n47, 352–55, 353n3, 354–55, 356n11, 357n13, 357n14, 358n15, 358n16, 362, 364n21, 367–8, 370, 371n31
Sosa, Ernest, 180n35, 260n21, 322n1, 324n8, 325–26, 332–36, 347–48
Speier, Richard, 29n4
Stalnaker, Robert, 105n7, 177, 191, 194, 242n45, 316, 318n71, 356n11
 on counterfactual statements, 163, 163n5, 211
 on presupposition, 354
Stanley, Jason, 241n41
stereotypes, truth and, 65–66
Stine, Gail Caldwell, 165–67, 327n17
stop cases, presupposition and, 361–63
Strawson, P. F., 83–84, 99–100, 120
 on presupposition, 352–53
 on truth-value gaps, 235–36, 235n28, 235n29
substitutivity principle, 140–2, 157–58, 157n42
supercredulous problem, 222–23
supervaluation
 disjunctions and, 94
 van Fraassen on, 94–95
surprise examination paradox, 28–45
synonyms, 20
synthetic a priori judgments, 1

Tarski, Alfred, 83. *See also* Gödel-Tarski theorem
  disquotational principle of, 140n26
  hierarchy of languages of, 79, 79n9, 82, 88n23, 93, 378
Thomason, Richmond, 243n45, 245n52, 353n3
"toy duck fallacy"
  philosophy of language and, 345–48
  unrestricted exportation and, 347
translation
  belief and, 139, 148–51, 157
  definite description and, 148–49
  disquotational principle and, 139–40
  homophonic, 140–42, 154, 154n37
  of natural kind terms, 152–53, 156n40, 158
  of proper names, 135n18, 150–51, 150n30, 281
  Quine's doctrine of indeterminacy of, 154–56
  sense and, 257–59, 282–83
truth-value gaps, 82, 82n13, 89
  controversy over, 98
  fixed points and, 93–94
  natural language and, 95
  Strawson on, 235–36, 235n28, 235n29
  universal language and, 97n34

unrestricted exportation, 322–48
  belief and, 328–29
  consequences of, 328
  contextual factors of, 334–35, 335n37
  Dennett on, 325–27, 336–44
  de re belief and, 325–26, 326n14, 330n25
  knowledge and, 331–32
  Quine on, 323–26, 335, 335n37, 344
  Sosa defending, 326, 334–37, 335n37, 347–48
  "toy duck fallacy" and, 347
  unnoticed consequences of, 328–32

vacuous names
  contingent identity statements and, 60–61
  counterfactual statements and, 57
  fictional entities and, 62–63, 68–69, 68n30
  necessary existence and, 56
  reference and, 60
  Russell on, 60–61, 60n14
  semantics of, 53
van Fraassen, Bas, 82
  supervaluation notion of, 94–95
Verstehen, 294
vivid designator, 326n16

Washington, Corey, 267n41
Weinberg, Stephen, 49
Weyl, Hermann, 250n60, 377n12
Wiggins, David, 2–3, 5, 26n19
Williamson, Timothy, 29n5
Wilson, George, 244–5, 244n48
Wilson, Neil, 156n40
Wittgenstein, Ludwig, 41n15, 53n3, 56n9, 60–61, 285, 288n91, 292n2, 295n10, 296n12, 299n20, 300n23, 303n27,
  as 'anti-scientific,' 293n4
  on "intellectual cramps," 28
  on 'I' pronoun, 311–12
  on knowledge, 165, 165n10
  self-consciousness and, 307–8
Woodruff, Peter, 83, 83n14, 95

Zermelo set theory, 373